Exceptional Children in the Schools

Special Education in Transition

Second Edition · Lloyd M. Dunn, Editor

University of Hawaii

Exceptional Children in the Schools

Special Education in Transition

Contributors:

Lloyd M. Dunn

Paul S. Graubard

Randall K. Harley, Jr.

Forrest M. Hull

Mary E. Hull

Ruth A. Martinson

Freeman McConnell

Dean K. McIntosh

Marguerite I. Wilson

HOLT, RINEHART AND WINSTON, INC.

New York Chicago San Francisco Atlanta Dallas Montreal Toronto London Sydney

Copyright © 1963, 1973 by Holt, Rinehart and Winston, Inc.
Library of Congress Catalog Card Number: 73-813
ISBN: 0–03–086293–0
Printed in the United States of America
    6 7 8 9 0   0 3 2   9 8 7

preface

The first edition of this book was published a decade ago when special education throughout the world had embarked upon an unprecedented period of expansion. Special education was looked to rather uncritically as the answer to educating children who are quite different from the average. In the last 10 years, however, profound changes have taken place in society which reflect a heightened awareness of the rights of the individual to be different in appearance and behavior. No longer are persons forced either to conform or be labeled, rejected, and even isolated. This increasing acceptance of diversity in individuals has had a profound impact upon society in general and upon the schools in particular. Perhaps in no area has it had a greater influence than in special education for children with unusual abilities and disabilities (whom we euphemistically have called *exceptional*). As a result, the field is much less sure of its premises and directions today than it was in 1963. But there is reason for optimism. Special educators in the 1970s are receiving more scholarly preparation than ever before. As a result, they are better equipped than in the past to search for and implement effective methods for educating children with special needs.

Four major trends have characterized the field of special education since the late 1960s. *First,* special educators are less inclined to group pupils by traditional handicapping labels originated by such noneducators as physicians and psychologists. *Second,* in place of such categories as the gifted, crippled, mentally retarded, emotionally disturbed, and juvenile delinquent, special educators are substituting an educationally relevant classification system that focuses on the special learning needs of these children. *Third,* special educators are concentrating more and more on pupils with major differences and on quality programs rather than on handicapped children from minority groups who in the past have often been placed in special education programs of undemonstrated effectiveness. *Fourth,* special educators are becoming much more integrative in their approach, pointing out that much of special education is not very different from general education—with a few exceptions, such as using braille with the blind and speechreading with the deaf. Thus, a capable regular teacher can do a remarkably effective job of teaching most exceptional children, especially when able special consultants and helping teachers are available to her on demand. This trend toward normalizing education even for those who are quite different, plus other important developments such as child advocacy, have moved special education into a turbulent *period of transition.* In place of a traditional, untested remedial technology oriented to the past, the field is becoming future oriented and research based with emphasis on the development of integrated and preventive programs of demonstrated effectiveness. All of these new directions demanded a revision of our original book.

This text represents a thorough overhaul of the 1963 edition. *First,* the emphasis is different. Instead of retaining the tone of complacency reflected in the first edition, this one examines critically traditional practices and suggests needed new directions. Unpleasant facts about past excesses in the field, as well as controversial issues, are treated forthrightly. *Second,* six new authors have contributed to this volume, bringing to it greater divergence in points of view. *Third,* due to the explosion of professional literature in the field during the past decade, this volume is 60 percent longer than the first edition. *Fourth,* in keeping with the emerging trend, the chapter titles stress special abilities and disabilities rather than traditional labels. *Fifth,* a chapter on the newest facet of the field, major specific

learning disabilities, has been added, replacing the original tenth chapter on exceptionality and adjustment, a subject which in this edition is handled within each
chapter.

This revision, as the original edition, contains 10 chapters. The first three chapters were written by the editor of this volume.

Chapter 1 provides *an overview of special education in transition.* This is followed by the nine chapters organized around the major ability and disability areas.
Chapter 2, on *children with moderate and severe general learning disabilities,* deals
with pupils who have been traditionally classified as nonadaptive educable, trainable, and severely mentally retarded. Chapter 3, on *children with mild general
learning disabilities,* examines the controversial topic of education for pupils traditionally classified as the adaptive, cultural-familial educable mentally retarded who
often come from ethnic minorities and suggests a blueprint for change in this area.
In Chapter 4, on *children with superior cognitive abilities,* Dr. Martinson discusses
students who are unusually creative or talented, but especially those who are
academically able. In Chapter 5, on *children with behavioral disorders,* Dr. Graubard
examines pupils who have been traditionally classified as emotionally disturbed
and socially maladjusted (juvenile delinquent) and includes a brief section on drug
abuse. In Chapter 6 on *children with oral communication disabilities,* the Hulls
discuss pupils with speech impairments and other oral language problems. Dr.
McConnell, in Chapter 7 on *children with hearing disabilities,* deals with pupils
who have been traditionally classified as deaf and partially hearing. In Chapter 8
on *children with visual disabilities,* Dr. Harley discusses children classified as
educationally blind and partially seeing. Dr. Wilson, in Chapter 9 on *children with
neuromotor and other crippling and health disabilities,* introduces cerebral palsied
and epileptic children and those having other crippling and chronic health conditions which reduce activity level; the chapter also deals briefly with pregnant
schoolgirls. Dr. McIntosh and Dunn, in Chapter 10 on *children with major specific
learning disabilities,* team up to provide an overview of pupils who do not fall
into any of the traditional areas, yet are in need of corrective education associated
with severe reading, writing, and arithmetic problems. Traditionally, these children
have often been considered to have minimal brain dysfunctioning problems, perceptual impairments, or related disorders.

As with the 1963 edition, the chapters were written by specialists in their
respective areas because we believe the body of information in special education
is now so extensive that no one person can write with equal potency on all of the
many facets of the field. Because of this *scholarly overview by specialists technique,* hopefully we have been able to obtain substantial depth of treatment in each
area. As a result, this revision is a basic text to orient students to the field of special education. It is aimed primarily at beginning graduate and fifth-year students in
special education, and perhaps the able upper-division undergraduate with a background of course work in education and psychology. Obviously the total special
education story can hardly be told in a survey text; therefore the student is repeatedly directed to fuller treatments of the various topics that we have attempted to
synthesize. In this way, we believe that this book will again serve not only to
orient students to the field but also provide a useful reference to advanced graduate students in special education, especially in the areas in which they have not
specialized. However, this book was written not only for special educators but also
for the other professionals who serve exceptional children in any capacity in the

schools. Thus we hope it will prove useful as a comprehensive overview of the field for general educators, including classroom teachers who work with large numbers of cases of exceptionality, and for school psychologists, social workers, and nurses.

I wish to extend special thanks for their flexibility to my colleagues who contributed chapters to this revision. Even though we worked as an editorial committee in the planning and execution of this revision, without some rather heavy editing by me I doubt if it would have been possible to arrive at a multiauthored text which we believe to be relatively free of overlap and inconsistencies and to have a fairly consistent style, format, and philosophy. The contributors had to compromise with me and with one another, yet get their own stories told. And they did it graciously—a measure of their humanism, if one is needed for people who have devoted their professional careers to advancing the education of exceptional children.

We wish to express our appreciation to the many people who contributed to the preparation of this revision. We thank the group of college instructors in special education across the United States who, before the revision began and through a detailed questionnaire, suggested changes that needed to be made in our original edition. In addition we are grateful to the scholars who reviewed penultimate drafts of chapters and provided innumerable helpful suggestions. Too, we thank our colleagues and students at our own various campuses across the United States who field tested early drafts of our revision and made innumerable helpful criticisms and suggestions. To these and to the many other unnamed persons who assisted in the preparation of this book we express our sincere appreciation.

Finally, I owe my wife, Leota M. Dunn, a special note of appreciation for her extensive technical and personal support during the three-year period this book was in preparation.

Honolulu, Hawaii
Spring 1973

L.M.D.
Editor

CONTRIBUTING AUTHORS

LLOYD M. DUNN, Ph.D., a former Canadian school teacher who obtained the first doctor of philosophy degree in special education from the University of Illinois, became affiliate professor of special education at the University of Hawaii in 1970. Before that he was at George Peabody College for Teachers from 1953, where he initiated doctoral programs in mental retardation for psychologists and special educators. He served first as chairman of the Department of Special Education and later as director of the Institute on Mental Retardation and Intellectual Development. Dr. Dunn has been president of the Council for Exceptional Children, a member of President Kennedy's Panel on Mental Retardation, editor of the CEC Research Monograph Series, and a researcher in the U.S. Office of Education. He is also a fellow of the American Association on Mental Deficiency and the American Psychological Association. Dr. Dunn is the author of the *Peabody Picture Vocabulary Test* and the senior author of the *Peabody Language Development Kits, Peabody Individual Achievement Test,* and the *English Picture Vocabulary Tests.*

PAUL S. GRAUBARD, Ed.D., who holds the doctorate from Yeshiva University, is now associate professor of education there, directing the teacher education program in the area of behavioral disorders. Before 1965, he worked at a residential treatment center and was an elementary school teacher in New York City. Dr. Graubard is a past president of the CEC Council for Children with Behavior Disorders, an associate editor of *Exceptional Children,* a fellow of the American Orthopsychiatric Association, and holds membership in the American Psychological Association and the American Educational Research Association. He has edited a book of readings on *Children against Schools;* co-authored *A Handbook for Applying Reinforcement Procedures in Classrooms;* and produced a film entitled *Dare To Do.*

RANDALL K. HARLEY, Ph.D., is associate professor of special education at George Peabody College for Teachers, where he obtained his doctorate in education for the visually impaired. From 1960 to 1964 he was principal of the North Carolina School for the Blind. Before that he was an elementary school teacher and principal and a teacher of multiply handicapped blind children. He is a past president of the CEC Division for the Visually Handicapped and a member of the publications board of the Association for the Education of the Visually Handicapped. He has served as a consultant for the American Foundation for Overseas Blind in Ceylon and as a visiting professor there. Dr. Harley is the author of a research monograph on *Verbalism among Blind Children* and was senior investigator of a study entitled *Comparison of Several Approaches for Teaching Braille Reading to Blind Children.*

FORREST M. HULL, Ph.D., who obtained his doctorate in speech pathology from the University of Illinois, is professor of speech pathology at Colorado State University in Fort Collins. Prior to 1963 he held appointments in special education at George Peabody College for Teachers and in speech science at Vanderbilt University Medical Center, while serving as coordinator of training for speech therapists at the Bill Wilkerson Hearing and Speech Center in Nashville, Tennessee. He is a fellow of, holds the certificate of clinical competency in speech pathology from, and is a member of the board of examiners of the American Speech and Hearing

Association. Dr. Hull has been president of the Tennessee Speech and Hearing Association and vice-president of the Colorado Speech and Hearing Association. Dr. Hull has served as a consultant in speech pathology to a number of organizations. He was project director from 1965 to 1972 of the *National Speech and Hearing Survey*, which probed into the prevalence of such conditions among school children.

MARY E. HULL, M.A., who holds her master's degree from Wichita State University, is head of speech correction services in the Poudre School District at Fort Collins, Colorado. Formerly she was a public school speech clinician in Nashville, Tennessee. She holds the certificate of clinical competency in speech pathology of the American Speech and Hearing Association. Mrs. Hull is a member of the Colorado Speech and Hearing Association, the Council for Exceptional Children, and the National Education Association. In Colorado she has instructed in several speech and language workshops, including a training program for speech aides, and has served as a member of the committee for comprehensive state planning for speech and hearing.

RUTH A. MARTINSON, Ed.D., who obtained her doctorate from the University of California at Los Angeles, is emeritus professor of education and psychology, California State College at Dominguez Hills, where she served as director of teacher education from 1964 to 1970. Previously she was a professor at California State College, Long Beach, a visiting professor at UCLA, and the director of a three-year, state-wide study of public school programs for gifted students in California. Before that she taught at the elementary and junior high school levels in the state of Washington. Dr. Martinson is a past president of the Association for the Gifted and a former member of the executive committee of the Council for Exceptional Children. In 1972 she received the first distinguished service award of the California Association for the Gifted. She is the author of *Curriculum Enrichment for the Gifted in the Primary Grades* and *Educational Programs for the Gifted* and the senior author of *The Abilities of Young Children* and *The Improvement of Teaching Procedures with Gifted Elementary and Secondary School Students*. She also contributed extensively to the 1972 report of the U.S. Commissioner of Education to Congress on the *Education of the Gifted and Talented*.

FREEMAN McCONNELL, Ph.D., who obtained his doctorate in audiology from Northwestern University, has been director of the Bill Wilkerson Hearing and Speech Center and chairman of the Department of Hearing and Speech Sciences at Vanderbilt University in Nashville, Tennessee, since 1951. In his earlier years he taught in Illinois public schools. Dr. McConnell is a fellow of the American Speech and Hearing Association, in which he has held a number of committee assignments, including the chairmanship of the Joint Committee on Audiology and Education of the Deaf and the Committee on the Clinical Fellowship Year. He has served as consultant to a number of programs on hearing, including the Bureau of Research of the U.S. Office of Education. He is past president of the Tennessee Speech and Hearing Association and of the Academy of Rehabilitative Audiology and has been active in the Council for Exceptional Children. He was co-editor of a book on *Deafness in Childhood* (1967) and is the author of more than 50 scientific and professional articles and chapters.

DEAN K. McINTOSH, Ed.D., who earned his doctorate from the University of California at Los Angeles, is chairman of the Department of Special Education at the University of Hawaii, where he has been on the faculty since 1966. Before that he taught in California junior high schools. Dr. McIntosh represents Hawaii on the board of governors of the Council for Exceptional Children and is a member of the Division for Children with Learning Disabilities of that organization. In Hawaii he has been chairman of the Governor's Committee on Learning Disabilities, is on the board of directors of the Hawaii Association for Children with Learning Disabilities, and is vice-president of the Variety Club School for Children with Learning Disabilities. He is a member of the U.S. Office of Education panel of experts on special education for the Trust Territories of the Pacific and a special education consultant to Taiwan, sponsored by the East-West Center for Cultural Interchange at the University of Hawaii.

MARGUERITE I. WILSON, Ed.D., who obtained her doctorate in special education from George Peabody College for Teachers, is associate professor of special education at Brigham Young University, Provo, Utah. She has been coordinator there of undergraduate programs in special education, of graduate teacher preparation in the related areas of the neurologically and orthopedically impaired, and of the Special Education Instructional Media Center. Before her appointment to Brigham Young University, she served as an elementary school teacher, a teacher of the physically handicapped, and the director of the Junior League program for homebound children in Salt Lake City. Dr. Wilson is a life member of the National Education Association, a member of the Council for Exceptional Children, and a past president of its Utah chapter. She also holds membership in the American Association on Mental Deficiency.

CONTENTS

Opposite: Exceptional children, who come from all strata of society, require teachers who possess high levels of competence, knowledge, and warmth.

chapter one / lloyd m. dunn

AN OVERVIEW

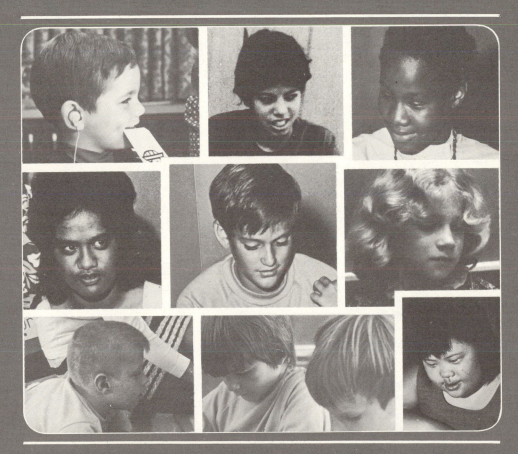

chapter outline

A key to excellence in teaching is an acceptance and understanding of all children and their individual differences. Most teachers recognize that each child is different from all others. Furthermore, they are aware that every individual has his own unique profile of characteristics. Consequently, educators are today making more provisions than ever before to individualize instructional programs to fit the unique needs of each pupil. While much remains to be done, a number of adjustments are being made in traditional school programs to accommodate differences *among* and *within* students. For example, courses of study are becoming more varied, thus providing a challenge for slow and rapid as well as average learners. More attention is being given to guidance, counseling, remedial education, and other ancillary educational services. The organization of the school is moving away from self-contained regular grades toward team teaching, open classrooms, ungraded schools, flexible grouping, schools without walls, and school parks. Coming into increased usage are such materials for self-instruction as programed texts, talking typewriters, and automated teaching machines, including computer-assisted instruction. And some traditional general education programs have been successfully recast to provide for the individual needs of children who deviate substantially from any typical pattern.

Yet it is widely recognized that a small number of students are so different from the average in one or more dimensions that it is unrealistic to expect regular educators alone to serve them adequately. These pupils with special abilities or unusual limitations are known as *exceptional children and youth*. For them, even such programs, procedures, and devices as those just cited do not provide appropriately for their educational needs. If these young people are to be given as great an opportunity to achieve their potential as more typical children, they require a program of *special education*, ranging from a short period of time to many years. The purpose of this book is to provide an orientation to exceptional pupils—both gifted and handicapped— and to the special education they need.

EXCEPTIONAL CHILDREN DEFINED

The term *exceptional* describes only that minority of pupils whose educational needs are very different from those of the majority of children and youth. That is, this group includes only those with deviations that require special teaching competence or unusual school services. For example, while many students have hearing losses, most can achieve adequately with a hearing aid and preferential seating; only those whose losses are great enough to produce a need for special instruction in communication skills are considered exceptional. An even larger number of pupils have visual impairments, but most cases can be corrected with glasses; only a small percentage require specialized perceptual training or help in learning braille and in using talking books, large print, and magnifiers. Similarly, there are many bright pupils, but only the few whose abilities are so outstanding that they are best served by special programs are classified as exceptional. (Actual prevalence estimates for children in need of special education will be presented later in this chapter.)

The first edition of this text (Dunn, 1963) defined exceptional children as those

> *(1) who differ from the average to such a degree in physical or psychological characteristics (2) that school programs designed for the majority of children do not afford them opportunity for all-round adjustment and optimum progress, (3) and who therefore need either special instruction or in some cases special ancillary services, or both, to achieve at a level commensurate with their respective abilities. [p. 3]*

This traditional definition has been criticized, with considerable justification, on three counts.

The *first* major complaint is that it is *too broad and subjective*, with the result that it is all too easy for some general educators to refer into special education children with quite mild learning and behavioral disabilities who are problems to them. And educators of exceptional children have been all too willing to accept these pupils—even though there is little evidence that they make greater progress in special programs. Reger, Schroeder, and Uschold (1968) have pointed out that special education is rendering a disservice to general education in following this practice:

> Special educational programming faces a critical danger today in becoming the vehicle for preventing change in the general curriculum. It is becoming increasingly easier, as programs multiply and our alertness to problems sharpens, to remove children who do not fit the general curriculum rather than to think in terms of making changes in the general curriculum to accommodate the child. If a school believes that its curriculum program is adequate it will never be proven wrong as long as any child who is unable to fit the pattern is removed and placed into a special educational program. [p. 13]

In a similar vein, Johnson (1969), a black special educator, has criticized general educators for using special education to rationalize away their guilt when they transfer out of their classrooms children they do not want:

> Special education is part of the arrangement for cooling out students. It has helped to erect a parallel system which permits relief of institutional guilt and humiliation stemming from the failure to achieve competence and effectiveness in the task given to it by society. Special education is helping the regular school maintain its spoiled identity when it creates special programs (whether psychodynamic or behavioral modification) for the "disruptive child" and the "slow learner," many of whom, for some strange reason, happen to be Black and poor and live in the inner city. [p. 245]

Criticisms of traditional referral practices have centered on children who are classified as marginally or mildly handicapped. The need for special education by the moderately and extremely handicapped has not been questioned.

The *second* and overlapping criticism of the 1963 definition has centered on *the effects of attaching disability labels* to children with learning problems, especially those of a marginal and mild variety. It is argued that such designations become destructive, self-fulfilling prophecies. When a pupil is labeled as handicapped, a logical explanation is provided for why he is not learning. As a result, the teacher does not expect him to learn very much, and he doesn't—largely because he is not stimulated and challenged to do so. Reger, Schroeder, and Uschold (1968) have stated the case against the labeling process and the circularity in logic which results:

> We as special educators step in with our curriculum deodorizers and spray everything with a heavy mist of fancy words inappropriately borrowed from medicine and everybody breathes a new aroma of pseudo-understanding. "No wonder that child couldn't read; he's brain injured!" And the reason the child was called brain injured was that he could not read. [p. 13]

Certainly, the traditional practice has been for school psychologists, social workers, physicians, speech and hearing personnel—and occasionally educators—to team up in designating children as learning disabled, minimal brain dysfunctioning, educable mentally retarded, behavior disordered, or some such term depending on the predispositions, idiosyncrasies, and backgrounds of the diagnostic personnel. Thus, there has been a tendency to take pupils the regular teacher cannot handle and find something wrong with them so they can be given a disability label. Following this, they are transferred into a special education program with other children who behave as they do. Then a special educator is expected to handle and teach this group. Understandably, the system has not worked well. Therefore the question arises, *How much damage is done by labeling a child with a disability?* Few people would argue that such labels are badges of distinction. As yet, however, the effects of the expectancies of teachers on pupils' self-concepts, behavior, and learning rates have not been well researched. Nevertheless, Rosenthal and Jacobson (1968) have provided a pioneering study which is having a profound impact on the field, in spite of its being severely criticized on methodological grounds by Thorndike (1968). Working with elementary school teachers across the first six grades, they obtained pretest measures on the intelligence of their pupils. A random sample of these pupils was drawn and arbitrarily classified as "late-bloomers" with hidden potentials. Their teachers were told that these randomly selected children would show unusual intellectual gains during the school year. All of the pupils were retested in the spring. Not all differences were statistically significant, but the gains of the children who had been arbitrarily designated as rapid learners were generally greater than those of the other pupils, with dramatic and statistically significant changes in the first two grades.

Anderson (1970), Gozali and Meyen (1970), and José and Cody (1971) were unable to replicate the Rosenthal and Jacobson findings, which should caution against overgeneralizing from the initial, landmark investigation. However, some compatible evidence has become available (Beez, 1968; Haskett,

1968; Heintz, 1968; McLean, 1968). For example, Beez (1968) studied the effects of teacher expectancy on the amount of reading material presented to five- and six-year-old Head Start children who were tutored by summer school teachers. The teachers of the randomly selected pupils who were labeled slow learners by the investigator taught only about half as many words as the contrast group of teachers whose pupils had been labeled rapid learners. Though it is still necessary to extrapolate considerably beyond the data presently available, teacher expectancies do appear to influence pupil progress, and the *self-fulfilling prophecy phenomenon* does appear to operate, at least under certain circumstances.

The potential for disability labels being self-fulfilling prophecies is having a traumatic effect on the field of special education, and is being much discussed (Meyen, 1971). How it will be resolved finally remains to be seen. However, it must again be kept in mind that this concern is directed primarily at the practice of classifying and referring for special education children who have been defined as having marginal or mild learning disabilities. For the moderately and extremely handicapped the label probably cannot be avoided, no matter what sleight of hand is used. Too, the special educational needs of such pupils are usually so apparent that the label is justified so as to provide the service. Nevertheless, one must be careful to recognize that *a physical, psychological, or legal impairment does not necessarily present an educational disability.* The two are not identical (Dolberg and Lenard, 1967).

The *third* related complaint about the 1963 definition of exceptional children is that *the blame for school failure is placed completely within the child* and is not shared by the teacher, the school, the parents, or the community. Under it, schools do not fail; only pupils fail. To counter this state of affairs, Lilly (1970) has suggested that educators move from defining "exceptional children" to defining "exceptional situations within the school."

An EXCEPTIONAL SCHOOL SITUATION is one in which interaction between a student and his teacher has been limited to such an extent that external intervention is deemed necessary by the teacher to cope with the problem. [p. 48]

This approach does not imply that the causative agent is specifically the child. Instead, it argues for a complete analysis of the situation before statements are made about the nature and cause of the problem and before steps are taken to bring about its solution. It may be noted, however, that the second aspect of the 1963 definition implies the need for an analysis of the total situation to determine if and how regular school programs can provide for the all-round adjustment and optimal progress of the pupil in question. Apparently, however, this evaluation has often been omitted.

How then should "exceptional children" be defined so as to avoid as much as possible (1) overreferring disruptive and slow-learning children out of general education simply to provide relief for the regular teacher and the other pupils; (2) the self-fulfilling effects of disability labels; and (3) placing sole blame for school failure on the child and none on the regular school setting? The following working definition, which is more restrictive than the original one, is proposed:

> An exceptional pupil is so labeled only for that segment of his school career (1) when his deviating physical or behavioral characteristics are of such a nature as to manifest a significant learning asset or disability for special education purposes; and, therefore, (2) when, through trial provisions, it has been determined that he can make greater all-round adjustment and scholastic progress with direct or indirect special education services than he could with only a typical regular school program.

Basic to the above definitions are the following three provisos. *First*, in cases where a child has been referred by a regular classroom teacher, the total school setting will have been analyzed carefully to determine if at least a partial fault lies in inadequate or inappropriate instruction, and, if so, the situation will be corrected and the pupil continued in the regular school program. *Second*, by trial provisions, special educators will have found an intervention superior to that provided in the regular school program before a more permanent special education arrangement is made. *Third*, the special education treatment—and therefore the label—will be retained only as long as there is evidence that the special education services are superior to the regular school program alone. In short, the advantages of the label and the consequent special education services outweigh the disadvantages. Clearly, the purpose of this definition is to caution educators to be more restrictive than before in classifying children as exceptional and providing special education for them.

SPECIAL EDUCATION SERVICES DEFINED

What is special about special education? This question is best answered by describing what is included in special education services. There are four types of provisions.

1. *Specially trained professional educators.* These include teachers, consultants, teacher educators, and administrators who possess additional competencies for serving a certain type or types of exceptional children over and above those possessed by regular classroom teachers. Their services may be made available to exceptional children directly or indirectly.

2. *Special curricular content.* Many exceptional children need a curriculum that differs in content from that which is offered in the regular school. Examples are speechreading for deaf and braille for blind pupils.

3. *Special methodology.* Certain exceptional children learn better with a particular teaching procedure, though relatively few unique techniques have as yet been designed and found effective. Perhaps the best example is special refinements in behavior modification techniques for those with severe learning disabilities.

4. *Special instructional materials.* These include specially designed electric typewriters for the uncoordinated cerebral palsied; braille and large-type books for the visually limited; inquiry-oriented teaching mate-

rials for the gifted; and programed materials for the retarded which may have many more small steps than is normal.

How many of the above four elements need to be provided before a pupil can be said to be receiving special education services? Would one, two, or three types be sufficient, or must all be available? There is no consensus on this issue. Some special educators would say that a child should be classified as exceptional when only special instructional materials are provided, such as braille books. More and more would argue that classification on this basis is undesirable because of the possible stigmatizing effect of a disability label. These persons would generally take the position that a child should be classified as exceptional only when he is receiving the direct services of a special educator—and there is much merit in this position. However, a child should not be given a disability label and be said to be receiving special education services when he is simply placed in a so-called special class and given a watered-down regular school program provided by a regular classroom teacher who has no special competencies. Similarly, fitting out a school with a ramp or providing a pupil with a wheelchair can hardly be called a special education service. Nor do such ancillary services as physical and occupational therapy and visiting teacher (school social worker) services constitute special education. The picture becomes even more clouded when one turns to public school speech therapists and remedial educators. Often for administrative purposes these personnel are included in special education, though many persons in these two fields consider that they belong to unique professions, each an entity in its own right. However, because of their close affinity to special education, they are included in the discussions in this book. In summary, there is a trend toward defining a special education program as one that provides a pupil with the direct (or perhaps even indirect) services of a trained special educator who uses a unique curriculum, a different method, and/or specialized instructional materials which are quite different from those traditionally available in the regular grades.

EXCEPTIONAL CHILDREN CLASSIFIED

By 1950, 12 types of exceptional children had been delineated: (1) gifted, (2) educable mentally retarded, (3) trainable mentally retarded, (4) emotionally disturbed, (5) socially maladjusted, (6) speech impaired, (7) deaf, (8) hard of hearing, (9) blind, (10) partially seeing, (11) crippled, and (12) chronic health cases. In fact, the 1963 edition of this text focused solely around these areas, with some chapters organized to include related categories, such as the deaf and hard of hearing; the blind and partially seeing; and the emotionally disturbed and socially maladjusted. What have the main new developments in this classification system in the last decade?

The 1960s saw special education for the gifted as the forgotten area of exceptionality. However, this state of affairs was reversed somewhat in 1970 when Congress mandated from the U.S. Office of Education a status report (Marland, 1972) on education of gifted and talented children. This national survey and the recent modest activity that has been generated by it are discussed in Chapter 4. Hopefully, both lay and professional persons will soon recognize more fully the need to make greater efforts at stimulating gifted children to realize their potential. This need is likely to become more apparent as a growing percentage of lower socioeconomic class, ethnic, and racial minority group children are integrated with other, more advantaged, pupils through busing, mixed housing, and school parks. This will create greater pupil heterogeneity than ever before in essentially every regular public school in the United States. As this occurs, the need will increase to utilize every conceivable procedure that is acceptable and effective to provide for this widened range of individual differences among students. One strategy that is likely to be used more is flexible grouping, which will insure that a cross section of pupils, including the gifted, will be grouped together for instructional purposes a good deal of the time. At the same time, this approach will allow very able students to come together as a homogeneous group for a portion of the school day to obtain extra stimulation through accelerated and enriched special education offerings, including the opportunity to be stimulated and challenged by their intellectual peers. Besides this emerging trend toward flexible grouping and away from inflexible grouping (including upper streams and special schools and classes for the gifted), two other developments are emerging. The traditional focus only on children with high scholastic aptitude and attainment is being broadened to include more emphasis on the areas of creative and productive thinking, leadership ability, the visual and performing arts, and even psychomotor ability. Thus the area of the gifted has been broadened to include an array of *superior cognitive abilities*. Finally, traditionally special education for the gifted has been reserved for children who scored among the top 3 percent or so on nationally standardized psychoeducational tests, especially in terms of IQ scores on individual intelligence tests. This identification strategy greatly favored white, native-born, Standard English-speaking children. Because of a heightened concern about talent loss among other elements of the population, there is a trend to redefine the group to include the top 3 percent or so of each ethnic, racial, and socioeconomic subgroup in the community who have unusual potential in any area of human endeavor that shows promise of making a lasting, meritorious contribution to society, though Martinson in Chapter 4 does not go quite this far in her definition. In short, the 1960s were an incubation period in the special education of those with superior cognitive abilities. The 1970s could see this area come from the shadows into the limelight.

The relatively dormant state of special education for the gifted during the 1960s cannot be reported about special education for the handicapped. As a result of unusually rapid growth during the last decade in these services there has been a critical re-examination of the 11 traditional disability labels. Five growing concerns have become apparent. *First,* even more than in the past, it is now widely recognized that related categories such as the blind and partially seeing are not discretely different. As a result, there has been a steady movement to break down the category walls and to combine and extend related areas. *Second,* the use of discrete disability labels has excluded from special education services many children with fairly serious learning problems who did not fall neatly into one of the 11 traditional categories. The most apparent omission has been children formerly said to have "minimal brain dysfunction" and now called children with "specific learning disabilities." These pupils do not fall into any one of the traditional areas yet have rather severe reading and other school problems. *Third,* the increased number of children with multiple handicaps has made barriers between the various areas of exceptionality even more indefinable than in the past. As will be pointed out time and again, disabilities are generally multiple. Dividing a field into narrow, discrete areas often denies such children a comprehensive special education program. *Fourth,* discrete categories have tended to create attitudinal problems among some narrowly trained specialists who feel capable of serving only pupils who have the one disability in which they have their preparation, a condition which seldom exists. For example, some speech therapists have been hesitant about working with a speech- or language-impaired child who is also mentally retarded. *Fifth,* there has been a recognition that the traditional labels have come largely from the diagnostic efforts of medicine and psychology and tend to emphasize the etiology and often pathology of children's handicaps rather than their educational needs. Typical of the dissatisfaction with medically and psychologically oriented categories have been the observations of Fisher (1967) in Canada:

> We seem to be possessed with categories and organizational designs which entrench the categories. Are we so sure that special classes, broken down into categories—slow learners, neurologically impaired, etc.— are doing the job? While the process may be administratively convenient, there is no doubt that the procedure has made special education special, isolated it and in so doing perpetuated isolationism and attending mysticism. [p. 10]

In the United States, Reger, Schroeder, and Uschold (1968) have voiced similar concerns:

> We are saying that grouping children on the basis of medically-derived disability labels has no practical utility in the schools. Children should be grouped on the basis of their education needs, and these needs may be defined in any number of ways. The notion that simple labels, applied by high-status authorities from outside the school, should serve as a basis for grouping children is basically nothing more than a refusal to accept responsibility for making educational decisions. It is educational laziness. [p. 19]

These are but two examples. Most spokesmen for the field agree that a new taxonomy of special education is needed, one based on educational needs (Meyen, 1971; Blatt, 1972).

In their search for a more appropriate system of terminology, special educators of the handicapped have turned to the term *learning disabilities* (or *learning problems*). Thus the total field can be conceptualized as dealing with pupils who have unusual learning abilities and disabilities, and this book was so organized.

PREVALENCE OF EXCEPTIONAL CHILDREN[1]

When educators are considering the development of special education services for handicapped and gifted pupils, they face the practical problem of estimating how many children are involved. In each of the subsequent chapters, the contributing authors deal with this topic for their own areas of exceptionality. The data are brought together here to provide an overview. Throughout, one will discover that this topic is fraught with problems. At the outset, it must be pointed out that numerous prevalence figures in the professional literature tend to be much too large for special educational purposes because they are based on noneducational frames of reference. Three examples will illustrate this. *First*, nearly all children with cerebral palsy may be counted by a private, voluntary agency for fund-raising purposes because most of these youngsters need some sort of medical or social services. Yet many such children do not have unusual educational needs and can and should be in the regular grades. Similarly, most pupils with chronic health problems such as epilepsy, diabetes, rheumatic fever, and other illnesses can function without special education after adequate medical treatment (U.S. Department of Health, Education and Welfare, National Health Survey, 1967). *Second*, Jones (1962) found that 82 percent of *legally* blind children in local school districts and 29 percent in residential schools read primarily by means of print, not braille, and therefore cannot be considered educationally blind. Harley discusses this situation in Chapter 8. *Third*, many very young children, even up through the primary grades, have trouble pronouncing certain speech sounds. But most acquire the ability to do so simply from good models, by maturation, and through informal assistance by their mother and the teacher, without speech therapy. Thus they should not be counted for purposes of planning special education services. Similarly, the number of medically, socially, and legally handicapped in other areas exceeds the number within the group who are educationally exceptional. These facts are forcing down-

---

[1] A distinction is made between prevalence and incidence figures. Prevalence is the meaningful figure for special education planning because it tells how widespread a condition is in a group. Incidence gives the rate of occurrence of a condition. For example, the incidence of occurrence of Down's syndrome (mongolism) is about 1.5 times in every 1000 (0.15 percent) live births. However, since a considerable number of such children die during their preschool years, the prevalence figure among school-age children is somewhat lower than 1.5 occurrences per 1000 pupils (see page 79 for a fuller discussion of Down's syndrome).

ward the traditional prevalence estimates, especially as increased efforts are made to "normalize" education for the handicapped.

At the same time, a major counterdevelopment, the increasing number of *multiply handicapped children*, may cause some prevalence figures to be too low. If a school system classifies each of its exceptional children only once in terms of his major special education needs, its figures will underestimate the true index of required special education services, since such children usually require more than one type of service. For example, a deaf-blind child needs instruction from a teacher of the deaf as well as from one trained to work with the blind or from someone with proficiency in both areas. Similarly, a moderately retarded child with a speech impairment will probably need the services of a speech correctionist as well as a teacher of the retarded. In both cases, the pupil needs to be counted twice in the prevalence estimates.

How many multiply handicapped children are there? Much attention and concern is being given to this group, as an examination of the *Exceptional Child Abstracts*[2] will attest. There is considerable speculation on their prevalence, yet no comprehensive study is available, although Wishik (1956) and Friedman and MacQueen (1971) have provided limited but useful ones. From these investigations and others, two generalizations are emerging. *First*, it would appear that *only about half of handicapped children have one educationally significant disability; another quarter have two; and the other quarter have three or more. Second*, the most frequent multiple disabilities with significance for special education are mental retardation, behavior disorders, and speech impairments. In the future there will probably be an even higher prevalence of complex problems, primarily as the result of three factors:

1. The fetus and embryo today are being endangered by many more damaging influences than in the past, including pollutants, drugs, and viruses to which the pregnant mother is exposed. The most glaring example has been maternal rubella, or German measles, which may produce visual, auditory, motor, and cognitive disabilities in combinations, depending on when the mother contracts the disease during the first trimester of pregnancy. This disease can now be controlled by immunization, but there will probably be other influences emerging that will produce similar results.

2. Medical advances[3] have resulted in preserving life in more and more babies with severe congenital problems who formerly spontaneously aborted or died at or near birth. Many of these difficulties, which are both genetically and environmentally determined, result in prematurity and other complications at birth.

3. Similarly, medical knowledge is being applied to save the lives of children who have severe infectious diseases, accidents, toxic conditions,

---

[2] See the *Resources* section at the end of this chapter for information on this and a number of other references covering exceptional children generally.

[3] Of course, medical advances have prevented many more handicapping conditions than they have created.

and other complications after they are born. Frequently, however, there are residual effects, and such children may be left with any combination of physical and/or psychological disabilities.

More attention will be given to the multiply handicapped throughout this book. Suffice it to say here that the increasing numbers of such children complicate the problem of arriving at valid prevalence estimates.

At the same time, prevalence figures cannot be accurately estimated from the number of pupils enrolled in special education services, since few school systems serve all of their exceptional children. Even the inclusion of those on waiting lists usually results in an underestimation. Because of these complications, only gross estimates are available. Table 1.1 presents the traditional prevalence figures, along with those cited by the U.S. Office of Education, plus some suggested goals for these figures by the years 1985 and 2000.

In column 1 are the traditional figures used in lobbying for special education services. *They now stand at 13½ percent.* These data are almost exactly the same as those used by the U.S. Office of Education when the 3 percent for the gifted (Marland, 1972) is added to the 10.035 percent estimate for the other handicapping conditions. But the total number of exceptional children cannot be found by adding up the percentages in column 1, since multiple exceptionalities are counted more than once. Therefore, when each such pupil is counted only once, *a traditional estimate is that perhaps 10 percent of the school population is now so exceptional in one or more areas as to need one or more types of special educational services.*[4] The traditional 10 percent figure is up 2 percent from the 8 percent figure used in the 1963 edition, mainly because the area of specific learning disabilities has been added to the field since then. These largely unchallenged estimates have been drifting around for years. They constitute a severe indictment of general educators, suggesting a grave inability on their part to deal with individual differences for approximately one tenth of the school-age population.

The present period, however, is one of transition for both general and special education, with more resources becoming available for serving children with special needs in the educational mainstream and with special educators becoming less willing to take all problem children off the hands of general educators. These developments mean that the traditional prevalence figures should move downward. Therefore, in column 2 of Table 1.1 are provided estimates to work toward up to 1985. Hopefully by then the total number of exceptional children, with multiple exceptionalities counted more than once, will have dropped from 13½ percent to approximately 10 percent. For persons planning services up until then, column 2 should be a more defensible one than the traditional figures in column 1. Column 3 suggests that more needs to be done to reduce still further the number of exceptional children to perhaps 8 percent by the year 2000. A major question is whether

[4] This 10 percent might be reduced even further if the first generalization concerning multiple handicaps presented on page 12 were rigorously applied.

TABLE 1.1 *Maximum Prevalence Estimates[a] for Pupils Classified as Exceptional for Special Education Purposes (Multiple Exceptionalities Counted More Than Once)*

	Percentages		
Areas of Exceptionality	*Traditional (1)*	*Goal up to 1985 (2)*	*Goal by 2000 (3)*
Total exceptional children (rounded numbers)	13½	10	8 (11½)[b]
Total handicapped children (rounded numbers)	10½	7	5 (8½)[b]
1. *Superior cognitive abilities* (intellectually gifted and creative)	3.0	3.0	3.0
2. *Moderate and severe general learning disabilities* (formerly nonadaptive, educable, trainable, and severe mental retardation)	0.8	0.5	0.5
3. *Mild general learning disabilities* (formerly adaptive, educable mental retardation)	1.5	0.8	0.5
4. *Behavioral disabilities* (emotionally disturbed and socially maladjusted)	2.0	1.5	1.0
5. *Oral communication disabilities* (major speech and language problems)	3.5	2.2	1.2
6. *Hearing disabilities* (deaf and partially hearing)	0.6	0.3	0.2
7. *Visual disabilities* (educationally blind and partially seeing)	0.1	0.08	0.05
8. *Neuromotor and other crippling and health disabilities*	0.5	0.3	0.2
9. *Specific learning disabilities* (reading, writing, and arithmetic problems, primarily)	1.5	1.5	1.5 (3.5)[b]

[a]For 1971-1972, the U.S. Office of Education was using a 10.035 percent prevalence figure for school-age *handicapped* children from five to nineteen (with the gifted excluded): mentally retarded, 2.3 percent; emotionally disturbed, 2.0 percent; speech impaired, 3.5 percent; deaf and hard of hearing, 0.575 percent; visually impaired, 0.1 percent; crippled and other health impaired 0.5 percent; specific learning disabled, 1.0 percent; multihandicapped, 0.06 percent. (U.S. Office of Education, 1971.) In another U.S. Office of Education publication (Marland, 1971), a prevalence figure of 3.0 percent for the gifted was cited.

[b]Additional prevalence estimates if tutoring of slow learning and remedial education are added into special education.

special education will be expanded to include remedial education and individual tutoring by specialists of slow learners in the regular classroom. If this happens, then another 3.5 percent would need to be added to the "specific learning disabilities" category, raising the total prevalence figure from 8 to about 11½ percent. Another major imponderable is the number of multiply handicapped children in the year 2000. Many more of these boys and girls could make the goal unattainable as well as distort the Table 1.1 estimates sharply in specific areas.

Two observations bear mentioning. *First*, of the 10½ percent in column 1 who are educationally handicapped, approximately only 1½ percent are severely disabled,[5] while the other 9 percent have milder disorders. These data add credence to the contention that as many as 90 percent of handicapped children should be able to remain at least part time in the mainstream of education when reasonably adequate provisions are made. *Second*, separate estimates should be provided at the preschool, elementary school, and high school levels. The problem is so complicated, however, that it must await good epidemiological surveys. On the one hand, early corrective special education for children with motor, visual, auditory, and communication learning disabilities should reduce the number of pupils needing special services in their later school years. On the other hand, differences among pupils in cognitive abilities tend to increase with age. Thus, in this area special services would appear to be needed more at the high school level than at the preschool level. Persons using the figures in Table 1.1 therefore need to apply corrective factors when projecting the need for special services at the different levels.

Two final notes of caution are needed concerning these estimates. *First*, all figures should be considered as broad estimates. While they should hold up fairly well when applied to a state, province, or very large school district, they would often be found lacking in specific instances, especially when applied to certain local communities. For example, the number of children classified as mildly retarded would be much greater in the slums than in the suburbs of a metropolitan area, while the reverse would hold true for the gifted. Certain parts of states, such as southern Arizona, Florida, and California, attract families with children who are chronically ill, thereby distorting the figures. Communities around large day and residential schools for the blind or for the deaf possess a greater number of these types of children because families move to be near such special services. *Second*, these figures cannot be well documented. Hopefully, the years ahead will make possible the cumulation of more accurate estimates, but for a variety of reasons precise national data may never become available. There are no universally accepted definitions of

---

[5] This 1½ percent is estimated by including the blind (0.01 percent), the deaf (0.05 percent), the severely emotionally disturbed and socially maladjusted (0.05 percent), the moderate and severely retarded (0.75 percent), the severely cerebral palsied (0.10 percent), and pupils with other severe conditions (0.09 percent) usually associated with multiple disabilities.

what constitutes the various handicaps for special education purposes. Precise objective appraisal measures are lacking. Innumerable difficulties would be encountered in any attempt to standardize case finding, identification, and reporting procedures across states. Manpower competencies for diagnosis vary in quality and quantity by geographical areas. Certain severe handicapping conditions still carry a stigma, so a number of cases would go unreported. All these factors caution against expecting accurate prevalence figures in the future.

EXTENT OF SPECIAL EDUCATION SERVICES

Rather extensive data are available on the numbers of exceptional children receiving specialized instruction throughout the world. The United Nations Educational, Scientific and Cultural Organization (1971) has published statistics on the nature of special education in 38 selected countries. Table 1.2 summarizes some of the information contained in the UNESCO bulletin for the 15 countries which tended to have the most extensive services, though a number of other countries serve about 1 percent of their school population. In terms of total school population (five to nineteen years of age), it will be seen that Sweden heads the list by far, serving 8.58 percent of its pupils in special education. Rated second and third are Denmark (4.67 percent) and the United States (3.98 percent), followed by Israel (3.47 percent) and Canada (3.42 percent). Far down the list is the U.S.S.R., with only 0.44 percent of its pupils in special education. Most of the other 23 nations in the report, but not listed here, would be recognized as developing ones in Asia, Africa, and South America. Clearly, the most extensive services tend to be in the countries of Europe and North America (excluding Mexico) and in such educationally advanced nations as New Zealand and Chile. However, it must be pointed out that information was presented for only 38 of the nations of the world. No doubt, had the information been available, certain other countries such as Japan and Australia would have made the list. In any event, the reader may wish to speculate on how heavily such factors as affluence, commitment to human equality, mixed ethnic and language backgrounds, educational standards, degree of socialized medicine, and so forth, contributed to the rankings. It is frequently stated that the United States and Canada entered the 1970s providing special education for about half of their exceptional children. If Sweden is used as the criterion of rather comprehensive services, and if adjustments are made for the fact that remedial reading, remedial mathematics, and tutoring of slow learners are included in special education in Sweden, then the comparative data in Table 1.2 add credence to this contention. The United States and Canada, in serving 3.98 and 3.42 percent respectively, of their pupils in special education, serve less than half the 8.58 percent so served in Sweden.

Table 1.2 also contains information on teacher/pupil ratios in special education. Provided are suggested maximum enrollments by authorities in the respective countries for special day classes. Included, as well, to provide

TABLE 1.2 Percentages of Handicapped Children Receiving Special Education (Multiple Disabilities Counted Once Only) and Suggested Maximum Enrollments in Special Day Classes in 15 Selected Countries in the Late 1960s[a]

Country	Percent of Pupils in Special Education	Suggested Maximum Enrollments in Special Day Classes							
		Blind	Partially Seeing	Deaf	Partially Hearing	Cerebral Palsied	Educable Mentally Retarded	Trainable Mentally Retarded	Behavior Disordered
1. Sweden	8.58	–	10	8	8	12	15	–	–
2. Denmark	4.67	–	–	10	10	6	10	10	–
3. U.S.A.	3.98	6	12	8	8	12	12	12	8
4. Israel	3.47	–	–	–	–	8	10	12	–
5. Canada	3.42	10	12	10	12	12	16	16	8
6. Netherlands	2.61	–	–	6	–	–	16	–	–
7. Czechoslovakia	2.06	15	15	15	15	15	12	12	–
8. France	2.06	15	15	15	15	12	15	15	15
9. Finland	1.88	–	–	–	–	–	20	15	10
10. New Zealand	1.45	–	15	7	12	–	17	17	10
11. Hungary	1.24	12	12	12	17	–	17	–	–
12. Italy	1.15	–	–	–	–	–	–	–	–
13. England	1.08	15	15	10	10	20	20	20	15
14. Chile	0.80	15	15	15	15	15	15	15	15
15. U.S.S.R.	0.44	12	12	12	16	–	16	–	–
Median suggested maximum enrollments		12	12½	10	15	12	15½	15½	10
Actual average U.S. teacher/pupil ratios, 1968–69[b]		6		8		10	11	11	9

[a] United Nations Educational, Scientific and Cultural Organization, *A Study of the Present Situation of Special Education.* Paris: United Nations Educational, Scientific and Cultural Organization, 1971.

[b] E. W. Martin, *Programs of the Bureau of Education for the Handicapped: U.S. Office of Education, Programs for the handicapped.* Washington, D.C.: U.S. Department of Health, Education and Welfare (Secretary's Committee on Mental Retardation), 1970.

Note: Other actual U.S. teacher/pupil ratios for 1968–1969 were: specific learning disabilities, 1/13; multiply handicapped, 1/4; the average case load for public school speech therapists was 1/82.

a frame of reference, are the actual average teacher/pupil ratios in the United States for 1968–1969. As for the suggested maximum enrollments, one would have expected to see a clearer pattern of lower teacher/pupil ratios for the more severely handicapped than for the more mildly handicapped. This happened only in the case of children with auditory disabilities. As for the actual U.S. figures, the ratios provide a far more realistic figure in planning services. Generally, the trend is toward lower figures for the more handicapped, with the lowest of all in cases of the multiply handicapped.

For a more detailed look at special education statistics in the United

TABLE 1.3 *Numbers of Pupils Enrolled in Special Education Services Provided by Local Public School Systems in the United States, 1922-1972*

Areas of Exceptionality	1971-72[a]	1968[b]
Total exceptional	–	–
1. Superior cognitive abilities (gifted)	(no data)	(no data)
Total handicapped	2,857,551	2,251,500
2. General learning disabilities (mentally retarded)	872,113	703,800
(moderate/trainable)	(no breakdown)	(55,000)
(mild/educable)	(no breakdown)	(648,800)
3. Behavioral disabilities (emotionally disturbed)	156,486	99,400
4. Oral communication disabilities (speech impaired)	1,360,203	1,122,200
5. Hearing disabilities (deaf and partially hearing)	79,539	65,200
6. Visual disabilities (blind and partially seeing)	30,630	22,700
7. Neuromotor and other crippling and health disabilities	182,636	109,000
8. Specific learning disabilities	166,534	120,000
9. Multiply handicapped	9,310	9,200
10. Other	–	–
Total K-12 school age population (in thousands)[e]	52,000 (est.)	50,500

[a]U.S. Office of Education, *Estimated number of handicapped children in the United States, 1971-1972.* Washington, D.C.: U.S. Office of Education, 1971.

[b]E. W. Martin, *Programs of the Bureau of Education for the Handicapped:* U.S. Office of Education. *Programs for the handicapped.* Washington, D.C.: U.S. Department of Health, Education and Welfare (Secretary's Committee on Mental Retardation), 1970.

[c]R. P. Mackie, *Special education in the United States: Statistics, 1948-66.* New York: Teachers College Press, Columbia University, 1969.

States and Canada, there are recurring reports by the U.S. Office of Education and by the Education Division, Dominion Bureau of Statistics.[6]

Over the past 50 years, the U.S. Office of Education has surveyed regularly the extent of special education services provided for exceptional children, especially by local public school systems. The returns have always been high. Of late, they have been essentially 100 percent, since federal aid to education is involved. Table 1.3 and Figure 1.1 present a historical view of the growth of special education in the United States between 1922 and 1972.

The following observations are drawn from Table 1.3, Figure 1.1, Figure 1.2, and reports on U.S. Office of Education surveys, especially a bulletin by Mackie (1969).

1. In 1971–1972, almost three million children were receiving special education services in local public school systems alone. Mackie (1969) found that approximately one child receives special education in public residential facilities for each ten in public day schools. This adds approximately another 300,000 children. An additional small number of handicapped children attend

[6] See Hardy et al. (1971) for a breakdown of special education services by Canadian provinces.

1958[c]	1948[c]	1940[d]	1932[d]	1922[d]
889,560	377,615	313,722	163,950	–
52,269	20,712	3,255	1,834	(no data)
837,291	356,903	310,467	162,116	26,163
223,447	86,980	98,416	75,099	23,252
(16,793)	(4,509)	(nil)	(nil)	(nil)
(206,654)	(82,471)	(98,416)	(75,099)	(23(252)
28,622	15,340	10,477	14,354	(no data)
494,137	182,344	126,146	22,735	(no data)
21,616	13,977	13,478	4,434	2,911
11,660	8,216	8,875	5,308	(no data)
57,230	47,227	53,075	40,186	(no data)
(nil)	(nil)	(nil)	(nil)	(nil)
–	–	–	–	–
579	2,819	–	–	–
39,500	28,600	28,250	28,400	25,000

[d]E. H. Martens, C. Harris, and R. C. Story, *Statistics of special schools and classes for exceptional children, 1947-48: Chapter 5, Biennial survey of education in the United States, 1946-48*. Washington, D.C.: U.S. Office of Education, 1950.

[e]K. A. Simon and W. V. Grant, *Digest of educational statistics: 1970 Edition*. Washington, D.C.: U.S. Office of Education, 1970.

private day and residential facilities. The number of gifted pupils in special education is unknown but may approximate 500,000, since over 300,000 were reported to be in such programs in 1965–1966. *Therefore, at the beginning of the 1970s it seems a safe generalization to say that almost four million U.S. children were in special education.*

2. Over the 50-year period, 1922–1972, that the U.S. Office of Education has been gathering special education statistics, the growth curves may best be viewed by dividing the period into the first versus the second 25 years (see Figure 1.1). From 1922 to 1947 the growth curves by areas of exceptionality tended to parallel those for the school-age population generally, except in the areas of general learning and oral communication disabilities (then called mental retardation and speech impairment), which were much accelerated in rate of growth even before 1947. However, in the last 25-year period, 1947–1972, the number of handicapped pupils in special education provided by public day schools increased over 700 percent, an increase almost nine times greater than that for the school-age population as a whole during the same period. As Figure 1.2 shows, for 1971–1972 versus 1968–1969, special education enrollments increased nine times as rapidly as those in general education, with the greatest percentage growths in the areas of neurological, behavioral, special learning, and visual disabilities.

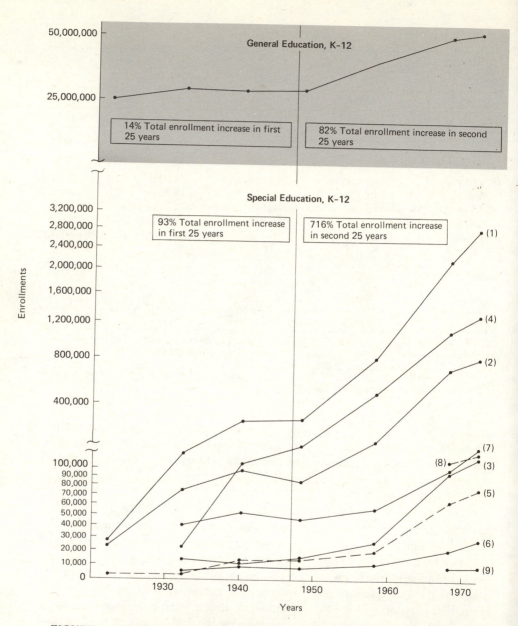

FIGURE 1.1 Number of pupils enrolled in special education for the handicapped provided by local school systems in the United States over the 50-year period 1922–1972, in contrast to general education enrollments, grades K–12. Percentage increases before and after 1947 calculated from the 1947 baseline enrollments. Key: (1) Total handicapped; (2) general learning disabilities; (3) behavioral disabilities; (4) oral communication disabilities; (5) hearing disabilities; (6) visual disabilities; (7) neuromotor and other crippling and health disabilities; (8) specific learning disabilities; (9) multiply handicapped.

3. Over the 50-year period, the three areas of slowest long-term growth have been (1) hearing; (2) visual, and (3) neuromotor and other crippling and health disabilities. Here medicine has probably made its greatest impact in reducing the prevalence of such disabilities by its preventative and curative techniques. Over this same 50-year period the areas of (1) general learning disabilities and (2) oral communication disabilities held up as the areas of greatest long-term growth.

4. The most recent areas of special education to be introduced were those designed for (1) the moderate or trainable mentally retarded in 1948; (2) pupils with specific learning disabilities in 1968; and (3) the multiply handicapped in 1968 (see Figure 1.1).

5. As for numbers of special educators, data in Martin (1970) reveal that about as many teachers were serving children in the one area of general learning disabilities in 1968–1969 as in all other areas combined. As one would anticipate, the smallest numbers of teachers work with children having visual and multiple disabilities.

6. The U.S. Office of Education reported 124,000 special educators employed by the local public schools in 1968–1970. Balow (1971) has noted that one half of these did not even meet minimal state certification standards for their positions. He estimated that 300,000 additional special educators would be needed to meet the differential between the handicapped served versus those needing to be served, using the traditional prevalence figures in Table 1.1. In addition, 8 percent (or 16,000) of existing teachers are lost each year by attrition, yet only about 18,000 new special educators are graduated annually for both classroom and leadership positions. In analyzing this supply/needs differential, Gallagher (1971) has estimated that it would take until the year 2770, at the least, to bridge the gap between manpower needs and training programs in the area of the mildly handicapped, assuming current special education prevalence figures and using current categories, instructional models, and teacher-education programs.

7. Special educators (except for speech therapists) have been serving very few pupils each (see Table 1.2). The median teacher/pupil ratio was 1/11 in 1968–1969. The lowest was 1/4 for teachers of the multiply handicapped; the highest was 1/13 for teachers of children with specific learning disabilities. Generally, it may be stated that special educators serve one half to one third as many pupils as regular teachers. This dramatically illustrates why special education is so costly. And there is essentially no research on the efficacy of different teacher loads in special education, though Vincent (1969) has reviewed a considerable body of literature on the topic for general education and concludes that class size, within broad limits, has little effect on pupil progress. On the average, public school speech therapists had a case load of 82. The Hulls in Chapter 6 point out the problems associated with such heavy loads, but again this variable has not been researched.

8. The sex ratio in special education is heavily weighted toward boys. Mumpower (1970) found overall that 70 percent of the pupils in special educa-

tion were boys versus 30 percent girls. This ratio held for the gifted; the retarded; those with special learning disabilities; the speech, hearing, and visually impaired; and the behavior disordered. As one would anticipate, the sexes were most evenly matched for neuromotor and other crippling and health disabilities.

9. Just as the gifted come from all levels of society but are concentrated in the higher socioeconomic strata, children with educational handicaps come from all levels but are concentrated among the poor and disadvantaged, including racial and ethnic minority groups. Among children with the milder learning and behavioral disabilities, over three quarters have come from the slums.

10. Recent information is not available on the number of special education pupils who spend at least part time in the regular grades. For 1957–1958, Mackie, Williams, and Hunter (1963) reported the following percentages of exceptional children integrated into the regular school program:

Speech impaired	100%	Gifted	32%
Partially hearing	71%	Deaf	23%
Partially seeing	52%	Educable mentally retarded	9%
Blind	50%	Crippling and special	5%
Socially and emotionally maladjusted	50%	health cases	
		Trainable mentally retarded	4%

More recent statistics would report much higher percentages than these, but the data are likely to be contaminated by those who consider participation in assembly, sports, and other nonacademic activities as constituting an integrated program. Therefore the picture may not be as optimistic as figures suggest.

11. More communities in more geographical areas are now serving more exceptional children than ever before under a greater variety of administrative strategies. In recent years the initiation of programs in smaller, more rural, and more sparsely populated regions has been heartening—even in the remote Rocky Mountain areas (Hensley and McAlees, 1969) and in the rural South (Fuddell, 1967). For 1970–1971, the U.S. Office of Education reported the following percentages of local school districts with special education services for the various types of handicapped children:

Speech impaired	85%	Partially hearing	34%
Mentally retarded	60%	Partially seeing	22%
Specific learning disabilities	52%	Deaf	5%
Behavioral disabilities	47%	Blind	4%
Crippling and other health disabilities	36%		

12. Special education for the mildly handicapped has tended to be "an exclusionary process masquerading as a remedial one" (Gallagher, 1972). U.S. Office of Education data indicate that far less than 10 percent of children placed in special education classes were ever returned to regular education.

13. Few data are available on special education programs that have been

cut back. However, during 1971–1972, California reported considerably fewer pupils in special day classes for the mildly retarded than in 1969–1970 (see Table 3.1). This trend is soon likely to spread to other states. However, for 1971–1972 versus 1970–1971, the increase in the number of children in special education classified as having general learning disabilities (mental retardation) for the United States as a whole was 144,500, as contrasted with the average annual increase of 30,902 for the 14-year period 1952–1966.

14. At the outset of the 1970s, nearly three quarters of all special education was at the elementary school level (Martin, 1972). Nevertheless, Mackie (1969) reported a trend for exceptional children to start school earlier and stay longer. Between 1948 and 1966 there was an eightfold increase in high

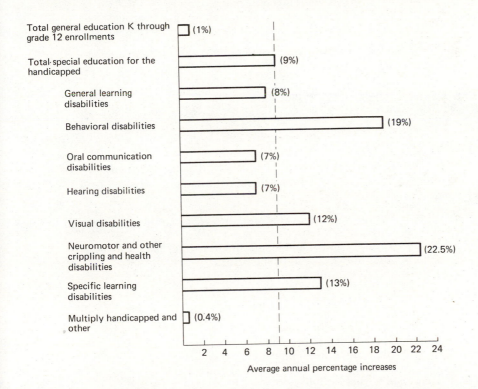

FIGURE 1.2 *Average annual percentage increases in special education enrollments in the United States from 1968–1969 to 1971–1972. SOURCES: K. A. Simon and W. V. Grant,* Digest of educational statistics: 1970 edition. *Washington, D.C.: U.S. Office of Education, 1970. E. W. Martin,* Programs of the Bureau of Education for the Handicapped, U.S. Office of Education. Programs for the Handicapped. *Washington, D.C.: U.S. Department of Health, Education and Welfare (Secretary's Committee on Mental Retardation), 1970. U.S. Office of Education.* Estimated number of handicapped children in the United States, 1971–72. *Washington, D.C.: U.S. Office of Education, 1971.*

school provisions, from 50,486 to 448,000 pupils. At the same time, by 1966, 53,000 handicapped children were enrolled in nursery and kindergarten special education programs. At least this is a beginning. However, the neglect of secondary special education programs has resulted in many handicapped adolescents having very little direct preparation for the world of work (Martin, 1972).

15. Concerning the postschool adjustment of handicapped adolescents, U.S. Office of Education statistics (Martin, 1972) suggest the following for the early 1970s:

21 percent will be fully employed or go on to college.
40 percent will be employed part time.
26 percent will be unemployed but employable.
10 percent will be employed in sheltered workshops.
 3 percent will be totally unemployed even in a sheltered setting.

The need for greater emphasis in *career education* for the handicapped at the secondary school level is obvious.

TYPES OF ADMINISTRATIVE PLANS AND OTHER STRATEGIES

The field of special education has been characterized by a wide variety of administrative organizations and plans. In this section these various plans, including their potentials and problems, are discussed in general terms. They are ordered from the most integrated to the most segregated.

I. Day school plans
    1. Special education instructional materials and equipment service only
    2. Special education consultants to regular teachers
    3. Itinerant or school-based tutors
    4. Resource rooms
    5. Part-time special classes
    6. Self-contained special classes
    7. Combination regular and special day schools
    8. Special day schools
    9. Diagnostic and prescriptive teaching centers
    10. Other day school plans and procedures
II. Residential or boarding school facilities
III. Hospital instruction
IV. Homebound instruction

Day School Plans

With approximately 90 percent of exceptional children in day schools, it is not surprising that a considerable range of types of services have evolved in such settings.

Special Education Instructional Materials and Equipment Service Only

The most minimal and marginal special education service is the provision of special instructional materials and equipment to students who can otherwise get along adequately in the educational mainstream. For example, an educationally blind high school student, as defined by Harley in Chapter 8, may need only brailled texts, a braille writer, and some talking books (recordings).

Special Education Consultants to Regular Teachers

Consultants are central office staff members who primarily provide indirect services to exceptional children by working with the regular classroom teachers. These consultants usually also instruct pupils in diagnostic and demonstration sessions, do some tutoring, and counsel with both pupils and parents. They often prepare specialized instructional materials and instruct the regular teacher and the handicapped child in the use of special equipment and materials. Consultants are defined as devoting 50 percent or more of their time to *indirect* services. In some cases, a distinction is made between the "teacher consultant" who spends 25–50 percent of her time in direct teaching and the remainder in consultative services and the "resource consultant" who provides less than 25 percent in direct services to children. As special educators become more and more reluctant to take problem children off the hands of general educators, this type of service is likely to expand as never before.

Under ideal circumstances, after observing the regular teacher working with the child who has a learning problem, the consultant does diagnostic teaching in an attempt to prescribe and provide the special instructional methods and materials the pupil needs. She assists in the continuous evaluation of the pupil and advises on the complex problem of making the necessary regular classroom adjustments for him to succeed. To serve in this difficult role effectively, consultants need to be master regular classroom teachers themselves, and, in addition, have a high level of expertise in teaching children in their area of specialization. Therefore, extensive advanced graduate preparation is implied. Clearly, a key to success for this type of service is to select productive, capable educators to whom the regular teacher will turn for help. However, special education consultants may encounter considerable resistance from a number of regular classroom teachers. As Smith (1972) has pointed out, special educators traditionally believed the best way to serve most of the mildly handicapped was through special classes. When this practice did not prove very effective, these educators of exceptional children then proposed to serve instead as consultants to the regular teachers. Smith went on to observe: "We special educators have failed to do anything measureable for these children so you get them back. However, we retain the right to tell you how and what to teach these boys and girls." The possibility of most regular classroom teachers being so gullible as to accept such a strategy on a drop-in basis would seem remote. However, when remarkably effective education consultants are made available who can demonstrate a sustained, continuous involvement, their acceptance should be generally assured.

Itinerant or School-based Tutors

This service differs in degree only from the special consultant plan just discussed. Pupils with special needs remain in general education where primary responsibility for their education is retained by the regular classroom teacher. However, here the specialist spends most of her time providing direct services to exceptional children. Under this scheme, the itinerant or school-based tutor spends 50 percent or more of her time in direct services to children. The remaining portion of her time is devoted to consultative services. Since she spends the major portion of her time tutoring pupils individually or in small groups, she may need a small tutoring room. *However, more and more such teachers do their specialized tutoring and small-group instruction in the regular classroom in a team-teaching situation.* In this way the regular teacher can observe what the specialist is doing, and vice versa. Thus the two programs can be integrated and coordinated. Therefore, the special tutor might be viewed as a *helping teacher*. In addition, these specialists observe, diagnose, prescribe, evaluate, and prepare and/or provide specialized instructional materials and equipment. In the future there are likely to be such specialists in each of the instructional areas covered by the chapters in this book.

This type of service plan is not new. Public school speech therapists have functioned as itinerant tutors for years. Too, under the "contact" or "itinerant teacher" plan in the areas of visual and auditory disabilities teachers have operated in a similar fashion. These specialists may serve one or many schools, depending on how many pupils need extra help. For example, each large school might have its own special tutor in specific learning disabilities. In such cases, the difference between a remedial teacher and a special education resource teacher might be insignificant. This type of service, too, is likely to grow substantially as more and more handicapped pupils are kept in general education. The effectiveness of these tutors will be hard to demonstrate. Furthermore, lack of close supervision makes selection and training particularly important. Four of the problems to be met are: (1) to keep the tutor's load within the limits which permit her to do a good professional job; (2) to avoid the assignment of pupils to the service who are in need of more help than it can provide; (3) to avoid accepting pupils who could be handled adequately by general educators with greater effort on their part; and (4) to avoid schedules which place an excessive demand on *travel* time—a major fault of an itinerant program.

Resource Rooms

Under this scheme the exceptional child is enrolled in the regular school program, but is provided with even more special help than the itinerant tutor is able to give. The pupil receives much of his instruction from general education, but, in addition, goes to a resource room to use specialized equipment and materials and/or to receive specialized instruction, either in a tutored situation or in a small group. The important difference between the itinerant-tutor plan and the resource-room plan is that the latter makes possible larger-group instruction. As with the itinerant tutor, the resource-room teacher, if she is to be successful, must function both as an instructor and as a consultant. This plan is suitable for any type of child who can succeed in the regular grades when provided with a reasonable amount of extra assistance.

The modified resource room is a combined special class and resource room. Some of the pupils have the resource room as their homeroom and spend essentially all their time in it. Others use it as originally intended. In either event, the usual procedure is for the resource teacher to serve the one single broad disability area in which she has expertise. However, occasionally, in some small communities, necessity may dictate that she serve children with a variety of learning disabilities. Such a resource-room service cannot be said to constitute a complete program of special education.

The basic problem with the resource-room plan is finding a proficient teacher. She must be a master diagnostic teacher. She must know how to organize her work. She must be an effective consultant with excellent human relations. And she must see herself as a helping teacher working as a team with the regular teachers. This is more difficult to achieve than under the itinerant or school-based tutor plan, since she does have her own classroom to manage. To be effective, her pupil load must be kept within bounds so she can spend sufficient time on each pupil to make an impact. Above all, there is the danger that the resource room will become largely a segregated program. While children may be enrolled in a regular homeroom, they may spend practically all of their time in the resource room. Such a practice, of course, violates the intent of the plan. Yet it is likely to happen often, especially with pupils who are frustrated in the regular grades but find the resource room less oppressive and demanding. They will soon learn that acting-out behavior in general education will gain them more time in special education.

Part-time Special Classes

Under this plan, exceptional children are enrolled in a special class but receive some, if not a great deal, of their *academic* instruction in the regular grades. In this way, exceptional children are to varying extents integrated into general education. Known as the *cooperative plan* in the area of visual disabilities, the system is growing in popularity in a number of areas of exceptionality. The major and important difference between this and the resource-room plan lies in where the pupil has his homeroom.

Like the resource-room teacher, the special-class teacher who integrates her pupils into regular instruction must be especially able. She needs to be good in human relations as well as a fine teacher. She must recognize that simply integrating her pupils physically into the regular grades neither assures their social acceptance nor adequate school progress.

Self-contained Special Classes

Until recent years, far more special teachers have served under this plan than under any other. The majority of them have been special-class teachers of pupils who have been labeled educable mentally retarded. Under this plan, usually pupils with only one type of exceptionality label are enrolled in one special class. Since these special classes traditionally have operated on a self-contained basis, the system has often been described as the *segregated plan,* meaning that the pupils are physically separated for academic instruction from so-called normal children. Under the special-class plan, pupils receive their academic instruction in the special class, but usually share with the children in the rest of the school such out-of-classroom activities as assembly, sports, school clubs, and dining. They may also take industrial arts, home economics, and physical education from the teachers who specialize in these fields at the school. In addition, they may also receive instruction from such system-wide, itinerant specialists as the music and art teachers and the speech therapist.

In some communities, especially in more rural areas, one special class may have enrolled in it children with a number of disability labels. While these classes may be better than no special education at all, it is difficult to see how one teacher could have all the competencies needed to work, for example, with crippled, hearing- and vision-impaired, and retarded children.

In general, the self-contained special-class plan has been most severely criticized when used with slow-learning and disruptive children. Too often the plan has been used to put out of sight pupils the regular teachers do not want. It is to be hoped, however, that this practice will not disguise the appropriateness of the plan, especially for children with severe learning disabilities and for younger children. Certain of these children may need an intensive, specialized curriculum to learn specific skills so as to take a greater part in the regular school program later in their school careers. Perhaps the best example is for young deaf children to learn speechreading and oral language. This plan is justified only where children need a special curriculum, and as yet essentially none has been devised for children with mild learning, behavioral, and intellectual disabilities.

Combination Regular and Special Day Schools

This type of facility serves the typical children of the immediate neighborhood within the given grade limits for the school, plus the exceptional children of a larger geographical area. One classical example is the Ann J. Kellogg School in Battle Creek, Michigan. Usually such schools serve a number of different types of exceptional children, with a broad range of general and special education programs provided. The special education services may be scattered throughout the school or concentrated in a specific portion of it. A large number of the plans already described may be employed in these settings. For example, consultants, special tutors, resource rooms, and self-contained special classes may be found in such schools. The degree of integration of exceptional children into general education varies from school to school. However, since exceptional children usually receive part of their academic instruction in the regular grades, this plan could be viewed as more integrated than the self-contained special day class plan discussed above.

A major problem in these facilities is to prevent "the tail from wagging the dog." The education of the other children may be disrupted by the abnormally high concentration of children with learning difficulties in the school. Another problem is to develop a staff of regular teachers with the interest and qualifications to serve average pupils and a large number of exceptional pupils as well. Inspired administrative leadership and in-service training are just two examples of what is needed to make this plan work smoothly. A constant problem will be to produce psychological, as well as physical, integration, since many of the exceptional children will not come from the immediate neighborhood where the average children reside.

Special Day Schools

A special day school usually serves only one type of exceptional children. These schools are most often found in large cities, since they would be uneconomical to operate for only a few children. Examples of such long-standing special schools include the Spaulding School for Crippled Children in Chicago, the Bronx High School of Science in New York City for the gifted and the Alexander Graham Bell School for the Deaf in Cleveland, Ohio. There are a few special schools, usually in small cities, which cater to the needs of a number of types of handicapped children. Typical of this type is the David W. Smouse Opportunity School in Des Moines, Iowa, which has been in operation for some time. Recently, most of the special day schools have been specifically for children with moderate and severe general learning disabilities, who have been traditionally labeled as trainable and severely mentally retarded. There are more special schools for such pupils than for all other types of exceptionalities combined.

Special day schools have the advantages of providing a physical plant especially designed for the type of handicapped children being served, a range of trained special educators, and a comprehensive array of ancillary medical, psychological, and social services. Two major problems associated with this type of school are isolation of the handicapped children from average children while at school and the long period of time which many pupils must spend on the bus each morning and afternoon. Therefore, this scheme contributes little to "normalizing" education for the children enrolled in these special schools.

Diagnostic and Prescriptive Teaching Centers

Perhaps the newest plan in special education is the *diagnostic and prescriptive teaching center*. These centers are staffed with a team of special educators, often supported by ancillary personnel from the field of psychology and sometimes even from social work and medicine. For short periods of time—usually about a month—the team works intensively with individual children who have learning problems. The goal is to develop a successful, specialized program of instruction for each pupil. Assembled at such centers are the most creative and clinically skilled special educators available. Often they must develop specialized instructional materials and programs needed by the child. In many ways these centers resemble the remedial reading and child-study centers of the past.

Other Day School Plans and Procedures

The nine administrative plans just described for providing public day school services for exceptional children do not exhaust the options in use.

One other such plan involves *team teaching* within one area of exceptionality. This strategy often emerges when a number of self-contained special classes in one area are located in one school. This plan has the distinct advantage of allowing teachers to concentrate on instructing in academic or other areas where they can best teach. In addition, the teachers involved have the opportunity to learn and be stimulated by their colleagues.

Another plan is to provide *boarding homes* for public day school students. In this way, for the school week, exceptional children who reside in rural areas are able to come to larger communities which have the special education facilities they need. The success of this plan depends on finding "houseparents" who are desirable individuals personally, who will accept the handicapped child into the family group, and who will take the time to furnish him with the social, recreational, and cultural activities needed for his out-of-school development. Good in-service training programs for these house parents and ample supervision are needed with this system.

A number of *interdistrict special education plans* have been initiated. An example is the Special School District for the Education and Training of Handicapped Children in St. Louis County, Missouri. This school district seems to have solved the complicated problems of tax structure, transportation, and other such mechanics. Its greatest advantage is in making available a broader array of carefully supervised special education services than could be provided by small local school districts individually. Here too major problems are segregation of handicapped children and the amount of time pupils must spend on the school bus.

Residential or Boarding School Facilities

About 10 percent of U.S. students receiving special education services are in residential settings. There are two basic types of residential units of concern to special educators. One is the traditional *boarding school*, which has been available for over a century, primarily to blind and deaf children. Its prime purpose is to provide special education services that are qualitatively or quantitatively superior to those available in local communities. The other is the traditional-type unit serving primarily the so-called mentally retarded and socially maladjusted. This latter type of facility is provided primarily (1) for the protection of society; (2) for corrective treatment of a non-educational nature; or (3) for the care of the child. In such cases, education is an adjunct to the total program. Such units have a variety of labels, such as training school, hospital and school, or detention home. In this text, these institutions will be called *residential facilities,* as contrasted to boarding schools. The major flaws of these facilities, which tend to be dehumanizing, are discussed in Chapters 2 and 5.

Boarding schools have also come under vigorous attack in recent years, primarily because they are the least effective plan for "normalizing" education and other services for children in need of special help. Children and parents are separated for much of the school year. Placement in such a setting may deprive an exceptional child of living with and learning from so-called normal children. These schools have traditionally not been available to preschool children or to school-age children without self-care skills, including, of course, the multiply handicapped. Another weakness is that boarding schools tend to be the most expensive of special education services. To counter these charges, boarding schools are enrolling increasingly both day and residential students. Furthermore, boarding pupils are encouraged to return home for weekends and for the conventional vacation periods, whenever possible. In an attempt to keep each pupil in intimate contact with his home, boarding school personnel encourage campus visits by parents and arrange for frequent correspondence or telephone conversations between the family and the child. Boarding school students often participate in recreational, church, and other activities in the community if the unit is not too isolated. Furthermore, more resident children than in the past are going to neighborhood public day schools for at least part of their instruction. In these ways, efforts are made to keep the pupils in the community as much as possible. The Oregon Cooperative Plan between the boarding school and the local school district for children with visual disabilities is perhaps best known.

Boarding schools do have a few potential advantages. They can provide a comprehensive program of instruction. Instead of a school program for six or so hours per school day, five days a week, theirs can be a twenty-four-hour day, seven days a week, and the school year can be extended when necessary. In addition, boarding schools are large enough to provide a comprehensive array of educational, vocational, and recreational services. Furthermore, they continue to provide about the only feasible public special education for some rural, isolated children. Too, boarding schools can mobilize specialized, comprehensive diagnostic and counseling services which would be difficult for any small community to provide. Finally, because of the large enrollments of pupils with a specific type of disability, they are able to provide a richer variety of special-subject teachers, especially in the upper grades.

Like day schools, boarding schools are going through a period of transition. As more and more children with mild, moderate, and single learning disabilities are being kept at home, and integrated into general education as much as possible, the boarding schools are being called upon to serve a greater number of multiply handicapped children. Here more intensive and comprehensive services can be provided for such children.

Great care needs to be taken to prevent boarding schools from becoming a haven for neglected, battered, abandoned, and orphaned children. In such cases, boarding homes with foster parents in cities with day school programs are often a better solution. Furthermore, pupil placement in such facilities should not be for the convenience of parents. The reason for placing a child in a boarding school should be because he can make greater progress in such a setting than in any other. (Material on the history of the special boarding school movement appears on page 41.)

Hospital Instruction

Provision for instruction of children confined to hospitals, sanatoria, and convalescent homes is a traditional service of special education. It usually is provided by a local school system, but may be a state- or county-wide program. Examples of types of exceptional children in need of prolonged hospitalization would be the severely emotionally disturbed who need extensive psychiatric care in a hospital setting and the profoundly retarded who are bedbound. In the area of neuromotor and other crippling and health disabilities, the trend is toward reducing to a minimum the length of hospitalization. However, children who are acute nephritics or hemophiliacs or who require extensive corrective measures for orthopedic and other conditions may need extensive hospitalization. Nonetheless, whenever possible they are sent home or placed in foster homes to convalesce between times of surgery and other hospital treatment.

The special teacher, in addition to serving the children who are more or less permanently on the register, works also with those who are hospitalized for shorter periods of time. This group includes the postoperative and children who have recovered sufficiently from an illness or accident to be ready for some engrossing scholastic activity. The effects of hospital instruction are usually psychologically therapeutic as well as educationally useful. Both bedside tutoring and group instruction are, of course, available. A satisfactory overall regimen for the child requires a team approach involving the physician, the nurses, the teacher, and other specialists in the hospital. More and more, especially when small numbers of pupils at any one level are on both homebound and hospital instruction, there is a growing tendency for specially trained teachers to serve children in both settings. Of course, the tele-class, discussed below, facilitates this arrangement.

Homebound Instruction

The most segregating of all special education services is traditional homebound instruction, since the child is not even able to associate with peers who have a disability similar to his own. Usually provided by local school systems, homebound instruction primarily serves two types of children: (1) the chronically ill—usually the bedridden—who will never be able to attend school and (2) those from the regular grades who are con-valescing from an operation, accident, or temporary illness. Sometimes disturbed and retarded pupils are also placed on homebound programs, but this should be viewed as an emergency measure.

Services are provided by either (1) a full-time, itinerant teacher who usually instructs each pupil in his home for one- or two-hour periods about three times a week or (2) the regular classroom teacher who after school instructs one of her regular pupils who is temporarily homebound. The provision of homebound instruction is based on the belief that children, even when confined to their homes, are entitled to an education and to the mental health values that learning activities provide.

It is necessary to reduce isolation to a minimum for pupils on home-bound instruction. News sheets are useful to help homebound children keep informed of as many school, community, and home activities as they possibly can. Whenever possible such children should participate in classroom discus-sions through the use of the home-to-school telephone. By participating in this way in a school group, the homebound or hospital-bound child feels less isolated from his peers. This teaching-by-telephone technique is being used increasingly as an adjunct to both homebound and hospital-school instruc-tion. This service works best for junior and senior high school pupils, but is also used by some schools for one or two of the upper elementary grades. Of course, the video telephone is a distinct improvement over the conven-tional voice-type machine and should work quite well for younger children. Recently, the Bell Telephone Company, in cooperation with the Oakland, California, public schools, developed a device which goes beyond the tradi-tional home-to-school telephone hook-up. By this means the specially trained teacher of the homebound and hospitalized Oakland pupils has been able to operate a *tele-class*. Every morning during the school week she inserts cards into a special telephone equipped with a headset to dial her pupils. Once all of the children are on the line and have their own headsets in place, the class begins. All ten children in the class can talk back and forth with their teacher and among themselves. Thus there can be discussions and question-and-answer sessions. Besides the tele-class sessions, the teacher makes bedside visits later in the day to tutor and test her students and to assign, pick up, and discuss school work. The School of the Air which serves the Australian children who live across the remote Australian out-backs suggests another procedure to bring homebound children into com-munication with each other and with their teacher. With this system, each pupil and teacher has his own transceiver. Educational television (ETV) is another means of supplementing homebound instruction which is becom-ing increasingly available.

A special responsibility is to make sure that home instruction never becomes a device for excluding from school children with unfortunate physical stigmata. It should be used only for children whose problems are so serious that school attendance is impossible or for those convalescing from an illness or accident. An excellent measure of the comprehensiveness and quality of a school's special education program is the degree to which its homebound instruction is kept to a minimum. This can be accomplished when the community provides a reasonably full range of special education programs, augmented by the necessary transportation, and makes frequent re-evaluation of pupils on its homebound program.

Some Final Words on Administrative Plans

1. Each plan that has been discussed has its special uses and limitations. Little scientific evidence exists which establishes one plan as more advantageous than another. Of greater importance than school organization is the quality of instruction. It is no doubt true that any arrangement may be good or bad for a particular pupil, depending on the quality of teaching, the type of curriculum offered, and the characteristics of the child.

2. Administrative plans at the early-childhood education level are just beginning to emerge on a fairly wide scale. Holding promise for the very young handicapped child are indirect services provided through parent instruction and consultation. Specialized nurseries offer hope for the deaf-blind and other multiply handicapped small children.

3. In secondary education for the handicapped, emphasis is strongly on career education for the world of work. Some successful plans of vocational education have evolved, especially the study-work programs, which are discussed in Chapter 3.

4. In higher education, the pioneer effort was made by Gallaudet College in Washington, D.C., a long-established institution of higher learning for deaf youth. Recently a technical institute for the deaf was also started. These examples are discussed in Chapter 7. Probably more higher education will emerge for the handicapped, including some form of institute for even the retarded, many of whom continue to increase in their ability to learn up into their twenties, if not early thirties.

5. It has been widely recommended that a variety of support systems be made available to both regular and special teachers to assist them in serving exceptional children more effectively. Gallagher (1972) has included in his list (1) research and development programs to determine more effective teaching procedures; (2) training programs to guarantee a flow of quality manpower, both paraprofessional and professional; (3) demonstration activities to illustrate the practical promise of new programs; (4) planning and evaluation efforts that will systematically help project future needs and evaluate current efforts; and (5) communication systems designed to keep educators in touch with the newest developments across the country and around the world (Gallagher, 1972).

6. *A special education contract* for mildly retarded, disturbed, or learning-disabled children has been proposed for pilot study by Gallagher (1972) as a means of holding special education more accountable. This contract would be drawn up and signed by general and special educators and by parents

and would be effective for a maximum of two years. Actual specific pupil progress to be attained would be detailed in the contract. It would be agreed that progress would be assessed every six months. The contract could be modified at such times by consent of the parents and educators. The contract would be nonrenewable after two years except by a quasi-judicial type of hearing. Otherwise the pupil would be completely removed from special education and returned to general education.

7. A voucher system has been offered as another alternative by Blatt (1972). Parents of a handicapped child would receive a voucher annually of two or three times the value of the basic expenditure for a regular-school child. They would then have a free choice in determining where to enroll their handicapped child—in public or private school, in general or special education.

8. Finally, an important emerging strategy is *child advocacy*. This concept is aimed at keeping in perspective, if not protecting, the civil rights of children who have not reached their majority. It is a part of society's move toward greater humanism with its heightened awareness of the rights of the individual to be different. This position argues that a child belongs to himself, first of all, and only secondarily—if that—to his society and his parents. Thus, this approach has an integrated, child-centered or child-development focus. To a considerable degree it is a new name to describe a focus that has been a central concern to both general and special educators for centuries. It is a force not only to counter child maltreatment in such classical areas as child beating and child labor, but in innumerable more subtle areas, including special education. The concept is introduced here because of its emerging role in protecting the child against such debilitating labels as mentally ill, mentally retarded, delinquent, and other such terms which often have the concomitant effect of segregating and even institutionalizing children because of their nonstandard behavior or exposing them to therapies and other interventions of questionable value. This concept of *child advocacy* has been included here because it is seen as benefiting the handicapped as well as the minority group and poverty-frozen child. This notion was spotlighted and advanced by the Joint Commission on Mental Health of Children (1970). As yet, there is no agreement on just who should be responsible for this protective function. Should it fall largely to the helping professions such as social workers, child psychologists, psychiatrists, and special educators? Or must the child be protected against these disciplines and their self-interests? Should the various separate services in the various separate departments be placed under one Office of Child Development which would have child-advocacy rights? If a prime function is to improve social services for children, can politicians or bureaucrats (or their appointees) be expected to attack the established systems and services? What role should children, their parents, and handicapped or other target-group adults play in child-advocacy strategies? Is child advocacy to be centered at the local, state, or national level or at all three? What types of child-advocacy agencies or

services should be established? These are the issues on which evidence may become available as a result of the joint efforts of the U.S. Office of Education and the National Institute of Mental Health. Together, at the outset of the 1970s, these agencies awarded six grants to develop different child-advocacy programs. In the meantime, the reader is directed to a series of enlightening articles on child advocacy in the October 1971 issue of the *American Journal of Orthopsychiatry,* which examines both the strengths and weaknesses of the notion. It seems probable that some legal or quasi-legal structure involving perhaps lawyers and judges will need to be devised to protect the child against the various vested interests. Failing this, perhaps a Child Advocacy Committee of interested, knowledgeable, and neutral lay-persons may be the most desirable procedure. In any event, the child-advocacy strategy could result in a new era of better coordinated, comprehensive, quality social services for children in which special education is bound to play an important part. Clearly, the more segregated the special education administrative plan, the more seriously is it likely to be questioned, criticized, and changed by the child advocates.

FACTORS INFLUENCING SPECIAL EDUCATION PLACEMENT

As a greater variety of special education programs become available, much greater flexibility is permitted in school placement. While it is true that the essence of special education is to provide effective individual instruction for each pupil with exceptional needs, the facts of life are that our schools operate largely by group instruction. While considerably more tutoring is and should be available in special education than in general education because of lower teacher/pupil ratios, it is still true that considerable grouping is necessary, given the available resources. Therefore, decisions must be made about (1) the school in which a child is to be enrolled; (2) the homeroom placement; and (3) where and when the pupil is to receive various aspects of his instructional program. In all three areas, placement should always be on a trial basis, after having reached the best possible tentative decisions based on a study of the pupil's own characteristics, his home and community situation, and the educational resources (or options) available. Some 20 influencing factors are listed on page 39. Nevertheless, a major guiding principle should be the concept of "normalization." The child should be integrated into his own home, community, and neighborhood school to the maximum degree possible. Figure 1.3 presents a schema for studying this factor.

Depicted as an inverted pyramid in Figure 1.3 is the array of major administrative plans described in the previous section. This conceptual model is based on the Reynolds framework (1962) and the Deno (1970) cascade model of special education services which elaborates on it. In describing the advantages of this approach, Deno (1970) stated:

The cascade system is designed to make available whatever different-from-the-mainstream kind of setting is required to control the learning variables deemed critical for the individual case. It is a system which facilitates tailoring of treatment to individual needs rather than a system for sorting out children so they will fit conditions designed according to group standards not necessarily suitable for the particular case. It acknowledges that the school system is a giant intelligence test involving multiple work samples and multiple performance judges who invoke highly variable criteria in making their judgments. It is designed to facili-

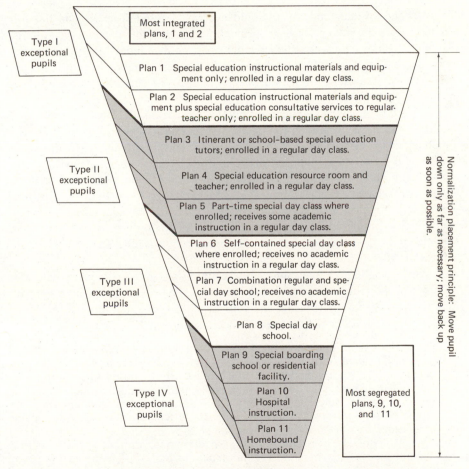

FIGURE 1.3 An inverted pyramid model to display 11 major administrative plans in special education from the most integrated to the most segregated, and from those that should serve the greatest numbers of pupils to those that should serve the least, classified for four types of exceptional children. Note: Plan 7 could shift up one category to serve Type II exceptional pupils when such children receive part of their academic instruction in a regular day class setting, as they often do.

tate modification based upon changing conditions and new assumptions.

The system is flexible and adaptable enough to make it possible to reduce essential special education enrollment while still retaining opportunity for those who require special education service. It can meet the objective of "community based facilities which will keep children as closely as possible within their normal routine setting." It can meet the anxiety of those who fear that the baby will be in danger of getting thrown out with the bath if we move from categorical programing to individualized programing tailored to the nature of the child's learning needs. It gives opportunity for a two-pronged approach—care for the already wounded while moving ahead at the mainstream boundary to help prevent further wounding. [p. 235]

The cascade system (and the pyramid system adapted from it) has the following characteristics. *First*, it projects an array of placement options. *Second*, it shows these options extending from the most integrated to the most segregated. *Third*, it points up that the largest number of pupils should be served in the most integrated programs and the smallest number in the most segregated plans.

In terms of special education placement within this system, the goal should be to move pupils as far upward as possible. Therefore there should be constant evaluation to determine if a pupil can be advanced. While some pupils will require one type of program for a school year or more, others may need it only for months. Furthermore, it should be possible to make large skips in placement. For example, a child may move from Plan 10 (hospital treatment) completely back into the general educational mainstream, or vice versa. Some pupils will require certain services for only part of a day. The goal is to keep the program as little special as possible for the adequate education of the child.

While labeling, categorizing, and grouping are not in keeping with the goal of special education, which is to individualize instruction, there may be some advantage to considering the four types of exceptional children identified in Figure 1.3. These types are defined as follows:

A Type I exceptional pupil is so classified for that segment of his school career (1) when he is enrolled in the regular program of the public day schools, (2) but the teachers in that program have failed in teaching him to such a degree (3) that special supplementary instructional materials and equipment have been made available to him and/or special education consultative services to the regular teachers who work with him; special educators are not directly teaching the child.

A Type II exceptional pupil is so classified for that segment of his school career (1) when the regular teachers have failed in teaching him to such a degree (2) that he is receiving direct instruction from one or more special educators, (3) though he continues to receive part of his academic instruction in the regular program and (4) may be enrolled in either a regular or special class.

A Type III exceptional pupil is so classified for that segment of his school career (1) when he is receiving no academic instruction in the regular program of the public day schools, (2) but is in a separate self-contained special education day program in the local school system.

A Type IV exceptional pupil is so classified for that segment of his school career (1) when he is unable to attend any type of day school program provided by the local school system, (2) but is in a special boarding school or on hospital or homebound instruction.

The major value in identifying these four types of exceptional children is to establish a major goal toward which special educators can aspire in their efforts to achieve maximum integration. One measure of the degree to which the United States and Canada have moved toward integrated special education will be to determine over a period of time the changes in the numbers of pupils classified in each of the four categories. The larger the proportion of pupils in the more integrated plans, the closer special education will have come to its objective.

As stated at the outset of this section, many considerations need to be taken into account in determining the best assignment for any individual exceptional child at any particular time. The more choices available, the greater the discretion that can be exercised. Influencing decision-making for a particular child are likely to be a number of factors related to the individual characteristics of the pupil, his school, his parents, and his community. Some of the major *pupil variables* are (1) type and degree of each learning ability or disability; (2) number of exceptionalities; (3) age at onset of condition; (4) present age; (5) scholastic attitudes, interests, and achievements; (6) behavioral characteristics; (7) social maturity; and (8) present wishes and goals. Among the *school-related factors* would be such items as (1) adequacy of the efforts of the pupil's regular school program if he has been in one; (2) alternate special education options available; (3) proficiencies of the available special educators; (4) types of special curriculum and instructional materials at hand; (5) related services available; (6) distances and travel time involved; (7) locations of the different programs; and (8) relative costs to possible gains. What effect the exceptional child has on the other children and teachers has not been included in this list, but reality suggests that it must be. Some of the *home and community considerations* would include (1) parent attitudes, interests, and wishes; (2) home conditions; (3) neighborhood conditions; and (4) pressures on the child and his family. Of course, any unusual factors peculiar to a given case would need to be considered.

SPECIAL EDUCATION IN PERSPECTIVE

At this point, it is appropriate to set in perspective the evolution of special education services for exceptional children. Perhaps there is no better way of viewing *special education in transition* than by examining the way society has treated deviant individuals over the years, especially over the last decade. In this undertaking four major groups of pupils must be considered. *First* are children with superior cognitive abilities (including the talented and creative as well as the academically able) for whom special education based on homogeneous grouping has not been widely accepted since the advent of mass education and the common school concept. *Second* are the noticeably handicapped such as the blind, deaf, and moderately retarded who historically were provided early with special residential schools and who currently are usually placed in special education programs at the outset of their school careers. *Third* are those with milder learning disabilities (including the marginally retarded and disturbed) for whom special education services have proliferated in recent years, and who usually are first enrolled in the regular grades and then referred for special education by regular classroom teachers when they become too troublesome to manage. *Fourth* are the relatively small number of profoundly handicapped children such as the severely retarded, the uncontrolled epileptic, the seriously cerebral palsied, and the extensively multiply handicapped, who largely continue to be excluded from any type of general or special school program. The social forces affecting the education provisions made for these four major groups have usually not been the same. No attempt will be made here to trace comprehensively the history of special education in any of the areas. A good history of the education of the handicapped is provided by Frampton and Rowell (1938). Furthermore, Hewitt and Forness (in press) have written a survey text from this point of view. In general, this section is intended only as an overview of the major concepts and developments in the growth of special education for exceptional children. However, the discussion tends to emphasize pupils with mild learning disabilities, since they comprise by far the largest group of pupils that constitute educational problems for the schools, and vice versa.

The history of man's treatment of his children, especially the gifted and the handicapped, is one that parallels our social evolution. Generally, over the ages, the able have been revered while the disabled have been rejected and exploited. The early history of the handicapped is particularly pathetic and tragic. In primitive and ancient times the unfit were often abandoned or destroyed, and examples of this practice continue to this day. Beginning in the Middle Ages such children were exploited to amuse others. For example, dwarfs were used as clowns and imbeciles as fools. With modern times a variety of forces have led very gradually to better treatment of the impaired. Perhaps the teaching of compassion by the various religions has been the most positive. Especially in Europe, special credit must be given to the clergy for early innovative efforts to educate the disabled, with physicians following in second place, well ahead of educators. The idea of survival of only the fittest began to fade out after the Industrial Revolution, which introduced such extensive evils as exploitation of child labor while at the same time ushering in an era of greater prosperity, education, leisure, and enlightenment than the world had ever known. For the first time, a fair number of people had time to be concerned about the less fortunate. Nevertheless, until relatively recent years, virtually all that was offered the handicapped by way of education came from private sources—from a few people of compassion who wished to help those less blessed than themselves.

Let us look briefly at the history of public education in the United States. It was not until after the War of 1812 that the free public school system as we know it became established in the United States (Pulliam, 1968). Before that time, education for both the typical and atypical was largely church sponsored, with the exception of private schools, which were available only to the intellectually able and socially elite. Clearly, at this stage, there was no commitment to the concept of equal educational opportunities for all children. In the first half of the nineteenth century, laws were enacted rapidly by the states requiring communities to establish public day schools supported by local taxation. This marked the beginning of the common school for the mass education of all U.S. children. But school attendance was permissive, not mandatory. A fixed academic course of study was offered to all, with the schools making little or no attempt to adjust to the needs of the pupils. Instead, it was up to the students to adjust to the school. Those who would not or could not dropped out, were pushed out, or were not sent to school by their parents. Therefore, the physically and mentally handicapped presented few, if any, problems for the schools. They were simply kept out of school with the other so-called misfits. At this point in the development of American public education, equality of educational opportunity was interpreted to mean simply making available but not requiring the same school program for all children. The picture changed dramatically with the advent of compulsory education laws, beginning in Rhode Island in 1840 and in Massachusetts in 1851. Finally, the mildly handicapped child and the schools "were forced into a reluctant mutual recognition of each other" (Hollingworth, 1923, p. 271). Never before had the schools been called upon to deal with such a broad range of individual differences. How would they deal with the situation? For well over a century since then, school authorities have been looking for solutions. Introduced below are the five major procedures which have emerged.

The Residential School Movement in Special Education

A boarding school for the deaf was established as early as 1817 in Connecticut, one for the blind opened in Massachusetts in 1829, and one for the moderately retarded began in the same state in 1848. By 1850, the residential school movement was expanding rapidly. By 1900, over 30 states had public boarding schools for the deaf, the blind, and the moderately retarded. These first units became the *modus operandi* for serving the handicapped. Today virtually every state has such facilities, and others have been established for the socially maladjusted (delinquent) and even a few for the cerebral palsied. These residential schools provided placement for many of the more severely but not profoundly handicapped. Often parents were required by court order to send such children to these residential units if the local school system would not enroll them in the regular grades and no special day school program was available (see Flowers and Bolmeier, 1964, for examples of rulings). Zedler (1953) also reports on an Iowa Supreme Court case which ruled in favor of the school board rather than the parents who wanted their deaf boy to remain in the regular school program of the local public school. The child was required to attend the state residential school for the deaf to which he had been assigned by the school authorities. After a more recent review of laws and court cases, Weintraub (1972) concluded:

> The Greeks of Sparta placed their cripples on the mountain sides; and the U.S. state governments, since the early 1800s, have placed their handicapped in institutions. Even today, "the general welfare" is often construed to legally sanction coercive methods of protecting society from the deviant. [p. 1]

Public School Exclusions and Exemptions

In every state, as Flowers and Bolmeier (1964) point out, local school authorities may exclude or exempt children from school on a number of grounds. The courts have consistently supported the position that attendance in the public schools is *not a guaranteed right for all, but a privilege* for those who meet a long list of criteria. For example, school authorities have traditionally had the authority to exclude from the public schools any child who is so seriously handicapped physically or mentally as to impede the progress of other pupils, disrupt classroom discipline, and present an undue number of problems for the teacher (Flowers and Bolmeier, 1964, p. 165). These authors reviewed a number of cases in which the court upheld local authorities in exempting cerebral palsied children who slobbered and drooled and retarded children who repeatedly obtained IQ scores around and below 50 on individual intelligence tests. Children have been excluded because of health and handicapping problems, as well as for willful misconduct, unconventional clothes and personal appearance, pregnancy, and a variety of other reasons. Recently, however, the courts have ruled that pupils cannot be excluded from school for marriage or denied graduation because they refuse to wear a cap and gown. At the same time, there has been a rapid progression of court actions making mandatory the provision of educational services for the handicapped, even the severely retarded (Weintraub, 1972). Thus decisions are shifting toward the civil rights of students and away from lending support to school authorities who enact rules that are unreasonably oppressive. Nevertheless, for some time to come the "exclusion and exemption" technique will enable local school systems in many communities to remove a variety of extremely deviant children from the educational mainstream, usually because they are believed to be uneducable or are considered severe behavior problems or disturbing influences upon the rest of the class because of unusual appearance. The perplexing problems are the many borderline cases who benefit little from regular instruction, who disturb the other members of the class, and who demand a disproportionate amount of the teacher's time. Obviously, there are two sides to the coin:

the civil rights of the problem child versus the rights of the other children and the teachers in the school. In the forseeable future, child advocates will meet this dilemma face to face. Perhaps by the 1980s some patterns will begin to emerge.

The Day School Movement in Special Education

By the middle of the nineteenth century, special day schools and classes were being founded as a means of providing handicapped children with a special education program separate from general education while at the same time keeping the youngsters at home rather than in a residential school. A day school for deaf pupils was established in Boston in 1871; a special day class for so-called educable mentally retarded children was founded in Providence, Rhode Island, in 1896; and a special class for crippled children opened in Chicago in 1899. By 1911, about 100 large cities were operating special day schools and classes. (The growth of this type of service for the 50-year period from 1922 to 1972 is depicted in Table 1.3 and Figure 1.1.) Today such facilities exist in even small communities and sparsely populated areas. Much of this movement has been most salutary. At the same time, there has been some undesirable and excessive usage of the strategy. In many cases these day schools and classes came about because parents recognized their children were so clearly handicapped that their educational needs could not be met in general education and so requested special programs. In other cases the pressure came from regular classroom teachers and principals who wanted their problem pupils placed elsewhere. In virtually every one of these latter cases the children ended up by being classified as educable mentally retarded, behavior disordered, specific learning disabled, or some such synonym. It has been these latter programs that have been most open to question. The major difficulty has been that, generally, only two options have existed—the pupil has either been completely integrated physically into the regular program or completely segregated into what was called the "self-contained" special day school or class.

Vignette 1.1 recounts the personal experience of Leonard Eaton, a cerebral palsied person who was segregated into a special class. His story depicts dramatically the hurt and bitterness which a school placement of this kind can produce in students. It raises, too, some serious ethical and moral issues for educators and school authorities.

Vignette 1.1 On Handicapped Education, by Leonard Eaton

You have asked that I explain my feelings on "civil rights" for the handicapped. I am now 29, married, and an attorney for the Federal Government. Although this is not a formula for overnight stardom, it has made me reasonably content. It is therefore difficult to recreate the bitterness and emotional anguish as well as the educational problems that developed for me as a result of a segregated educational system. However, in the hope that I can benefit other handicapped individuals who are still victimized by the same outmoded educational concept, I will try.

My education was segregated because I did not attend class with the non-handicapped student until I entered high school. All disabled students were lumped together in what was called a "special class." Indeed, we were a "special class," since our academic workload was geared to the intelligence level of the lowest achiever in our grade. My non-handicapped friends, all of whom I met outside of school, were learning geometry while I was doing simple arithmetic; they were reading *Ivanhoe* while I was reading "See Spot Run." It was tacitly assumed that since we all were physically handicapped, we also all had the same mental ability. This philosophy of education caused the brighter handicapped students to give up on education. They often became academically lazy. If some instructor did try once or twice to give them grade-level work, by then the student often did not perform because he or she had never developed good work habits. This failure on the part of the bright student was used as further evidence of his incapacity to do grade-level work.

It is obvious that in giving the handicapped student separate and unequal treatment, society is saddling him with an educational disability to add to his physical one.

But this system of learning creates a third burden far greater than the other two. This third burden is intense self-hate. These students often thought of themselves as inferior beings, not so much for their crutches and braces but because of the different treatment these devices brought on. Many students spent their entire academic day dreaming of being with the "norms" (non-handicapped) upstairs, because they were "better" people. Of course, the "norms" never came downstairs to be with us. If by chance there was a meeting on the ground-floor level, it was accomplished with shy embarrassment.

What I am saying here is that much of the argument which led to the outlawing of racial segregation in the schools could be applied in the case of the handicapped. To be treated as inferior makes one feel inferior, and unfortunately leads to inferiority.

Indeed, just as the black man developed his caste system based on the degree of blackness, so the handicapped students develop a system based on the degree of disability. The more disabled you are, the worse you are. In the case of both the black man and the handicapped, it is really society's attitude that engenders this feeling in the individual and creates these hierarchies.

The reasons given for our separation were many. The one most often heard was "they can't manage stairs." (All special classes were on the ground floor.) Doubtless, no one in the educational hierarchy had heard the old saw about Mohammed and the Mountain. The second favorite shibboleth was that we would "upset" the other children. To this can be answered that so does anything which is at first physically strange and different, but that human compassion gained by the non-handicapped child would far outweigh his initial fear.

Integrated classroom work need not be on a full-day basis. It is obvious that the handicapped child has special physical needs which cannot be fulfilled in a normal classroom setting. But some integrated classroom activity can and should be arranged for the benefit of both groups of children. School guidance personnel should become attuned to what areas the handicapped child can participate in and enjoy with the physically normal. Perhaps a girl has exceptional artistic or musical ability. Perhaps a boy can manage an athletic team or be a member of the chess team.

My suggestions may not be easy to implement—but then neither was Brown v. Board of Education, the Supreme Court case which made racially segregated schools illegal. (Eaton, 1970, pp. 1–3)

Sorting and Tracking Pupils in the Public Schools

Traditionally, the schools grouped primarily by grades—which meant by achievement levels—and sometimes by sex. With the advent of the compulsory education laws in the middle of the nineteenth century, under the pressure of serving a broader range of individual differences than ever before, the schools became more sophisticated and more inventive in the processes of classifying, sorting, and streaming and began to take account of such variables as age, socioeconomic status, skin pigmentation, and, especially, the propensity to learn factor, which resulted in *ability grouping*—usually derived from some combination of intelligence and achievement test scores. Even before the 1940s, Harap (1936) reported that ability grouping was the "most common method of adjusting learning to individual differences in the elementary school." And after that, this system, called multitracking and streaming, became even more fashionable, especially in the high schools. By relegating the less able and the nonconforming into the lower track, educators had found a way of setting such children aside. And it must be recognized that a self-contained special class is just another name for this lower track.

Of late, both research and court actions have raised serious questions about tracking. Passow (1962), Heathers (1969), Dahllof (1971), and Findley and Bryan (1971) have reviewed the literature on grouping, including research on its efficacy. From more recent U.S. studies, it would appear that *homogeneous grouping works to the disadvantage of slower children* in most of today's schools. Apparently, in a heterogeneous group, such pupils learn considerably from their somewhat more able peers, teacher expectancies tend to be higher for them, and teachers devote a substantial amount of time in attempting to bring them up to group norms in school achievement. Conversely, *homogeneous grouping works to the advantage of more able students.* Such pupils appear to be more stimulated by and to learn more from their intellectual peers. In addition, in such settings, teachers make the curriculum more demanding and challenging. In the United States, currently, when teachers of heterogeneous groups of pupils are pushed to the limit and must make choices and so neglect some children, their compassion generally leans to limited learners. They work with them to the neglect of the gifted.

It is interesting to note that U.S. studies on homogeneous versus heterogeneous grouping conducted before the 1954 Supreme Court ruling against "separate but equal" schools showed different results. The benefits of homogeneous groupings then accrued to slow learners. In those days, at a time of more rigid academic standards, U.S. teachers, in a heterogeneous setting, as a group, when forced to make choices, concentrated on average and able learners, neglecting the dull by leaving them largely to sit out their school days.

In Sweden, Dahllöf (1971) has recently found streaming to create somewhat different results. As in the United States, he found homogeneous grouping to have moderate benefits for the more able learners. However, he found there was no corresponding disadvantage for slow learners. Perhaps Swedish teachers in lower tracks, in their stress on scholastic accomplishments, push their pupils harder than their counterparts in the United States. Another possible explanation may be that the range of individual pupil differences is not so great in general education in Sweden. In this connection, it will be recalled that Sweden has twice as much special education as any other country in the world surveyed in the UNESCO study reported earlier in the chapter (see Table 1.2), including the United States and Canada. Much of this was to assist children with mild general and specific learning difficulties in the 3R's, through both special classes and itinerant tutors who supplemented the regular teachers, including those teaching a lower track. It would appear that one strong result in the rapid growth of ancillary special education services in Sweden has been to counter the possible negative effects of homogeneous grouping of slow-learning pupils.

The literature is further complicated by a study of streaming in the primary schools of England (Barker-Lunn, 1970). Generally, the data were unfavorable to streaming for any group. However, little learning of any kind took place when teachers who believed in streaming were assigned a heterogeneous group of pupils. Clearly, the prevailing educational philosophy of the school system, as well as the individual teacher's own priorities, greatly influences what happens to slow and rapid learners in a nonstreamed school setting.

The relevant court actions, of which there are a growing number, have been reviewed by Ross, DeYoung and Cohen (1971) and Weintraub (1972). Only a few of the landmark ones will be presented here. The first was the historic Supreme Court decision in 1954 concerning racial segregation (Brown versus Topeka, Kansas, Board of Education). The court ruled against the dual, separate but equal school-system concept. Even about a quarter of a decade later, its full impact has yet to be realized in general and special education because so many *de facto*, if not *de jure*, segregated schools still exist. However, widespread "busing" began by court orders in 1971, aimed at hastening the pace of integration. This too would appear to be only one stop-gap measure, an alternate for comprehensive housing and social integration. Eventually, the Supreme Court decision of the 1950s will have the same dramatic effect on the schools as the compulsory education acts of the 1850s had a century before. Again the schools are being faced with an increase in heterogeneity of pupils, many of whom cannot keep up to grade standards. And again school authorities have been responding with a resurgence of their established practices of using multitracks—and increasing the numbers of special classes which become the lowest track. This practice is encouraged by teachers' associations, which have become more militant and more unionistic. To improve working conditions for their members, these groups frequently demand *more* special classes for disruptive and slow-learning children. Thus, with racial integration, to an even greater degree than ever before, lower tracks, including special classes, have been becoming repositories for unwanted, minority group children. But two court cases are changing the picture. In the 1967 case of Hobson versus Hansen, Judge J. Skelly Wright (1968) ruled that the track system must be abolished in the District of Columbia because it is unconstitutional in that it discriminates against black *as well as poor children generally*. According to this ruling, the system violated the equal protection clause of the Constitution. Since then, the ruling has been appealed and upheld by a four to three decision of the U.S. Court of Appeals (Smuck versus Hobson, 1969). The second landmark litigation was brought to the California District Court of Northern California in behalf of Mexican-American children labeled educable mentally retarded and placed in special classes in Monterrey County (Diana versus State Board of Education). It was argued that the intelligence tests used as a basis for placement were inappropriate in that they were culturally biased, used standard English, and were standardized largely on native-born Americans. In a 1970 stipulated agreement order signed by both parties, it was agreed that (1) intelligence testing will be conducted in the primary language of the child, using interpreters when bilingual examiners are not available; (2) Mexican-American and Chinese children in special classes will be re-evaluated and removed when misclassified; (3) special efforts will be made to aid misplaced children to readjust to regular classrooms; and (4) the state will undertake to develop and standardize more appropriate intelligence tests. Other court cases, especially in California and Massachusetts, are being conducted, which may be traced through the bibliographical aids found in the back of Flowers and Bolmeier (1964) and through Ross, DeYoung, and Cohen (1971) and Goldberg and Weintraub (1972). These involve (1) the rights of other minorities, especially blacks; (2) parent involvement and/or approval for special class placement; (3) the establishment of a child advocacy commission, including members who are parents to oversee testing and classification; and (4) punitive damages for misplacement. It will likely be years before these litigations converge on the U.S. Supreme Court. Nevertheless, it can be anticipated that neither segregated special schools and classes nor any other form of tracking will be viewed as a substitute for schools that are integrated in terms of ethnic background, race, and socioeconomics. What if the Supreme Court ruled against tracks and all self-contained special classes across the nation which serve primarily ethnically and/or economically disadvantaged children were forced to close? Passow (1967) has answered this way: "If tomorrow morning, every child could be placed in an integrated school, many are so seriously retarded academically that they would still need, as they do now, a great deal of special help". The challenge of the future is to obey the laws of the land, yet provide equality of educational opportunity for the large numbers of children from the slums and rural pockets of poverty who make up such a substantial percentage of our handicapped children. Such a program will likely involve as-yet-unforeseen innovations in both special and general education, but a number of practices are evolving which would appear to be constitutionally acceptable. Clearly there must be special services for deviant pupils without segregation.

Special Services for Deviant Pupils without Segregation

What the future holds for the education of exceptional children is closely tied to society's interpretation—through the courts—of what constitutes equality of educational opportunity for all children. The courts today are saying that only in the most severe cases of disability, if then, is it permissible to segregate deviant pupils from so-called normal boys and girls. Therefore, it would appear that *the role of special education is to enable handicapped and gifted children to learn to the maximum of their potentialities in integrated programs wherever possible*. The problem is, how do we best attain this goal?

It will be hard indeed to realize our objective. For one thing, unfortunately, not all educators have caught up with the courts in their concepts of what constitutes equality of educational opportunity. Furthermore, some educators fail to appreciate the full extent of the individual differences which exist among school children. Others believe that regular teachers alone are capable of dealing with essentially all pupil deviations. Still others feel that difficult and different children are someone else's job—often without specifying who that someone else might be. There are educators, too, who fail to recognize that negative teacher attitudes toward exceptional children result in the ostracism and even the rejection of such children in school, even though they are physically integrated. Finally, there are the extreme environmentalists, who believe that identical school programs for all children will best help to overcome economic and social inequalities. In view of these and other attitudinal problems that we face, it would be hazardous simply to place children with marked deviations in the regular school program and let them sink or swim. There would likely be far too much of the former and not enough of the latter.

Individual differences in pupils are real, and they need to be dealt with adequately, responsibly, and constitutionally. In our search for ways to do this we can examine the many excellent publications in the literature on individualizing instruction and on individual differences, including Gagné (1967); Goodlad (1966); Henry (1962); Thomas and Thomas (1965); and Tyler (1965). These publications, however, tell us little about what to do concerning the unique profile of qualities of each exceptional pupil. We have little evidence as to whether we should teach (1) to remedy weaknesses; (2) to accentuate strengths; or (3) to develop each dimension considered important by the schools in a balanced fashion. Certainly, the latter has been the approach in general education—supplemented sometimes by remedial education to correct weaknesses, especially in reading. Conversely, special educators of the handicapped have tended to concentrate on correcting weaknesses, placing secondary concern on the other aspects of a comprehensive curriculum. A few general and special educators talk of teaching through strengths to weaknesses. A classic example is to use strengths and interests in the manual and motor areas to teach weak academic skills. Even fewer special educators of the disabled favor teaching to accentuate strengths. Only in the area of the gifted has there been concern about developing outstanding attributes. Again, essentially no research has focused on comparing the relative effectiveness of these various strategies. It would appear that our current practice in special education for the handicapped of attempting to remedy disabilities was borrowed from the *medical model* of diagnosing the trouble and trying to cure it. Our tendency of holding exclusively to this strategy needs to be critically examined. *How much human potential has been squandered because we have drummed away at a weakness when there was a hidden strength to be nurtured!*

In spite of our limited knowledge about how to group and teach children with marked individual differences, some practices appear to be emerging that should be acceptable, morally and legally. With each advancing decade, regular classroom teachers have devoted more attention to individual instruction and have done more and more small-group teaching. Perhaps the strategy of working within the regular classroom holds the greatest promise of all. Much more individualized and small-group instruction should be possible within the ungraded classroom as more special educators become available to serve as helping teachers and consultants, as more team teaching is practiced, as more extra teachers are provided through such plans as the *three on two* (three teachers for two classrooms), and as more paraprofessionals and others are brought into the classroom. In short, *since segregated grouping will not be permitted, individualizing of instruction will need to be done within the educational mainstream through flexible within-classroom grouping, team teaching, tutoring, computer-assisted instruction, and special edu-*

cators serving as helping teachers and consultants. Segregated special class placement will likely be permitted when it can be demonstrated that exceptional children make greater progress in such facilities. And it will be up to the special educators to demonstrate this, not to assume it. Accountability is here to stay. We probably will be able to make three main cases. *First*, as general education becomes more heterogeneous, the gifted are likely to be slowed down more and more. We should be able to show that ability grouping with their intellectual peers for part of the day enhances their scholastic progress. *Second*, we should be able to remove children with major specific disabilities from the regular classroom for a small part of the day for special instruction from a special tutor. *Third*, segregated special education will probably be permitted for the more severely handicapped who need a very different instructional program.

Emerging Dimensions for Special Education

The preceding discussion demonstrates dramatically why trends in the education of exceptional children are more difficult to discern today than ever before. Turmoil and profound changes are taking place in society, in the schools, and in special education. For these reasons, this textbook is focused on *special education in transition.* Described below are 12 major developments that will affect the field of special education as it moves toward the twenty-first century.

1. *Nothing is likely to affect special education more than social change.* Every area of American society today is in a state of flux, as Reich (1970) points out in *The Greening of America.* Serious questions are being raised concerning the adequacy of our present politics, institutions, and professions (Wallia, 1970). Today, too, people who formerly lived in silence with poverty, poor health, pollution, inadequate schools, and the population explosion are raising their voices and demanding attention. Modern man is setting higher values on human dignity, including the right to be different. Ethnic and racial minorities are becoming more and more proud of their heritage, language, and mores. At the same time, public education is being challenged as never before. People are tired of the limited menu offered by most schools— on which pupils must exist or be labeled misfits and discarded. Fitting pupils to the schools must finally stop, many people are saying. Furthermore, as never before, citizens are questioning our priorities in committing our resources.

Despite all of these forces, the establishment, including the educational establishment, is resisting change. With this state of affairs it is not possible to predict the future of special education. What we must recognize is that well over half of all handicapped children come from the slums. Thus what happens to the disadvantaged will profoundly affect what happens to special education. Perhaps the best way to reduce the need for special education is to improve the conditions of the poor. We need to eliminate urban decay and deterioration, poverty, insensitive public education, prejudice, and lack of opportunity for all if we are to remove some of the root causes for much of special education. Therefore, special education programs, especially for the handicapped, will be greatly strengthened by coordinated and cooperative efforts with other social services working to improve the home, school, and community environment of children. Without a total ecological approach special education is likely to fail in its ultimate purpose.

2. *Noticeable changes are taking place in the diagnostic, prescription determining, and placement processes in special education.* Traditional procedures have been characterized by three phenomena. *First,* psychologists and physicians have had responsibility for diagnosing disabilities, giving pupils labels, and declaring them eligible for a specific type of special education. *Second,* we have supported a multidisciplinary team, case-study approach for gathering comprehensive information about the problems of the child, his family, and his milieu. *Third,* pupils have been placed in special education usually without real parent involvement and often without even parental consent. Only after placement—if then—have attempts been made to arrive at an effective instructional program for them.

We are now committed to the premise that the profession which provides the treatment must do its own diagnosis, though information may be requested from the other disciplines. Therefore educators, not members of other professions, must have prime responsibility for educational diagnosis and school placement. Similarly, the multidisciplinary team approach is falling into disfavor. Much of the information gathered by the team has been valueless for educational treatment; the team has tended to vie in finding as much as possible wrong with the defenseless child; and the team has proven to be more costly and time consuming than it was worth for educational purposes. In addition, there is now a growing commitment to involve parents in the placement process. The prime purpose of educational diagnosis is no longer seen as simply a labeling and placement process. Instead, its first aim is to determine the levels at which a child is functioning—baseline data, if you will. Then interventions are tried out on him by prescriptive-clinical teachers until effective ones are found. Only then is the initial diagnostic process terminated and a determination made of where the pupil might best be placed to receive the instructional program he needs. In addition, we now recognize that the pupil and his instructional program need continuous evaluation to assure that the best match has been found. Finally, there is a continuous need for special education to be highly flexible so as to meet the changing needs of exceptional children at different times in their school careers.

3. *Traditional practices of categorizing exceptional children by means of medical, psychological, and social criteria and terminology are slowly being replaced by a system that has significance for special education.* Conventional terms such as "epileptic," "psychotic," and "mentally deficient" have little or no meaning for purposes of educational treatment. Even such milder terms as "brain injured," "emotionally disturbed," and "mentally retarded"

have little significance. In addition, such labels are stigmatizing and reduce the expectancy for pupil progress. Furthermore, we have found that children with different handicapping labels are receiving or need to receive the same general and special education programs. Too, wide individual differences exist among children in each area of exceptionality, a fact which is sometimes overlooked, resulting in stereotyping. Two new principles have evolved: (1) the learning requirements of exceptional pupils—not their etiology or medical classification—should determine the organization and administration of special education services (Reynolds, 1971); and (2) exceptional children should not be so identified for special education purposes unless a special education program is available which in all probability will be more effective than general education. These concerns have led to two major developments concerning the classification process. *First,* if labels must be used, there seems to be emerging an agreement that a series of special learning ability and disability categories be derived from distinctive, special education interventions which have been found uniquely effective for a group of children with similar characteristics. *Second,* there is a trend away from labeling children and toward designating different types of special educational treatments, such as those in the motor, visual, auditory, language, affective, cognitive, and academic domains.

4. *With today's emphasis on respect for the individual, the practice of segregating children with learning disabilities into self-contained special education programs are about to be markedly reduced.* In their efforts to expand special education, those in the field have welcomed whatever children the regular schools have chosen to reject as misfits, usually placing such pupils in a segregated special program. Both the parents through the courts and special educators because of a new moral and ethical awareness are demanding that children with mild learning disabilities not be stigmatized either by labels or by segregation into separate programs. Our long-term belief that unequal, extra, separate special education promotes equal opportunity is being challenged from within and without. Educational segregation by race, ethnic group, sex, or disability label will no longer be accepted except where the special needs of the child are clearly demonstrated. Thus segregated special education is likely to be reduced sharply as we approach the twenty-first century. Concurrently, a larger number of exceptional children than ever before will be retained in regular education for longer periods of time. All educators, both general and special, need to live up to the basic principle that each exceptional child is primarily a child with the same rights to acceptance, understanding, and education as any other child. One current objective is to loosen state laws having to do with exceptional children. As the Policies Commission of the Council for Exceptional Children stated: "Regulatory systems which enforce rigid categorization of pupils as a way of making allocations of children to specialized programs are indefensible" (Reynolds, 1971). Three broad principles now determine our action. *First,* we reaffirm that broad goals of special educators are not different from those of other educators. The

focus is on the individual and his optimal development as a skillful, free, and purposeful person, able to plan and manage his own life and reach his highest potential in society (Reynolds, 1971). *Second*, exceptional children need individualized instruction to develop their personal skills and knowledge and also group instruction with a cross section of their age mates to develop their social effectiveness. *Third*, and therefore, exceptional children should be integrated into the educational mainstream to the maximum extent possible and provided with special education services only when necessary. Whenever possible special education should be made available through team teaching of regular and special teachers in the regular classroom.

5. *We can anticipate a drop in the number of special education programs in some areas of exceptionality in favor of quality.* In the past, we have operated on the philosophy that there is something about special education which makes it better than general education, even for children with mild behavior and learning problems. Therefore, the number of special education services has far outstripped the supply of trained, capable special educators to staff them. In the future, however, we will be less likely to place children with mild disabilities in special education programs. And only to the degree that we can secure quality personnel and demonstrate that we have effective instructional programs are we likely to expand our services. A guiding principle is that special education programs should be initiated only when proficient personnel are available and discontinued when they are not. But we are far from implementing this principle. In 1971, it will be recalled, Balow (1971) reported that one half of the 125,000 special educators in the United States were not even certified for their positions and that only 15,000 annually were getting some updating and upgrading, much of it very minimal.

6. *The various groups of special education and other professional personnel are becoming less isolated from each other.* There have been far too many gaps, barriers, and feuds among different professional groups. Society, which pays the bill, cannot be expected to tolerate these divisive forces. Educators are developing a greater respect for each other and are beginning to work in cooperation. Special education for the learning disabled; remedial education; compensatory education for the disadvantaged; psychological services for children with behavior disorders; and public school speech therapy are all ancillary services to general education and are all related. They require coordination and cooperation to be productive. Competition at the expense of the other professions and the consumer has no place in humanistic programs aimed at assisting our fellow man. It is rewarding that these groups are starting to coordinate their efforts. It is also encouraging that all ancillary personnel and programs are growing in their recognition that they are wholly owned subsidiaries of general education.

7. *We can anticipate major changes in teacher-preparation programs in special education as we approach the twenty-first century.* During the 1950s and 1960s, the trend was toward undergraduate and fifth year preservice training programs. This development represented a reaction against the inadequacy

of add-on, marginal graduate preparation usually conducted through summer sessions for regular teachers shifting over to special education. Many of these teachers had been away from teaching for years while raising a family and were enticed into special education by its attractively low teacher/pupil ratios, by nondemanding classroom teaching regimens, and by traineeships to take a few retread courses in summer sessions. The product was not always satisfactory. As a substitute, undergraduates with no classroom teaching background were recruited and trained, often through fifth-year programs. Essentially all of these new teachers found employment in segregated special education settings where they as well as their pupils were sheltered. But today the pattern is changing. More and more special educators are required to work in integrated situations (1) as consultants to regular educators; (2) as team teachers with the regular teacher; (3) as diagnostic-prescription specialists; and (4) as tutors for complex cases. To be effective, this consultant-resource-helping-clinic teacher requires a high level of expertise. For such persons we will probably move toward selecting young, experienced master teachers from the regular grades providing them with leave with pay, fellowships, and other inducements such as wage increases to encourage them to take *at least two-year graduate training programs.* The undergraduate and fifth-year programs will be reserved for the narrow specialties such as for speech therapists or teachers of the blind, deaf, and moderately retarded. It does not seem likely that enough of these high-level specialists can be recruited and trained to serve pupils with quite mild learning problems. Instead, the field of special education will probably be narrowed to those with major learning disabilities, and a variety of paraprofessional personnel will be trained to assist these master special educators.

8. *The number of children with multiple disabilities continues to increase, making barriers among the various areas of exceptionality even more indefensible than in the past.* The implications of this trend are still unclear. Apparently as many as one half of children with moderate and severe disabilities have them in multiplicities. On the one hand, it is possible that educators will be trained more comprehensively so as to work with essentially all of the several serious learning disabilities of multiply handicapped pupils. On the other hand, schools may be organized to bring together teachers, each with different, narrow specializations to work with these children. This latter plan is likely to be a more practical one.

9. *Special education for children with learning disabilities is being profoundly influenced by behavior-modification and behavioral-objectives movements.* These strategies have been discussed in detail in an array of books, including one by Becker, Engelmann, and Thomas (1971). As a result, one sees special education as moving away from the era characterized by a philosopher of "give us your defective, defeated, and unwanted: we will cherish and shelter them" (Deno, 1970). Perhaps we are overreacting to the charge that we have not taught enough. In setting down narrow and specific objectives and in shaping children toward them by rewarding the responses we

favor, we may be force feeding too much. The challenge of these strategies is to assure that the pupil is not treated as a mindless object to be molded as educators see fit. There may be things a child does not want or need to learn and others that he does. In all probability, a balance among mental health, discovery, and behavior-shaping teaching approaches is necessary to enable each pupil to grow in self-esteem, self-actualization, and self-proficiency. In the meantime, the behavior-shaping techniques have given us a procedure for teaching effectively children formerly considered uneducable and untrainable. Special education is thus moving to implement its basic position that no child should be excluded or expelled from school except under extraordinary circumstances.

10. *There is likely to be an increase in pre-, high-, and post-school programs in the years ahead.* In the past, most special education was offered at the elementary school level. Many exceptional children, however, need to begin their education at an early age if they are to make optimal progress in school and more nearly approach their potentials. Therefore early education is provided to more such children today than ever before so as to give them the necessary tools to succeed in general education. On the increase are specialized nurseries and kindergartens and specialized components of regular early education programs which serve handicapped children. Home-training programs are also being developed for parents of infants with special needs. In addition, since individual differences in scholastic aptitude and achievement increase with age, high school programs are being increased as never before. Finally, a follow-up of each exceptional student after he leaves school, placement assistance, and postschool education where needed are responsibilities of the school. A beginning is being made at providing such programs.

11. Since the first edition of this volume appeared in 1963, *there has been a good accumulation of behavioral research applicable to the education of exceptional children.* Summaries of the status of knowledge up to the 1970s are given, for example, in the *Encyclopedia of Educational Research* (Ebel, 1969), in the *Review of Educational Research* (Reynolds, 1969), and in the *Exceptional Children Research Review* (Johnson and Blank, 1968). It has long been known that most educational practices are based on tradition and philosophy and not on scientific evidence. In special education particularly, progress toward correcting this deficiency has been accelerated recently. The years ahead could constitute a bright era for the exceptional child if the shift continues from practice based on tradition to practice based on sound experimentation. We need to know much more than we do about educating pupils with special learning abilities and disabilities. Research on developing and evaluating specialized instructional approaches should have the highest priority. However, since behavioral research can never be expected to prove anything conclusively, there will always be a need to use, as well, the best common sense available in establishing, maintaining, modifying, and discontinuing school policies and procedures when appropriate.

12. *There has not been nearly as great an increase in concern for special education for the gifted in the past decade as there has been for the handicapped.* Priorities have been given to the disadvantaged and the learning disabled. It is unfortunate that educators cannot seem to give equal emphasis to both ends of the continuum at the same time. Surely if we are to find a better way of life, our philosophy of equality of educational opportunity for all students demands that the most creative, innovative, and critically able of our youth be given every chance to advance to the maximum of their capacities. As more and more disadvantaged and learning-disabled pupils are integrated with middle class and normally learning students, the gifted are going to be more and more penalized. Some people would take the position that the less able should have an opportunity to learn from the more able. Others would argue that such a view represents a belief in mass education through a common school with standard treatment for all students. Still others would say that the gifted should not be exploited at all to assist the less able. In any event, certainly for part of their school day and at other times outside of regular school hours, gifted children should have an opportunity to be optimally stimulated by their peers and by resource persons, both educators and informed and talented persons in the community. Hopefully, as we move toward a common public school for all, as we must, this opportunity will be provided as the school fits itself to the pupils through making available an array of options and enrichments for each child.

SUMMARY

Since compulsory education laws were enacted over a century ago, most school systems have increased the number and kinds of provisions offered for dealing with individual differences among students. This is well illustrated by the expanding numbers of *special education services for exceptional children* that have become available, especially in recent years. These pupils include both the educationally gifted and the educationally handicapped. In addition to those with superior cognitive abilities, classified as exceptional are pupils with motor, visual, auditory, communication, behavioral, cognitive, and specific academic learning disabilities. Special education services utilize differently trained educators; different curricular content; different methodology; and/or different instructional materials and equipment than are traditionally provided in the educational mainstream.

A pupil should be classified as exceptional and provided with special education as a supplement to, or as a replacement for, the regular school program only after all attempts have failed to adjust the general education program for the child. Such a student should be labeled exceptional only for that segment of his school career when it has been determined through trial provisions that he can achieve greater scholastic progress with direct or indirect special education services than he could with only an adequate regular school program. Therefore, only a very small percentage of the school population should be so classified. Traditionally, in addition to the 3 percent in the area of the gifted, 1½ percent have been considered as severely handicapped and 9 percent as having mild behavioral and learning disabilities.

By 1970, approximately 4 percent of U.S. and Canadian children were in special education—3 million in the United States and about 120,000 in Canada. About 90 percent were in day schools and 10 percent in boarding schools. Education for exceptional children is today in a state of transition; the trend is toward greater integration of special and general education services. The most integrated special education strategies enroll the exceptional children in the regular grades and provide only needed special instructional materials and equipment and consultative services. The next most integrated plans also allow the exceptional pupils to receive all or at least part of their academic instruction in the mainstream of education but supplemented with special education tutors who serve as helping teachers to regular instructors or who preside over resource rooms or special classes. Quite segregated are self-contained special day schools and classes. The most segregated plans are boarding schools and hospital and homebound instruction. Not only is the press toward greater integration of all special education into general education, but major efforts are underway in this period of transition to "normalize" education for many of the 9 percent who have mild behavioral and learning disabilities. The principal means are removing stigmatizing labels and seeking heterogeneity in the regular schools with respect to student background.

There is general agreement among both general and special educators that each pupil should be encouraged to achieve to the maximum of his abilities. While general educators tend to adopt an across-the-board teaching strategy, teachers of the gifted interpret this to mean an emphasis on teaching to strengths, while teachers of children with behavioral and learning disabilities concentrate on correcting, alleviating, or circumventing weaknesses. No research is available on the relative effectiveness of these three strategies, suggesting that a balanced approach may be advisable until evidence to the contrary is forthcoming.

In their efforts to correct pupil shortcomings and to counter past charges of not setting their expectancies sufficiently high, special educators of the handicapped have turned to the determination of specific behavioral objectives and to the use of behavior-modification techniques for attaining these objectives. While these techniques appear to be dramatically effective, concerned persons have pointed out that these procedures need to be balanced with individualized opportunities, so that the handicapped may discover and learn what is of interest to them, and with group activities, so that they can test and perfect their social skills.

In the years ahead, both general and special educators are likely to be molded by a variety of changes which are taking place in society today. One force is a heightened awareness of the right of the individual to be different and to pursue his own goals in his own way. This new humanism should augur well for integrating more deviating students into general education. But all is not blue sky ahead, since many militant teacher organizations are demanding that disruptive and slow-learning children be removed from general education and placed in segregated special education programs. Thus, if more children with unusual education characteristics are to be accepted into the educational mainstream, it is imperative that teacher attitudes change. To accomplish this, all educators need to become familiar with the characteristics and educational needs of such pupils, to find there is little that is mysterious about education for exceptional children, and to discover that they can be effective in dealing with a much wider range of individual differences than they encountered in the past. In a real sense, exceptional children provide every educator with an opportunity to test the degree to which he believes in accepting and serving all boys and girls regardless of intellectual capacity or socioeconomic, racial, or ethnic background. Each educator needs to ask, "To what degree do I believe that the only thing of lasting value one receives in this life is what one gives to others?"

Resources

The information below covers exceptional children generally. At the end of each chapter in this book has been included a short section similar to this one. In the subsequent ones are outlined the agencies, organizations, professional literature, and other resources that the reader will find most helpful for the particular areas of exceptionality under consideration.

The *Council for Exceptional Children* (CEC), first known as the International Council for the Education of Exceptional Children, observed its fiftieth anniversary in 1972, having been formed in 1922 by 12 founding members from the United States, Canada, and India. It is the one professional organization that draws together special educators from all the areas of exceptionality. In 1941, CEC became a department of the National Education Association (NEA), but in 1969 it chose to become independent again, retaining an affiliation with NEA as an associate organization. Thus it is able to work more easily with the American Federation of Teachers (AFT) as well. The CEC headquarters in the early seventies was at Suite 900, Jefferson Plaza, 1411 S. Jefferson Davis Highway, Arlington, Virginia 22202, though a move to Reston, Virginia, is planned. By 1972, its membership had grown to over 40,000, up from 17,000 in 1962. It subsumes 47 state and provincial federations and over 700 local chapters, as well as the international organization. There are nine CEC divisions: (1) the Association for the Gifted (TAG); (2) the Council of Administrators of Special Educators (CASE); (3) the Council for Children with Behavior Disorders (CCBD); (4) the Division for Children with Communication Disorders (DCCD); (5) the Division for Children with Learning Disabilities (DCLD); (6) the Division on Mental Retardation (CEC-MR); (7) the Division on the Physically Handicapped, Homebound, and Hospitalized (DOPHHH); (8) the Division for the Visually Handicapped (DVH); and (9) the Teacher Education Division (TED). In addition to a special publication series, CEC headquarters publishes three journals: *Exceptional Children*; *Education and Training of the Mentally Retarded*; and *Teaching Exceptional Children*. Published also are the *Exceptional Child Education Abstracts*, a product of the CEC Information Center (CEC-ERIC Clearinghouse). In addition, the Canadian members of CEC publish *Special Education in Canada* (c/o 81 Ranleigh Avenue, Toronto 12, Ontario, Canada).

The *U.S. Department of Health, Education and Welfare* (DHEW) includes many public agencies concerned with exceptional children. The most important to special education is the Bureau of Education for the Handicapped in the U.S. Office of Education (USOE), which has three divisions: (1) Education Services; (2) Training Programs; (3) Research. Other DHEW units which provide public services for the handicapped include the U.S. Public Health Service; the U.S. Social and Rehabilitation Service; the U.S. Social Security Administration; and the U.S. Office of Child Development. Mail addressed to Washington, D.C. 20201, will reach the various DHEW units.

Articles on special education appear in a rich array of journals. For the broad field, in addition to the CEC publications, the following are suggested: *Journal of Special Education; Focus on Exceptional Children; Journal of Learning Disabilities; Behavioral Research and Therapy; Children; Journal of Applied Behavioral Analysis; Journal of Individual Psychology; Special Education* (12 Park Crescent, London W1, England); *Understanding Children. The Exceptional Parent* is a journal for parents. Perhaps the next most useful abstracting services after *Exceptional Child Education Abstracts* are *Education Index; Current Literature; Dissertation Abstracts; Perceptual-Cognitive Development Abstracts;* but especially *Rehabilitation Literature* published by the National Easter Seal Society for Crippled Children and Adults, 2023 West Ogden Avenue, Chicago, Illinois 60612. This monthly publication is a major secondary source for current articles and books of interest to all disciplines concerned with rehabilitation of the handicapped in its broadest sense.

Persons with a problem about the education of an exceptional child may also communicate with the director of special education in their state or provincial departments of education. Some of these departments have consultants in a number of areas of exceptionalities whose services are available upon request. These departments also provide a wide range of other services. Of course, increasing numbers of local school systems are also employing consultants in special education who can render invaluable assistance.

References

Anderson, P. J. Teacher expectancies and pupil self-conceptions. Unpublished doctoral dissertation, University of California, 1970.

Balow, B. Teachers for the handicapped. *Compact*, 1971, **5(4)**, 43–46.

Barker-Lunn, J. C. *Streaming in the primary school: A longitudinal study of children in streamed and non-streamed junior schools.* Slough, England: National Society for Educational Research in England and Wales, 1970.

Becker, W. C., Engelmann, S., and Thomas, D. R. *Teaching: A course in applied psychology.* Chicago: Science Research Associates, 1971.

Beez, W. V. Influences of biased psychological reports on teacher behavior and pupil performance. Unpublished doctoral dissertation, Indiana University, 1968.

Blatt, B. Public policy and the education of children with special needs. *Exceptional Children*, 1972, **38**, 537–545.

Dahllöf, U. S. *Ability grouping, content validity, and curriculum process analysis.* New York: Teachers College Press, Columbia University, 1971.

Deno, E. Special education as developmental capital. *Exceptional Children*, 1970, **37**, 229–237.

Dolberg, M., and Lenard, H. M. The concept of disability and handicap revisited. *Cerebral Palsy Journal*, 1967, **28**, 3–6, 9.

Dominion of Canada Bureau of Statistics. *Statistics of special education for exceptional children, 1953–54.* Ottawa, Canada: Queen's Printer, 1959.

Dominion Bureau of Statistics, Education Division. *Statistics of special education for exceptional children, 1966.* Ottawa, Canada: Queen's Printer, 1967.

Dunn, L. M. (Ed.) *Exceptional children in the schools.* (1st ed.) New York: Holt, Rinehart and Winston, 1963.

Eaton, L. On handicapped children. *Performance*, 1970, **20(9)**, 1–3.

Ebel, R. L. (Ed.) *Encyclopedia of educational research.* (4th ed.) New York: Macmillan, 1969.

Findley, W. G., and Bryan, M. M. *Ability grouping: 1970 status, impact, and alternatives.* Athens, Ga.: Center for Educational Improvement, University of Georgia, 1971.

Fisher, H. K. What is special education? *Special Education in Canada*, 1967, **41**, 9–16.

Flowers, A., and Bolmeier, E. C. *Law and pupil control.* Cincinnati, O.: W. H. Anderson, 1964.

Frampton, M. E., and Rowell, H. G. *Education of the handicapped.* New York: Harcourt Brace Jovanovich, 1938.

Friedman, R. J., and MacQueen, J. C. Psychoeducational considerations of physically handicapped conditions in children. *Exceptional Children*, 1971, **37**, 538–539.

Fuddell, S. E. *The South's handicapped children: 1945/65.* Atlanta, Ga.: Southern Regional Education Board, 1967.

Gagné, R. M. (Ed.) *Learning and individual differences.* Columbus, O.: Charles E. Merrill, 1967.

Gallagher, J. J. The future special education system. In E. Meyen (Ed.), *The Missouri Conference on the categorical/non-categorical issue in special education.* Columbia, Mo.: University of Missouri, 1971.

Gallagher, J. J. The special education contract for mildly handicapped children. *Exceptional Children*, 1972, **38**, 527–535.

Goldberg, I. I. Human rights for the mentally retarded in the school system. *Mental Retardation*, 1971, **9(6)**, 3–7.

Goodlad, J. I. *School curriculum and the individual.* Waltham, Mass.: Blaisdell, 1966.

Gozali, J., and Meyen, E. L. The influence of the teacher expectancy phenomenon on the academic performance of educable mentally retarded pupils in special classes. *Journal of Special Education*, 1970, **4(4)**, 417–424.

Harap, H. Differentiation of curriculum practices and instruction in elementary school. In G. M. Whipple (Ed.), *The grouping of pupils.* Thirty-fifth Yearbook, Part I, National Society for the Study of Education. Chicago: University of Chicago Press, 1936.

Hardy, M. I., McLeod, J., Minto, H., Perkins, S. A., and Quance, W. R. *Standards for educators of exceptional children in Canada.* Downsview, Ont.: National Institute on Mental Retardation, 1971.

Haskett, Sister M. S. An investigation of the relationship between teacher expectancy and pupil achievement in the special education class. Unpublished doctoral dissertation, University of Wisconsin, Madison, 1968.

Heathers, G. Grouping. In R. L. Ebel (Ed.), *Encyclopedia of educational research* (4th ed.) New York: Macmillan, 1969.

Heintz, P. The relationship between teacher expectations of academic achievement and current school achievement of educable mentally retarded pupils in special classes. Unpublished doctoral dissertation, Teachers College, Columbia University, 1968.

Henry, N. B. (Ed.) *Individualizing instruction.* Sixty-first Yearbook, Part I, National Society for the Study of Education. Chicago: University of Chicago Press, 1962.

Hensley, G., and McAlees, D. *Special education in the West.* Boulder, Colo.: Western Interstate Commission for Higher Education, 1969.

Hewett, F. M., and Forness, S. *Education of exceptional learners.* Boston: Allyn & Bacon, in press.

Hollingsworth, L. S. *The psychology of subnormal children.* New York: Macmillan, 1923.

Johnson, G. O., and Blank, H. D. (Eds.) *Exceptional children research review.* Arlington, Va.: Council for Exceptional Children, 1968.

Johnson, J. L. Special education in the inner city: A change for the future or another means for cooling the mark off? *Journal of Special Education,* 1969, **3**, 241–251.

Joint Commission on Mental Health of Children, *Crisis in child mental health: Challenge for the 1970's.* New York: Harper & Row, 1970.

Jones, J. W. Problems in defining and classifying blindness. *New Outlook for the Blind,* 1962, **56**, 115–121.

José, J., and Cody, J. J. Teacher-pupil interaction as it relates to attempted changes in teacher expectancy of academic ability and achievement. *American Educational Research Journal,* 1971, **8**, 39–49.

Lilly, M. S. Special education: A teapot in a tempest. *Exceptional Children,* 1970, **37**, 43–49.

Mackie, R. P. *Special education in the United States: Statistics, 1948–66.* New York: Teachers College Press, Columbia University, 1969.

Mackie, R. P., Williams, H. M., and Hunter, P. P. *Statistics of special education for exceptional children and youth, 1957–58.* Washington, D.C.: Government Printing Office, 1963.

Marland, S. P. *Education of the gifted and talented.* Washington, D.C.: U. S. Office of Education, 1972.

Martens, E. H., Harris, C., and Story, R. C. *Statistics of special schools and classes for exceptional children, 1947–48: Chapter 5, Biennial survey of education in the United States, 1946–48.* Washington, D.C., U.S. Office of Education, 1950.

Martin, E. W. Programs of the Bureau of Education for the Handicapped: U.S. Office of Education. *Programs for the handicapped.* Washington, D.C.: U. S. Department of Health, Education and Welfare (Secretary's Committee on Mental Retardation), 1970.

Martin, E. W. Individualism and behaviorism as future trends in educating handicapped children. *Exceptional Children,* 1972, **38**, 517–525.

McLean, R. The effects of teacher expectations on the achievement of educable mentally retarded pupils. Unpublished doctoral dissertation, University of Kansas, 1968.

Meyen, E. (Ed.) *The Missouri conference on the categorical/non-categorical issue in special education.* Columbia, Mo.: University of Missouri, 1971.

Mumpower, D. L. Sex ratios found in various types of referred exceptional children. *Exceptional Children.* 1970, **36**, 621–622.

Passow, A. H. The maze of the research on ability grouping. *Educational Forum,* 1962, **26**, 281–288.

Passow, A. H. *Toward creating a model urban school system: A study of the Washington, D.C. public schools.* New York: Teachers College Press, Columbia University, 1967.

Pulliam, J. D. *History of education in America.* Columbus, O.: Charles E. Merrill, 1968.

Reger, R., Schroeder, W., and Uschold, D. *Special education: Children with learning problems.* New York: Oxford University Press, 1968.

Reich, C. A. *The greening of America.* New York: Random House, 1970.

Reynolds, M. C. A framework for considering some issues in special education. *Exceptional Children*, 1962, **28**, 367–370.

Reynolds, M. C. The education of exceptional children. *Review of Educational Research*, 1969, **39**, whole issue.

Reynolds, M. C. Policy statements: Call for response. *Exceptional Children*, 1971, **37**, 421–433.

Rice, M. C., and Hill, A. S. *Statistics of special education for exceptional children, 1952–53: Chapter 5, Biennial survey of education in the United States, 1952–54.* Washington, D.C.: U.S. Office of Education, 1958.

Rosenthal, R., and Jacobson, L. *Pygmalion in the classroom: Teachers' expectations and pupils' intellectual development.* New York: Holt, Rinehart and Winston, 1968.

Ross, S. L., DeYoung, H. G., and Cohen, J. S. Confrontation: Special education placement and the law. *Exceptional Children*, 1971, **38**, 5–12.

Simon, K. A., and Grant, W. V. *Digest of educational statistics, 1970 edition.* Washington, D.C.: Government Printing Office, 1970.

Smith, J. O. *Personal communication.* Seattle, Wash.: University of Washington, 1972.

Thomas, R. M., and Thomas, S. M. *Individual differences in the classroom.* New York: John Day, 1965.

Thorndike, R. L. Review of R. Rosenthal and L. Jacobson, Pygmalion in the classroom. *American Educational Research Journal*, 1968, **4**, 708–711.

Tyler, L. E. *The psychology of human differences* (3d ed.) New York: Appleton-Century-Crofts, 1965.

United Nations Educational, Scientific and Cultural Organization. *A study of the present situation of special education.* Paris: UNESCO, 1971.

U.S. Department of Health, Education and Welfare. *National health survey, 1965.* Washington, D.C.: Government Printing Office, 1967.

U.S. Office of Education. *Estimated number of handicapped children in the United States, 1971–72.* Washington, D.C.: U.S. Office of Education, 1971.

Vincent, W. S. Class size. In R. L. Ebel (Ed.), *Encyclopedia of educational research* (4th ed.) New York: Macmillan, 1969.

Wallia, C. S. (Ed.) *Toward Century 21: Technology, society, and human values.* New York: Basic Books, 1970.

Weintraub, F. J. Recent influences of law regarding the identification and educational placement of children. *Focus on Exceptional Children*, 1972, **4(2)**, 1–11.

Weintraub, F. J., Abeson, A. R., and Braddock, D. L. *State law and education of handicapped children: Issues and recommendations.* Arlington, Va.: Council for Exceptional Children, 1971.

Wishik, S. M. Handicapped children in Georgia: A study of prevalence, disability, needs and resources. *American Journal of Public Health*, 1956, **46**, 195–203.

Wright, J. S. The Washington, D.C. school case. In M. Weinberg (Ed.), *Integrated education: A reader.* Beverly Hills, Calif.: Glencoe Press, 1968.

Zedler, E. Y. Public opinion and public education of the exceptional child—court decisions 1873–1950. *Exceptional Children*, 1953, **19**, 187–198.

Opposite: While they seldom reach literacy level in written language, most typical pupils with Down's syndrome can learn to count, group, and do simple addition. (Photo courtesy Hawaii State Department of Public Instruction; photographer, Robin Kaye.)

children with moderate and severe general learning disabilities

CHAPTER OUTLINE

PART 1: AN ORIENTATION TO INTELLECTUAL INADEQUACIES
  Mental Retardation Broadly Defined
  Mental Retardation Redefined
  General Learning Disabilities Defined
  Classification
  Prevalence
  Causes
    Unknown Etiologies
    Pathological Etiologies
    A Final Note on the Terms "Exogenous" and "Endogenous"
  Other Literature
PART 2: SPECIAL EDUCATION FOR CHILDREN WITH MODERATE
        AND SEVERE GENERAL LEARNING DISABILITIES
  Terminology
  Definitions and Descriptions
  Prevalences
  Identification
  Classification
  Educational Provisions for the Moderately Retarded
    Early Curricular Approaches
    Traditional Curricular Approaches
    Present-day and Emerging Curricular Approaches
  Educational Provisions for the Severely Retarded
    Traditional Practices
    Future Directions
  Effects of Moderately and Severely Retarded Children on Families
  Residential Facilities
  Postschool Occupational Services for the Moderately and Severely Retarded
  Emerging Directions in Special Education
        for Moderately and Severely Retarded Children

PART 1: AN ORIENTATION TO INTELLECTUAL INADEQUACIES

For a good part of his history man has been searching for new and more appropriate terms by which to designate persons with intellectual inadequacies. One reason for this quest is that as civilization advances, intellectual competence becomes increasingly prized, so that negative values are soon attached to any term used to describe persons with cognitive limitations. Thus there has been a continuous pursuit for new terms, which, at least when they first come into use, are more socially acceptable than the old ones— although before too long they too acquire negative connotations. Another reason for the continuing search is that the condition known as mental retardation is so complicated, with so many different causes and levels of manifestation, that it is virtually impossible to include such diversity under one rubric. Yet we continue to search for a term that will do the job. Finally, each of the many disciplines responsible for different aspects of the field, including education, psychology, sociology, medicine, speech pathology, and social service, is inclined to coin a term or develop a definition suited to its orientation. Even more confusion is generated when a broad approach is taken to nomenclature in an attempt to satisfy all lay and professional groups with one set of terms and criteria. This is what has happened with the generic term "mental retardation." Recently, special educators have been asking whether the term has utility for them.

Mental Retardation Broadly Defined

For over a decade, the field of mental retardation has been dominated by the broad, socioeducational definition prepared by Heber (1961) for the American Association on Mental Deficiency (AAMD). Recognizing that only a very inclusive description could encompass the diversity of the field, the many disciplines involved, and all ages and levels of retardates, Heber arrived at the following logical[1] definition: "Mental retardation refers to (1) subaverage general intellectual functioning, (2) which originates during the developmental period, and (3) is associated with impairments in adaptive behavior" (p. 499). According to this definition, three criteria must be met before a person may be labeled mentally retarded.

In terms of his criterion 1, Heber defined *subaverage general intellectual functioning* operationally as performance that is greater than *one standard deviation below the population mean* for the age group involved, as measured by an individual test of general intellectual functioning. Since such well-known individual intelligence tests as the 1960 edition of the Stanford-Binet Intelligence Scale, the 1955 edition of the Wechsler Adult Intelligence Scale, the 1949

---

[1] A *logical* definition is descriptive in nature, using well-reasoned statements which can be confirmed by observation. An *operational* definition is more specific, utilizing quantified values.

edition of the Wechsler Intelligence Scale for Children, and the 1967 edition of the Wechsler Preschool and Primary Scale of Intelligence use a mean IQ score of 100 and a standard deviation of 16 or 15 IQ points, persons with IQ scores below 84 on the Stanford-Binet scale and 85 on the Wechsler scales could be classified as mentally retarded. (See Figure 2.1 for the distribution of deviation IQ scores.)

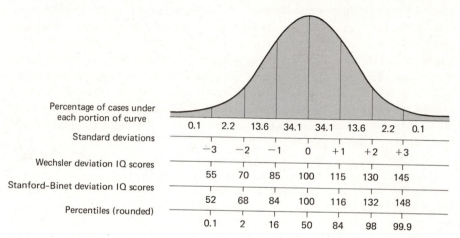

Percentage of cases under each portion of curve: 0.1   2.2   13.6   34.1   34.1   13.6   2.2   0.1

Standard deviations: −3   −2   −1   0   +1   +2   +3

Wechsler deviation IQ scores: 55   70   85   100   115   130   145

Stanford–Binet deviation IQ scores: 52   68   84   100   116   132   148

Percentiles (rounded): 0.1   2   16   50   84   98   99.9

FIGURE 2.1 *The theoretical normal probability curve of intelligence test scores showing the distribution of deviation IQ scores and percentages of cases under each segment of the curve.*

Heber's second criterion, namely, that mental retardation must have to have *originated during the developmental period*, applies approximately through the first 16 years of life. Under this operational definition, persons whose intelligence in childhood was normal but who obtained low IQ scores in adulthood due to neurological damage or mental illness are not to be classified as mentally retarded.

Heber's third criterion, an impairment in *adaptive behavior*, was defined logically only, and differently at different age levels. During the preschool years, it means a slow rate of growth in such developmental or maturational skills as walking, talking, and other sensory-motor-cognitive accomplishments. During school years, impaired "learning" ability is the unadaptive behavior which qualifies a pupil for classification as mentally retarded for special education purposes. Among adults, poor "social" adjustment in terms of an inability to maintain oneself independently or to earn a living in competitive employment is the prime criterion for designation as a mental retardate.

Of course, many factors other than mental retardation can cause children to be slow in learning to talk or to experience difficulty learning in school or cause adults to have problems in getting and holding a job. Persons cannot be labeled mentally retarded just because of an impairment in adaptive behavior. Furthermore, they cannot be so classified just because they have IQ scores below 85. To be designated mentally retarded, an individual must meet both of these criteria, and must have had the condition before his sixteenth birthday. *This cannot be overemphasized.* If an IQ score below one standard deviation were the sole criterion, approximately 16 percent of the population could be classified as mentally retarded (see Figure 2.1).

Mental Retardation Redefined

For purposes of this text, the all-purpose Heber-AAMD definition is replaced by two more specific ones.

The term "mental retardation" is restricted to its classical *sociolegal meaning* of social incompetence. Therefore, a more precise terminology would be "sociointellectual inadequacy," though it is unlikely that this cumbersome nomenclature will ever be adopted. An adequate sociolegal definition would need to elaborate on old English laws in this area which have strongly influenced legal actions in the area in both the United States and Canada. By 1959, in Great Britain, the term *mental deficiency* was replaced with *mental subnormality* and defined as follows:

> A state of arrested or incomplete development of mind so severe that the patient is incapable of leading an independent life or of guarding himself against serious exploitation or, in the case of a child, that he will be so incapable when an adult. [Tredgold and Soddy, 1970, p. 7]

As early as 1944, the Education Act of Great Britain was amended to abolish the application of the terms "mental deficiency-mental subnormality" to children on the basis of their scholastic inability. Since then, the only types of persons designated by such terms in that country have been those who are socially incompetent, or are destined to be. Thereafter, children with severe enough intellectual inadequacies to require special education services with an academic emphasis have been known as the educationally subnormal (ESN). Perhaps, more than 25 years later, it is time the United States and Canada followed the lead of Great Britain and divorced scholastic inability from mental retardation.

The following logical, sociolegal definition elaborates on the British one. It will be the one used in this text, but hopefully it will find broader usage. It is designed to prevent a child from being called mentally retarded for educational purposes, and to restrict the usage of this term.

> *Mentally retarded individuals include not more than that 1 percent of each ethnic or racial subgroup who are so deficient in general intellectual ability that their inability to care for themselves, coupled with their disruptive behavior in some cases, is so severe, when compared with their age mates in the community, that they require assistance, care, and protection in excess of that which average parents can be expected to provide during their childhood, or that which average communities should be able to provide during their adulthood.*

Unfortunately, it is not possible to operationalize precisely this definition as yet. Criterion-referenced tests are not available designating minimum standards of intellectual functioning and of social maturity for each age group in each cultural milieu in which an individual is likely to find himself.

Instead, we must rely on our broad and nationally standardized, *norm-referenced* appraisal devices. To be classified as mentally retarded, a person would need to score below the 1.0 percentile for his age and cultural group on both such individual tests of intelligence as the Stanford-Binet administered in his native tongue and on such individual tests of social maturity as the Vineland Social Maturity Scale and the AAMD Adaptive Behavior Scale.

The reader may wonder why even a restrictive sociolegal definition for mental retardation is retained. It is because it appears unrealistic to expect it to be completely abandoned by society. By some label, the condition has existed since the beginning of man and will continue to exist. Furthermore, society will increasingly be called upon to protect individuals who have inadequate intellect and to assist them to function independently. Such services might include placement in residential facilities, sheltered workshops, halfway houses, or foster homes; making available vocational rehabilitation and other training programs; having the courts serve as advocates, guardians, or custodians; and providing Social Security support funds. Thus the concept of mental retardation and its restrictive operational definition needs to be retained to enable qualifying individuals to receive social services to which they are entitled, while protecting some persons from being wrongly labeled.

General Learning Disabilities Defined

It is proposed that the term "mental retardation" no longer be applied to pupils for special education purposes. It is not educationally relevant, and it is associated with the stigmatizing condition of social incompetence. In its place, the term *general learning disabilities* is substituted. Beginning on page 84, this terminology is discussed more fully. For now, it is defined as follows:

> *Pupils with general learning disabilities are those who require special education because they score no higher than the second percentile for their ethnic or racial subgroup on both verbal and performance types of individual intelligence test batteries administered in their most facile language.*

Classification

For over a century, throughout Europe and North America, the field of mental retardation has been divided into three levels according to degree of intellectual inadequacy. The changing nomenclature over the years for these three categories and for the generic terms is traced in Table 2.1. Just as it has been proposed that the term "mental retardation" be dropped from educational parlance, so it is now proposed that "educable," "trainable," and "custodial" no longer be used for reasons that will be discussed later in this chapter and the next. (It should be noted that there has always been a fourth group, with IQ scores approximating 75–85, who have been known as "borderline mental retardates" to professional persons in residential facilities and generally as "slow learners" to educators, although one state, Ohio, has used for years the term "slow learner" as a synonym for the "educable" mentally retarded.)

TABLE 2.1 Descriptive Terminology for Retarded Persons Classified into the Three Classical Levels of Intellectual Inadequacy

Intellectual Levels	Approximate IQ Ranges (for White, Native-born)	United States and Canada			Great Britain			Rest of Europe
		Recent Traditional	Early 1900s	Late 1800s	Recent Traditional	Early 1900s	1800 and Before	Traditional
I	50±5 to 75±5	Mild (semi-independent) (educable)	High grade	Moron	Mild	Feeble-minded	Simpleton	Debile
II	25±5 to 50±5	Moderate (semidependent) (trainable)	Middle grade	Imbecile	Moderate	Imbecile	Fool	Imbecile
III	Below 25±5	Severe (dependent) (custodial)	Low grade	Idiot	Severe	Idiot	Idiot	Idiot
Generic terms	Below 75±5	Mental retardation	Mental deficiency	Feeble-mindedness	Mental subnormality	Mental deficiency	Amentia	Oligophrenia

Not only did Heber (1961) develop an astoundingly broad definition of mental retardation for the American Association on Mental Deficiency, he also developed, to accompany it, a five-level classification system based on measured intelligence. Table 2.2 describes these five levels, including their descriptive terminology and IQ characteristics. They are psychometric divisions based upon the standard deviation demarcations of our traditional intelligence test. Since they are not logical divisions based on differential treatments, their prime use is for statistical analysis and epidemiological studies. For this reason, Heber's five levels have not been widely adopted by practitioners. However, they have served the useful purpose of shifting us away from the three traditional categories.

TABLE 2.2 *Five-Level Classification System of the American Association on Mental Deficiency Based on Intelligence Test Scores*

Descriptive Terminology	Levels of Impairment	Standard Deviation Ranges	Corresponding Range in IQ Scores for National Sample on Whom Test Was Standardized	
			Stanford-Binet (SD = 16)	Wechsler Scales (SD = 15)
Borderline	-1	-1.01 to -2.00	68-83	70-84
Mild	-2	-2.01 to -3.00	52-67	55-69
Moderate	-3	-3.01 to -4.00	36-51	40-54
Severe	-4	-4.01 to -5.00	20-35	25-39
Profound	-5	Below -5.00	Under 20	Under 25

SOURCE: Adapted from Heber, 1961, pp. 58-59.

What adaptive behavior can be expected of persons who are classified into the various categories of retardation? Clearly, there are no sharp distinctions between persons falling on either side of the various demarcation lines. However, some general descriptions are outlined in Table 2.3 for the four levels of intellectual functioning. These have emerged over the years as having more meaning for persons involved in behavioral (educational, psychological, social, and vocational) interventions than either the conventional three categories or Heber's five-level system. For this reason, they are retained in this textbook to organize the material in this and the next chapter, although it is recognized that advocates of the removal of all labels and categories would consider these descriptions limiting and therefore harmful.

Prevalence

How many people are mentally retarded? The most frequently quoted figure in the United States is the 3 percent estimate contained in the report of President Kennedy's Panel on Mental Retardation (Mayo, 1962). In Canada, Shaw (1962) has used a figure of 3.4 percent. Are these estimates defensible? To help us answer these questions, Heber (1970) has summarized 28 prevalence surveys conducted in Europe, Japan, and the United States between 1906 and 1966. The median value is *one per hundred* (1 percent), with a range from 0.16 percent to 23 percent. In general, the number has moved upward from about a modal figure of 0.5 percent at the turn of the century to the present 1 percent. The appallingly high figures, such as the 23 percent, are based on studies of school-age children using the dual criteria of an IQ score

TABLE 2.3 *Typical Adaptive Behavior Expectancies for Persons with General Learning Disabilities by Four Levels of Intellectual Functioning*

Intellectual Levels (Approximate IQ Scores for National Sample on Whom Test Was Standardized)	Age Levels		
	Preschool (under 6)	*School Age (6-18)*	*Adult (over 18)*
Mildly retarded (60 ± 5 to 75 ± 5)	Slightly slow in walking, talking, and caring for self; but usually indistinguishable from average children and therefore unidentified before entering school	Capable of learning academic skills between the 3d- and 6th-grade levels only; therefore literate	Capable of vocational, personal, and marital independence; thus most lose identification in adulthood. The more retarded may need some supervision and guidance
Moderately retarded (35 ± 5 to 60 ± 5)	Noticeably slow in learning self-help skills; but usually do learn to walk, feed self, and speak simply; toilet training will be minimal at this age	Capable of school learning between kindergarten through 3d grade; therefore still typically illiterate	Capable of employment in supervised unskilled occupations, often only in sheltered workshops; very rarely attempt marriage or unsupervised independent living
Severely retarded (20 ± 5 to 35 ± 5)	By 6 may finally have learned to walk and feed self, but very little toileting, speaking, or other self-help skills at this age	Capable only of rudimentary learning of nonacademic skills in areas of self-care, and elementary speech	Some capable of performing chores and other simple tasks even in home or sheltered workshop; need permanent care from parents, relatives, or society
Profoundly retarded (below 20 ± 5)	Usually learn at best minimal ambulatory skills; rarely any feeding, speaking, toileting, or other self-help skills; many permanently bedbound	Some capable of some ambulation and feeding; many continue permanently bedbound and helpless; never learn to speak	Incapable of any self-maintenance or vocational usefulness; need permanent nursing care

SOURCE: Adapted from Sloan and Birch, 1955, p. 262.

of 75 or 80 and below and learning problems in school. When such criteria are applied to metropolitan school districts with heavy concentrations of slums and minority groups, it is not surprising that such inflated estimates result. As already pointed out, using such loose and inappropriate criteria, one could get a figure even closer to 50 percent if one selected black slum children or poor youngsters from selected ethnic minority groups such as Indians, Mexican-Americans, and Puerto Ricans. These inflated estimates point out the inappropriateness of defining mental retardates as persons with IQ scores below 70, 75, 80, or 85, based on norms derived from a cross section of the population, since the large preponderance would be represented by middle class whites.

Heber (1970) has provided other interesting data on the prevalence of mental retardation. When mental retardation is defined broadly, as in the Heber-AAMD socioeducational definition, evidence is provided for the following three points. *First,* prevalence rises dramatically as children enter school, reaches a peak at 14 years, and falls off sharply as children leave school. This pattern demonstrates that the majority of persons designated as mentally retarded have been so labeled only for the latter part of their school years. *Second,* for the United States, the high prevalence figures tend to be associated with the South, with blacks and other racial and ethnic minority groups, with low socioeconomic class, and with large families. *Third,* there is a considerable risk of mental retardation recurring in the same family. For example, among institutionalized retardates, the risk of siblings being retarded ranged from a high of 74.9 percent for the so-called cultural-familial to a low of 13.6 percent for Down's syndrome (mongoloid), with a median of about 36 percent.

From this vast and carefully compiled array of data amassed by Heber (1970), the following recommendations are made:

1. When mental retardation is defined restrictively in sociolegal terms meaning social incompetence due to intellectual inadequacy, a prevalence figure of 1 percent of the population seems defensible. The 3 percent figure of the Panel on Mental Retardation (Mayo, 1962) and the 3.4 percent figure used in Canada by Shaw (1962) are 300 percent too high.

2. The approximate ratio of cases of mild to moderate to severe-profound mental retardation based on this restricted sociolegal definition is 12:3:1, or 75, 20, and 5 percent, respectively, but the trend is toward fewer mild and more severe cases. For example, while it is recognized that there is a movement toward only the more retarded being placed in public residential facilities, the population of these institutions, based on the five-level Heber-AAMD classification system, at the outset of the 1970s, was mild and border-line, 18 percent; moderate, 22 percent; severe, 33 percent; and profound, 27 percent.

3. These estimates need constant, critical examination. They should be adjusted to suit specific local conditions and populations.

For use in special education, prevalence figures for pupils with mild, moderate, and severe learning disabilities will be presented later in this chapter and in the next.

Causes

When one adopts the broad Heber-AAMD socioeducational definition of mental retardation with its 3 percent prevalence estimate, one arrives at a very different etiological (causation) picture than if one uses the narrower sociolegal definition with its 1 percent prevalence estimate. The more one broadens the definition, the more unknown causes of retardation result. Based on the Heber-AAMD definition, not more than 6 percent of mental retardation conditions have known etiologies, while 94 percent are classified as unknown and unclassified (many presumed multigenetic in nature). Based on the restricted sociolegal definition, the ratio becomes approximately 15 percent known to 85 percent unknown. For the even more restricted sample of retarded persons in state residential facilities, the ratio is 25 percent known to 75 percent unknown etiologies. Therefore, in spite of active research efforts in recent years, very little is yet known about the causes of mental retardation. The larger group, persons with unknown etiologies, tend to be mildly retarded. Other terms for unknown causation are *nonpathological, aclinical, endogenous,* and *cultural-familial.* Persons making up the small group with known etiologies are spread across the full IQ range for retardation, but are concentrated among the moderately, severely, and profoundly retarded. Terms used to describe this small percentage are *pathological, clinical, exogenous,* and *brain damaged.* Many of these latter persons are said to have clinical types of mental retardation, by far the most prevalent one being Down's syndrome, which will be discussed shortly.

For years it has been recognized that the theoretical normal probability (Gaussian) curve of intelligence shown in Figure 2.1 is a hypothetical one. There is strong evidence that intelligence is not normally distributed but skewed to the lower end. This is due to an overlay of the pathologically or neurologically impaired who pile up at the bottom end of the curve, as shown in Figure 2.2. Dingman and Tarjan (1960) have calculated the proportions under the normal probability curve and in the overlay or excess. Overall, they estimated that 6 percent of those with IQ scores below 70 would fall outside the regular curve and 94 percent under it. This excess would be only 1 percent of the 50–70 IQ group, but would be 55 percent of the 20–50 group and over 99 percent of the below 20 group.

Unknown Etiologies

There is much debate about the causes of retardation among the 94 percent with IQ's below 70 who fall under the Gaussian curve. These persons have been labeled nonpathological because no evidence of organic brain damage can yet be detected. On the one hand, many workers in the biological sciences hold to the *biological hypothesis,* contending that future research

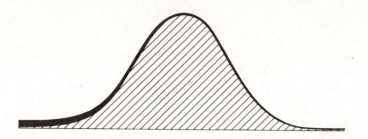

FIGURE 2.2 *Illustration of skewness of the normal probability curve for intelligence test scores due to brain injury, including biochemical disorders resulting in minimal brain dysfunction. Note: This figure is schematic and not intended to depict the actual configuration. See Dingman and Tarjan (1960) for more precise characteristics.*
Shaded portion: brain-damaged cases, including biochemical disorders resulting in minimal brain dysfunction. Hatched portion: non-brain-damaged cases, presumably resulting from nonpathological environmental events interacting on inherited characteristics, multigenetically determined.

will reveal subtle physiological abnormalities among this group due to genetic, biochemical, malnutritional, and other defects. On the other hand, most persons in the behavioral sciences advance the *environmental-deprivation hypothesis,* contending that this type of retardation is due in large measure to lack of appropriate early stimulation, cultural disadvantages, maternal deprivation, and emotional stress. Still others hold to the *interaction hypothesis,* believing that the depressed intellectual functioning is due to a combination of biological weaknesses and environmental deprivation. This last argument probably best states the case, given our present state of knowledge. In any event, major research breakthroughs will be needed to advance our knowledge on this topic. In the meantime, educators usually call this large group of persons *cultural-familial,* which also suggests that causation is due to a complex interaction of both environmental and hereditary factors. These retardates run in families who live in severely underprivileged conditions in city slums or rural areas in which deficiencies in intellectual, social, and emotional stimulation abound. Such conditions are brought on by a vicious cycle. To begin with, a number of persons appear at the lower end of the continuum on most human traits, including intelligence, probably as a result of a complex of hereditary factors, theorized as a multiple-gene phenomenon. Since these persons are less well endowed intellectually, they have difficulty in competing for good-paying jobs. As a result, they find their way into underprivileged areas of the community, including inner-city ghettos, because they cannot afford anything better. Here their offspring are born into an inadequate environment with some inherited predisposition to intellectual subnormality. Here they experience poor health, malnutrition, lack of educational opportunity, and so on. Thus causation appears to be due to both familial and cultural factors. Even though many researchers have concerned themselves with the effects of environment on intelligence, it cannot be inferred that this type of retardation is due to cultural factors alone, especially for white, native-born children with low IQ scores and no biological problems. While many studies show that environmental conditions play an important part in intellectual development for such children, a more realistic statement would be that heredity sets limits on intellectual functioning while environment facilitates or hinders the fulfillment of an individual's inherited potentialities. Clearly, environmental conditions and the nature of our intelligence tests alone are sufficient to explain why about half of the black population in the United States receive IQ scores below 80 or 85. But even among this group, there must be many cases of cultural-familial retardation among the 1 percent who obtain the lowest IQ scores. Whatever the IQ demarcation level may be, those who have been called cultural-familial retarded tend to be more average in appearance, coordination, and adjustment than the pathological group. However, such students experience great difficulty in school. In addition to inadequate home and community conditions, these children have been made to attend schools in the slums where teachers, curricula, library facilities, and physical plants are often inadequate. With this combination, one cannot expect such children to be intellectually curious, stimulated, or interested in conventional school work. According to Zigler (1967), cultural-familial children have the same developmental patterns as normal children and represent the lower tail of the normal probability curve of intelligence. Since their developmental patterns evolve at a slower rate, their educational programs should follow normal patterns but with slower pacing. Further discussion of cultural-familial retardation follows in Chapter 3, which deals with mild general learning disabilities.

Vignette 2.1 illustrates a rather typical case of what is considered to be cultural-familial retardation. Of course, rather than hold to the interaction, cultural-familial hypothesis, one can argue that the probable cause is due to a single recessive gene, or solely to cultural deprivation. At this point we do not have the tools to be sure.

Vignette 2.1 An Apparent Cultural-Familial Family Living in Rural Poverty

The following is a sketch to illustrate what we mean by cultural-familial retardation. I first met this family when consulting at a residential facility for the retarded. An old truck pulled in one Saturday driven by a poor, white farmer of about 50 years of age. A neat, fairly attractive pregnant lady in her late thirties sat beside him, and three young children were in the back of the truck. Upon inquiring, I learned this was at least the sixth man with whom she had lived, all of whom would be classified as slow and in the lower class, but this one was a notch above the others. The staff considered her intelligence to be probably in the slow-learner range or below. She lived on welfare except when she could find a man to support her, augmented by income from housework, especially cleaning, at which she was good. While she led a marginal life of bare subsistence, at least she had managed to remain in society. By her various men, including the first one whom she had married but who disappeared, she had given birth to a rather large number of children, some of whom had died. Two boys, 14 and 16 years of age, were residents of the facility where I was working. Both were classified as having mild retardation, cultural-familial in nature. They were strong, healthy fellows who were assigned to yard work and did a good job of it. Both could read a little, and the younger one was still going to the school on the grounds. They had been institutionalized three years earlier, precipitated by some petty thievery which brought the case before the courts, with the resulting commitment by the judge. The newest man in the mother's life did not want them living with him but at least would bring the mother to visit the boys and give them a little spending money once a month. Two of the three youngsters who lived at home were of preschool age and had no obvious signs of a handicap. The third was a nine-year-old. He had been tried in the regular grades, but was slow in learning, was unclean and unkempt, was frequently in fights, wasn't liked, and didn't like school. He had recently been found to have an IQ of 67 by the school psychologist and had been placed in a self-contained special class for the educable mentally retarded. He liked it better there because he had more time to work at puzzles and do school work, at which he found he could succeed.

How many such families are there in the United States and Canada? We must in all candor report that there are thousands in every state and province. While some specific genetic defect may be operating in this case, they generally represent the lower end of the intellectual continuum. They tend to drift down into the lower class, just as those who are gifted tend to shift upward into the upper class. More and more the community is attempting to deal with and help these multiple-problem families. Therefore, less and less often are the offspring institutionalized. What are the solutions? Probably there are no complete ones but many partial ones—including family planning and birth control, foster homes, and a wide variety of community encouragement, financial support, and a wide array of health, education, and welfare services.

Pathological Etiologies

There are innumerable causes of retardation for the 6 percent of the below 70 IQ group who have recognizable *pathological* conditions. Heber

(1970) has provided an excellent overview of these. Some of them include chromosomal anomalies; abnormalities of gestation; maternal dietary deficiencies; metabolic disorders; virus infections of the mother and newborn; blood-type incompatability; and poisoning of the fetus due to lead, carbon monoxide, drugs, and other substances ingested by the mother. In past years it was thought that most cases of brain damage resulted primarily from birth injuries. However, after a careful review of the literature, Masland (1958) concluded that the predisposing problem is more likely to have arisen early in the gestation period, primarily by the end of the third month of pregnancy. The resulting fetus, being abnormal, produces an abnormal pregnancy which results in birth difficulties. Therefore no longer are anoxia at birth, prematurity, and instrument births assumed to be major causes of retardation. In recent years there has been a renewed interest in genetic determinants, cell division problems, biochemical disorders, and maternal insults. Nevertheless, birth traumata and children's diseases which result in severe infections of brain tissue (meningoencephalitis), as well as accidents, occasionally can and do cause retardation. However, the relative occurrence of these is rare indeed.

The biochemical disorders which result in brain damage are just beginning to be researched and include such conditions as galactosemia (a genetic defect resulting in an inability of the body to metabolize galactose, a sugar found in milk), and phenylketonuria (a genetic defect resulting in the lack of an enzyme needed to digest phenylalanine, an amino acid in proteins). In these two cases, a special diet is prescribed which, when given early enough, reduces markedly the damage to the brain which would result from an accumulation of the poison (such as phenylpyruvic acid) in the body. There appears to be a rather consistent link between metabolic disorders and genetic determinants. The future will likely find a number of the other causes of retardation similar to galactosemia and phenylketonuria.

Wilson in Chapter 9 points out that cerebral palsy is motor incoordination due to brain injury. It is not surprising that brain damage severe enough to result in readily discernible motor dysfunction can also result in intellectual inadequacy. In fact, as Wilson indicates, research shows that about 50 percent of cerebral palsied children have IQ scores below 70. Similarly, many cases of pathological retardation could be labeled cerebral palsied. The designating terminology is often arbitrary.

Not only can brain injury result from a large number of factors, but very different types of central nervous system damage may occur. In most cases, the injury is diffused and general. In other cases, a specific area of the brain may be much more damaged than other. Therefore, the behavioral characteristics of children with brain damage vary greatly. Depending on the area and extent of the brain which has been damaged, these children may be hypoactive (lethargic), hyperactive (hyperkinetic), or normal in activity level. Some may be skinny and bony, some flabby and fat; still others may have average bodies. Some may be grossly uncoordinated while others have normal body movements. Some may be susceptible to epilepsy while others are not. Therefore, as is pointed out in Chapter 10, it is impossible to talk about brain-injured children as a homogeneous group. However, this group is generally much more retarded in intellect and more multiply disabled than the cultural-familial group. They do appear in homes which extend from the very poor to the very wealthy, with most of them coming from average or above-average socioeconomic settings, simply because these groups represent the largest percentage of the population.

The Strauss syndrome. At this point, it is important to introduce the terms "Strauss syndrome" and "Strauss-type child." Concern for this type of child has been high among educators and psychologists since the publication of Volume I of *Psychopathology and education of the brain-injured child* by Strauss and Lehtinen (1947). These authorities labeled children as brain injured or exogenous when they had one or more of the following specific behavioral characteristics: (1) hyperactivity; (2) lack of coordination; (3) uninhibited behavior; (4) perseveration; and (5) perceptual disorders. Prior to 1960 they were most often found in special classes for so-called educable retarded children in well-to-do localities. During the 1960s these children were relabeled as perceptual disordered, minimal brain dysfunctioning, and educationally handicapped. Now, in the 1970s, they are classified as pupils with specific learning disabilities, and a wider array of special education services are provided them. If one were to obtain IQ scores on all such children, probably about half would score below 75 or so and half above. A very few would have scores well above 100, but a fair number would fall in the normal range of 85 to 115. It is unfortunate that Strauss and Lehtinen named their pupils brain injured or exogenous. This Strauss-type child is recognized by his behavior characteristics, not by his brain injury.

In Chapter 10, the role of special education is examined in serving the Strauss-type child. The term and its definition are briefly introduced here for two reasons: *first,* to make the point that special education for these children grew out of services for the retarded; and, *second,* to facilitate a discussion of the condition both when presenting children with mild general learning disabilities (formerly labeled educable mentally retarded) in Chapter 3 and children with neuromotor impairments in Chapter 9.

Clinical types, including Down's syndrome. In the past, much has been made of the many "clinical types" of retardation in texts for teachers, reflecting probably a preoccupation with medical labels. Each of these types has a distinctive set of characteristics. There is not space in this survey text to dwell on these, but they are well described in a number of sources (Heber, 1961; Robinson and Robinson, 1965; Tredgold and Soddy, 1970). As already stated, these clinical types are relatively rare, except for Down's syndrome, which represents about one third of the moderately retarded. Therefore, the condition is singled out for considerable attention. However, in addition to it, brief descriptions are first given of three of the slightly more common, but still rare, clinical types.

Hydrocephalus is "water on the brain," or, more correctly, pressure on the brain and skull from cerebral-spinal fluid. This pressure results from blockages in the brain passages, defective absorption of the fluid, or over-secretion of it. Hydrocephalus can frequently be arrested when it is detected early and a surgical shunt inserted (a tube from the cerebral cavity to the jugular vein or some other part of the body). Uncorrected hydrocephalus results in progressive brain deterioration, a greatly enlarged skull, loss of ambulation, confinement to bed, and death. Early arrested hydrocephalus may result in only a slight loss in intellectual functioning, and average school progress may even be possible. In other arrest cases, where considerable brain damage has resulted, a special education program may be indicated.

Microcephaly is characterized by a small head, with the skull portion being especially reduced in size. The forehead is often receded and the back of the head flattened. The scalp is often wrinkled. This rare condition is usually inherited, but may result from unusual environmental factors such as X-ray radiation of the pregnant mother. The child is usually born severely retarded, but occasionally children with this condition are found in special day classes for the moderately retarded. More often they are found at home or in a residential facility.

Cretinism (or *hypothyroidism*) results from thyroid deficiency which may be due to a lack of iodine in the diet or to a defective thyroid. Now that iodine is regularly added to salt, one seldom sees a person with all the clinical signs of this condition. Severe thyroid deficiency reduces the body metabolism to such a degree that the child becomes dwarfish and bloated. Dry, scaly, sallow skin and severe retardation are other clinical signs. (Superficially, children with cretinism and Down's syndrome resemble one another in their short stature and sallow skin.) Iodized salt cannot prevent hypothyroidism caused by a structurally defective thyroid gland. Thyrozine dosages given at an early age will greatly reduce the physical stigmata and appreciably reduce intellectual retardation. In fact, early detection and medical treatment has practically eliminated full-fledged cretinism.

Down's syndrome (*mongolism*) was identified in 1866 by J. Langdon Down, a British physician, who labeled people with this condition mongo-loids because of their superficial resemblance to the Mongolian physical type in such characteristics as slanting eyes, flattened skull, and broad nose. However, this clinical type is associated with a chromosomal anomaly which occurs in all races, and in recent years the condition has become known as Down's syndrome rather than mongolism. The abbreviation "Dowsyn," coined by D'Amelio (1971), will be used in this book.

In a study of 100 Dowsyn children from 5 to 19 years, Gibson and Frank (1961) listed the 13 most common physical signs of this condition. Ranking these anomalies from most prevalent to least prevalent, they cited (1) large, fissured tongue; (2) short, squared hands; (3) epicanthal fold at inner corner of the eye; (4) single transverse crease across a flabby hand; (5) inward-curving little finger; (6) nose with flat bridge and upturned nostrils; (7) fused ear lobules; (8) deep cleft between big toe and second toe; (9) small, flattened skull; (10) short fifth finger; (11) smooth, simple outer ear lobe; (12) congenital heart problems; and (13) little fingers with one lateral crease rather than two per finger. Few Dowsyns have all these symptoms, and some people with a number of these signs do not have the condition. The grave danger of making a diagnosis on the basis of physical signs alone cannot be overstressed. Identification should be based on a combination of physical signs, measures of intellectual development, and, especially, study of chromosomal matter. Chromosome study is the only certain means of diagnosis.

Prior to the discovery of antibiotics and other improved medical treatment, Dowsyn children usually died at an early age from respiratory infection and heart defects. Rarely did one live past 10 years of age. Today their life expectancy has been greatly extended, and it is not unusual to find persons with this condition living into their forties, fifties, and even sixties.

The cause of Down's syndrome has puzzled scientists since the condition was first identified. The major cue for research has been the discovery that incidence rates increase with maternal age. With this phenomenon in mind, a number of early speculations were advanced to explain the condition, a popular one having to do with endocrine dysfunction. A major breakthrough came in 1959 when a group of French investigators published their discovery that three persons with Dowsyn carried an extra chromosome (Lejeune, Gautier, and Turpin, 1959). The next year British scientists reported the same extra chromosome in six more cases (Penrose, Ellis, and Delhanty, 1960). Instead of the normal complement of 46 human chromosomes (23 pairs), persons with Down's syndrome had 47. Three types of the syndrome have now been identified:

1. In the *standard trisomy 21* type, the 21st set of chromosomes contains three rather than the conventional two chromosomes; the extra chromosome is free and distinct. This condition is known as nondysjunction. This is the most common type; it is associated with increasing maternal age and it is not inherited.

2. In the *13–15 translocation* type, the extra 21st chromosome attaches itself to another chromosome, usually in pairs 13 or 15; this leaves a count of 46 chromosomes, although the extra material of the 47th is present. This is a much less common type; it occurs in mothers of all ages and it is inherited. Younger mothers tend to account for more of this type because more young women than older ones have children. Translocations have been found in fathers, mothers, grandparents, and other relatives who are carriers.

3. In the very rare *mosaicism* type, the extra chromosome is found in some cells of the body and not in others. Children with this type usually have fewer physical signs of the condition and higher intellect. The extra chromosome may be translocated or in nondysjunction.

Scientists are still not sure why the syndrome is associated with maternal age, but a number of hypotheses have been advanced. Lilienfeld (1969) considers the Penrose postulate the most promising. It states that the incidence of the syndrome increases with maternal age as a result of progressive deterioration of the egg cell due to natural aging. Other possibilities include (1) malfunctioning body chemistry associated with the menopause, which effects early cell division, and (2) a reduction in selectivity of the uterus in accepting a good fertilized egg.

In terms of psychological characteristics, Dowsyn children vary considerably, a phenomenon easier to accept since the identification of the three subtypes. In the years ahead, major advances can be expected in determining the behavioral characteristics peculiar to each of these types. Already Gibson and Pozsonyi (1965), in comparing 10 cases of the standard trisomy 21 type with 10 cases of the translocation type, have found distinguishing differences in their behavior. However, until large samples and replicated findings are available, it appears safer to hold to the following generalizations:

1. In terms of *intelligence,* Dowsyn children range from the very severely retarded to the near normal. The majority achieve between one quarter to one half of normal intelligence. Those who live at home generally score above those in residential facilities. For example, McNeill (1954) found a mean IQ of 33 for those who remained at home and a mean IQ of 22 for those in residential schools. Wunsch (1957) showed a mean IQ of 38 points for his community sample and a mean IQ of 30 points for his institutionalized cases. Parenthetically, Gibson and Pozsonyi (1965) found a mean IQ of 43.5 for their translocation type and 40.1 for their trisomy type, the difference being statistically significant; and Rosecrans (1968) found a mean IQ score of 65 for 30 rare cases of mosaicism with a range from below 30 to above 90.

2. In terms of *personality,* research has somewhat dispelled the stereotype that all Dowsyn children are cheerful, affectionate, and docile, although Johnson and Abelson (1969) found such children to have greater social competence than other retardates of comparable intelligence. Wunsch (1957) found that many are happy and lovable, especially when young, but that others are aggressive and hostile, particularly those who have reached adolescence and adulthood. Nevertheless, Dowsyn children as a group fit in better at home and in the community than do retarded children with organic brain injury. Whether their personality traits are acquired or innate or derive from some combination of inheritance and environment has yet to be demonstrated. On the one hand, it can be argued that children with the syndrome are recognized at birth, so parents have a better chance to accept and love them. On the other hand, it may be contended that the distinguishing characteristics are innately determined and associated with the early aging process.

3. In terms of *coordination and motor skills,* Dowsyn children are believed to have unusual dexterity. However, Semmel (1960), in comparing the teacher ratings of 59 matched pairs of moderately retarded children in community day classes (half Dowsyn and half brain injured), found the two groups to be remarkably similar in motor skills, although those with Down's syndrome tended to scatter more.

4. In terms of the belief that Dowsyn children have high ability in *mimicry and rhythm*, Cantor and Girardeau (1958) found that they were not significantly different in these traits from normal boys and girls of the same mental age.

5. In terms of *speech and language*, Dowsyn children were found by Johnson and Abelson (1969) to be significantly inferior to non-Dowsyn retardates of comparable intelligence. Their large tongue and/or small mouth combine to add to their unintelligibility. Clearly these children need speech therapy.

6. In terms of *learning characteristics*, Cantor and Girardeau (1958) found that Dowsyn children did not differ significantly from other children of the same mental age. Therefore, there appears no justification for grouping children with Down's syndrome homogeneously for instructional purposes.

There is growing optimism that the incidence of Down's syndrome can be reduced sharply and that the condition may be ameliorated when prevention is not possible. Theoretically, due to a recent breakthrough, it is possible today to eliminate the condition regardless of type. Steele and Breg (1966) credit Fuchs of Scandinavia for pointing out the practicability of diagnosing Down's syndrome in the fetus by chromosomal studies (*karyotyping*) of the cells in the amniotic fluid which surrounds the fetus and is of fetal origin. The fluid is usually drawn off by a process known as *amniocentesis* (membrane pricking) in the third to fourth month of pregnancy. As yet this process of fluid removal entails some slight risk to both the mother and the unborn. Theoretically, however, if every pregnant woman were to have this test made and then underwent a therapeutic abortion when chromosomal anomalies were discovered, the condition could be eradicated. At this point this approach is not practical for both moral and technical reasons. For one thing, karyotyping has been a slow, painstaking, and expensive task. Only recently has research begun on computer-assisted chromosome analysis, with the aim of developing a five-minute heredity test by the analysis of one drop of fluid on a computer-controlled microscope. By such means not only Down's syndrome but a variety of other genetic defects could be detected.

With the rare translocation type of the syndrome, which is inherited, chromosome studies can be made of tissues from the suspected carrier. In a family with an affected child or where a mother or father carries a translocated extra chromosome, the chances of having a child with Down's syndrome are about 33 percent. Here is an area in which genetics counseling, cytogenetic screening methods of detecting carriers, and classical, pedigree methods of tracing back through the family tree are paying off more and more.

Once a baby with Down's syndrome is born there is no known "cure." However, perhaps some chemical supplement will be found to reduce the effects of the syndrome, just as thyroxine has reduced the effects of cretinism. Until some medical treatment is found, however, the care of Dowsyn children rests on instruction and training. The goal is to guide each such child to optimal use of his limited potential. As will be seen later in this chapter, we have as yet had only minimal success in this endeavor, but the future looks brighter.

Persons desiring a fuller treatment of Down's syndrome are referred to such sources as Benda (1969); Lilienfeld (1969); and Penrose and Smith (1966). Vollman (1969) and Stedman and Olley (1969) have provided comprehensive bibliographies on the condition. Too, the CEC Information Center on Exceptional Children has a selected bibliography on the topic (see the Resources section at the end of this chapter for the address).

Vignette 2.2 is a case history of a teen-aged girl who has Down's syndrome. Sarah's story illustrates the problems, fears, and concerns such a person often generates for the family.

Vignette 2.2 A Retarded Teenager with Down's Syndrome

Sarah, now 16 years old, was born when her mother was 45. She has two bright older sisters, both married, in their thirties with able children. No other cases of Down's syndrome are known to exist in the extended family. Both of her parents are college graduates, the father being a successful executive who has been the president of the local parents' association for retarded children. For the past 10 years, they have devoted their lives to their retarded daughter, moving from an exclusive community to a lower-middle class, interracial one near a day care and sheltered workshop center which Sarah now attends. But they find Sarah is still not very well accepted. For this reason, they have dropped most of their outside activities.

Sarah has developed intellectually at about one third the normal rate, so she is estimated now to be like a five-year-old cognitively. Her highest skills are in caring for herself. She is well groomed, well dressed, and has good manners. Her speech is primitive and distorted by her large tongue, but those who know her well can usually understand what she wants. She has essentially no academic skills even after years in a special school and can do very few household chores adequately. After much training at the center, she has been taught to sweep the floor fairly well. At home she does no work. Sarah is somewhat stubborn. She forms strong likes and dislikes toward her peers and the staff, but is generally quite affectionate and cheerful. She loves her father, but expects her mother to care for her constantly. She is rather overweight and is neither good at physical exercise nor does she like it.

Her parents are now both in their sixties, with the father soon to retire. They are deeply worried about what will happen to Sarah when they are too old to care for her. The sisters will not take on the job. Furthermore, they feel that Sarah should have been institutionalized years ago and that the parents' estate should be divided between them to enable their very able offspring to have greater educational opportunities. If the parents honor the sisters' wishes, they are fearful their Sarah will end up in the large state residential facility unless a small, public, special-purpose boarding home is established where the emphasis would be on recreation and continuous care.

A Final Note on the Terms Exogenous and Endogenous

In concluding this section on etiology, it must be pointed out that the terms "exogenous" and "endogenous" have been used differently by different authorities in the field. Under endogenous some include only the genetic causes of mental retardation and under exogenous all known and unknown causes from conception and on. Others have equated endogenous with cultural-familial cases and exogenous with all pathological conditions, even when predetermined by heredity. As already pointed out, Strauss restricted exogenous to his own Strauss syndrome and appeared to classify all other cases as endogenous. Thus, when confronted by these terms, one needs to ascertain the particular writer's definitions of them.

Other Literature

This brief orientation to the field of retardation provides only a setting for a discussion of special education for children with mild, moderate, and severe general learning disabilities. There are a number of textbooks devoted completely to this topic. Some of the better-known ones include Baumeister (1967); Clarke and Clarke (1965); Ellis (1963); Jordon (1972); Kolstoe (1972); Robinson and Robinson (1965); Rothstein (1971); Sarason and Doris (1969); Smith (1971); Stevens and Heber (1964); and Tredgold and Soddy (1970). For a deeper appreciation of this complex subject, the reader is directed to these useful references, as well as to a detailed listing of approximately 400 textbooks on retardation to be found in Appendix D of Rothstein (1971).

PART 2: SPECIAL EDUCATION FOR CHILDREN WITH MODERATE AND SEVERE GENERAL LEARNING DISABILITIES

Terminology

The term "general learning disabilities" (GLD) was defined on page 68. At that time, it was explained why this nomenclature, rather than the traditonal term "mental retardation," should be used with school children in need of special education.

The traditional descriptive terms for levels of intellectual impairment in special education, namely, "educable," "trainable," and "custodial," are abandoned because the latter two are derogatory and imply a defeatist position. Instead, this text uses the nomenclature outlined in Table 2.3. Children with moderate GLD's obtain IQ scores of about 35 ± 5 to 60 ± 5, while those in the severe category score between 20 ± 5 and 35 ± 5. As abbreviations, the terms "mildly," "moderately," "severely," and "profoundly retarded" will be used in this chapter and the next.

Definitions and Descriptions

Since children who are classified as *moderately* retarded for special education purposes have IQ scores from about 35 ± 5 to about 60 ± 5, they develop intellectually at approximately one third to six tenths the rate of the average child. Therefore, at six years of age, they are cognitively like children of between two and almost four years. In adulthood, their intellectual development approaches five to nine years, which implies that the most able of the group can be expected to achieve academically at about the third-grade level. If one defines literacy as reading at the fourth-grade level and beyond, then only rarely would a moderately retarded person qualify. This is the main reason such persons have been considered uneducable in the academic sense. Now, using new methods and materials that will be presented later in the chapter, there is a good chance that a fair number will be able to read simple materials for enjoyment, safety, and information. Even in the past there have been a number of case studies (Seagoe, 1964; Hunt, 1967) of moderately retarded persons who could read and write quite well. Usually these individuals were born into rare, culturally stimulating conditions, or reading instruction was pushed almost exclusively. This raises the issue of how much time and energy should be expended on getting a child up to the literacy level when so many other areas of his development need attention.

The typical adaptive behavior of the moderately retarded was outlined in Table 2.3 for three age levels. Such persons have at least sufficient ability (1) to develop self-care skills in such areas as dressing, toileting, and eating; (2) to learn to talk and carry on a simple conversation, though they will have little verbal skill during their early preschool years; (3) to guard themselves against common dangers in a protective environment or in familiar community settings; (4) to perform simple chores in such sheltered and closely supervised environments as the home, a workshop, and even occasionally a factory or business; (5) to learn a considerable range of social graces so they can function in public places; and (6) to travel unattended about the immediate neighborhood and over familiar routes. However, as adults they will generally be semi-independent all of their lives. They seldom if ever marry, raise families, or set up their own homes. Instead, they usually continue to live with parents, relatives, or friends or are cared for eventually by some social agency which has usually taken the form of a residential facility. More recently, however, halfway houses and other forms of semi-independent living units, such as supervised boarding homes which cater to this group, have become available in some communities.

Since children who are classified as *severely* retarded for special education purposes have IQ scores between 20 ± 5 and 35 ± 5, they develop intellectually at only about one fifth to one third the rate of average children. Therefore, at age six, they will function between approximately the one- and three-year levels; in adulthood, they will reach a three- to five-year intellectual level. This means they will always perform at the preacademic level. Nevertheless, they have the potential to develop the adaptive behaviors outlined in Table 2.3. They have the ability (1) to walk, toilet, dress, and feed themselves; (2) to speak in a very elementary fashion; and (3) to perform simple chores in the home or in a very protective environment. Of course, as adults they are always dependent on others for protection and support. As will be pointed out later in the chapter, special educators are just beginning to assume responsibility for this subgroup of retardates. As yet, we have not completely identified their range of potential.

Prevalences

As the basis for planning both day and residential services for children who are moderately and severely retarded, combined prevalence figures are suggested of a minimum of 0.5 percent and a maximum of 0.80 percent (see Table 1.1).

This would break down as follows: (1) children with IQ scores in the 50's, traditionally described as nonadaptive educable retardates, 0.25–0.55; (2) children with IQ scores of 35–50, traditionally described as trainable retardates, 0.20; (3) children with IQ scores of 20–35, known as severely retarded, 0.05. How does one arrive at these estimates?

Our most accurate data are provided by five surveys of school-aged children with IQ scores below 50. Three of these studies were conducted in the United States and two in Great Britain. They are summarized in Table 2.4. The results are remarkably consistent, with a median value of 0.25 percent. The slight inconsistencies can be readily explained. For example, three of the surveys included all children with IQ scores below 50 while two restricted the population to those with IQ's between 30 and 50. The highest total percentage of all was found in the Michigan survey (Wirtz and Guenther, 1957) because it was conducted in a local community that had a small residential facility in it which attracted more than an average number of families with retarded children. If one estimates that there are at least four children with IQ's between 35 and 50 for each child with an IQ score below 35 (ratio, 4:1), then the prevalence figure for the 35–50 IQ subgroup would be 0.20 and for the below 20 IQ subgroup 0.05. (Only rare cases fall below 20.)

It is much more difficult to justify the 0.25–0.55 percent prevalence estimate for children with IQ scores in the 50's. This figure is based on the Dingman and Tarjan (1960) distributions, which shows only slightly more cases with IQ's in the 50's as contrasted with the 40's. However, experience may indicate this 0.25–0.55 percentage figure needs to be increased up to as

TABLE 2.4 *Summary of Prevalence Surveys of 1950s and 1960s School-age Retarded Children with IQ Scores below 50*

| Survey | Total | Percentages | |
		In Community	In Residential Facilities
1. New York[a]	0.280	0.110	0.170
		(included those severely retarded)	
2. Illinois[b]	0.234	0.149	0.085
		(included only IQ 30-50 group)	
3. Michigan[c]	0.330	0.170	0.160
		(included only IQ 30-50 group)	
4. United Kingdom[d, e]	0.253	–	–
		(included those severely retarded)	
Rounded medians	0.25	0.15	0.10

[a]Bienenstock and Coxe, 1956.
[b]Wirtz and Guenther, 1957.
[c]Wirtz and Guenther, 1957.
[d]Goodman and Tizard, 1962.
[e]Kushlick, 1964.

high as perhaps 0.75. Assuming the figure remains 0.25–0.55 percent, for every 10,000 school-age children one can estimate that between 50 and 80 will have IQ scores between approximately 20 and 60. This breaks down as 5 pupils in the IQ 20–35 range, 20 in the 35–50 range, and 25–55 in the 50–60 ± 5 range. At least 60 percent will need to be served in the community and no more than 40 percent in residential facilities, including boarding schools, judging from the data in Table 2.4.

In the two surveys conducted in Great Britain (Goodman and Tizard, 1962; Kushlick, 1964), investigators found 0.253 percent of the school population to have IQ scores below 50 (or 2.53 per 1,000). However, some 35 years earlier, Lewis (1929) found four "imbeciles" per 1,000 of the population in that same country.[2] This would suggest that the prevalence has been cut almost in half in this short period of time. It was found that the numbers of every type of retardate had decreased sharply with the exception of Dowsyn children. In this case there was a fourfold increase because so many more persons with this condition are being kept alive today. The implications appear to be that medical advances are preventing many more cases of moderate retardation than in the past.

What does the future hold? While a number of insults to mothers today, such as drugs and pollutants, are resulting in children being born retarded, and while improved medical services are keeping alive many of these youngsters, still it would appear that potent developments in the biological sciences are more than countering these negative factors as far as the child

[2] Lewis also found the proportion of "idiots" to "imbeciles" to be 1:4.

with an IQ between 20 and 60 is concerned. There is no reason to suggest that this trend of lower prevalence figures will not continue. A major breakthrough in preventing Down's syndrome would sharply reduce these figures.

Identification

While most children with mild learning disabilities have few obvious physical and psychological disabilities, a large number of the moderately retarded, and even more of the severely retarded, demonstrate such signs at an early age. Therefore, the vast majority of these children are identified either at birth or during their preschool years. For example, because of their physical stigmata, Down's syndrome children are usually identified by the attending obstetrician at birth. Other children in these categories demonstrate various symptoms in their early years. In most cases, the children lack coordination and exhibit a slowness in learning to sit, walk, and talk. By late in the child's first year or shortly thereafter the suspicions and concerns of the family are aroused, whereupon the parents look to the family physician to identify the difficulty. In some cases, in cooperation with a child psychologist, he soon makes the diagnosis. However, since the family doctor is seldom an authority on retardation, he often refers the family to an inter-professional clinic for diagnosis and evaluation. These clinics are becoming increasingly available. In some cases they are designed solely for the retarded, but they may serve a variety of handicapped children. Here a physician, psychologist, social worker, and others who have special competence in the field cooperate in the identification process. However, it may take many years before a diagnosis of moderate or severe retardation is accepted by the parents. In the meantime, they often shift from one professional person to another, hoping against hope that some label other than retardation will be given their child.

Classification

A number of surveys have been made of moderately and severely retarded children in special day schools and classes (Hottel, 1956; Wirtz and Guenther, 1957; Connor and Goldberg, 1960; and Cain and Levine, 1963). A fairly safe generalization is to consider these children as falling into three classification categories, as follows: (1) about one third are *clinical types,* with all but the rare case being Down's syndrome; (2) another one third have diagnosed *organic brain injury;* and (3) the remaining one third include a *miscellaneous group* of undifferentiated and as yet unknown conditions which are probably due largely to endocrinological, biochemical, and/or genetic defects. While surveys of the 1970s are not available, it is probable now that slightly more cases of Down's syndrome would be present and slightly fewer of the second category. Too, by shifting the upper demarcation line from IQ 50 to IQ 60 ± 5, the number of cases in the third category would be up sharply. A major breakthrough in the prevention of Down's syndrome would shift these proportions dramatically.

**Educational Provisions
for the Moderately Retarded**

Today, moderately retarded children go to school in a variety of community and residential facilities, but the genesis of many of our modern-day practices can be traced back to developments in Europe some 150 years ago. Not only will these early curricular approaches now be explored, but the traditional provisions of the 1950s and 1960s, as well as emerging present-day strategies, will also be examined.

Early Curricular Approaches

Three European physicians—Itard, and later Seguin and Guggenbühl—provided the major early contributions to the field. The work of these pioneers and their disciples during the nineteenth century may well be viewed as the first golden age for moderately retarded children (Kanner, 1964; Doll, 1967; Ball, 1971).

Jean Marc Itard (1774–1838) is recognized as the first person to use systematic methods in teaching a retarded child. For five years he worked with a young boy, the so-called Wild Boy, Victor, who was captured at the age of 12 years in the forest of Aveyron in southern France about 1800. Itard (a sensationist, environmentalist, and physician at the Institute for the Deaf in Paris) considered that the boy's animal-like behavior was due only to lack of human stimulation resulting from years of isolation in the forest and therefore gave him remedial education. Victor was his instrument for testing his theory and shedding light on the nature-nurture controversy.

Even though Itard had considerable success in training Victor, he viewed his experiment as a failure, since his goal was to bring the boy up to normalcy through appropriate stimulation and training, but Victor never approached that level. However, most authorities have since come to believe that the boy was retarded and was therefore abandoned by his parents not too long before he was captured. Thus, in this context, Itard's accomplishments may be viewed as remarkable. His goals were to develop Victor's language, self-help, and socialization skills. These are recognized today as three of the major goals in special classes for the moderately retarded. Much of his initial work with Victor involved "sense training." For example, he taught Victor heat discrimination by plunging his hand into hot and then cold water. Itard taught him other sensory discriminations, for example, by exposing him to foul versus sweet smelling materials and by presenting loud sounds followed by soft sounds. Itard believed that Victor could not be expected to acquire more complex skills until he was better able to discriminate among concrete stimuli. Perhaps his greatest contribution came when he began to teach Victor more complex tasks. He developed a systematic set of basic learning strategies which are essentially the same as those used today in behavior modification. The following account illustrates his technique in teaching a rudimentary academic skill.

One morning when he was waiting impatiently for the milk which he always had for breakfast, I carried to him his board which I had specially arranged the evening before with the four letters L A I T. Madame Guérin, whom I had warned, approached, looked at the letters and immediately gave me a cup of milk which I pretended to drink myself. A moment after I approached Victor, gave him the four letters that I had lifted from the board, and pointed to it with one hand while in the other I held the jug full of milk. The letters were immediately replaced but in inverted order, so that they showed T I A L instead of L A I T. I indicated the corrections to be made by designating with my fingers the letters to transpose and the proper place of each. When these changes had reproduced the sign, he was allowed to have his milk. [Itard, 1962, p. 47; translated by George and Muriel Humphrey]

Here we see that Itard's teaching procedures demonstrated the effectiveness of (1) individualized instruction; (2) systematic programing of learning experiences; and (3) immediate reinforcement.

Edward O. Seguin (1812–1880), a student of Itard and also a Parisian physician, carried on from where Itard left off in the development of instructional procedures for the moderately retarded. Instead of working with a single boy like Victor, he established the first public residential facility in France for moderately retarded children and devised a curriculum for them. Seguin's *Physiological Method* (1907) was based upon the belief that the blocked or damaged nervous systems of the retarded could be re-educated to normalcy by motor and sensory training. He developed extensive didactic materials, insisting that his teachers use these and follow his training procedures in a systematic fashion. He advocated training of gross motor movements followed by finer movements, leading on to perceptual-motor exercises. Furthermore, he used colors, music, and other devices to motivate the child. His training procedures relied heavily on imitation. Like Itard, he was a sensationist and environmentalist. (Talbot [1967] has an excellent description of Seguin's procedures and contributions.)

Samuel Gridley Howe was instrumental in getting Seguin to move to the United States so that he could introduce his particular curriculum and teaching procedures into the first state residential facility for the retarded in the United States. This was created in Massachusetts in 1848 and is now known as the Walter E. Fernald State School. In the later half of the nineteenth century, a number of residential schools were opened in the United States, all of them established under the Seguin influence, with high public anticipation that retardation would be cured by his approach. His book on the physiological method (Seguin, 1907) became the syllabus for residential-school training programs. Unfortunately, Seguin was not successful in stimulating moderately retarded children to normal functioning. As a result, early hope for the residential school in the United States soon faded. At the beginning of the twentieth century, a wave of pessimism swept the country. No longer were residential schools viewed as *training* institutions for the habilitation of the moderately retarded. Instead, they became *custodial* facilities for retarded children and adults who got into trouble, taking in a broad IQ spectrum, including both the mildly and profoundly retarded. As will be discussed later in this chapter, only in recent years, due largely to the behavior-modification movement, has there been a strong resurgence in training.

Johann J. Guggenbühl (1816–1863), another physician who lived his 47 years during the same period as Seguin, is famous for his treatment of cretins at Abendberg, a residential facility located in the Swiss Alps, where thyroid deficiences were common due to a lack of iodine in the diet (Kanner, 1964). Like Itard and Seguin, he believed that a combination of medical and educational therapies would habilitate his patients to normalcy. His regimen consisted of open air; a milk and meat diet supplemented with iodine; and aromatic baths and massages. His goal was to change cretins from vegetating objects of pity into objects of therapy. Especially creative were his sense-training exercises. He used Chinese gongs and phosphorus pencils in darkened rooms to establish and focus attention. Because of his optimism and ideas, Guggenbühl was influential in establishing his concepts of teaching in residential facilities throughout Europe. Like Seguin, Guggenbühl was unable to attain his lofty goal of remediating retardation, probably largely because he did not fully understand the role of iodine, and, of course, began iodine therapy too late. Too, no doubt not all of his patients were cretins as he thought; a number probably had Down's syndrome, which was not recognized as a specific clinical type until after Guggenbühl's death. In any event rumors began to spread in Europe that he was faking cures to retain his popularity. Finally, his followers rejected him, investigations were conducted, and Abendberg was closed. Thereupon, Europe went through the same pendulum swing from overoptimism to overpessimism as did the United States.

Traditional Curricular Approaches

Historical perspectives. Traditionally, educators have valued highly the ability of pupils to succeed academically in school. In fact, as already pointed out in Chapter 1, even after the advent of compulsory school attendance laws in about the middle of the nineteenth century, with some rare exceptions, only students of "educable mind" were allowed to attend school. And the slower of these were accepted and retained only reluctantly—a condition which still exists today. A legal demarcation line for educability was generally considered to be an IQ of 50–55, and this figure was adopted uncritically throughout the United States and Canada. Until the 1950s when they banded together to change the system, parents of children with scores below this point had three choices: (1) they could keep their children at home; (2) they could place them in private or public residential facilities; or (3) they could set up their own parent-sponsored schools. And they went through all three options in turn.

During most of the 1800s and well into the 1900s, parents simply kept their moderately retarded children at home. But gradually state *residential* facilities were established and a number of these children were placed in them. Soon, however, the early emphasis on training in these facilities became minimal and mediocre. As a result, parents became less and less interested in sending their children to these institutions, which had become largely custodial. In their search for better alternatives, parents joined together to establish and operate parent-sponsored day schools. While this day school movement for the moderately retarded was largely a phenomenon of the 1940s and beyond, a few programs were in operation much earlier. Classes were opened in St. Louis as early as 1914, in New York City by 1929, and in St. Paul, Minnesota, by 1934 (Wallin, 1966). A few were publicly supported, but most were operated by private donations. By the late 1940s the private day school movement was widespread. Although these services proved expensive both in terms of time and money, the parents felt they were worthwhile and far superior to large residential institutions.

Next, parents became vocal in their demands that local public school systems assume responsibility for operating these private day schools, which were usually located in church halls and basements. The turning point came in 1950 in the United States when parents established their own organization, now known as the National Association for Retarded Children (NARC). One of the chief aims of this organization was to foster the development of public day school services for the moderately retarded. As never before, parents wished to keep their children at home and in the community, yet they hesitated to do so unless every opportunity was given them to develop intellectually. This implied formal training by qualified teachers, and the parents had had great difficulty in recruiting, holding, and paying such instructors. Parents contended that they were taxpayers, that their children could learn, and, therefore that the schools had as great a responsibility toward a moderately retarded child as toward any other child. They carried their demands to state legislators, and, as a result, legislation was passed in most states authorizing local school systems to establish or take over special day schools and classes for this group of children. With legal authority and the promise of state reimbursement for a considerable proportion of the costs of these programs, parents petitioned local school boards and superintendents to extend their services. After considerable initial debate and resistance by educational authorities (Goldberg and Cruickshank, 1958), the moderately retarded became widely recognized as a responsibility of the public school. Thus the public day school movement gained its impetus during the 1950s and became solidly established during the 1960s.

The concept behind the phrase "of educable mind" lingered, however. The children were known as "trainable" retardates, as contrasted with "educable" retardates, and were considered to be uneducable in terms of the 3 R's. Only recently has this term been changed from "trainable" to "moderately retarded" and more academic instruction, including cognitive development, added to the curriculum. At the same time, by 1970, the term "of educable mind" had been dropped from the statutes of all but two states.[3]

[3] These statutes define local public school special education services for handicapped children that are legally eligible for state financial support (Abeson and Trudeau, 1970).

Even in these two states, local school programs for so-called trainables are supported by state funds, the term "of educable mind" simply remaining on the statutes as a vestige of the past. Therefore, it has become an academic if not a dead issue as to whether the moderately retarded are the responsibility of the public schools and/or the teaching profession. However, these children are still far from being universally accepted by school personnel. In addition, educators have shown little or no inclination to extend services downward to the severely, but not profoundly, retarded—even though more and more is being learned about how they may be taught self-help skills.

Growth, extent, and nature of special educational services. An overview of the growth and extent of special education services for the moderately retarded in special day schools and classes provided by local school systems in the United States was presented in Table 1.3. More complete U.S. Office of Education statistics on numbers of pupils enrolled are reported in Table 2.5 for the period 1948–1973, along with percentages of estimated numbers of such children served and not served in such programs.

TABLE 2.5 *Numbers of Moderately Retarded Pupils Enrolled in Special Day Schools and Classes in Local School Systems in the United States, 1948-1973, Plus Estimates of Percentages Served and Not Served*

Year	Number of Pupils Enrolled[a]	Estimated Number in U.S.[b] (0.20%)[c]	Percent Enrolled (rounded)	Percent Remaining at Home or in Residential Facilities[d]
1948	4,509	66,800	7	93
1953	6,453	79,200	8	92
1958	16,793	94,500	17	83
1963	30,022	109,600	27	73
1968	55,000 (est.)	119,000	46	54
1973	70,000 (est.)	122,500	53	47

[a]Derived from a number of U.S. Office of Education statistical reports, plus Mackie (1969); estimated values for 1968 and 1973 obtained by extrapolating the growth curve.
[b]Based on total U.S. population in 5-19 age bracket.
[c]A prevalence estimate of 0.20 percent was used in these calculations.
[d]A few could also be in privately sponsored day-care centers, and so forth.

Less extensive are the data available on the growth of special education services for the moderately retarded in public residential facilities in the United States. Occasionally the U.S. Office of Education has collected such data. For example, in 1963 (see Mackie, 1969) 18,689 moderately retarded children were in such services while 30,022 of these youngsters were enrolled in local school systems (see Table 2.5). It appears that in the late 1950s or early 1960s, the number of special education services in local school systems surpassed those in residential facilities for the first time, and clearly the trend has continued. As for the number of special educators on the staff of public residential facilities, over the last 25 years the total has risen from about 650 in 1948 to 850 in 1953 to 1,175 in 1958 to 1,580 in 1963 to 2,200 in 1968 to 3,000 in 1973. However, until very lately, the size of the population in public residential facilities for children of all IQ levels, ages 5 to 19, has increased at about the same pace over the same period, resulting in a ratio of approximately 35 such children per teacher. Finally, as a rough rule of thumb, it may be stated that at the outset of the 1970s, approximately 50 percent of moderately retarded pupils in the United States were in special education programs provided by local school systems; another 25 percent were in such programs in public residential facilities; and the remaining 25 percent were in a variety of other home, community, and residential settings.

In the community, most of the services have taken the form of self-contained special day classes in neighborhood regular public schools. There have also been a number of special day schools in operation, some serving only the moderately retarded, others serving a variety of handicapped children. Few efforts have been made to integrate the moderately retarded into the regular school program except for such noninstructional activities as lunch and assembly.

At the large, multipurpose state residential facilities there is usually a school building for special education teachers and their classes. Usually the institutionalized moderately retarded attend school five days a week for about the same number of hours as the local community school operates, but more half-day sessions are in evidence because of teacher shortages. Occasionally, when distances permit, the moderately retarded in institutions are taken by bus to community facilities.

Traditional curricular objectives. Since the moderately retarded have been considered to be only semi-independent, the broad goals for their education have been different from those for the mildly retarded. Program objectives have emphasized the development of the minimal skills needed to live and work in sheltered environments. In broad terms, the goals of the 1950s and 1960s were threefold while the children were considered only "trainable." These were (1) self-help; (2) socialization; and (3) oral communication. Very little academic preparation or vocational training was included.

Traditional curricular content. Hudson (1960a,b) has provided the most comprehensive survey of curriculum ingredients emphasized during the late 1950s. Over a school year, she observed in some 29 special day classes for younger and older moderately retarded pupils operated by local school systems. Below are listed, in rank order, the 15 major lesson areas she identified, along with the percentage of time each received and some of the ingredients contained under each.

    1. *Language development*—18 percent of time. For the younger children in the primary classes, emphasis was on oral communication, including listening to the teacher, following directions, building vocabulary, giving one's name and address, talking in sentences, speaking

clearly, talking about pictures, using the telephone, explaining one's needs, and storytelling. For the older pupils, there was some time devoted, as well, to writing (copying words) and reading (recognizing labels, traffic and safety signs, and so on).

2. *Motor development*—10.2 percent of time. For younger children, manipulation of objects, ball throwing, and free play were stressed. Older pupils had more organized games and physical education.

3. *Cognitive development*—8.8 percent of time. For both younger and older groups, memory training, following directions, and puzzle solving (form boards) were included in the syllabus.

4. *Sensory training*—8.5 percent of time. For both younger and older groups, visual and auditory discrimination, matching exercises, and gaining information through the various senses were included.

5. *Music*—7.7 percent of time. Keeping time to music, using rhythm sticks, and listening and singing along to music were the focus for the younger children. Musical games were added for the older pupils.

6. *Health and safety*—7.6 percent of time. Cleanliness, rest, and safety rules were stressed most with the younger children. Health habits, proper diet, teeth cleaning, and posture were added for the older boys and girls.

7. *Social studies*—6.9 percent of time. This area was provided only for the older group and emphasized lessons about home and community.

8. *Arithmetic concepts*—6.6 percent of time. With younger children, quantitative vocabulary was stressed. Older pupils learned to group, count, do simple addition facts, and use money.

9. *Self-help*—5.2 percent of time. Included were feeding, dressing and undressing, toileting, hair combing, and caring for belongings. Older pupils learned more advanced grooming, including make-up and hair care, and traveling skills.

10. *Occupational education*—4.8 percent of time. This area was stressed more with teenagers. Some attention was given to the use and care of tools and the production of objects typically made in sheltered workshops.

11. *Socialization*—4.7 percent of time. Lessons included taking turns, obeying rules, sharing, learning greetings, manners, and etiquette, and getting along together while working and playing.

12. *Arts and crafts*—3.8 percent of time. This lesson area included coloring, drawing, painting, pasting, cutting, and making simple objects. With older pupils, simple woodworking was added.

13. *Dramatization*—3.0 percent of time. Activities included accompanying songs with gestures, playing house, pantomiming actions, and dramatizing simple stories.

14. *Science concepts*—2.2 percent of time. Lessons in this area were mostly for older children, the emphasis being on understanding how to use tools and utensils, but exploring the environment through field trips was carried out in both primary and older classes.

15. *Practical arts*—2.0 percent of time. As the children grew older, some slight attention was given to washing and drying dishes, setting and clearing the table, serving, making beds, room cleaning, yard care, errand running, and other household tasks. (One might ponder why this aspect of the curriculum was given less time than any other.)

It will be noted that language development consumed almost one fifth of the time. The next highest-ranking activity, motor development, received just over half as much emphasis. As Hudson (1960b) has pointed out, too much time was spent on language development to the neglect of other areas. For example, no doubt the lack of attention to practical arts was due partially to the backgrounds and values of the instructors, who generally had prior experience as regular classroom teachers. It may also have been due to the fact that all of the special classes were located in regular public schools. One cannot help but wonder how much more emphasis would have been placed on the practical arts had the program been housed in a cottage which as nearly as possible replicated a typical home in the community. Also missing from the above list is the development of academic skills other than the very rudimentary ones. The traditional view has been that academics are beyond the abilities of the moderately retarded. Furthermore, the older youngsters were not taught specific occupational skills for outside employment. Instead, the concern—limited as it was—was on developing skills that would be useful in the sheltered environments of the home, immediate neighborhood, and workshops.

Traditional educational procedures. During the 1950s and early 1960s, American and Canadian special educators of the moderately retarded were influenced more by the "progressive education" philosophy and the "group play" procedures of the regular kindergarten rather than by the intensive, individualized instructional techniques of Itard, Seguin, or Guggenbühl. This is not surprising, since most of these teachers had little or no special experience with moderately retarded children. Thus they had to rely on their background of training and experience in early childhood and elementary education. Few had any special training beyond summer courses and workshops. The programs were largely day-care operations. The teachers were so busy attempting to control some 10 or 12 pupils in their self-contained special classes that they had little time for individual tutoring, even when teacher's aides were provided. Furthermore, few if any had training in determining specific behavior objectives for individual pupils or in implementing the behavior-modifying procedures necessary to achieve them. Finally, the teachers often found themselves in regular classrooms which had been converted for special class use but retained chalkboards, individual desks or tables, and other such nonfunctional equipment. Practical necessity and their own proclivities resulted in most of them emphasizing group activities, including oral language and group play, to keep their pupils occupied.

Effectiveness of traditional special education treatments. In the educational programs described above, were the appropriate ingredients chosen or emphasized in the curriculum? Did informal group-teaching procedures produce positive results? Might it have been better to concentrate on such specific areas as perceptual-motor training and cognitive development? Should behavior-modification procedures be widely adopted? To answer such questions, it is necessary to examine the research on the effectiveness of the programs of the 1950s and 1960s. Relevant investigations have been carried out in Minnesota, Illinois, Michigan, New York, Tennessee, Texas, California, and England. They are reviewed in considerable detail by Kirk (1964). Only the major findings are summarized here.

1. In Minnesota, the survey study of the opinions of parents and teachers by Reynolds, Ellis, and Kiland (1953), with no contrast groups, found that (1) the teachers believed retarded children had profited from the special day schools and classes in terms of socialization and self-care but not in the 3 R's; (2) higher-IQ children profited more than those with lower IQ scores; and (3) parents lessened their expectancies as the program continued.

2. In *Illinois,* using rating scales and psychometric tests, Goldstein (1956) conducted a two-year study of moderately retarded children in special classes. He found that (1) both children with Down's syndrome and those with other types of conditions made equal progress in adaptive behavior, the larger gains occurring in the first year rather than in the second; (2) children with IQ's below 35 had to be excluded because of extreme disruptive behavior; and (3) after a period of time, parents realized their children would not become self-sufficient.

3. In *Michigan,* Guenther (1956), over three years, used a case study approach in a small, rural special school serving a heterogeneous group of retarded children; in a small, urban special school for young children; and in an itinerant-teacher, home-training program for adolescents. He found that (1) pupils in the rural special school made slight to considerable progress in adaptive behavior; (2) the young children in the urban setting were too immature to profit from instruction; and (3) the home-instruction program did not seem to profit the adolescent pupils appreciably.

4. In *New York,* Johnson and Capobianco (1957) and Johnson, Capobianco, and Blake (1960), by pre- and post-testings over a two-year period, contrasted moderately retarded children in full-day special day classes, in half-day special day classes, and in residential facilities. They found that (1) both day and residential subjects made equal progress in self-care and socialization; (2) the improvements were no greater than could have been expected from mental age growth alone; and (3) children with IQ's below 30 could not profit from the school program.

5. In *Tennessee,* Hottel (1958), over a one-year period, compared the gains of high-IQ (40–50) and low-IQ (30–40) moderately retarded children in special day classes with those remaining at home. He found that (1) the high-IQ group at school gained significantly more *intellectually* than the high-IQ group at home; (2) the high-IQ group at school gained more *intellectually* than the low-IQ group at school, and (3) there were no significant differences on the many other measures of self-care and socialization.

6. In *Texas,* Peck and Sexton (1961) contrasted four groups over two years, namely, a special class in a regular public school; a segregated community class; an institutional class; and a control group at home. They found (1) no significant differences in IQ or SQ (social quotient) change

scores for any of the four groups; (2) significant gains for all three experimental groups over the control group on the subjective behavior-rating scale; and (3) no significant differences among the three experimental groups on either the objective tests or subjective ratings.

7. In *California,* Cain and Levine (1963) contrasted four groups of moderately retarded children, namely, a special day class experimental group; a home (no training) control group; an institutional special class experimental group; and an institutional (no classes) control group on measures of social competence and parent adaptability. They found that (1) both the experimental and control groups in the community made significantly more progress in social competence than either of the institutional groups; (2) the experimental groups in both settings did not make significant gains over their own controls; (3) a major portion of time in both community and institutional special classes was wasted on noninstructional activities; and (3) in terms of adaptability, parents in both community groups decreased in flexibility and empathy over time. These findings suggest that placement of moderately retarded children in present-day, large, multipurpose residential facilities will reduce their social development, but may be justified in taking pressure off the parents.

8. In *England,* Tizard (1964) and his associates conducted a two-year "Brooklands" experiment which contrasted an experimental group of moderately retarded children in a small, rural special boarding school operated by child care workers under the direction of an experienced and able nursery school teacher with a control group in a large London institution. They found that (1) the experimental group made significantly greater gains over the controls in intelligence, verbal skills, social and personal adjustment, and even motor coordination; and (2) the costs ran considerable higher in the small, family-group–oriented boarding school located in a private home on a pleasant estate.

All of these studies reflect many weaknesses: training periods were short; sample sizes were small; attrition was high; controls were inadequate; measuring instruments were insensitive; heterogeneous groups of subjects were usually used; specific curriculum and teaching methods were not detailed; and teacher variables were not systematically manipulated. Significantly, too, in the main, the U.S. studies were conducted just as the public schools were assuming responsibility for such programs. Thus this was a period of inexperience and uncertainty concerning what and how to teach the moderately retarded. Nevertheless, with the exception of the Brooklands boarding school experiment, the findings were largely negative. There is little evidence from these studies to suggest that special day classes are effective *as they have been constituted,* emphasizing as they have the development of self-care and socialization by informal, total-group instruction for groups of children with IQ's over the full range from about 25 to about 50. However, the ultimate effectiveness of these traditional programs rests on the evidence from follow-up studies on what happens to these moderately retarded pupils after they leave the special schools and classes.

Follow-up studies. Some evidence is now presented on what has happened to the graduates of various special day class programs as well as to a group of children who were kept at home.

1. Delp and Lorenz (1953) followed up 84 individuals formerly enrolled in the St. Paul, Minnesota, special day class program.[4] The subjects had a median age of 22 years when the study was made. Of these 84 former students, 41 (about 50 percent) were still residing at home; 25 (about 30 percent) were already in residential facilities; 9 (about 10 percent) were deceased; and 9 (about 10 percent) had moved out of the state. None had established their own homes. Only 2 had ever held full-time jobs, and only 10, all males (about 12 percent), had ever been gainfully employed. Most of those still living at home were fairly well accepted in the immediate neighborhood and were useful about the house.

2. Saenger (1957) followed up some 2,640 adults formerly enrolled in special classes for the moderately retarded in New York City during the period 1929–1955. He found two thirds of the graduates living at home, compared with the one half noted by Delp and Lorenz. Of the remaining one third, 26 percent were institutionalized and 8 percent had died since leaving school. Those who were employed tended to be older (over 30 years), brighter (IQ scores in the high 40's and low 50's), and were usually men. Many of the jobs were found with (or through) relatives. Saenger went on to say that one in five of his subjects assumed major responsibility for such household chores as cleaning the apartment, helping with the dishes, and running errands. Over half took responsibility for taking care of their own things and cleaning their rooms.

3. Tisdall (1960) followed up 126 children who had been enrolled in special day classes for the moderately retarded in Illinois during the previous five years, and so were younger than either the Delp and Lorenz or Saenger samples. Too, their IQ scores were lower. Twelve percent had been institutionalized. Only one subject was gainfully employed for pay in the community outside of a sheltered workshop. Interviews with the parents suggested they believed that the school curriculum, which had stressed self-care, social adjustment, and economic usefulness, had been effective, since the children were not disturbing influences in the family and were self-sufficient in eating, washing, and dressing.

4. The three studies just described need to be evaluated in the light of a study conducted by Jewell (1941) on 190 children from the District of Columbia who, in the 1930s, were excluded from school because of low intelligence, their IQ scores ranging from 30 to 50. The majority of these subjects were reported to be getting along well at home, but only a few were employed for pay. These young people, *without any special education training,* appeared to have become as effective in later life as those who graduated from the Minnesota, New York, and Illinois special classes. The follow-up

---

[4] These classes were initiated in 1934.

studies, then, must be viewed as not lending much support for special classes in terms of adult preparation.

What conclusions can one draw from these investigations? On the one hand, one might argue that special classes are not doing the job that might be done and that changes are needed. On the other hand, one could say that considerable evidence suggests that moderately retarded pupils will never become socially and economically self-sufficient, and, therefore, the curriculum should be restricted to teaching practical skills that will be useful in the restricted environment of the home and sheltered workshops. Furthermore, many moderately retarded individuals will be placed in residential facilities as they become older and relatives are not available to care for them. If special education cannot prevent this from occurring, what can it do to prepare individuals for such placement? Certainly neither the efficacy nor the follow-up studies indicate that the special day schools and classes of the 1950s and 1960s were adequate for the education of moderately retarded boys and girls.

Present-day and Emerging Curricular Approaches

Effects of specific treatments. Studies addressed to specific aspects of teaching the moderately retarded are becoming the present research approach. These should provide more useful information than the broad investigations just described. References to these narrower studies can be obtained in the *Mental Retardation Abstracts* (see Resources section, Chapter 3) and the *Exceptional Child Education Abstracts* (see Resources section, Chapter 1). Only a few examples are presented here.

1. Brown and Perlmutter (1971), in 60 instructional hours, demonstrated that moderately retarded teen-aged children could be taught to read, with understanding, the following 17 words arranged into nine different sentences: "The penny is (on top of, on the bottom of, under, over, on the right side of, on the left side of, in front of, in back of, inside) the box." Their refreshing success was due, in large measure, to use of imaginatively developed educational materials, including a box mounted in a frame, wherein the subjects could verify their reading by checking on the location of the penny. This is but one example of a series of studies conducted by Brown and his associates at the University of Wisconsin on the teaching of functional academic skills to the moderately retarded.

2. Apffel (1969) found that the moderately retarded could be taught a mini-sight vocabulary equally well using the *rebus* (see Chapter 10) and traditional orthography approaches and that those taught by the teacher made significantly greater gains than those taught by machine instruction.

3. Weber (1966) used music as a teaching aid (*Musicall*) with moderately retarded children and found they improved in visual perception, auditory discrimination, reading, writing, and number concepts.

4. With moderately retarded subjects, Daw (1964) observed improve-

ments in body image and Kershner (1968) in intellectual functioning following motor-training programs. Richardson (1970) found equally positive results when he compared a conventional physical fitness program with a specially designed psychomotor training program.

These are but a few examples of the newer sorts of studies appearing in the literature. Still largely absent are investigations of concept formation and cognitive development, and there are few studies on the training of attention, concentration, and memory. No doubt these topics will be more thoroughly investigated in the years ahead as research on the moderately retarded continues.

Present-day curricular objectives and references. Since the 1950s and 1960s, the demarcation line between the mildly and moderately retarded has shifted upward toward IQ scores of 55, 60, and 65. Accompanying the trend to integrate so-called educable retardates into general education has come the realization that most children from standard English-speaking homes with IQ's in the 50's cannot function in an academically oriented class. Thus more and more of these students are likely to be reclassified as moderately retarded and placed in self-contained special education facilities. Concurrently, children with IQ's in the 20's and low 30's, who are usually unsuccessful in special classes for the moderately retarded, are increasingly being placed in *day-care centers* and other services for the severely retarded. At the same time, behavior-modification techniques are enabling us to teach more than was previously thought possible to this middle group. As a result, instead of calling the moderately retarded semi-dependent, they are now referred to as semi-independent, reflecting a subtle but important attitudinal change. Therefore, curricular objectives have been broadened considerably to include the following four rather comprehensive goals:

1. Self-help, basic readiness, and independent living skills development.
2. Communication, language, and cognitive development.
3. Socialization and personality development.
4. Vocational-, recreational-, and leisure-skills development.

These shifts can easily be seen by examining the text books in the field over the years. The first generation ones were those by Baumgartner (1960); Perry (1960); and Rosenzweig and Long (1960). These were followed by the second generation of texts on the topic, including Neale and Campbell (1963); McDowall (1964); Frankel, Happ, and Smith (1966); and Morgenstern, Low-Beer, and Morgenstern (1966). There has been a third, more recent, collection of publications: Alpern and Boll (1971); Bradley, Hundziak, and Patterson (1971); D'Amelio (1971); Gardner (1971); Molloy (1972); Stephens (1971); Stevens (1971); Thompson and Grabowski (1972); and Waite (1972). Evans and Apffel (1968) have also contributed a comprehensive survey of developments during the 1960s in education for the moderately retarded. These sources constitute a rather complete collection of the books focusing on special education for the moderately retarded.

Present-day curricular contents. Figure 2.3 depicts the specific ingredients included under each of the four educational objectives listed above.[5] In interpreting the figure, the reader should keep in mind that most of the specific ingredients listed receive attention over a broad age span of the children and not at one age level, as this pictorial representation suggests.

Effects of present-day behavior-modification techniques. Earlier it was pointed out that the moderately retarded could be taught more than previously had been thought possible, largely through the use of behavior-shaping techniques. Proponents of these techniques see little value in such diagnostic instruments as psychometric tests which label and categorize persons into IQ groups. They take the position that a child is not retarded, only his behavior is retarded by the standards which we hold for him. Their approach, therefore, is to obtain baseline data on a particular type of behavior that is to be modified and then set up an individualized instructional program of small sequential steps designed to raise a pupil's level of functioning. Successful performances are immediately rewarded, since this increases the likelihood that the desired behavior will reoccur when the child is placed in a similar situation. Of course, the instructional program is continuously revised to insure a pattern of pupil successes. Behavior-modification advocates believe that the limits of achievement for the retarded are largely determined by the ingenuity of the instructor in designing and carrying out the training program, contending that any skill or knowledge may be taught, at least in some preparatory version, to all but the most profoundly retarded.

No attempt will be made here to summarize the over 100 studies on the topic. Watson (1967, 1970) has excellent reviews of the area for institutionalized subjects. A comprehensive, three-part discussion of behavior modification for the retarded is provided by Nawas and Braun (1970), and Wiesberg (1971) has published an even more recent paper on the topic. Gardner (1971) has written a complete book on the use of behavior modification in the education and rehabilitation of the retarded adolescent and adult, Thompson and Grabowski (1972) have edited a volume on the same topic applicable over the full age range, and Girardeau (1971) has a very helpful chapter in the area. There is little doubt but that the body of knowledge on the topic has grown to the point where it could revolutionize the teaching of the more retarded. Already the area of teacher training is focusing heavily on teaching behavior-modification techniques. Hopefully, the application of these procedures, in the last quarter of the twentieth century, will replace the generally unsuccessful traditional efforts of the past in teaching the moderately retarded. However, as Nawas and Braun (1970) have cautioned: "Probably nothing is more lethal to the progress of a novel approach than unbridled

[5] These ingredients were gleaned from personal experience plus an examination of the program areas listed in Evans and Apffel (1968); Campbell (1968); Frankel, Happ, and Smith (1966); D'Amelio (1971); Stephens (1971); and Molloy (1972). For a detailed description of the curriculum content in each topic, the reader should consult these sources.

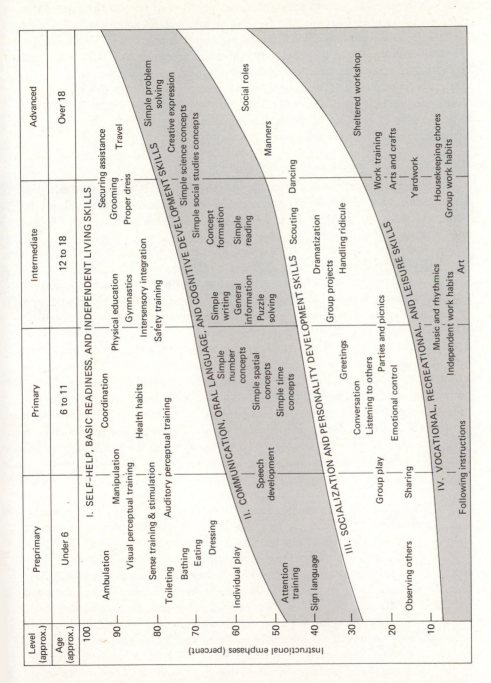

FIGURE 2.3 *Specific ingredients in four broad curricular areas by age levels for moderately retarded children and youth.* (Adapted from Campbell, 1968.)

zeal." Therefore, students of the field need to read such critical reviews of the research to date as Gardner (1971), who points out that studies have been plagued by many methodological flaws, making it dangerous to adopt whole-heartedly and uncritically behavior-modification procedures in the classroom. Nevertheless, these procedures cannot be ignored. If they are particularly suited for any one group, it is for the moderately and even the more retarded. Therefore, the teacher of the moderately retarded needs herself to become an experimenter in the use of these instructional techniques as she discovers which ones work best for her and for her pupils.

Educational Provisions for the Severely Retarded

Severely retarded pupils were defined as having IQ scores within the range 20 ± 5 to 35 ± 5. We focus now on special education for these children, who have been excluded or dismissed from special day schools and classes for the moderately retarded.

Traditional Practices

At one time, parents of severely retarded children who were excluded from programs for the moderately retarded had two options open to them: (1) to keep their children at home or (2) to place them in a residential facility. However, again through the efforts of parents, a third alternative became available, the *day-care center*. At first these were parent sponsored, but in the late 1960s they began to be supported by public funds, though generally not through the local school district, since severely retarded children were not considered to be a public school responsibility. These day-care centers did not usually employ teachers. Instead, they were served by day-care workers whose main goals were to provide custodial and recreational services. A prime function of these centers was to provide a respite for mothers from the constant care of their severely retarded children.

Future Directions

A dramatic breakthrough has been the effectiveness of behavior-modification techniques with severely retarded children. Finally, special educators have an effective method of teaching such youngsters. Typical of the many excellent guidelines in this area that have appeared is Bensberg's (1965) practical guide to help ward attendants teach the severely retarded using behavior-shaping techniques. These procedures should be even more effective when provided by trained instructors. Similarly, Larsen and Bricker (1968) have released a fine handbook on the topic for parents and teachers of the severely retarded. Such instructional materials as these should revolutionize the field.

At the same time, parents, through their National Association for Retarded Children, have taken vigorous action, by two strategies, to implement a bill of rights for all retarded persons. One approach is through court actions and the other is through state legislation making mandatory education for all retarded children. In 1971, in response to legal action by the organization of parents, a federal court in Philadelphia ordered Pennsylvania to assume responsibility for the education of all retarded children in the state. It gave the state 90 days to identify every retarded child denied an education and ordered it to begin programs for these excluded children by September 1972 or be liable for contempt of court action. Struck out of the state public school code were a number of provisions, including (1) exclusion practices based on a psychologist finding a child "ineducable and untrainable"; (2) the requirement that beginners have a mental age of five years; and (3) the interpretation of compulsory school age to mean only 8 through 17 years. Education departments can no longer turn over their unwanted pupils to welfare departments or other state agencies. However, apparently tuition grants so parents can send their children to private schools and homebound instruction are legally acceptable forms of special education. In any event, similar court action is likely to occur in other states if state education agencies do not comply with this ruling. By 1972, over 10 states had taken the necessary steps to avoid court action. For example, Rhode Island passed legislation making the state responsible for the education of *all* retarded persons without exception between the ages of three and twenty-one. Whether all states will follow this example remains to be seen. In any event, the 1970s should be the decade of special education for the severely retarded. The following editorial from the *New York Times* (October 13, 1971) summarizes it well:

> The ruling by a three-judge Federal court in Philadelphia that the State of Pennsylvania must provide free public education to all retarded children constitutes a historic step in an area that has suffered from public and professional neglect. Similar court tests will inevitably be instituted unless school systems across the country move toward voluntary compliance with what will surely become the universal legal requirement.
>
> The education of retarded children is a difficult task, but it is clearly a responsibility to be borne by school and society. For parents it is, under present chaotic and often callously inadequate provisions, both a personally heartbreaking and financially ruinous problem. School systems apply widely differing standards in categorizing youngsters ineducable. Even where districts nominally accept the responsibility for keeping such children in school, they often fail to provide effective instruction, thus adding frustration to disability. Yet the few existing private institutions of acceptable quality are beyond the financial reach of most families of even comfortable means.
>
> The court ruling is humane and socially sound. Whatever the cost of educating retarded children, the cost of setting them adrift in the world without giving them the means to lead useful lives is far higher. It is also morally indefensible. With only about three percent of the school-age population in the retarded category, the nation is surely able to provide the means to point these youngsters on a productive course.
>
> A court order alone, however, is not enough. To translate the law into educational policy requires fully trained personnel and adequate staffing in existing schools and in special facilities. United States Education Commissioner Sidney P. Marland Jr. urges that 1980 be set as the target year for assuring all retarded children a free public education. The

Pennsylvania ruling provides a new legal basis for eliminating a glaring neglect.[6]

It will be interesting to observe the pattern of special education services which evolve for the so-called ineducable and untrainable child. No doubt a variety of options will need to be tried to serve such a wide diversity of youngsters in so many different communities and family situations. Homebound (including parent) education would appear to be most minimal but could be useful for very young and immature children. Public tuition grants to attend private boarding schools cannot be ruled out. Hopefully, the route will not be toward an uncritical initiation of special day classes with the characteristics of nursery, kindergarten, and primary-grade classes for normal children. Instead, even more than with the moderately retarded, there is a need to follow the Russian practice of establishing *special boarding schools* for these children on a five-day week (Dunn and Kirk, 1963). Such a plan would provide an around-the-clock program of intensive instruction for developing self-help and other skills. Failing this, it is hoped that *special day cottages* will be operated where the setting is as similar to a regular home as possible. Ideally, a combination of these two plans should be available so as to provide the flexibility to serve pupils on both a day and boarding basis. It will be interesting to see how rapidly public school authorities are induced to accept responsibility for the severely retarded and provide them with such programs as these.

Effects of Moderately and Severely Retarded Children on Families

A number of investigators have studied the effects that retarded children have on their families. Included here are only a few highlights from the rather extensive research that has been done on this topic. It is data such as these which suggest the likelihood that such children will be kept at home and in the community in the future versus the extent to which some type of residential placement will be demanded by parents and relatives. More extensive treatment of this topic is provided by Ross (1964); Farber and Ryckman (1965); and Farber (1968). The generalizations presented here are drawn from the classical studies of Edgerton (1967) in California; Farber (1968) in Illinois; Saenger (1960) and Grossman (1972) in New York; Braginsky and Braginsky (1971) in the New England states; Schonell and Rorke (1960) in Australia; Tizard and Grad (1961) in England; and Fotheringham, Skelton, and Hoddinott (1971) in Canada.

1. Obviously, keeping a moderately or severely retarded child at home puts pressure on the family, but this does not always make home "hell on earth." For example, Tizard and Grad (1961) found that one third of such children presented mild management problems, one third moderate, and one third severe.

[6] © 1971 by the New York Times Company. Reprinted by permission.

2. Placement in a large, traditional, multipurpose residential institution will have a harmful effect on the person so placed, but will reduce the pressure on the family.

3. When there is such a child in the home, the family tends to restrict its community contacts. Conflict results in the family when one of its members finds major interests outside the home.

4. Parents with a moderate or even a more retarded child in the home tend not to have additional children.

5. The retarded child, regardless of his birth order, tends to be treated as the youngest child.

6. The moderately and severely retarded child at home has a deleterious and restrictive effect on an older sister who has to care for him and is hesitant about bringing dates home. Older brothers, on the other hand, are given extra freedom, since the parents are focusing their attention on the retarded child. The closer the age of the siblings to that of the retarded, the more they are negatively affected.

7. Siblings who associate a good deal with their retarded brother or sister tend to become more concerned about improving the lot of man in society than those who do not.

8. There is some evidence that Catholic homes are better able to tolerate and integrate a retarded child than Protestant and Jewish ones. In general, close ties to the church are a positive factor for preventing disintegration of the family unit which includes a noticeably retarded child (Stedman, undated). However, socioeconomic conditions and ethnic background may play as important a part as religion. Apparently a combination of Catholicism; old central European mores; and upper lower and lower middle class living conditions—combined with good, sound, family solidarity—are the conditions most likely to result in a severely retarded child being accepted at home.

9. Upper and middle class parents who place their child in a state residential facility tend to maintain much less contact with their retarded child than lower class families and are less likely ever to take him home again.

10. Parents who keep a retarded child at home tend to drift downward socially, but institutionalization tends to inhibit this process.

11. There is consensus that the more severely retarded are more likely to be institutionalized.

12. Institutionalization is related to such factors as family disintegration, broken and overcrowded homes, parental inadequacy, financial problems, and lack of professional support. Tizard and Grad (1961) and Braginsky and Braginsky (1971) also found this positive relation to hold for large family size and low income, but Saenger (1960) did not.

Obviously, there is no simple answer to the twofold question, what is it like to have a retarded child, and should he be placed in a residential facility? It has been pointed out that residential placement in the typical large, multipurpose institution will have a harmful effect on the person so placed, but will reduce the pressure on the family. Therefore, the decision to institutionalize results in a conflict between what is in the best interests of the child and what is best for the rest of the family. As long as institutionalization is the only option open, each family will need to evaluate its own situation and plan its own course of action. In the past, much institutionalizing was done by the courts, who tended to commit delinquent young people who were not too bright. Today, it is more frequently the parents of the visibly retarded who face this decision. The major research findings just presented should be helpful to professionals as they counsel parents about whether their moderately or severely retarded child should remain at home or be placed in a residential facility.

One can find little reason for complacency about either our traditional special day schools and classes or our traditional, large, multipurpose institutions for the retarded. Clearly, comprehensive changes are needed in both types of services.

Residential Facilities

The historical origins of residential facilities for retarded were presented earlier in this chapter. We consider now the kinds of services offered in these institutions as well as their current and future status. Good overview statistics on them are available in annual editions of *Statistical Abstracts of the United States.* Furthermore, these abstracts list more detailed sources of information.

In 1970, 186,743 U.S. citizens were in 180 public residential facilities, down slightly for a third consecutive year from the high of 193,188 reached in 1967 (U.S. Department of Health, Education and Welfare, 1972). About another 20,000 were in some 500 private institutions. Therefore, the average population was still over 1,000 per institution in the public facilities and about 400 in the costly private ones. Thus, approximately 0.1 percent of the general population was in these two types of residences. The number of public facilities has steadily increased for many years, more than doubling from 1940 to 1970. In fact, during the sixties more new state residential facilities were opened than in any other decade in our history. The proportion of moderately retarded in them has remained constant at about one third since the early 1920s. The number of mildly retarded has dropped from over 50 percent to under 20 percent since the 1920s, while the proportion has reversed for the more severely and profoundly retarded. Approximately one half of the residents are under 20 years of age, and about 55 percent are males. Some good comprehensive references on these institutions in the United States include Baumeister and Butterfield (1970) and Kugel and Wolfensberger (1969), which treat the topic in detail.

It is difficult to place appropriately in this text the topic of residential facilities, since these institutions serve persons of all ages with all levels of retardation. The subject is treated here only because most residents are now moderately or more retarded. But the reader is cautioned to consider the discussion which follows in the total context of the topic.

Since well over 90 percent of retarded persons in residential facilities are in large, multipurpose institutions operated by state and provincial governments, these will be the focus of this discussion. These units are asked to provide all types of care and treatment for retardates of all ages and all levels of intellect. Typically, these facilities are understaffed, underfinanced, and overcrowded. For example, only about 11 dollars per day per patient was available in state residential facilities in 1970 for care and treatment. However, these large, multipurpose residences have some advantages. They are less expensive to operate than small ones; they permit an interdisciplinary approach to treatment; and they provide a large population of retardates for research. Notwithstanding, they have overshadowing disadvantages which have been widely illustrated by Blatt and Kaplan (1967) and extensively described by Kugel and Wolfensberger (1969). They are so large that a mass, dehumanizing, deindividualizing approach to treatment usually prevails. Often they are oriented toward custodial care rather than intensive treatment. In these institutions interdisciplinary rivalry is frequently evident. Much of the service is provided by untrained attendants while the professionals engage in administrative tasks, including attending case conferences and other meetings. They often are unable to attract capable professional personnel. Funds are frequently spent on expanding the physical plant at the expense of the staff and services. Even the President's Committee on Mental Retardation described them as a disgrace to the nation, stating in its 1969 report that institutionalized retarded persons continue to be "warehoused in de-humanizing residential programs that make no serious attempt to rehabilitate residents."

The question arises as to whether these residences can be improved significantly or whether they should be abandoned in favor of different types of residential services designed to serve populations with different treatment needs, degrees of retardation, and ages.

According to the 1970 report of the President's Committee on Mental Retardation (1971), for the first time, a concerted, national effort is being made to improve these facilities. A federally funded Council for the Accreditation of Mental Retardation Facilities is working at this task, as are the International League of Societies for the Mentally Handicapped and the National Association for Retarded Children. The last two organizations urge that the reasons and goals for an individual's admission to a residential facility be specified and that the intervention program be geared to the attainment of these goals. The President's Commission has proposed the following nine-point platform for fundamental change and improvement. Parenthetical comments are added so the reader can better debate whether these proposals are likely to do the job.

1. The *primary* purpose of residential services is to enable the retarded individual to develop his capacities to the fullest extent possible and whenever possible learn skills, habits, and attitudes for return to community living. (This statement fails to recognize that placement is made *primarily* to take pressure off the parents and society; it is not in the best interests of the individual. Furthermore, institutional placement prepares one for institutional living, not community living.)

2. It is the obligation of the residential facility to develop each individual's economic potential. (This is unrealistic, since more and more

institutionalized persons are too severely retarded to be gainfully employed in even a sheltered environment.)

3. The residential facility should be used for programing, not punishment. (The fact is that essentially all institutionalized persons are incarcerated in such facilities by parents, guardians, or the courts, although the movement has been away from commitment by the courts.)

4. Good residential programs provide both long- and short-term services. (State residential facilities are doing a much better job in this regard; but in the end the program largely is a long-term one, since parents take the child out less and less and since the more severely retarded who need constant health care are enrolled. Furthermore, many facilities are located in rural areas far from the large cities, making short-term services unworkable.)

5. It is essential that a residential facility coordinate its programs with other regional and community mental retardation services for the development of a full range of comprehensive services. (Such cooperation is improving and will be increasingly possible as a fuller range of community services become available. However, before long this recommendation is likely to result largely in a one-way street, with the community seeking to get the profoundly retarded cases off its hands.)

6. The model residential environment should provide a warm, stimulating social setting, devoid of dehumanizing conditions. (This goal would seem to be unattainable in large warehouses for thousands of human beings; furthermore, essentially all staff contacts are provided by poorly educated attendants who are often only slightly more intelligent than some of the residents.)

7. Staff must reflect attitudes and behaviors consistent with the concept that they serve as family surrogates while the retarded are in their care. (Here is the major flaw. Generally, these well-organized, if not unionized, attendants seldom invest this much of themselves. Negative attitudes are so firmly implanted that they cannot be changed significantly.)

8. Administrative policies should recognize the importance of the interrelation of parents, volunteers, staff and residents. (Generally this has been the case, but policies and practices have traditionally been at variance.)

9. The mentally retarded shall have the same constitutional rights and guarantees as other American citizens. (This laudable goal has been espoused for some time, especially in the report of President Kennedy's Panel on Mental Retardation (Mayo, 1962) and by the members of the Joint Commission on Mental Health of Children [1970]. The fact remains that retarded persons are incarcerated in such facilities by others, are not free to come and go as they wish, are not allowed to marry or cohabit, and so on.)

In summary, it is suggested that the above nine goals are largely unattainable, pious platitudes.

A growing number of concerned professionals, parents, and politicians are coming to realize that these large, multipurpose facilities cannot be salvaged. First, it must be recognized that they are dumping grounds for society's misfits. Institutional placement of a problem person is often the easy way out. What is needed is a comprehensive ecological approach aimed at determining why the parents and the community were unable to tolerate the individual. The needed adjustments could then be made so the person could remain outside the institution. Second, the negative attitudes and practices of ward attendants in the large facilities are so entrenched that they are not likely to be changed appreciably. Thus for these two reasons especially, many people believe that these multipurpose institutions should be phased out as soon as possible.

Since residential services for retarded persons appear to be a necessity, what form should they take? A number of models are presented in Kugel and Wolfensberger (1969). Tizard argues for a wide continuum of community and residential services. Wolfensberger proposes an even broader human service system based on a cost-benefit rationale, which would include a wide array of community-based "retardation" services. Clearly, a trend is beginning. Already in a few states a fairly good variety of community and alternate residential services are available. In these states, the large institutions no longer have waiting lists. In fact, in 1967, for the first time, the total number of persons in state residential facilities for the retarded dropped slightly. In addition, Ross (1972) reported that 67 percent of the male and 73 percent of the female patients classified as mildly retarded at Fairview State Hospital in California were on nonresident status in 1970, a pattern that is spreading across the nation.

Dunn (1969) has proposed a series of small, single-purpose, intensive-treatment boarding units to replace the large, multipurpose residences. The medically-oriented ones would include short-term specific medical treatment centers, long-term general medical care centers, and long-term nursing care units. As nonmedical ones, child-development centers, boarding schools, habilitation centers, foster homes, hostels, rest homes, and so forth, would be included. Six principles would underlie the operation of these small units. (1) The number of residents in these facilities would be as small as possible, seldom if ever exceeding 100 or so. (2) All except the profoundly retarded would spend at least a day or two a week out in the community. (3) A flexible, open-door policy would exist to permit persons easy movement among spe-cial-purpose units, community services, and relatives. (4) The profession primarily trained to provide the needed specialized treatment would be in charge of the facility. (5) Every resident would receive extensive intervention treatment provided by professional and paraprofessional personnel; attend-ants (if employed) would always work at simple routine chores under a pro-fessional person who would always be present. (6) These units would be geographically distributed as close to population centers as possible.

Canada, with a population of about one tenth that of the United States, appears to be making a more vigorous attempt to phase out, reduce, and/or change the emphasis of its large residential facilities, especially in the west-ern and middle provinces. By 1972, British Columbia had established: (1) three short-stay-hostels with 10 to 15 beds each where parents could place their retarded children to have a period of respite up to 30 days; (2) three farm-training centers for mildly retarded boys from 17 to 21 years, each serving 18 to 40 young men; (3) seven *group boarding homes* for the moderately retarded serving 8 to 30 children each; and (4) three *group hostels* serving 8 to 18 retarded adults each. Alberta had five of these small, special-purpose community residences in operation, with five more under construction and another four on the drawing board. Saskatchewan had six, Manitoba had five, and Ontario had twelve in operation, and as many more were under construction or planned. Too, as in the United States, many residents are being placed in individual boarding or foster homes. With these two developments, the number of persons in the large residential facilities is dropping quite rapidly. Clearly, a major anticipated trend is that in both the United States and Canada large, multi-purpose residential facilities will be largely phased out by the end of the century.

Postschool Occupational Services
for the Moderately and Severely Retarded

In our attempts to retain the maximum number of retarded persons in the community, one important consideration will be to find as many opportunities as possible to develop and utilize their vocational skills. From the follow-up studies described earlier, it was seen that very few moderately retarded pupils, upon reaching adulthood, become economically self-sufficient. It has therefore been important to find employment for them in a protective environment. This has largely taken the form of sheltered workshops, which have been of the three types: type 1—*training oriented* to prepare individuals for competitive employment; type 2—*terminal oriented* for those who cannot compete in the marketplace; and type 3—a *combination* of the first two. There are a number of type 2 workshops which serve only the retarded. The type 1 and 3 workshops usually serve disabled adolescents and adults with a variety of handicapping conditions.

The literature is extensive on sheltered workshops and other vocational rehabilitation programs for both residential and day school programs. Good reviews are available by Windle (1962), Cohen (1966), Eagle (1967), Huddle (1967a), Wolfensberger (1967), and Cobb (1972). A look at the British scene is provided by Gunzburg (1965). As Wolfensberger (1967) pointed out, many middle-level retarded persons in Europe are performing tasks believed by most American professionals in the field to be beyond their capacities. For example, Tizard (1967) has found that persons with IQ's as low as 25 can be taught routine industrial jobs. This finding is supported in the United States by such studies as Appell, Williams, and Fishell (1962), who discovered that retardates with good work habits and good social adjustment could go from a workshop setting into certain forms of competitive employment. Huddle (1967b) reached the following conclusions from his and other studies:

1. Moderately retarded persons are usually much slower in *initial* level of performance than subjects of higher IQ, but their *final* performance is equal on routine tasks when proper training procedures are provided.

2. Such individuals generally appear to work best in small-group situations.

3. Most moderately retarded adults respond better to monetary incentives than to the effects of competition or cooperation, although social approval is also very important.

4. Most properly motivated and trained moderately retarded adults finally need only minimal supervision.

5. In addition to inadequate training and supervision, the major reasons for lack of job success on the part of the moderately retarded are poor work habits, poor interpersonal relations, and insufficient motor skills. The more skills the moderately retarded develop in these areas, the more likely they are to become gainfully employed.

6. With the moderately retarded, IQ score of itself is not the major reason for lack of occupational success.

7. A few moderately retarded adults will not even succeed in a terminal-type sheltered workshop and will need other organized community activity programs to entertain and care for them.

Clearly, we have a long way to go in providing optimal vocational preparation and occupation for moderately and severely retarded persons. Three directions are suggested. (1) The school curriculum for the older, moderately retarded pupils should be revised to put a much greater emphasis on occupational education than has been the case in the past. In fact, a presheltered workshop program should dominate for adolescents who have a prognosis of occupational success. (2) Sheltered workshops need to improve markedly. A U.S. Labor Department report (1967) has pointed out that many of them have poor productivity because of low skill levels of the workers, small capacity, primitive production techniques and equipment, and poor management training and supervision services. Suggested is experimentation with better training, more careful programing, and significant financial incentives. (3) Industry, government, and other agencies need to examine attitudes toward middle-grade retarded persons with a view toward making more routinelike jobs available to them. But the schools and vocational-rehabilitation agencies have a responsibility to do a better job than ever before of preparing, placing, and supervising such persons in community positions. Too, relatives or society will need to continue to provide sheltered, home-living facilities for them, especially for the severely retarded, who may be able to do only household and yard chores under supervision.

A final word of caution needs to be injected. As automation and technology reduce job opportunities for all persons, it is clear that the traditional lifetime of work will not be expected of everyone, much less the moderately and more retarded. Because of this, it would be unfortunate if there was a preoccupation with training for and making or finding work for these persons. Instead, a balance is suggested. Of prime importance is the provision of opportunities for them to develop into well-adjusted, socially-accepted adults who can care for themselves as much as possible and occupy their leisure time to their own satisfaction.

Emerging Directions in Special Education
for Moderately and Severely Retarded Children

As special education goes through a period of transition during the 1970s, the following would appear to be the most promising directions with respect to the moderately and severely retarded.

1. The terms "educable," "trainable," "nontrainable," and even "mentally retarded" need to be abolished by educators because of their stigmatizing effects. If undesirable labels must be retained, then "mildly," "moderately," and "severely retarded in general learning ability" are recommended.

2. The *moderately* retarded need to be redefined upward to include the IQ range 35 ± 5 to 60 ± 5, thus dropping out the lower end of the former "trainable" category and adding in the lower end of the former "educable" category who have been found to be nonadaptive to an academic school program.

3. The potential of the *moderately* retarded appears to be considerably higher than was thought earlier, thanks to the use of specific behavioral objectives and behavior-modification techniques. Therefore, the school curriculum needs to be upgraded to include more academic as well as social and vocational instruction. While few of these individuals are likely to become completely literate or completely socially independent, most should be able to achieve between the first- and third-grade levels and be gainfully employed in semi-independent settings.

4. For the *moderately* retarded, small combined day and boarding school units are recommended. These should bring together the features of a special school or class, a typical home and yard, and prevocational and sheltered workshop facilities. Self-contained special day classes in regular public schools should be phased out. Traditionally, these have not been very different from a regular kindergarten or primary grade, and even the special schools have looked too much like regular schools. This situation is understandable when it is realized that most of the buildings used are abandoned regular elementary schools, that most of the special teachers have backgrounds in regular education, and that most parents want their retarded children to go to "school" as they knew it. More appropriate would be *community cottages* furnished, in part, like regular homes. Here the children could look after the lawns, shrubs, and garden. They could care for the house, cook in the kitchen, and clean up afterwards. They could learn how to wash a car, use a bathroom, change beds, and store materials in and get them from cupboards. They could have their own bedrooms, linen closets, and a washer and dryer. They could live in a living room, eat in a dining room, and play in back and front yards. And a place for academic and vocational instruction could still be provided.

5. State or local public school systems need to assume responsibility for the *severely* retarded with IQ scores in the 20 ± 5 to 35 ± 5 range who have so far been considered uneducable and untrainable. These children have

either had to remain at home, attend a parent-sponsored day-care center, or be institutionalized. It is imperative that special *five-day–week boarding schools* be established for these severely retarded children where the curriculum would emphasize self-care and socialization. The facility should also duplicate a typical home, yard, and neighborhood setting, but would not have the classroom or vocational components of the somewhat similar facilities for the moderately retarded. Furthermore, the severely retarded need a 24-hour–day instructional setting, so the day option would not generally be available. Under no circumstances should we attempt an educational program in special day classes in the regular public schools. The cottage training program proposed by Girardeau and Spradlin (1964) would appear to have much promise.

6. Day-care nurseries and centers should be extended to serve the moderately and severely retarded *preschool* child through his first five or six years. These should be under the aegis of a variety of child developmentalists, including educators. Nurses or other members of the medical profession should assume a supportive role.

7. There is a need for a rich array of community services such as more and better sheltered workshops, camps, hostels, halfway houses, temporary crisis residences, counseling services, and recreational and other programs, so that parents and relatives will not have to "go it alone," a situation which too often finally results in a desperate decision to institutionalize. In this regard, respite facilities to provide intervals of relief for families of the retarded such as those described by Paige (1971) should be helpful. The emphasis is on providing a broad collection of community services so that the vast majority of retarded individuals will not be placed in residential facilities, except as a last resort.

8. Large, multipurpose state residential facilities should be phased out as soon as possible and replaced with small, special-purpose residential units (or combined day and residential units). It is generally recognized that public institutions have a dehumanizing effect on individuals and, in addition, are mainly custodial in nature. But any form of residential placement should be kept at an absolute minimum and used only when all else has failed.

SUMMARY

Until the second half of this century, retarded children with IQ scores equivalent to 50 and below for white, native-born, standard English-speaking youngsters were believed ineducable and unable to profit from classroom instruction. Due to parent pressure, in the 1950s and 1960s, the public school assumed responsibility for the IQ 25–50 group, largely through providing special day schools and classes, but pupils were considered only trainable. In the past decade, teaching procedures for these moderately retarded children have been revolutionized by the application of behavior-modification techniques. As a result, it has been demonstrated that such pupils can be taught much more than was previously thought possible, which suggests that special education could be extended downward to those who are somewhat more retarded.

To provide a springboard for improved special services for the moderately and more retarded in the future, it is suggested that such pupils be reclassified as having "general learning disabilities (GLD's)," which describes them educationally rather than labeling them mentally retarded, a term which is restricted to its sociolegal usage to convey social incompetence. Further, it is proposed that the terms "trainable" and "custodial" be dropped in favor of "moderate" and "severe" GLD's, with the IQ range for the former group being 35 ± 5 to 60 ± 5 and for the latter group 20 ± 5 to 35 ± 5. (Individuals with IQ's below 20 ± 5 are seen as "profoundly" retarded, and for them no effective special education has yet been devised.) IQ equivalents would need to be adjusted for other than white, middle class, native-born children who speak standard English. No more than the lower ½ percent of any ethnic or racial group would be classified as moderately or more severely retarded.

The initial special day schools and classes of the fifties and sixties were found to be of limited value in promoting pupil progress. With improved instructional procedures and materials, there have been more positive results. As a result, the traditional objectives of developing a few self-help, socialization, and oral-communication skills have been broadened to the following four rather comprehensive goals: (1) self-help, basic readiness, and independent living skills development; (2) communication, language, and cognitive development; (3) specialization and personality development; and (4) vocational, recreational, and leisure skills development. It is proposed that self-contained special day classes for the moderately retarded in regular public schools be phased out in favor of community cottages with day and boarding school services. By court action, the next decade will see a variety of special education services extended to children with severe GLD's, including five-day boarding schools where the curriculum will emphasize self-care and socialization. Hopefully, by the end of the century, large, multipurpose residential facilities will be largely phased out in favor of a rich array of small, special-purpose community and residential services for retarded individuals of all ages and levels of functioning. These will be needed because as yet no effective special education methods have been found to enable those with moderate GLD's to become more than semi-independent and those with severe GLD's to become more than semidependent.

Resources

There has been a gratifying increase in resources in retardation in the last half of this century. These will be presented here and at the end of the next chapter. The parent organizations are singled out for attention here. The professional organizations and publications are described at the end of Chapter 3.

The present National Association for Retarded Children (NARC) in the

United States was founded in 1950 with a membership of 40 individuals. By 1960, this number had grown to more than 50,000 persons. By 1970, it was up to 211,000, but had dropped back to 210,000 by 1972. Its periodical, *Mental Retardation News* (formerly *Children Limited*), is widely circulated. The address of NARC is 2709 Avenue E East, Arlington, Texas 76011. NARC works through more than 1,300 state and local affiliates to advance the welfare of retarded persons of all ages and all levels of intellect.

The Canadian Association for the Mentally Retarded (CAMR) was incorporated in 1958. It, too, is a parent organization dedicated to helping retarded persons regardless of race, color, creed, or age. It is a federation of the 10 provincial and 351 local associations, plus a number of associate organizations, including some in the West Indies. By 1972, the CAMR membership had grown to over 25,000. Its quarterly publication is *Deficience Mentale/Mental Retardation*. CAMR has established a National Institute on Mental Retardation (NIMR) to serve as a technical training program development, research, and information service on mental retardation for Canada. The address of CAMR and its NIMR is Kinsmen Building, York University Campus, 4700 Keele Street, Downsview (Toronto), Ontario, Canada.

The headquarters for the International League of Societies for the Mentally Handicapped is located at 12 rue Forestière, 1059 Brussels, Belgium. Dybwad (1971) has provided us with an *International Directory of Mental Retardation Resources* covering 60 countries, including their parent organization. These organizations have had a great impact on the field of retardation. Their strength in fostering more adequate legislation, funds, research, and services have made the second half of the twentieth century a brighter age for the moderately and severely retarded, not only in Canada and the United States but around the world.

References

Abeson, A., and Trudeau, E. Handicapped children defined—legal eligibility for services expanded. *Exceptional Children*, 1970, **37**, 305–311.

Alpern, G. D., and Boll, T. J. (Eds.) *Education and care of moderately and severely retarded children.* Seattle, Wash.: Special Child Publications, 1971.

Apffel, J. A. A comparison of rebus symbols and traditional orthography in the teaching of rudimentary reading skills to children classified as trainable mentally retarded. Unpublished doctoral dissertation, Peabody College, Nashville, Tenn., 1969.

Appell, M. J., Williams, C. M., and Fishell, K. N. Significant factors in placing mental retardates from a sheltered situation. *Personnel and Guidance Journal.* 1962, **41**, 260–265.

Ball, T. S. *Itard, Seguin, and Kephart: Sensory education—A learning interpretation.* Columbus, O.: Charles E. Merrill, 1971.

Baumeister, A. A. (Ed.) *Mental retardation: Appraisal, education and rehabilitation.* Chicago: Aldine-Atherton, 1967.

Baumeister, A. A., and Butterfield, E. C. *Residential facilities for the mentally retarded.* Chicago: Aldine-Atherton, 1970.

Baumgartner, B. B. *Helping the trainable mentally retarded child.* New York: Teachers College Press, Columbia University, 1960.

Benda, C. E. *Down's syndrome: Mongolism and its management.* New York: Grune & Stratton, 1969.

Bensberg, G. L. (Ed.) *Teaching the mentally retarded: A handbook for ward personnel.* Atlanta, Ga.: Southern Regional Education Board, 1965.

Bienenstock, T., and Coxe, W. W. *Census of severely retarded children in New York State.* Albany, N.Y.: New York State Interdepartmental Health Resources Board, 1956.

Blatt, B., and Kaplan, F. *Christmas in purgatory.* Boston: Allyn and Bacon, 1967.

Bradley, B. H., Hundziak, M., and Patterson, R. M. *Teaching moderately and severely retarded children: A diagnostic approach.* Springfield, Ill.: Charles C Thomas, 1971.

Braginsky, D. D., and Braginsky, B. M. *Hansels and Gretels—Studies of children in institutions for the mentally retarded.* New York: Holt, Rinehart and Winston, 1971.

Bricker, D. D. Imitative sign training as a facilitator of word-object association with low-functioning children. *American Journal of Mental Deficiency,* 1972, **76**, 509–516.

Brown, L., and Perlmutter, L. Teaching functional reading to trainable level retarded students. *Education and Training of the Mentally Retarded,* 1971, **6**, 74–84.

Cain, L. F., and Levine, S. Effects of community and institutional school programs on trainable mentally retarded children. *CEC Research Monograph,* Series B. No. B-1. Arlington, Va.: Council for Exceptional Children, 1963.

Campbell, L. W. *Study of curriculum planning.* Sacramento, Calif.: California State Department of Education, 1968.

Cantor, G. N., and Girardeau, F. L. *An investigation of discrimination learning ability in mongoloid and normal children of comparable mental age.* Nashville, Tenn.: Peabody College, 1958.

Clarke, A. M., and Clarke, A. D. B. (Eds.) *Mental deficiency: The changing outlook.* (Rev. ed.) New York: Free Press, 1965.

Cobb, H. V. *The forecast of fulfillment: A review of research in predictive assessment of the adult retarded for social and vocational adjustment.* New York: Teachers College Press, Columbia University, 1972.

Cohen, J. S. Vocational rehabilitation of the mentally retarded. The sheltered workshop. *Mental Retardation Abstracts,* 1966, **3**, 163–169.

Connor, F. P., and Goldberg, I. I. Opinions of some teachers regarding their work with trainable children: Implications for teacher education. *American Journal of Mental Deficiency,* 1960, **64**, 658–670.

D'Amelio, D. *Severely retarded children: Wider horizons.* Columbus, O.: Charles E. Merrill, 1971.

Daw, J. F. The effect of special exercises on body image in mentally retarded children. *Slow Learning Child,* 1964, **11**, 109–116.

Delp, H. A., and Lorenz, M. Follow-up of 84 public school special class pupils with IQ's below 50. *American Journal of Mental Deficiency,* 1953, **58**, 175–182.

Dingman, H. F., and Tarjan, G. Mental retardation and the normal distribution curve. *American Journal of Mental Deficiency,* 1960, **64**, 991–994.

Doll, E. E. Trends and problems in the education of the mentally retarded: 1880–1940. *American Journal of Mental Deficiency,* 1967, **72**, 175–183.

Dunn, L. M. Small, special purpose residential facilities for the retarded. In R. B. Kugel and W. Wolfenberger (Eds.), *Changing patterns in residential services for the mentally retarded.* Washington, D.C.: President's Committee on Mental Retardation, 1969.

Dunn, L. M., and Kirk, S. A. Impressions of Soviet psychoeducational service and research in mental retardation. *Exceptional Children,* 1963, **29**, 299–311.

Dybwad, R. F. International directory of mental retardation resources: A publication issued by the President's Committee on Mental Retardation. Washington, D.C.: Government Printing Office, 1971.

Eagle, E. Prognosis and outcome of community placement of institutionalized retardates. *American Journal of Mental Deficiency*, 1967, **72**, 232–243.

Edgerton, R. B. *The cloak of competence: Stigma in the lives of the mentally retarded.* Berkeley, Calif.: University of California Press, 1967.

Ellis, N. R. (Ed.) *Handbook of mental deficiency: Psychological theory and research.* New York: McGraw-Hill, 1963.

Evans, J. R., and Apffel, J. A. Educational procedures for the trainable mentally retarded. *IMRID Papers and Reports*, Vol. 5, No. 1. Nashville, Tenn.: Peabody College, 1968.

Farber, B. *Mental retardation: Its social context and consequences.* Boston: Houghton Mifflin, 1968.

Farber, B., and Ryckman, D. B. Effects of severely mentally retarded children in family relations. *Mental Retardation Abstracts*, 1965, **2**, 1–17.

Fotheringham, J. B., Skelton, M., and Hoddinott, B. A. *The retarded child and his family: The effects of home and institution.* Toronto, Ontario: Ontario Institute for Studies in Education, 1971.

Frankel, M. G., Happ, F. W., and Smith, M. P. *Functional reaching of the mentally retarded.* Springfield, Ill.: Charles C Thomas, 1966.

Gardner, J. M., and Watson, L. S. Behavior modification of the mentally retarded: An annotated bibliography. *Mental Retardation Abstracts*, 1969, **6**, 181–193.

Gardner, W. I. *Behavior modification in mental retardation.* Chicago: Aldine-Atherton, 1971.

Gibson, D., and Frank, H. F. Dimensions of mongolism; I. Age limits for cardinal mongol stigmata. *American Journal of Mental Deficiency*, 1961, **66**, 30–34.

Gibson, D., and Pozsonyi, J. Morphological and behavioral consequences of chromosome subtype in mongolism. *American Journal of Mental Deficiency*, 1965, **69**, 801–804.

Girardeau, F. L. The systematic use of behavioral principles in training and teaching developmentally young children. In B. Stevens (Ed.), *Training the developmentally young.* New York: John Day, 1971.

Girardeau, F. L., and Spradlin, J. E. Token rewards in a cottage program. *Mental Retardation*, 1964, **2**, 345–351.

Goldberg, I. I., and Cruickshank, W. M. The trainable but noneducable: Whose responsibility? *National Education Association Journal*, 1958, **47** 622–623.

Goldstein, H. *Report number two on study projects for trainable mentally handicapped children.* Springfield, Ill.: Superintendent of Public Instruction, 1956.

Goodman, N., and Tizard, J. Prevalence of imbecility and idiocy among children. *British Medical Journal*, 1962, **5273**, 216–219.

Grossman, F. K. *Brothers and sisters of retarded children.* Syracuse, N.Y.: Syracuse University Press, 1972.

Guenther, R. J. *Final report of the Michigan demonstration research project for the severely retarded.* Lansing, Mich.: State Department of Public Instruction, 1956.

Gunzburg, H. C. Vocational and social rehabilitation of the subnormal. In A. M. Clarke and A. D. B. Clarke (Eds.), *Mental deficiency: The changing outlook.* (Rev. ed.) New York: Free Press, 1965.

Heber, R. A manual on terminology and classification in mental retardation. *Monograph Supplement of the American Journal of Mental Deficiency.* (2d. ed.) 1961.

Heber, R. *Epidemiology of mental retardation.* Springfield, Ill.: Charles C Thomas, 1970.

Hottel, J. V. *The Tennessee experimental program of day classes for severely mentally retarded (trainable) children: Interim report of the study.* Nashville, Tenn.: Peabody College, 1956.

Hottel, J. V. *An evaluation of Tennessee's day class program for severely mentally retarded children: Final report.* Nashville, Tenn.: Peabody College, 1958.

Huddle, D. D. Sheltered workshops for the trainable mentally retarded: Research implications. *Education and Training of the Mentally Retarded,* 1967, **2**, 65–69. (a)

Huddle, D. D. Work performance of trainable adults as influenced by competition, cooperation, and monetary reward. *American Journal of Mental Deficiency,* 1967, **72**, 198–211. (b)

Hudson, M. An exploration of classroom procedures for teaching trainable mentally retarded children. *CEC Research Monograph,* Series A, No. 2. Arlington, Va.: Council for Exceptional Children, 1960. (a)

Hudson, M. Lesson areas for the trainable child. *Exceptional Children,* 1960, **27**, 224–229. (b)

Hunt, N. *The world of Nigel Hunt: The diary of a mongoloid youth.* New York: Garrett, 1967.

Itard, J. M. G. *The wild boy of Aveyron.* Translated by George and Muriel Humphrey. New York: Appleton-Century-Crofts, 1962.

Jewell, A. M. A follow-up study of 190 mentally deficient children excluded because of low mentality from the public schools of the District of Columbia. *American Journal of Mental Deficiency.* 1941, **45**, 413–420.

Johnson, G. O., and Capobianco, R. J. *Research project on severely retarded children.* Albany, N.Y.: New York State Interdepartmental Health Resources Board, 1957.

Johnson, G. O., Capobianco, R. J., and Blake, K. An evaluation of behavior changes in trainable mentally deficient children. *American Journal of Mental Deficiency,* 1960, **64**, 881–893.

Johnson, R. C., and Abelson, R. B. The behavioral competence of Mongoloids and non-Mongoloid retardates. *American Journal of Mental Deficiency,* 1969, **73**, 856–857.

Joint Commission on Mental Health of Children. *Crisis in child mental health: Challenge for the 1970's.* New York: Harper & Row, 1970.

Jordon, T. E. *The mentally retarded.* (3d ed.) Columbus, O.: Charles E. Merrill, 1972.

Kanner, L. *A history of the care and study of the mentally retarded.* Springfield, Ill.: Charles C Thomas, 1964.

Kershner, J. R. Doman-Delacato's theory of neurological organization applied with retarded children. *Exceptional Children,* 1968, **34**, 441–450.

Kirk, S. A. Research in education. In H. A. Stevens and R. F. Hever (Eds.), *Mental retardation: A review of research.* Chicago: University of Chicago Press, 1964.

Kolstoe, O. P. *Mental retardation: An educational viewpoint.* New York: Holt, Rinehart and Winston, 1972.

Kugel, R. B., and Wolfensberger, W. (Eds.) *Changing patterns in residential services for the mentally retarded.* Washington, D.C.: President's Committee on Mental Retardation, 1969.

Kushlick, A. The prevalence of recognized mental subnormality of I.Q. under 50 among children in the South of England, with reference to the demand for places for residential care. *International Copenhagen Congress on the Scientific Study of Mental Retardation.* 1964, Vol. 2, 550–556.

Larsen, L. A., and Bricker, W. A. A manual for parents and teachers of severely and moderately retarded children. *IMRID Papers and Reports,* Vol. 5, No. 22. Nashville, Tenn.: Peabody College, 1968.

Lejeune, J., Gautier, M., and Turpin, R. Etude des chromosomes somatique de neuf enfants mongoliens. *Comptes Rendus Academie demie Sciences,* 1959, **248,** 1721–1722.

Lewis, E. O. *Report of the mental deficiency committee, Part IV.* London: His Majesty's Stationery Office, 1929.

Lilienfeld, A. M. *Epidemiology of mongolism.* Baltimore, Md.: The Johns Hopkins Press, 1969.

Mackie, R. P. *Special education in the United States: Statistics, 1948–66.* New York: Teachers College Press, Columbia University, 1969.

Masland, R. L. The prevention of mental subnormality. In R. L. Masland, S. B. Sarason, and T. Gladwin (Eds.), *Mental subnormality: Biological, psychological, and cultural factors.* New York: Basic Books, 1958.

Mayo, L. W. (Chairman) A proposed program for National action to combat mental retardation: A report by President Kennedy's Panel on Mental Retardation. Washington, D.C.: Government Printing Office, 1962.

McDowall, E. B. *Teaching the severely subnormal.* London: Edward Arnold, 1964.

McNeill, W. D. D. Developmental patterns of mongoloid children: A study of certain aspects of their growth and development. Unpublished doctoral dissertation, University of Illinois, Urbana, 1954.

Molloy, J. S. *Trainable children: Curriculum and procedures.* (Rev. ed.) New York: John Day, 1972.

Morgenstern, M., Low-Beer, H., and Morgenstern, F. *Practical training for the severely handicapped child.* Kingswood-Tadworth, Surrey, England: William Heinemann Medical Books, 1966.

Nawas, N. M., and Braun, S. H. An overview of behavior modification with the severely and profoundly retarded: Part III, Maintenance of change and epilogue. *Mental Retardation, 1970* **8(4),** 9.

Neale, M. D., and Campbell, W. J. *Education for the intellectually limited child and adolescent.* Sydney, Australia: Ian Novak, 1963.

Paige, M. *Respite care for the retarded: An interval of relief for families.* Washington, D.C.: Government Printing Office, 1971.

Peck, J. R., and Sexton, C. L. Effects of various settings on trainable children's progress. *American Journal of Mental Deficiency,* 1961, **66,** 62–68.

Penrose, L. S., Ellis, J. R., and Delhanty, J. D. A. Chromosomal transformations in mongolism and in normal relatives. *Lancet,* 1960, **2,** 409–410.

Penrose, L. S., and Smith, G. F. *Down's anomaly.* Boston: Little, Brown, 1966.

Perry, N. *Teaching the mentally retarded child.* New York: Columbia University Press, 1960.

President's Committee on Mental Retardation. MR69. *Toward progress: The story of a decade.* Washington, D.C.: Government Printing Office, 1969.

President's Committee on Mental Retardation. MR70. *The decisive decade.* Washington, D.C.: Government Printing Office, 1971.

Reynolds, M. C., Ellis, R., and Kiland, V. R. *A study of public school children with severe mental retardation.* St. Paul, Minn.: Minnesota State Department of Education, 1953.

Richardson, R. E. Effects of motor training on intellectual function, social competency, body image, and motor proficiency of trainable mentally retarded children. Unpublished doctoral dissertation, Peabody College, Nashville, Tenn., 1970.

Robinson, H. B., and Robinson, N. M. *The mentally retarded child: A psychological approach.* New York: McGraw-Hill, 1965.

Rosecrans, C. J. The relationship of normal/21-trisomy mosaicism and intellectual development. *American Journal of Mental Deficiency*, 1968, **72**, 562–565.

Rosenzweig, L. E., and Long, J. *Understanding and teaching the dependent retarded child.* (2d ed.) Darien, Conn.: Educational Publishing Corp., 1960.

Ross, A. O. *The exceptional child in the family.* New York: Grune & Stratton, 1964.

Ross, R. T. Behavioral correlates of levels of intelligence. *American Journal of Mental Deficiency*, 1972, **76**, 545–549.

Rothstein, J. H. (Ed.) *Mental retardation: Readings and resources.* (2d ed.) New York: Holt, Rinehart and Winston, 1971.

Saenger, G. *The adjustment of severely retarded adults in the community.* Albany, N.Y.: New York State Interdepartmental Health Resources Board, 1957.

Saenger, G. *Factors influencing the institutionalization of mentally retarded individuals in New York City.* Albany, N.Y.: New York State Interdepartmental Health Resources Board, 1960.

Sarason, S. B., and Doris, J. *Psychological problems of mental deficiency.* (4th ed.) New York: Harper & Row, 1969.

Schonell, F. J., and Rorke, M. A second survey of the effects of a subnormal child on the family unit. *American Journal of Mental Deficiency*, 1960, **64**, 862–868.

Seagoe, M. V. *Yesterday was Tuesday, all day and all night: The story of a unique education.* Boston: Little, Brown, 1964.

Seguin, E. *Idiocy and its treatment by the physiological method.* New York: Columbia University Press, 1907.

Semmel, M. I. Comparison of teacher ratings of brain-injured and mongoloid severely retarded (trainable) children attending community day-school classes. *American Journal of Mental Deficiency*, 1960, **64**, 963–971

Shaw, R. Every 25 minutes. . . . *Canada's Mental Health*, 1962, 10, ii.

Sloan, W., and Birch, J. A rationale for degrees of retardation. *American Journal of Mental Deficiency*, 1955, **60**, 258–259.

Smith, R. M. *An introduction to mental retardation.* New York: McGraw-Hill, 1971.

Stedman, D. J. *The decision to institutionalize.* Chapel Hill, N.C.: University of North Carolina, undated.

Stedman, D. J., and Olley, J. G. Bibliography of world clinical and research literature on Down's syndrome: Behavioral, social, and education studies through 1968. *IMRID Papers and Reports*, Vol. VI, No. 2. Nashville, Tenn.: Peabody College, 1969.

Steele, M. W., and Breg, W. R. Chromosome analyses of human amniotic fluid cells. *Lancet*, 1966, **1**, 383–385.

Stephens, B. (Ed.) *Training the developmentally young.* New York: John Day, 1971.

Stevens, H. A., and Heber, R. (Eds.) *Mental retardation: A review of research.* Chicago: University of Chicago Press, 1964.

Stevens, M. *The educational needs of severely subnormal children.* Baltimore, Md.: Williams and Wilkins, 1971.

Strauss, A. A., and Lehtinen, L. E. *Psychopathology and education of the brain-injured child.* Vol. 1. New York: Grune & Stratton, 1947.

Talbot, M. E. Edouard Seguin. *American Journal of Mental Deficiency*, 1967, **72**, 184–189.

Thompson, T., and Grabowski, J. *Behavior modification of the mentally retarded.* New York: Oxford University Press, 1972.

Tisdall, W. J. A follow-up study of trainable mentally handicapped children in Illinois. *American Journal of Mental Deficiency*, 1960, **65**, 11–16.

Tizard, J. *Community services for the mentally handicapped.* London: Oxford University Press, 1964.

Tizard, J. *Survey and experiment in special education.* London: George G. Harrap, 1967.

Tizard, J., and Grad, J. C. *The mentally handicapped and their families: A social survey.* London: Oxford University Press, 1961.

Tredgold, R. F., and Soddy, K. *Tredgold's mental retardation.* (11th ed.) London: Bailliere, Tindall & Cassell, 1970.

U.S. Department of Health, Education and Welfare. *Programs for the handicapped.* Washington, D.C.: Office of Mental Retardation Coordination, March 23, 1972.

U.S. Department of Labor. *Sheltered workshops: A pathway to regular employment.* Washington, D.C.: Government Printing Office, 1967. (Manpower Research Bulletin, No. 15.)

Vollman, R. F. *Down's syndrome (mongolism): A reference bibliography.* Washington, D.C.: National Institutes of Health, 1969.

Waite, K. B. *The trainable mentally retarded child.* Springfield, Ill.: Charles C Thomas, 1972.

Wallin, J. E. W. Training of severely retarded, viewed in historical perspective. *Journal of General Psychology*, 1966, **74**, 107–127.

Watson, J. S. Application of operant conditioning techniques to institutionalized severely and profoundly retarded children. *Mental Retardation Abstracts*, 1967, **4**, 1–18.

Watson, J. S. Behavior modification of residents and personnel in institutions for the mentally retarded. In A. A. Baumeister and E. C. Butterfield, *Residential facilities for the mentally retarded.* Chicago: Aldine-Atherton, 1970.

Weber, R. W. An approach to the use of musical instruments in the education of the "trainable" mentally retarded. Unpublished doctoral dissertation, Teachers College, Columbia University, 1966.

Wiesberg, P. Operation procedures with the retarded: An overview of laboratory research. In N. R. Ellis (Ed.), *International review of research in mental retardation.* Vol. 5. New York: Academic Press, 1971.

Windle, C. Prognosis of mental subnormals. *American Journal of Mental Deficiency, Monograph Supplement*, 1962, **66**, 1–180.

Wirtz, M. D., and Guenther, R. J. The incidence of trainable mentally handicapped children. *Exceptional Children*, 1957, **23**, 171–172, 175.

Wolfensberger, W. Vocational preparation and occupation. In A. A. Baumeister (Ed), *Mental retardation: Appraisal, education, and rehabilitation.* Chicago: Aldine-Atherton, 1967.

Wunsch, W. L. Some characteristics of mongoloids evaluated at a clinic for children with retarded mental development. *American Journal of Mental Deficiency*, 1957, **62**, 122–130.

Zigler, E. Familial mental retardation: A continuing dilemma. *Science*, 1967, **155**, 292–298.

Opposite: A difficult but important independent living skill for young people with mild general learning disabilities to acquire is the ability to handle money wisely, including the figuring out of correct change. (Photo courtesy Hawaii State Department of Public Instruction; photographer, Robin Kaye.)

children with
mild general learning disabilities

CHAPTER OUTLINE

Ever since public school education was made compulsory at the middle of the nineteenth century, teachers have been confronted with the problem of what to do about slow-learning pupils. In large measure these children have been kept in the educational mainstream where an increasing variety of strategies for teaching them have evolved. At the same time, from the turn of the century through the 1960s, there was a parallel tendency to eject from the regular grades the most troublesome of them if they had IQ scores between 50 and about 75 or 80—especially if their parents had little influence in the community. *Traditionally*, these rejected pupils have been labeled educable mentally retarded and placed in self-contained, or segregated, special day classes in regular public school buildings, though a few have been enrolled in special day and residential schools.

By late in the 1960s, this process of labeling, ejecting, and segregating came under intensive review. The result was the development of a sharp trend to declassify, normalize, and return to general education many of these slow-learning pupils, particularly the excess of those from ethnic minority groups who had been placed in these special classes. Thus *present-day* and *emerging* placement practices are very different from traditional ones. Yet the controversy is far from over concerning which of these pupils should be taught by regular versus special educators. And should the pattern be the same or different at the preschool, elementary, and high school levels? Such other basic questions as the following have also arisen: What are the characteristics of these pupils? What are reasonable scholastic expectancies for them? What and how should they be taught? If more are to remain in the educational mainstream, what special help, if any, should be provided for them there?

This chapter provides a critical examination of *traditional* special education practices and explores *present-day* and *emerging* services for these mildly retarded pupils. Also included here is material to help teachers deal with the kinds of questions raised above.

DEFINITION AND TERMINOLOGY: TRADITIONAL, PRESENT-DAY, AND EMERGING

Traditionally, *educable mentally retarded* children were defined as

> *those pupils who experienced so much difficulty progressing through general education because they developed intellectually at only about one half to three quarters the rate of average children (IQ 50–75) that they required special education services.*

In late adolescence, upon leaving school, their scholastic aptitude (mental age) ranged from about 8 to 12 years. Upon reaching maturity, then, they had the ability to achieve at between the third and seventh grades academically. A rough rule of thumb was that by late adolescence *most* mildly retarded pupils would have the capacity to achieve at the fourth-grade level or above. Since this is the recognized point of literacy, it was also said that, as a group, they generally had the ability to be *literate*. For this reason the term "educable" was adopted.

The special education crisis of the late 1960s was precipitated because this definition was not operational and was not applied restrictively. Largely on the basis of teacher opinion concerning what constituted inadequate school progress, plus an IQ score of between 50 and 75 obtained on a nationally standardized verbal-type individual intelligence test, administered in standard English, a child could be classified as educable mentally retarded and segregated into a special class. Furthermore, it did not assure that each ethnic group would be represented proportionately. In addition, this stigmatizing term was applied only to children while they were attending school. The vast majority who were found to have IQ scores between 50 and 75 in school were not recognized as intellectually inadequate in their preschool years. While they may have been slightly slow in learning to walk and talk, the signs were not obvious enough to cause the parents to have the child examined for intellectual endowment. Only when these children were enrolled in school and began to fail in academic learning did they call attention to themselves. Furthermore, the majority of them lost their labels upon leaving school, becoming at least marginally self-sufficient. As a result, the President's Committee on Mental Retardation (1970) called them "six-hour retarded children," since they were retarded only for school purposes.

As discussed on pages 68–70 in Chapter 2, it is proposed that the schools discard both the terms "educable" and "mentally retarded"; in their place it is suggested that these children be designated as those with "mild general learning disabilities." The following new definition for children with mild general learning disabilities[1] is recommended, since it would appear to have utility for present-day and emerging special education programs:

> To be classified as having a mild general learning disability for purposes of receiving special education services, a pupil (1) must have reached the age of six years; (2) must score no higher than the second percentile for his ethnic subgroup based on local school district norms on both verbal and performance types of individual intelligence tests administered in his most facile language, yet not in the lower one half of 1 percent; and (3) must be achieving in all basic school subjects, as measured by age norms on an individual, nationally standardized test of school attainment administered in the language of instruction, no higher than his capacity as determined by the average mental age expectancy score derived from his scores on both the verbal and performance types of nationally standardized intelligence tests administered in the language of instruction.

In terms of the first condition, it is recommended that even the milder MGLD label not be applied to preschool children, since no useful purpose and possible damage could result (Moore and Moore, 1972). Instead, it is suggested

---

[1] For the sake of simplicity, the term "mildly retarded" and the abbreviation "MGLD" are used throughout the chapter.

that their preschool education—which is crucial for them—be provided through Home Start, Head Start, and other such programs. In their early years these youngsters are less different intellectually from average children than they will ever be again. As for the second condition, the upper IQ limit for this group would revert back to the equivalent of about 70 for native-born Anglo children based on nationally standardized intelligence tests normed to yield a mean IQ of 100 and a standard deviation of 15 (see Fig. 2.1). However, to insure fairness for pupils from ethnic minorities, local norms, by ethnic groups, are substituted for national ones. Computers make this derivation now feasible. Until these local norms are forthcoming, national or state norms by ethnic groups could be used, or selection could be based on the 1½ percent just above the lower ½ percent of pupils in each ethnic group in the local school district who display the greatest discrepancy between achievement and capacity specified in the third condition. As for the third criterion, the use of nationally standardized individual achievement and intelligence tests should reduce the opportunity for subjective opinion on the part of the classroom teacher and serve as a check against the use of group tests, which may yield invalid scores. (Under this restricted definition, other behaviors which are troublesome to the teacher and/or the other children are not to become the prime triggers for pupil referral in this area. Instead, they should be seen as an indication of an *exceptional child situation* which needs attention; see page 6 in Chapter 1.) Finally, the reader will need to study the materials to follow in this chapter to determine the degree to which he or she can accept these proposed restricted definitional and terminological suggestions for *present-day* and *emerging* special education programs which serve mildly retarded girls and boys.

PREVALENCE ESTIMATES: TRADITIONAL, PRESENT-DAY, AND EMERGING

Traditionally, the most frequently quoted figure for the number of educable mentally retarded pupils in need of special class placement has been 2 percent of the school population. For example, in 1971–1972, the U.S. Office of Education cited 2.3 percent as mentally retarded, with 2 percent classified as mildly retarded and 0.3 percent as moderately retarded (see footnote 1, Table 1.1). The traditional figure given in column 1 in Table 1.1 for MGLD children is 1.5 percent, since only children formerly classified as *adaptive* educable mentally retarded were included. Of the inclusive traditional 2 percent in the EMR category, 1.5 percent were classified into this adaptive category because they had the ability to become independent in adulthood and thereby lose their identity as mentally retarded. Conversely, the remaining 0.5 percent who have usually had IQ scores in the 50s or low 60s have been considered nonadaptive EMR because they will require somewhat sheltered environments as adults.[2]

---

[2] The reader will recall from Chapter 2 that it was recommended that these children traditionally classified as nonadaptive educable mentally retarded be shifted over into the category of moderate general learning disabilities.

The present-day prevalence estimate which follows directly from the second condition of the definition of MGLD children on page 128 is also 1.5 percent of the school population, which would be a maximum figure for each ethnic and racial subgroup. But the *emerging* estimate to be attained by 1985 or sooner is shown in column 2 in Table 1.1 to be 0.8 percent overall. It is further suggested that this estimate be broken down by levels, as shown in Table 3.1. The zero percentage for the preschool years obviously follows

TABLE 3.1 *Maximum Suggested Emerging Prevalence Estimates of Pupils in Each Ethnic and Racial Subgroup in a Local School District To Be Classified as Having Mild General Learning Disabilities for Special Education Purposes*

Preschool years	0%
Elementary school years	0.6%
High school years	1.0%
School-age average	0.8%

the recommendation that no child be labeled MGLD before entering the first grade. The differential between 0.6 percent at the elementary school level and 1.0 percent at the high school level is based on the fact that mildly retarded pupils, as measured against average children, become more retarded in intellectual functioning and school achievement as they grow older. Therefore, more of them will need special education at the high school level.

By way of discussion, it needs to be pointed out that neither the traditional 2 percent figure nor the 0.8 percent emerging estimate follows from the definitions already presented. These definitions allow for, or suggest, higher values. For example, as will be seen from Figure 2.1, nearer to 5 percent of the total school population would obtain IQ scores between 50 and 75, and nearly 9 percent between 50 and 80, rather than the traditional 2 percent. For certain ethnic subgroups the situation is even worse. Since black children, as a total group, regularly obtain mean IQ scores of about 85 on nationally standardized intelligence tests, it follows that one half of such pupils obtain IQ scores below 85, one third below 75, and about 16 percent below 70. For black children in the slums, about 50 percent score below 70 by the time they reach their teens. The percentages for Chicanos, American Indians, and a number of other minority groups are also far higher than the traditional 5 and 9 percent figures for the school population as a whole, though not as dramatically high as the percentages for blacks. Clearly, the traditional 2 percent prevalence figure has not followed from the traditional definition. Similarly the suggested emerging 0.8 percent figure is about half of the 1.5 percent that follows from the proposed new definition. The same basis can be used to explain both of these low figures, namely, that about half or even more of these low IQ children make adequate enough progress and are accepted well enough in the regular program that they avoid being referred for special education services.

Overall, the new definition and the 0.8 percent prevalence figure suggest that special education for MGLD pupils be sharply reduced, at least for the next decade. This retrenchment seems to be the only defensible way to reorder this field of special education after the many problems that have plagued it. Finally, the reason for the selection of the 0.8 percent estimate will become more obvious when Table 3.2 is discussed later in the chapter. It will then be seen that by 1971–1972, as a result of the most energetic program in the nation to remove labels from and normalize educational experiences, California had reached the point where only 0.8 percent of its school enrollment was classified as mildly retarded and placed in special education programs. And, indeed, there would appear to be a trend for this figure to go even lower. Perhaps, as improvements are made in general education to serve the slow learner, it is not unrealistic to anticipate that the prevalence rate will have fallen to 0.5 percent by the year 2000, as it was suggested it should be in Table 1.1.

TRADITIONAL GENERAL CHARACTERISTICS

What are the general characteristics of children who have traditionally been classified as educable mentally retarded and placed in special day classes? The following *modal* descriptions of such pupils are an elaboration on a list drawn from Rothstein (1971). Of course, there have been many exceptions to these 12 generalizations. However, as contrasted to the general school population, these children were more likely (1) to have met defeat, frustration, and rejection in the regular grades where they were first placed; (2) to have exhibited substantial behavior disorders in general education; (3) to be from racial or ethnic minority groups; (4) to have parents who place little value on education; (5) to have inadequate health and nutritional provisions; (6) to be unclean and unkempt; (7) to live in poverty and deprivation; (8) to be boys rather than girls; (9) to come from broken or disorganized homes; (10) to be seriously retarded in school achievement; (11) to have restricted oral language skills in standard English; (12) to have obtained IQ scores ranging between 65 and 78 on individualized tests of verbal intelligence administered in standard English.

These traditional general characteristics of special class mildly retarded pupils should change dramatically in the next decade or so if the proposed definition on page 128, as well as the recommended screening and placement procedures outlined later in the chapter, are accepted.

TRADITIONAL SUBGROUP CHARACTERISTICS

The 12 general characteristics just presented give an incomplete picture of traditional special class mildly retarded pupils, who have been lumped together on the basis of global IQ scores for too long. Figure 3.1 depicts the three main types of such children, along with the five subgroups into which they have fallen.

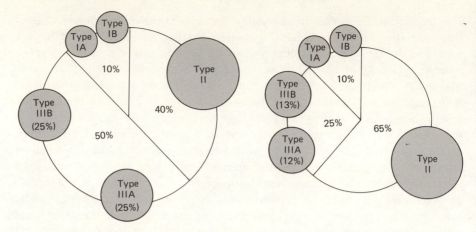

FIGURE 3.1 *Traditional and proposed emerging proportions among the three major groups and five subgroups of pupils classified as mildly retarded for special education purposes.*

I. Traditional Proportions:
Type I—Noncultural-familial of all ethnic groups (Type IA—Neurologically impaired; Type IB—Multiply handicapped).
Type II—Anglo cultural-familial.
Type III—Linguistically and culturally different (Type IIIA—Black, predominantly poor; Type IIIB—Nonblack bilingual ethnic minorities, predominantly poor).

II. Proposed Emerging Proportions:
Type I—Noncultural-familial of all ethnic groups (Type IA—Neurologically impaired; Type IB—Multiply handicapped).
Type II—Anglo cultural-familial.
Type III—Non-Anglo cultural-familial (Type IIIA—Black cultural-familial; Type IIIB—Nonblack ethnic minorities cultural-familial).

The Noncultural-Familial Type

The Neurologically Impaired Subgroup

The children represented in Figure 3.1 as Type IA have been variously diagnosed and classified as neurologically impaired, brain injured, or exogenous and come from all strata of society (see page 76). They comprise one of the two smallest subgroups of special class retardates. For example, Dingman and Tarjan (1960) calculated that only 1 percent of pupils in the IQ 50–70 group are pathological. Thus it would seem safe to say that not more than 5 percent, and perhaps only about 1 percent, of mildly retarded pupils in special classes can be classified as neurologically impaired. Of course, rare special class programs in Anglo middle and upper class neighborhoods would be composed of essentially all brain-injured pupils, because one would not expect to find the cultural-familial or poor minority groups in such communities.

The specific pathological conditions of Type IA children are sometimes identified, but usually the damage to the central nervous system is assumed.

Not surprising, this subgroup is a heterogeneous one with many different types of brain injuries resulting in a wide variety of different behavioral characteristics. A fair number exhibit the hyperactive and distractible characteristics of the Strauss syndrome (see page 78). Others are lethargic due to the nature of their brain damage or to sedation. Still others are epileptic.

The specific educational interventions these pupils require have yet to be determined, but in no way is it suggested that a separate special education program be set up for pupils who are usually classified into this category by physicians.

Elaine, in Vignette 10.1 on page 535, is an example of a Strauss-syndrome pupil. She exemplifies a girl who might have been classified borderline MGLD, as emotionally disturbed, or, more likely, as having a specific learning disability.

The Multiply Handicapped Subgroup

Another relatively small subgroup of children who have been classified as mildly retarded is represented in Figure 3.1 as Type IB. These are pupils with multiple handicaps, one of their conditions being low intellectual functioning. Since mental retardation is the disability that is most often associated with other disabilities, it is not surprising that it combines with all known handicaps. Most physically handicapped mildly retarded pupils have not been classified with retardation as their major disability. Instead, they have tended to be classified by their physical conditions, probably largely because these have been less stigmatizing. In addition, there exists a long tradition of parents first taking their multiply handicapped children to physicians, who have tended to attach medical labels based on physical characteristics. For many years special education accepted unquestioningly this medical classification, with the result that relatively few of these children have been placed in special day schools and classes for the mildly retarded.

In spite of the innumerable combinations of disabilities which exist, mild retardation associated with emotional disturbance has been the one most frequently found in special classes for the mildly retarded. In these cases, lack of academic progress and low intelligence may often have been secondary to adjustment problems. Often these children have come from broken or disorganized homes or had otherwise inadequate parents. As already indicated, essentially all pupils who have been referred by the regular teacher for special class placement for the educable mentally retarded have displayed disruptive classroom behavior and negative attitudes toward themselves and others. Of course, drawing the line between a mentally retarded child and one who is behaviorally disordered has been difficult indeed, and the distinction has often been arbitrary. This same problem of diagnosis has existed and continues to exist with essentially all Type IB children. Since each of their multiple disabilities exists in varying degrees, it is difficult to arrive at the major handicapping condition which needs priority in terms of special education intervention. One of the major challenges of the 1970s is to find better ways of educating children with multiple learning disabilities. As shown in Figure 3.1, the relative proportion of Type IA and Type IB pupils will probably remain somewhat constant in the future, collectively accounting for not more than 10 percent of MGLD pupils.

Sally, in Vignette 3.1, is an illustration of the complexities encountered in classifying multiply handicapped pupils who are mildly retarded.

> **Vignette 3.1 Sally: An Apparent Case of a Multiply Handicapped Mildly Retarded Pupil (Type IB)**
>
> Since infancy Sally, an only child, has been of considerable concern to her parents, who are both professional persons; her mother is a teacher and her father a lawyer. She has always appeared withdrawn, inattentive, and slow in learning. Sally has been taken to many medical specialists. Vision, hearing, and brain-injury disorders have been ruled out as the major cause of her problem, and she appears normal in other physical respects. She has also been seen repeatedly by school and clinical psychologists and by speech pathologists. Rather consistently, Sally obtains IQ scores in the low 70's, doing better on performance-than on verbal-type tests. These experts have variously labeled her as autistic, emotionally disturbed, aphasic, auditorially perceptually impaired, and educable mentally retarded. In the early 1970s, Sally had her twelfth birthday. At that time she was reading at the second-grade level. In the small town where she lived, the only special education program was two special classes for the educable retarded. She was transferred from a regular fourth grade into one of these so as to obtain more individualized and specialized instruction, and hopefully make greater progress in school.

The Anglo Cultural-Familial Type

The complex phenomenon known as cultural-familial (or familial) retardation was discussed briefly in Chapter 2. Since intelligence appears to be multigenetically determined and fairly normally distributed for every ethnic group and every culture, it follows that each such group has a small proportion of individuals who fall at the lower end of the normal probability curve. These have become known as cultural-familial retardates. Those from native-born, white, standard English-speaking (Anglo) backgrounds are designated as Type II in Figure 3.1. The four criteria for designation as cultural-familial retarded are: (1) the child displays intellectual inadequacy; (2) he has one or more parents or siblings who are also subnormal intellectually; (3) he shows no evidence of an inherited or acquired specific pathological condition that could explain his intellectual deficit; and (4) he lives in a non-intellectually stimulating slum environment. About 40 percent and probably nearer to 50 percent of all special class mild retardates in the United States have probably been of the Anglo cultural-familial type, though no national survey has been made. This means that this group has been underrepresented by about half, since approximately 80 percent of U.S. children come from Anglo backgrounds. As Figure 3.1 suggests, the proportion of this group is likely to go up to approximately 65 percent, probably even higher.

Teachers may have special difficulty in accepting the cultural-familial group because the mores and values in such families are vastly different from their own. Since educators come primarily from the middle class, they are shocked when they see the conditions in which a majority of these children live.[3]

Failure to recognize the inheritance of a poor genetic pool for intelligence in the case of such children may result in placing too much blame for the retardation on an inadequate society, home, and/or school. Similarly, too much pressure might be put on the pupils by holding unrealistically high expectancies for them, considering their inherited lower capacities. To date, however, the actual tendency has been to expect too little of them.

Vignette 2.1 on page 75 provides a brief sketch of a family living in rural poverty; two of the three boys who had been classified as cultural-familial retarded were residents in a state residential facility and the other was enrolled in a special day class.

The Linguistically and Culturally Different Type

The Black Slum Subgroup

Black slum mildly retarded native-born children are depicted as Type IIIA in Figure 3.1. Since cultural-familial retardation is present in all ethnic groups, and since black pupils represent about 12 percent of the U.S. school population, we would expect to see about 12 percent of special class retardates fall into this category. However, conversely to the Anglos, who have been underrepresented, the blacks have been overrepresented. In the late 1960s and early 1970s, about 25 percent of the special class retarded have generally been black children from the slums, and in some communities the numbers have been much higher. Implementation of the definition on page 128 would correct this situation. In the meantime, if a school system decided to provide special education for the lowest 5 percent of this population, it would need to set the upper IQ limit for black MGLD pupils at about 62–65 rather than 75. To include only 2 percent, the upper limit would need to be lowered to about 57–59. To include only 0.8 percent, the upper limit would need to be

---

[3] In a fair number of cultural-familial cases, it must be pointed out that the family members do well with their limited resources. Especially when one parent is reasonably intelligent, they keep a clean, well-managed home, live together harmoniously, and follow the standard mores of the community.

dropped still further to about 50 on nationally standardized intelligence tests.

Jensen (1969) raised a furor by suggesting that the cognitive processes of black children are different from those of whites. He noted, for example, that blacks appear to have far superior short-term rote memory and psychomotor skills, though they obtain inferior scores in abstract reasoning. Should we teach to these strengths or weaknesses? Jensen says to the strengths. Perhaps such intervention studies as the one by Heber and Garber (1970), described later in this chapter, will shed some light on the subject. To what degree these differences are due to environment or inherited factors is not likely to be settled soon, if ever. For example, two geneticists, Bodmer and Cavalli-Sforza (1970), have concluded that the genetic basis for differences between blacks and whites cannot be established from existing evidence. However, rather than become preoccupied with etiology, the challenge for educators is to determine whether certain approaches are more effective than others for teaching black children from the slums, and, if so, to structure instructional programs to take advantage of such findings.

Joe, in Vignette 3.2, is an example of a Type IIIA special class pupil.

Vignette 3.2: Joe: A Black Slum Mildly Retarded Pupil (Type IIIA)

Joe, who was black, had his fourteenth birthday in 1968. He was born and raised in a ghetto of a large northern city, where he practically lived on the streets. His mother had moved north in 1940 with her parents when she was 12 years old. She married young and had three children by her husband before he left her. She then moved back in with her parents and went to work on an assembly line to support herself and her offspring. The grandmother watched over the children as best she could in their out-of-school hours. In school, Joe was always a slow learner and a problem for his regular classroom teachers. When he was 10 and had reached only a third-grade placement, he was referred for special class placement and was so placed when the school psychologist found he had a Wechsler IQ score in the low 60s. Even after four years, the special education teachers were still trying unsuccessfully to teach him minimal word-attack skills.

The Bilingual Slum Subgroup

Represented in Figure 3.1 as Type IIIB is the fifth and last subgroup of children who have been placed in substantial numbers in special classes for the mildly retarded. Like black slum children, this group is also linguistically and culturally different from Anglo boys and girls. It comprises a variety of bilingual children who live largely in poverty, including Chicano, Tex-Mex, Puerto Rican, and other so-called Spanish-American children. However, depending on the region, included also are pupils from a variety of backgrounds, such as American Indians, Eskimos, Orientals, Hawaiians, and

Filipinos, to mention a few.[4] Recognizing that cultural-familial retardation occurs proportionately in all ethnic groups, and knowing that about 13 percent of the U.S. school population is made up of these bilingual slum groups, we could anticipate that about 13 percent of special class retardates would come from these ethnic categories. However, these groups have been over-represented, with the number nearer to 25 percent, but with great variability from community to community.

To succeed in regular school programs, where standard English is the language of instruction, bilingual boys and girls of average intelligence need special help to acquire standard English at an early age, although this single emphasis is not likely to be enough. Changes will need to occur in a variety of conditions associated with their poverty and life-style if they are to compete successfully with Anglo pupils. Yet even for youth of average intelligence from these minority groups, there is an increasing hesitancy to encourage life-style change. Further, there is growing pressure to provide early instruction in the language of the home. Even more than for these average youth, an educational program to foster the existing life-style and vernacular would seem to be justified for those who are less well endowed intellectually. This basic issue is likely to affect special education in as yet unforeseeable ways. In the meantime, it is now recognized that it has been unjust to label the non-standard English-speaking children as educable mentally retarded on the basis of individual intelligence test scores where the items are culturally loaded and the instructions are given in English.

A Type IIIB pupil is illustrated by José in Vignette 3.3.

Vignette 3.3: José: A Bilingual Slum Mildly Retarded Pupil (Type IIIB)

During the 1960s, as they are now, José's parents, who came from Mexico, were migrant farm workers. The family, which spoke border Spanish, wintered in the South and worked northward in the summer. José, an eight-year-old boy who had not learned to read, was the youngest of seven children. He did not like school and showed it. After he had been in the first grade for two years, the teacher where the family wintered referred him for psychological testing. His IQ score on the Stanford-Binet was in the high 60s, so he was enrolled in a special class whenever the family returned to its home base. Even there he continued to learn very little from the special class teachers, who used standard English as the language of instruction. When on the road with his family, he was a very infrequent school attender.

[4] Historically, a disproportionate number of children of recent non-English-speaking immigrants were routed into special classes for the educable mentally retarded. In some communities it was the Polish, in others the Chinese, and in others the Italians. This is not surprising. It takes a good command of English to succeed in U.S. schools and on nationally standardized tests of intelligence.

THE CALIFORNIA ETHNIC SURVEYS: AN EMERGING PATTERN

While no national survey has been made in either Canada or the United States of the proportion of special class retardates in each of the five categories just described, one state survey provides information on ethnic balance. As a result of mounting litigation on the disproportionate numbers of minority group children assigned to special classes for the educable retarded, the California State Department of Education (1970) first analyzed the ethnic backgrounds of such pupils in 1969–1970. Similar surveys for all aspects of the California general and special education programs were made in subsequent years (California State Department of Education, 1971). The

TABLE 3.2 *Ethnic and Racial Surveys of Pupils Classified as Educable Mentally Retarded as Contrasted with Proportions in the Total School Population in the Public Day Schools of California*

Category	Total	Spanish Surname	Other White	Negro	Oriental	American Indian	Other Nonwhite
Percentage of Pupils in Each Ethnic and Racial Group							
1. Total school enrollment:							
1969-70 (enrollment— 4,597,687)	100	15.2	72.4	8.9	2.3	0.3	0.9
1971-72 (enrollment— 4,545,279)	100.1	16.0	71.1	9.3	2.2	0.4	1.1
2. Pupils classified as educable mentally retarded:							
1969-70 (enrollment— 56,349)	99.9	28.3	44.3	25.5	0.7	0.5	0.6
1971-72 (enrollment— 38,208)	100	23.9	47.4	26.7	0.7	0.6	0.7
3. Percent of total school enrollment of each ethnic or racial group diagnosed educable mentally retarded:							
1969-70	1.2	2.1	0.7	3.3	0.4	1.9	0.9
1971-72	0.8	1.2	0.5	2.3	0.3	1.2	0.5

SOURCES: California State Department of Education, *Placement of underachieving minority group children in special classes for the educable mentally retarded, 1969* (Sacramento, Calif.: California State Department of Education, 1970); and California State Department of Education, *Racial and ethnic survey of California public schools grade distribution, Fall, 1971* (Sacramento, Calif.: Bureau of Intergroup Relations, California State Department of Education, 1971).

data for 1969–1970 and for 1971–1972, summarized in Table 3.2, suggest that there was a sound basis for the court action.

In analyzing the table, which speaks largely for itself, three highlights to be especially noted are:

1. By the use of more appropriate diagnostic procedures (Burgener, 1971) California was able to reduce the number of pupils in special classes for the mentally retarded in the two-year period by 32 percent, bringing the percentage down to 0.8 percent overall.

2. Black children especially, followed by Spanish-American youngsters, were seriously overrepresented. Even in 1971–1972 they comprised 50.6 percent of the special class pupils as contrasted with only 25.3 percent in the total school population.

3. The other whites (Anglos, largely) were most dramatically underrepresented. While there were 71.1 percent in the total school population, only 47.4 percent of the special class pupils were of this ethnic group. While lesser numbers were involved, the same pattern held for children from Oriental backgrounds.

These California surveys, more than any other single set of data, formed the basis for the new definition of MGLD children, the terminology associated with it, and the prevalence estimates proposed earlier in the chapter. While other states and some Canadian provinces have also made progress in correcting inequities in this area, generally they are half a decade behind California.

TRADITIONAL AND EMERGING PLACEMENT PRACTICES

As was stated at the outset of the chapter, traditionally, prime responsibility for selecting and referring pupils to be classified as educable mentally retarded for special class placement purposes has rested with regular classroom teachers. Placement has usually occurred in the primary grades when such children have failed to learn to read. Once a referral form for a particular child was filled out by the homeroom teacher and routed through the principal to the central special education office, a case was usually processed through the following steps:

1. The child was given an individual psychometric examination by a school psychologist or psychometrician. Typically, only one or two hours were available per pupil to administer and interpret a test battery and write up a report. Considering the shortage of such diagnosticians, the child was usually given only (a) an individual intelligence test such as the Stanford-Binet or one of the Wechsler scales and (b) an individual screening test of school achievement such as the Peabody Individual Achievement Test or the Wide Range Achievement Test. These are all norm-referenced tests based on a cross section of the U.S. population, which makes them biased toward the white middle class culture. Too, the instructions are in standard English.

2. The diagnostician may also have screened the pupil to rule out

emotional disturbance as the major disability. However, school psychometricians who actually do the testing have seldom been experts in this area, usually having no more than a master's degree in school, clinical, or educational psychology. In more affluent school systems, selected children were referred to mental health clinics, clinical psychologists with Ph.D.'s, or child psychiatrists for such diagnostic information.

3. The child may also have been referred to medical or paramedical people to rule out sensory deficits (vision and/or hearing losses) as the prime cause of his general learning disability. At best, testing of this kind was done by physicians. However, usually school nurses or technicians simply administered the audiometric and vision-screening devices discussed in Chapters 7 and 8, respectively.

4. The reports were then submitted to the director of special education or a special education placement committee for action. This committee has traditionally been made up of such persons as the coordinator of special classes for the retarded, the pupil's regular teacher, a special education teacher, the school psychologist, the school principal, and sometimes a nurse or physician and a school social worker who may have gathered family information. The duty of the committee was to decide on the best possible educational placement and program for the child. This case-conference approach was viewed as the ideal procedure. Often, because of time considerations, system pressures, and manpower shortages, no such conference was convened. The director of special education, or one of his central office staff, simply placed the pupil in a special education program on the basis of his being declared eligible by a psychometrician—a casual practice indeed!

5. An additional controversial step was followed in some school systems and not in others. In some, a signed parent consent was obtained before special class placement was made. In others, the parents and child were counseled about (and talked into) the placement. Sometimes the parents were allowed to see the information used to justify the pupil's special class placement, though in other cases they were not. In some schools, they were simply given notice of what was being done. For example, Kolstoe (1970) has recommended that both the parents and the child simply be told about the transfer, and that the special class be described as "an opportunity, not a punishment for poor accomplishment or bad behavior" (p. 42). This procedure is expedient. Certainly the process might be delayed for years and much controversy generated if parents were given access to the records and could question the data. Many pupils might never be placed in special classes if parental approval were required. Regardless of what procedure educators may consider desirable, court actions, such as the 1971 Pennsylvania ruling, are requiring parental involvement and/or approval in special education placement (Weintraub, 1972).

In an eight-year study conducted in a suburb of Los Angeles, Mercer

(1971a; 1971b) demonstrated that in this one community three quarters of the pupils classified as special class mildly retarded by these traditional practices were mislabeled because the cultural and linguistic family backgrounds of the children were not taken into consideration. This is an even bleaker picture than the data for California as a whole presented in Table 3.2, which suggests that nearer to 50 percent were mislabeled. Mercer compared a random sample of black and Spanish-American elementary school children in special classes for the mildly retarded with a contrast group eligible for such placement but not so placed; the two groups were equated for racial background, intelligence, and school achievement. Among a number of factors investigated, three differentiated significantly between the groups. Those placed in special classes displayed disruptive behavior, were disliked by their classmates, and used poor English. These were the traits which caused the teachers to overrefer these two types of minority group children. The study raises serious questions as to whether initial referral can remain with regular classroom teachers, many of whom are no doubt tempted to turn over to special education those pupils who display these behaviors which they view as undesirable.

In contrast to the traditional selection and placement procedures which have just been discussed and evaluated, the following are a set of practices recommended for the identification of MGLD children to fit the definition on page 128. These draw upon but go beyond those outlined by Weintraub, Abeson, and Braddock (1971).

1. Instead of subjective selection by regular teachers, initial referral should be based on the screening of all first-grade pupils, with periodic rescreening thereafter, at least in the fourth, seventh, and tenth years in school, by means of individual screening tests of intelligence and achievement administered in the language of instruction by educational diagnosticians, or technicians working under their direction. (This practice will result in much overreferral and should include a number of children who will be found to fall in such other special education areas as specific learning disabilities).

2. All referred cases should be intensively studied to rule out other disabilities and to rule in a general learning disability. The study should include the administration of both verbal and performance types of individual tests of intelligence given in the language of instruction as well as in the language with which the subject is most facile, if the two are different. Local norms for the subject's ethnic group need to be available for these tests.

3. A diagnostic test battery for the basic school subjects should next be administered in the language of instruction to those who meet the second condition of the definition on page 128. This will determine whether the subject is achieving in each area no higher than his mental age expectancy score. (If the number of eligible pupils still exceeds the prevalence guidelines for the school level given in Table 3.1, those with the most severe intellectual deficits and those who are underachieving to the greatest degree should be given priority to receive special education services.)

4. The determination of the most appropriate school placement and

educational program should be based on a study of the problems of the school situation from which the pupil was referred as well as on the child's own problems. The case-conference procedure just described should be used for decision-making.

5. Parents should be given the opportunity to meet with school officials to determine appropriate placement and/or general and special education services to be received. In this regard, parents should be entitled to advance notification, to access to appropriate school records, including all test scores and reports, and to representation by legal counsel.

6. Furthermore, parents should have the right to obtain an independent evaluation of their child at public expense if necessary.

7. In addition, parents should be provided with an official transcript of the due process hearings and should have the right to appeal decisions resulting from such hearings to the state education agency or directly to the appropriate court.

8. Every MGLD pupil provided with special educational services should be thoroughly reevaluated at least each year; parents should also have the right to reassess their concurrence with the school services being provided their child.

Taking courses of action on the basis of these eight guidelines should do much to correct traditional inequities.

TRADITIONAL SPECIFIC BEHAVIORAL CHARACTERISTICS

In this section, the behavioral characteristics of mildly retarded children are outlined for six areas of child development relevant to education. These are based on the extensive body of research literature which has accumulated for the past two decades or so. In fact, more such data have been gathered for the mildly retarded than for any other group of exceptional children. Generally, the findings are derived from comparative studies of a group of mildly retarded children and a group of pupils possessing average or above average intelligence who may have been matched on either chronological or mental ages. Sometimes the comparisons were made against specific samples of retarded children, such as cultural-familial white boys or neurologically impaired children, but usually the groups were constituted solely on the variable of intelligence test scores. Thus, the statements to follow hold for pupils who, as a group, have possessed the 12 traditional general characteristics outlined on page 131. Nevertheless, when data are available for the cultural-familial versus the neurologically impaired, this fact will be pointed out.

The task of listing the behavioral characteristics of the mildly retarded is complicated because these children vary greatly in most dimensions. That this is true is hardly surprising in light of the previous discussion of the subgroups of such pupils, which were depicted in Figure 3.1. While it can be stated that the mildly retarded, as a group, have compared unfavorably on essentially all traits with pupils of average and above-average intellect, many individuals so classified are exceptions. Further, it is important to consider how these lists of characteristics to follow will change with the implementation of the new definition and identification procedures proposed earlier. Since they tend to be restrictive, one can anticipate that children classified as MGLD in the future will display even more inferior characteristics than has traditionally been the case.

Motor Development

In motor development more than in any other area, the mildly retarded, as a group, have been found to be more nearly like children with average and above-average intelligence. This finding is based upon much research. (See Cratty, 1969; Kral, 1972; Malpass, 1963; Stein, 1963; Rarick, Widdop, and Broadhead, 1970; see also a report by the American Association for Health, Physical Education and Recreation [1966], which contains a 490-item bibliography of research reports.) The following conclusions are also drawn from these publications:

1. Even though mildly retarded children, as a group, look almost normal in height and weight, both girls and boys lag one to four years behind national norms on most tests of gross motor proficiency and physical fitness, the differential increasing with age.
2. The mildly retarded are even more behind the standards for normal children on fine and more intricate motor skills, including hand-eye coordination.
3. Cultural-familial retardates and those from ethnic minority groups are markedly superior in motor proficiency to those who are neurologically impaired and multiply handicapped.
4. There is a low positive correlation between intelligence and motor skills among the mildly retarded; the lower the intelligence, the lower the proficiency.
5. The mildly retarded respond well to structured training programs of physical education, sometimes approaching national norms in motor proficiency (Soloman and Pangle, 1967).
6. Some studies have shown that structured programs of physical education have also resulted in modest increases in measured intelligence and social-personal adjustment in the mildly retarded, probably because of their improved feelings of well-being (Oliver, 1958; Corder, 1966; Corder and Pridmore, 1966; Soloman and Pangle, 1967).
7. The types of motivational incentives used influences performance, with continuous verbal encouragement plus material (monetary) rewards being generally the most effective (Soloman, 1968).

Clearly, mildly retarded children are in need of assistance and can profit from instruction in the motor area. Cratty (1969) has provided a good guide for bringing this about.

Speech, Hearing, and Oral Language Development

Language sets mankind above all other forms of life. It is the key to human communication and the major tool to human thought. Language involves reception, association, and expression. The integrator for the individual is the brain, where the association and generation of ideas take place. It is not surprising that a close relation exists between language and intellectual development. In fact, since the original Binet scale was published, size and complexity of vocabulary in one's native tongue have been recognized as one of the best single measures of verbal intelligence. The greater the extent of intellectual inadequacy, the greater the degree of speech and language disability. Within the last decade or two, a vast amount of research activity and instructional material has been generated in this area. Excellent reviews of the literature are available in Lloyd (1972), in Schiefelbusch, Copeland, and Smith (1967), and in Webb and Kinde (1967). Peins (1969) has provided an extensive bibliography on the topic, and McLean, Yoder, and Schiefelbusch (1972) have edited a fine volume on language interventions for the retarded. The following are some of the major conclusions drawn from these studies and reports:

1. Speech and language are moderately delayed among the mildly retarded, but seldom are these delays severe enough to result in a diagnosis of retardation in the pre-school years.

2. The prevalence of hearing losses of 15 dB's or more among special class retardates approximates 11 percent (Lloyd, 1970).

3. Studies indicate that the prevalence of speech defects range from 8 to 37 percent among special class retardates, with articulation disorders the most prevalent. However, the mildly retarded have no unique configuration or pattern of speech problems (Keane, 1972).

4. Special class retardates generally profit from speech therapy, including practice to correct articulation errors, voice management, and auditory training.

5. Retarded oral language development becomes an increasingly serious problem for mildly retarded pupils as they grow older. In fact, lack of ability to manipulate language is a more serious problem than difficulties in hearing or in correctly making the various speech sounds.

6. Oral language stimulation appears to be modestly effective with mildly retarded special class children. For example, using the Peabody Language Development Kits, Dunn, Nitzman, Pochanart, and Bransky (1968) conducted a two-and-a-half-year efficacy study with special class educable retardates and found verbal intelligence and psycholinguistic processes significantly improved over those of the controls, but not school achievement.

While speech and hearing therapists have an important instructional role to play in helping the retarded hear and speak better, the teacher has an equally, if not more, important one in the overall field of language development. The teacher needs to provide a comprehensive language-development program as a major part of her curriculum. This must go far beyond the development and correction of speech sounds. Furthermore, oral language instruction is probably even more important than instruction in reading and writing. Three programs appear to be most popular for stimulating the oral language of MGLD pupils. Kirk and Kirk (1971) have devised a comprehensive manual for the diagnosis and remediation of specific psycholinguistic learning disabilities identified by the Illinois Test of Psycholinguistic Abilities

(ITPA); Engelmann, Osborn, and Engelmann (1969) have prepared a Distar Language program aimed at young black children; Dunn and Smith (1965, 1966, 1967) and Dunn, Smith, and Horton (1968) have developed four levels of the Peabody Language Development Kits aimed at stimulating oral language and cognitive development. It has been heartening to see a new emphasis on group oral language instruction for the mildly retarded, since so many of these children have come from bilingual or nonstandard English-speaking homes. At the same time, Goldman and Lynch (1972) have prepared a Goldman-Lynch Sounds and Symbols Development Kit which enables teachers and others to stimulate and correct articulation, or speech-sound production, through group instruction.

Learning and Motivational Characteristics

Nothing is more central to teaching the retarded than understanding their learning processes. Prior to 1958, very few studies on the topic were found in the literature. Since that time there has been a wealth of investigations dealing with learning characteristics of MGLD pupils. Comprehensive reviews of the literature are available (Ellis, 1963, 1966a, 1966b, 1968, 1970, 1971; Estes, 1970; Prehm, 1968). MacMillan (1971a) has examined the problem of motivation among the mildly retarded. Educators ask such questions as the following: How are the learning processes of retardates different from those of normals? How can we teach to reduce the learning deficits? It is difficult to find answers to such questions as these. The psychologists have usually conducted laboratory rather than classroom studies, and therefore neither the conditions nor the tasks approximate those with which the teacher is confronted. Today, however, a large number of behavior-modification studies are becoming available, many of which have more relevance for classroom instruction. Greene (1966), Weisberg (1971), and Gardner (1971) have done comprehensive reviews of the work in this area.

The following conclusions are drawn from the literature on learning, memory, and motivation. These might be viewed as speculations not inconsistent with the preponderance of research literature, though for almost each point there are contradictory findings.

1. Retardates demonstrate a deficit in learning both meaningful and nonmeaningful materials when compared with their brighter age mates. However, they do a better job when learning concrete rather than abstract materials.
2. Retardates and younger normals matched on mental age learn verbal tasks at comparable rates, whereas the retarded learn much more slowly than normals of the same chronological age.
3. Nonblack retardates have both short- and long-term memory deficits.
4. Black retarded children are superior to white retarded children in rote memory.
5. Retardates rather consistently are much better able to recall the last part of materials learned than the earlier portions. This suggests

that they should be asked to learn and retain materials in very small units or sequences.

6. Distributed practice, as contrasted with massed practice, facilitates learning for retardates even more than for normals.

7. One way to foster learning among the retarded is to find devices to encourage them to pay attention and focus on the task. They tend to have an arousal deficiency or attention lag. Reducing distractions, drawing attention to the task, and motivating the pupil should all help.

8. Retardates generally have more trouble than normals in avoiding distractors such as negative and extraneous cues in learning tasks, suggesting that this skill needs to be taught specifically to the retarded.

9. Retardates tend to continue to use a learning strategy even when it is not effective. The teacher should deal with this "rigidity in changing sets" by pointing out to the pupil why he should shift to another approach to problem-solving.

10. The retarded have more difficulty than normals in dealing with materials that are reversed or otherwise changed from the order in which they were originally learned, suggesting that they either be placed in tasks where they do not need to reorganize or be taught specifically how to recognize and deal with reordered materials.

11. Failure of retardates to store information permanently appears to be due to inferior rehearsal (mediational) strategies. Apparently, retardates need to be taught how to memorize by silently repeating many times what they are asked to retain. Too, they need to be taught how to organize material into "clusters" or "chunks." With more abstract materials for which they do not have common labels or other descriptive devices to aid in rehearsal, these should be provided. Exposure of materials to be learned for longer periods of time will facilitate acquisition by the retarded.

12. There is considerable, but not consistent, evidence that much *overlearning* will compensate considerably for the poor memories of the white retardates.

13. Motivating consequences, that is, praise plus monetary and other concrete incentives, will facilitate initial learning but have little effect on the memory processes.

14. While punishment deters and inhibits learning for all children, the mildly retarded have a history of and an expectancy for failure. MacMillan (1971a) has argued cogently that successful experiences must be provided these pupils to counter their failure expectancy. He stresses the need of the mildly retarded for teachers with *positive reaction tendencies* (those who generally find reasons to approve) versus those with *negative reaction tendencies* (those who generally find reasons to criticize). Furthermore, he points out that retarded children come to distrust their own solutions to problems and seek guidance from others because of their repeated failure. The challenge for teachers is to convert this *outer-directedness* to an *inner-directed* problem-solving style. It may be that pupil attitudes and motivation are greater detriments to school learning than intellectual incapability.

Finally, teachers should know that mildly retarded pupils are able to learn, retain, and transfer quite complex motor and verbal skills. Some educators have rationalized that it is not in the best interests of either the teachers or the pupils to expect them to acquire appreciable knowledge, since their learning abilities are limited. Such an escape is not tenable.

Reading Characteristics

Almost as much debate is waged over the appropriate curriculum for the mildly retarded as over their school placement. While most authorities oppose a strictly academic program, there is almost complete agreement that these pupils need to learn to read as well as possible for their social and vocational success in adulthood. Since about 1920, a considerable body of literature has been accumulated on the reading characteristics and methods of teaching the mildly retarded. The findings have been summarized by Dunn (1954), Kirk (1964), Quay (1964), and Cegelka and Cegelka (1970). The following conclusions can be drawn from this body of literature:

1. The mildly retarded, as a group, do not read up to mental age expectancy, but come closest to doing so in the regular grades, followed by special day schools and classes and then residential facilities.
2. Retarded girls tend to be superior readers to retarded boys and less variable in their performance.
3. It is not unrealistic to expect the mildly retarded to read up to mental age expectancy; in programs where reading is stressed, they approach this goal. Generally, the mildly retarded should make at least two thirds of a year's progress for each year spent in school when adequate attention is given to the subject.
4. The findings are mixed on the relation between reading achievement and emotional adjustment. Generally, there is a modest positive correlation, but causation cannot be assumed; each contributes to the other.
5. The mildly retarded tend to be more retarded in reading comprehension than in any other school subject, including oral reading (reading recognition). They are least retarded in general information.
6. In reading comprehension, the retarded are especially inferior to normals of the same mental age in locating relevant facts, in recognizing main ideas, and in drawing inferences and conclusions.
7. In oral reading, the retarded are inferior to normals of the same mental age in word-attack skills. They make significantly more faulty vowel and omission of sound errors, make significantly less addition of sound and repetition errors, and require that more words be pronounced for them. They are also inferior in the use of context clues.
8. Generally, there are no significant differences in the reading processes of cultural-familial (endogenous) and neurologically impaired (exogenous) mildly retarded children. Whatever superiorities exist are in favor of the exogenous group.
9. Mildly retarded children who are given an extended period of reading readiness and oral language stimulation until they have a mental age of six to eight tend to catch up to those whose formal reading instruction was begun at the chronological age of six years.
10. The evidence is very mixed on the effectiveness of teaching machines and programed instruction in teaching reading to the mildly retarded. The value of this approach appears to depend on the proficiency of the teachers, the superior ones having less need for it. A

combination of tutoring plus programed instruction appears to hold greatest promise for average teachers.

11. Each of the media has produced reading gains for the mildly retarded when the teacher is committed to and competent in using it, including the standard 26-letter Roman alphabet known as traditional orthography, the Rebus (pictorial) symbols, and the Initial Teaching Alphabet (ITA), in which a different written symbol stands for each of the 40 or so standard sounds of English.

12. Research has not demonstrated that one method of teaching reading to the mildly retarded, as a group, is universally superior to another— phonic, look and say, or kinesthetic. Probably the method is not as important as the teacher. What appears to be necessary is to find the best method for a particular child. A superior teacher needs to know and use a variety of methods to serve adequately a variety of MGLD pupils with very different backgrounds and characteristics.

Mathematics Characteristics

Much less systematic research has accumulated on the teaching of mathematics than on the teaching of reading to the mildly retarded. However, during the 1960s more useful studies appeared on the topic than in all previous decades combined. Reviews of the early literature will be found in Kirk (1964) and Quay (1964). More recent studies are abstracted in *Exceptional Child Education Abstracts* and *Mental Retardation Abstracts.* There tend to be many more conflicting findings in this area than in reading. Furthermore, the subject gets more complex when it is seen to include studies on quantitative thinking and concept formation. The following conclusions are drawn from the research to date:

1. The mildly retarded, as a group, tend to work up to mental age expectancy in arithmetic fundamentals, but not in arithmetic reasoning, where reading and problem-solving are involved.

2. As with reading, retarded girls tend to be superior to retarded boys in mathematics.

3. The research on the relation of motivational and personality variables to achievement in mathematics is replete with contradictory data, but there does appear to be some positive relation between good adjustment and mathematical proficiency, with failure accompanied by anxiety. Higher achievers have higher expectancies for success, and vice versa.

4. While it depends on job, role, and sex, mildly retarded adults need very little mathematics beyond that required for handling money to function adequately in society.

5. The mildly retarded develop quantitative concepts in the same order and stages as normal children, but considerably later. They acquire them by a combination of teaching and maturation. When drilled early to perform more advanced Piagetian-type quantitative tasks, they may appear to have the skills but will not understand the concepts, such understanding coming later after adequate intellectual growth has taken place.

6. When compared with younger normal children of the same mental age, mildly retarded children make more careless errors in working out problems, have more reading difficulties, use more primitive habits such as counting on the fingers, get more confused by superfluous data, and

have more difficulty selecting the appropriate computational skill to use.

7. Few significant differences in mathematics skills have been found between the cultural-familial (endogenous) and neurologically impaired (exogenous) mildly retarded, although there is a slight tendency for the neurologically impaired to have more problems with mathematics.

8. Concrete materials for teaching mathematics, such as colored Cuisenaire rods, Distar Arithmetic, and Stern's Structured Arithmetic materials, appear to work well with the mildly retarded.

9. The considerable body of literature on the use of programed instruction in teaching mathematics to the mildly retarded has generated more confusion than order, with little clear evidence for the superiority of either programed instruction or teaching machines over individualized teacher tutoring. Programed instruction appears to be superior for the lower IQ pupil when small-step sequences and a small error rate are built into the program and when branching is not used. As with reading, a combination of programed instruction and good teacher tutoring appears to produce the best results.

Social and Emotional Characteristics

The body of literature on the social and emotional adjustment of the mildly retarded has grown substantially in the last decade. Many of the studies reported up through the 1960s have been carefully reviewed by Gardner (1966; 1968), Goldstein (1963), and Schurr, Joiner and Towne (1970). More recent literature may be searched out by consulting *Psychological Abstracts, Exceptional Child Education Abstracts*, and *Mental Retardation Abstracts*. The following conclusions concerning the characteristics of the mildly retarded may be drawn from the literature:

1. There is a moderate positive correlation between intelligence and social acceptance. Generally, the lower the intelligence, the lower the social status (Dentler and Mackler, 1962).

2. Retarded children in the regular grades tend to be rejected or ignored. This is not so much due to their stupidity as to such negative characteristics as belligerence, dirtiness, and aggressiveness. In short, retarded children in the regular grades are socially segregated even though they are physically integrated. For example, Goodman, Gottlieb, and Harrison (1972) found, in a suburban elementary school, that mildly retarded pupils integrated academically into the educational mainstream were more rejected than comparable children segregated into self-contained special classes, but both retarded groups were less accepted and more rejected than their nonretarded peers. Younger retarded children and girls of all ages were less rejected than older retarded children and boys of all ages. Since all the mildly retarded were bused in from other neighborhoods, this factor may have contributed to the results. The reason the integrated mildly retarded pupils were more rejected than those who were segregated may have been because the latter were clearly labeled retarded and were therefore not expected to conform to the behavioral standards of those perceived to be nonretarded. Furthermore, attention was called to the integrated retarded, since they were regularly called out of the class for remedial tutoring. Similarly, Monroe and Howe (1971) found, in an integrated high school setting, that mildly retarded adolescents were rejected by their nonretarded peers.

Too, the longer the retarded had been enrolled in the school, the more they were rejected. Also, higher social class retardates were better accepted than lower class retardates. These findings should caution against wholesale integration into the educational mainstream of the mildly retarded—especially older, lower class pupils—without careful attention to improving their acceptance in that setting.

3. Some studies have shown that pupils with IQ's of 50–75 in the regular grades are more fearful of failure than their special class counterparts. In the past, this point and the previous one were used as strong arguments for special class placement, but further complications have come to light.

4. Among special class retardates, the lower IQ pupils were less accepted than the higher IQ ones (Jordan, 1961). In short, the pecking order extends into the special class. MacMillan (1971b) argues by extrapolating from the Edgerton and Sabagh (1962) study that certain high-grade special class retardates may derive aggrandizements by comparing themselves favorably with their lower IQ classmates—an opportunity they did not have in the regular school program.

5. While the findings are mixed, it appears that special class retardates tend to become overconfident and unrealistic about their abilities as their self-concept improves; this is accompanied by an increased dislike for the special class and by feelings of self-derogation about placement in special classes (Meyerowitz, 1962; 1967; Schurr and Brookover, 1967).

6. It has not been possible to demonstrate that children with IQ's of 50–75 develop a more positive self-concept when placed in special classes earlier as opposed to later in their school career (Mayer, 1966).

7. There is evidence that mildly retarded children in a partially integrated setting show greater improvements in self-concept over an academic year than pupils in a totally segregated special class program (Carroll, 1967).

8. Former special class retardates, freed of their label and returned to a regular school program (a new ungraded elementary school), displayed significantly more favorable attitudes toward themselves and school and considered themselves to be viewed by other pupils in the school as less deviant than a contrast group of retarded children still segregated into special classes (Gottlieb and Budoff, 1972).

9. In any event, whether in England (Chazan, 1967) or in the United States (Collins, Burger, and Doherty, 1970), special class retardates demonstrate more hostility than children of comparable IQ's in the regular grades. This should come as no surprise when it is recalled that IQ 50–75 children have been referred for special class placement selectively in the first place—as much or more for their behavior problems as for their academic failures (Mercer, 1971a).

Of greater interest to teachers should be the intervention studies which have attempted to improve the social status of the mildly retarded. To date, the following four have been reported in the literature:

1. Diggs (1964) attempted unsuccessfully, over a six-week period, to improve the social status of rejected pupils with IQ's below 70 in the regular grades by informing the regular teacher about the social status of these pupils and instructing her on methods of bringing about changes in that status.

2. Chenault (1967), using black special class retardates, paired low-status pupils with popular pupils, and for five weeks these pairs were removed from the room twice weekly for 15-minute sessions to practice a skit for presentation to the special classes. As a result of this intervention, on immediate posttesting the low-status subjects gained significantly more in peer acceptance and self-perceived status than did the controls.

3. Rucker and Vincenzo (1970) attempted to test the permanence of the Chenault effect. An experimental group of unpopular special class retardates was paired with popular classmates to plan and put on a class carnival for their peers. At the conclusion of the carnival the experimental subjects had become significantly more popular than their unpopular controls. However, on a follow-up test one month after the treatment terminated, significant differences no longer existed.

4. Lilly (1971) worked with low-status, low-achieving pupils in upper elementary grades in urban slum schools to improve their social acceptance, using five experimental groups and one full control group. Three of the experimental groups, each made up of a number of pairs of popular and unpopular children, met twice weekly for 15-minute periods, with various amounts of experimenter involvement, to produce and star in an 8 mm silent color movie which was finally shown in class. A fourth group made a movie on one Saturday that was shown to the class but did not get to leave the class during the week. The fifth experimental group had a within-class treatment wherein the unpopular pupils were paired with popular ones by seating them close together and having them work as pairs on projects which they presented to the class. In terms of an immediate posttest after the five-week period, all of the intervention groups made greater gains than the control group. However, the gains were no longer present after a six-week follow-up.

This led Lilly (1971a) to conclude that future sociometric research efforts should focus on classroom interventions carried out by the teacher, since such procedures would be more feasible and could be extended over a longer period of time. He recommends that the behaviors associated with low social acceptance be identified and specific treatments devised to correct them:

> Low acceptance children would be identified, and their behavior patterns analyzed to determine the specific behaviors underlying their low social acceptance. Then attempts would be made to modify problem behaviors, and the effects of changes in behavior on level of social acceptance would be determined. It is the present investigator's opinion that when we begin dealing with the particular behavior problems of individual children, in the manner outlined above, our intervention methods will be both more appropriate and more effective. (p. 347)

PIONEERING AND TRADITIONAL SPECIAL EDUCATION PROVISIONS

Growth, Extent, and Nature of Traditional Services

In the United States, mildly retarded children have been enrolled in special education programs in residential schools since the first such facility began operating in Massachusetts in 1848, and in special day classes since the first one opened in Providence, Rhode Island, in 1896. The growth and extent of these two types of services provided by state and local government are shown in Table 3.3 for the 20-year period 1953–1973. Additional information on special education for MGLD pupils provided by local school districts was presented in Table 1.3 and Figure 1.1. On the basis of these and other corroborative data, the following two observations can be made:

1. Since the 1920s, the number of pupils in special day classes for the mildly retarded has increased in an accelerated fashion, so that by 1973 almost one million such pupils were involved. This growth curve is likely to flatten out or even reverse directions by the 1980s if the national trend follows that already established in California (see Table 3.2). Conversely, as alternate strategies to special classes, such as use of special consultants, helping teachers, and resource-room tutors are extended to pupils without the use of the stigmatizing label mental retardation, the number of pupils receiving special education interventions should increase dramatically.

2. The extent of special education services for the mildly retarded in public residential institutions has always been relatively limited, building up to only about 20,000 pupils so served in 1963 and dwindling gradually since then. As far as large multi-purpose facilities are concerned, this trend is likely to continue. It is anticipated, however, that increased numbers of MGLD pupils will receive special education in a variety of small boarding schools in the future.

TABLE 3.3 *Extent and Growth of Special Education Services for Mildly Retarded Children and Youth in U.S. Public Day Schools and Residential Facilities, 1953-1973 (rounded to the nearest thousand)*

Year	Total in Special Education	Public Day Schools		Public Residential Facilities (estimates)	
		Pupils[1]	Percentages	Pupils	Percentages
1953	119,000	109,000[a]	92	10,000	8
1958	221,000	207,000[b]	94	14,000	6
1963	380,000	361,000[b]	95	19,000	5
1968	665,000	649,000[c]	98	16,000	2
1973	823,000 (est.)	809,000 (est.)[d]	98	14,000	2

[1]Earlier data[e]: 1922–23,000; 1927–52,000; 1932–75,000; 1938–100,000; 1940–98,000; 1948–82,000.

[a]M. C. Rice and A. S. Hill, *Statistics of special education for exceptional children, 1952-53: Chapter 5, Biennial survey of education in the United States, 1952-54.* Washington, D.C.: U.S. Office of Education, 1958.

[b]R. P. Mackie, *Special education in the United States: Statistics, 1948-66.* New York: Teachers College Press, Columbia University, 1969.

[c]E. W. Martin, *Programs of the Bureau of Education for the Handicapped: U.S. Office of Education, Programs for the handicapped.* Washington, D.C.: U.S. Department of Health, Education and Welfare (Secretary's Committee on Mental Retardation), 1970.

[d]This estimate was obtained by extrapolating the growth curve and utilizing tentative 1971-1972 U.S. Office of Education statistics which showed 872,213 mild and moderately retarded children combined in special education provided by local school systems. For 1973, a minimum total of 879,000 was assumed: 809,000 mildly retarded and 70,000 moderately retarded.

[e]E. H. Martens, *Statistics of special schools and classes for exceptional children, 1947-48: Chapter 5, Biennial survey of education in the United States, 1946-48.* Washington, D.C.: U.S. Office of Education, 1950.

Pioneers in Curriculum Adjustment

Kirk and Johnson (1951), Rothstein (1971), and Kolstoe (1972a) have described the approaches of pioneers to the education of the mildly retarded. A brief overview of the main contributions of these early leaders is presented here.

D. Maria Montessori (1964—first translated and published in the United States in 1912), the first female Italian physician, who lived from 1870 to 1952, developed an instructional program built upon Itard's and Seguin's sense-training procedures for children who were probably mild to moderately retarded. Her system stressed *autoeducation* (self-teaching), utilizing such *didactic materials* as blocks, cutouts, dressing frames, and embossed letters. Later, and continuing to this day, her program was extended to academics and was utilized extensively with young children of average intelligence. The chief criticisms of her approach include (1) not enough socializing experience; (2) lack of evidence on transfer of learning to real-life situations; (3) lack of attention on oral language and literature; (4) lack of field trips, dramatic plays, and outdoor activity; (5) rigidity of content; and (6) lack of follow-through above the primary school level. Gitter (1970) has written a book on the Montessori way of teaching young children with intellectual inadequacies and an article on the promise of Montessori for special education (Gitter, 1967).

Alice Descoeudres (1928), a Belgian physician, contributed the first comprehensive curriculum guide for the mildly retarded, thus beginning a movement away from sense training. While Montessori emphasized self-teaching through didactic materials, Descoeudres emphasized educational games in a natural, group setting, though individual instruction was also provided to compensate for specific sensory and perceptual defects.

Annie K. Inskeep (1926), the first American educator to provide a textbook devoted exclusively to teaching dull and mildly retarded children, proposed an academic curriculum emphasizing the three R's and geared to the mental ages of the pupils. In addition to academic instruction, she recommended group activities in such areas as vocational training, social living, and health. Further, she proposed that more recreational activities and arts and crafts be provided than were used in the regular grades. Hers has become known as the "watered-down regular curriculum."

Christine P. Ingram (1935—third revision in 1961) is recognized as the foremost U.S. advocate of her day of the "unit" plan built on the project method. This strategy was advocated somewhat earlier by J. E. W. Wallin (1924) and popularized later by Elise H. Martens (1950). Units of work were centered around such real-life situations as food, dress, child care, and shopping. In contrast to Inskeep's approach, Ingram proposed that academics be brought in incidentally, as needed, to carry out units of instruction.

Richard Hungerford (1948) and his associates, including Chris J. De Prospo and Louis E. Rosenzweig in New York City and Marcella Douglas in Detroit, extended Ingram's "units of instruction" approach, which they called "cores of instruction." The focus was on occupational education, with the emphasis throughout on preparation for employment, the management of a home, and the development of social competence.

John Duncan (1943), in England, developed a boarding school program in the country for mildly retarded boys which emphasized school learning through using one's hands on concrete materials. He argued that his pupils were better at performance-type tasks than at abstract, verbal-reasoning tasks. In place of the unit or core approach that integrated across subject matter, Duncan's curriculum covered 13 subject areas: (1) paper and cardboard construction work; (2) woodwork; (3) needlework; (4) art; (5) domestic arts; (6) physical education; (7) folk dancing; (8) gardening; (9) rural science; (10) English; (11) arithmetic; (12) history; and (13) geography.

Alfred A. Strauss, with *Laura E. Lehtinen* (1947) and *Newell C. Kephart* (1955), in the United States, developed a school program for the hyperactive Strauss-type exogenous child in a classroom setting designed to reduce perseveration, hyperactivity, distractibility, and emotional and perceptual disturbances. The Strauss syndrome was described in Chapter 2 and the methods of Lehtinen and Kephart are discussed in Chapter 10.

Samuel A. Kirk and his associate *G. Orville Johnson* (1951), while at the University of Illinois, developed a comprehensive "eclectic" curriculum for special class mildly retarded pupils. For the first part of the day, the academic subjects of reading, writing, spelling, and arithmetic were taught in their own right as proposed by Inskeep. The project, core, or unit method was then used for the other part of the day to develop social studies, science, and social adjustment skills, as proposed by Ingram. Occupational education, as proposed by Hungerford, was stressed at the high school level.

Traditional Special Class Curriculum

What the pioneers proposed and what special class teachers have practiced have often been very different. Part of the reason, no doubt, has been that many of these teachers were recruited unselectively and were only minimally trained for their job—if at all. What have actually been the curricular approaches emphasized at different times since 1900? The four major *traditional* emphases have been (1) the arts and crafts, (2) the units of instruction with rudimentary academics, (3) the mental health, and (4) the occupational education approaches.

1. For the first quarter of the century, the focus was on *arts and crafts.* Since the physical skills of retarded pupils appeared to excel their mental skills, it seemed natural that early special classes would have a handicraft emphasis. Thus they were filled with weaving looms, sewing machines, woodworking benches, tools, and so forth. By the 1930s, this focus, which none of the pioneers had advocated, though Duncan came as close as any to doing so, came under criticism. It was discovered that many of these pupils also had problems of incoordination. Further, the program became largely busy work.

With technological advances it became clear that shop skills were not very saleable. Thus the arts and crafts phase began to fade, though remnants of it exist to this day.

2. In its place came the second stage, which combined *units of instruction with rudimentary academics.* It was argued that retarded pupils could learn sufficient skills to be literate and needed this knowledge to become independent and self-supporting adults. Equally important, it was believed, they needed to develop social living skills. This approach is still the curriculum of choice at the elementary school level for trained, competent teachers.

3. While it permeates the whole special class movement, the *mental health* approach reached its peak in the fifties and extended into the 1960s. During that decade, as Johnson (1962, 1964) said, many of the programs were little more than "happiness" classes—again an approach not advocated by any of the pioneers. The argument was that the children had faced frustration and failure in the regular grades and therefore could not be expected to learn until their self-confidence was restored. Thus nothing much was expected of the pupils themselves or of the teachers that taught them. With special classes proliferating, administrators recruited essentially untrained teachers, many of whom were told that they needed only to keep their pupils happy, busy, and out of trouble. While fading at the outset of the 1970s, much of this approach remains. In fact, in 1970, one state director of special education reported that 89 percent of his teachers of the retarded were not adequately prepared—39 percent were not certified and 50 percent needed upgrading, and this was probably a rather typical picture. However, with an oversupply of teachers for the first time in almost 50 years, standards should rise appreciably in the years ahead. When the right teacher has taught the retarded, beautiful things have happened. Unfortunately, this was too often the exception during the 1960s.

4. The *occupational education approach* advocated early by Hungerford (1948) and his associates, and more recently by Thiel (1972), has been with us throughout the special class movement. While this emphasis is seen even in the elementary school, it has been reflected more in the prevocational and vocational programs of junior and senior high schools.

Even into the seventies one could find all of these four traditional curricular emphases in special classes throughout Canada and the United States. The course of study followed by the teacher depended on her own philosophy, background, and training, plus the particular strategy favored by the special education leader in the school system. Since the special classes were self-contained, the teacher did not need to be concerned with integrating her curriculum into that of the educational mainstream.

Traditional Special Class Organization

Special class teacher-pupil ratios have tended to run about one half those in general education. Pupils in these special classes were not usually organized by IQ, sex, etiology, or environmental background during the fifties and sixties, except as the last two factors were influenced by the location of the neighborhood school. Instead, they were grouped by levels according to a combination of the chronological and mental ages of the pupils, primarily the former. Table 3.4 lists the chronological age, mental age, and grade capacity ranges of mildly retarded pupils in traditional special classes at four school levels with a postschool stage added. Approximately two thirds of the special classes have been at the elementary school level and one third at the secondary level. Less than 1 percent of services have been at the preschool and postschool levels combined (Mackie, 1969).

TABLE 3.4 *Traditional and Proposed Intellectual Characteristics of Pupils Classified as Having Mild General Learning Disabilities at Four School Levels Plus Postschool*

| School Level | CA Range (years) | MA Range (years) | | Grade Capacity Range[c] | | Average Pupil Grade Placement |
		Traditional[a]	Proposed[b]	Traditional	Proposed	
1. Preschool	under 6	below 4½	below 4	Nursery	Nursery	K and below
2. Elementary	6–11	3[d]-8[e]	3½–8	N–3	N–3	1–6
3. Junior high school	12–14	6–10½	7–10	1–5½	2–5	7–9
4. Senior high school	15–17	7½–12	9–11	2½–7	4–6	10–12
5. Postschool	18 and over	8–12½	9½–11½	3–7½	4½–6½	Beyond 12

[a]Assuming a traditional IQ range equivalent to 50–75 and a mean of 70 for mildly retarded Anglo pupils:

[b]Assuming a proposed IQ range equivalent to 60–70 and a mean of 67 for mildly retarded Anglo pupils.

[c]*Rule of five* used to estimate grade capacity range; that is, subtract five from mental age.

[d]Lower limit obtained by using IQ 50 for one half of six years (or a mental age of three).

[e]Upper limit obtained by using IQ 75 for three quarters of 11 years (or a mental age of 8¼ rounded to eight).

Effectiveness of Traditional Special Day Classes

Today as never before the value of special day classes for the mildly retarded is being questioned on both sides of the Atlantic. This challenge has been stimulated in part by the results of a series of studies comparing the effectiveness of special class versus regular class placement. These investigations, which have been conducted over the past 50 years in the United States and Europe, have been reviewed by Kirk (1964), Osterling (1967), and Guskin and Spicker (1968). Compared to laboratory investigations, they have many weaknesses. Nevertheless, the results have been so uniform that the following conclusions seem justified:

1. As a group, mildly retarded pupils retained in the regular grades

make as much or more progress in school achievement as special class retardates, but this is slightly less true for adolescents.

2. Neither special class nor regular class retardates, as a group, work academically up to even their mental age expectancy.

3. Even when placed in special classes upon entering school at the age of six; having carefully selected, trained, and supervised teachers; being in small classes; and being given a balanced curriculum and excellent instructional materials, special class retardates, as a group, do not achieve academically above randomly selected regular class retardate controls (Goldstein, Moss, and Jordan, 1965).

4. Lower IQ special class retardates appear to gain more in school achievement than higher IQ ones in such a setting.

5. As noted earlier, mildly retarded pupils in the regular grades, as a group, tend to be rejected and isolated by their more average peers. While the evidence is somewhat mixed on the adjustment of retardates in the sheltered environment of the special class, generally, it has been found to be superior to that of those left in the regular grades. Apparently, the self-concept of the higher IQ pupils goes up somewhat with success, but at the expense of the low IQ pupils who are rejected and isolated by them. With their increase in status and confidence, the higher IQ retardates grow in their dislike of the special class placement and increase in their feelings of self-derogation about such placement.

6. Special class retardates appear to be superior to regular class retardates in brainstorming and other aspects of free thinking, apparently because they are less inhibited.

7. Retarded pupils make more progress in school districts that employ central office specialists to consult with and supervise the special class teachers than in situations where special class teachers are unsupervised.

8. Special classes appear to be best suited for (1) the white, native-born, slum, low IQ children from unstable homes; (2) the behavior-disordered, aggressive, acting-out pupils; and (3) the hyperactive, neurologically impaired children.

9. Low IQ children who make the best progress in the regular grades are those who come from ethnic minorities where nonstandard English is spoken in the homes and who are reasonably well adjusted and accepted in that setting.

This mixed picture of more failures than successes leaves us little choice but to question traditional special day class placement for many mildly retarded pupils. As Kirk (1964) has commented:

> Special classes for educable mentally retarded children in the United States increased in enrollment nearly tenfold between 1922 and 1958. This increase would indicate an acceptance of the advantages of special classes over the retention of the mentally retarded in the regular grades. To date, however, research has not justified the faith on which this acceptance is based. (p. 62).

There are some who justifiably would ignore this accumulation of a half century of research findings because of the weaknesses of these field studies, which have included (1) selection factors, with the more troublesome pupils referred for special class placement; (2) insensitive measures of pupil progress; (3) few follow-ups into later years; (4) small sample sizes; (5) short treatment periods; and (6) little control of teacher, curriculum, or method variables. No doubt poorly prepared teachers washed out the effects of capable teachers in a number of studies. And no doubt selected pupils may have profited from special class placement even though overall positive effects were not demonstrated. Further, since essentially all the studies were conducted at the elementary school level, they tell us nothing about the efficacy of special education at either the preschool or high school levels. In addition, since mostly self-contained special day classes were investigated, little is yet known about the effectiveness of the more integrated plans outlined in Chapter 1. Finally, no study has contrasted boarding school with day school placement, which would seem desirable in light of the appalling home and community conditions from which many mildly retarded children come; perhaps a 30-hour school week for only 40 or so weeks a year is just not enough. In spite of the lack of rigor of much of the past research and the clear need for additional studies, it would appear prudent to give serious consideration to the negative results of traditional special class placement obtained by a variety of investigators in a variety of communities.

Adult Status of Former Traditional Special Class Pupils

Before examining options other than special classes, it would appear desirable to examine the evidence from follow-up studies on what happens to graduates of special classes upon leaving school. Numerous such investigations have been made over the last 50 years. Reviews of the literature are given by Goldstein (1963), Wolfensberger (1967), Sparks and Younie (1969), and Heber and Dever (1970).

The follow-up studies conducted up to 1950 provide a very optimistic picture that special class retardates do lose their identity in adulthood, becoming independent, self-supporting citizens. These findings have been widely used in support of special education. The following conclusions can be drawn from a review of the early literature:

1. From 61 to 98 percent of former special class retardates became economically self-sufficient in adulthood, with a median of 82 percent.
2. Former special class retardates tended to be more fully employed during periods of high employment and to do less well during periods of recession and depression, with blacks and young persons experiencing the greatest problems.
3. While most retarded persons found employment in the service and unskilled occupations, a surprising number from recent-immigrant homes located work further up the economic ladder.
4. Former special class retardates tended to shift jobs frequently during their early work careers before gaining maturity, learning job expectancies, and finding their niche.
5. Personal qualities of good work habits—getting along with others, taking criticism, and profiting from mistakes—appeared to be more related to job success than intelligence or achievement test scores. Furthermore, vocational failures were due to such factors as labeling, preoccupation with sex, problems with work skills, and poor family living conditions.

6. Female graduates of special classes tended to have about as adequate work-adjustment histories as male retardates.

7. Most graduates of special classes who married tended to wed higher IQ spouses and have children with somewhat higher intelligence than their own. A higher percentage of girls than boys married, with the latter marrying later, after they had developed more independent living skills.

8. The crime records of former mildly retarded pupils were very high, ranging from 40 to 60 percent, with a median of 50 percent. The crimes tended, however, to be minor ones involving sex offenses, drunkenness, vagrancy, and petty thievery.

The follow-up studies since 1950 do not provide such an optimistic picture as the earlier investigations. For example, Lee, Hegge, and Voelker (1959) followed up graduates from Detroit special classes and from the Wayne County Training School, a boarding facility outside Detroit which serves that community. Only 61 percent of the special class and 29 percent of the residential training school graduates had achieved even minimal social and economic adequacy in young adulthood. Dinger (1961) found that 40 percent of his former special class retardates were earning less than $3,000 annually, with a median income for the group of $3,327.

The findings of the two studies contrasting the adult adjustment of former regular and special class retardates were at variance. Porter and Milazzo (1958) compared 12 such pairs matched on age and intelligence. In the unusual setting of a small midwestern city where the special classes were in a demonstration school on the university campus, a greater percentage of the special class group were gainfully employed and had fewer arrests. Since no inferential statistics were used, and since the groups were small, it is not possible to generalize from this study. In contrast to Porter and Milazzo, Carriker (1957) found no significant differences between the groups using such measures as number with full-time employment, wages earned, or law violations after leaving school. However, the former special class retardates were rated higher by their employers. This record can be viewed as good in light of their poor prognosis, since during their school years they had more referrals to juvenile courts, were placed in foster homes more often, and had fathers more often involved in major law violations. This study suggests that special classes are more necessary for troubled children from poor family backgrounds.

The studies comparing former special class retardates with regular-grade graduates of normal intellect but similar socioeconomic backgrounds also obtained somewhat opposite results. Peterson and Smith (1960) compared 45 such pairs matched on similar low socioeconomic backgrounds. They found that the retarded had substantially more problems in adulthood than their nonretarded peers of similar backgrounds and were employed more in the unskilled and service areas. The female retardates earned less than half the amounts earned by the normal females. (Similarly, Gorelick [1968] found that female retardates were less realistic about their occupational prospects, held fewer jobs, worked fewer hours, and earned much less than male retardates.) Kennedy (1962) too, in following up well into adulthood mildly retarded and non-retarded children initially matched on age, sex, religion, and ethnic background, found the retarded significantly inferior on some important aspects of vocational, social, and marital adjustment, but not too different on many others. Martin (1969) obtained different results from Peterson and Smith and from Kennedy when he compared 40 retarded male graduates from special classes with 60 normal males of similar socioeconomic backgrounds who had graduated from the regular grades. No significant differences existed between the groups in employment rate, extent of self-support, method of obtaining employment, job stability, or degree of job satisfaction. However, the higher IQ regular class group did earn more, got a job more quickly, had higher occupational ratings, and had taken more additional training after leaving school. Since the evidence is so mixed, more such comparative studies are needed.

Useful information is provided by the Baller, Charles, and Miller (1967) study on the mid-life attainment of former special class pupils. They found that the most successful members of the group did not have the highest IQ scores. Instead, they (1) had more middle class patterns of dress, speech, and personal habits; (2) either worked for a big, paternal business such as the railroads or had learned a simple skill such as barbering and had stuck to it; or (3) as children knew some adult (teacher, employer, relative) who gave them a sense of their own worth.

In summary, the recent analyses of the status of graduates of special classes suggest that most such individuals are leading a marginal existence near or below the poverty line. Therefore, there is little reason for complacency concerning the fate of pupils classified by the schools as mildly retarded. The differential between the recent studies and the earlier ones may be due to a number of factors, not the least being the increasingly complex society in which we live, the technological advances in industry, including automation and the population explosion, all of which make it more difficult for the retarded to be competitively employed.

Arguments for and against Traditional
Special Class Placement

Should traditional special day classes for the mildly retarded be retained, abandoned, or used selectively? As late as 1970, this issue headed the list of then-current controversies in special education (Jordan and McDonald, 1971). Articles defending special classes have included those by Engel (1969), Miller and Schoenfelder (1969), Harvey (1969), Kidd (1970), MacMillan (1971b), and Kolstoe (1972b), who have made such telling arguments as the following:

1. Because studies to date on the effectiveness of special classes have had so many methodological weaknesses and have measured largely academic progress, one cannot rely on them as a basis for making changes. Furthermore, the effectiveness of alternative plans needs to be demonstrated before they are adopted in a wholesale fashion.

2. More than general educators, special class teachers are trained (1) to set realistic expectations of achievement commensurate with the mental abilities of their retarded pupils, (2) to use more concrete materials, (3) to insure relevance by making the everyday experiences of the pupils the content for lessons, (4) to preserve the integrity of each child by making him feel successful and worthwhile, and (5) to stress realistic practical work skills (Kolstoe, 1972a, p. 201).

3. Class size in special classes, being about half that in the regular grades, allows for more individualized instruction.

4. The retarded pupil meets academic failure and social rejection in the regular grades, whereas in the special class he finds greater success and acceptance; if returned to the regular grades, he will again face scholastic failure and social rejection.

5. Separate special programs are justified, especially as retarded pupils grow older, because they slip further behind their intellectually normal peers and the curriculum becomes increasingly more inappropriate with each advancing year.

6. By removing retarded pupils from the regular grades, the range of individual differences is reduced and teachers can be more effective with the remaining average and bright students, as research on heterogeneous versus homogeneous grouping has demonstrated (see page 45).

7. Teacher associations are going to increase their demands that the most burdensome and troublesome pupils, many of whom are slow learners, be removed from the regular program, and these demands cannot be ignored.

8. Special educators have for years been successfully selling special classes to school administrators and legislators, and now that all three parties are so involved in this area, it will not be easy to reverse their orientations. Further, special class teachers who have devoted their professional careers to this field cannot be abandoned.

A number of articles critical of special classes have appeared in the United States, Canada, and abroad, including Blatt (1960), Johnson (1962), Fisher (1967), Dunn (1968), Johnson (1969), Christoplos and Renz (1969), Jansen, Ahm, Jensen, and Leerskov (1970), and Cormany (1970). Those who favor reducing our commitment to special classes argue as follows:

1. While it is recognized that the efficiency studies have many weaknesses, the remarkably consistent findings over the years pointing to the limited value of such facilities cannot be ignored.

2. The recent follow-up studies which indicate that graduates of special classes are leading a marginal existence near or below the poverty line suggest that better alternatives are needed to prepare the mildly retarded for a successful adulthood.

3. The vast array of research on homogeneous versus heterogeneous grouping indicates that most slow children profit from a classroom setting with a broad range of individual differences (see p. 45).

4. Although the research is far from conclusive, the studies on the self-fulfilling prophecy phenomenon of disability labels cannot be ignored (see p. 5).

5. The regular versus special class placement issue is no longer a meaningful one in light of recent court rulings. Ability grouping, the basis for special classes, is unconstitutional.

6. Unless their superiority can be demonstrated, special classes need

to be abandoned because they cost at least twice as much per pupil as the regular school program.

7. The special class track was devised in an era when there was a prevailing belief in the constancy of an individual's intellect; which meant that retardation was irreversible. Much research indicates, however, that intelligence can be stimulated, especially by early interventions for the culturally different. This finding suggests the abandonment of special classes as the sole alternative to the regular grades in favor of a wide range of intervention strategies aimed at stimulating the cognitive processes.

8. Special classes were initiated at the turn of the century when regular classroom teachers were poorly prepared to handle individual differences and had few ancillary resources. Now they are better prepared and have more assistance in dealing with slow learners. Furthermore, to take such pupils off their hands will reduce their need to effect additional improvements in individualizing instruction for the intellectually inadequate.

9. The sheltered, protective environment of the segregated special class does not prepare the mildly retarded for the realities of the competitive world.

10. There is little or no logic in grouping pupils in special classes on the basis of intelligence test scores when these children vary so greatly on so many other educationally relevant dimensions and when the major goal of the special class program has not been to stimulate the cognitive processes.

The present trend seems to be neither to continue to uncritically sponsor special classes nor to abandon them completely. Such articles as those by Nelson and Schmidt (1971) and Hammons (1972) attempt to balance the controversy. As a result, there is a movement toward providing an extensive array of options for MGLD pupils in school placement and programing. A consensus appears to be emerging that special class placement makes sense for selected pupils at certain stages in their school career.

PRESENT-DAY AND EMERGING
SPECIAL EDUCATION PROVISIONS

For an up-to-date, in-depth analysis of emerging practices in teaching MGLD pupils, the reader is directed to the professional journals and abstracts in the field which are listed in the Resources section at the end of this chapter. As for textbooks of the late 1960s and early 1970s on the topic, Smith's (1968) explores the clinical teaching of the retarded while Kolstoe's (1970) is not substantially different from the earlier classic of Kirk and Johnson (1951) published some 20 years earlier, except for giving a more balanced treatment to all four levels: the preschool, elementary, prevocational, and vocational. Gardner's (1971) focuses on the education and rehabilitation of the retarded adolescent and adult, emphasizing a behavior-modification approach.

Present-Day and Emerging Diagnostic and
Prescriptive Teaching Practices

The most dramatic changes to follow in the wake of the special class placement controversy have come in the area of *how to study and teach* mildly retarded pupils, not in what to teach them. This is the move toward the *clinical diagnostic,* or *prescriptive teaching* process. This approach has two interacting facets. One has to do with the educational diagnostic process and the other with the educational prescriptive process. Therefore, it combines the tools of the diagnostician, the behavior modifier, and the clinical teacher. The total process includes seven steps: (1) a general area of behavior is designated for attention; (2) the child is studied to find out what behaviors he has acquired along this dimension; (3) specific behavioral objectives which need to be acquired next are identified; (4) the relative effectiveness of different motivators and reinforcers are investigated; (5) the most effective modalities for reaching the child are identified; (6) the needed materials for implementing the instructional program are assembled; and (7) the best strategy is determined to teach the child the identified specific behaviors. Since the instructional program itself becomes the diagnostic device, this procedure can be called *diagnostic teaching.* Failures can then be recognized as program and instructor failures, not pupil failures. When an effective prescription of instruction has been found, the pupil is placed in the most appropriate general and/or special education programs to implement the ongoing program. Clearly, the major weakness of this approach is that it demands individualized instruction. It is best suited, therefore, to self-teaching and individual tutoring. The challenge is to utilize the strategy effectively in a classroom situation where one teacher is responsible for a substantial group of pupils .

How can the diagnostic teaching process best be put into practice? Rather obviously desirable would be for all regular and special education teachers to attain their maximum efficiency in carrying out the seven-step sequence just described. But many are not likely to acquire the high level of expertise needed to design creatively a series of successful interventions in a variety of instructional areas for a divergent group of MGLD pupils who have failed repeatedly in school, even though they might very effectively implement such programs. Two patterns for establishing a successful regimen are emerging. One procedure which large school districts, or two or more small cooperating ones, are following is the *special education diagnostic and pre-scription-generating center* described on page 29. Unfortunately, there are not enough trained clinical educators and behavior shapers available today to assemble teams to man these facilities, and even if there were, the operation is often viewed as too costly. An alternative, and a far less expensive procedure than a center with its cadre of educational specialists, is a single expert in diagnostic teaching who performs the diagnostic and prescriptive functions alone. She might operate on an itinerant basis or in a self-contained diagnostic class which would enroll pupils on a short-term basis only. The problem with this plan is that one teacher could hardly be expected to have the array of proficiencies of a diagnostic teaching team.

After a successful intervention has been established by the specialists, it needs to be put into an ongoing operation. The ideal means to accomplish this would be for one or more of the diagnostic teachers involved in the preliminary work to continue to tutor the pupil as helping teachers in the regular or special class or in a separate resource-room setting. Since this would often not be the best use of their time, an alternative would be for diagnostic specialists to serve as continuing consultants and crisis teachers to the regular or special teacher with whom the pupils are enrolled.

As the next decade will demonstrate, for better or for worse, diagnostic teaching will become the preferred strategy for teaching MGLD pupils. Preoccupation with diagnostic teaching would discount reliance on other strategies, including one that has been handed down as the preferred strategy by a number of the pioneers in this field—the unit, core, or group-project approach. Too, this technique lends itself to a focus on correcting pupil weaknesses rather than to a comprehensive program. Thus, hopefully in the years ahead, diagnostic teaching will be seen as only one very useful procedure among many to employ in a comprehensive program of instruction for the mildly retarded.

The reader is directed to Peter (1965) for the earliest general book on prescriptive teaching for handicapped children and to the same author for a later, more detailed system (1972). Those who support the widely held position that this procedure is appropriate for all children with learning problems regardless of their disability label will find a text by Becker, Englemann, and Thomas (1971) to be very much on target. Many others on behavior modification in the classroom will be found in the literature.

Present-Day and Emerging Curricular Objectives, Content, and Organization

Curricular Objectives

Unfortunately, special educators have been so preoccupied with the issues of special class placement and diagnostic teaching that they have given very little attention in recent years to curricular objectives and content for MGLD pupils. Since the vast majority of these individuals lose their label in adulthood, it is not surprising that most authorities continue to agree that the broad educational aims for children with normal intellect apply equally to MGLD pupils. The widely cited four broad objectives for public education listed by the Educational Policies Commission of the National Education Association (1938) (self-realization, economic efficiency, civic responsibility, and good human relations) have also been viewed as the key goals for special education for mildly retarded children. The objectives listed in the three most widely used textbooks on special education for the mildly retarded (Kirk and Johnson, 1951; Smith, 1968; Kolstoe, 1970) elaborate on these basic ingredients. After reviewing the literature on objectives, Kolstoe (1970) concluded that the entire program should be aimed at developing practical skills for independent living, including homemaking and earning a living at unskilled and semiskilled employment. This goal is not incompatible with the following four broad curricular areas which form the basis for the discussion to follow: (1) basic readiness and practical academics development; (2) communication, oral language, and cognitive development; (3) socialization, family living, self-care, recreational, and personality development; and (4) prevocational and vocational development, including housekeeping. The reader will need to consider two important questions. Can these objectives be best achieved in an integrated, segregated, or partially integrated school setting? A consequence of integrating more MGLD pupils into general education will also be the need to integrate curriculum more. The second question is, Are these objectives too general to have utility in determining needed curricular content for an individual retarded pupil? The advocates of diagnostic teaching would argue "yes" and recommend, instead, the use of specific, narrow, operationalized instructional objectives.

Curricular Content and Organization

Figure 3.2 organizes present-day curriculum content under the four broad curricular objectives just presented. An examination of this figure will reveal that the attention devoted to each of these areas changes considerably as a pupil advances from preschool through elementary, junior high, and senior high school. Present-day and emerging curricular patterns at each of these four levels will now be examined in historical perspective.

Preschool level. Traditionally, only a handful of preschool, special education programs have existed for MGLD pupils because they were not usually identified until they reached first grade. However, increasing numbers of low IQ children have been receiving kindergarten education in neighborhood schools that serve all youngsters in the community. In fact, the sixties was the decade for kindergarten education for four- and five-year-old preschoolers from the slums, thanks to Head Start and other federally sponsored projects. Mildly retarded children were included because the large proportion of IQ 50–75 children come from poverty-stricken areas.

This preschool movement was generated by a reawakening to the fact that cognitive development is depressed by adverse environmental conditions. It was hypothesized that slum children would progress more rapidly in language and cognitive development with a stimulating preschool program. This idea was not new. In fact, a number of studies on the topic were conducted in the twenties and thirties and are reported in the Thirty-ninth Yearbook of the National Society for the Study of Education, edited by Stoddard (1940). Perhaps the most famous one for the field of retardation is that of Skeels (1966), who followed up on his groups into adulthood, after a 21-year lapse. Involved were 25 children who were under three years of age at the outset of the study and who had been placed in an unstimulating orphanage environment. Thirteen of these children who were considered unplaceable were selected to be the experimental group. Their initial mean IQ score was 64.3, with a range of 35–89. They were transferred from the orphanage to become house guests of mildly retarded women at a state residential facility. In this way, each experimental subject was paired up with a mother surrogate who gave him much care and attention. The other 12 children remained in the orphanage as a contrast group. They were a more able group at the outset,

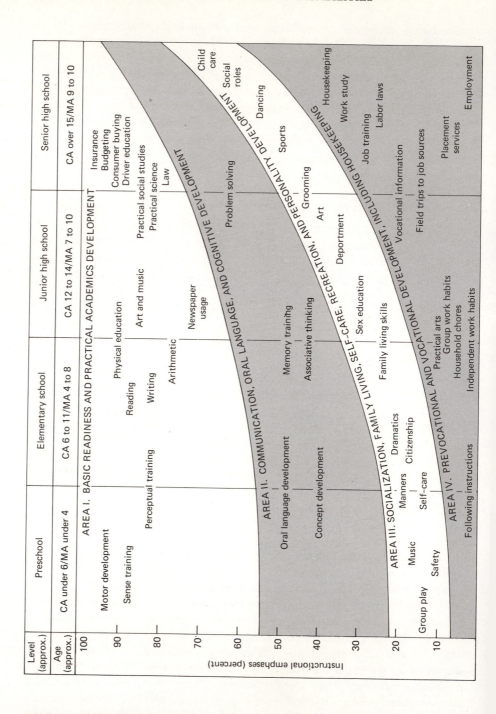

FIGURE 3.2 Present-day curriculum content areas by levels for children with mild general learning disabilities. (Adapted from Campbell, 1968.)

considered as possibly adoptable, and had a considerably higher initial mean IQ of 86.7, with a range of 50–103. After a two-year period, the children received their first posttests. The experimental group had made an average gain of 28.5 IQ points while the contrast group had lost an average of 26.2 points. Then, following variable periods with their retarded foster mothers, the members in the experimental group were placed in foster homes. The contrast group was exposed to the nonstimulating orphanage environment over a prolonged period of time. Skeels (1966) summarized as follows the differences between the groups in adulthood:

> The two groups had maintained their divergent patterns of competency into adulthood. All 13 children in the experimental group were self-supporting and none was a ward of any institution, public or private. In the contrast group of 12 children, one had died in adolescence following continued residence in a state institution for the mentally retarded, four were still wards of institutions, and one was in a mental hospital, while the other six were in the community—five doing menial jobs while one was the exception, being married and earning a good living as a compositor and typesetter.
>
> In education, disparity between the two groups was striking. The contrast group completed a median of less than the third grade. The experimental group completed a median of the twelfth grade. Four of the subjects had one or more years of college work, one received a B.A. degree and took some graduate training. (pp. 54–55)

The early studies of the influences of environment upon intelligence were severely criticized for their weaknesses in experimental design[5] by McNemar (1940) and others. However, Kirk (1958) conducted another classic study which supported the Skeels investigation and which anticipated Head Start. Very enriching preschool programs were provided for experimental groups of children with IQ scores of 50–75 in both community and residential school settings over a period of up to three years. Each such subject received both group instruction and individual tutoring based on his diagnosed needs, the teacher-pupil ratio being 1:4. At the same time, contrast groups were identified that remained at home and on the wards of the residential facilities. Some children were even placed in foster homes to determine the effects of that variable. The various groups were then followed into their later school careers. The general conclusion was that preschool education is desirable for retardates who live in conditions of extreme cultural deprivation, whereas the age of six is not too late to begin formal schooling for pupils from more adequate environments.

After Kirk found substantial positive effects of an enriched preschool program upon the intelligence and later school success of children reared in inadequate environments, Hunt (1961) wrote an influential book in which

---

[5] Skeels was partially rewarded for his landmark study just before his death in the late 1960s by receiving a Kennedy Scientific Award, at which time his degree-holding experimental subject made an appearance that greatly impressed the audience.

he presented a scholarly review of the literature on the influences of environment on intelligence. He concluded that the idea of intelligence being fixed is no longer tenable. Instead, he proposed the now-popular "interaction hypothesis," arguing that measured intelligence results from a complex interaction of genetic and environmental factors. By the early 1960s, three positions were widely held by professionals interested in early childhood education: (1) IQ scores are far from constant; (2) the preschool years appear to be especially important for cognitive growth; and (3) others, in addition to natural mothers, can provide a warm, enriching environment conducive to intellectual development.

During the sixties more studies than ever before were conducted on the effects of nursery school experiences on three-, four-, and five-year-old children, in large measure as a part of Head Start programs. This literature is well reviewed in such sources as Gray and Miller (1967), Lichtenberg and Norton (1970), LaCrosse, Lee, Litman, Ogilvie, Stodolsky, and White (1970), and Spicker (1971). Much of the work was done on inner-city slum preschoolers rather than specifically on the mildly retarded. However, about a third of the subjects had IQ scores below 75 at the outset of the various interventions.

Perhaps the most crucial and classic study on the degree to which retardation can be prevented by education among the black population living in inner-city ghettos was that of Heber and Garber (1970). Identified was a slum tract in the inner-city of Milwaukee that had provided a large number of mildly retarded special class children. In fact, in the tract, the mean IQ of the children in the total survey sample was 86.3, with 22 percent of them having IQ's below 75. Mothers with IQ's below 80 accounted for four fifths of the children who had scores below 80. In fact, a major finding of the initial survey was that maternal intelligence is the best single predictor of the level of cognitive functioning of children. Forty mothers with IQ scores below 70 were drawn from the pool and assigned to the experimental and control groups. A third contrast group was constituted from the survey sample, apparently of older siblings of the experimental subjects. The experimental group of infants was stimulated intensely commencing at birth and continuing through their preschool years to determine whether mental retardation can be prevented in this group. There were three thrusts to this comprehensive intervention program. During early infancy, an especially trained woman, through home visits, worked with the child directly and indirectly through the mother. Next, at four months, the child was enrolled in an infant education center. Third, throughout, a training program was provided the mothers to improve their child care and homemaking techniques. The final effectiveness of this combined infant and mother education program will not be known for some time. However, as they approached their fourth birthday, the average IQ score of the experimental subjects was 128, while the mean scores of the control and contrast groups were 94 and 85, respectively. Thus the experimental group exceeded the control group by 34 IQ points and the contrast group by 43 IQ points. Heber and his group are aware that their experimental infants are being intensively trained on skills sampled by the tests. No doubt the discrepancy between the experimental and reference groups will diminish as the children grow older. But it is difficult to conceive of the experimental children slipping down to IQ scores in the 60's and 70's. Therefore, the preliminary data from this study suggest that it is possible to prevent by education the kind of mental retardation that occurs in children reared in ghettos by minority-group parents who are both poor and of limited intellectual ability. However, even these large IQ gains for seriously impoverished young children do not refute the overwhelming evidence that intelligence is largely an inherited human trait (Jensen, 1969).

Preschool studies on children from impoverished environments, such as the three just described, have provided a foundation for the growth of early childhood education for boys and girls from the slums. Traditionally, nurseries and kindergartens for middle class youngsters used the *natural unfolding* approach, which stressed informal socialization and exploration in a play-like setting. Influenced by the writings of such persons as Bereiter and Engelmann (1966), preschool programs of the sixties for children of the poor became largely *preventative* and *compensatory*. This approach stressed the systematic teaching of cognitive and linguistic rules in a standard English format. There was much less emphasis in this setting than the traditional one on play, field trips, and so on. It was argued that field trips would not help a child much if the child did not have the cognitive skills to analyze, classify, and store the information he observed.

Of late, especially for young black boys and girls, there has been growing resistance to these structured, compensatory programs in standard English aimed at increasing their proficiency in Anglo-oriented regular school programs and on Anglo-oriented tests of intelligence. One argument centers on whether standard white English or the black English vernacular (BEV) should be used. A number of authorities argue that nonstandard English represents a deficit among these children that must be corrected or supplemented for intellectual development to proceed. Others contend that nonstandard English is only different and that it is equally capable of conveying complex semantic messages and equally useful for logical thought, reasoning, and other complex intellectual processes. Williams (1971) has provided a useful reference on this "difference-deficit issue." (Clearly, to date, special educators have tended to favor the "deficit" argument.) Other fundamental issues about early childhood education in general have been raised by Moore and Moore (1972); these caution against making inflated claims about the paramount importance of early childhood education, though clearly the strongest case is for impoverished children who are likely to suffer intellectual deficits unless enriching experiences are provided for them early.

Figure 3.2 highlights the areas of instruction which need additional emphasis for children from this group who are destined to have a mild general learning disability unless appropriate interventions are begun early. For the first year or two, the initial importance of motor development and sensory training cannot be overstressed. Then, in the second and third years, the emphasis should shift to oral language stimulation combined with cognitive development of a variety of types, including early concept formation. Throughout, sharing, playing together, and conforming to accepted social standards are important, but not of the first priority for the potential mildly retarded. Self-care and habit training need to be learned by low IQ children, including personal cleanliness, neatness, care of property, and safety. In a comprehensive curriculum, music, art, and dramatics are also important.

Finally, what is special about education for preschool children who are, and who are destined to be, mildly retarded? The answer is that very little is special when heterogeneous groups of children are placed in more conventional day-care centers, nurseries, and kindergartens and where the curriculum consists largely of play, socialization, informal chats, storytelling, sleeping, and eating under the direction of typical preschool teachers and day-care workers. To the degree that activities are added to stimulate the cognitive and linguistic processes of impoverished children, there could be much that is special for this latter group. In light of the value of more able children to serve as models for the less able, what is probably needed are nursery and kindergarten programs that serve a broad socioeconomic cross section, with flexible grouping to give each child the type of program he most needs—in keeping with the needs of the group. Under such a strategy, if it can be accomplished without labeling or stigmatizing any child, there would be a place for both general and special educators to team up.

An important value of universal nursery and kindergarten education would be that many MGLD children could be identified before they experience failure in the regular grades. Through a combination of readiness and intelligence tests administered to all preschool children, the preschool educational history, and a case study by at least special diagnostic teachers, essentially all such potential pupils could be recognized.

Elementary school level. It is at the elementary school level that the greatest amount of reform is needed in special education for MGLD pupils, since this is where special classes have been concentrated. In Chapter 2 it was recommended that the relatively small number of children who obtain scores equivalent to 50–60 ± 5 for Anglo youngsters be reclassified as moderately retarded and be provided with separate day and boarding schools resembling conventional homes. Similarly, it was argued earlier in this chapter that pupils of ethnic minorities who obtain scores above the second percentile, based on local norms for that subgroup, on either verbal or performance types of individual intelligence tests be declassified as retarded and returned to the educational mainstream. Thus, the focus of this section is on the remaining 0.6 percent of the elementary school population (see Table 3.1) (1) who fall between the intellectual endowment limits of the two groups just described; (2) who will be no more than 10 percent neurologically impaired and multiply handicapped, and probably more than 90 percent cultural-familial, proportionately distributed as to the ethnic nature of the community, of which 65 percent will be poor whites (see Fig. 3.1); and (3) who will have approximately the scholastic characteristics outlined in the appropriate columns of Table 3.4.

In terms of the various special education plans shown in Figure 1.3, one finds some research which cautions against the wholesale abandonment of special classes for such strategies as the resource room, helping teacher, and consultant plans for MGLD pupils. For example, during the 1950s, Ainsworth and his associates (1959) compared the relative effectiveness of three approaches with groups of traditional IQ 50–75 pupils: (1) an itinerant-teacher service; (2) the traditional, self-contained special class plan; and (3) a regular school plan where the mildly retarded were left in the regular grades without any special instruction. The investigators found that the group of children in the itinerant plan made no more and no less progress academically than the group of special class pupils or the control group of retarded children who received only regular classroom instruction. (Unfortunately, no subanalysis was conducted to determine the characteristics of individual pupils who made the greatest progress in each of these three settings.) Nevertheless, this investigation indicates that the efficacy of the itinerant-teacher plan has yet to be demonstrated for mildly retarded pupils.

Similarly, in studying the effectiveness of partially integrated plans for traditional IQ 50–75 pupils, often utilizing a resource-room teacher, neither Carroll (1967), Smith and Kennedy (1967), nor Flynn and Flynn (1970) found evidence to support the partially integrated plans in terms of the self-concept or school achievement of the mildly retarded subjects. For example, Flynn and Flynn (1970) found that removal of these pupils for 45 minutes a day of individual tutoring in a special resource room did not enhance their school achievement and was detrimental to their social adjustment. They recommended, therefore, that a program of individualized instruction *for both normal and retarded students* in need of help be provided *within* the *regular class setting*. In their view, such a practice might well remove the stigma which becomes attached to the mildly retarded child by his being sorted out by the teacher for special resource-room attendance.

Adamson and Van Etten (1972) evolved a "fail-safe" school placement model that needs serious consideration. They evaluated the relative effectiveness of the teacher-consultant, resource-room, and special class plans over a three-year period. For every 100 traditionally defined pupils, 70 were adequately served by the teacher-consultant and another 21 by the resource room, leaving nine potential special class candidates. The first step in their flexible placement program was to utilize the teacher-consultant for up to about half a school year, in 10-week blocks, with in-service training and close collaboration between the specialist and the regular teacher. If the child did not respond, a resource-room–regular class placement was tried for up to an additional school year, in about 20-week units. If the child still did not respond, a special classroom–resource-room placement was made for up to an additional school year. At the end of this time, if more rapid progress was not attained with special education service than in the regular program alone, the pupil was recycled back through the system, starting with regular classroom placement. All this time the regular teacher, the teacher-consultant, the resource-room–special class teacher, and the parents continued in conference sessions. They shared in the diagnostic information, the instructional programing, and the placement decisions. One value of this model is that it does not allow a regular classroom teacher, as in the past, to take the initiative for referring a pupil directly into a self-contained special class. All she can do is call in a teacher-consultant to help her. After that she is only one member of the team that is responsible for initiating a move even to a resource-room plan, let alone a special class placement. Further, if a pupil does end up in a self-contained special class after going through the various steps, he cannot be retained there for the remainder of his school career. This four-option flexible placement model, the effectiveness of which needs to be further studied, would seem to have greater relevance at the elementary school level, where a more standard curriculum is offered MGLD pupils, than at the high school level. But one should not expect to find the 70-21-9 Adamson-Van Etten split among the group of 0.6 percent of elementary school pupils who meet the restricted MGLD definition. Many of these young people will have already fallen so far behind their normal peers by the time they reach the upper elementary school that they will require a program very different in level of difficulty from that provided in the regular grades. Perhaps all or nearly all of these children will need to obtain essentially all of their more academic instruction separate from regular education. Perhaps the courts will not rule segregated special schools and classes illegal for this restricted, ethnically balanced subgroup. If they continue to do so, then the only option open would appear to be to implement a flexible grouping plan within an ungraded regular elementary school. In any event, all of this should caution against the wholesale adoption of any one administrative plan at this point in our knowledge. Research, including field study of individual cases, should make it possible in a few years to predict the kind of setting in which an individual pupil is likely to make the most progress and to estimate what proportion of MGLD pupils will need what type of service at a particular age level.

On the subject of grouping within the traditional special class, as Heber and Dever (1970) have cogently argued, there has been too much one–total-group instruction. There will be much more special about special education of the various types for MGLD pupils in the elementary school as programs are individually designed to achieve specific behavioral objectives and as individual tutoring is used to attain these goals. The challenge is to find a better balance than in the past among total-group instruction, small-group instruction, individual tutoring, and self-instruction, since all have an important place.

In terms of the elementary school curriculum, besides the content that was introduced at the preschool level, other ingredients are now added in each of the four broad areas of instructional emphasis depicted in Figure 3.2. In terms of Area I, which should have about 50 percent of the instructional emphasis at this stage, the initiation of more formal instruction in reading, writing, and arithmetic at about a mental age of six is a major event, though continuing attention needs to be given to perceptual training and physical education. As for Area II, about 25 percent of the time needs to be devoted to oral language and cognitive development. If one accepts Piaget's theory of intellectual development, then much remains to be done with MGLD pupils from 6 through 11 to stimulate their cognitive processes. Books by Inhelder (1968) and Kolstoe (1972a) should be helpful in this regard. Relative to Area III, approximately 15 percent of the instructional emphasis should be on self-care, family living, and social and personal development. The remaining 10 percent of the time should be devoted to Area IV, with the emphasis on the development of good individual and group work habits, as well as the practical arts related to housekeeping. Again it will be recognized that for MGLD pupils, at this point, the curriculum is not too different from that in mainstream education, except that somewhat more time is devoted to practical skills. Further, it will also be recognized that what has just been proposed is essentially the classical curriculum advocated by Kirk and Johnson (1951).

Junior high school level. By the time more normal 12-year-old youngsters are doing seventh-grade work, the average 12-year-old MGLD pupil will have accumulated a mental age equivalent of about eight years (two thirds of 12) and, if he is working up to capacity, is doing only third-grade work (see Table 3.4). He is now so scholastically retarded that the regular academic junior high school curriculum is far too difficult for him. Furthermore, few regular high school teachers have the time, energy, or ability to meet the needs of MGLD pupils within a heterogeneous group of adolescents. It will be recalled that more than 90 percent of the restricted group labeled MGLD in this chapter will be cultural-familial. No matter how good the elementary school program has been, it is unrealistic to expect the majority of these children to return to the educational mainstream at the junior high school level and proceed satisfactorily. The quandary is a serious one. On the one hand, adolescents, probably more than any other group, learn from and follow their peer models. The mildly retarded, therefore, need to be integrated as much as possible with students who are desirable models. Yet they need practical and meaningful instruction at their own level. Given these conditions, these young people require both adjustments in curriculum content and in the regular school organization if they are to make reasonable progress at the junior high school level.

In terms of school organization, since segregated special classes and streaming are illegal, it would seem that implementing the same plan as at the elementary school level, namely, a flexible grouping plan within an ungraded setting, would be the most feasible. It must be observed that the restricted group of MGLD pupils differ only in *degree* and not in kind from the other children who fall along the full spectrum of scholastic aptitude. The demarcation line is arbitrary. There are pupils just across the line who differ only in slight degree from the 1 percent that are the focus of this section (see Table 3.1). While MGLD youngsters may see a good deal of one another in the classes they attend, other pupils who are functioning at the same level in a particular area of instruction should be there as well. Thus, what is not recommended is streaming, to the degree it is permitted by the courts, solely on the basis of intellectual level.

What type of instructional program is desirable for MGLD pupils at the junior high school level? As shown in Figure 3.2, the emphasis on academics should fall off considerably in favor of greater attention on such more practical skills as life adjustment, home management, and occupation education. As indicated earlier in this chapter, a focus on academics at this level does not appear to be as profitable as attention on social skills, work habits, and job training (see p. 158). Smith (1968) has recommended that approximately 50 percent of school time be given to occupational instruction at the junior high school level, even more than that shown in Figure 3.2. Obviously, this leaves limited time for the other curricular ingredients. Again no hard and fast rules can be made. For example, the few pupils who were socially promoted through the elementary school who are not reading near their capacity and who were not provided with special services until junior high school may need intensive work in remedial reading. Because of their increased maturity, with appropriate instruction and motivation they should acquire basic skills in this area rather rapidly.

The prevocational, work-training program for MGLD boys and girls should begin much earlier than the junior high school level, even though it culminates there. From the outset of their school careers these pupils must be taught good work habits, including doing assignments well and in a reasonable amount of time. However, by the time they reach junior high school, retarded youngsters need to engage in more formal work experiences within the school. Retarded youths, therefore, need to spend part of each day at supervised yard, janitorial, and housekeeping chores around the school, largely to improve general work habits. Kolstoe (1970) has included on his list of such chores ground and building maintenance, food service, office service, and library chores.

Additional ingredients for the junior high school and the emphasis to be given to them will be determined from an additional study of Figure 3.2. In terms of Area III, since essentially all MGLD pupils will have their own homes eventually, both the boys and the girls need training in homemaking, home management, and family living. Therefore they all need experience with cooking, cleaning, care of clothing, and child care as well as with the simple maintenance of the equipment of the home, with simple plumbing and electrical repairs, and with yard care. Since essentially all of these mildly retarded pupils will date and marry, they need concrete information on the reproduction processes and family planning, including birth control and abortion. Since they tend to run into trouble with the law, they need instruction on the laws and the consequences of breaking them, as well as where to turn when they do have trouble. In addition, they need instruction and concrete experiences in understanding themselves and others.

Senior high school level. Traditionally, MGLD pupils have experienced their greatest problems when they reached senior high school age. By that time they lag even further behind their normal peers scholastically. Furthermore, senior high school teachers have a remarkably low tolerance for academic ineptness. It is not surprising, then, that the mildly retarded have been kept in elementary and junior high schools as long as possible, if not throughout their school years. Even vocational and technical schools have tended to bar low IQ pupils because of their alleged tarnishing effects on the status of these facilities. Furthermore, short of some revolutionary changes, and with some excellent but rare exceptions, these schools will no doubt continue to bar MGLD adolescents. Therefore, these pupils must find their place in comprehensive senior high schools if special day and boarding schools are found to be illegal.

The scholastic characteristics of mildly retarded youth over 15 years of age are shown in Table 3.4. These pupils have the capacity to do only about fourth- to sixth-grade work, and, on the average, they are six years/grades in capacity behind average students. The gap has widened considerably.

For MGLD pupils at the senior high school level, the relative emphasis given to each of the four broad curriculum areas is shown in Figure 3.2. By far the greatest proportion of time is devoted to vocational training, ranging from about 40 percent at the outset to 70 percent at the conclusion of this phase of the pupils' schooling. By the time these young people reach 15 to 18 years of age, hopefully they will have sufficient work, social, and personal skills to be ready for part-time competitive work placement on selected jobs in the community. This work-study program is one of the most innovative features of the senior high school program that has become popular in the last decade. Until their last year in school, pupils usually spend half of the day on a specific job in the community and the other half in study at school. It is customary, at first, to move a student to a variety of different jobs to discover his strengths and weaknesses. However, in the future, with improved diagnostic procedures such as work samples, this may not be as necessary. To provide close cooperation between the school and employers, a work-study coordinator is often provided who arranges and supervises the work experiences. Too, he feeds back to the other teachers information about areas in which the pupils need assistance in school. He usually also counsels the young people. By their last year of senior high school, pupils may be spending essentially all of their time on the job in the community, returning to school only when they need specific help. Ideally, this might occur before or after work hours. Kolstoe (1970) has suggested such ingredients as the following for the study portion of a retarded youth's senior high school course of study: (1) timetable usage; (2) traveling; (3) grooming and personal hygiene; (4) banking; (5) dating, marriage, divorce, and family planning; (6) home and family living; (7) car buying, insurance, and care; (8) the law, police, and drunkenness; (9) citizenship, including voting; (10) job applications, interviews, expectancies, and failures; (11) leisure and recreation; and (12) personal and social effectiveness.

The success of these work-study programs, which are still in short supply, depends in large measure on how well the coordinator works with community agencies other than the schools. State vocational-rehabilitation agencies have the responsibility to assist in the job training of retarded youth of 16 and over and usually like to begin the process as early as 14. The Wage and Hour Division of the U.S. Department of Labor has usually allowed schools to offer work-study programs to retarded pupils under 16 years of age. Furthermore, close liaison with the labor unions is usually necessary for a variety of service jobs. In many school districts, when a retarded pupil is able to hold a full-time job he is encouraged to do so and is excused from day school, although one condition of his taking the job may be that he attend school one evening a week. Thus cooperation within the school system is also needed.

In the past, educators have stressed the development of good work habits and attitudes rather than the teaching of a specific job. This approach is understandable if one takes the position that the retarded will move from casual job to casual job where few specific skills are needed. However, this approach may not now necessarily be the best one. In some communities, there are certain specific jobs which the retarded are most likely to be able to fill satisfactorily. For example, these might be on assembly lines, in the hotel trades, or in the food industry. With changes in the labor field and with more vocational counselors available to assist the retarded in the transition from school to work, preparation for specific employment will probably become the pattern. Some of this special training could be done by the schools through work-study programs. A study by Strickland and Arell (1967) lends support for this practice. They found that 80.2 percent of their mildly retarded subjects had found initial employment in the jobs for which they had been trained. Furthermore, Chaffin (1967) found that 91 percent of adolescents in work-study programs secured employment as contrasted with only 65 percent of comparable youth who did not get such training. The reader is directed to Kolstoe and Frey (1965) and Freeland (1969) for more information on the work-study approach of retarded adolescents.

After-graduation school services. It has long been recognized that even after retarded young people leave school their need for school services does not cease. A few progressive school systems have offered personal counseling, night school, and other such services to retarded graduates through an "open-campus" policy with considerable success. However, these have indeed been few in number. Generally, upon leaving school, the young people are turned over to vocational counselors employed by the state vocational-rehabilitation agency.

Postschool programs would seem to be professionally, economically, and ethically sound. When the school continues to keep its doors open to him, the retarded adolescent or adult has a haven and a source of information in his time of need and stress. In such programs the major emphasis should probably be placed on personal and vocational counseling. However, individual tutoring should also be made available. Too, young people who fail on the job need the opportunity to return to school to be recycled through the work-study program. The special teacher-counselor should be available not only to give help in night school but also to follow up on former students and to counsel with parents or parent surrogates. In this way the schools derive the fringe benefits of gathering data on the effectiveness of their programs. Hopefully schools of the future will not wash their hands of former pupils when they complete senior high school.

The Future for Mildly Retarded Adults

What does the future, with its automation, mechanization, urbanization, increased longevity, and the population explosion, hold for mildly retarded adults? More than a decade ago, Fraenkel (1961) argued that the picture ahead was bright. With automation would come a shortened work week, more leisure, and greater affluence. These developments, in turn, would combine to produce a greater demand for services, the area in which the mildly retarded are most likely to find employment. Other authorities argue that the job future for the retarded will darken. For example, Albizu-Miranda, Matlin, and Stanton (1966) concluded that the more complex the society, the more difficult it is for the retarded individual to adjust, since he does not have the ability to meld into a technically complex way of life. Certainly the job opportunities are changing dramatically for the mildly retarded. While service jobs will probably increase somewhat, unskilled positions will fall off sharply by 1980. Taken together, in fact, by 1980 only about 18 percent of the jobs in the United States will be of the unskilled and service types. By that year, for the first time in U.S. history, there will be more white and blue collar workers than unskilled workers. As people retire earlier from their major life work, and as the U.S. population continues to grow, there will be more competition for these less intellectually demanding jobs, especially from older persons but also from members of minority groups of all ages. Too, more and more women are entering the labor market. In 1972, 65 percent of the U.S. labor force was composed of men and 35 percent of women. At the same time, the minimum wage threatens to rise to the point where it will become unprofitable for an employer to hire a marginal worker. Furthermore, pressures for consumer protection and accountability will raise work standards. In addition, trade unionism protects the established worker. Therefore, there does not seem to be room for complacency about the future of the mildly retarded in competitive employment. Furthermore, while most will do so, it must be recognized that not all mildly retarded individuals will be able to find and hold competitive community jobs or become fully independent members of society—especially the restricted group on which this chapter has focused. Thus it rests with the community to provide a comprehensive range of services for retarded adults, including some of a more sheltered variety.

A number of proposals in the competitive employment field deserve consideration. Should a percentage of certain competitive jobs be reserved for the retarded? Should specific roles be assigned to the retarded, just as certain newsstands are reserved for blind persons? Should government-subsidized jobs be provided? Should government induce industries that can accommodate them to take their fair quota of retarded adults? How much on-the-job work training should private business be expected to provide, and how should the remainder be subsidized? Should labor laws be changed to reduce the work week and restrict moonlighting so everyone can have the opportunity to work a little?

As for habilitation by government agencies, should state and federal vocational-rehabilitation agencies do more for the mildly retarded? In 1969, for example, retardates accounted for only about 10 percent of their case load, and in that year they were habilitating only about 100 per state—a mere drop in the bucket. Furthermore, the amount of federal vocational-rehabilitation funds annually being spent on research and demonstration projects for the habilitation of the retarded had dropped alarmingly from a high of over three million dollars in 1965 to well under one million in 1970 (Garrett, 1971).

Perhaps these questions are largely academic ones. It is becoming less necessary for essentially all persons to work and be productive in our increasingly computerized technological society. Perhaps all citizens in the future will not be afforded the right and dignity of gainful employment. Perhaps a life of leisure with a guaranteed minimum income for many mildly retarded citizens is the easiest solution for society. In any event, for those who do not acquire competitive employment skills, such community facilities and services as the following would appear to be minimal: adult counseling, guidance, and placement services; sheltered workshops of both the transitional and terminal variety; and boarding homes and halfway houses. Only the future will determine the courses of action we elect to follow in dealing with the retarded adult in our emerging society. One would hope that the rights of the retarded to the "good life" will be better protected than they have been in the past.

SUMMARY[6]

Traditionally, a referral by a regular classroom teacher plus an IQ score of 50–75 on a nationally standardized individualized test of verbal intelligence has been sufficient to label a child as educable mentally retarded (EMR) and to place him in self-contained special classes for the remainder of his school career. This system resulted in as many as three quarters of such pupils being mislabeled because their ethnic and linguistic backgrounds handicapped them in their school work and on the intelligence tests. In about 1970, changes were initiated to correct these practices.

In this chapter it was recommended that EMR pupils be reclassified as having mild general learning disabilities (MGLD) for special education purposes and that the category be restricted to boys and girls who score below the second percentile, yet not in the lower one half of 1 percent for their ethnic subgroup in the community, on both verbal and performance types of intelligence tests. Children so selected would thus be proportioned equally across all ethnic groups and would be noticeably slow learning, with the retardation in 90 percent or more of the cases being due, in varying degrees, to inherited characteristics. Thus effective family planning, including genetic counseling and birth control, should help in preventing some such cases. Since essentially all of this group live in conditions of poverty, an ecological approach to eradicate slum conditions should also be effective.

As they advance through school, MGLD pupils lag progressively further behind children of average intelligence. Thus their need for a different educational program increases with age. It has therefore been recommended that the ratio of heterogeneous to homogeneous grouping and individual tutoring in school be shifted for them in approximately the following proportions: preschool, more than 95 percent heterogeneous to less than 5 percent homogeneous and tutorial; elementary school, 75 percent to 25 percent; junior high school, 50 percent to 50 percent; and senior high school, 25 percent to 75 percent. Of course, the goal should be to attain the maximum amount of homogeneity possible for each individual student commensurate with his abilities and curriculum needs, as well as with his ability to fit in.

It was recommended that slow children, at the preschool level, not be labeled MGLD and placed in special education. Instead, the focus should be on parent education, on highly stimulating infant, nursery, and kindergarten education programs for heterogeneous groups of children, and on special readiness tutoring for those in need, regardless of their IQ scores. At the elementary school level, since the broad instructional goals are the same for MGLD children as for other children, and since MGLD pupils do not lag dramatically behind other children at this point, many of them should be able to function adequately in the educational mainstream, when special educator-

[6] A section on emerging directions was omitted from this chapter even though it was included in all others because the approach throughout has been to trace through from traditional and present-day practices to emerging ones.

consultants and tutors team up with regular teachers to provide the extra attention these boys and girls need. In high school, even those MGLD pupils who have received excellent general and special education services earlier will have dropped so far behind average students that they cannot profit from the typical secondary school curriculum. However, in comprehensive high schools where departmentalization and flexible grouping are practiced, and when a rich array of vocational and homemaking options are provided for mildly retarded adolescents, most of them can be taught sufficient vocational, homemaking, social, and practical academic skills to become at least marginally self-supporting adults in casual service and unskilled employment. This is most likely to occur when adequate governmental and industrial support is provided during periods of need. For those few who do not acquire competitive employment skills, a comprehensive array of community services, including boarding homes, halfway houses, and sheltered workshops, will be needed.

Resources

In the Resources section at the end of Chapter 2 organizations primarily for parents of the retarded were outlined. Here professional organizations and journals and federal agencies with services for the retarded are described briefly. For additional information see Rothstein (1971).

The best-known professional association centrally concerned with the field of mental retardation is the American Association on Mental Deficiency (AAMD), which had its inception in 1876 and which has a joint Canadian and American membership. It is a multidisciplinary organization with members from the fields of education, psychology, medicine, nursing, rehabilitation, administration, religion, physical therapy, social work, and speech and hearing, plus a general section. By 1973, its membership had grown to approximately 10,000 persons. The Association publishes *Mental Retardation* (bimonthly) and the *American Journal of Mental Deficiency* (bimonthly). It also publishes directories of its membership and of state and private residential facilities for the retarded, as well as special monographs. The AAMD headquarters is at 5201 Connecticut Avenue, N.W., Washington, D.C. 20012.

A growing number of journals deal with retardation. Included among American journals, in addition to those published by AAMD, are *Education and Training of the Mentally Retarded*, published by the Division on Mental Retardation of the Council for Exceptional Children (see Chapter 1 Resources for address); *Journal for Special Educators of the Mentally Retarded*, 107-20 125 Street, Richmond Hill, New York, N.Y. 11419; and *Training School Bulletin*, published quarterly by the American Institute for Mental Studies, Vineland, N.J. 08360. There are four British journals in the field: *Journal of Mental Deficiency Research; Journal of Mental Subnormality; Forward Trends*, a quarterly journal of the Guild of Teachers of Backward Children; and *Teaching and Training*, a quarterly journal of the National Association of Teachers of the Mentally Handicapped. Another professional journal written in English is the *Australian Journal of Mental Retardation*. Canada has no professional journal focusing on the mentally retarded, but pertinent articles often appear in such journals as *Education Canada, Special Education in Canada,* and *Canada's Mental Health.*

The *International directory of mental retardation resources* (Dybwad, 1971), mentioned in Chapter 2, also lists international and national professional organizations around the world, and their journals.

In the United States, federal government activities are monitored by the President's Committee on Mental Retardation (PCMR). This committee submits annual reports to the President and the citizenry generally on progress that has been made in serving the retarded and issues special reports from time to time. Inquiries concerning federal affairs in the area may be addressed to the PCMR, Washington, D.C. 20201. Most retardation activities are housed in the Department of Health, Education and Welfare (DHEW), which formed an Office of Mental Retardation Coordination in 1972 to replace the Secretary's Committee on Mental Retardation. In 1971, the Division of Mental Retardation in the Rehabilitation Services Administration Service became the Division of Developmental Disabilities to administer broader legislation; it also encompasses such closely related areas to mental retardation as cerebral palsy, epilepsy, and neurological disabilities. This division has responsibility for a quarterly publication, *Mental Retardation Abstracts*, one of the most useful references in the field, which is available from the U.S. Government Printing Office. Other major federal government services for the retarded are provided by such DHEW components as the U.S. Office of Education; the U.S. Health Services and Mental Health Administration; and the National Institutes of Health. The U.S. Office of Child Development and the Office of Economic Opportunity serve the poor generally, into which category many of the mildly retarded fall.

References

Adamson, G., and Van Etten, G. Zero reject model revisited: A workable alternative, *Exceptional Children*, 1972, **38**, 735–738.

Ainsworth, S. H., et al. *An exploratory study of educational, social and emotional factors in the education of mentally retarded children in Georgia public schools.* Athens, Ga.: University of Georgia, 1959.

Albizu-Miranda, C., Matlin, N., and Stanton, A. *The successful retardate.* Hato Rey, Puerto Rico: University of Puerto Rico, 1966.

American Association for Health, Physical Education and Recreation. *Bibliography on research in psychomotor function, physical education, and recreation for the mentally retarded.* Washington, D.C.: National Education Association, 1966.

Baller, W. R., Charles, D. C., and Miller, E. L. Mid-life attainment of the mentally retarded: A longitudinal study. *Genetic Psychology Monographs*, 1967, **75**, 235–329.

Becker, W. C., Engelmann, S., and Thomas, D. R. *Teaching: A course in applied psychology.* Chicago: Science Research Associates, 1971.

Bereiter, C., and Engelmann, S. *Teaching disadvantaged children in the preschool.* Englewood Cliffs, N.J.: Prentice-Hall, 1966.

Blatt, B. Some persistently recurring assumptions concerning the mentally subnormal. *Training School Bulletin*, 1960, **57**, 48–59.

Bodmer, W. F., and Cavalli-Sforza, L. L. Intelligence and race. *Scientific American*, 1970, **223(4)**, 19–29.

Burgener, C. W. Diagnosing handicaps and language deficiencies in California. *Compact*, 1971 **223(4)**, 19–29.

California State Department of Education. *Placement of underachieving minority group children in special classes for the educable mentally retarded, 1969.* Sacramento, Calif.: California State Department of Education, 1970.

California State Department of Education, *Racial and ethnic survey of California public schools grade distribution, Fall, 1971.* Sacramento, Calif.: Bureau of Intergroup Relations, California State Department of Education, 1971.

Campbell, L. W. *Study of curriculum planning.* Sacramento, Calif.: California State Department of Education, 1968.

Carriker, W. R. A. A comparison of postschool adjustments of regular and special class retarded individuals served in Lincoln and Omaha, Nebraska public schools. *Dissertation Abstracts,* 1957, **17,** 2206–2207.

Carroll, A. W. The effects of segregated and partially integrated school programs on self-concept and academic achievement of educable mental retardates. *Exceptional Children,* 1967, **34,** 93–99.

Cegelka, J. A., and Cegelka, W. J. A review of research: Reading and the educable mentally handicapped. *Exceptional Children,* 1970, **37,** 187–200.

Chaffin, J. D. Production rate as a variable in the job success or failure of educable mentally retarded adolescents. Unpublished doctoral dissertation, University of Kansas, 1967.

Chazan, M. Recent developments in the understanding and teaching of educationally subnormal children in England and Wales. *American Journal of Mental Deficiency,* 1967, **72,** 224–252.

Chenault, J. Improving the social acceptance of unpopular educable mentally retarded pupils in special classes. *American Journal of Mental Deficiency,* 1967, **72,** 455–458.

Christoplos, F., and Renz, P. A critical examination of special education programs. *Journal of Special Education,* 1969, **3,** 371–379.

Collins, H. A., Burger, G. K., and Doherty, D. Self-concept of EMR and nonretarded adolescents. *American Journal of Mental Deficiency,* 1970, **75,** 185–189.

Corder, W. O. Effects of physical education on the intellectual, physical, and social development of educable mentally retarded boys. *Exceptional Children,* 1966, **32,** 357–364.

Corder, W. O., and Pridmore, H. Effects of physical education on the psychomotor development of educable mentally retarded boys. *Education and Training of the Mentally Retarded,* 1966, **1(4),** 163–167.

Cormany, R. B. Returning special education students to the regular grades. *Personnel and Guidance Journal,* 1970, **48(8),** 641–646.

Cratty, B. J. *Motor activity and the education of retardates.* Philadelphia, Pa.: Lea & Febiger, 1969.

Dentler, R. A., and Mackler, R. Ability and sociometric status among normal and retarded children: A review of the literature. *Psychometric Bulletin,* 1962, **59,** 273–283.

Descoeudres, A. *The education of mentally defective children.* New York: Heath, 1928.

Diggs, E. A. A study of change in the social status of rejected mentally retarded children in regular classrooms. *Dissertation Abstracts,* 1964, **25,** 220–221.

Dinger, J. C. Post-school adjustment of former educable retarded pupils. *Exceptional Children,* 1961, **27,** 353–360.

Dingman, H. F., and Tarjan, G. Mental retardation and the normal distribution curve. *American Journal of Mental Deficiency,* 1960, **64,** 991–994.

Duncan, J. *The education of the ordinary child.* New York: Ronald Press, 1943.

Dunn, L. M. A comparison of the reading processes of mentally retarded boys of the same mental age. In L. M. Dunn and R. J. Capobianco, Studies of reading and arithmetic in mentally retarded boys. *Monograph of the Society for Research in Child Development*, 1954, **19(1)**, 7–99.

Dunn, L. M. Special education for the mildly retarded: Is much of it justifiable? *Exceptional Children*, 1968, **35**, 5–22.

Dunn, L. M., Nitzman, M., Pochanart, P., and Bransky, M. Effectiveness of the Peabody Language Development Kits with educable mentally retarded children: A report after two and one-half years. *IMRID Papers and Reports*, Vol. V, No. 15, Nashville, Tenn.: Peabody College, 1968.

Dunn, L. M., and Smith, J. O. *Peabody Language Development Kits*. Circle Pines, Minn.: American Guidance Service, Level #1, 1965, Level #2, 1966; Level #3, 1967, Level #P (with K. B. Horton), 1968.

Edgerton, R. B., and Sabagh, F. From mortification to aggrandizement: Changing self-conceptions in the careers of the mentally retarded. *Psychiatry*, 1962, **25**, 263–272.

Educational Policies Commission. *The purposes of education in American democracy*. Washington, D.C.: National Education Association, 1938.

Ellis, N. R. *Handbook in mental deficiency: Psychological theory and research*. New York: McGraw-Hill, 1963.

Ellis, N. R. (Ed.) *International review of research in mental retardation*. New York: Academic Press, Vol. 1, 1966 (a); Vol. 2, 1966 (b); Vol. 3, 1968; Vol. 4, 1970; Vol. 5, 1971.

Engel, M. The tin drum revisited. *Journal of Special Education*, 1969, **3**, 381–384.

Engelmann, S., Osborn, J., and Engelmann, T. *Distar Language 1: An instructional system*. Chicago: Science Research Associates, 1969.

Estes, W. K. *Learning theory and mental development*. New York: Academic Press, 1970.

Fisher, H. K. What is special education? *Special Education in Canada*, 1967, **41**, 9–16.

Flynn, T. M., and Flynn, L. A. The effects of part-time special education programs on adjustment of EMR students. *Exceptional Children*, 1970, **36**, 680–681.

Fraenkel, W. A. *The mentally retarded and their vocational rehabilitation: A resource handbook*. Arlington, Tex.: National Association for Retarded Children, 1961.

Freeland, K. H. *High school work-study programs for the retarded*. Springfield, Ill.: Charles C Thomas, 1969.

Gardner, W. I. Social and emotional adjustment of mildly retarded children and adolescents: Critical review. *Exceptional Children*, 1966, **33**, 97–105.

Gardner, W. I. Personality characteristics of the mentally retarded: Review and critique. In H. J. Prehm, L. A. Hamerlynck, and J. E. Crossen (Eds.), *Behavioral research in mental retardation*. Eugene, Ore.: University of Oregon, 1968.

Gardner, W. I. *Behavior modification in mental retardation*. Chicago: Aldine-Atherton, 1971.

Garrett, J. F. Economic benefits of programmes for the retarded. *Programs for the Handicapped*, 1971, **71(2)**, 1–8.

Gitter, L. L. The promise of Montessori for special education. *Journal of Special Education*, 1967, **2**, 5–13.

Gitter, L. L. *The Montessori way*. Seattle, Wash.: Special Child Publications, 1970.

Goldman, R., and Lynch, M. E. *Goldman-Lynch Sounds and Symbols Development Kit*. Circle Pines, Minn.: American Guidance Service, 1972.

Goldstein, H. Issues in the education of the educable mentally retarded. *Mental Retardation*, 1963, **1**, 10–12, 52–53.

Goldstein, H., Moss, J. and Jordan, L. J. *The efficacy of special class training on the development of mentally retarded children.* Urbana, Ill.: University of Illinois, 1965.

Goodman, H., Gottlieb, J., and Harrison, H. Social acceptance of EMRs integrated into a nongraded elementary school. *American Journal of Mental Deficiency*, 1972, **76**, 412–417.

Gorelick, M. C. Assessment of vocational realism of educable mentally retarded adolescents. *American Journal of Mental Deficiency*, 1968, **73(1)**, 154–157.

Gottlieb, J., and Budoff, M. Attitudes toward school by segregated and integrated retarded children. *Studies in Learning Potential*, 1972, **2(35)**, 1–10 (Research Institute for Exceptional Problems, 12 Maple Avenue, Cambridge, Mass.).

Gray, S. W., and Miller, J. O. Early experiences in relation to cognitive development. *Review of Educational Research*, 1967, **37(5)**, 475–493.

Greene, F. M. Programmed instruction techniques for the mentally retarded. In N. R. Ellis (Ed.), *International review of research in mental retardation.* Vol. 2. New York: Academic Press, 1966.

Guskin, S. L., and Spicker, H. H. Educational research in mental retardation. In N. R. Ellis (Ed.), *International review of research in mental retardation.* Vol. 3. New York: Academic Press, 1968.

Hammons, G. W. Educating the mildly retarded: A review. *Exceptional Children*, 1972, **38**, 565–570.

Harvey, J. To fix or to cope: A dilemma for special education. *Journal of Special Education*, 1969, **3**, 389–392.

Heber, R., and Dever, R. Education and rehabilitation of the mentally retarded. In H. D. Haywood (Ed.), *Social cultural aspects of mental retardation.* New York: Appleton-Century-Crofts, 1970.

Heber, R., and Garber, H. An experiment in the prevention of cultural-familial mental retardation. Paper presented at the Second Congress of International Association for the Scientific Study of Mental Deficiency, Warsaw, Poland, August 25–September 2, 1970.

Hungerford, R. H. Philosophy of occupational education. *Occupational Education.* New York: Department of Special Education, New York City Public Schools, 1948.

Hunt, J. M. *Intelligence and experience.* New York: Ronald Press, 1961.

Ingram, C. P. *Education of the slow-learning child.* (3d ed.) New York: Ronald Press, 1961.

Inhelder, B. *The diagnosis of reasoning in the mentally retarded.* New York: John Day, 1968.

Inskeep, A. L. *Teaching dull and retarded children.* New York: Macmillan, 1926.

Jansen, M., Ahm, J., Jensen, P. E., and Leerskov, A. Is special education necessary? Can this program possibly be reduced? *Journal of Learning Disabilities*, 1970, **3(9)**, 11–16.

Jensen, A. R. How much can we boost IQ and scholastic achievement? In *Environment, heredity and intelligence.* Cambridge, Mass.: Harvard Educational Review, 1969. (Reprint Series No. 2.)

Johnson, G. O. Special education for the mentally retarded—a paradox. *Exceptional Children*, 1962, **29**, 62–69.

Johnson, G. O. A reply to a critique of Johnson's paper. *Exceptional Children*, 1964, **31**, 68–70.

Johnson, J. L. Special education in the inner city: A challenge for the future or another means of cooling the markout? *Journal of Special Education,* 1969, **3**, 241–251.

Jordan, J. B. Intelligence as a factor in social position—a sociometric study in special classes for the mentally handicapped. *Dissertation Abstracts,* 1961, **21**, 2987–2988.

Jordan, J. B., and McDonald, P. L. *Dimensions: Annual survey of exceptional child research activities and issues—1970.* Arlington, Va.: Council for Exceptional Children, 1971.

Keane, V. E. The incidence of speech and language problems in the mentally retarded. *Mental Retardation,* 1972, **10(2)**, 3–8.

Kennedy, R. J. A Connecticut community revisited: A study of the social adjustment of a group of mentally deficient adults in 1948 and 1960. Washington, D.C.: U.S. Office of Vocational Rehabilitation, 1962 (Project 655).

Kidd, J. W. Pro—The efficacy of special class placement for educable mental retardates. Paper presented at the 48th Annual Convention, Council for Exceptional Children, 1970.

Kirk, S. A. *Early education of the mentally retarded: An experimental study.* Urbana, Ill.: University of Illinois Press, 1958.

Kirk, S. A. Research in education. In H. A. Stevens and R. Heber (Eds.), *Mental retardation.* Chicago: University of Chicago Press, 1964.

Kirk, S. A., and Johnson, G. O. *Educating the retarded child.* Boston: Houghton Mifflin, 1951.

Kirk, S. A., and Kirk, W. D. *Psycholinguistic learning disabilities: Diagnosis and remediation.* Urbana, Ill.: University of Illinois Press, 1971.

Kolstoe, O. P. *Teaching educable mentally retarded children.* New York: Holt, Rinehart and Winston, 1970.

Kolstoe, O. P. *Mental retardation: An educational viewpoint.* New York: Holt, Rinehart and Winston, 1972. (a)

Kolstoe, O. P. Programs for the mildly retarded: A reply to the critics. *Exceptional Children,* 1972, **39** 51–56. (b)

Kolstoe, O. P., and Frey, R. M. *A high school work-study program for mentally subnormal students.* Carbondale, Ill.: Southern Illinois University Press, 1965.

Kral, P. Motor characteristics and development of retarded children. *Education and Training of the Mentally Retarded.* 1972, **7(1)**, 14–21.

LaCrosse, R. E., Lee, P. C., Litman, F., Ogilvie, D. M., Stodolsky, S. S., and White, B. L. The first six years of life: A report on current research and educational practices. *Genetic Psychology Monographs,* 1970, **82**, 161–266.

Lee, J. J., Hegge, T. G., and Voelker, P. H. *A study of social adequacy and social failure of mentally retarded youth in Wayne County, Mich.* Detroit, Mich.: Wayne State University, 1959.

Lichtenberg, P., and Norton, D. G. *Cognitive and mental development in the first five years of life.* Chevy Chase, Md. National Institute of Mental Health, 1970.

Lilly, M. S. Improving social acceptance of low sociometric status, low achieving students. *Exceptional Children,* 1971 **37**, 341–347.

Lloyd, L. L. Audiologic aspects of mental retardation. In N. R. Ellis (Ed.), *International review of research in mental retardation.* Vol. 4. New York: Academic Press, 1970.

Lloyd, L. L. (Ed.) Communications issue. *Mental Retardation,* 1972, **10(2)**, whole issue.

Mackie, R. P. *Special education in the United States: Statistics, 1948–1966.* New York: Columbia University Teachers College Press, 1969.

MacMillan, D. L. The problem of motivation in the education of the mentally retarded. *Exceptional Children,* 1971, **37**, 579–586. (a)

MacMillan, D. L. Special education for the mildly retarded: Servant or savant. *Focus on Exceptional Children,* 1971, **2(9)**, 1–11. (b)

Malpass, L. F. Motor skills in mental deficiency. In N. R. Ellis (Ed.), *Handbook of mental deficiency.* New York: McGraw-Hill, 1963.

Martens, E. H. *Curriculum adjustments for the mentally retarded.* (2d ed.) Washington, D.C.: U.S. Office of Education, 1950.

Martin, A. W. The vocational status of former special class and regular class students from lower socioeconomic backgrounds. *Dissertation Abstracts,* 1969, **29**, 4330–4331.

Mayer, C. L. The effects of early special class placement on the self concepts of mentally handicapped children. *Exceptional Children,* 1966, **33**, 77–81.

McLean, J., Yoder, D. E., and Schiefelbusch, R. (Eds.) *Language intervention with the retarded: Developing strategies.* Baltimore, Md.: University Park Press, 1972.

McNemar, Q. A critical examination of the University of Iowa studies of environmental influences upon the IQ. *Psychological Bulletin,* 1940, **37**, 63–92.

Mercer, J. R. The meaning of mental retardation. In R. Koch and J. C. Dobson (Eds.), *The mentally retarded child and his family.* New York: Brunner-Mazel, 1971. (a)

Mercer, J. R. The eligibles and the labels. *Behavior Today,* 1971, **2**, 2. (b)

Meyerowitz, J. H. Self-derogation in young retardates and special class placement. *Child Development,* 1962, **33**, 443–451.

Meyerowitz, J. H. Peer groups and special classes. *Mental Retardation,* 1967, **5**, 23–26.

Miller, J. D., and Schoenfelder, D. S. A rational look at special class placement. *Journal of Special Education,* 1969, **3**, 397–403.

Monroe, J. D., and Howe, C. E. The effects of integration and social class on the acceptance of retarded adolescents. *Education and Training of the Mentally Retarded,* 1971, **6(1)**, 20–24.

Montessori, M. *The Montessori method.* New York: Schocken Books, 1964. (first published in U.S.A. in 1912)

Moore, R., and Moore, D. The dangers of early schooling. *Harper's Magazine,* 1972, **245**, 58–62.

Nelson, C. C., and Schmidt, L. J. The question of the efficacy of special classes. *Exceptional Children,* 1971, **37**, 381–384.

Oliver, J. N. The effects of physical conditioning exercises and activities on the mental characteristics of educably sub-normal boys. *British Journal of Educational Psychology,* 1958, **28**, 155–165.

Osterling, O. *The efficacy of special education: A comparative study of classes for slow learners.* Uppsala, Sweden: Almqvist & Wiksells Boktryckeri, 1967.

Peins, M. *Bibliography on speech, hearing, and language in relation to mental retardation: 1900–1968.* Washington, D.C.: Maternal and Child Health Services, U.S. Public Health Services, 1969.

Peter, L. J. *Prescriptive teaching.* New York: McGraw-Hill, 1965.

Peter, L. J. *Prescriptive teaching system, Vol. 1: Individual instruction.* New York: McGraw-Hill, 1972.

Peterson, L., and Smith, L. L. The postschool adjustment of educable mentally retarded adults with that of adults of normal intelligence. *Exceptional Children,* 1960, **26**, 404–408.

Porter, R. B., and Milazzo, T. C. A comparison of mentally retarded adults. *Exceptional Children,* 1958, **24**, 410–412.

Prehm, H. J. Rote verbal learning and memory in the retarded. In H. J. Prehm, L. A. Hamerlynck, and J. E. Crossen (Eds.), *Behavioral research in mental retardation.* Eugene, Ore.: University of Oregon, 1968.

President's Committee on Mental Retardation. *The six-hour retarded child.* Washington, D.C.: U.S. Government Printing Office, 1970.

Quay, L. C. Academic skills. In H. A. Stevens and R. Hever (Eds.), *Mental retardation: A review of research.* Chicago: University of Chicago Press, 1964.

Rarick, G. L., Widdop, J. H., and Broadhead, G. D. The physical fitness and motor performance of educable mentally retarded children. *Exceptional Children,* 1970, **36(7)**, 509–519.

Rothstein, J. H. (Ed.) *Mental retardation: Readings and resources.* (2d ed.) New York: Holt, Rinehart and Winston, 1971.

Rucker, C. N., and Vincenzo, F. M. Maintaining social acceptance gains made by mentally retarded children. *Exceptional Children,* 1970, **36**, 679–680.

Schiefelbusch, R. L., Copeland, R. H., and Smith, J. O. (Eds.) *Language and mental retardation: Empirical and conceptual considerations.* New York: Holt, Rinehart and Winston, 1967.

Schurr, K. T., and Brookover, W. B. *The effect of special class placement on the self-concept-of-ability of the educable mentally retarded child.* East Lansing, Mich.: Michigan State University, 1967.

Schurr, K. T., Joiner, L. M., and Towne, R. C. Self-concept research on the mentally retarded: A review of empirical studies. *Mental Retardation,* 1970, **5**, 39–43.

Skeels, H. M. Adult status of children with contrasting early life experiences. *Monograph of the Society for Research in Child Development,* 1966, **31(3)**, 1–65.

Smith, H. W., and Kennedy, W. A. Effects of three educational programs on mentally retarded children. *Perceptual and Motor Skills,* 1967, **24**, 174.

Smith, R. M. *Clinical teaching: Methods of instruction for the retarded.* New York: McGraw-Hill, 1968.

Soloman, A. H. Motivational and repeat trial effects on physical proficiency performances of educable mentally retarded and normal boys. *IMRID Behavior Science Monograph No. 11.* Nashville, Tenn.: Peabody College, 1968.

Soloman, A. H., and Pangle, R. The effects of a structured physical education program on physical, intellectual, and self-concept development of educable retarded boys. *Exceptional Children,* 1967, **33**, 177–181.

Sparks, H. L., and Younie, W. J. Adult adjustment of the mentally retarded: Implications for teacher education. *Exceptional Children,* 1969, **38**, 13–18.

Spicker, H. H. Intellectual development through early childhood education. *Exceptional Children,* 1971, **37**, 629–640.

Stein, J. U. Motor function and physical fitness in the mentally retarded: A critical review. *Rehabilitation Literature,* 1963, **24**, 230–242.

Stoddard, G. D. (Ed.) Intelligence: Its nature and nurture. Comparative and critical exposition. *39th Yearbook, Part II.* National Society for the Study of Education, 1940.

Strickland, C. G., and Arell, V. M. Employment of the mentally retarded. *Exceptional Children,* 1967, **34**, 21–24.

Strauss, A. A., and Kephart, N. C. *Psychopathology and education of the brain-injured child.* Vol. II. New York: Grune & Stratton, 1955.

Strauss, A. A., and Lehtinen, L. E. *Psychopathology and education of the brain-injured child.* Vol. 1. New York: Grune & Stratton, 1947.

Thiel, E. A. *Design for daily living: A framework for curriculum development for children and youth with mental retardation.* Quincy, Fla.: Thiel Enterprises, 1972.

Wallin, J. E. W. *The education of handicapped children.* Boston: Houghton Mifflin, 1924.

Webb, C. E., and Kinde, S. Speech, language, and hearing of the mentally retarded. In A. A. Baumeister (Ed.), *Mental retardation: Appraisal, education, and rehabilitation.* Chicago, Ill.: Aldine-Atherton, 1967.

Weintraub, F. J. Recent influences of law regarding the identification and educational placement of children. *Focus on Exceptional Children,* 1972, **4(2)**, 1–11.

Weintraub, F. J., Abeson, A. R., and Braddock, D. L. *State law and education of handicapped children: Issues and recommendations.* Arlington, Va.: Council for Exceptional Children, 1971.

Weisberg, P. Operant procedures with the retarded: An overview of laboratory research. In N. R. Ellis (Ed.), *International review of research in mental retardation.* Vol. 5. New York: Academic Press, 1971.

Williams, F. (Ed.) *Language and poverty.* Chicago: Markham, 1971.

Wolfensberger, W. Vocational preparation and occupation. In A. A. Baumeister (Ed.), *Mental retardation: Appraisal, education, and rehabilitation.* Chicago: Aldine-Atherton, 1967.

Opposite:
Primary gifted students study air navigation. They are using a flight computer and plotter to plot a course from one airport to another. Principles of geometry, physics, and mathematics are involved in the computation of distance, time, and speed of the airplane. (Photo courtesy Garden Grove, Calif., Unified School District; photographer, Trudy Pridham.)

children with
superior cognitive abilities

cHApTER ouTliNE

DEFINITION, PREVALENCE, AND EXTENT OF SERVICES
IDENTIFICATION PROCEDURES
   Teacher Observation and Nomination
   Group Achievement and Intelligence Tests
   Previous Demonstrated Accomplishments
   Individual Intelligence Tests
   Creativity Tests
   Racial, Ethnic, and Socioeconomic Factors
   Some Final Observations on the Identification Process
CHARACTERISTICS
   Physical Characteristics
   School Achievement Characteristics
   Personal and Social Adjustment
     Personal Adjustment
     Social Adjustment
EDUCATIONAL PLANNING AND PROGRAMS
SPECIAL EDUCATIONAL GROUPINGS
EARLY SCHOOL ADMISSION AND ACCELERATION
CURRICULUM ENRICHMENT IN THE REGULAR CLASSROOM
INSTRUCTIONAL PROCEDURES AND MATERIALS
CURRENT CURRICULUM PLANNING FOR THE GIFTED
   Program Support
PROVISIONS FOR THE GIFTED IN OTHER COUNTRIES
FUTURE DEVELOPMENTS FOR THE GIFTED, TALENTED, AND CREATIVE

The optimal education of children with superior cognitive abilities is recognized increasingly as a major priority for the schools of the United States (Marland, 1972) and many other countries of the world (see page 233). Today, few general or special educators would hold to the position that the proper education of the gifted can be accomplished under a philosophy of the same education for all. Instead, teachers are becoming aware that students of high ability need a variety of special educational opportunities to develop, utilize, and enjoy their potentials. Unfortunately, *traditionally* the demands on the schools to provide even an adequate education for the large majority, including the moderately bright and those with learning disabilities, have precluded any significant attention to the small minority of students who have very special abilities. It appears that increasing efforts to correct this condition are to be taken in the public schools of the United States during the 1970s. Through the U.S. Office of Education, the federal government is supporting more personnel, projects, and research than in the past, aimed at improved special educational opportunities for all unusually able boys and girls.

Not only has the traditional talent waste denied the rights of the ablest to function at full potential; it has also deprived society of needed persons of high ability. The formulation of creative, altruistic means for attaining essential social goals will rest largely with those of superior abilities. The greater involvement of young people in social problems provides an unusual opportunity to reduce the distinct cleavage that has existed in the past between school and society and enables adults to collaborate with youth in mutually valuable community learning experiences. The present and future rewards to the gifted individual, as well as to society, should be great.

The purpose of this chapter is to provide an overview of the nature and characteristics of children with a variety of different superior cognitive abilities, as well as a view of traditional and emerging educational procedures for stimulating their special gifts and talents. In doing so, it is hoped that the reader who studies this material will have a better understanding of gifted students and their special educational needs, and thus be able to assist them to use their abilities properly.

This chapter deals with a variety of children in the schools, all of whom have one characteristic in common; *superior cognitive abilities*. Their common element includes outstanding promise, or an unusual level of ability, whether in academic attainment, in creative performance, in talent, in ability to deal with advanced concepts and generalizations, or in the generation of ideas of uncommon merit. Because the term "superior cognitive abilities" is cumbersome to use repeatedly, the term *gifted* will also be used interchangeably with it throughout this chapter. To the writer this poses no problem, because the term "gifted" has always been used and understood generically. It encompasses creativity as well as many other talents and abilities, including high intelligence and high scholastic attainment.

DEFINITION, PREVALENCE, AND EXTENT OF SERVICES

In the past, definitions of gifted persons were based largely on precocious accomplishment. The principal criterion was *actual achievement*. If their talents in intellectual or artistic areas were apparent, children were singled out for special tutorial experiences, usually at the expense of wealthy parents or sponsors. They were later called prodigies if their performance reached remarkable heights. The criterion for designation as prodigy, gifted, or genius did not depend on promise but upon concrete evidence of actual production.

Definition of persons displaying *unusual promise* has not concerned educators until rather recently. The substantial positive correlation between socioeconomic class and intelligence has been well documented (Terman, Baldwin, and Bronson, 1925; Terman and Oden, 1959). Nevertheless, it is erroneous to assume that the gifted and talented come only from privileged environments. Even though the Terman group was not based on an exhaustive search, there were some children in it from minorities and from lower socioeconomic groups. Gifted children come from all ethnic, racial, social, and economic groups, though in fewer numbers from the disadvantaged. As early as the 1930s, Jenkins (1964) found substantial numbers of black intellectually gifted children in the segregated slum schools of Chicago. With the growing recognition that giftedness is found in all walks of life has come a realization that a satisfactory definition of giftedness must include children who show promise, even though they are living in unstimulating environments and are functioning far below their capacity. The need in the 1970s is therefore to define the gifted as including those with *potential* for lasting or significant contributions, as well as those who are actually achieving at a high level.

A number of sources of confusion complicate the definition of giftedness. A *first* source lies in the wide choice among the group and individual tests of intelligence, special aptitudes, and creativity available on the market today. The problem is compounded when one considers possible combinations of measures. A *second* problem is that of terminology. Whether one defines intelligence narrowly or broadly, whether one separates intellectual ability conceptually from specific talents, whether one regards creativity as distinct from intellectual capacity, and whether one concentrates on specific capabilities in definition, all affect the meaning attached to superior cognitive powers. A *third* source of confusion arises simply from the numbers included. Prior to the 1950s, writers and experts generally referred to the gifted as the upper 2 or 3 percent of the general population in intellectual ability. Beginning in that decade, a number of persons advocated the inclusion of larger and larger numbers under the rubric "gifted," and extended the descriptive terminology, sometimes to ridiculous proportions. The well-meaning purpose behind the extension was to include every potential individual under the classification. The result was that students with superior abilities were assumed to include the entire college-potential population, or approximately the upper 15 to 20 percent in intelligence of the general population. Thus DeHaan and Havighurst (1957) designated the upper one fifth of a community as gifted. Cutts and Moseley (1957) agreed that a restrictive definition is neither necessary nor desirable. The National Education Association during the late 1950s and early 1960s referred to the "academically talented" as a group comprising the upper 15 to 20 percent of the school population. This broad approach was due largely to the influence of Conant (1959) during his studies of the high schools of the United States. Added extension of the concept of giftedness came with widespread use of tests in the identification of creativity, from the 1950s to the present. The confusion widened with the assertions of some people that high intellectual ability is not necessarily present in persons of high "creative" ability, or that *all* persons are creative (Taylor, 1964). While great furor would arise if 10 or 15 percent of children were classified as handicapped, no parent is likely to resist the notion that his child is part of the "gifted" population; this inclusiveness, rather, was commonly regarded as democratic. And the result was that those with very remarkable abilities did not receive the special educational opportunities they should have had.

The report to the U.S. Congress by the U.S. Commissioner of Education (Marland, 1972), entitled *Education of the Gifted and Talented*, once more restricted the gifted to 3 to 5 percent of the general population, including children capable of high performance in one or more of the following six areas: (1) general intellectual ability; (2) specific academic aptitude; (3) creative or productive thinking ability; (4) leadership ability; (5) ability in the visual or performing arts, and (6) psychomotor ability. The report also specified that these individuals, identified by professionally qualified persons, require special educational programs and/or services beyond those normally provided by the regular school program in order to realize their proper contribution to self and society. Since the writer of this chapter believes that the easy temptation to avoid definition, or to be overinclusive, is a profound disservice to a population of children with special needs, a definition is given here, with some brief amplifying comments:

> Students with superior cognitive abilities include approximately the top 3 percent of the general school population in measured general intelligence and/or in creative abilities or other talents that promise to make lasting contributions of merit to society. These students are so able that they require special provisions if appropriate educational opportunities are to be provided for them.

This definition assumes that intensive and special efforts will be made to assure proper representation of all ethnic and racial minorities, as well as economically deprived groups. The proportions of identified gifted from these segments of society can be increased substantially through careful search, individual study and testing, and, ultimately, through the development of tests that adequately identify the qualities of giftedness without cultural penalties.

The group is limited to a small segment of the total population rather than including all of those with potential for success in college. This restricted definition is used so as to designate only those with truly unusual learning needs and outstanding potential. In the scholastic areas the group comprises those who go beyond mere easy success with advanced academic fare to those who function at unusually high levels of ideational production, generalization, and application, and/or give evidence and promise of uniquely outstanding and original creative performance. These are the individuals who have the capacity to sense and solve important problems and issues at high levels of abstraction.

In the creative and talent areas the group includes those who function at unusually high levels of originality and/or artistry. The skilled technician whose performance level has been attained through special advantages but whose ability is chiefly imitative, would not be included here. The proficient but mechanical accompanist, for example, would be differentiated from the Rubenstein, the writer of commercial jingles from the Sandburg, and the skilled draftsman from the Lipschitz. The determination of talent is a matter of degree. Many can learn to play an instrument; few learn to the level of potential or actual performance of recognized merit. Many persons can compose music, but few produce works that endure. Two tests for inclusion on the basis of creative ability or talent are advocated: (1) that the talent be one that gives evidence or *promise* of contributions of *lasting merit* with proper nurture, and/or (2) that the talent be so unusually advanced that special arrangements are needed for its full development.

Physical skills and social leadership as *ordinarily* conceived are not included in the definition above. At present, physical skills are generally recognized within school athletic programs and the student who has athletic talent usually receives highly specialized attention. Social leadership, in the ordinary sense, requires that the leader not be too far apart ideationally from the group he leads. The inclusion of the physical-social dimensions requires analysis of other relevant factors within the individual, such as ability, power of conceptualization, and originality. The test lies in *potential contribution of lasting merit to society.*

The leadership exhibited by the class chairman or student officer, though commendable, is commonplace; the leadership of the student who devises a worthwhile plan for conquest of aggravated human relations problems is not. The skills of the able quarterback may produce considerable temporary status; the skill of the individual who uses his physical and mental talents for invention of a machine or for beautiful, poetic dance interpretation may provide physical leadership in an enduring sense. Martin Luther King was a social leader whose ideas have lasted beyond his lifetime; Huey Long was not. Similarly, a young Robert Frost, a young Maria Tallchief, a young Marian Anderson, or a young and creative Leonard Bernstein will require more special attention than the young reporter, the young choral participant, or the young orchestra member.

The use of the criterion of potential for contribution of lasting merit eliminates the whimsical or bizarre. Productive capacity or creative products must necessarily meet the criteria of lasting beauty, originality, and value.

Let us now apply our restrictive 3 percent prevalence estimate. At the outset of the 1970s, with a substantial drop in preschool children (under four years of age) in the United States to about 17 million; with elementary school children (5 to 13 years) easing back to about 32 million and high school students leveling off at about 15 million, the total estimated number of gifted pupils was 1,935,000 (Table 4.1).

TABLE 4.1 *Estimated Number of Gifted Children in the United States Public Schools, Early 1970s, Based on a 3 Percent Prevalence Estimate*

Level	Number
Preschool	510,000
Elementary school	960,000
High school	465,000
Total	1,935,000

Even based on the restricted prevalence estimates of 3 percent, special education services have reached a very small percentage of gifted pupils. For example, as Dunn reported in Chapter 1 (see Table 3), only 52,269 gifted pupils in 1958, in all of the United States, were in special education at the combined elementary and secondary school levels, when the total enrollment approximated 42 million. A 3 percent prevalence estimate for the gifted would yield 1,260,000 such students in need of special education, and, therefore, approximately 4 percent were served. These services included only special schools and classes, not enrichment, acceleration, or upper tracks in schools that practiced streaming. The last U.S. Office of Education survey of special education services for the gifted was conducted in 1966, when 312,100 pupils were reported as being served (Mackie, 1969). Based on the 3 percent prevalence figure on 49 million pupils in the elementary and secondary schools at that time, the number in need of such services had risen to 1,470,000. This would suggest that 21 percent were being provided with special education. However, this sharp increase may have been due, in part, to the inclusion of some students who were only in enrichment, acceleration, and upper track programs. It is interesting to note that the U.S. Office of Education has not chosen to gather statistics on the extent of special education services since 1966, not even in connection with the 1972 Congressional mandate that the U.S. Office of Education conduct a national survey on education of gifted and talented children (Marland, 1972).

The situation in Canada is even gloomier. The last available statistics were also for 1965–1966 (Dominion Bureau of Statistics, 1967). At that time, 8,390 gifted pupils were receiving special education. Using the 3 percent prevalence estimate and a school population of approximately five million, 150,000 gifted children were in need of services. Therefore, only 6 percent were receiving them. This 8,390 figure did not include gifted children in the upper track or stream, those who had been accelerated, or those in an enrichment program. None of these children were in special schools. All were in full- and part-time special classes or otherwise receiving the services of special teachers-consultants of the gifted. (The need to exclude streaming, enrichment, and acceleration indicates the difficulties in surveying the extent of special education services for the gifted.)

Finally, while new statistics are unavailable in either the United States or Canada, there is no evidence that more than 25 percent of our gifted children are receiving special education services, while at least 50 percent of the handicapped are being so served. On the one hand, one might observe that both the gifted and handicapped should be receiving equal attention. On the other hand, questions arise about the attitudes of educators, parents, and the public concerning the degree to which they believe in and support special educational services for the gifted. In reading the rest of this chapter, one needs to consider seriously the question, *To what degree should special education services be provided for students with superior cognitive abilities, and in what forms?*

IDENTIFICATION PROCEDURES

One of the most challenging facets of work with gifted and talented students is that of identification. Many people believe that it is easy to recognize giftedness. Certainly, many gifted students reveal themselves by their highly advanced talents, concepts, interests, and outstanding performance. These qualities often are readily observed by teachers, parents, and acquaintances. An equal number, however, are very difficult to identify because they conceal or do not have opportunities to reveal their true abilities. Though they are unrecognized, they, too, deserve special educational attention.

Table 4.2 provides an overview of the six major procedures used and recommended in the screening and final identification process. The three procedures most used are teacher nomination, group school achievement test scores, and group intelligence test scores, in that order. The order recommended by experts was (1) individual intelligence tests; (2) teacher observation and nomination; (3) previous accomplishments; (4 and 5) group achievement and creativity tests; and (6) group intelligence tests. Other less used procedures are tests of special aptitudes and talents; peer and parent judgments; measures of social and personal adjustment; self-selection (pupil volunteers); and rank in performance. The six major identification procedures will now be discussed in turn.

TABLE 4.2 *Major Procedures Used and Recommended in the Identification of Gifted Students*

Major Identification Procedures	Percent Using (and Rank) Order (1)	Percent Recommending (and Rank) Order (2)	Rank Order Difference (3)
Teacher observation and nomination	93 (1)	75 (2)	−1
Group school achievement test scores	87 (2.5)	74 (4.5)	−2
Group intelligence test scores	87 (2.5)	65 (6)	−3.5
Previous demonstrated accomplishments (including school grades)	56 (4)	78 (3)	+1
Individual intelligence test scores	23 (5)	90 (1)	+4
Scores on tests of creativity	14 (6)	74 (4.5)	+1.5

SOURCE: S. P. Marland, *Education of the gifted and talented.* Washington, D.C.: U.S. Office of Education, 1972. Column 1 data are drawn from page 261 of this report on identification practices in the local school systems of Illinois and are reported as averages of elementary and secondary school practices; column 2 data are from page 122 of the report and are based on what was considered important by 204 experts in the education of the gifted.

Teacher Observation and Nomination

Teacher nomination is used more extensively than any other approach in identifying gifted students. Yet a number of studies have shown it to be successful only about 50 percent of the time in identifying children with outstanding scholastic ability (Pegnato and Birch, 1959; Terman, Baldwin, and Bronson, 1925; Walton, 1961). The same accuracy occurs when teachers attempt to nominate children as creative (Martinson and Seagoe, 1967). Even when the criterion group is limited to those highly gifted in intelligence who presumably would be most evident in a classroom group, Barbe and Horn (1964) found that teachers failed to recognize approximately 25 percent. The classroom teacher fails to nominate a large number of children who are gifted while naming others who are not but who are hard-working and enthusiastic.

Because of the problems in teacher nomination, numerous checklists have been devised to improve screening procedures. Usually such lists have been compiled by individuals or committees on the basis of observation, personal beliefs, and descriptions from the literature. An evaluation of various teacher checklists by Walton (1961) indicated that the items vary in predictive value. While all of her items were useful, some were of more value than others in identifying children who later were found to have IQ's beyond 130 on the Stanford-Binet. The seven items that best discriminated the intellectually gifted from the nongifted were:

1. Who learns rapidly and easily?
2. Who uses a lot of common sense and practical knowledge?
3. Who retains easily what he has heard?

4. Who knows about many things of which other children are unaware?
5. Who uses a large number of words easily and accurately?
6. Who recognizes relations, comprehends meanings?
7. Who is alert, keenly observant, responds quickly?

Even with checklist items such as these, which focus attention on higher cognitive processes, the teacher misses many bright children who are not motivated to display their abilities and talents. Despite the loss, teachers are able to nominate many gifted children, and experts value their judgment as an important facet of the screening and identification process (Marland, 1972).

Group Achievement and Intelligence Tests

The major method by which the teacher has supplemented her own observations is the use of scores on group achievement and intelligence tests, given routinely and rather regularly in most schools. A number of studies have shown that these group tests are only about as successful as teacher nomination in identification of those with outstanding ability. The level of success in each instance is about 50 percent (Pegnato and Birch, 1959; Terman, Baldwin, and Bronson, 1925. A combination of teacher nomination and group tests is somewhat better than either alone, but still very inadequate. Group tests tend to underrefer. The higher the level of achievement or ability, the greater will be the penalty. For example, Table 4.3 provides data on individual versus group intelligence test scores for 56 bright pupils. These data were developed by the California Test Bureau and were reported in the California State Study (Martinson, 1961). For the individual intelligence test group who obtained IQ's of 160 to 169, group test IQ's were about 34 points lower, on the average. This huge differential reduced to about 11 points for the individual IQ group 130 to 139. In another aspect of this same California study, the group test IQ's of 332 high school pupils who had Binet IQ's of 130 or more were examined. If a criterion IQ of 125 or above on a group test had been applied, 25 percent of the pupils would have been eliminated, and if the IQ of 130 had been used, 51.5 percent of the gifted pupils would have been eliminated. The range of IQ's among those who might have been disqualified was considerable. Of the total, 70 had group IQ's below 120 and 10 had IQ's between 100 and 110. It is not likely that many of these would have been referred for individual testing. Pegnato and Birch (1959) obtained similar results. They pointed out that 49 of 84 gifted junior high school students with individual Binet IQ's above 125 had group IQ's of less than 125, including nine whose Binet IQ's ranged from 146 to 161. By implication, more than half of their gifted, as identified through the individual Binet test, would not have been recognized as gifted with group tests.

Similarly, group achievement tests, such as the Stanford, California, and Metropolitan achievement test batteries, and the Sequential Tests of Educational Progress (STEP), are widely used in the schools. They too underestimate the attainment of many bright pupils, often because tests suitable for

TABLE 4.3 *Differences in Test Scores between Group and Individual Tests of Intelligence at Various IQ Levels*

Individual Test IQ Range	Number of Pupils	Mean Algebraic Differences[a]
160–169	6	33.83
150–159	11	18.27
140–149	11	13.91
130–139	28	10.61

[a]In favor of the individually administered Stanford-Binet Intelligence Scale.
SOURCE: R. A. Martinson, *Educational programs for gifted pupils.* Sacramento: California State Department of Education, 1961.

the majority fail to provide items to measure the actual achievement of the gifted. A gifted child may be capable of achievement far beyond the ceiling of the test he is given, and tests for an older population would be more suitable and challenging for him.

Group tests, universally employed because of economy factors, have four serious limitations. *First*, most of them are organized by levels, and therefore are of restricted range. Because they have few difficult items to truly test the gifted, they fail to measure the actual scholastic achievement or aptitude. Some group intelligence tests in wide use would convince school personnel that they had no gifted pupils, since the tests do not yield IQ's beyond 125. *Second*, it is difficult to motivate all children to optimal effort when giving a group test. *Third*, most group tests depend on reading proficiency to score well, even in other academic subjects. *Fourth*, group tests are chiefly useful above the primary grades after the children have developed some of the skills necessary for efficient performance. Therefore, the identification of very young gifted children is often neglected. Yet the need for early identification is great, since it is at the point of school entry that children who need unusually advanced or different learning opportunities experience their greatest difficulties. With careful screening, it is possible to attain 50 percent accuracy even at this level.

While tests underrefer seriously, a combination of group achievement and intelligence test scores correct somewhat for biases that affect teacher nominations. Therefore their wise use is advocated.

Previous Demonstration Accomplishments

Teachers and the schools are understandably preoccupied with school achievement and verbal skills. But the emphasis in schools is increasingly directed toward the development of other talents in leadership, in the visual and performing arts, and in added creative fields. One method for recognizing these talents is through individual study. Here specialists in a given area should be involved in the study of the child's potential; for example, musicians who are also knowledgeable in child development can best identify the potentially musically talented. To date such persons are seldom utilized by the schools, but this strategy should not be overlooked.

Individual Intelligence Tests

At present, the best single method available for the identification of children with superior cognitive abilities is standardized individual intelligence tests such as the Stanford-Binet or the Wechsler scales. The chief limitation in their use is the expense involved in time and services. Nevertheless, they should be used whenever possible by trained psychologists to avoid the loss incurred by group tests and teacher nomination and to identify children from minorities or economically deprived groups. A trained psychologist can make judgments concerning a child's capabilities from his total performance and the quality of his responses and often can recommend inclusion of a child who otherwise would be omitted on the basis of score alone.

To reduce the expense of error, added screening instruments such as the Harris-Goodenough Draw-a-Person, the Peabody Picture Vocabulary Test, the Raven Coloured Progressive Matrices, and the Slosson Intelligence Test have been used. As rough screening instruments they are of value, but they should not be regarded as substitutes for the more comprehensive individual examination. They are short, easy to administer, and serve as cues to recommend further testing. Validation studies have been conducted more frequently on the handicapped than on the gifted, and little evidence is available that they are useful in minority or deprived groups, a criticism also frequently leveled at the Binet and Wechsler tests.

Creativity Tests

The past decade has seen a great deal of attention in the professional literature focused on creativity and its measurement. Yet tests of creativity are ranked last in terms of use as major identification procedures, and their extensive use is not highly ranked by experts in the field (see Table 4.2). A list of available tests will be found in Kaltsounis (1972). These tests tend to measure divergent thinking in the areas of fluency, flexibility, and originality. Many of them have grown out of measures first designed by Guilford (1966). The unique nature of these tests of creativity as opposed to conventional intelligence tests has been seen as the production of *multiple answers*, rather than as making a choice of a single appropriate answer (Thorndike, 1963).

Only an overview of the topic of creativity can be included in this chapter. Therefore, no attempt will be made here to summarize comprehensively the extensive literature on the identification of creativity. For one thing, the vast majority of studies have been conducted on adults. Space will permit only a review of some of the major developments and the best-publicized studies on school-age children. Following this, some suggestions will be tendered for the use of the knowledge we now have regarding identification of creativity.

Prior to the era of factor analysis the identification of creativity was relatively simple. By general agreement, the term applied to a person who had demonstrated exceptional productivity in some valued way. Thus, such disparate producers as Lister, Da Vinci, Raphael, Goethe, Helmholtz, and Franklin were considered to be creative. To the present day, the product referent is still used when one designates outstanding artists, composers, conductors, inventors, and others. Little quarrel would result from the nomination as creative of such adults as William Lear, Jonas Salk, or Grandma Moses. The problem arises in identifying children with budding creativity who have the potential for creative production in adulthood such as these persons have displayed. In this regard, there is much discussion concerning whether or not conventional tests of intelligence and the newer tests of creativity measure overlapping attributes, or if either of them really identify creativity.

The debate on creativity and its relation (if any) to measured intelligence began as a result of the efforts of Guilford and others to identify aptitudes beyond those measured by traditional intelligence tests. Thus, the work of Guilford probably has had more direct influence on the current search for measures of creativity than that of anyone else. His now familiar *Structure of Intellect* model portrayed 120 different kinds of intellectual abilities of all types (Guilford, 1966). The basic operations, as seen in Figure 4.1, are *cognition*, involving discovery, awareness, recognition, comprehension, or understanding; *memory*, involving retention and storage of information; *divergent thinking*, which involves the generation of information from given information; *convergent thinking*, where the emphasis is on use of given information to produce the best response; and *evaluation*, or reaching decisions or making judgments concerning the correctness, suitability, adequacy, and/or desirability of information in terms of criteria of identity, consistency, and goal satisfaction. Within the *Structure of Intellect*, 24 divergent thinking abilities that are believed to be closely relevant to creative thinking have been identified. Of the 24, 16 were demonstrated in adult and ninth-grade populations and 6 at the fifth-grade level (Guilford, 1967).

Early studies on the relation between traditional tests of intelligence and new-type tests of creativity were conducted by Getzels and Jackson (1962) and replicated by Torrance (1962). In the main, Getzels and Jackson concentrated on two small groups: (1) $H_{IQ}L_C$—High on IQ and low on creativity measures (28 adolescents); and (2) $L_{IQ}H_C$—low on IQ and high on creativity (26 adolescents). But *both* groups were bright. The $H_{IQ}L_C$ had a mean IQ of 150, and the $L_{IQ}H_C$ had a mean IQ of 127. $H_{IQ}L_C$ was defined as the top 20 percent in IQ but not in creativity; $L_{IQ}H_C$ was defined as in the top 20 percent in creativity as measured by some Guilford divergent thinking items, supplemented by some of their own. The major finding was that not all children with high IQ scores obtained high creativity test scores, or vice versa. In short, scores on tests of creativity, while positively correlated with scores on tests of intelligence, appeared to measure something else as well.

These studies stimulated a decade of avid research into creativity. This literature has been well reviewed by Wallach (1970), Buros (1972), and Crockenberg (1972), and all serious students of superior cognitive abilities are encouraged to read these reports. Especially important, too, are earlier

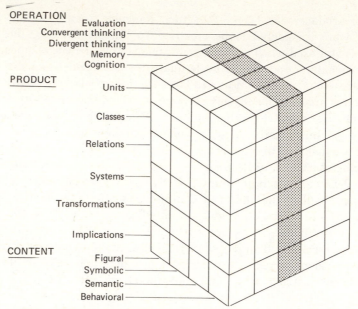

FIGURE 4.1 *The Guilford structure-of-intellect model (SI), showing the 24 divergent thinking abilities considered most closely related to creative thinking. Divergent thinking is shaded to emphasize its difference from other Operation categories. From J. P. Guilford,* The nature of human intelligence. *New York: McGraw-Hill, 1967. Used with the permission of McGraw-Hill Book Company.*

reviews by deMille and Merrifield (1962); Thorndike, (1963); and Barron, (1968).

The following are some generalizations about this controversial topic:

1. Correlations between creativity and IQ scores are quite high, approximately 0.50, which still leaves considerable variance in creativity scores to be determined by other than IQ score. In short, creativity tests do not measure identically what IQ tests measure.

2. A high degree of intelligence (120 or more) is required as a threshold for substantial creativity test scores. Above that point the degree of intelligence does not influence significantly the degree of creativity.

3. No increase in predictability of school achievement is obtained by adding creativity scores to IQ scores. Further, intelligence tests are better predictors of school success than tests of creativity.

4. Test-retest reliability coefficients are highly variable for various tests of creativity and their subtests, ranging from nonsignificant values up into the 0.90's. Generally, reliabilities are higher for verbal tests and for fluency and flexibility measures. Overall, while they are less reliable than intelligence tests, *batteries* of creativity tests tend to have fairly good reliability, but individual subtests do not.

5. There are extremely low correlations among subtests of creativity, yet they are pooled to imply a high relation—a questionable practice.

6. Added research is needed to establish the predictive value of crea-

tivity tests. Martinson and Seagoe (1967) found that high intelligence test scores predict creative production in elementary school children, as rated by expert judges, better than scores on creativity tests. Torrance (1972) used ratings by judges of self-reports by young adults, who had been nominated by peers and selected by tests as creative 12 years earlier, to confirm that creativity can be identified. One persistent problem, however, is in measuring the *quality* of production.

7. Increasingly, the contradiction between testing factors, such as timing, group administration, mood of the child, instant demand for production, and the necessary conditions for true creative production have been pointed out. The need for observers capable of understanding the complexity and originality of the creative act, the inadequacy of mechanical scoring systems, the problem of distinguishing eccentricity from originality, the difficulty of measuring nonverbal creativity, the annoyance that creativity tests evoke in some highly creative persons, and the difficulty of scoring all have been cited as problems by Barron (1968).

8. In conclusion, it is to be hoped that added research and improvements will make creativity tests more effective than they have been. At this time, they have tentative value, and the low ratings in Table 4.2 for the use in the schools as an identification procedure appear to be justified.

Some of the labeling of certain tasks as "creativity tests" was done in advance of the evidence. Gallagher (1969) stated it well:

> The value lies in the development of theoretical models which serve as a hypothetical road map for cognition. We must, however, keep in mind that these models should be sketched in light pencil, with a large eraser nearby. They are not constructed to be "right". . . . the models of Piaget and Guilford are not stone pillars set in concrete; they are springboards or launching pads for a more sophisticated understanding of productive thinking in the future (p. 542).

Racial, Ethnic, and Socioeconomic Factors

The literature dealing with failures to seek giftedness in children from minorities or from economically depressed groups is extensive, and the failures are producing mounting concern. Very few efforts have been made to search systematically for giftedness, using the best available instruments. Much of the dissatisfaction with identification procedures and their ineffectiveness with different cultural and socioeconomic groups has been based upon the use of *group* tests. Although efforts to produce "culture-free" tests have met with little success, research to develop tests of value continues at an increasing rate. At least some of the impetus has come from the resistance of minorities to tests based upon the cognitive developmental patterns of middle class white populations. While the pressure has mounted in recent years, it is not of recent origin. The problems of adequate measurement instruments for children from different racial, economic, social, and language backgrounds have troubled psychologists ever since Binet.

The early work of Witty and Jenkins (1936), which gave clear evidence that highly gifted black children could be found in substantial numbers, *given the effort to find them*, has been largely ignored. Their work pointed out the need for active efforts on the part of educators for identification of minority-group children. While this comment may seem trite, it is significant to note that in a national survey conducted in the United States in 1970, *57.5 percent of elementary and secondary school principals reported that they had no gifted students in their schools.* (Marland, 1972).[1] The figures for segregated schools undoubtedly are far worse.

Eleven years after a study by Witty and Theman (1943) which located many black children with high IQ's in urban communities, Miles (1954) commented that Indians and blacks were insufficiently represented among the gifted. Her comment was underscored by Ginzberg (1956), who described the black potential as the largest untapped talent pool. During the 1960s, Plaut (1963) estimated that only one tenth of the eligible black population entered college and that they accounted for only 1 percent of the total college population. Despite the fact that increasing numbers of black students were enrolling, Plaut found that the vast majority were attending segregated southern colleges with poor endowments. The need for continuing identification of able students in nonaffluent communities also is evident in the report of the National Merit Scholarship Corporation, which revealed that black students who qualified for scholarships came chiefly from higher socioeconomic levels and from well-equipped large public schools (Blumenfeld, 1969).

What is said about the black student is applicable to other groups as well. Vernon (1969) has made the same point in his comment about American Indian children withdrawing into apathy and *learning to be unintelligent*. The writer believes that, up through the early 1970s, it is fair to say that little effort was made in many communities with large minority populations to identify those with outstanding cognitive abilities. The failure to do so means that the capacities remain invisible because they are not given opportunities to develop; instead, they remain dormant and waste away.

The problem of identification through traditional measures is not one of *transfer* of emphasis from the middle class white population but rather one of *broad extension* of efforts. Such efforts produce samples representative of the total community, as Walton (1961) has shown. Since more than half of U.S. school principals believe that they have *no* gifted children in their schools, the task is obviously one of enormous proportions in all groups. In certain communities, however, the primary emphasis in education is on compensatory education, and the practices, accordingly, are largely remedial and terminal. In such communities, in effect, the existence of a range of human potential is ignored and the ablest suffer through an inadequate education.

Even without economic deprivation of a severe nature, the promises and expectations of society have a powerful impact on gifted young people from minority groups. Minority students—yellow, brown, or black—frequently express fears of stepping into an unknown occupational environment (white)

---

[1] Based on national statistics.

and still contend that the B.A. degree will serve only to make them literate custodians! The self-doubt apparent in their conversations often makes the likelihood of completion of college seem doubtful.

The effect of educational deprivation on bright minority persons is described in Vignette 4.1 on Dorothy J. This gifted, but inadequately educated, American Indian, who lives in a meagerly furnished house on a reservation, has sought opportunities to learn all her life. Not many persons would apply for college admission at the age of 42, nor would they continue to maintain the level of intellectual curiosity that she manifests to her friends, many of whom are college and university professors. The very psychological resilience and potential of gifted persons should motivate educators to seek them out in less favored environments. Even when gifted college students come from poor economic conditions, they rank much higher on favorable attributes of personality, attitudes, and interests than do the rest of college students from similar backgrounds (Nichols and Davis, 1964).

Vignette 4.1 How Far Could She Have Gone?

Dorothy J. is a middle-aged member of the Cahuilla Indian tribe. When she started school at age eight, she experienced immediate difficulties because of her lack of knowledge of English and her fear of teachers. Eventually she succeeded in learning English, with no special help, and she finally finished high school at 19.

In school she and other Indian children encountered teachers who regarded Indians as "dumb" and incapable of learning. Many Indian children believed this, and of a dozen Indian children who entered school, Dorothy was the only one to finish. She maintained her interest in learning, but her only opportunity to apply for a college scholarship for Indians (when she was 42) was denied.

Dorothy's favorite subject in school was history, but she found that the contributions of Indians were either denied or ignored, and their culture was denigrated by teachers. On the other hand, persons like Andrew Jackson, who was responsible for the slaughter of countless Indians, were presented as heroes.

Dorothy, largely self-taught, has compensated well for her lack of opportunity. She is co-author, with university professors, of several books in linguistics, ethnobotany, and music and has served as a university lecturer both in the United States and abroad. Meanwhile, because she lacks formal higher education, she earns a living on an assembly line in a factory near her reservation home.

The responsibility is great for locating the gifted and providing appropriate education for them in all groups, and the problem is complex. One method might be arbitrarily to designate as the gifted the upper 3 percent of each group within the general population, with different IQ's for each group. But such a practice poses several problems. One is that the unique qualities of giftedness described earlier do not necessarily come in fixed percentages by subgroup; that is, certain groups, by virtue of both hereditary and environmental factors, may have more than 3 percent. Another problem is the patronage implied in assuming lower intelligence and assigning lower IQ's to certain populations in order to include them. The implications of this to the general public are unhealthy, in the perpetuation of nonvalid stereotypes. A third is the assumption that ability is determined by color or wealth, which is questionable, to say the least.

Better search, better measures, careful judgments of trained examiners, and belief in potential in all human groups will improve representation of minorities greatly. Systematic annual ethnic, racial, and socioeconomic surveys of gifted children, as conducted in California, will serve to reduce underreferral and neglect in certain groups.

To improve the identification of minority-culture children research should be directed toward the development of new measures of ability. These measures should not be predicated on the adjustment upward or downward of existing measures but on the suitability of content to the identification of superior cognitive abilities in a given culture. Such measures, when available, will mean that the identification process will be based on results from several validated measures rather than from a single measure. Meanwhile, as Ausubel (1965) put it, we ought not to castigate intelligence tests as unfair to deprived children because they score poorly any more than we should say the tuberculin test is invalid or unfair because the environment predisposes the child to the illness. The intelligence test does measure *functional* ability. Rather than the measuring instrument itself, what should be attacked are (1) the indiscriminate and inappropriate use of group measures rather than more discriminating measures; and (2) the environmental problems that create intellectual deprivation.

Some Final Observations
on the Identification Process

The basic needs in identification remain the use of adequate measures, careful interpretation of measures, and complete accompanying information regarding all special skills, interests, and aptitudes. Gifted children tend to be complex, and identification of their many capabilities is an important responsibility. Search for those of high ability should extend to all groups, regardless of economic level, race, or other factors. Minority groups, whose mean incomes are appreciably lower than those of whites, continue to be ignored in many localities, as if children with superior abilities were not present.

For the identification of gifted children, the individual intelligence test is the best single means we have at present for *measuring cognitive abili-*

ties. This is especially true at the elementary school level. Intelligence tests are used because they *do* furnish useful information. As Thorndike (1963) pointed out, the various subabilities measured are linked together by appreciable correlations and do provide estimates of general intelligence that are of value in educational planning. Much of the criticism of intelligence tests has been made of the mere IQ as a single and relatively meaningless score. Yet Guilford (1967) pointed out that the Stanford-Binet scale probably encompasses 28 factors, which expands its interpretation considerably from the single score. When used in the context of an accompanying interview and complete case study, its value is, of course, enhanced.

Current agreement seems to be that a series of valid and reliable measures to identify added components of ability will be useful *when they are developed, tested,* and found to have *predictive validity.* The availability of computers should speed the process. Meanwhile, it will be useful to refer to tests of traits accurately and specifically, rather than globally. There is no question of the value of identifying specific special abilities as fully as possible; some skepticism has been expressed concerning the possibility of implementing the added knowledge, particularly in the schools. That remains to be seen.

CHARACTERISTICS

A great deal is known about the gifted, chiefly through biographical accounts of eminent individuals and through major group studies. Of the latter, the five-volume work *Genetic Studies of Genius* by Terman and his associates stands out as the most important by far (Terman, Baldwin, and Bronson, Vol. 1, 1925; Cox, Gillan, Livesey, and Terman, Vol. 2, 1926; Burke, Jensen, and Terman, Vol. 3, 1930; Terman and Oden, Vol. 4, 1947; Terman and Oden, Vol. 5, 1959). His longitudinal studies over a 40-year period, beginning in 1921, did much to provide information about persons with high IQ's and their remarkably diverse abilities and talents. It is through his work and through some later biographical and group studies that we find recurrent descriptions of giftedness and creativity.

Physical Characteristics

The 1,528 gifted children in the Terman group, defined as having a Stanford-Binet IQ of 140 or more (the top 1 percent of the population), were thoroughly studied in 1921 and again in 1928, 1940, and the middle 1950s. The general picture, from complete initial developmental histories and medical examinations, was one of comprehensive advanced early development for the group (Terman, Baldwin, and Bronson, 1925). Age by age, they exceeded the norms for average children in height, weight, general bodily development, strength, and in energy and general neuromuscular capacity. They had fewer physical problems and exhibited fewer emotional problems than the average. The physicians who conducted the studies noted that major and minor defects were less common in the group of gifted and commented that superior physical health seemed to accompany superior ability in the group.

Studies during the 1920s and 1930s by Hollingworth (1926), Hildreth (1938), Witty (1940), and others confirmed the findings of Terman. All of these writers noted individual variations within groups, of course, and different patterns of development. Hollingworth (1942) later pointed out that children with very high IQ's often have problems with games and tasks requiring close coordination, such as writing. The rapidity and level of mental functioning may produce impatience and conflict when game rules or requirements for precision and neatness interfere with ideas. Another source of potential difficulty is the preference for older playmates and for games that normally interest older children.

The early excellent health and superior physical traits were maintained by the Terman group into adulthood and mid-life (Terman and Oden, 1959). While Terman was unable to finance repeated physical examinations, considerable information was made available by the subjects and their parents. In a follow-up study, 91 percent of the men and 83 percent of the women rated their health as "very good" or "good," while only 1.9 percent of the men and 3.7 percent of the women rated their health "poor" or "very poor."

On the basis of extensive work with preschool gifted children at the City and County School in Michigan, Roeper (1963) made some comments about the physical characteristics of these children. Contrary to Terman, who found that the children slept longer than the average, Roeper observed that many needed little sleep. Various parents commented on children who never went to sleep before ten o'clock and were up at six, "raring to go." Roeper's opinion was that life is so stimulating for many gifted children that they find it hard to relax. She found they have unusual physical and mental energy. Her other comments supported the reports of Terman and Hollingworth regarding walking, talking, and disparities between mental and physical skills.

The advanced status in physical development reported by Terman and others was confirmed by Martinson (1961). In that study, which involved nearly a thousand pupils, it was found that the parents of the gifted reported earlier development in such physically related factors as first steps and first teeth than reported by the Terman parents. This may reflect some of the medical and nutritional advances during the last 40 years.

In all of the studies, no support is found for the caricatured spindly, puny, bespectacled, physically inept gifted child. The true portrait that emerges is one of physical superiority on the whole. Many of the high school pupils in the Martinson study (1961) were outstanding athletes, and many won letters in several sports.

Finally, some slight caution about these findings is suggested from a study by Laycock and Caylor (1964). When socioeconomic status and other cultural and familial factors are controlled by using less gifted siblings for a contrast group, there are less marked differences in physical characteristics between intellectually gifted and nongifted children. At least some of the physical superiority of the gifted may be ascribed to the fact that the majority have come from homes in which they had superior physical care. This bears further research.

School Achievement Characteristics

The gifted as a group develop reading skills early. Of the California children studied by Martinson (1961), 92 percent could read by the age of 70 to 73 months (5–10 to 6–1). Thirty-three percent did their first reading by the time they were 58 to 61 months (4–10 to 5–1). When children have taught themselves to read and to function in other areas of learning, they are at odds with classroom norms and expectations from the outset. As they go through school, given reasonable learning opportunities, their deviation from the norm should increase because of their greater aptitude for learning. However, the tendency to group children in school on the basis of chronological age can easily handicap the gifted child unless special provisions are made. The actual or true level of performance is typically several years beyond that of the age group, and individuals sometimes deviate upward by eight or more years in measured achievement, even as primary-grade pupils. Thus the California kindergarten group of gifted children equaled second-grade norms in reading and mathematics. As Figure 4.2 shows, the mean total average score on the STEP of the fourth- and fifth-grade gifted children was 271.1, which approached the mean for average ninth-graders of 272. The mean for seventh-grade gifted subjects was above the average for twelfth grade. The gifted children in both the tenth and eleventh grades were well above the average performance of college sophomores.

High school seniors performed in similar advanced fashion on the Graduate Record Examinations in the social sciences, humanities, and natural sciences. A randomly selected group of 75 gifted students surpassed college-senior norms on all three examinations and exceeded the scores of college seniors who had majored in the social sciences.

This same level of excellent scholastic attainment was noted by Hermanson (1970) in using the Graduate Record Examinations with highly gifted high school sophomores, juniors, and seniors. Their *average* achievement was beyond that of two thirds of college seniors in all of the areas tests, and in the natural sciences they exceeded 85 percent of the college seniors.

The Terman, Baldwin, and Bronson (1925) population exhibited similar patterns of advanced learning achievement. The highest levels of school achievement were found in areas that required verbal comprehension and usage, while the fields requiring primarily manual dexterity, such as writing, art, and handwork, were areas of relative weakness. When the Terman children were rated in other areas of learning, the pattern tended to be uniformly higher than for average children, although there were wide individual variations. The high performance in academic areas was accompanied by wide extracurricular interests. More than half of Terman's group studied music, art,

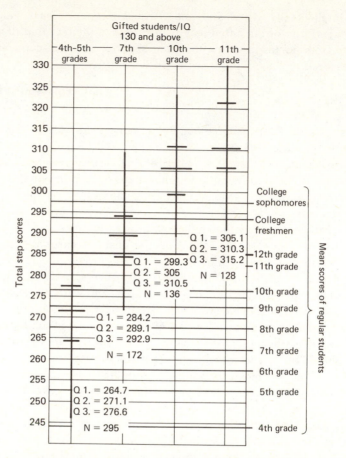

FIGURE 4.2 *Variation between the average performance of regular pupils and the actual performance of the gifted—mean results on the Sequential Tests of Educational Progress (STEP). From R. A. Martinson, Educational programs for gifted pupils. Sacramento: California State Department of Education, 1961.*

dancing, and other topics outside of school. They read far more books than the average and exhibited more diverse interests. The traits described by the parents most frequently as indicators of superior learning ability were excellent memory, curiosity, quick understanding, early and advanced speech, and extensive information.

From Project Talent, a massive national survey of 450,000 secondary students conducted in 1960 by Flanagan and Cooley (1966), data were extracted comparing the top 2.5 percent with the 2.5 percent closest to the mean in aptitude. Certain data emerged that indicated the expected high-learning potential in the upper group, but learning problems as well (Marland, 1972). Of the high group, some 20 percent received grades that would jeopardize them for admission at many universities and colleges. Nearly one fifth

of the high group did not enter college and, although college is not a necessary avenue to intellectual satisfaction, five years after high school 17 percent found themselves in jobs that were not satisfying to them. Many
expressed dissatisfaction and intended to leave their occupations at the first
opportunity.

Personal and Social Adjustment

The personal and social adjustment of the gifted has been studied in
considerable detail both at child and adult levels. The brief review here will
include that information which is chiefly relevant to children. Many of the
references at the end of the chapter contain extensive reviews and accounts
of major studies.

Personal Adjustment

General agreement can be found in various studies that intellectually
gifted children, as a group, have superior emotional adjustment. Terman and
his associates (1925) found this, using a wide range of tests and rating devices
on 500 gifted children versus an unselective control group. In a follow-up
study of the Terman group during high school, the same picture prevailed
(Burke, Jensen and Terman, 1930). Similarly, in adulthood they rated well
(Terman and Oden, 1959). They were more self-sufficient, more dominant,
and less neurotic. Since then many studies have replicated these findings—
in an overwhelming fashion. However, an overcommitment to the generalization that gifted children are *all* well adjusted is unsound.

The problem of different levels of intellectual giftedness must be recognized. In a classic study, Hollingworth (1942) examined in detail the problems
of highly gifted children. Many had adjustment problems, due no doubt in
part, to the difficulty of "accepting fools gladly." Hollingworth pointed out
the inevitable frustrations of the highly gifted child in seeking satisfactory
play relations with other children and his very early concern with problems
of origin, destiny, and evil in the abstract sense. The problems of coping with
authority created in some children attitudes of rebellion, contentiousness,
and general negativism. And the attitude of cynicism, coupled with lack of
suitable associations, produced feelings of isolation, inferiority, shyness, and
general anxiety in relation with others. Children with IQ's in the 120's and
130's appear to have far better adjustment patterns than those with much
higher IQ's. Both Terman and Hollingworth regarded the major problems of
gifted children as isolation from contemporaries, frustration of learning needs,
boredom, and concern with ethical and moral problems.

Differences among intellectually gifted children were emphasized by
Drews (1963). She hypothesized four types of gifted students on the basis of
their self-classification and her study of the individuals: (1) the high-achieving
studious, (2) the social leader, (3) the creative intellectual, and (4) the rebel.
She described the *high achievers* as conformers, hard-working, conscientious,
and rule-oriented; the *social leaders* as peer-oriented rather than teacher-

oriented, handsome, materialistic, and hedonistic; the *creative intellectuals* as fluent, original, nonconformists, low in social responsibility. Drews noted the difficulty with her categorizations of children and adolescents in the fact that 30 percent of the rebels changed to other categories within one year.

Bonsall and Stellfre (1955) added still another complication. When they controlled for social class, the differences in personality dimensions were less marked. Much of the research ignores this important variable.

Martinson (1961), in her California study of children with individual Stanford-Binet scores above 130, studied their personal and social maturity by means of the California Psychological Inventory. Some of the data are presented in Figure 4.3. They show the following: (1) the eighth-grade group possessed social and emotional security far above their randomly selected eighth-grade age mates; (2) while the pattern of a sample of business executives with whom they were also compared was slightly higher overall, generally the gifted eighth-graders were much more nearly like these executives than their average age mates; and (3) the gifted eighth-graders appeared to excel most in measures of socialization and communality. More specifically, their positive qualities included being tactful, reliable, sincere, patient, steady, realistic, honest, and conscientious, and they tended to use common sense and good judgment.

The gifted student is not the psychological counterpart of his age peers. This commonly held view undoubtedly adds to the frustrations, personality problems, and failures to perform adequately experienced by too many gifted, particularly those of the highest ability. Although projection of these specific findings into the lower grades is hypothetical, nevertheless, it is the judgment of the writer that many gifted children should be freed from much of the usual classroom supervision from kindergarten onward. If advanced psychological growth is characteristic of gifted youth at the eighth-grade and high school levels, it is reasonable to assume that many younger gifted children are similarly advanced.

Despite the above, it is nonetheless true that subgroups of children with superior cognitive abilities need to be examined more carefully by ethnic and racial classifications, by socioeconomic class, by levels and types of giftedness, by achievement versus underachievement, and by intellectual versus artistic talent. At this point, two stereotypes would appear to be equally unacceptable: that instability and high intelligence are closely related; and that high intelligence guarantees good personal and social adjustment. While there appears to be more truth to the latter than the former, it is hardly an infallible rule.

Social Adjustment

As for social status, the gifted as a group have been found to be very well accepted by others. Contrary to some beliefs, the typical gifted child is not an isolate; rather, he relates very well to others. Early studies which indicated that twice as many gifted students as others are leaders and hold

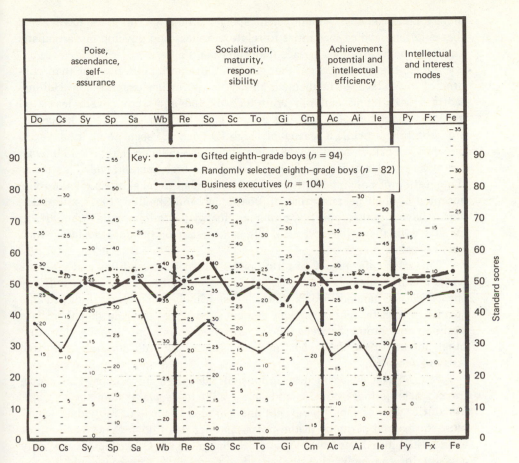

FIGURE 4.3 *Comparison of California Psychological Inventory Profiles of gifted eighth-grade boys, randomly selected eighth-grade boys, and business executives, based on male norms. From R. A. Martinson, Educational programs for gifted pupils. Sacramento: California State Department of Education, 1961. Code: The 18 scores in the inventory and the symbols representing them are as follows: dominance (Do); capacity for status (Cs); sociability (Sy); social presence (Sp); self-acceptance (Sa); sense of well-being (Wb); responsibility (Re); socialization (So); self-control (Sc); tolerance (To); good impression (Gi); communality (Cm); achievement via conformance (Ac); achievement via independence (Ai); intellectual efficiency (Ie); psychological-mindedness (Py); flexibility (Fx); femininity (Fe).*

elective offices have been substantiated in recent studies and in reviews of them (Barbe, 1965; Gallagher, 1966; Marland, 1972). The gifted student often finds time for extensive involvement in school government, clubs, athletics, cultural events, creative endeavors, and scholastic pursuits. While the gifted tend to spend time with others like themselves if they have the choice (O'Shea, 1960; Barbe, 1965), they enjoy favorable status with others even when in completely heterogeneous situations. In special groupings, teachers have noted that children have opportunities to relate to others and develop more realistic and wholesome attitudes toward themselves and others.

Again, the generalization that gifted children are more popular than children of lower level of intellectual ability needs further examination. Hollingworth (1942) found children with IQ's of 180 and above were less well accepted than the 130 to 150 IQ group. They are too brilliant to be understood by others, while a reasonably high IQ does not seem to be a barrier to popularity. Further, Martyn (1957) has provided evidence that gifted students are more popular at the elementary than at the high school level. This raises the question of how much gifted adolescents need to mask their talents to be accepted by their peers. Zorbaugh, Boardman, and Sheldon (1951) and others since, have pointed out the problems for gifted adolescents who are in conflict with the values, ways of life, and behavior of adult society which they regard as unworthy.

The sheer infrequency of gifted peers with similar abilities and interests poses another dilemma. Mann (1957) found that gifted students in half-day special classes tended to pick their closest friends from among those in this special setting. In light of present evidence, one can conclude that there is a positive correlation between social acceptance and intelligence, but that other potent forces play a part in determining how well children with high IQ's are accepted.

For the last 50 years descriptions of the gifted have consistently portrayed them as more popular and better adjusted socially than the average. Yet stories persist about the exceptions, perhaps because of individual examples, stories and cartoons in the press, and articles that present accounts of maladjusted gifted persons (Witty and Lehman, 1930). Other factors that may account for the belief that the gifted are not well accepted could be the hostility of some adults (including teachers) toward them and the belief of many in the law of compensation. For example, Gilbert and Jones (1972) found that a group of more than 200 undergraduates and teachers perceived the gifted as mainly Caucasian, intelligent, possibly talented, privileged economically, and liberal politically, as those who read or played intellectual games in their spare time, and as persons who would work in the humanities or physical sciences. The undergraduates perceived the gifted as inferior physically, weak in both hearing and vision; teachers regarded them as arrogant, superior, and bossy. Socially the gifted were seen as unsatisfactory in their peer relations, as arrogant, formal, distant, and authoritarian, as stodgy and shy, as anxious, introverted, and morose. Many of these perceived traits are totally incorrect, of course, when checked against the research evidence.

Interests, Social Pressures, and Values

As one would expect, gifted children have a wider range of interests than their less well-endowed peers. While they enjoy individual hobbies and solitary activities, they are quite social, enjoying especially games that require skill and thought. They tend to persist at worthwhile, difficult activities longer than other children (Terman et al., 1925; Burke et al., 1930).

Pressures from peer and adult groups on gifted students restrict the development of their accomplishments and personalities in many ways. Gifted adolescents have reduced their academic performance, have neglected class work, and have sought social activities so as to maintain social status with their peers. Unless brilliant students also were outstanding athletes, Tannenbaum (1960) found that they suffered group pressures from their peers. Many have found the problems of academic and social conformity unbearable. In one state study, 17.6 percent of the high school dropouts were classified as academically talented (Green, 1964). Almost twice as many girls as boys quit school. Despite the fact that the dropouts ranked high on standardized achievement tests, they received lower grades and participated in fewer activities than did students who remained.

Studies of underachievement are based on differing criteria, and thus generalizations are difficult. The use of grades rather than more meaningful measures of academic knowledge as a criterion of underachievement is just one case in point. Although the consensus is that a poor self-concept is a major factor differentiating the student with low academic achievement from the high achiever (Shaw and Alves, 1963), the very measurement of self-concept continues to be a difficult problem. Self-concept is affected by both internal and environmental forces. Some interesting studies have been made that reveal certain pressures which affect gifted girls and boys differently, and which probably affect their social and academic behavior.

Family and societal expectations have differed traditionally for boys and girls. Without doubt, these have served to limit the aspirations of many girls with ability to venture into many fields. D'Heurle and Haggard (1959) found marked differences between gifted boys and girls in academic performance and psychological behavior. Gifted girls have been found to be more docile, less independent, less venturesome, more inhibited, and more responsive to authority. Boys have been found to have healthier egos, greater spontaneity, better task orientation, and greater capacity for leadership than girls. Gifted girls are more independent than average girls, but less independent than gifted boys (Bachtold, 1968).

In adulthood, the women in the Terman sample lagged far behind the men in fully utilizing their potential occupationally (Terman and Oden, 1959). A total of 38 percent of the approximately 700 women were engaged in some type of office work, while only 1.6 percent were in medicine. Very few went beyond the master's degree. None was in law, engineering, and other fields that recently have started to open for women. While their status was somewhat better than that of comparable women in 1930, when only 1 woman in 28 entered graduate school, their occupations in the majority of instances did not challenge their potentials. There is little doubt that this picture has begun to change, but the change has been slow in coming. Many of the early problems of gifted women still persist (Helson, 1961; Bayley, 1970; Bachtold and

Werner, 1970b). The impact of the total civil rights movement on the status and opportunities for gifted women should be an interesting subject for research in the decade ahead.

With regard to values, the gifted tend as a group to be remarkably sensitive to human problems, even at the elementary school level. Hollingworth (1942) and many subsequent writers noted the acute concern of gifted children on moral and social issues and their worries over poverty, injustice, and lack of ethical behavior in adults. Gifted children identify with heroes who have contributed to humanity through discoveries, political action, the arts or through outstanding exemplary activity, often in the face of great difficulty. They contrast sharply with other children in their concern for others rather than for themselves (Martinson, 1961).

The values, aspirations, and occupational choices of students are affected by society, of course. Much has been made of the fact that the Terman group produced no eminent artists or musicians. When the Terman gifted were young, their principal avocations were creative and artistic (Terman and Oden, 1959). When they grew up, however, their chosen occupations were those that produced economic rewards greater and more stable than those available in the arts. In an excellent article, Pressey (1955) compared the nurture and production of eighteenth-century European musicians with the nurture and production of twentieth-century American athletes. He pointed out the impact of social and economic pressure on young persons who have many alternatives. No doubt this pressure still exists today. New studies of gifted and talented adolescents are needed to determine whether the ethics of modern-day youth have served to insulate them from the imposed values of adult society.

Postschool Adjustment

Follow-up studies of the Terman group (Terman and Oden, 1959), of the Ford Foundation accelerates (Fund for the Advancement of Education, 1957), and a later study of the "Fordlings" (Pressey, 1967) indicate that gifted individuals, as a group, make more satisfactory adjustments and accomplish more than the general population. Not all gifted students, however, are successful. The adult male Terman subjects who were most successful were compared to those who were least successful (Miles, 1954). Of the 167 most successful and 146 least successful in the group, the most successful were rated as better adjusted, from better-educated parents, and from more stable home environments. Their fathers were more successful; they won more fellowships; they had better academic records; and they earned appreciably more income at mainly professional occupations.

At mid-life, the Terman population, as a group, was both productive and versatile in accomplishments, with contributions ranging across the arts, sciences, social sciences, and humanities (Terman and Oden, 1959). The men produced nearly 2,000 scientific and technical articles; 60 books and monographs in science, literature, the arts, and the humanities; 230 patents;

33 novels; 375 short stories, novelettes, and plays; more than 60 essays; and 265 miscellaneous articles. The women, while less productive, produced 5 novels; 5 volumes of poetry; 70 poems; 32 scholarly books; some 50 short stories; 4 plays; more than 150 essays, critiques, and articles; over 200 scientific papers; and 5 patents. The extent of their productivity becomes apparent when compared to the production of an average cross section of 700 men and 700 women.

Many gifted persons start their contributions at a very early age and continue them far past the usual retirement age. Lehman (1953) has pointed out the accomplishments of young people in such fields as mathematical theory, and the early childhood contributions of a number of musicians. Significant discoveries in science often were made by children of school age. These same individuals continued their productivity into adulthood. The study of Pressey and Pressey (1967) of eminent persons of old age found that many made contributions when they were in their sixties, seventies, and eighties. Michelangelo was chief architect of St. Peter's Basilica from age 72 to 89, Goethe completed *Faust* at 82, Churchill was Prime Minister of England from 77 to 81, and Franklin helped to write the Declaration of Independence at 70.

In general, the pattern of postschool adjustment and productivity of gifted adults is excellent. Many gifted individuals find great satisfaction in their work and absorb themselves in their pursuits intensively by choice. They involve themselves in their work with greater intensity and dedication and often contribute far more to society than the average person.

EDUCATIONAL PLANNING AND PROGRAMS

Educational planning and programs for the gifted must be based directly on their needs, interests, and actual levels of academic and creative performance. The advanced levels of academic performance by the gifted were described in an earlier section of this chapter and do not need repetition here. The general advancement gives only partial insight into the scholastic and creative functioning of the gifted, however. Possibly the greatest challenge to education is posed by this group if their needs are to be met. In a very real sense, meeting their needs properly compounds the problem of the educator, because the adequate program can result only in increasing deviation from the norm, increasing versatility and complexity of a given group, increasing diversity of interests from the content of the usual curriculum, and increasing need for added teaching personnel and situations in which to learn.

Gifted children, even when given no attention, do very well and reflect credit upon the school. Regrettably, this may diminish any sense of urgency to plan needed educational experiences for them. But such an attitude serves only to retard their progress. When young gifted children are in the usual "good" schools, they make little more than the progress of the norm group on academic tests. When they are able to pursue interests, read independently, and select books freely at any level, they exceed the progress of equally gifted children to a significant degree (Martinson, 1961).

From the time they enter school, gifted children often develop special interests and pursue the interests avidly. They frequently become "experts" on topics unfamiliar to their teachers, and in some instances they follow the topics for an extended period of time. The topics may have nothing to do with classroom activities, although they are of great interest to the child. Often teachers assist the child by allowing private time and by giving him access to materials and resource personnel.

Some gifted children absorb content on certain subjects to the extent that it is available; thus a child may read the entire collection in mythology at one point, read all of the materials on sea life at another, and then immerse himself in the study of biography, mathematics, or archaeology. Because of his accumulated information and skills, the typical gifted child has little need for the drill and routine that some other children require. On the contrary, he may upset his teacher because of his ready insight and ability to solve a problem that is programed to consume more time. Many bright children are impatient with detail, and dislike writing because their ideas outpace their ability to put them down properly and neatly. Some will express themselves with calculated parsimony in order to avoid having a great deal of material to correct. Gifted children enjoy working with broad questions, ideas, and issues. The opportunity to relate problems that they encounter in textual materials to relevant parallel problems, and to analyze possible solutions, appeals to them far more than working as recipients and regurgitators of knowledge.

The ability of gifted children to involve themselves in many activities simultaneously and to manage all of them with relative success implies a need for access to rich and varied opportunities. A young gifted child may spend his time at experiments in animal nutrition, intensive violin practice, reading on prehistoric animals, construction, writing a play for neighborhood performance, and editing a weekly one-page neighborhood "newspaper," in addition to performing excellently in all areas of classroom activity. This kind of versatility is common at all school levels.

These examples from one secondary school group of 21 students are typical. Seven students were simultaneously attending classes at a large university. One boy received the Harvard Book Award and was chosen as school representative to a state government study group. Another placed eighth in a group of approximately one thousand contestants in the American Chemical Society contest, was chosen for a special summer program by the Committee for Advancement of Scientific Training from a total school population of more than one million, and received repeated honors. A girl was chosen also to be the second school representative to the state government study group; one was nominated for the National Council of Teachers of English Achievement Award. Another student also was nominated for this award, had his poetry published in a national anthology, and was accepted for an advanced honors course in advanced literature and composition. One had her poetry published in the National Anthology of High School Poetry; one had highest mention in a national poetry contest; and another was finalist in a speech contest that was open to thousands of potential contestants. This is not the usual level of performance in a high school class.

The basic difficulty in planning programs for the gifted lies in the often implicit assumption that the word "program" describes an administrative arrangement for a group with similar attributes. Anyone who has worked with gifted children is acutely aware of their intense individuality and versatility. Their interests, knowledge, and abilities are wide-ranging, far beyond those of other children in both scope and level. The real need, therefore, in the conceptualization of programs is for educational *planning* that is based on knowledge of the capacities, talents, interests, and psychological needs of a group of individuals who are more heterogeneous and advanced in their accomplishments than most. The program planner in a very real sense seeks to accommodate the educational establishment to suitable learning opportunities for these children. Such planning is difficult because of time schedules, class periods, curriculum requirements, established levels of progression, legal requirements, class groupings, and other factors. These schedules, requirements, and regulations are not suited to the gifted child with his curiosity and spirit of inquiry, his independence, his self-education in many fields, and his advanced knowledge. Clearly, the need for planning and innovation is great if our most able students are to realize their true potentials.

The need for better planning is apparent when one considers the waste of human potential and the resultant unworthy functioning of individuals. Though we should apply knowledge from studies of underachievement to prevent hostility and waste of abilities, we still turn out many underachievers. Despite increasing awareness of the problems of gifted girls and women, we know that recent studies during the 1960s still found girls to be more dependent, more imitative, less analytic, and more hesitant to tackle "male" subjects such as science and mathematics, and that their occupational choices were constricted and less ambitious (Bachtold, 1968; Bachtold and Werner, 1970b). Problems for the gifted are created by the demands of society for conformity. The feelings of loneliness, ostracism, difference, and isolation described by Roe's scientists (1953) still are the lot of many children when adults regard the responsibilities for adaptation to be only those of the child rather than, also, of the adults who work with him.

The need for planning is apparent, too, when we look at the gifted in the light of promised social contribution. The numbers who waste themselves and fail to make a proper social impact can only be guessed. One clue may be found in examining the world population increments over a period of time and speculating that these increments would produce proportionate significant individual contributions. From the birth of Christ up to 1850 the world population increased from 250 million to one billion. Today it approaches four billion, a fourfold increase in a little more than a century. The prevalence of gifted persons should be proportionate to the increment, and gifted and creative individuals of stature should be increasingly evident. In order to provide for the gifted, such factors as uniform requirements, pressure toward occupations with economic rewards, pressures that restrict development or alter aspirations, pressure toward conformity, and discouragement of individuality must be eliminated. To counter many of these difficulties, special programs have been developed. Because more continuity and consistency are found historically in program development than is apparent in the matter of identification, somewhat less reference will be made in this section to past studies; studies will be used selectively as examples of major trends and developments. This does not deny the value of many other studies. One of the major problems in the development of meaningful provisions for the gifted, indeed, has been the neglect of available past literature. Many repeated errors could be avoided through study of materials written by past leaders in the field. One of the impressions from such study would be that the available information has not been systematically employed to the advantage of gifted children, and that many "current" notions regarding giftedness and creativity were presented in past decades.

In early public school programs in the United States, arrangements for the gifted generally included special classes, grade skipping, and/or accelerated content. These three major aids, more recently referred to as special groupings, acceleration, and/or enrichment (including provisions in the regular classroom), are common today. Separation into these categories is an oversimplification of educational planning, however, as we will see in this section.

SPECIAL EDUCATIONAL GROUPINGS

Special groupings for the gifted vary widely. They may range from small groups of two or three children to completely segregated specialized schools, such as the New York high schools in science and in the performing arts. The groupings may be part time or full time. They may concentrate on a specific subject or may cover a range of subjects. They may be formed either in the school or in the community. They may meet daily or periodically. A given child or group of children may be involved in several special groupings at one time. For example, a child may be in a special class and an advanced astronomy club; another may be in several honors classes and be a member of a small cluster working with a community artist; another may be in a regular class and meet semiweekly in half-day special interest groups; still another may attend the Bronx (N.Y.) High School of Science full time. Many other arrangements are also found. The principal purpose of any special educational grouping, if it has merit, is to provide an adequate setting for learning and the kinds of curriculum content and teaching procedures appropriate for the gifted. Educators of the gifted over more than a 50-year period have employed ingenious means to provide for the wide range of abilities they face.

Even during the 1920s special groups of gifted pupils were established to work at their own pace, to deal with major questions, to do extensive research on their own interests, to do creative work and have specialized teaching in the arts, to work with social issues, and to use wide community resources (Stedman, 1924). Reactions during the 1930s to special groupings were generally favorable. Persons who worked in programs found that gifted children were significantly superior in achievement, had fewer failures, participated in more activities, and were rated higher by their teachers than were control groups. Reports in the 1936 *Yearbook* of the National Society for the Study of Education and in the *Manual of Child Psychology* (Miles, 1954) summarized various early studies and pointed out that special groupings produced favorable academic and psychological results. Hollingworth (1938) evaluated the impact of special classes on the personal adjustment of bright children and concluded that claims of conceit, poor health, or social unadaptability made by critics were not based on evidence or direct experience. Passow (1958), in the *Yearbook* of the National Society for the Study of Education, concurred that studies found generally beneficial academic and psychological results for the gifted in special classes. Although many of the programs during the 1920s and 1930s were carried on without accompanying evaluative procedures found in some later studies, a fair amount of evidence was collected in support of special groupings.

Follow-up studies (Terman and Oden, 1947) of children in the Terman group who were in special classes, and of the graduates of the Cleveland Major Work Classes (Barbe, 1953), pointed out favorable results. The Terman special class participants received highly favorable ratings from their teachers. In a follow-up study of the Cleveland Major Work participants from 1938 to 1952, Barbe found that only 8 percent of the former students disapproved of the program, from a 77 percent return.

Why, then, in view of the evidence, have special groupings been subject to so much debate and controversy? Numerous reasons can be found in the literature, some of which are extant today. Two major ones were (1) concern about the establishment of a meritocracy and (2) the fear of snobbery within an elite group. Others included (3) fear of pressures on children and (4) the deprivation of gifted and average children of contact with one another. While it is true that average and below-average children can benefit from contact with the gifted, the reverse does not necessarily follow. Gifted children who are given opportunities to work with other gifted children in good programs have been found to develop better attitudes toward learning, toward themselves, and toward others (Passow, 1958; Martinson, 1961). Research to the contrary is meager, but the lack of evidence has not prevented expressions and reiteration of resistance to special groupings. Determined and vocal opposition of some prominent educational leaders has been based mainly on resistance to grouping as undemocratic, and articles on this theme have appeared in teacher journals from time to time.

Elimination of classes for the gifted occurred despite their success during the 1930s and the early 1940s, due in part to fiscal retrenchment but probably also because of the growing belief that teachers could care for the gifted in regular classrooms. Important, as well, may have been competing priorities and the persistent belief that the gifted can care for themselves without any special considerations.

In the middle and late 1950s, concern about the gifted began to increase. Although the Cold War rivalry is credited for much of this concern, many groups and individuals had devoted their efforts to the problem before this period. Publications by educational groups and numerous individuals all preceded Sputnik. The spreading awareness of neglect resulted in an increase in both research and programs. Modern-day special groupings are characterized by much more variability and different emphases than was true of groupings in the 1920s and 1930s. Earlier groupings generally were formed on a total-day basis, and pupils were assigned to a given teacher. Present-day groupings may include any of the following, singly or in combination: special classes, honors classes made up of gifted and high-achieving pupils, Saturday classes, before- or after-school groups or classes, seminars, community-based groups or classes, summer programs, part-time special interest groups, clusters of gifted in heterogeneous classes, and others. The greater flexibility in current programs is due to an increasing emphasis on pupil study and planning arrangements appropriate for the individual pupil based on such study, rather than establishing an administrative grouping *first* and then fitting the pupil into that grouping. Present-day programs also are incorporating careful and complete study of pupil needs; preparation of teachers, both on a prestudy and inservice basis; planning for individual pupils; continuous consultant help; provision of appropriate curriculum experiences both in and out of school; the use of many community resources, and close cooperation with parents. Administrative arrangements that are planned carefully by school personnel to afford logical arrangements for the identified gifted children tend to succeed because they have the understanding and endorsement of those working with them.

The support of school personnel is important, indeed fundamental, to the success of any type of grouping arrangement. Typically, increasing varieties of groupings occur as personnel consider alternatives to existing arrangements for learning. Typically, also, teachers at the elementary school level favor assignment of the gifted to the regular classroom initially; it is after they experience frustration in providing for them that they begin to seek alternatives. Recent studies have centered on the effects of specific intervention rather than on the assessment of administrative arrangements, per se. In such studies the results generally have been favorable. In a study by Bent and others (1969), an experimental group of nearly 500 third-grade children, placed in special classes ranging from grades 4 through 8 and taught by teachers who were prepared for their assignments, were found to equal or surpass control groups in achievement, despite the fact that their regular classroom activities were cut in half. Their skills grew in foreign languages, research, creative thinking, social awareness and concern. leadership, creativity, interests, and self-reliance. Teachers and parents approved of the program.

In an assessment of both cognitive and affective behaviors, Steele and others (1970) found significant differences between children in regular classes and those in gifted classes in the extent of emphasis on higher thought processes, classroom focus, and classroom climate. Steele also found differences in such factors as application, synthesis, enthusiasm, independence, and retention. These differences were ascribed to the preparation of teachers for differentiated instruction.

In a follow-up study of five special groups Arends and Ford (1964) found the experimental groups significantly higher than control groups in 10 of 21 instances. Their results indicated that the program needed improvement, that it hurt no one, and that both students and teachers liked to work in special groups better than in traditional groupings. The impact of contacts for rural youth also was found to be of benefit. More than 90 percent of those who had attended weekly seminars at the state university subsequently entered college, although large numbers initially had no intention to do so (New York State Department of Education, 1961). Even the use of media for direct teaching has produced favorable results for the gifted (although the writer believes that media serve their best purpose as *tools* for the gifted). Programed instruction produced significant gains in vocabulary skills in 42 fourth- and fifth-grade gifted pupils, and televised units in astronomy, mathematics, and geography produced significant gains in learned content (Gotkin and Massa, 1963; Hennes, 1965).

Teaching for creativity in a three-year program designed to test the influence of a creative aesthetic approach in beginning academic areas on creative development resulted in significantly higher scores by kindergarten children on tests of creative thinking, problem-solving, and originality (Torrance, 1969). Bachtold and Werner (1970a) found mixed results from teaching based on the Guilford structure and Myers and Torrance workbook lessons. For a small group they found that eight months of training produced a greater openness in considering alternatives, but also greater inhibition in decisions. The gifted appeared more inhibited, less spontaneous, and more cautious after the training in productive thinking, and the girls were more cautious than the boys.

McFee's study (1968), which used a creativity-based curriculum in design, produced significant gains in tests of fluency, adaptive flexibility, and originality in another class group. Gains were significant in divergent areas, and attitudes toward creativity were better than those of control students. She concluded that gifted young people need aesthetic experiences as an important part of their total curriculum.

The growing move to allow young people to study in fields of their own choosing has resulted in programs devoted to special interests and to programs combining independent study and seminars jointly designed by students and faculty. One such program that extended far beyond the standard curriculum in many areas was recently found especially effective for the diverse interests and talents of highly gifted high school students (Hermanson and Wright, 1969).

Available evidence suggests that grouping, accompanied by learning content that is suitably designed for the gifted, enables them to escape from previous limitations and to improve in interest in school, achievement, attitudes, and psychological adjustment. Programs that have not produced results have been those centered on a given administrative arrangement, without accompanying attention to the teaching-learning aspects.

A well-publicized study by Borg (1964) of the use of different grouping patterns produced no differences in achievement. In this study the curriculum in the various groups was not differentiated. Goldberg, Passow, and Justman (1966) found similar results in New York groupings, where grouping per se did not affect academic achievement. In other words, when nothing was done change did not occur. Other large-scale studies where curricular changes were made produced different results.

In summary, ability grouping as such is not very productive in and of itself, just as Jacobs (1959) found identification alone to be nonproductive. To insure the best results in special groups, specific planning of learning opportunities must follow knowledge of the student's real capacities and interests.

EARLY SCHOOL ADMISSION
AND ACCELERATION

As an administrative device, acceleration may include early entrance at school at any level, grade skipping, curriculum acceleration within a given grade, simultaneous attendance at schools of different levels, intensive acceleration in one or more subject fields, or compression of curriculum content into shorter-than-normal time periods. Any one of these has been a traditional remedy for the deficits in the regular classroom curriculum for the gifted. How effective has it been?

As with homogeneous grouping, opposition to acceleration appears founded on emotion rather than on evidence. The interested student may wish to examine summaries by Shannon (1957), Pressey (1949, 1967), and Worcester (1956). Children in Nebraska admitted to school early on the basis of mental age did as well or better than their older classmates, were socially and emotionally as well or better adjusted than their classmates, and had as good or better physical coordination (Worcester, 1956). Birch (1954) found similar results in follow-up studies, during the primary grades, of kindergarten children who had been admitted to school early. Hobson (1956) followed a group of kindergarten children who were admitted to school early and found that they also maintained and increased their scholastic superiority and distinction in honors and athletics over others. Despite the fact that these findings have been confirmed in later studies, less than 20 percent of U.S. schools accelerate children, and teachers continue to resist the practice (Braga, 1972).

Most of the studies mentioned were based on comparisons of young gifted children with older classmates. A more exacting comparison can be made by comparing gifted accelerants with gifted nonaccelerants. Rusch and Clark and Klausmeier found no difficulties for accelerated gifted as compared to gifted controls who had progressed normally through the grades (Gallagher, 1966).

One study critical of early entrance was made of a group of 32 children, only eight of whom were gifted (Klein and Breneman, 1965). Aside from this study, it is difficult to find reports of negative results on bases other than opinion.

Results from studies of older pupils at the secondary and college levels also favor acceleration. Major studies by Justman (1954) of curriculum acceleration, of early entrance into college (Fund for the Advancement of Education, 1957), and of curriculum acceleration and simultaneous high school and university enrollment (Martinson, 1961) all pointed out the advantages of acceleration. Students who entered college early under sponsorship of the Ford Foundation reported little or no harm from skipping high school work, some initial but fleeting social difficulty because of their youth at the point of college entrance, and a gain of time in launching a career. Some were found to have demonstrated early outstanding promise in their vocations (Pressey, 1967).

In summary, the precocious early development of highly gifted individuals suggests that their school progress should differ from that of their chronological peers. If adequate learning experiences were provided, the need for grade-skipping theoretically should cease. Many highly gifted young children would profit from programs at the preschool level. There are occasional highly gifted individuals who absorb college curricula with ease before they reach adolescence (Grost, 1970). And many gifted high school students are able to succeed in college classes. With the current academic structure a reality, acceleration at least enables children to learn at a more realistic level than otherwise would be possible.

CURRICULUM ENRICHMENT
IN THE REGULAR CLASSROOM

This mode of dealing with the learning needs of the gifted is a favorite, particularly at the elementary school level. It requires no administrative adaptation, is regarded as democratic, and intraclass provisions can be made for individuals. Advocates also cite the advantage to children in learning to work with all others and to benefit mutually from contacts with different persons.

Those who favor other approaches do so because they believe that the gifted in the regular classroom are neglected in favor of others with more pressing needs and because of the dearth of opportunity for the gifted, the lack of stimulation, and the possible development of poor attitudes and work habits.

Actually, *enrichment* is a term describing practices that should prevail in any administrative arrangement. It is common in all programs where education is differentiated for the gifted, whether in the regular classroom, in any special group, or in any kind of accelerated program. If the program is worthwhile it is because of differentiated curriculum provisions.

Enrichment is increasingly understood as central to any curriculum plan for the gifted. Content that is enriched should carry the student to higher levels of competence and understanding. It should be at an appropriate ideational level, dealing with major concepts and ideas, should extend conceptualization and understanding, and should provide for transfer, generalization, and application. For example, a gifted child may apply research on learning from animal experiments to his own learning processes in the classroom, or his readings on the causes of pollution to suggested solutions to the urban smog problem. Another may apply his study of artistic style to his own creations, while still another gifted student may work within a small group to analyze barriers to remedies for social problems.

INSTRUCTIONAL PROCEDURES AND MATERIALS

Instructional materials and procedures for gifted children are difficult to describe. If study of the individual student, including his current status, accomplishments, and interests, is the basis for curriculum development, the provisions and procedures are highly individualized. Curriculum adaptation and modification are immediately necessary, but provisions are highly differentiated.

Some of the efforts that have been successful have taken several approaches: (1) self-determination of learning activities by the student, with the teacher providing time, counsel, resources, and (if qualified) evaluative guidance; (2) the development of study kits based upon key questions and resources, on topics of known appeal to gifted children (prehistoric animals, space, insects, or biography for younger children; man's inhumanity to man or the concept of the hero throughout history for the older students, for example); (3) the establishment of a course of study with alternative choices for long-range study, all based on topics and questions of appropriate conceptual level; (4) precourse testing on comprehensive content of a course, with evaluation and planning of procedures by teacher and students; (5) assignment of students to special mentors for individual study.

The instructional materials developed for individual and group use that have been of greatest appeal have provided pupils with opportunities for comparative studies and discussion of issues of concern to them. Suggestions in such materials are marked by such words as "discuss," "compare," "trace," "analyze." Options for reporting of findings are left open; often students are asked to find means *other* than the traditional term report, and media resources are made available to them.

Resource units have changed from earlier listings of single ideas for gifted students to units such as those based on major questions, major contributions and their contributors, social problems, significant aesthetic experiences, and recurrent events in history. The trend is from many isolated ideas to fewer significant ideas.

CURRENT CURRICULUM PLANNING FOR THE GIFTED

Although some people believe that progress in education for the gifted has been minuscule in recent years, changes and improvements have been made. In many instances, more flexibility and increasing options are apparent in the schools. Through specially financed projects and workshops teachers are learning how to work effectively with the gifted. Some local and state programs were developed and maintained during the 1960s despite meager funds. And the commitment of the U.S. Office of Education to a permanent effort for the gifted and talented augurs well. But much remains to be done.

The magnitude of the task is seen in the reactions of 204 national experts (Fig. 4.4). At all grade levels from kindergarten through the twelfth grade, over 75 percent of state and local programs were considered inadequate or nonexistent (Marland, 1972). Translated into numbers based on 1969 estimates of gifted and talented children, the neglect of gifted students in the United States has been appalling. Between one and two million gifted students receive little attention beyond the regular program, according to the experts.

In systems where programs do exist, changes are occurring in many areas—program structure, curriculum, teaching styles, teaching personnel, and types of activities. The trend in general is a departure from the single-program structures of the past to increasing variability and flexibility of structure. Changes that particularly affect curriculum are the following:

1. *From single and specific modes of administrative organization to flexible, multiple, and changing organization.* School organization increasingly reflects the diversity of the students. As educators attempt to provide for the special needs of the gifted, such students are given open access to courses rather than being limited to specific class-level offerings. Transition between school levels is increasing so that students who need to take courses at a higher-level institution can do so. Increasing opportunities for independent study and seminars are available at both elementary and secondary levels, and traditional time schedules are not as sacred as formerly. Students who

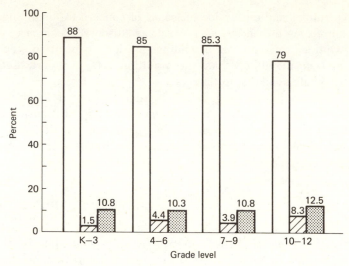

FIGURE 4.4 *Existence of school programs for the education of gifted and talented children in the United States, 1960, as viewed by 204 national experts in the field. From S. P. Marland,* Education of the gifted and talented. *Washington, D.C.: U.S. Office of Education, 1972. Key:☐Rare, few, or none; ▨ mostly adequate or complete; ▦ not ascertainable, or don't know, or other.*

no longer need certain curricula are excused from those requirements and are given opportunity for independent study instead; in some instances this type of program occupies all or nearly all of the student's time.

Arrangements are made for student contacts with teachers as needed, and no longer are students with specialized interests limited to single teacher contacts. Adults with special knowledge work with children individually and in small groups for varying periods of time. Students are sent into the community for special studies and for work experiences with adults who share their interests. Those with special talents are given contacts with artists and specialists in different fields.

Within schools, student and teacher competencies are matched, as well as student-student competencies. On a small group and individual basis, children are paired with adults and older students with whom they can share interests and from whom they can learn. For example, a high school student who is a computer specialist may teach other high school students, or a 10-year-old may work on an experiment with a 6-year-old. The principal may serve as the mentor of a child whose mathematical background exceeds that of his teacher, and a musician-teacher may work with a young musician from another class.

Weekly and daily schedules arranged to cover X minutes of time for each subject are changing to afford both latitude and private time for the gifted. Although acceptance of the idea that the gifted waste much of their time in school has been slow, it is increasing, and teachers are willing to allow the child to devote blocks of time to his interests.

2. *Increased emphasis on conceptually advanced learning for the gifted.* Instead of content that is advanced a year or two, the trend is toward topics of major importance and the identification of central concepts and ideas. Grade-level content that is found unnecessary is eliminated. Quantity and rote learning are out; the latter is used when necessary for consolidation of skills, but much of this type of learning may occur via programed materials without any teacher contact. Teachers and students select a key question or idea and deal with it through interdisciplinary study. For example, a group of secondary students may devote an entire year to the topic "The Individual in Society" and examine interrelations from a variety of standpoints, including the aesthetic (with ramifications), the political, social, racial, and others, as one class did. Similarly, elementary school children in a study of slavery may investigate the political, historical, international, and psychololocal aspects of the system.

3. *Less reliance on exercises and workbooks and on artificially contrived curriculum.* Various taxonomies, principally those of Bloom (1956) and Guilford (1967), have been influential in curriculum building. Although educators and psychologists have for many years espoused the importance of development of hypotheses, examination of alternatives, critical thought, transfer, application, and pupil initiative, these psychologists conceptualized levels and types of learning in a way that is more easily translated into practice by educators. Bloom's cognitive domain at the higher levels is especially relevant in the consideration of key questions and issues, and Guilford's divergent-thinking domain is important to mental health, openness, hypothesizing, and creativity.

The taxonomic approach can be helpful to teachers in examining the relevance of activities. The same approach can be limiting if too literally applied. If teachers use any taxonomy as a rigid *model* rather than as a *guide,* the end result can only be artificial. Children do not need to touch base with equal frequency in all taxonomic categories, nor is one part of a taxonomy necessarily more valuable than another. If taxonomies are unnecessarily complex, as sometimes happens when they are interrelated by model builders, the danger lies in excessive time being spent in filling taxonomic cells rather than in identifying and dealing with important ideas and learnings.

4. *From the teacher as sole designer of curriculum to involvement of the student.* The student at every level is designing many aspects of his curriculum, both as an individual and as a member of a group. As an individual he may center on his own interest topic, no matter how esoteric. As a group member he may be very active in the determination of topics within a central subject of study. He also is given more latitude, especially at the elementary school level, to work independently rather than as a committee member and thus frequently is freed from the necessity of consensus or of adaptation to the group.

5. *From creativity as a separate dimension to creativity as a cognitive style of learning and a function of personality.* Studies in creativity and in the identification of traits important to creativity have been done largely at the adult level. The advantage held by psychologists who have studied adults is that they have been able to conduct their studies of persons who already had attained eminence. The tentativeness in childhood creativity research thus can be avoided. Since many of the adult studies have identified important characteristics that can be nurtured during childhood and should be, and since many creative adults have related childhood experiences of special significance, it is possible to use adult-level reports to advantage.

It is the belief of the writer that the current application of present-day creativity research at the childhood level can be based more securely on the psychological climate espoused than on the use of testing and identification. Complete agreement should be found among all those interested in children with superior cognitive abilities, when it comes to discussion of required psychological conditions in the classroom.

All would agree that the task of both teacher and parent is the creation of an environment in which the child can be a fully effective human being, in which his belief in himself and his self-understanding will grow rather than diminish, in which he can extend his curiosity and interests, and experiment without fear of failure or censure, in which no bars are placed on his search for knowledge, and in which he is given any needed access to resources in the development of his abilities and talents, regardless of age.

All might also agree that creativity in the sense of lasting original contributions to humanity is a phenomenon of development, and that the general atmosphere conducive to originality and to the full expression of unusual ideas is important to maintain.

Studies in creativity have served to strengthen understanding of positive mental health principles that are germane to full effectiveness of the individual and to point out some of the barriers to creativity, such as structure, schedules, timing of activities, imposition of requirements, and insistence on conformity to teacher-imposed standards. We know that first-order cognitive production does not always come easily within a time schedule or under preordained conditions!

It is not necessary or desirable to foster creativity separately from curriculum. Wide opportunities for creativity are present in the curriculum if it is used as it should be. Children who have ample opportunity for experiences in the arts, drama, music, dance, dramatic play, creative writing, experimentation, construction, folklore, poetry, the sciences, and literature need not be deprived or uncreative. The use of exercises to develop creativity, as sometimes advocated, holds two dangers: (1) that natural opportunities for creativity will not be employed or regarded as desirable, and (2) that teachers will assume that this basically artificial and contradictory approach does indeed produce "creativity." Some exercises may improve performance on tests that contain identical elements, but creativity is a much more personal, private, and uncommon occurrence than exercises permit. The production of creativity cannot occur by assigning time to it. Attention must be given instead to those conditions that encourage or inhibit creativity, and this can be a major goal of the sensitive teacher.

Studies to promote and test creativity within the curriculum have produced mixed results. Skipper (1972) reported growth over a control group in ideational fluency, flexibility, originality, elaboration, inventiveness, and sensitivity toward aesthetics in young adolescents in a three-year after-school program in the arts. Kaltsounis (1971) found discovery learning in mathematics to be a suitable teaching method for creative children. Intervention through exercises or intensive programs to develop creativity, however, produced little or no improvement in studies by Anastasi (1970) and Warren (1971). Again, these various studies seem to favor the development of climate and opportunities for learning rather than applied exercises or intensive training programs, at least at the elementary school level.

Program Support

Program costs are difficult to ascertain because cost data are incomplete. Data from the U.S. Office of Education Study (Marland, 1972) indicate that all of the states except one provide sums ranging downward from an average of $28 per gifted pupil per year for programs. Several states with well-publicized programs actually provide for 20 percent or less of the known gifted.

Federal reports indicate that current provisions for gifted students relative to special education for the handicapped are meager. As Figure 4.5 shows, the programs in 27 model school systems are far more numerous for any handicapped children than for the gifted. The lone exception is the multiply handicapped population, which fared slightly worse than the gifted. Similarly, expenditures for the gifted in the same school systems are low. The intellectually gifted are allocated only a small fraction of the amount allotted to the mentally retarded and other groups of handicapped children (see Fig. 4.6).

The effect of limited funds is evident also in the fact that only 10 of the 50 states have even one state consultant assigned responsibility for the gifted for the major portion of his time. Typically, consultants are found in a few states with legislative support and in large school systems with a long history of commitment to the gifted.

The national survey by the Commissioner of the U.S. Office of Education revealed that educational provisions for the gifted and talented hold very low priority at all levels of government (Marland, 1972). While marginal support is provided in some sections of the country, the needs of most talented youth are unrecognized. State governments have provided verbal support without funds in all but a few instances. Both apathy and hostility among educators and laymen have been strikingly evident. The waste of abilities and misplacement of priorities are clear.

Other Commissioners of the U.S. Office of Education, as early as 1915,

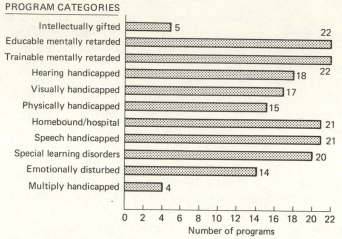

FIGURE 4.5 *Number of programs, by categories of exceptionality, reported by 27 model school districts in five states with generally superior special education services for children with exceptional learning needs. From S. P. Marland,* Education of the gifted and talented. *Washington, D.C.: U.S. Office of Education, 1972.*

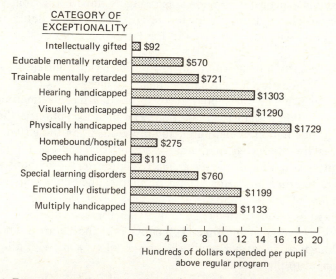

FIGURE 4.6 *Excess expenditures over that for the regular program, by categories of exceptionality, in 27 model school districts in five states with generally superior special education services for children with exceptional learning needs. From S. P. Marland,* Education of the gifted and talented. *Washington, D.C.: U.S. Office of Education, 1972.*

had also expressed concern. The 1972 report was unique in the addition of specific and immediate actions, many of which will enhance opportunities for the gifted and talented nationally during the 1970s and beyond.

PROVISIONS FOR THE GIFTED
IN OTHER COUNTRIES

Meager as provisions in the United States seem at the present, educators in other countries look forward to the development of programs in their countries that can emulate ours.

Individual educators in New Zealand provided leadership in some instances and conducted some excellent studies in the past. While interest has been high among Japanese educators, crowded schools and other problems have limited their efforts. Australia provides minimal opportunity for the gifted per se. In India, certain individuals rose above the clerical level assumed by the former British educational system, but massive improvements have been slow because of economic and political problems. Education in England and France has slowly changed from the selective secondary education pattern for the privileged to more comprehensive programs for the total population. Special educational opportunities for talented children in England are available in art classes, through prizes and subsidies won in competitions and through the royal music and ballet schools. Other countries attempt to provide for the gifted, but largely do so on the basis of competition and evidence of performance (Bereday and Lauwerys, 1961).

Efforts for the gifted in Canada have in many respects paralleled those in the United States. Laycock (1963), who has been one of the leaders in Canadian special education, referred to problems related to identification, terminology, inadequate research data, and inadequately financed research studies. As he pointed out, many types of administrative arrangements have been utilized in various Canadian cities, but careful studies are lacking on the impact of specific curriculum practices. Efforts for the gifted in Canada, as in the United States, have been carried on despite severely limited financial support.

The stages of revolution have had some philosophical impact on programs in Communist countries. China makes no acknowledgment of giftedness, concentrating rather on education that is largely applied and practical in nature for the masses (Richman, 1971). Russia, on the other hand, provides many opportunities for the gifted and talented to develop their skills. Special music schools, ballet schools, theatrical schools, art schools, schools of architecture and design, and centers for young naturalists and young technicians are provided. Special competitions are held, auditions are held, ensembles are organized, and special skills are subsidized and rewarded. In Russia, ability is identified through performance, then nurtured (Bereday and Lauwerys, 1961).

FUTURE DEVELOPMENTS FOR THE GIFTED,
TALENTED, AND CREATIVE

The future for the gifted may be viewed with considerable optimism. Although progress has been marginal, and while some programs have actually diminished or disappeared, there has been steady growth in a number of areas. The gifted do not carry the emotional appeal conveyed to many by the handicapped, but their problems nevertheless are receiving gradually expanding attention. The extension of concern in the United States is marked when one examines progress over the past half-century.

Fifty years ago the very few programs that existed were sponsored chiefly by outstanding educators and psychologists and were centered in relatively large urban centers. Today, while services for the gifted are still meager, the awareness of need does exist, and active efforts are being made to improve provisions for this group. Fifty years ago state efforts were non-existent. Currently 24 states have designated an individual to develop and improve programs, even though in only 10 of the 50 states does this individual devote full time to the gifted. While the majority of gifted children in the United States still receive little or no attention, the public hearings on the needs of the gifted (Marland, 1972) pointed out the neglect and caused school personnel at all levels to be aware of the need to use all available resources at the local, state, and federal levels for this group. Existing leadership should improve opportunities for this particular population more effectively than has been the case in the past. A number of trends can be predicted.

1. *There will be an increasing emphasis on improved programs of screening and identification and on the search for varied talents in all groups.* Emphasis will be placed on early screening and identification and on complete data as a basis for individual planning. The identification of exceptional abilities and talents in all segments of society, regardless of economic, racial, or ethnic factors will be expanded.

2. *Continued research to develop and validate instruments for the identification of added human abilities will go on.* Efforts will be made to develop instruments that identify capacities relevant to originality and to make these instruments efficient for use with groups of children in the schools.

3. *The writings of the 1960s, which often stressed programs for the gifted and/or creative separately, will change from stress on programs to concern for those conditions of learning that foster full potential.* As Lucito (1963) noted so well, the single fact that the gifted have both qualitatively different modes of intellectual functioning and different adult role expectations should justify differentiated educational procedures for them. Awareness of the intensely advanced, complex, and diverse needs of the gifted will be reflected increasingly in the writings dealing with their education. Programs will be seen chiefly as a point of departure for arrangements.

4. *Extended efforts will be made to develop appropriate education for the gifted.* The programs for the gifted in the 1960s were highly diverse and imaginative in many instances. We can look to increasingly differentiated arrangements for this population as school personnel seek to adapt to their true educational needs. Pace-setting developments in education should occur as educators move to use the broad community, including industry, tech-

nology, the arts, learning centers, research facilities, and specialist personnel as resources for the gifted, without limitations on either subject matter or materials. Arrangements for learning will be made in multiple settings rather than in just the school, and opportunities for learning will be enhanced by student mobility, extended use of communication media, and contacts with any needed human and material resources.

5. *Increasingly, it will be recognized that teaching the gifted requires special preparations, as does the teaching of any child with unique learning needs.* Teachers who work with the gifted in various types of groups will be expected to prepare for the assignment. The special preparation of teachers will necessitate the selection of those who possess the requisite intellectual and psychological attributes to understand and work with the gifted successfully and will center particularly on the proper role and relation of the educator to the pupil. Preparation of special resource personnel other than certified teachers will also be carried on through intensive institutes and special study groups.

6. *The concern for the gifted will increase (as Dunn hopefully states in Chapter 1), but not on the basis of social need as in the past.* Much of the added attention will come through the increasing militance of parent groups. Parent associations are growing rapidly, and their members are determined that provisions for gifted and talented children will be extended and improved.

7. *Longitudinal studies of the impact of full educational opportunity for the gifted, talented, and creative, particularly with respect to populations that have suffered neglect in the past, will increase understanding of the relations among factors that enhance or hinder growth.* Emphasis will expand to include psychological and social elements that affect the total cognitive functioning of individuals in all segments of society.

SUMMARY

Children with superior cognitive abilities are defined in this chapter as those who possess capacities for contributions of outstanding merit across the total spectrum of human achievement. That population is recognized as a small segment who require specialized provisions either in or outside of the school setting if they are to be educated adequately. Differentiation into categories of giftedness is not made, in recognition of the fact that the gifted do not fit neatly into discrete isolated segments of excellence. The likelihood instead is that, with sufficiently discriminating means for identification and pupil study, basic data on a complex array of unusual strengths and talents will emerge. Since understanding of the potential for achievement in the child is essential to intelligent planning of his education, a fairly lengthy treatment is included of problems that have impeded identification of the gifted in the past, the current status of identification, and elements beyond tests that are useful to educators in understanding the pupil.

Data from various studies, both past and current, are presented to portray the psychological and educational differences in the gifted that are of importance in planning. They are shown to be a population differing to a marked degree from their age peers, so that often traditional education is completely irrelevant for them. Problems that particularly confront the young gifted child at the point of school entry are emphasized, and the pressures for adaptation to the norm that have been the lot of the gifted at various levels of education are described. Special problems that stem from the role expectations of society, from minority status, from unusual interests, and from sheer psychological and academic advancement are discussed.

Although the concern for the gifted in the past has not been great, school personnel increasingly understand that the gifted have adapted to limited opportunities successfully and have been perceived as successful while they actually were failing to exercise their capacities to any appreciable extent. The emphasis on provisions for the gifted is gradually changing from various types of programs such as special groups or acceleration (which often offer limited curricular change) to higher flexible planning for individuals. Programs per se are seen as convenient administrative arrangements, within which teachers and pupils may be more appropriately matched than is the case with completely heterogeneous arrangements; they also are understood as basic structures within which curricular individualization must occur. Thus, while the chapter reviews the evidence on several common approaches to educating the gifted, space is also given to those elements of educational planning that are important to the gifted in *all types* of educational settings.

Progress in educating the gifted has been far less than spectacular during the past half-century. A good deal more is known about the problems of children with superior cognitive abilities than is being done to alleviate them. The educator who is sensitive to the problems and frustrations of the gifted is still the exception. Improvements and changes are occurring steadily, nevertheless, and growing numbers of educators and laymen are aware of the rights of the gifted and the contributions they make to humanity. A continued expansion of efforts made for them can produce untold benefits to both the individual and his society.

Resources

The American Association for Gifted Children (AAGC), 15 Gramercy Park, New York, New York 10003. Activities include publication of books and articles.

The Association for the Gifted (TAG), Jefferson Plaza, 1411 South Jefferson Davis Highway, Arlington, Virginia 22202. A division of the Council for Exceptional Children. Sponsors national and regional conventions, issues periodic publications.

The Information Center on Exceptional Children, Council for Exceptional Children, Jefferson Plaza, 1411 South Jefferson Davis Highway, Arlington, Virginia 22202. This center provides bibliographies of research on the gifted without charge.

The Council of State Directors of Programs for Gifted Children. State Department of Education, 721 Capitol Mall, Sacramento, California 95814. This association can provide information on state programs and resource materials.

National Association for Gifted Children, 8080 Spring Valley Drive, Cincinnati, Ohio 45236. Sponsors national convention and publishes the *Gifted Child Quarterly.*

Office of Gifted and Talented Education, U.S. Office of Education, Room 2100, ROB-3, 7th and D Streets, S.W., Washington, D.C. 20202. Clearing house for information on programs. Sponsors studies and projects and assists in research planning.

Publications are available at cost from various state departments of education and local school systems. Information regarding publications can be obtained from the systems directly or from the state department of education. Finally, another useful source is the *Journal of Creative Behavior,* published by the Creative Education Foundation, Buffalo, N.Y.

References

Anastasi, A. Correlates of creativity in children from two socioeconomic levels. Final report, Project no. 1-7-062868, U.S. Office of Education, 1970.

Arends, R., and Ford, P. M. *Acceleration and enrichment in the junior high school: A follow-up study.* Springfield, Ill.: Illinois State Department of Public Instruction, 1964.

Ausubel, D. P. The influence of experience on the development of intelligence. In M. J. Aschner and C. Bish (Eds.) *Productive thinking in education.* Washington, D.C.: National Education Association, 1965.

Bachtold, L. M. Interpersonal values of gifted junior high school students. *Psychology in the Schools,* 1968, **5**, 368–370.

Bachtold, L. M., and Werner, E. D. Evaluation of teaching creative students in grades 5 and 6. *Journal of Educational Research,* 1970, **63**, 253–256. (a)

Bachtold, L. M., and Werner, E. D. Personality profiles of gifted women: Psychologists. *American Psychologist,* 1970, **25**, 234–243. (b)

Barbe, W. B. A follow-up study of the graduates of special classes for gifted children. Unpublished doctoral dissertation, Northwestern University, 1953.

Barbe, W. B. *Psychology and education of the gifted: Selected readings.* New York: Appleton-Century-Crofts, 1965.

Barbe, W. B., and Horn, R. A. One in a thousand: A comparative study of moderately and highly gifted elementary school children. Columbus, O.: State Department of Education, 1964.

Barron, F. The measurement of creativity. In *Handbook of measurement and assessment in the behavioral sciences.* Reading, Mass.: Addison-Wesley, 1968, pp. 348–366.

Bayley, N. Development of mental abilities. In P. H. Mussen (Ed.), *Manual of child psychology* (3d ed.) New York: Wiley, 1970, pp. 1163–1209.

Bent, L. G., et al. Grouping of the gifted: An experimental approach. Peoria, Ill.: Bradley University, 1969.

Bereday, G. Z. F., and Lauwerys, J. A. (Eds.) Concepts of excellence in education. *The Yearbook of Education.* New York: Harcourt Brace Jovanovich, 1961.

Birch, J. W. Early school admission for mentally advanced children. *Exceptional Children,* 1954, **21**, 84–87.

Bloom, B. S. (Ed.) *Taxonomy of educational objectives.* New York: McKay, 1956.

Blumenfeld, W. S. Research report on selecting talented Negro students:

Nominations vs. test performance. Evanston, Ill.: National Merit Scholarship Corporation, 1969, **5**, 1–13.

Bonsall, M., and Stellfre, B. The temperament of gifted children. *California Journal of Educational Research,* 1955, **6**, 195–199.

Borg, W. R. An evaluation of ability grouping. Cooperative Research Project No. 577, U.S. Office of Education, 1964.

Braga, J. L. Early admission: Opinion versus evidence. *Elementary School Journal,* 1972, **72** (1), 35–46.

Burke, B., Jensen, D., and Terman, L. M. The promise of youth. *Genetic studies of genius.* Vol. 3. Stanford, Calif.: Stanford University Press, 1930.

Buros, O. K. (Ed.) *The seventh mental measurements yearbook.* Highland Park, N.J.: The Gryphon Press, 1972.

Conant, J. B. *The American high school today.* New York: McGraw-Hill, 1959.

Cox, C. M., Gillan, L. O., Livesey, R. H. and Terman, L. M. The early mental traits of 300 geniuses. *Genetic studies of genius.* Vol. 2. Stanford, Calif.: Stanford University Press, 1926.

Crockenberg, S. B. Creativity tests: A boon or boondoggle for education. *Review of Educational Research,* 1972, **42** (1), 27–45.

Cutts, N., and Moseley, N. *Teaching the bright and gifted.* Englewood Cliffs, N.J.: Prentice-Hall, 1957.

DeHaan, R., and Havighurst, R. *Educating gifted children.* Chicago: University of Chicago Press, 1957.

D'Heurle, A., and Haggard, E. A. Personality, intellectual and achievement patterns in gifted children. *Psychological Monographs,* **73** (13), 1959.

deMille, R., and Merrifield, P. R. Review of J. W. Getzels and P. W. Jackson, Creativity and intelligence. *Educational and Psychological Measurement,* 1962, **22**, 803–808.

Dominion Bureau of Statistics, Education Division. *Statistics of special education for exceptional children 1966.* Ottawa: Queen's Printer, 1967.

Drews, E. The four faces of adolescents. *Saturday Review,* 1963, **46**, 68–71.

Flanagan, J. C., and Cooley, W. W. *Project talent one-year follow-up studies.* Pittsburgh, Pa.: University of Pittsburgh, 1966.

Fund for the Advancement of Education. *They went to college early.* New York: The Fund, 1957.

Gallagher, J. J. *Research summary on gifted child education.* Springfield, Ill.: State Department of Public Instruction, 1966.

Gallagher, J. J. Gifted children. *Encyclopedia of educational research.* New York: Macmillan, 1969, pp. 537–544.

Getzels, J. W., and Jackson, P. W. *Creativity and intelligence.* New York: Wiley, 1962.

Gilbert, V. S., and Jones, R. Stereotypes of the gifted. Unpublished study, University of California, Riverside, 1972.

Ginzberg, E. *The Negro potential.* New York: Columbia University Press, 1956.

Goldberg, M. L., Passow, H., and Justman, J. *The effects of ability grouping.* New York: Teachers College Press, Columbia University, 1966.

Gotkin, L. G., and Massa, N. *Programmed instruction and the academically gifted.* New York: Columbia University Institute for Educational Technology, 1963.

Green, D. A study of talented high school drop-outs. In J. L. French (Ed.), *Educating the gifted: A book of readings.* (Rev. ed.) New York: Holt, Rinehart and Winston, 1964.

Grost, A. *Genius in residence.* Englewood Cliffs, N.J.: Prentice-Hall, 1970.

Guilford, J. P. Intelligence: 1965 model. *American Psychologist,* 1966, **21**, 20–26.

Guilford, J. P. *The nature of human intelligence.* New York: McGraw-Hill, 1967.

Helson, R. M. Creativity, sex, and mathematics. In *Proceedings of conference on the creative person.* Berkeley, Calif.: University of California Institute of Personality Assessment and Research, 1961. Ch. iv, 1–12.

Hennes, J. D. The Illinois television project for the gifted: A combined experiment and demonstration project to test and demonstrate televised enrichment units for students at upper elementary levels. Springfield, Ill.: Illinois State Department of Public Instruction, 1965.

Hermanson, D. *Evaluation of achievement of highly gifted students.* San Diego, Calif.: San Diego Unified School District, 1970. (mimeographed)

Hermanson, D., and Wright, D. Perceptual change of student and staff toward learning by participation in a seminar program for the gifted learner. Unpublished doctoral dissertation, San Diego, Calif.: International University, 1969.

Hildreth, G. Characteristics of young gifted children. *Journal of Genetic Psychology,* 1938, **53,** 287–311.

Hobson, J. R. Scholastic standing and activity participation of under age high school pupils originally admitted to kindergarten on the basis of physical and psychological examinations. Presidential address, APA Division 16, September 1956. (mimeographed)

Hollingworth, L. S. *Gifted children: Their nature and nurture.* New York: Macmillan, 1926.

Hollingworth, L. S. An enrichment curriculum for rapid learners at public school 500 (Speyer School). *Teachers College Record,* 1938, **39,** 296–306.

Hollingworth, L. S. *Children above 180 IQ.* New York: Harcourt Brace Jovanovich, 1942.

Jacobs, C. Formal recognition of mentally superior children: Its effect on achievement and achievement motivation. Unpublished doctoral dissertation, Stanford University, 1959.

Jenkins, M. D. The upper limit of ability among American Negroes. In J. L. French (Ed.), *Educating the gifted: A book of readings.* (Rev. ed.) New York: Holt, Rinehart and Winston, 1964.

Justman, J. Academic achievement of intellectually gifted accelerants and non-accelerants in junior high school. *School Review,* 1954, **62,** 143–150.

Kaltsounis, B., and Stephens, H. G. Learning mathematics by discovery: Implications for a creative child. *Perceptual and Motor Skills,* 1971, **33** (3), 884–886.

Kaltsounis, B. Instruments useful in studying creative behavior and creative ability. *Journal of Creative Behavior,* 1972, **5** (2), 117–125.

Klein, J., and Breneman, E. R. *Longitudinal study of children in Somerset County who were permitted to enter school early under Act 312 of 1949 Pennsylvania General Assembly,* Somerset County, Pa.: Special Education Department, 1965.

Laycock, S. R. *Special education in Canada.* Toronto: W. J. Cage, Ltd., 1963.

Laycock, F., and Caylor, J. S. Physiques of gifted children and their less gifted siblings. *Child Development,* 1964, **35,** 63–74.

Lehman, H. C. *Age and achievement.* Princeton, N.J.: Princeton University Press, 1953.

Lucito, L. J. Gifted children. In L. M. Dunn (Ed.), *Exceptional children in the schools.* New York: Holt, Rinehart and Winston, 1963.

Mackie, R. P. *Special education in the United States: Statistics, 1948–66.* New York: Teachers College Press, Columbia University, 1969.

Mann, H. How real are friendships of gifted and typical children in a program of partial segregation? *Exceptional Children,* 1957, **23,** 199–201, 242.

Marland, S. P. (Submitter) *Education of the gifted and talented.* Washington, D.C.: U.S. Office of Education, 1972.

Martinson, R. A. *Educational programs for gifted pupils.* Sacramento: California Department of Education, 1961.

Martinson, R. A., and Seagoe, M. V. The abilities of young children. *CEC Research Monograph B4.* Arlington, Va.: Council for Exceptional Children, 1967.

Martyn, K. A. The social acceptance of gifted students. Unpublished doctoral dissertation, Stanford University, 1957.

McFee, J. K. *Creative problem solving abilities in art of academically superior adolescents.* Washington, D.C.: National Art Education Association, 1968.

Miles, C. C. Gifted children. In L. Carmichael (Ed.), *Manual of child psychology.* New York: Wiley, 1954.

New York Department of Education. Research report on the Saturday seminars at the State University College of Education. Oneonta, N.Y.: New York State University, 1961.

Nichols, R. C., and Davis, J. A. Characteristics of students of high academic aptitude. *Personnel and Guidance Journal,* 1964, **42**, 794–800.

O'Shea, H. E. Friendship and the intellectually gifted child. *Exceptional Children,* 1960, **26**, 327–335.

Passow, A. H. Enrichment of education for the gifted. In N. B. Henry (Ed.), *Education for the gifted. National Society for the Study of Education,* 57th Yearbook, Part III, 1958, 193–221.

Pegnato, C. W., and Birch, J. W. Locating gifted children in junior high schools: A comparison of methods. *Exceptional Children,* 1959, **25**, 300–304.

Plaut, R. *Searching and salvaging talent among socially disadvantaged populations.* New York: National Scholarship Service Fund for Negro Students, 1963.

Pressey, S. L. *Educational acceleration: Appraisals and basic problems.* Columbus, O.: Ohio State University Press, 1949.

Pressey, S. L. Concerning the nature and nurture of genius. *Scientific Monthly,* 1955, **81**, 123–129

Pressey, S. L. Fordling accelerates: Ten years after. *Journal of Counseling Psychology,* 1967, **14** (1), 73–80.

Pressey, S. L., and Pressey, A. Genius at 80; and other oldsters. *The Gerontologist,* 1967, **7** (3), 183–187.

Richman, B. Inside Red China. *The Center Magazine,* 1971, **4**, 29–38.

Roe, A. *The making of a scientist.* New York: Dodd, Mead, 1953.

Roeper, A. Some observations about gifted preschool children. *Journal of Nursery Education,* 1963, **18**, 177–180.

Shannon, D. C. What research says about acceleration. *Phi Delta Kappan,* 1957, **39**, 70–73.

Shaw, M. C., and Alves, G. J. The self-concept of bright academic underachievers. *Personnel and Guidance Journal,* 1963, **42**, 401–403.

Skipper, C. E. A longitudinal study of creative abilities in adolescents. Paper presented at American Educational Research Association, April 1972.

Stedman, L. *Education of gifted children.* New York: Harcourt Brace Jovanovich, 1924.

Steele, J. M., et al. Instructional climate in Illinois gifted classes. Urbana, Ill.: University of Illinois Center for Instructional Research and Curriculum Evaluation, 1970.

Tannenbaum, A. Adolescents' attitudes toward academic brilliance. Unpublished doctoral dissertation, Teachers College, Columbia University, 1960.

Taylor, C. W. (Ed.) *Creativity: Progress and potential.* New York: McGraw-Hill, 1964.

Terman, L. M., Baldwin, B. T., and Bronson, E. Mental and physical traits of a thousand gifted children. *Genetic Studies of Genius.* Vol. 1. Stanford, Calif.: Stanford University Press, 1925.

Terman, L. M., and Oden, M. H. The gifted child grows up. *Genetic Studies of Genius.* Vol. 4. Stanford, Calif.: Stanford University Press, 1947.

Terman, L. M., and Oden, M. H. The gifted group at mid-life. *Genetic Studies of Genius.* Vol. 5. Stanford, Calif.: Stanford University Press, 1959.

Terman, L. M., and Merrill, M. *Stanford-Binet intelligence scale.* (3d ed.) Boston: Houghton Mifflin, 1960.

Thorndike, R. L. The measurement of creativity. *Teachers College Record,* 1963, **64**, 422–424.

Torrance, E. P. *Guiding creative talent.* Englewood Cliffs, N.J.: Prentice-Hall, 1962.

Torrance, E. P. *A three-year study of a creative-aesthetic approach to school readiness and beginning reading and arithmetic on creative development.* Athens, Ga.: University of Georgia Research and Development Center, 1969.

Torrance, E. P. Career patterns and peak creative achievements of creative high school students twelve years later. *The Gifted Child Quarterly,* 1972, **16**, (2), 75–88.

Vernon, P. E. *Intelligence and cultural environment.* London: Methuen, 1969.

Wallach, M. A. Creativity. In P. H. Mussen (Ed.), *Manual of child psychology.* (3d ed.) New York: Wiley, 1970.

Walton, G. Identification of the intellectually gifted children in the public school kindergarten. Unpublished doctoral dissertation, University of California, Los Angeles, 1961.

Warren, T. F. Creative thinking techniques: Four methods of stimulating original ideas in sixth grade students. Final report, Project no. TR-169; Bureau no. BR 5-0216, U.S. Office of Education, 1971.

Witty, P. A. A genetic study of 50 gifted children. In N. B. Henry (Ed.), *Intelligence: Its nature and nurture. 39th Yearbook, National Society for the Study of Education,* Part I. Chicago, Ill.: University of Chicago Press, 1940.

Witty, P. A., and Jenkins, M. D. Inter-race testing and Negro intelligence. *Journal of Psychology,* 1936, **1**, 179–192.

Witty, P. A., and Lehman, H. C. Nervous instability and genius: Some conflicting opinions. *Journal of Abnormal Social Psychology,* 1930, **23**, 486–497.

Witty, P. A., and Theman, V. A follow-up study of the educational attainment of gifted Negroes. *Journal of Educational Psychology,* 1943, **34**, 35–47.

Worcester, W. *The education of children of above-average mentality.* Lincoln, Neb.: University of Nebraska Press, 1956.

Zorbaugh, H., Boardman, R. K., and Sheldon, P. Some observations of highly gifted children. In P. Witty (Ed.), *The gifted child.* New York: American Association for Gifted Children, 1951.

Opposite: Art can be an effective medium to reach behaviorally disordered children. It can be used to teach specific skills and to foster improved interpersonal relationships. (Photographer, Gary Pedersen.)

children with
behavioral disabilities

chapter outline

DEFINITION AND CLASSIFICATION
  Definitions
  Classifications
PREDICTIVE AND IDENTIFICATION PROCESSES
  Prediction
  Initial Screening and Identification
  Diagnosis
PREVALENCE ESTIMATES
  Behavioral-Disability Figures
  Juvenile Delinquency Figures
ETIOLOGICAL FACTORS
  Causes of Behavioral Disabilities
    Biological Factors
    Psychological and Environmental Factors
  Causes of Juvenile Delinquency
  Drugs and Maladaptive Behavior
ACADEMIC AND SOCIAL MANIFESTATIONS
EXTENT AND NATURE OF SPECIAL EDUCATION PROGRAMS
PROGRAM EVALUATION
FOLLOW-UP STUDIES
TEACHER PREPARATION AND SELECTION
CURRICULAR AND INSTRUCTIONAL APPROACHES
  The Psychodynamic Approach
  The Behavioral-Deficit Approach
  The Behavior-Modification Approach
  The Ecological Approach
A VOCATIONAL APPROACH TO DELINQUENT YOUTH
MOTIVATION AND PUNISHMENT
EMERGING TRENDS
  Legal Decisions and Civil Rights
  Legislation, Financing, and Decentralization
  High School Graduation Requirements
  Child-Advocacy Programs
  Technology, Innovation, and Accountability

Deviancies in behavior do not exist in and of themselves. They are largely social phenomena which must be viewed in that context. The problems of educating a child perceived as having behavioral disabilities can be as concrete as struggling to hold and restrain an angry adolescent intent on hurting a fellow student or a teacher, or as abstract as asking if mental illness really exists. Whether the result of grappling with abstract questions or concrete pupils, the kinds of answers developed largely determine the definition of behavioral disabilities and, ultimately, how such disabilities will be handled.

Presented in this chapter is an examination of different approaches to defining, classifying, and identifying children considered behaviorally disordered as well as a discussion of the prevalence of such perceptions. Salient characteristics of the target population and the active processes which result in the labeling actions will be described, as well as causes of deviancy (including a brief section on drug abuse). Methods of educational treatment are discussed in the second part of the chapter. The approach taken is primarily behavioral and proceeds from the bias that deviancy is more a function of societal expectations than of intrapsychic phenomena.

DEFINITION AND CLASSIFICATION

Definitions

This chapter deals with children whom educators have classified *traditionally* as "emotionally disturbed" and "socially maladjusted." The term "emotionally disturbed" has been borrowed primarily from psychiatry and clinical psychology and is seen as including both children who are seriously "withdrawn" and those who are "acting out." Other terminology for extreme forms of this condition have been "mental illness," "psychosis," "childhood schizophrenia," and "autism." These labels have been applied to children and youth of all ages. The term "socially maladjusted" is a less noxious synonym for "juvenile delinquent." Its usage is usually restricted to adolescents or preadolescents who break the law and thus has a legal derivation.

The emerging pattern in special education is to abandon these two terms which were assumed from other professions in favor of the inclusive category "behavioral disability." Among the reasons for this terminology shift was the growing recognition that it is possible for some youngsters to fit into either category. For example, what different interpretations might be given to the truant behavior of a physically well pupil who has been absent from school for 50 days out of a 75-day term? If the school favors a mental health approach and refers the child for a psychiatric examination, he might be classified as "emotionally disturbed." In another school a truant officer might refer the offending pupil to the courts, where he could be treated as a "juvenile delinquent." Members of the clergy might view the behavior as "amoral" and insist that the child be given moral lessons. Sociologists might see it as congruent with the norms of a "subculture at variance with the larger culture." Members of a counterculture might admire the behavior, considering it legitimate opposition to oppressive school-attendance laws. Since all of these designations might be made for one kind of behavior on the part of one pupil, it becomes clear that *what is viewed as deviant behavior and how it is designated, interpreted, and treated are as much a function of the perceiver as they are of the behaver.*

In the sixties, Rhodes (1967) was among the first to explicate this ecological approach for defining maladaptive behavior. He observed that such behavior lies, in substantial measure, in the sanctions and behavioral prohibitions of the culture. He pointed out that there is an agitated exchange which creates a disturbance in the environment when the culture bearer and the culture violator meet. Thus Rhodes saw maladaptive behavior as a reciprocal condition in which both the "exciter" and the "responder" bear relation to the problem. Further, he considered the "dis-ease" as much a condition in the responder as in the elicitor.

This modern conceptualization by behavioral scientists is not new. In a classic cross-cultural study, Benedict (1934) noted that certain types of people considered "sick" and "abnormal" in the United States fitted readily into other cultures. She examined many types of "abnormality," ranging from extreme instability to sadism and delusions of grandeur. If a specific behavior is neither good nor bad, neither healthy nor pathological, but rather adaptive or maladaptive for a given culture, then such terms as "maladaptive," "nonnormative," and "socially deviant" become equivalents. Use of this conceptualization demands examination of (1) the specific behaver and his behavior, (2) the viewpoint of the perceiver, and (3) the effect of the behavior on the perceiver.

In keeping with the trend in special education, for purposes of this chapter, both the categories emotionally disturbed and socially maladjusted are subsumed under the broader category "behavioral disabilities" or "behavioral disorders." Important distinctions can be made between selected children falling into these groupings. Not all, but a considerable number of children who are labeled emotionally disturbed by mental health personnel would be considered socially maladjusted by those associated with the law, and vice versa.

The following definition of behavioral disabilities to be used in this chapter is an adaption of an earlier one by Graubard and Miller (1968).

> *Behavioral disabilities are defined as a variety of excessive, chronic, deviant behaviors ranging from impulsive and aggressive to depressive and withdrawal acts (1) which violate the perceiver's expectations of appropriateness, and (2) which the perceiver wishes to see stopped.*

It will be seen that this definition arises from an ecological bias. In the case of the schools, the perceivers are the educators, the teachers and principals who want the behavior of the pupil changed or his removal from general education into special education. Although there are varying degrees of behavioral deviation, the key to eventual classification and to the provision of special education services is a combination of the severity, offensiveness, and chronicity of the child's acts.

The terms "socially maladjusted" and "juvenile delinquent" continue to be used as synonyms in this chapter. Most such children are adept in social intercourse on the streets and many join with other youths in their opposition to authority. While some people designate their behavior as socially maladjusted and others prefer the label juvenile delinquent, the behavior on the part of the child is usually the same.

Varying expectations also complicate the problem of definitions. Thus the label emotional disturbance is usually applied when children engage in actions that are not easily understood. For example, if a poor child from the inner city stole a car, most people could comprehend his action and would term him a juvenile delinquent or socially maladjusted. However, if a middle class youngster, whose parents would buy him a car, proceeded to steal one, people could not so easily understand his behavior, and he would more likely be labeled emotionally disturbed. The distinction between emotional disturbance, and social maladjustment or delinquency can also be made quantitatively. Delinquent acts are really quite commonplace, and therefore no one is really surprised when such acts are committed. The label emotionally disturbed is more frequently used for children who engage in actions that are less common and more surprising.

There are several important exceptions to the interchangeability of the labels emotionally disturbed and juvenile delinquent. The courts will seldom adjudicate a youngster as delinquent unless he has been involved in a serious crime which hurts other people, such as rape or mugging, or unless the child is an offender who has come before the authorities several times. The behavior necessary for a child to be labeled a juvenile delinquent must usually be in violation of the law. However, many laws apply only to children, such as compulsory school attendance, and a child who absents himself from school could be adjudged as delinquent.

Classifications

Those attempting to deal with behavioral disabilities often try to classify people perceived as deviant into different categories. Classification is probably a natural human endeavor; certainly it is an important scientific endeavor that can lead to increased understanding of natural phenomena. Classification of deviants is often done without their knowledge or consent, and the classification label can profoundly and often deleteriously affect their lives. During the Inquisition heretics were defined and classified by Inquisitors. Currently clinicians and special educators classify others so their behavior may be more readily changed, even if those who are to be changed do not feel that they require change.

Those educators with a behavior-modification bent prefer to disregard classification schemes entirely. They look solely at the behavior of the individual and take frequency counts of specific behaviors without typing the individual. Those with an ecological orientation observe both the child *and* the teacher in order to isolate faulty interactions, rather than attempt to classify the child. In both cases these educators are intent on dealing with individual children.

Reality dictates that educators recognize the need for at least some group instruction in the schools. Three choices would appear open. One would be for children with a variety of behavioral disorders to be retained in the educational mainstream in all but the most extreme cases, based on the belief that the maladaptive would learn acceptable behaviors from their normally acting peers in such a heterogeneous setting. Another would be for children with a variety of behavioral disorders and a common label to be grouped together in a special education program, a rather frequent traditional practice, the primary logic for which would appear to be relief for the other pupils. The third choice would be to group together pupils with a similar maladaptive pattern of behavior. Here the approach would be to give intensive corrective instruction to change the common behaviors in question. Clearly what is needed is a classification scheme that is pedagogically relevant. As yet, research is not available to indicate which of the above-mentioned electives create the greatest pupil progress. It would be evidence for the third choice that could create the greatest justification for a classification system for subgrouping children and youth with behavioral disabilities. We are a long way from having such a system to report or advocate. Instead, only historical developments in the field can be provided.

Classification schemes for children perceived as having behavioral disabilities have been heavily influenced by a traditional application of the medical model, which looks at and attempts to sort individual "pathology." In education, however, there are several reasons for questioning the use of the medical model of emotional or behavioral disturbance: (1) it has been of dubious value in aiding educators to boost achievement and change pupil behavior; (2) illness models tend to lead toward over-diagnoses; (3) such models work with a person's weaknesses rather than strengths (Scheff, 1966); and (4) diagnostic labels tend to overshadow the whole person, obscuring needs—thus, while a *specific behavior or syndrome* leads to the act of labeling, in practice the total person is invariably labeled and responded to socially in terms of his label (Ullmann and Krasner, 1969).

Aided in their development by computer processing, factor-analytic approaches to classification schemes have more successfully avoided the criticism of low reliability characterizing psychiatric classification. Using repeated factor analyses of a multitude of behavioral and psychological traits, for example, Quay (1969) developed a classification system which shows some promise for educational practice. He drew a parallel between the lack of educational relevance in classifying groups of mentally retarded children and the newer field of behavioral disorders. He thought that the absence of a clear-cut and useful classification scheme on which prescribed instructional techniques and tactics could be specifically based might underlie the absence of significant effects in comparing special classes for the retarded with regular classes, and that, by analogy, programs for the behaviorally disordered will also fail to show demonstrated effects in the absence of clear-cut classification. The special education programs might be more effective for certain *types* of pupils, but this would be obscured by treating the handicapped children as one group. The four Quay dimensions (with only their salient characteristics included here), are:

1. *Conduct Disorder.* Behavior including attention-seeking, boisterousness, rudeness, hyperactivity, and physical and verbal aggression.

2. *Anxious-Withdrawn.* Principal components are hypersensitivity, feelings of inferiority, lack of self-confidence, fear, and anxiousness. This dimension reflects the characteristics of a child who underbehaves rather than misbehaves.

3. *Inadequate-Immature.* While not showing up in as many studies as the previous two dimensions and accounting for a lesser percentage of variance, according to Quay, this dimension appears frequently enough to suggest that it is not an artifact and warrants continued investigation. Children falling within this dimension show lack of interest, sluggishness, daydreaming, reticence; they make noise with objects, play with toys in class, mark furniture, and fail to complete work. When found in older children this behavior probably represents delayed behavioral maturity.

4. *Socialized Delinquent.* The socialized or subcultural delinquent child displays behavior such as group delinquent acts, gang activities, loyalty to a delinquent peer group, truancy, and failure to abide by middle class school ethics. Such children are capable of loyalty and of subscribing to ethical codes. They are more frequently located in urban areas, particularly in deteriorating portions of the city.

Two other dimensions might be included in such a classification scheme: (1) autistic, childhood schizophrenic, or otherwise psychotic and (2) adjudicated juvenile delinquent. However, public day schools are usually not called upon to serve these latter two groups.

Quay (1969) has suggested that differential educational programing can be developed for his four-way classification system, but one of the difficulties with this approach is that children are seldom "pure" conduct disorders or socialized delinquents. Often they are representative of a mixture of all kinds of traits. Furthermore, the efficacy of different special education programs for each of these four groups has yet to be demonstrated empirically. Nevertheless, Quay's system does permit the reliable classification of children with behavioral disabilities, and if research can demonstrate the efficacy of different programing for different groupings, instruction will be placed on a more scientific basis than is presently the case.

Most ecological psychologists believe that it is not yet possible to promulgate classification systems, since, by definition, such activity limits the field of study and does not take into account the ecosystem with its myriad interactions. Perhaps even more strongly opposed to such schemes are many advocates of reinforcement theory—both psychologists and special educators—who believe that since every child is unique, grouping is neither necessary nor desirable. Lindsley (personal communication, 1970) called for use of the term "uniques" to eliminate the problems of people trying to group other people, or using averages. Many reinforcement practitioners will record data only on individuals, believing that group norms are misleading. Nevertheless, educators must group children for instructional purposes in the public schools as they are now constituted. It is inconceivable for the foreseeable future that groupings will be disbanded.

PREDICTIVE AND IDENTIFICATION PROCESSES

The distinction between prediction and identification is important to special education programing. Prediction is used primarily for actuarial purposes and gives general guidelines for program planning and evaluation. Identification is usually used for administrative reasons and implies a specific intervention program.

Prediction

Substantial objections have been voiced about making diagnostic predictions in the earlier grades, particularly with reference to delinquency. These concerns are partly based on the invasion of privacy engendered when extensive dossiers on children are kept. Such files, necessary for conducting and validating research projects, are seen as a violation of civil liberties. In addition, the possibility of exposing children to self-fulfilling prophecy is feared. The compilation of information on research subjects, testing, and the confidentiality of the information obtained is an extremely thorny issue.

A number of standardized prediction instruments have been developed in the field of delinquency, the Glueck Prediction Scale (Glueck and Glueck, 1950) being the most effective and widely known. (Details about such scales can be found in Kvaraceus [1966]; Kvaraceus [1953] has also established his own prediction scale of delinquency.) The Glueck Prediction Scale (Glueck and Glueck, 1950) uses family interviewing to measure family cohesiveness, affection, supervision, and discipline. While the Glueck scale tends to predict too many false positives (that is, too many children are identified as potential delinquents who do not become delinquent), its accuracy is substantial—few children in the sample used became delinquent in the absence of a delinquency prediction.

Kvaraceus (1961) has stated that teachers can predict potential delinquents from observation of student behavior as effectively as standardized prediction instruments, and possibly his statement can be broadened to include a greater range of behavioral problems.

Initial Screening and Identification

Many school systems attempt to use measures that can be administered by teachers for the initial screening. Based on their classroom observations, teachers are often asked to identify children perceived as having behavioral disabilities. Harth and Glavin (1971) report that teacher ratings of "disturbed" behavior correlated significantly with a self-report measure of personality—the California Test of Personality.

While numerous studies have been conducted (Hodges and Tait, 1963; Meyer, Borgatta, Jones, Anderson, Grunwald, and Headly, 1965) showing that early identification and programing did not lead to a reduced prevalence of "behavioral disability" later, the treatment program of Cowen, Zax, Izzo, and Trost (1966)—including remedial help and the use of aides to establish relations with the target children—was begun in the early grades and was successful in reducing "behavioral disabilities" in comparison with a control group that was identified but not treated.

An observation matrix, adapted from Becker, Madsen, Arnold, and Thomas (1967), which can aid the teacher in detailing the specifics of a child's behavior plus the frequency of its occurrence, is shown in Figure 5.1. Using a stopwatch taped to a clipboard holding the observation matrix, periodically throughout the school day observers watch a particular child for 20 seconds and use the next 10 seconds to record classes of behavior exhibited by the child. This observation device, however, examines only pupil behavior. A more sophisticated version of it is an interaction matrix, which notes teacher behavior in reaction to pupil behavior. Such a matrix was developed by Spence (1972), and an example is presented in Figure 5.2. In Spence's matrix tally marks are made by the observer as the specific teacher and pupil behaviors being monitored are emitted. This method has the advantage of identifying difficulties, or at least patterns, in interaction and does not always put the onus on the child. It also makes it easier to devise intervention programs, since more knowledge is available than if the child alone were observed. That is, the teacher will learn whether it seems advisable to shift her own behavior—how and in which direction—and then the data on the individual child can be used to compare the child's behavior with himself, with peers in the same class, or with any other normative data that the teacher wishes to use.

No. of 20–second intervals / Names of pupils	1st	2d	3d	4th	5th	6th	etc.
REIS, R.	SNT	XA	BS	X-AB	X-AB X	SNT	
Etc.							

FIGURE 5.1 A sample observation matrix showing codification of child's behavior over time. Adapted from Becker, Madsen, Arnold, and Thomas (1967). Key: A—disturbing others directly and aggression; B—blurting out, commenting, and vocal noise; AF—fighting; L—looking; N—disruptive noise made by striking objects; S—relevant behavior; T—talking; X—gross motor behaviors; X-AB—walked out of room.

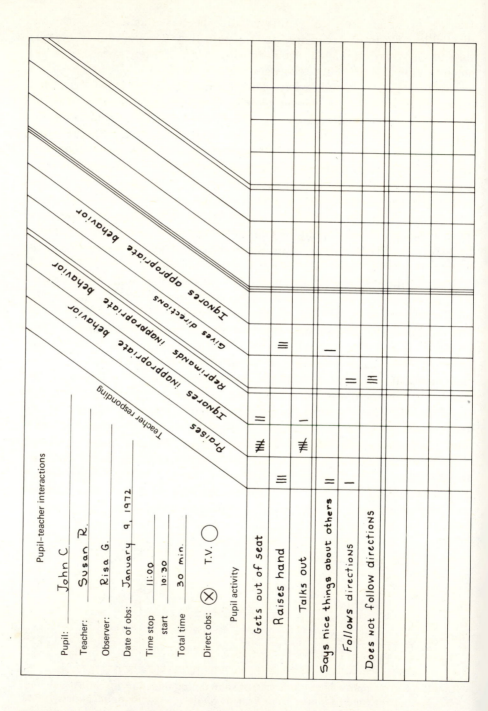

FIGURE 5.2 A sample interaction matrix showing John's behaviors and teacher behaviors during one half hour.   Adapted from Spence (1972).

Diagnosis

Many special education programs still legally require examination and certification by a psychiatrist or psychologist before a child can be placed in a program for children with behavioral disabilities. Behavior that is primarily of educational concern is thus transferred outside the realm of education. Many psychiatric and/or psychological reports merely label the subject and tell the teacher what she already knows: the child is extremely withdrawn or hyperactive. Psychiatric diagnostic interviews should not be confused here with psychiatric treatment; psychiatrists are physicians and only they can prescribe medication which can be helpful in the treatment of certain kinds of behavioral disorders. Both psychologists and psychiatrists use clinical interviews, and most psychologists use psychometric tests as well. These instruments include intelligence tests such as the Wechsler Intelligence Scale for Children and the Stanford-Binet, and instruments purporting to measure language characteristics such as the Illinois Test of Psycholinguistic Abilities. Tests like the Rorschach and the Children's Apperception Test are also used, as well as the House-Tree-Person and Draw-a-Man tests. All these latter four tests are intended to uncover the child's inner dynamics and illuminate personality structure, but the reliability and validity of such measures have yet to be satisfactorily documented. It is difficult to translate these tests results into specific recommendations for practice.

From the point of view of special education, psychiatric and psychological examinations suffer from the same weaknesses and do not substitute for sustained observation of the child and the teacher in the classroom. It is well documented that children function differently in different situations and at different times, and these differences can be modified by the responses, perceptions, skills, and tolerances of different teachers. Placement decisions should therefore be based on a child's classroom behavior rather than on interviews or tests administered outside that specific context. Psychometric and sociometric instruments are thus probably better suited to long-range research projects involving many children than they are to specific intervention programs for individual pupils. Viewing behavioral disabilities as a reciprocal condition between two people and disturbance as a result of specific behaviors manifested by at least one of them leads to the conclusion that those involved are in the best position to state what specific behaviors caused the disturbance. In the classroom the teacher and the child can, ideally, agree upon behaviors that are to be accelerated or decelerated. Then the teacher, the teacher's aide, or the child can take a rate measure of the behavior's occurrence over time. Noted frequencies can then be compared as to the child's behavior before and after an intervention program is put into effect. External opinions and elaborate screening procedures are not necessary to tell teacher or pupil what they already know: that they are having a difficult time together in the classroom or that certain teacher expectations are not being met. Nevertheless, as things still stand, final diagnosis and labeling for special education purposes does not rest exclusively with regular classroom teachers. This is probably just as well if "pupil exclusion" is included as an option, since the temptation would be great to remove the troublesome. General educators, however, are gaining an increased voice in deciding which pupils are to be provided with special education services. This is in keeping with the trend to view educational diagnosis in this area of exceptionality as the primary responsibility of educators and not mental health specialists such as psychiatrists, psychologists, and social workers. As mentioned repeatedly throughout this textbook, final diagnosis needs to rest with the personnel responsible for the intervention. More and more, this will need to be made on the basis of the effectiveness of trial treatments rather than either diagnostic interviews and tests or classroom observations of pupil behavior.

PREVALENCE ESTIMATES

Prevalence figures for behavioral disabilities are extremely difficult to ascertain. Given the differences in terminology and definitions that are used by various agencies, it is not surprising to find estimates · varying widely and sometimes changing abruptly. Such estimates are largely guesswork given the looseness of terms like "emotionally disturbed" and "socially maladjusted."

Behavioral-Disability Figures

Estimates compiled by the U.S. Office of Education are set at 2 percent of school-age children presumably in need of special education (see Table 1.1). This 2 percent figure is not specifically broken down into the kinds of services needed.

According to Schultz, Hirshoren, Manton, and Henderson (1971), prevalence figures for special education purposes vary widely according to states. In a survey they found that 18 states used a prevalence estimate of 2 percent and 7 states one of 3 percent, while 6 states used a prevalence figure of 5 percent. The range reported was from 0.05 percent to 15 percent, while 7 states had no figures available at all. It is plausible to conceptualize the need for different programs for many children, with perhaps 10 percent of school-age children needing only slight modifications of existing school practices, which might vary from additional reading help to more judicious use of aides in the classroom and home and school-based contingency programs. Of the school-age population, 2 percent might need considerably different educational programing than they now receive, for example, special classes, intensive remedial work, guidance services, and work-study programs. Probably less than 1 percent of children need intensive care or occasional residential placement.

Pate (1963) stated that "emotional disturbance" is not *distributed* evenly throughout the population. While "disturbed children can be *found* in all social classes, lower socio-cultural classes *produce* far more than their share" (pp. 244–245). Most teachers and mental health workers come from the middle and upper classes, and most of these professionals, particularly those with advanced training and therefore real power in the school and mental health hierarchies, are also white. The behavior of lower class minority-group children is in many ways foreign to these professionals. In addition there are different expectations of what children should do and differences of opinion concerning which child is a suitable candidate for help. This issue has been systematically examined and discussed in a number of studies. In a classic study Hollingshead and Redlich (1953) describe two cases of almost identical sexual behavior. Psychiatry was called upon in the case of a girl from an upper class family to protect her from the law, while a girl from a lower class family was sentenced to a woman's reformatory. McDermott, Harrison, Schrager, and Wilson (1965) found that children from lower class groups receive the poorest prognosis and are assigned to the least favorable diagnostic categories, while children from middle and upper classes with similar behavior are classified in considerably more benign diagnostic categories. Moreover, children from the lower social classes were not referred for treatment. Casual inspection of institutions and special classes reveal that they are filled with low-achieving male minority-group members, far out of proportion to their number in the general population. The fact that males predominate in school difficulties both in terms of academic and social behaviors has been noted in numerous studies (McCaffrey and Cummings, 1967, 1969; Werry and Quay, 1969).

White and Charry (1966) studied differential treatment for cases referred to school psychologists in Westchester County, New York. They found that psychological treatment was given to upper class groups but not to lower class groups; the schools had to cope as best they could with the latter untreated youngsters. Special class placement, attended by all the problems of labeling, usually results in difficulties of reintegrating children into the mainstream of education. Mackler (1967), in a study of New York City's schools for maladjusted children, found that almost all the children in these classes were black, Puerto Rican, and poor and were represented in these classes far out of proportion to their representation in the population at large.

Juvenile Delinquency Figures

Several federal agencies collect delinquency statistics. The data most frequently used for reporting are the juvenile court statistics. There is an assumption that a fairly constant ratio exists between court and arrest statistics and prevalence of hidden delinquency where violations are not reported. No one, however, has been able to ascertain successfully what this ratio is. What is clear is the steady increase in prevalence of adjudicated delinquency cases, to a point that by 1968 almost 3 percent of youth had been found guilty of delinquent acts (U.S. Juvenile Court Statistics, 1970).

There is little question that arrests and juvenile court appearances are particularly high in deteriorated urban neighborhoods. An educationally significant aspect of the prevalence problem of delinquency is the fact that arrest rates rise sharply from junior high school age to about age 16. Approximately four boys are arrested for each girl, with type of offense differing sharply between the sexes. Boys are more often convicted of crimes involving aggression, such as rape, robbery, and vandalism; girls are more often convicted of sex-related crimes, such as prostitution or being "incorrigible," which is a euphemism for being considered sexually promiscuous (U.S. Juvenile Court Statistics, 1970). In 1970 boys comprised 77 percent of all children in public training schools. In terms of overall figures, 154 out of every 100,000 American children (or 0.15 percent) were confined to institutions, with the average length of commitment 8.4 months. In 1966 there were 170 children out of every 100,000 in institutions (National Center for Social Statistics, 1970). The downward trend probably reflects attempts at alternatives to incarceration rather than any real shift in delinquency.

ETIOLOGICAL FACTORS

Causes of Behavioral Disabilities

Aberrant behavior can be divided into two primary etiological categories: (1) biological factors and (2) psychological and environmental factors. In practice, when examining the development of specific individuals, these distinctions are more difficult to make than they are in theory, since there is an interaction effect among the two factors. Even in terms of resultant characteristics, so much overlap exists between the behaviorally disabled child and his "normal" peer that generalizations are made with great difficulty. That is, to discuss the characteristics of *any* group—whether an ethnic group or a behaviorally disabled group—we end by discussing stereotypes when each person is unique. Any discussion of characteristics of behavioral disability necessarily includes studies where means were calculated, and in almost all cases of such studies standard deviations are high enough to preclude statements such as *all* behaviorally disabled children have shorter attention spans than *all* children who are perceived as "normal." Studies of causes of behavioral disorders are based on similar statistical grounds, and thus our present understanding of the etiology of such disturbances provides many more questions than answers. Presented here are highlights of current etiological studies, referring the reader to the extensive and most relevant review of literature on the topic compiled by Rhodes and Tracy (1971).

Biological Factors

Some behavioral disorders, especially the more severe types, are caused by genetic, constitutional, or organic factors. Rutter (1965) reviewed the research in this area and concluded that psychogenic factors usually constitute only a secondary role in the development of childhood psychosis.

Meehl (1969) concluded that it is sometimes possible to make reliable diagnoses of schizophrenia without ever having seen the patient. If the diagnostician knows that the subject's monozygotic twin is schizophrenic, for example, the chances can be as high as 85 percent that the patient has schizophrenia or will become similarly afflicted (Sagor, 1971). Some "psychoses" can be caused by toxic substances affecting the brain. Lead poisoning is a common example of a toxic substance causing permanent behavioral disability, a phenomenon most common in deteriorated urban areas where babies eat lead-based paint which causes damage to the central nervous system (CNS).

Instances of behavioral disabilities caused by *organic* factors were uncovered by Gittelman and Birch (1967) in a study of relations among IQ, evidence of organicity (including evidence of perinatal CNS damage), and family psychopathology. They discovered that perinatal complications were frequent in a sample of children labeled childhood schizophrenics, and the IQ was inversely related to evidence of CNS dysfunction while directly related to age of onset of clinical symptoms. They concluded that the prevalence of organicity in their sample, along with the failure to find a correlation between degree of family pathology and subject characteristics, supported the view that many cases of "childhood schizophrenia" were of organic etiology. (Their study clearly points out the difficulties of labeling— children in their sample were frequently later rediagnosed as brain injured or mentally retarded rather than childhood schizophrenic.)

Characteristics of physiological disorders often are manifested in classroom behavior and academic results. One generalization in this area can be made: the more grossly aberrant the behavior of the child, the more likely there is to be some evidence of physiological involvement. Abnormal EEG patterns have been noted by many researchers in the field of childhood behavior disorders (Stevens, Sachder, and Milstein, 1968). In a review of the literature on hyperkinesis, Marwit and Stenner (1972) suggested that at least one type of hyperkinetic child showed evidence of neurological difficulties.

Psychological and Environmental Factors

Psychological disturbances are caused by interactions between a child and significant others in his life. In a well-designed study Jenkins (1966) attempted to determine the relation between family background factors presumed to be causal in the evolution of psychiatric symptom clusters. Five clusters were differentiated: (1) shy seclusive; (2) overanxious neurotic; (3) hyperactive distractible; (4) undomesticated; and (5) socialized delinquent. These clusters were then correlated with family background factors presumed to have substantial etiological significance, such as: (1) education; (2) condition of the home; (3) supervision; (4) regularity of meals; (5) maternal rejection; and (6) prolonged illnesses. Chronic illness was frequent in mothers of shy children, and one sixth of these mothers were considered mentally inadequate. Most of the overanxious neurotic group had a history of serious illness and often came from middle class homes; the mothers of these inhibited children were not likely to be hostile toward their children, who generally did not feel rejected, while mothers of aggressive children were often openly hostile toward them. In addition, the inhibited children tended to come from homes with both parents present, which was less likely in the case of the hyperactive or aggressive children. The undomesticated children characteristically came from backgrounds showing lack of sufficient maternal love and acceptance in early life, while socialized delinquents were found to be generally products of both neglect and a deteriorated neighborhood.

The interaction of constitutional and environmental factors is most clearly shown in the work of Thomas, Chess, and Birch (1968), where the authors postulate that children are born with certain clearly identifiable temperamental characteristics and response approaches which influence behavior independently of the task being performed. While there is no one-to-one relation between specific patterns of temperament and the emergence of behavior problems, children with a "culturally negative" temperament are likely to develop maladaptive behavior patterns. Substantial numbers of children with this behavior do not develop maladaptive patterns, and a small percentage of children from a group with culturally favorable temperament did develop maladaptive behavior patterns. Thus, an "interaction effect" was identified, and the authors concluded that a child with any kind of temperament could develop behavior abnormalities under "wrong" environmental conditions.

Psychodynamic theorists, heavily influenced by Freud, are of a deterministic philosophy in that they believe that behavior—"healthy" or "unhealthy"—is predicated upon past experiences and influenced by external forces that impinge on the growing personality of the young child. They believe in the unconscious—that is, that experiences, memories, or feelings of which the subject may be unaware nevertheless determine to a large extent the course of his daily life. While there are many psychodynamic theorists, Rogers' work (1961, 1969) is most directly applicable to education. He perceives "emotional disturbance" as a state of incongruence between the self and experience. The person defends himself through the mechanisms of rationalization and projection at times, such as when he has experiences incongruent with his self-concept as a "good" person. When the incongruent experience becomes patently clear to the individual, he is open to severe processes of psychological disorganization. The aim of education, according to Rogers, is "self-actualization," in which a person fulfills himself and his self-perception is not marred by external standards. Rogers has tried to apply dynamic considerations to education; defining full personal functioning as congruence between the self and experience, he advocates an educational process which stays close to the experience of students. Learning should have the quality of pervasive personal involvement, should be self-initiated, and should be evaluated only by the learner. The teacher's role emerges from the concept of the teacher as a facilitator rather than as an instructor.

Rezmierski and Kotre (1971) point out that the major emphasis of the advocates of psychoanalytic and psychodynamic principles for education has been on the destructive effects of regulations that are imposed too early in the child's life. For the most part these prescriptions have come from persons who were basically theoreticians and not practitioners. A good description of *psychodynamic theories* applied to education can be found in the work of Bower and Hollister (1967).

Behavioral psychologists believe that maladaptive behaviors are learned behaviors that do not differ in either development or maintenance from any other behavior manifested. They believe that there is no discontinuity between either "desirable" and "undesirable" behaviors or between "healthy" and "sick" behaviors. Because in most cases there are no organisms within individuals that produce "maladaptive behavior," societal mores determine which behaviors are to be considered aberrant, and there are a full range of reinforcers available for people who fill particular roles. For example, Ullmann and Krasner (1965) describe maladaptive behavior in the following way:

> The person whose behavior is maladaptive does not fully live up to the expectations for one in his role, does not respond to all the stimuli actually present, and does not obtain the typical or maximum forms of reinforcement available to one of his status. The difference between the types of reinforcement that maintain adaptive and maladaptive behavior is that the latter is maintained by more direct and immediate forms of reinforcement than the former. Behavior that one culture might consider maladaptive, be it that of Shaman or paranoid, is adaptive in another culture if the person so behaving is responding to all the cues present in the situation in a manner likely to lead to his obtaining reinforcement appropriate to his status in that society. Maladaptive behavior is behavior that is considered inappropriate by those key people in a person's life who control reinforcers. Such maladaptive behavior leads to a reduction in the range or the value of positive reinforcement given to the person displaying it. (p. 20)

Like psychodynamic theorists, then, learning theorists are determinists, believing that behavior is caused by and is subject to laws—such as that when a behavior is reinforced it tends to occur again. Learning theorists believe that the causes of human behavior are so complex that we never fully understand them because of our necessarily incomplete history of the organism, and thus that people must be worked with ahistorically, first by identifying which behaviors need to be accelerated or decelerated and subsequently finding appropriate stimuli or reinforcers to change that behavior. They also believe that "healthy" and "unhealthy" responses develop similarly, since they are subject to the same laws.

In an interesting experiment Hall, Lund, and Jackson (1968) demonstrated how teacher attention "caused" what was described as aberrant behavior. They noticed that teacher attention followed inappropriate student behavior, although when a child was "on task" he was ignored. They then cued the teacher to reverse his procedures and to reinforce appropriate behavior and ignore inappropriate behavior. They found that the child's appropriate behavior increased and his inappropriate behavior decreased. The teacher then reversed the procedures again, returning to the original conditions. The child's behavior at that point reverted to approximately the same ratio of appropriate to inappropriate behavior that he had originally displayed. It can therefore be concluded that teacher attention "caused" the given behaviors. This study is consonant with Skinner's (1938) theory that it is not what is "inside" the organism that is important but, rather, that the response occurring after any given behavior is manifested will determine the direction, strength, and magnitude of that behavior.

Causes of Juvenile Delinquency

There are many theories about the causes of juvenile delinquency, but proponents of all of them are usually in agreement that the delinquent or socially maladjusted child is a product of his social environment. The delinquent is neither a congenital criminal nor is he prompted by some emotional pathology to commit crimes against society. Rather, he has *learned* precepts that are normal and behavior that is normative within his social milieu, although these behaviors are defined as criminal or in need of reform by the dominant society. We lack an effective technology with which to ameliorate delinquent behavior patterns, but theories of the genesis of delinquent behavior—such as those summarized by Scarpitti and Scarpitti (1969)—are extremely important if we are to evolve preventive programs. Five of the major theories are briefly discussed here.

1. *The theory of social disorganization* evolved from the pioneer work of Shaw and McKay (1942). They divided Chicago into concentric zones based on ecological characteristics and discovered the highest delinquency rates in or adjacent to industrial and commercial zones which were characterized by high mobility rates, dense population, welfare dependency, physical deterioration of the neighborhood, and high rates of *adult* crime. They postulated that such areas had an absence of social solidarity and little sense of community that could function as an effective means of social control and that consequently individuals developed delinquent patterns of behavior.

2. Sutherland (1947) proposed a *theory of differential association.* He postulated that behavior perceived as delinquent is learned through association and interaction with others who are already delinquent—that is, that children become delinquent when they internalize the skills, attitudes, and values of a group in which they have an intimate, almost primary, relation. He also felt that learning criminal behavior includes the division of legal codes into those that are favorable (that is, those that should be observed) and those that can be violated. Since delinquency is seen here as imitative behavior, it follows that more lower class youth will become delinquent, since there is more opportunity for criminal associations in disorganized areas than in more stable ones. However, Sutherland does not discuss what prompts the norm-violating behavior in the first place.

3. Cohen (1955) also contended that delinquency is primarily a lower

class phenomenon. He saw it as emergent when children are frustrated by being unable to function successfully in middle class institutions, basing his *theory of social class difference* on the fact that the middle class value system emphasizes ambition, individual responsibility, skill, deferred gratification, and respect for property. Lower class children find it hard to internalize these values, which are not exemplified in their environment. Only a few adjustment options are open to working class youth: acceptance of lower class status is the most common response; another alternative is to gain upward mobility through education; finally, a response can occur toward the delinquent subculture that provides criteria of success and status for the working class youth.

4. Miller's (1959) *subculture theory of delinquency* is distinguished from Cohen's in that Miller does not believe that lower class children must necessarily be frustrated in their status ambitions before taking on the values of delinquent subcultures. Miller says that a society can contain several value systems of unequal dominance. Adhering to a subordinate value system can evoke punishment from agents of the dominant value system. Miller believes that trouble, toughness, smartness, excitement, fate, and autonomy are positive values of the lower class culture. Smartness means the ability to outwit others. Excitement is found in thrills, danger, and adventure. Fate is comprised of the acceptance of luck. Autonomy, for the lower class child, means that he or she will not be "bossed around" or controlled by anyone. Thus, like Cohen, Miller sees delinquency as a natural consequence of adherence to lower class norms.

5. A theory of *differential opportunity* was developed by Cloward and Ohlin (1960), who explain delinquency as a function of a limited opportunity system. They believe that pressures toward the formation of a delinquent subculture come about because of a disparity between aspirations and legitimate means for achieving them.

Drugs and Maladaptive Behavior

Another factor in behavioral disability, probably directly related to much delinquent behavior, is the use of drugs. Teachers must know a great deal about drugs if they are to help youngsters with drug-related problems—what drugs look like, their effects on users, and available methods for helping children (which will be discussed in a later section of this chapter). Drug abuse in the United States is a phenomenon of which we are increasingly aware. Drug use now occurs at an earlier age, and some illicit drug use is part of the social fabric of most schools, its extent and specifics usually not well known to faculty.

The Federal Food and Drug Administration defines drugs as "substances used to diagnose, treat, or prevent illness; or *substances (other than food) which modify* body function" (italics added). The term "dangerous drugs" is often used to refer to nonnarcotic drugs that are habit forming or that have a potential for depressing or stimulating hallucinogenic effects. Eddy, Halbach, Isbell, and Seevers (1965) have begun to use the term "drug depend-ence" to designate the point where drug use becomes a problem, even though there may be no physiological addiction.

Because nonmedical drug use is illicit, it is difficult to ascertain the actual extent to which drugs are abused. The sale of narcotics in the public schools, however, has been well documented by journalists (*New York Post*, February 2, 1972). Reports of children taking pills in school lavatories and smoking marijuana between classes are quite common. Inhalants such as glue and paint thinner are often "sniffed" by preteenage children. Users of "softer" drugs such as marijuana, hallucinogens, stimulants, depressants, and under-age users of alcohol are not well known to the police. The Department of Justice estimates that there may be as many as 20 million users of marijuana in this country, and many of these are school-age children.

Thus, child drug abuse is anxiety provoking and not well documented. Almost all teachers will need to deal with children who take drugs, some of whom take them on a casual, experimental basis while others become pre-occupied with drugs to the exclusion of almost everything else in their environment. (See pages 556–557 for a discussion of the problems in the use of drugs to control hyperactivity.)

What should a teacher do about drug usage by her pupils? The neces-sity of making immediate decisions concerning specific drug problems within the classroom is complicated by the fact that drug use is illegal. Drug taking in many cases is a police problem, and only sustained coopera-tion between school and police authorities can lead to elimination of organ-ized drug rings within schools. In some cases, however, calling in such authorities only leads to gross mistrust between the teacher and the child, with the result that a situation which might have been therapeutically handled and resolved becomes one where dialogue is aborted. Although primary re-sponsibility for drug treatment must be assumed by outside agencies, teachers can exert enormous influence over such children both by precept and educa-tion. Teachers can also talk with children and help them with the problems of "keeping up with the crowd," which is probably a major reason for the spread of drug use. Usually it is quite apparent when a youngster is taking drugs: puncture marks on arms and bloodstains on clothing are often obvious clues, as is the wearing of long sleeves during hot weather; other signs are nodding and drowsiness, which often follow some drug taking, and sudden changes in mood and behavior—for example, the euphoric mood and garru-lous behavior resulting from use of marijuana and amphetamines may be unusual for particular students. An extremely large percentage of youth in training schools for maladjusted children have used drugs, and obtaining the drugs or especially obtaining enough money to obtain the drugs becomes a major preoccupation for the user; thus, the drug-dependent child will steal, extort, or turn to prostitution (regardless of sex of the addict) in order to obtain money for drugs. The following list states several principles usable by teachers in such situations.

1. Avoid Panic and Scare Techniques:
   Children, often from first-hand observation of the effects of smoking marijuana, know that it does not inevitably lead to psychoses or addiction. If parents and teachers lie (e.g., by saying marijuana use will lead to heroin addiction) children will tend not to listen to *anything* from such sources about drugs.
2. Listen to Your Children:
   It is recommended that drugs should not be focused on as a single issue with children, but should be discussed parallel with such issues as disrespect for property, accident-proneness, acting on impulse.
3. Use Full and Factual Information:
   The little information we know about drug effects should be shared factually with children.
4. Education Should Start Young:
   Children should be taught to take medicines only as needed and to follow specific directions when they do. They should know that overdoses, even of aspirin, can lead to death.
5. Firm and Fair Discipline:
   It is stressed by specialists that youths want authority but not tyranny. Clear and consistent guidelines are needed with assurance about the reasons for saying "No".[1]

ACADEMIC AND SOCIAL MANIFESTATIONS

Since variation in children labeled with behavioral disabilities is so great, assessments of a child's school achievement based solely on such labels cannot be made. Some behaviorally disordered children are brilliant or talented, while others have difficulty in learning to read and write and do not demonstrate skill in any area of endeavor. The majority of children labeled as behaviorally disordered are often behind their peers both in grade and level of achievement. This finding has been reported in many studies (Bower, 1962; Rubin, Simpson, and Betwee, 1966). Graubard (1971) differentiated children in special classes on a variety of behavioral dimensions and found that statistically derived groups of behaviorally disordered children could also be significantly differentiated on academic achievement. Several groups were retarded in reading relative to chronological age, but all groups were reading commensurate with mental age. Given a normal IQ, the study found that the higher the score on the conduct-disorder dimension, the lower was the score of reading measures.

In a classic study by Morse, Cutler, and Fink (1964) of special education programs for the behaviorally disordered, over 50 percent of their national sample were considered to be neurotic, with a great deal of antisocial behavior displayed. The next largest groups were considered to be "primitive neglected" and immature. The study also found that over 83 percent of the children in special programs were boys and the majority had IQ's over 100.

---

[1] From A. Blakeslee, What you should know about drugs and narcotics. In B. Hafen (Ed.), *Readings in drug use and abuse.* Provo, Utah: Brigham Young University Press, 1970.

Many studies have shown a strong relation between school experiences and delinquency. Kvaraceus noted the extent to which overt aggression was related to the stress of school experiences, finding that delinquents generally had to repeat school grades and received very low school marks. In his "Delinquency Prone Check List" Kvaraceus (1958) lists 18 characteristics of "socially maladjusted" children that can be found in school, including: (1) shows marked dislike for school; (2) resents school routine and restrictions; (3) is uninterested in school program; (4) is failing in a number of subjects; (5) has repeated one or more grades, and so forth. Spiegelman (1968) found a significant negative correlation between grades completed in school and the probability of being arrested for juvenile crime even when race, income, IQ, and parental presence were held constant. High school dropouts were three to five times more likely than high school graduates to be arrested for juvenile crime. While delinquents are not significantly less intelligent than the general population when social class is held constant, they are considerably more likely to fail in school (Prentice and Kelly, 1963; Graubard, 1971).

Thus, many children perceived as having behavioral disabilities manifest academic retardation. Many of these same children are considered to have learning disabilities. (The definition of specific learning disabilities used in the the U.S. Learning Disabilities Act of 1969 is given in Chapter 10, page 539.) Despite the disclaimer that children who are emotionally disturbed (behaviorally disordered) are excluded from the above definition, the difficulties of diagnosis and definition are so paramount that one can readily see the overlap between learning disabilities and behavioral disabilities. Many programs for behaviorally disordered children include, in fact, many children with severe learning deficiencies and consequently have built into them intensive remedial efforts, often using materials and curriculum that were developed for other areas of exceptionality such as brain-injured and mentally retarded children. In practice, then, labels become less and less meaningful, and it is most important, especially in intervention programs, to look at the specific behavior of *each* child in order to avoid stereotyping the individual.

Teachers are likely to find that many behaviorally disordered children have short attention spans, oppose authority, fight more frequently than the average child, have substantial fears and phobias, and avoid structured learning situations. Some behaviorally disordered children, however, may display exactly the opposite characteristics. The specific characteristics and problem areas of the individual child must be discovered and noted—not to medically diagnose or characterize the child but to gain information necessary for planning educational activities.

EXTENT AND NATURE OF SPECIAL EDUCATION PROGRAMS

We must not confuse the number of children with behavioral disabilities actually receiving special education services with the number of such children in need of such services. For 1971–1972, the U.S. Office of Education estimated that there were 1,388,000 behaviorally disordered children and adolescents. As Dunn pointed out in Table 1.3, an estimated 156,486 such children were receiving special education services in local school systems that school year. Schultz, Hirshoren, Manton, and Henderson (1971) reported that in 1948 there were only 90 public school programs in the United States which serviced approximately 15,300 behaviorally disordered children. In 1966 this number had increased to 875 public school systems serving approximately 32,000 children. The same authors estimated that in 1970 there were probably 100,000 children enrolled in day programs and more than 65,000 under the age of 18 enrolled in residential programs. These data speak only to the question of needed versus provided special education. They say nothing about the quality of such services.

Schultz et al. (1971) found that the majority of special education programs offered by the states was provided on a permissive basis. Although 19 states required a psychiatric evaluation for placement, this was used as the single criterion in only five states. At least one state required return to regular classes after one year, while several states required return to the educational mainstream after two or three years of special services. Mandating specific return dates to regular classes can prevent abuses when children, because of administrative inertia and other factors, are left in the special education track. (It is imperative that more adequate criteria be developed for both placement and discharge from special education so that children's rights are protected.)

Schultz et al. identified 12 types of special school services: (1) special class program; (2) resource-room program; (3) crisis intervention; (4) itinerant-teacher program; (5) academic tutoring; (6) homebound instruction; (7) guidance counselors; (8) school social workers; (9) psychotherapy by school psychologist; (10) psychiatric consultation; (11) public school transportation to nonschool agency; and (12) payment by public school for private school. Special classes were offered by most states (47), followed by resource-room programing (40 states) and then by homebound instruction (38 states). Ten students was the modal class size permitted by most of the states. Figures for children returned to regular classes from special education classes ranged from 5 percent to over 90 percent.

School districts frequently offer only one or two special education options. This produces a Procrustean bed where the child must be fitted into the limited programs available. When a school and a child have more options, both are usually better off. In all of the approaches mentioned systematic evaluation of their effectiveness on the child is crucial, but unfortunately this is accomplished in too few programs. None are necessarily always good or always bad. Clearly, the value of each rests on the caliber of the professional manpower and services provided. That is, the virtue or evil of any one program does not rest in the administrative plan per se.

PROGRAM EVALUATION

Program evaluation is a current, vital concern for special education. Special education classes in even the least developed programs have lower pupil-teacher ratios and higher per capita costs than regular classes; thus, high taxes and difficulties in meeting school operating costs make evaluation of program effectiveness and justification of expenditures especially important. Since a social stigma is attached to children receiving special education for the behaviorally disordered, such programs must demonstrate their effectiveness or run the risks of needlessly forcing children to lose prestige and be further burdened by the labeling process.

It is often said that evaluation gets in the way of good teaching. However, teaching that cannot be evaluated is often fuzzy and global. Evaluation provides a way of knowing whether a teaching strategy has been successful. It is an aid in specifying desirable outcomes and in ascertaining effectiveness in reaching these outcomes. Collecting ongoing data, such as a pupil's academic response rates (as opposed to pre- and posttesting), enables a teacher to make appropriate shifts in technique and content based on empirical observation rather than on hunches.

Continuous measurement of a child's progress through the curriculum can be an excellent method for evaluating program effectiveness when a stated program objective is to increase reading or arithmetic competence. The rate of work accomplished can be assessed by recording the time work started and stopped for each class session, and then counting and graphing the number of correct responses. Pupils can also collect and graph this kind of information. The curriculum would be used as the dependent variable, and the teaching method, the reinforcement contingencies, or the seating arrangements would be the independent variable.

A study by Cook, Cort, Flocco, and Sanford (1972) reported that only 103 programs out of 272 queried had collected data on academic or behavioral gains indicating program effectiveness. Less than 12 programs in the sample had sufficient data and information on their procedures to enable them to be replicated. It appears that teachers and administrators have grave difficulties in evaluating their own work. Consultation assistance should be sought, if necessary, in designing evaluation procedures, with careful consideration given to experimental design and methods of analysis. The following guidelines were prepared by Cook et al. to help educators:

Attitude rating should not be equated with actual improvement in behavior, since the correlation between perception of change and actual change (as documented by specific recording of behavior) is by no means a perfect one. Evaluators should be cautious in citing indirect evidence, such as reduction of referrals to special services, without using control groups as evidence of program effectiveness. The rate of referral is often caused by other than program factors, and correlational studies are always of dubious validity. Causal statements about treatment effects are on a better foundation when designs such as the multiple baseline or reversal design are used (Baer, Wolf, and Risley, 1968), or when control groups with at least one placebo treatment are included. In addition, program and evaluation objectives must coincide. Certain program objectives are not amenable to empirical evaluation. When objectives are loosely stated—for example, "to develop self-respect" or "to maximize motivation of children"—adequate evaluation is difficult. Operational definitions must be given for program objectives.

Direct observation of behavior can supply data to be used in good evaluation design *if* observations are systematic and of sufficient duration so that stable rates of behavior emerge. On a given task if behavior ranges from 20 percent to 80 percent over a time period, collecting observational data to determine which figure is typical is crucial. Anecdotal records and questionnaires are more helpful when used to ascertain which behaviors should be systematically studied than when used as ends in themselves. (A good discussion of research and evaluation as it applies to educating behaviorally disordered children can be found in Miller, 1969.) In evaluating the success of programs for children with behavioral disabilities, the most difficult questions are what criteria shall be used to judge success and when and where the behaviors constituting these criteria should be examined. Whether change in overt behavior is as important as reported improved feelings of self-worth is a question that each investigator must answer for himself.

FOLLOW-UP STUDIES

Methodological problems and questions of what criteria constitute success make it difficult to assess the long-range effect of treatment programs. Most treatment programs are so generally described that it is not possible to attribute changes to treatment procedures. Whether gains made during treatment are subsequently sustained should not be left to chance. It is more sensible to think of behavioral disabilities as a long-range problem.

McKinnon (1969) conducted a follow-up of 88 elementary school children placed in special day classes for the behaviorally disordered in two urban school districts. Classes were psychoeducationally oriented and were staffed by certified teachers of the emotionally disturbed. The average placement lasted one and one-half years. Follow-up was conducted three years after termination of the special class placement. At that time, maladjustment had increased from levels noted at the end of special class placement. Furthermore, progress in reading and arithmetic attainment had decreased. Thus, although behavior was considered to be slightly improved after treatment, such gains were not sustained.

In a follow-up of 71 children diagnosed as "infantile autistic" (42 treated, 29 untreated), Havelkova (1968) studied the effects of a residential treatment program. The children were diagnosed during the preschool period and followed for 4 to 12 years. Assessment procedures included observations made in different life situations, daily reports by a therapist, and family assessment based on interviews and home visits. Individual treatment in a playroom conducted by a clinician preceded the introduction of the treated child to a normal nursery school environment, while the untreated group received no formal treatment, although regular contact was maintained. Comparisons of intellectual functioning on various criteria revealed a general tendency toward intellectual deterioration for both groups at follow-up. Havelkova concluded that childhood psychosis results in an intellectual deficit only partially preventable by residential treatment. Changes in the clinical form of psychosis appeared to occur on a maturational basis irrespective of therapeutic procedures.

The results of psychotherapy for children have been ambiguous. In a review of the literature in this field, Lewis (1965) reported five studies that compared follow-up data on more than 1,000 treated children with data on a similar number of children who defected from clinic waiting lists. There were no significant differences in the rate of improvement between the treated and the untreated groups. Similarly, in a classic study by O'Neal and Robins (1958a; 1958b), 525 consecutive admissions to a child guidance clinic, made 30 years prior to follow-up, were compared to a sample of normal subjects matched on the bases of sex, race, age, and socioeconomic status. At follow-up social and psychiatric status was determined through interviews and a search of public records, with the group that had received psychotherapeutic treatment showing a significantly higher order of psychiatric problems than did the contrast group. Hodges and Tait (1963) showed that it was possible to identify potential delinquents, but that psychotherapeutic treatment did not decrease delinquency. From these studies it would appear that identification and prediction measures have outstripped our ability to effectively intervene with psychotherapy in the lives of children to prevent aberrant behavior.

During the first half of this century, professional and legal thought generally placed the responsibility for the treatment of behaviorally disordered children with the medical profession, but the available numbers of psychiatrists, clinical psychologists, and social workers have simply proved inadequate to the task. This lack, coupled with the equivocal results of child psychotherapy (Lewis, 1965) and the growing acceptance of models other than psychoanalytic, have resulted in a return of the main responsibility for educating and changing the behavior of conduct-disordered children to educators, with clinical personnel assuming a secondary role in program planning and instruction. Furthermore, it appears that distinctions among therapy, therapeutic teaching, and regular teaching are breaking down. Ullmann and Krasner (1965) have summarized an approach that specifically looks at overt behavior: when a child's behavior is considered from the point of view of the question, "What behavior do I need to accelerate or decelerate?" intervention on a *functional* level by teachers and others sharing environmental situations with him becomes possible. In this context what is therapeutic can be achieved by various professionals, and differentiations between disciplines have less meaning.

TEACHER PREPARATION AND SELECTION

Numerous training programs exist to prepare teachers to work with children perceived as having behavioral disabilities. In programs which it funds, the U.S. Office of Education has mandated (1971) that outcome data, as opposed to input variables, must be emphasized in program evaluation. This requirement will undoubtedly lead to an upgrading of training programs, and a more systematic and rigorous examination of the training process and the net effect of training on special education teachers can be anticipated. Gersh and Nagle (1969) surveyed special education teachers and found them highly critical of their training. Respondents felt that they had been inadequately prepared to manage obstreperous behavior, and they were not as interested in theory as in learning specific techniques such as remediation and behavioral management. Respondents were also interested in increasing their self-awareness and were concerned about the lack of communication between disciplines.

Dorward (1963) had teachers of children with behavioral disabilities and teachers of "normal" children contrast approximately 100 teaching competencies, drawn from a study by Mackie, Kvaraceus, and Williams (1957). There were significant differences in comparing the two groups on only two items. More important for teachers of the behaviorally disabled were: (1) the ability to work with extremely aggressive children and (2) the ability to work on a team with clinicians. The Mackie, Kvaraceus, and Williams competency checklist was also readministered by Bullock and Whelan (1971). Teachers were asked to evaluate the significance of the original competencies and to rate their own degree of skill mastery. This study suggested that teachers need to emphasize individualized and sequenced programing procedures and to develop a comprehensive overview of curriculum materials for all grade levels and a thorough knowledge of remediation procedures. Too, teachers need good comprehension of behavioral principles and a better understanding of how to work with a team. Finally, the study suggests that teachers need to have a working knowledge of various kinds of handicapped youth, since a substantial increase of multihandicapped children in the schools is predicted. Table 5.1 shows how the Bullock and Whelan teachers rank ordered competencies needed to be successful in teaching children with behavioral disabilities.

While there has been little empirical evaluation of competency hierarchies or other models for teacher training, Hewett (1968) developed a competency hierarchy proposing the following skills: (1) objectivity—the ability to evaluate teaching progress and to separate the problems of the teacher from those of the pupil; (2) flexibility—the ability to make rapid shifts and adjustments to meet the pupil's needs; (3) structure—the ability to set and maintain reasonable standards; (4) resourcefulness—the ability to innovate and try new approaches when old ones are not working; (5) social reinforcement—the ability to deliver positive social reinforcement to pupils; (6) curriculum expertise—the ability to match the appropriate curriculum content and methods to the pupil; and (7) intellectual model—the ability to serve as a model to stimulate creativity and the acquisition of knowledge. From this list it would appear that what the teacher does with the child is more significant than any personality characteristic of the teacher. However, Bruno (1968) reported that teachers with high nurturance needs left the classroom after about two years while those with high needs for dominance remained; thus,

TABLE 5.1 *Competencies Rated as Very Important in Their Teaching by Teachers of Children with Behavioral Disabilities*

Rank Order	Very Important Items
1	*A knowledge or understanding of the advantages of providing experiences in which pupils can be successful.
2	A knowledge or understanding of the education and psychology of various types of exceptional children.
3	The ability to tolerate antisocial behavior, particularly when it is directed toward authority.
4	A knowledge or understanding of basic human physical and psychological needs.
5	*A knowledge or understanding of techniques adaptable to classroom situations for relieving tensions and promoting good mental health.
6	*A knowledge or understanding of the advantages of flexibility of school programs and schedules to permit individual adjustment and development.
7	The ability to establish "limits" for social control (neither overprotective nor overrestrictive).
8	*The ability to develop self-imposed social control within the pupils.
9	The ability to establish and maintain good working relations with other professional workers, such as social workers and psychological personnel.
10	The ability to teach remedial reading.
11	*The ability to avoid identical, stereotyped demands of maladjusted pupils.
12	A knowledge or understanding of curriculum and methods of teaching the "normal" pupil.

*Items that were also rated as "Very Important" in the Mackie, Kvaraceus, and Williams study (1957).

SOURCE: Adapted from L. Bullock and R. Whelan, Competencies needed by teachers of the emotionally disturbed and socially maladjusted: A comparison. *Exceptional Children,* 1971, 37, 7.

the more authoritarian teachers remain teaching, while those with less need to dominate others leave the field. Teachers leave because of general dissatisfaction with pupil progress and the extreme physical and psychological strain of working in special education classrooms.

Piaget (1972) examined the teaching styles, which presumably can be linked to personality traits, of 36 special class teachers of aggressive children along with the concurrent classroom behavior of over 200 boys. He used the Amidon-Flanders Interaction Analysis, which measures direct (that is, authoritarian) and indirect (that is, student-receptive) teacher style. Children's behavior was measured by the Werry-Quay classroom observation instrument. Piaget found a significant relation between teacher style and pupil behavior, the indirect teacher having the greatest degree of acceptable pupil behavior. It should be possible to devise screening instruments which would predict teacher success in this direction.

CURRICULAR AND INSTRUCTIONAL APPROACHES

The goal for too many school programs is simply to reduce disruptive behavior. The inhibition of behavior rather than the learning of new responses is frequently emphasized. Disruptive behavior can be suppressed, but if additional responses are not added to the child's repertoire, the chances of maintaining the "nondisruptive behavior," except in isolated and circumscribed circumstances, are slim.

Appropriate curricular content can be a major vehicle for working with behaviorally disordered youth. Proper placement and appropriate curriculum materials can help eliminate many incipient behavior problems. The number of responses in a child's behavioral repertoire can be widened considerably through the medium of curriculum. Many children with maladaptive behavior patterns respond predictably and negatively to curriculum they cannot master. When they are presented with interesting material within their competence, discipline problems subside, and frequently such children cannot be distinguished from "normal" children in terms of school behavior. The need to choose appropriate curricular ingredients and to teach each child at his own level are essential components of less stressful and positive teaching situations, especially when goals are set in consultation with the child rather than imposed upon him. Few curriculum guides are specific enough for classroom use in changing children's social behavior. In most cases the teacher must construct the curriculum after observing the given behavior in which change is desired.

In terms of instructional approaches many programs, except when research is involved, are more eclectic in practice than they are on paper. Some programs, however, are based on specific and clearly defined, identifiable strategies: (1) the psychodynamic approach; (2) the behavioral-deficit approach; (3) the behavior-modification approach; and (4) the ecological approach. This section will describe the application of each of these approaches. It will be seen that they are not mutually exclusive in that they do not represent clearly different options for what or how to teach pupils perceived as disturbed.

The Psychodynamic Approach

The psychodynamic approach is used principally in day treatment centers and psychiatric hospitals. Because of its expense and shortages of personnel this model has not been used extensively in schools, and since the primary emphasis is given to clinicians' and teachers' understanding of unconscious factors for each child, research to evaluate the success of this method is extremely difficult to conduct.

In commenting on Roger's work (1961, 1969) (mentioned on page 258 in the discussion of psychodynamic factors in the etiology of behavioral disability), Rezmierski and Kotre (1971) say:

> A climate of learning is not created by lesson tasks, assigned readings, lectures (except upon request), evaluation and criticism on the part of the teacher (again, except upon request), and required examinations. Programmed instruction in which the student sets his own pace, simulations of experience and events, and work in small groups are methods that promote experiential learning. Rogers suggests the use of student-teacher contracts and is not opposed to the notion of basic encounter work in the

classroom. The teacher, in his view, is like the therapist in non-directive therapy and the parent of the child on the way to maturity. He is not an authority or an evaluator. He provides the warm, accepting climate which facilitates significant learning. (p. 40)

Thus, the educator is generally placed in an ancillary therapeutic role by this approach, which considers overt behavior to be symptomatic of underlying and intrapsychic conflict. The basic assumption of much psychodynamic treatment is that the basic causes of maladaptive behavior need to be diagnosed, treated, and corrected in order for education to be optimally effective. Treatment is often directed to making unconscious conflicts accessible to the individual so they can be worked with therapeutically in order to strengthen the individual's ego functioning. Therapy is based on diagnosis by a clinician and can include a variety of techniques, such as play therapy with neurotic children, holding and rocking children with severely aberrant behaviors, or discussion designed to bring insight to those—generally more verbal children —who can use it.

Berkowitz and Rothman (1960) described their educational procedures for disturbed children. Their psychodynamically oriented approach emphasizes the teacher's role in acceptance of the child and the establishment of a close and positive interpersonal relation. Their techniques encouraged children to express thoughts and feelings and emphasized teacher acceptance of these thoughts and feelings. Techniques such as sentence completion, finishing unfinished stories, making up pictures about stories, and round-robin stories were used to encourage children to reveal their fantasies (which is considered therapeutic) while they were concurrently learning academic skills. Thus, even the Berkowitz and Rothman strategy can be viewed as an eclectic one.

In summary, the psychodynamic approach is essentially child centered. Determining *why* a child behaves as he does is the key. It indicates *what* is to be emphasized, namely, dealing with the underlying forces hypothesized to be the cause of the maladaptive behavior. Further, it suggests somewhat *how* to teach, usually to provide a permissive environment, ancillary and supportive to the psychotherapy which will aim at giving the child greater insights into himself. (Some indication of the effectiveness of this procedure can be gained by referring back to page 268 where the results of psychotherapy were presented; not surprising, only remnants remain of this traditional approach.)

The Behavioral-Deficit Approach

The behavioral-deficit approach is again largely child centered. It argues from the premise that the pupil's maladaptive behavior is primarily a result of frustration and failure in school, and perhaps elsewhere. The strategy is to determine the academic and/or social behavior deficits and to correct them. With success will come improved feelings of self-worth with a resulting diminution in the aberrant behavior. There is far from agreement on how to implement this approach. (The options are extensively discussed in Chapter 10.)

Just briefly, most special educators have favored the classical remedial education paradigm. Psychoeducational diagnostic instruments are administered to the child as a central part of a more complete child study. Weaknesses are thus identified. The role of the special educator is to tutor to correct these deficits, usually academic in nature. Kirk (1972) has labeled this the "learning disability" strategy. But if engendering feelings of success to attain the end product of more acceptable behavior is the chief goal, it is remarkable that advocates of this approach have drummed away at weaknesses. Why not ascertain the pupil's strengths, academic or otherwise, and concentrate on these? Perhaps the foundation for this procedure is more straightforward, namely, that the pupil is going to compensate for poor academic progress with aggressive or withdrawn behavior until his achievement is up to standard for his peers. If so, an emphasis on remedial education makes sense.

The behavior-modification approach to be presented next is primarily a teaching procedure; it does not tell the teacher what to teach. However, in practice, advocates of this procedure generally also share a deficit-correction predisposition. But they are opposed to standardized psychoeducational tests. Instead, they substitute a detailed, individualized, hand-tailored analysis of the pupil's behavior along a dimension they consider important. Generally, they too choose problem areas, be they academic or social behaviors. While the words used by the advocates of the learning-disability and the behavior-modification strategies may be different, each group first determines the level at which the pupil is functioning. Then tutoring is initiated to advance his competencies, in a step-by-step fashion. Both of these *modus operandi* are concerned with *what* the child does rather than *why* he does it.

Morse (1967) has identified another variation of this same behavioral-deficit theme which he has entitled the "psychoeducational" strategy. It is concerned not only with *what* behavior deficits the child has but also with *why* he has them. In this sense he is an eclectic, but the causation is usually not couched in psychodynamic terms. The life-space examination is an important diagnostic technique in this approach. Teachers and other professions on the team consider, moments after a crisis, the meaning of the child's maladaptive behavior. Hypotheses are determined and an education intervention is then devised and implemented, aimed at correcting the target behavioral deficit, be it academic or social. This could lead to a variety of interventions, including (1) reducing the pressure placed on the child; (2) teaching the child coping strategies; (3) focusing on teacher-pupil relations; (4) centering on peer-group relations; (5) changing the child's motivations; and (6) enhancing his self-concept. A description of how to implement these options can be found in Morse (1967).

The Behavior-Modification Approach

As stated a number of times throughout this text, the behavior-modification approach deals primarily with how to change overt student behavior. It does not tell us what behavior to modify yet the delineation of what specific behaviors are to be increased or decreased is the first step. Behavioral objectives are then spelled out. This requires a subjective judgment. The teacher or behavior modifier must explicitly state what these are, and they must be measurable. For example, the degree to which a pupil is establishing "meaningful" relations with the teacher may be measured by counting how many times a child approaches her and the length of time spent with her. The child is reinforced after performing the given act that the teacher wants to strengthen, or when behavior approximates the terminal behavior that the teacher wants to shape, as is illustrated in Vignette 5.1 (The reader is referred to *Preparing Instructional Objectives* by Mager (1962) for an extended discussion of how to set and write specific behavioral goals.)

Vignette 5.1 Teaching a Child by Behavior Modification

Martha was placed in a day treatment center affiliated with a hospital at the age of seven. Her suicidal threats, slapping herself, and uncontrollable screaming in her regular school class prompted the placement. In kindergarten, Martha had refused all year to enter class unless her mother was present. Martha rarely spoke to anyone and spent most of her time playing alone. She was promoted with the hope that she would mature with time. In the first grade, her mother was permitted to wait in the hall, but could not accompany Martha into the classroom. Martha had temper tantrums for several days but then went into class. She cried quietly and did only a minimum of school work. She was also hypochondriacal and often absent. Toward the end of the year she began to scream and the school suspended her to spare the other children. She was placed on home instruction until there was an opening in the treatment center.

After her placement in the day treatment center, a family counselor met with the parents once weekly. They were given basic instruction in child management. Furthermore, the parents observed the teacher working with Martha through a one-way vision glass. The teacher's instructional procedures included ignoring Martha's tantrums and sobbing and responding to her appropriate behavior with praise and more tangible rewards such as snacks and reading stories. These snacks and other reinforcers were made contingent upon appropriate school behavior such as sitting quietly and completing school work. When Martha cried, the teacher turned her back and worked with another child. When Martha did not cry, the teacher returned to her.

Martha became quite attached to the teacher after two months, following her around, and often trying to hold her hand and kiss her. The teacher explained to Martha how much she really cared for her, but that too much hand holding and kissing is inappropriate. They arranged a private signal of touching each other on occasion to symbolize the affection. The teacher made a point of going over to Martha when she was with other children, but not when she was alone. Martha soon began to spend more time with other children.

The parents learned a great deal about child-management techniques from observing the teacher. Too, they learned how they had been, in a sense, manipulated by Martha's crying and threats. The counselor and the teacher reinforced the parents when they did not give in to Martha's threats and temper tantrums. Martha was able to respond satisfactorily to the academic curriculum and was able to return to a regular class after one year in the day treatment program.

The behavior-modification approach is ahistorical and does not examine the past for causative explanations of a child's behavior. This strategy seeks for those stimuli in the environment that will maintain or strengthen a behavior and for consequences in the environment that can serve to suppress, extinguish, or develop specific behaviors. The key to the behavioral approach can be found in the word "contingency." Positive or negative reinforcers are delivered contingent upon pupils' behavior. A careful analysis is made of the effects of the contingency on the behavior until the behavior modifier is satisfied that there is a functional relation between the contingency and the behavior; after a functional relation has been established the behavior modifier can manipulate the contingencies to accelerate or decelerate a given behavior.

It is possible to conquer the problem of emphasizing the inhibition of behavior by concentrating on accelerating new responses. Lindsley (1968) has suggested the use of the "dead man's test" as a criterion measure which should be used to avoid falling into the trap of striving to create non-behavior such as sitting passively. This rule states that *if a dead man can do it, it is not behavior and therefore should not be used as a goal by teachers.* Thus, getting into a seat would be an acceptable response on the part of the child, but merely sitting would not. Recording answers to arithmetic problems is an acceptable goal for a teacher to work toward with a pupil, but having eyes on the task is not. This problem has been given particular cogency by a study of Winett and Winkler (1972), who reviewed the papers published in the *Journal of Applied Behavior Analysis* and concluded that the dependent variable in the majority of the studies dealing with behaviorally disordered children has been behaviors such as "attending," which Lindsley would view as too passive a behavior to strengthen. Using a reinforcement program, one finds that it is relatively easy to shape "attending behavior," but reinforcing "in seat behavior" or "eyes on task" will not teach a child academic or social skills unless specific teaching situations are set up with appropriate instructional materials and goals.

A project that taught social behavior was conducted by Minuchin, Chamberlain, and Graubard (1967), using curriculum to remediate some hypo- thesized deficits in the learning style of disorganized children from multi- problem families, often found in inner cities. The children involved seemingly did not expect to be heard and developed a style of communication in which they asserted themselves by yelling. They were not trained to elaborate ques- tions, gather information, or garner the nuances of degree. The children had also not been taught to develop themes to their logical conclusions or to achieve closure on conflicts. To counteract these deficits this study devel- oped a curriculum which consisted of *listening*, which was taught through the medium of games, such as "Simon Says." Winners in this game were explicitly commended for knowing how to listen. In another activity children listened to messages over the telephone and were later asked to repeat the message exactly. Differences between guessing and careful listening were made explicit and the results of each were contrasted. Taking turns at reciting stories was included in lessons. Discussion centered on the difficulties of listening for one's part, talking in turn, and waiting for the other person to speak. The novel device of having the children judge each other, was also explored. Points were awarded on the basis of specific, cogent criticisms, which had to be positively phrased. The judges (children who acted as ob- servers) were themselves rewarded according to the degree of correspondence between their observations and those of adult judges. It appeared that im- portant gains were made by children as a result of this instructional se- quence, since they were able to modify their own behavior and that of others as well, though no contrast group was involved.

Another experiment by Graubard, Rosenberg, and Miller (1971) designed to change social behaviors taught special class children the content as well as some of the methods of applied behavior analysis. The content included re- cording of data and how to establish baselines and evaluate intervention procedures. Some of the specifics included: (1) *extinction*, or walking away from children when teased or ridiculed, breaking eye contact, and ignoring behavior which they wished to decrease; (2) *reinforcement* of behaviors which they wished to increase through the sharing of toys and candy con- tingent upon desired behaviors or approximations to the terminal behavior; (3) *reinforcement of incompatible responses*, or initiating and reinforcing participants in activities which did not lend themselves to participants teas- ing each other or fighting with each other, and (4) *setting contingencies*, such as helping other children with homework, crafts, and in school activities, contingent upon the other children displaying behavior which the special edu- cation children wished to build. The *methods* employed to teach these skills included role playing, simulating, extensive use of videotape recordings and feedback on performance from peers and teachers, and data collection and analysis. In the process of changing other people's behavior it was learned that the special education children changed their own behavior as well. These reinforcement techniques were used by the special education children

to change the behavior of those teachers the children perceived as being punitive. By reinforcing appropriate teacher behavior the children were able to
change the amount of positive reinforcement the teachers gave. These same
special class children were also able to change the behavior of "normal"
children so that clashes between groups of children were significantly decreased. An extension of this same experiment involved teachers who had
highly structured their classrooms and had permitted children little freedom
of movement. The teachers, praised by supervisors for the freedom of movement which they now permitted children, were requested to use their classrooms as models for new teachers, to demonstrate how freedom and noise
could be tolerated. The teachers were praised in front of visitors for the
tolerance of freedom of movement and noise. Decibel readings, surrepti-
tiously taken, showed significant increases in noise level and that greater
freedom was allowed the children.

The development of the behavior-modification technology is responsible
for much success in teaching children with behavioral disabilities. Included
are teaching machines and programed instruction because they utilize successive approximations and positive reinforcement. The procedures used
in behavior-modification programs can be replicated and are sufficiently
technologically explicit to be packaged for any user. The effect of this
technology on classroom practice is shown as increasing numbers of studies
demonstrate the efficacy of such procedures. For instance, O'Leary and
Drabman (1971) reported that they were unable to find one published study
failing to find a routine positive effect of token-reinforcement programs, one
particular form of behavior modification.

Token economies are special systems based on reinforcement principles,
although they have not been as successful in raising academic levels as they
are reported to be in controlling social behavior. In a token system a unit
of exchange (token, poker chip, gold star, green stamp, and so on) is delivered contingent on a specified response. The token acquires the properties
of a conditioned reinforcer which can later be exchanged for a backup
reinforcer, usually selected from various items, since in children what constitutes a reinforcer is idiosyncratic. Because of the quest for novelty, certain
stimuli may in time lose their reinforcing properties for any individual child,
and teachers may find that they do not know which things will act as reinforcers at any given time. In a classroom one token might be given for each
correct response in a programed reading series during a work period, and
then during an exchange period the pupil could surrender his tokens and
purchase available items. Ayllon and Azrin (1968) have presented an extended discussion of token economies so explicit in its treatment of procedures that it can be very helpful to teachers.

Token reinforcement contingent on academic behavior has been successfully used to improve academic performance (Staats and Butterfield, 1965;
Tyler and Brown, 1968). Also, research has shown that with certain delinquents such extrinsic reinforcements are far more powerful than social

reinforcement (Quay and Hunt, 1965). The most explicit set of procedures for teaching delinquents has been detailed by Cohen, Filipczak, and Bis (1967), who describe a program conducted at the National Training School in Washington, D.C. Inmates were allowed to perform educational tasks for points, each of which was worth 1 cent, which could be applied toward the purchase of items from a Sears Roebuck catalog or to purchase time in the lounge or visiting time with friends. Students needed 90 percent accuracy on programed material to receive points. When they had enough points they could rent private offices, move into a general study area where they could also receive help, go to the library, or use the store. The points were displayed visually, and each inmate was responsible for his own addition and subtraction of points. Students paid tuition for tutoring and for taking advanced courses which could help them to earn even more points as their skill levels increased. Work was always corrected in front of the student, and an objective scoring key was used. The academic gains shown were substantial, and a disproportionate number of students in this project were placed in honors cottages and showed considerably improved social behavior as well.

Group incentives have also been found effective in changing academic behavior of juvenile inmates (Graubard, 1969). The group is extremely important to the juvenile delinquent. For example, Polsky (1962) found that the group in a residential school determined what was acceptable behavior for its constituents. When children threatened the homeostasis of the group by violating the delinquents' mores, the group persecuted the norm violators until one was eventually transferred to a mental hospital; no one child was powerful enough to withstand the group.

Educators can establish group incentives so that learning is a permissible activity for its members. Using a token system for children with elective mutism, for instance, Straughn, Potter, and Hamilton (1965) made class parties contingent on the children gaining enough points, by speaking, to earn the party. Wolf, Giles, and Hall (1968) set up an after-school group in which they used competition between teams of students for the best test grades. The winning team received a bonus of candy bars. The children in the group showed substantial improvement in reading achievement.

Csapo (1971) used peer recorders and peer models to change the behavior of primary school children considered disturbed by teachers involved in the study. The peer recorder was responsible for collecting the data, which proved reliable; the role of the peer model was to exhibit teacher-designated appropriate behaviors in the presence of the emotionally disturbed child, and to give tokens to the disturbed child when his behavior resembled the model's behavior. The tokens were coupled with social approval as well. Csapo's investigations show that peers were clearly able to modify the behavior of their classmates.

It is apparent that the place and format for modifying counterproductive modes of interaction can vary considerably. Given sufficient reinforcers and technical knowledge, the *behavior modifier* can be child, parent, or teacher. Using the appropriate incentive system, it should also be possible for entire school systems to work on a contingency basis. Many problems inherent to behavior-modification approaches remain: methods of fading out reinforcement systems have not yet been adequately investigated, nor have the long-term effects of motivational systems been followed up; in addition, behavior modification emphasizes how to change behavior and does not consider what should be changed; furthermore, there are many ethical considerations that arise whenever behavior is being controlled. Thus, although the behavior modification approach appears quite promising, much more research and thought needs to be devoted to the efficacy and wisdom of depending on this strategy.

The Ecological Approach

An ecological approach allows the practitioner to use the psychodynamic, behavioral-deficit, and behavior-modification techniques as well as to manipulate interpersonal relations and other aspects of the environment. It is the only approach that is not almost exclusively child centered. It differs from the other models in that it looks at the behavior of a least two people. Ecologically oriented teachers consider a child only in the context of the ecosystem in which he operates. The difficulty with this approach is that it is hard to ascertain just where the ecosystem of any individual stops. Although most ecological programs reported in the literature have had extensive research support, the feasibility of them as a method of treatment in any large-scale program has yet to be demonstrated.

As stated at the outset of this chapter, this approach is based on the definition of behavioral disability as an agitated exchange beween the culture violator and the culture bearer. Community child dissonance is considered to be a part of the "disturbed" condition and therefore must be considered in the intervention procedures (Rhodes, 1970). Treatment is not directed solely at the child but at the community as well. A major goal of ecological approaches is to change what is considered deviant by the community. Rhodes (1967) has called for the school to be divided into two equal components: the first focus should be concerned with cognitive development and the mastery of academic skills; and the second focus involves entering the world of the child, whether that world is found in the child's academic classrooms, his family, or the streets. The teacher dealing with the second aspect of the child's education would be charged not only with teaching the child behaviors to minimize community-child conflict but also with teaching the community to be more tolerant of "deviant" behavior. Such a teacher would help people to avoid being triggered into retaliatory reactions which create "dis-ease."

One of the most successful programs with an ecological approach is Project Re-Ed, developed by Hobbs (1969). In this program the child is removed from the family for approximately six months and placed in a boarding school, although treatment is directed to the family as a unit. The referring school and community are also included. A special teacher (the liaison teacher-counselor) works full time with the referring schools and agencies. The philosophy of Re-Ed has been expressed in a Tennessee State Department of Mental Health (1963) publication as follows:

> We assume that the child is an inseparable part of a small social system, of an ecological unit made up of the child, his family, his school, his neighborhood and community. . . . The Re-Ed school becomes a part of the ecological unit for as brief a period of time as possible, withdrawing when the probability that the system will function appears to exceed the probability that it will not. (p. 32)
> The following are some of the goals of Project Re-Ed:
> 1. Restoring to the child some trust in adults, some confidence in self, and some joy in the morrow.
> 2. Helping a child maintain normal·progress in school when possible and providing him with remedial work when needed.
> 3. Helping the child to unlearn some specific habits that cause rejection by family, school, and friends, and to acquire some specific habits that make him more acceptable to the people who are important in his life. (p. 32)

Teachers strive to meet these goals through a combination of goal setting, group process, and contingency management. Each child, along with his teacher and group, is responsible for setting explicit goals for himself at school and for his weekend at home. Goals are also set for each group by a council of peers and teachers which assesses each child's progress nightly at a "pow-wow." In addition to the feedback and contingency-management system, Re-Ed attempts to engage children in exciting, adventurous activities, such as wilderness camping, construction, caring for younger children in a therapeutic manner, and trips. The Re-Ed philosophy includes the belief that ceremonies and rituals give order and meaning to life and that pleasurable physical activities also promote growth of a positive self-concept. This strategy is an outcome of Hobbs' contention that "There should be some joy in every day and for the morrow." Several evaluations of Re-Ed (Weinstein, 1969; 1971) have generally found it to be an effective program, with approximately 80 percent of its graduates maintaining improved behavior at least six months after discharge.

A VOCATIONAL APPROACH TO DELINQUENT YOUTH

The education of delinquent children is an extremely difficult task for any teacher. A paucity of research exists in this area, and teachers have very few guidelines to follow. Whether academic instruction helps to reduce a delinquent life-style is simply not known at this time, but if youngsters learn marketable skills and good work habits it seems probable that they will at least have options open to them other than crime.

The vocational approach to rehabilitation uses a curriculum with an occupational emphasis as an integral part of attempts to prepare adolescent delinquents for the world of work. Many training schools and day schools for predelinquents structure their academic programs around job demands. For example, arithmetic problems will be geared around measuring lumber to make cabinets, or reading exercises will be concerned with how to order supplies and read blueprints. Writing exercises will revolve around composing business letters and how to fill out job applications. But academics usually occupy a minor part of the school day. Most of the child's time will be spent at shop work. Instructors in such programs are usually skilled auto mechanics, carpenters, or electricians.

Shore and Massimo (1966) described in detail their program of working with delinquent adolescents. In one experiment a group of boys were given psychotherapy and remedial education as well as vocational education. This group showed significant gains in skills as well as positive work records. An untreated control group continued to have difficulty with school, the law, and job placements. This writer finds their approach sensible, especially in working with adolescents who do not have aspirations for college education, but it is important that youngsters in vocational programs receive training on new and not obsolescent machinery and that they not be trained for nonexistent jobs. Adequate staff should be provided to work with the community and employers.

In general, when dealing with education for "delinquent" youth, what seem to be the most important factors are role clarification, individualized instruction, and an adequate instructional system, which—as emphasized in the discussion of behavior modification—takes the group into account, as illustrated in Vignette 5.2.

Vignette 5.2 Teaching a Delinquent Child by an Ecological Approach

John was placed in a residential center by the court when he was 12 years old for turning in false fire alarms, stealing, and being beyond the control of the school. At the residential treatment center John experienced much difficulty and continued his fighting and truancy. Other children avoided him, and teachers wanted him transferred from their classes after a day or two of attendance.

John was extremely powerful for his age and was known as a good fighter. Usually he responded to any perceived threat by striking out blindly. This also happened whenever he got excited while watching television or during active games. John's thinking was extremely concrete. Direct teaching had to be given him in how to argue, what phrases to use, and how to appeal to reason. Instructions such as "Be sure you pay attention to what he is saying before you answer" and "Be sure to ask a question if you're not sure of the meaning" served to enlarge his attention span. He was reinforced for not "letting the other guy sucker you into a fight." Adults taught him a signal system which helped him to lower his voice before he got angry, so that adults were perceived as guiders and not solely as controllers.

When he was taught in a group, systems had to be set up to help him. Specific peers had to be assigned to help John if he did not understand an assignment. It had to be made clear to him just what steps he was to take if the teacher was not immediately available to him. These procedures were rehearsed many times, and he was guided through these steps as part of his school work.

Although his reading skills were minimal, his listening skills were better and were used as the initial primary method of instruction. Large supplies of arts and crafts materials were made available to John. Because he was very vulnerable to provocation by teasing and had frequent temper outbursts, a group incentive was introduced. The group received a reinforcement such as a movie trip if John was able to go through specified lengths of time without fighting one of them.

An individualized reading program using the Hegge, Kirk, and Kirk Remedial Reading Drills was introduced, with card games and Cokes provided him on a contingent basis. He was not given a book to read until he had worked for over four months on the phonics drills—an unusually long time, but since his tolerance for failure was minimal, success had to be guaranteed before books were introduced. Since jokes appealed to him, his first reader was a *Book of Riddles* by Bennett Cerf.

Having entered the residential center a nonreader, after a year's placement in the center John achieved at the 2.8 grade reading level, according to the Metropolitan Reading Test.

MOTIVATION AND PUNISHMENT

Motivation is a key factor in teaching children successfully. Every teacher finds it much easier to work with a motivated student. However, such comments as "He just doesn't care," and "He doesn't have the proper attitude" are frequently heard. Furthermore they are sometimes used to dismiss teacher failure. Motivation, operationally defined by the degree of engagement in a particular behavior, is subject to change. The teacher can create motivation by the judicious use of contingencies. Premack (1959) developed some of the most salient principles of motivation for educators, stating that "Any response A will accelerate any response B, if and only if the independent rate of A is greater than that of B, and if the high probability behavior A is made contingent on the low probability behavior B." Acts of high probability (for example, ice cream eating) will reinforce low-probability behavior (spinach eating), but only if the availability of the ice cream cone is contingent on eating the spinach. This principle is no different from that used by mothers serving dessert only *after* the main meal is eaten. It has been followed intuitively by teachers and parents throughout the ages.

The systematic use of Premack's principle has been demonstrated to result in substantial improvements in academic progress and social behavior in conduct-disordered children (Haring and Phillips, 1962) and with children in residential treatment (Graubard, 1969). Many reinforcers are available in classrooms, for example, recess, gym periods, games, and jobs as monitors, which can be systematically programed according to Premack's principle. Token economies and contingency contracting incorporate the Premack principle in their operation by making access to high-probability behaviors such as play contingent upon the acceleration of low-probability behavior such as reading. It is necessary to ascertain the relative "strengths" of the ongoing behaviors, which can best be done through direct rate or frequency measurement of the child's behavior. The Premack principle can be easily applied by teachers to their pupils and does not depend upon outside "experts" for implementation.

Punishment of behaviorally disordered children is frequently observed in a variety of situations and settings. James (1969) conducted a survey of conditions in detention centers, mental hospitals, and training schools and noted that physical abuse was common. Some children were physically damaged permanently by some of the punishment procedures invoked. Children were locked in solitary confinement or sat idle for over 20 hours a day in a cell. The inmates of schools and institutions, with the tacit consent of the administration, sometimes terrorize and brutalize each other. Claude Brown's *Manchild in the Promised Land* (1965) vividly describes life in a residential treatment center where he was an inmate. While the extreme instances noted by these two writers are not common in public day school programs, most teachers employ punishment, their most frequent form being scoldings or ridicule.

Punishment can be empirically defined as a procedure that, when applied contingently to a behavior, decreases the frequency of that behavior. If used contingently on other classes of behavior, it will decrease the frequency of their occurrence as well. Punishment may be effective on a short-term basis and can be understood as an outgrowth of the extremely taxing situation in which many teachers work. While not a great deal is understood about punishment and its effects, it is important to examine what information is available.

Skinner (1968) feels that the use of punishment is counterproductive because it causes the learner to pay more attention to the punishment than to the material to be learned. Thomas, Becker, and Armstrong (1968) found that, when the number of disapproving remarks made by the teacher was tripled, the amount of disruptive behavior was increased. Teacher attention is usually contingent upon disruptive behavior. Theoretically, what is viewed as punishment by the teacher may increase the frequency of disruptive behaviors because the child learns that he must be "bad" in order to get teacher attention.

After reviewing the literature, Lipe and Jung (1971) concluded that if punishment is to be used, it is better to administer it without emotions such as rage, expressions of revenge, or disgust. O'Leary and Becker (1969) found soft reprimands to be more effective in reducing disruptive behavior than loud ones. Soft reprimands may serve as cues to the pupil to return to work. Reprimands sharply and publicly delivered provoke emotional reactions, and the child becomes concerned with "saving face" and opposing the teacher's authority.

Electric shock has been used, with equivocal results, in cases of serious self-destructive behaviors such as head banging and eye gouging. Birnbrauer (1968) used response-contingent electric shock to eliminate infrequent but unpredictable biting behavior of a retarded adolescent. Although the initial results were dramatic, the objectives of permanently eliminating this behavior were not achieved. Risley (1968) unsuccessfully tried to use ignoring procedures and positive reinforcement to eliminate a particularly dangerous behavior (climbing) in a child who had been labeled autistic. Punishment with electric shock was then used successfully to eliminate this behavior. Long-term follow-up was not reported for this study, so the permanence of the effects is a moot question.

An alternative to punishment (although many critics consider it a form of punishment), is the "time-out" procedure. During "time out" the child is removed from the scene of the misbehavior and cannot earn positive reinforcers. "Time out" is usually brief, and the child is ignored until the specific time period is over. This has been found to be quite effective in reducing certain kinds of disruptive behavior. This technique is directly applicable to classrooms and does not have to disrupt normal school routines.

In this writer's opinion, punishment—including "time out"—should be used only when behavior is extremely dangerous to the child or others. In the interests of protecting children, it is desirable to establish systems permitting the use of punishment only after more than one person, such as a review committee, has evaluated the factors involved. When a teacher feels punishment is indicated, it is often because the child has not been given an appropriate curriculum, or the teacher has not attempted to reinforce positively behaviors incompatible with the specific behavior she wishes to suppress.

EMERGING TRENDS

A number of emerging developments in both general and special education will undoubtedly have strong repercussions for the education of the behaviorally disabled child. Some of these are outlined below.

Legal Decisions and Civil Rights

Most of the recent landmark legal decisions concerning ethnic minorities have concerned the field of the mildly retarded and were discussed by Dunn in Chapters 1 and 3. These will probably soon begin to influence special education programs for the behaviorally disordered as well. A casual inspection of training schools and other special schools and classes for

behaviorally disordered children reveals that minority groups are dispro-
portionately represented. Schools will have to justify this practice. The courts
have already ruled that parents must be a part of the placement decisions.
Much of the litigation necessary to effect change will probably be initiated
by civil rights organizations. Urban centers with large black populations have
had demonstrations against the overwhelming proportion of black and Puerto
Rican students in "schools for maladjusted children." Concern has also been
expressed about the professional staff, which is predominantly white, especially at the leadership level.

Court decisions favoring children have been initiated by the American
Civil Liberties Union on issues such as arbitrary disciplinary procedures
involving dress codes, locker searches, and rules prohibiting children from
exercising their constitutional rights. The American Orthopsychiatric Association recently served as a "friend of the court" in a case where the decision
determined that adults could not be incarcerated in mental hospitals without
treatment. Thus, the trend for schools, agencies, and hospitals will be that
they must begin to provide educational treatment, eliminate institutional
racism, and scrupulously follow procedures that are neither arbitrary nor
culturally biased. There will thus be legal checks on the power of school
administrators and mental health personnel. Special education will be forced
to establish effective programs or be challenged on placement decisions.
Social action and litigation in this area will probably increase in the next
decade.

Legislation, Financing, and Decentralization

Although many states have permissive legislation concerning the education of behaviorally disordered children, there has been a sharp trend toward
mandatory laws regarding special education for severely disturbed youth.
Several state legislatures have now decreed that schools must provide
suitable education for these children. In cases where classes are not available, school districts must either establish them or provide transportation to
suitable facilities. A stipend may be awarded by the state to the parents,
who are then free to find their own private schools. The idea of giving
parents direct payments or vouchers to select programs closer to the needs
of their children has been frequently discussed. Such legislation will help
private schools. The development of a plethora of such schools with vastly
different philosophies and educational practices is likely. Teachers will also
be able to choose schools with educational philosophies similar to their own.
As a result of states mandating services, or providing the funds for parents to
purchase such services, geography will be less important in determining
whether children receive the services they need. Formerly, children in rural
or overcrowded urban areas were unlikely to receive special services. Opportunities for them have now been increased.

Consistent with a general pattern of voter rejection of local bond issues, especially for education, mental health services—both within and outside schools—have been drastically reduced. Special education budgets have also been pared in several communities, and federal funding has either been reduced or has remained static. Because of lack of demonstrated efficacy, programs for the behaviorally disordered have been quite vulnerable to budget cutting. During the late 1960s there were many more jobs than teachers available, but beginning in 1971 it became increasingly difficult for special educators to find jobs in their areas of specialization because entire programs were dismantled in certain school districts. Several factors are involved in abandoning classes for the behaviorally disordered, and financial reasons are more and more significant in such decisions. Programs will be stringently financed and much of the ancillary help on which programs depended in the past will be eliminated.

In very large cities there has been a trend toward decentralization, allowing local school boards to start tackling problems afresh, without cumbersome bureaucracies or vested interests pushing for particular programs. In many cases such a trend will probably end certain special education programs for at least two reasons: special education programs are expensive, and there is a growing reluctance to accept the "illness" model upon which much of special education rests. Thus, there will be a concerted effort to keep more children in the mainstream of education. This means that the itinerant-teacher model, rather than the special class, will be increasingly used in teaching the behaviorally disabled.

High School Graduation Requirements

High school offerings will be more diverse in the future. Furthermore, the passing of appropriate examinations will be accepted for graduation in lieu of school attendance. In addition, students will be able to earn high school diplomas through successful employment in industry and business. This will also affect special education programs for the behaviorally disordered at the high school level. With a greater diversity of programs and requirements in the regular schools, there will be less stress on many students and possibly a consequent reduction in social deviancy.

Child-Advocacy Programs

The Joint Commission on Mental Health of Children introduced the concept of child advocacy, which was discussed in Chapter 1. Its objectives include obtaining more responsive, adequate, and effective services from agencies, including the schools, and developing more sophistication within families to control their own destinies.

These programs will affect special educators of the maladjusted in many ways. Some will be asked to report to the pupils' advocates on the effectiveness of their interventions. In addition, child advocates will hopefully make bureaucracies more responsive to the people they are supposed to serve.

Technology, Innovation, and Accountability

The development of educational technology for behaviorally disabled children should enable teachers to become more efficient and effective. Procedures to reduce the frequency of antisocial behavior will be tried out and then disseminated to the field. Methods of evaluating these procedures will also be developed, so that teachers will be able to anticipate the effects of procedures with some degree of certainty. Computer-assisted instruction will be the rule rather than the exception. Much of the anxiety associated with learning will be reduced in behaviorally disordered children. Data analysis and printouts from computers will help teachers plan instruction and will assist in monitoring the performance of individual children.

Programed instruction and curriculum materials that accommodate individual differences will become increasingly popular and effective, enabling teachers to deal with diverse academic groups so that more time can then be devoted to building constructive social patterns for students. This will probably lessen the number of children placed in special classes for the behaviorally disordered for academic reasons, and members of such special classes will include only the more aberrant behavers.

Several educational programs are becoming sufficiently explicit in their procedures and methods of operation to be replicable by trained personnel. Complete models, coming with instructional procedures, curriculum, trainers, and consultants, will soon be available in toto to school districts.

Several school systems have begun the practice of performance contracting. Payment is predicated upon the actual performance of the children in basic school subjects. Several such contracts have been entered into between the U.S. government and industrial corporations or other organizations. The results have been equivocal, but we can expect to see corporations contracting with school boards to provide services for behaviorally disabled children. Since reimbursement will be contingent on student performance, such corporations will have a vested interest in innovation and will pay more attention to the end products than has been normal practice.

One innovation of recent influence is the British Infant School model, which has received considerable attention and popularity. In this country open classrooms are an outgrowth of this model. They are structured to eliminate individual desks and assigned places. There are tables for activities such as art, sand play, science and mathematics, library corners, and a doll house. In such a space children are given options for learning, and within ideal classrooms there is no real difference between work and play. The curriculum is individualized. The rules are few and simple: the child may not hurt others and must clean up after each activity. Emphasis is placed on peer tutoring. While evidence of successful scholastic achievement of children from the open classroom is equivocal, there is some evidence that children in these programs run afoul of authority fewer times than they do in conventional classrooms. Thus, this type of school could reduce the prevalence of children classified as maladjusted.

Finally, in the technological realm, there seems to be little doubt that drug treatment, when properly used, has resulted in benefits to some behaviorially disabled children. While considerable controversy still reigns (for instance, in the area of drug treatment for hyperkinetic children—see Chapter 10), its contribution to the control of behavioral problems should increase. Furthermore, drug addiction will tend to be better controlled in the future. This should reduce the need for education programs for the behaviorally disordered, especially for the juvenile delinquent, since drug addiction is the cause of much of the incarceration and special programing that takes place today.

SUMMARY

In this chapter the term "behavioral disability" or "behavior disorder" is defined as a chronic display of deviant behaviors that violate the perceiver's expectation of appropriate behavior and which the perceiver wishes to see stopped. The term "behavioral disability" is used to include both the "emotionally disturbed" and "socially maladjusted" (or "juvenile delinquent"). Quay has provided a four-way classification system for pupils usually enrolled in public school special education, namely, children with (1) conduct disorders, (2) personality problems, (3) inadequate-immature behavior, and (4) socialized delinquency. Two other groups—(5) schizophrenic, psychotic, or autistic children and (6) adjudicated juvenile delinquent—have also been considered in this chapter, although usually the public schools are not called upon to serve these latter groups. These six classifications may have some use for educational grouping, although many reinforcement theorists oppose any type of classification, and ecological theorists believe that behavioral disability is not the exclusive property of the behaver but rather is an agitated exchange between the behaver and the responder.

This chapter took the stance that aberrant behavior should be observed in the place and with the people where the problems actually occur, rather than in examination rooms. An efficacious way to measure and rate behavior is through direct observation, using behavioral checklists. This method is the most specific and relevant to classroom teachers. There are few if any behavioral characteristics exclusive to behaviorally disordered children. The overlap between different types of behaviorally disabled children and "normal" children is substantial. It is therefore imperative to look at the individual without stereotyped notions about behaviorally disordered children.

The U.S. Office of Education has stated that 2 percent of children need special education programing for behavioral disabilities. Probably 10 percent of the school-age children in this country need some type of program shift. Much of this could be accomplished in regular classrooms with the assistance of remedial specialists, home and school cooperative arrangements, or through the use of aides. One half of 1 percent of school-age children probably need some type of residential or other intensive service.

Special education instructional approaches for these pupils include psychodynamic, behavioral-deficit, behavior-modification, and ecological approaches. The primary administrative arrangements for delivering the above were discussed in Chapter 1; these include self-contained special day classes, resource rooms, itinerant teachers, residential schools, and homebound instruction.

Evaluation is a major problem in programs for the behaviorally disordered. Program objectives must be stated in behavioral terms that are measurable. Evaluation will become more important as budgets become more stringent and the demand for accountability grows. A number of trends in general and special education will begin to have greater impact in the years ahead on education programs for behaviorally disabled children and youth. Placement into special education programs will have to be soundly justified and parental cooperation must be assured. Legislation mandating special education programs will increase, and the more severely aberrant behavers will have to be provided with effective services. Technology will have an increasing impact on programs, and cost will be a major factor in program planning.

Resources[2]

There are many resources available for teachers of children with behavioral disabilities. Described in this present section are professional organizations and journals concerned with such children.

Although many organizations serve children with behavioral disorders, there are few concerned primarily or exclusively with this population. The Council for Children with Behavioral Disorders, a division of the Council for Exceptional Children, Suite 900, Jefferson Plaza, 1411 S. Jefferson Davis Highway, Arlington, Virginia 22202, is one of the most noteworthy organizations in the latter category. Additional relevant organizations are the Association for Mentally Ill Children, 12 West 12th Street, New York, New York 10003; the National Society for Autistic Children, 621 Central Avenue, Albany, New York 12206; and the National Council on Crime and Delinquency, 411 Hackensack Avenue, Hackensack, New Jersey 07601. The following are organizations serving more general populations but devoting a significant proportion of their resources to serving the behaviorally disordered: American Orthopsychiatric Association, 1775 Broadway, New York, New York 10019; American Public Welfare Association, 1313 East 60th Street, Chicago, Illinois 60637; Child Study Association of America, 9 East 89th Street, New York, New York 10028; Child Welfare League of America, 44 East 23rd Street, New York, New York 10010; Family Services Association of America, 44 East 23rd Street, New York, New York 10010; National Association for Mental Health, 1800 North 10th, Rossalyn Station, Arlington, Virginia 22209; and American Schizophrenia Foundation, 230 Nickels Arcade, Ann Arbor, Michigan 48108.

[2] This section was compiled with the aid of Mrs. Gwen Zeichner from the Henry Ittleson Center for Child Research, Jewish Board of Guardians, Bronx, New York.

One of the few professional publications that deals exclusively with behaviorally disabled children is the *Newsletter of the Council for Children with Behavior Disorders*. Two others are the *Journal of Autism and Childhood Schizophrenia* and the *Journal of Abnormal Child Psychology*. There are key journals of a more general nature in which articles dealing with behaviorally disordered children can most frequently be found. Included in this category are *American Journal of Orthopsychiatry, Behavior Research and Therapy, Exceptional Children, Journal of Abnormal and Social Psychology, Journal of Applied Behavior Analysis*, and the *Newsletter* of Division 12 for Clinical Child Psychology of the American Psychological Association. The American Schizophrenia Foundation publishes a journal, *Schizophrenia*, and the *Schizophrenia Newsletter* of the ASF. The National Council on Crime and Delinquency publishes two journals, *Crime and Delinquency* and the *Journal of Research on Crime and Delinquency*, plus a newsletter.

Finally, the National Institute of Mental Health, located at 5454 Wisconsin Avenue, Chevy Chase, Maryland 20015, deals with problems such as delinquency and child mental health. It has numerous publications that will be of interest to special educators. Additional publications can be obtained from the U.S. Office of Education, Bureau of Education for the Handicapped, 7th and D Streets, Washington, D.C., 20202. Answers to questions about specific services for children with behavioral disorders can be had from the U.S. Office of Education by writing to Project Closer Look, P.O. Box 1492, Washington, D.C. 20013.

References

Ayllon, T., and Azrin, N. *The token economy*. New York: Appleton-Century-Crofts, 1968.

Baer, D., Wolf, M., and Risley, T. Some current dimensions of applied behavior analysis. *Journal of Applied Behavior Analysis*, 1968, **1** (1), 91–97.

Becker, W. C., Madsen, C. H., Arnold, C. R., and Thomas, D. R. The contingent use of teacher attention and praise in reducing classroom behavior problems. *Journal of Special Education*, 1967, **1** (3), 287–307.

Benedict, R. Anthropology and the abnormal. *Journal of General Psychology*, 1934, **10**, 59–82.

Berkowitz, P., and Rothman, E. *The disturbed child*. New York: New York University Press, 1960.

Birnbrauer, J. S. Generalization of punishment effects—a case study. *Journal of Applied Behavior Analysis*, 1968, **1**, 201–211.

Blakeslee, A. What you should know about drugs and narcotics. In B. Hafen (Ed.), *Readings in drug use and abuse*. Provo, Utah: Brigham Young University Press, 1970.

Bower, E. M. Comparison of the characteristics of identified emotionally disturbed children with other children in classes. In E. P. Trapp, and P. Himmelstein (Eds.), *Readings on the exceptional child*. New York: Appleton-Century-Crofts, 1962.

Bower, E. M., and Hollister, W. G. *Behavioral science frontiers in education*. New York: Wiley, 1967.

Brown, C. *Manchild in the promised land*. New York: Macmillan, 1965.

Bruno, F. Life values, manifest needs, and vocational interests as factors influencing professional growth satisfaction among teachers of the emotionally disturbed. Unpublished doctoral dissertation, Wayne State University, 1968.

Bullock, L., and Whelan, R. Competencies needed by teachers of the emotionally disturbed and socially maladjusted: A comparison. *Exceptional Children*, 1971, **37** (7), 485–490.

Cloward, R. and Ohlin, L. *Delinquency and opportunity*. Glencoe, Ill.: Free Press, 1960.

Cohen, A. K. *Delinquent boys: The culture of the gang*. Glencoe, Ill.: Free Press, 1955.

Cohen, H., Filipczak, J., and Bis, J. *Case I: An initial study of contingencies applicable to special education*. Washington, D.C.: Education Faculty Press, 1967.

Cook, C., Cort, H., Flocco, E., and Sanford, J. A study of exemplary programs for emotionally disturbed children. Final report in fulfillment of Contract No. OEC-0-70-4922. New York: General Learning Corporation, 1972.

Cowen, E. L., Zax, M., Izzo, L., and Trost, M. Prevention of emotional disorders in the school setting. *Journal of Consulting Psychology*, 1966, **30**, 381–387.

Csapo, M. G. Utilization of normal peers as behavior change agents for reducing the inappropriate behavior of emotionally disturbed children in regular classroom environments. Unpublished doctoral dissertation, University of Kansas, 1971.

Dorward, B. A. A comparison of the competencies for regular classroom teachers and teachers of emotionally disturbed children. *Exceptional Children*, 1963, **30**, 67–73.

Eddy, N. B., Halbach, H., Isbell, H., and Seevers, M. H. Drug dependence: Its significance and characteristics. Geneva, Switzerland, *World Health Organization Bulletin*, 1965, **32**, 721–733.

Gersh, M., and Nagle, 'R. Preparation of teachers for the emotionally disturbed. *Exceptional Children*, 1969, **35** (8), 633–642.

Gittelman, M., and Birch, H. G. Intellect, neurologic status, perinatal risk and family pathology in schizophrenic children. *Archives of General Psychiatry*, 1967, **17**, 16–25.

Glueck, S., and Glueck, E. *Unraveling juvenile delinquency*. New York: Commonwealth Fund, 1950.

Graubard, P. S. Utilizing the group in teaching disturbed delinquents to learn. *Exceptional Children*, 1969, **36**, 267–272.

Graubard, P. S. An investigation of reading correlates of emotionally disturbed and socially maladjusted children: The relevance of a classification scheme to educational characteristics. *Exceptional Children*, 1971, **37**, (10), 755–757.

Graubard, P. S., and Miller, M. B. Behavior disorders. In G. O. Johnson and H. D. Blank (Eds.), *Exceptional children research review*. Arlington, Va.: Council for Exceptional Children, 1968.

Graubard, P. S., Rosenberg, H., and Miller, M. Ecological approaches to social deviancy. In B. Hopkins and E. Ramp (Eds.), *A new direction for education: Behavior analysis 1971*. Lawrence, Kan.: Department of Human Development, University of Kansas, 1971.

Hall, R. V., Lund, D., and Jackson, D. Effects of teacher attention on study behavior. *Journal of Applied Behavior Analysis*, 1968, **1** (1), 1–12.

Haring, N., and Phillips, L. *Educating emotionally disturbed children*. New York: McGraw-Hill, 1962.

Harth, R., and Glavin, J. Validity of teacher rating as a subtest for screening emotionally disturbed children. *Exceptional Children*, 1971, **37** (8), 605–606.

Havelkova, M. Follow-up study of seventy-one children diagnosed as psychotic in pre-school age. *American Journal of Orthopsychiatry*, 1968, **38**, 846–857.

Hewett, F. M. *The emotionally disturbed child in the classroom.* Boston: Allyn & Bacon, 1968.

Hobbs, N. Helping disturbed children: Psychological and ecological strategies. In H. Dupont (Ed.), *Educating emotionally disturbed children.* New York: Holt, Rinehart and Winston, 1969.

Hodges, E. F., and Tait, C. D. A follow-up study of potential delinquents. *American Journal of Psychiatry*, 1963, **120**, 449–453.

Hollingshead, A. B., and Redlich, J. C. Social stratification and psychiatric disorders. *American Sociological Review*, 1953, **18**, 163–169.

James, H. *Children in trouble: A national scandal.* New York: Mackay, 1969.

Jenkins, R. Psychiatric syndromes in children and their relation to family background. *American Journal of Orthopsychiatry*, 1966, **36**, 450–457.

Kirk, S. A., *Educating Exceptional Children* (2d. ed.) Boston: Houghton Mifflin, 1972.

Kvaraceus, W. C. *KD proneness scale and check list.* New York: Harcourt Brace & Jovanovich, 1953.

Kvaraceus, W. C. *Juvenile delinquency. What research says to the teacher.* Washington, D.C.: American Educational Research Association of the National Educational Association, No. 15, 1958.

Kvaraceus, W. C. Forecasting juvenile delinquency: A three-year experiment. *Exceptional Children*, 1961, **28**, 429–435.

Kvaraceus, W. C. *Anxious youth: Dynamics of delinquency.* Columbus, O.: Charles E. Merrill, 1966.

Lewis, W. W. Continuity and intervention in emotional disturbance: A review. *Exceptional Children*, 1965, **31**, (9), 465-476.

Lindsley, O. R. *Training parents and teachers to precisely manage children's behaviors.* Lawrence, Kan.: University of Kansas Bureau of Child Research, 1968.

Lindsley, O. R. Personal communication, 1970.

Lipe, D., and Jung, S. Manipulating incentives to enhance school learning. *Review of Educational Research*, 1971, **41**, (4), 249–280.

Mackie, R., Kvaraceus, W., and Williams, H. Teachers of children who are socially and emotionally maladjusted. Washington, D.C.: U.S. Office of Education, 1957.

Mackler, B. A report on the "600" schools: Dilemmas, problems, and solutions. In D. A. Dentler, B. Mackler, and M. Warshauer (Eds.), *The urban R's.* New York: Praeger, 1967.

Mager, R. F. *Preparing instructional objectives.* Palo Alto, Calif.: Fearon, 1962.

Marwit, S. J., and Stenner, A. J. Hyperkinesis: Delineation of two patterns. *Exceptional Children*, 1972, **38**, 401–406.

McCaffrey, I., and Cummings, J. Behavior patterns associated with persistent emotional disturbances of school children in regular classes of elementary grades. Onandaga County, N.Y.: Mental Health Research Unit, New York State Department of Mental Hygiene, 1967.

McCaffrey, I., and Cummings, J. Persistence of emotional disturbances reported among second and fourth grade children. In H. Dupont (Ed.), *Educating emotionally disturbed children.* New York: Holt, Rinehart and Winston, 1969.

McDermott, J. F., Harrison, S. I., Schrager, J., and Wilson, P. Social class and mental illness in children: Observations of blue collar families. *American Journal of Orthopsychiatry*, 1965, **35**, 500–508.

McKinnon, A. A follow-up and analysis of the effects of placement in classes for emotionally disturbed children in elementary school. *Dissertation Abstracts*, 1969 (5-A), 1872.

Meehl, P. Schizotaxia, schizotypy, schizophrenia. In A. Buss (Ed.), *Theories in schizophrenia*. Chicago: Aldine-Atherton, 1969.

Meyer, H., Borgatta, E., Jones, W., Anderson, E., Grunwald, H., and Headly, D. *Girls at vocational high—an experiment in social work intervention.* New York: Russell Sage Foundation, 1965.

Miller, M. Behavioral research: A modest primer for teachers. In P. S. Graubard (Ed.), *Children against schools.* Chicago: Follett, 1969.

Miller, W. Lower class culture as a generating milieu of gang delinquency. *Journal of Social Issues*, 1959, **14**, 5–19.

Minuchin, S. H., Chamberlain, P., and Graubard, P. S. A project to teach learning skills to disturbed, delinquent children. *American Journal of Orthopsychiatry*, 1967, **37**, 558–567.

Morse, W. The education of socially maladjusted and emotionally disturbed children. In W. Cruickshank and O. Johnson (Eds.), *Education of exceptional children and youth.* Englewood Cliffs, N.J.: Prentice-Hall, 1967.

Morse, W. C., Cutler, R. L., and Fink, A. H. *Public school classes for the emotionally handicapped: A research analysis.* Arlington, Va.: Council for Exceptional Children, 1964.

National Center for Social Statistics. Report No. 6. Statistics on Public Institutions for Delinquent Children, U.S. Department of Health, Education and Welfare, 1970.

New York Post. How a five-year-old gets his start: Road to drugs, February 2, 1972, p. 5.

O'Leary, K. D., and Becker, W. The effects of the intensity of a teacher's reprimands on children's behavior. *Journal of School Psychology*, 1969, **7**, 8–11.

O'Leary, K. D., and Drabman, R. Token reinforcement in the classroom: A review. *Psychology Bulletin*, 1971, **75** (6).

O'Neal, P., and Robins, L. N. The relation of childhood behavior problems to adult psychiatric status. *American Journal of Psychiatry*, 1958, **114**, 961–969. (a)

O'Neal, P., and Robins, L. N. Childhood patterns predictive of adult schizophrenia. *American Journal of Psychiatry*, 1958, **115**, 385–391. (b)

Pate, J. E. Emotionally disturbed and socially maladapted children. In L. M. Dunn (Ed.), *Exceptional children in the schools.* New York: Holt, Rinehart and Winston, 1963.

Piaget, A. Teacher style and pupil behavior in special classes for acting-out, disturbed children. Unpublished doctoral dissertation, Yeshiva University, 1972.

Polsky, H. W. *Cottage six.* New York: Russell Sage Foundation, 1962.

Premack, D. Toward empirical behavior laws: I—positive reinforcement. *Psychology Review*, 1959, **66**, 219–233.

Prentice, N., and Kelly, F. J. Intelligence and delinquency: A reconsideration. *Journal of School Psychology*, 1963, **60**, 327–339.

Quay, H. C., and Hunt, W. Psychopathy, neuroticism, and verbal conditioning: A replication and extension. *Journal of Consulting Psychology*, 1965, **29**, 283.

Quay, H. C. Dimensions of problem behavior and educational programming. In P. S. Graubard (Ed.) *Children against schools,* Chicago: Follett, 1969.

Rezmierski, V., and Kotre, J. A limited literature review of the theory of the psychodynamic model. In W. C. Rhodes and M. L. Tracy (Eds.), *A study of child variance: Conceptual project in emotional disturbance.* Ann Arbor, Mich.: University of Michigan Institute for the Study of Mental Retardation and Related Disabilities, 1971.

Rhodes, W. C. The disturbing child: A problem of ecological management. *Exceptional Children*, 1967, **33**, 449–455.

Rhodes, W. C. A community participation analysis of emotional disturbance. *Exceptional Children*, 1970, **36**, 309–316.

Rhodes, W. C., and Tracy, M. L. (Eds.), *A study of child variance: Conceptual project in emotional disturbance*. Ann Arbor, Mich.: University of Michigan Institute for the Study of Mental Retardation and Related Disabilities, 1971.

Risley, T. The effects and side effects of punishing the autistic behaviors of a deviant child. *Journal of Applied Behavior Analysis*, 1968, **1**, 21–34.

Rogers, C. *On becoming a person*. Boston: Houghton Mifflin, 1961.

Rogers, C. *Freedom to learn*. Columbus, O.: Charles E. Merrill, 1969.

Rubin, E. Z., Simson, C. B., and Betwee, M. C. *Emotionally handicapped children and the elementary school*. Detroit: Wayne State University Press, 1966.

Rutter, M. The influence of organic and emotional factors on the origins, nature, and outcome of childhood psychoses. *Developmental Medicine and Child Neurology*, 1965, **7**, 120–129.

Sagor, M. Biological bases of childhood behavioral disorders. In W. E. Rhodes and M. L. Tracy (Eds.), *A study of child variance: Conceptual project in emotional disturbance*. Ann Arbor, Mich.: Institute for the Study of Mental Retardation and Related Disabilities, 1971.

Scarpitti, F., and Scarpitti, E. The social origins of delinquency. In P. S. Graubard (Ed.), *Children against schools*. Chicago: Follett, 1969.

Scheff, T. *Being mentally ill*. Chicago: Aldine-Atherton, 1966.

Schultz, E. W., Hirshoren, A., Manton, A., and Henderson, R. Special education for the emotionally disturbed. *Exceptional Children*, 1971, **38** (4), 313–320.

Shaw, C. R., and McKay, H. D. *Juvenile delinquency and urban areas*. Chicago: University of Chicago Press, 1942.

Shore, M., and Massimo, J. Comprehensive vocationally oriented psychotherapy for adolescent delinquent boys: A follow-up study. *American Journal of Orthopsychiatry*, 1966, **6**, 609–615.

Skinner, B. F. *Behavior of organisms*. New York: Appleton-Century-Crofts, 1938.

Skinner, B. F. *The technology of teaching*. New York: Appleton-Century-Crofts, 1968.

Spence, I. Counting the teacher reactions to pupil behaviors: A tool for teacher training. Unpublished doctoral dissertation, Yeshiva University, 1972.

Spiegelman, R. *A benefit-cost model to evaluate educational programs*. Menlo Park, Calif.: Stanford Research Institute, 1968.

Staats, A. W., and Butterfield, W. H. Treatment of nonreading in a culturally deprived juvenile delinquent: An application of reinforcement principles. *Child Development*, 1965, **36**, 925–942.

Stevens, J., Sachder, K., and Milstein, V. Behavior disorders of children and the electroencephalogram. *Archives of Neurology*, 1968, **18** (2), 160–177.

Straughn, J., Potter, W., and Hamilton, S. Behavior treatment of an elective mute. *Journal of Child Psychology and Psychiatry*, 1965, **6**, 125–130.

Sutherland, E. *Principles of criminology*. Philadelphia: Lippincott, 1947.

Tennessee State Department of Mental Health. Project Re-ed: A demonstration project for teachers of emotionally handicapped children. Nashville, Tenn.: Department of Mental Health, 1963.

Thomas, D. R., Becker, W. C., and Armstrong, M. Production and elimination of disruptive classroom behavior by systematically varying teacher's behavior. *Journal of Applied Behavior Analysis*, 1968, **1**, 35–45.

Thomas, A., Chess, S., and Birch, H. *Temperament and behavior disorders in children.* New York: New York University Press, 1968.

Tyler, V. O., and Brown, G. D. Token reinforcement of academic performance with institutionalized delinquent boys. *Journal of Educational Psychology*, 1968, **59**, 164–168.

Ullmann, L., and Krasner, L. (Eds.) *Case studies in behavior modifications.* New York: Holt, Rinehart, and Winston, 1965.

Ullmann, L., and Krasner, L. *A psychological approach to abnormal behavior.* Englewood Cliffs, N.J.: Prentice-Hall, 1969.

U.S. Juvenile Court Statistics, Department of Health, Education and Welfare Publication No. 72-03452.

U.S. Office of Education. Preparation of personnel in the education of the handicapped—Public Law 71-230. Program Administration Manual, 1971. Washington, D.C.: U.S. Office of Education.

Weinstein, L. Project re-ed schools for emotionally disturbed children: Effectiveness as viewed by referring agencies, parents, and teachers. *Exceptional Children*, 1969, **35**, 703–711.

Weinstein, L. The zoomer class: Initial results. *Exceptional Children*, 1971, **38**, 58–65.

Werry, J., and Quay, H. Observing the classroom behavior of elementary school children. *Exceptional Children*, 1969, **35**, 461–470.

White, M., and Charry, J. (Eds.) *School disorders, intelligence, and social class.* New York: Teachers College Press, 1966.

Winett, R., and Winkler, R. Current behavior modification in the classroom: Be still, be quiet, be docile. *Journal of Applied Behavior Analysis*, 1972, **4**, 499–504

Wolf, M. M., Giles, D. K., and Hall, R. V. Experiments with token reinforcement in a remedial classroom. *Behavior Research and Therapy*, 1968, **6**, 51–64.

Opposite: The most frequent speech disability found in primary grade pupils is articulation problems such as producing the "sk" sound correctly. (Photographer: Jack Pearson, Colorado State University Photographic Department.)

chapter six / forrest m. hull and mary e. hull

children with
oral communication disabilities

cHApTER OuTliNE

The central theme of this text emphasizes the urgent need to improve the quality of education for the exceptional child. It is argued that the educational needs of the exceptional child can be met more efficiently if we concentrate on ways of keeping him in the mainstream of education while providing him with the special services he needs to assure educational success. As in the other areas of exceptionality, many new trends have emerged in the field of speech and oral language since 1963, when the first edition of this book was published. Therefore, in many respects, this revision is viewed by us as a report on a transitional phase in the honing of our skills in helping children with oral communication disabilities.

Human communication has been of major interest to society since man's early history. Oral speech is probably the most universally used form of communication among all societies. Interest and fascination with this process deepen to concern when the ability of one individual to communicate orally with another is impaired in any way. For example, the problem of stuttering has been recognized for many centuries and a variety of procedures have been prescribed to alleviate the condition, but despite all "cures," approaches, techniques and some advances, the problem remains unsolved. The concern for stuttering and other speech disorders shown in the past by philosophers and physicians continues into the modern-day classroom where the teacher may be faced with the challenge of a child who cannot satisfactorily ask his questions nor express his ideas.

Until 1960, the emphasis on the alleviation of communication disturbances was restricted to speech problems such as articulation, voice, and stuttering and to language impairments due to central nervous system damage, including aphasia, dyslexia, dysgraphia, and auditory imperceptions. During the 1960s, the field broadened to include language differences generally referred to as "nonstandard English," which are associated with children from economically disadvantaged environments, and those from various ethnic and racial minority groups. Some behavioral scientists hold to the view that nonstandard English interferes with cognition and learning and thus is detrimental to education. As discussed later in this chapter, others tend to disagree with this concept. In any event, nonstandard English came in for much attention in the 1960s.

Increased knowledge concerning normal language acquisition and concern with the effects of language deficit on educational success are bringing about a new direction for the speech clinician[1] in the schools. The traditional role was one of the clinician selecting large numbers of children with mild or moderate speech problems, as well as those more severely handicapped, for individual or small group therapy. In the 1970s, there is a trend in the

---

[1] Throughout this chapter, the term "speech clinician" will be used. Other titles commonly used to denote this individual are "speech therapist," "speech correctionist," "speech pathologist," and "speech specialist." These terms are often used interchangeably.

schools away from the self-contained classroom toward the concept of "open school." Such a trend may necessitate a changed role for the speech clinician. In this new role the speech clinician would serve as a consultant to teachers for children whose speech and language deviations do not require individual attention and highly specific techniques. As a consultant, the speech clinician would be one member of a team (which includes the teacher, the counselor, and perhaps others) whose purpose is to keep the child in the classroom and solve the problem there. Thus, the selection of any child for individual therapy away from the classroom would be made only after other possible alternatives had been explored and rejected. The primary goal is to keep the child with a communication problem in the mainstream of education as much as possible. In order to do this classroom activities must be structured in such a way that the teacher can provide for the increased responsibility of handling oral communication problems. This is seen as a truly cooperative effort on the part of the teacher, the speech clinician, and any other team members involved if all children with speech and language disabilities are to enjoy maximum benefits from the total educational program.

This chapter is divided into two broad sections. Approximately the first half of the chapter deals with the normal development of speech and oral language expression with definitions and classification of the various types of speech and oral language disabilities, prevalence, and social and vocational implications. The latter part of the chapter deals mainly with identification and remediation procedures for each type of disability, including suggestions for the classroom teacher.

DEVELOPMENT OF SPEECH AND ORAL LANGUAGE

The normal acquisition of speech and language is orderly and at times appears to be operating in accordance with some sort of predetermined time schedule, which varies to a certain degree for individual children. However, normal speech and language development are closely associated with chronological age and normal physical and intellectual maturation, so that a broad timetable which reflects the sequential acquisition of some important indicators of development can be devised. Although numerous measures have been used to describe speech and language development, the information shown in Table 6.1, which was compiled from the works of Berry (1969), Carrow (1968), Davis (1937, 1938), Irwin (1947, 1948), Lee (1966), McCarthy (1954), Metraux (1950), and Templin (1957), illustrates the patterns of change beginning with the use of crude undifferentiated vocalizations during the first few months following birth, to the use of complex grammatical structures in communicating ideas as the child approaches adulthood. The category of *general characteristics* provides information about the way language elements (vocabulary, rules of grammar, and parts of speech) are used in com-

TABLE 6.1 *Summary of Early Normal Speech and Oral Language Developmental Stages*

Age	General Characteristics	Usable Speaking Vocabulary (Number of Words)	Adequate Speech Sound Production
Months			
1–3	*Undifferentiated crying.* Random vocalizations and cooing.		
4–6	*Babbling.* Specific vocalizations. Verbalizes in response to speech of others. Immediate responses approximate human intonational patterns.		
7–11	Tongue moves with vocalizations (lalling). Vocalizes recognition. Reduplicates sound. Echolalia (automatic repetition of words and phrases).		
12	*First word.*	1–3	All vowels
18	*One-word sentence stage.* Well-established jargon. Uses nouns primarily.	18–22	
Years			
2	*Two-word sentence stage.* Sentences functionally complete. Uses more pronouns and verbs.	270–300	
2.5	*Three-word sentence stage.* Telegraphic speech.	450	h, w, hw
3	Complete simple-active-sentence structure used. Uses sentences to tell stories which are understood by others.	900	p, b, m
3.5	*Expanded grammatical forms.* Concepts expressed with words. Speech disfluency is typical. Sentence length is 4–5 words.	1200	t, d, n
4	Excessive verbalizations. Imaginary speech.	1500	k, g, ng, j
5	*Well-developed and complex syntax.* Uses more complex forms to tell stories. Uses negation and inflexional form of verbs.	2000	f, v
6–8	*Sophisticated speech.* Skilled use of grammatical rules. Learns to read. Acceptable articulation by 8 years for males and females.	2600+	l, r, y, s, z, sh, ch, zh, th, consonant blends

munication; *usable speaking vocabulary* denotes the number of meaningful words that are available to the child; and the *speech sound production* category indicates the level of intelligibility that can be achieved when accurate production of the speech sound elements are incorporated into expressive language behavior. This way of looking at development says nothing about receptive language ability. However, it has been well established that comprehension (reception) precedes meaningful production (expression). Thus, observation of a given level of expressive language behavior implies that comprehension had developed earlier.

The birth cry, which many consider to be the first speech sound (not necessarily language), marks the beginning of a series of complex changes in linguistic behavior that will cover a period of several years; indeed, it continues to develop in complexity to adulthood, although there is very little available information in the literature describing the development of oral language progress beyond eight years of age. Language development beyond that point is influenced by many factors that did not play a predominant role in the early years. As children continue to mature, they become increasingly mobile and are influenced more and more by experiences that extend beyond the home environment. The growing child continues to experiment with the grammatical rules, developing more complex forms of language usage as the need arises. His vocabulary will continue to expand with the development of his reading skills. Students at the junior high and senior high school levels begin to develop specific academic, vocational, and social interests which will affect the oral-language developmental process. Motivation and opportunity to learn are also important determinants for the development of language skills. If a person is physically, intellectually, and emotionally healthy, he probably will acquire language skills that are compatible with his environment. Thus, if his environment changes so will his language, and one may then conclude that oral language is a constantly changing phenomenon throughout life.

DEFINITION AND CLASSIFICATION

Oral language may be defined as the distinctively human use of spoken symbols arranged systematically for the expression and comprehension of ideas. For example, in the sentence "I see the house," the words are arranged in a system or order which expresses a meaningful idea. If words thus arranged mean what the speaker intended, then he has demonstrated oral language expressive ability. If the listener understands the meaning of this arrangement of words, then he has demonstrated oral language receptive ability. *Speech* is the major means used by man to express language, and it may be defined as the production of the unique audible utterances which serve as the basic symbols for oral language. These utterances used to form "words" consist of sound units that are usually identified broadly as phonemes (speech sounds). In the American English dialects of the United States approximately 22 vowel and diphthong phonemes and 25 consonant and consonant-blend phonemes are used. Vowels are voiced phonemes and are characterized by a "tonal" or "musical" quality. Typical vowels are the "a" in *cat* and "oo" in *good*. Consonants, considerably more important to speech intelligibility than vowels, are phonemes which may be voiced or unvoiced. Note, for instance, that the consonants "c" and "t" in *cat* are unvoiced while the "g" and "d" in *good* are voiced.

Oral language expression can be differentiated from speech in that the former term refers to the information (idea) which is transmitted and the latter to the vehicle (spoken words) used to transmit the information. Under certain circumstances, it is conceivable that connected words can be spoken without expressing an idea meaningful either to the speaker or listener. The result may be "speech," but not "language." From the foregoing definitions, corollary definitions may be drawn for disabilities of oral language and speech.

ORAL LANGUAGE DISABILITIES

Disability in oral language occurs when an individual is unable to comprehend meaningful ideas which have been spoken or when he is unable to use spoken words to effectively express meaningful ideas.

There appear to be two relatively distinct categories of language expression disabilities which can be considered: (1) language problems which are related to some form of central nervous system malfunction, and (2) those related to lack of experience because of environmental factors which provide an inadequate linguistic model (nonstandard English).

Language Disabilities Related to Central Nervous System Impairment

When normal function of the central nervous system has been impaired, many types of behavioral disorders may be manifested. One of the most important of these is the language disturbance which is frequently accompanied by other kinds of deviant behavior. In the broad sense, language disturbances include disorders of oral comprehension and expression as well as deficiencies in reading and writing that involve the use of written symbols for communication. The term *aphasia* is frequently used in a restrictive sense to designate deficiencies in the ability to use linguistic symbols (spoken words) for oral communication (Wood, 1964). The terms *dyslexia* and *dysgraphia* are used to designate disturbances of reading and writing, respectively. Although many children exhibit impairment in the use of both auditory and written symbols, the discussion here will be confined to the consideration of aphasia.

Aphasia in adults. The term "aphasia" has been used to describe the language and certain other behavioral disturbances associated with brain injury in adults for over one hundred years (Broca, 1861; Wernicke, 1874). Several years later "aphasia" was adopted as an appropriate term to be used in connection with children who displayed disturbances similar to those observed in adult aphasia.

Weisenberg and McBride (1935) used a four-category system to classify the predominant linguistic disturbances of adult aphasia, which includes *predominantly expressive aphasia, predominantly receptive aphasia, mixed expressive-receptive aphasia,* and *amnesic aphasia.* The *predominantly expressive* class is characterized by major disturbances in the ability to express ideas with written or spoken words, although comprehension may be affected to a much lesser degree. In *predominantly receptive aphasia* the ability of the individual to comprehend the meaning of written or orally expressed ideas of others is disturbed. One characteristic which distinguishes between expressive and receptive aphasia is that the person with an expressive language deficiency may attempt to correct errors in expression because he is aware of them while those with receptive deficiencies usually do not attempt to make corrections because they are not aware that an error has been made. Typically *mixed expressive-receptive* aphasia is characterized by severe disturbances in both expressive and receptive areas of language function. Obviously the ability to communicate is affected to an extreme degree when both receptive and expressive functions are seriously affected. In *amnesic aphasia,* a type of expressive language involvement, the ability of the individual to name objects, qualities, or conditions is reduced, although receptive ability may be intact. The four-category classification does not denote mutually exclusive categories of behavior, as there is usually some overlap of the observed characteristics; however, this system of classification does provide some useful information about the nature of language disturbances generally.

Aphasia in children. Similar to adults who have aphasia caused by brain damage, there are some children who are unable to use symbols adequately for communication; therefore it is convenient to use the same terminology. The four types of language behavior described for adult aphasics are also found, although it must be remembered that there is much overlap among the types.

Aphasia among children is variously termed *childhood aphasia* and *congenital* or *developmental aphasia. Childhood aphasia* usually refers to language dysfunction related to central nervous system damage (an extremely high fever, a severe blow to the head) which occurred after language had begun to develop. The terms *developmental* or *congenital aphasia* imply that damage to the central nervous system occurred prior to the development of language, so that the child has a disability in learning the language rather than in a loss of language already learned, although the specific cause of this condition cannot be readily identified.

Eisenson's (1972) detailed discussion of developmental aphasia is helpful in distinguishing the behavioral characteristics of these children from others who may be delayed in the development of language skills. As emphasized by Eisenson (1972), the child with developmental aphasia is one who (1) is not mentally retarded, (2) is not deaf or may not have even a moderate loss of hearing, although he does not seem to hear as well at one time as another, and (3) is not severely emotionally disturbed to the point that he is not able to relate to others. Children with developmental aphasia do *at times* appear to be mentally retarded, deaf or partially hearing, or emotionally disturbed. Such inconsistent behavior is one of the important differential-diagnostic clues of which teachers should be aware. For example, if a child in the classroom appears to be mentally retarded, the teacher should observe him carefully to determine if he is consistently inept academically or if he seems to have periods of "academic alertness."

There are a number of specific linguistic characteristics of developmental aphasia which are important to the understanding of such children, especially those in the classroom. Because spoken language may have little meaning for them, some children apparently ignore it or seem confused when placed in a highly verbal environment, such as a group of children in a school setting. Under such circumstances these children may be considered to be inattentive or possibly partially hearing. Occasionally deficiencies in the child's ability to produce oral language is profound enough that he is relatively silent. Therefore if the child's ability to produce language is impaired, there is a strong implication that the underlying factor is that he is not able to comprehend spoken language. Thus it seems safe to assume that if a child is not able to comprehend oral symbols, he has no basis for learning to produce them. If he does talk, his sentences are short and characterized by deficiencies in syntactic structure. His vocabulary is often limited in sheer quantity of words, but even when the vocabulary is of sufficient size, its use may be restricted. Another feature of developmental aphasia is the frequent presence of many errors in articulation or production of speech sounds that comprise the words. However, some apparent articulation errors are, in reality, an impairment in the child's ability to generate adequate grammatical structures. For example, in the sentence "It's a dog," one child consistently omitted the contracted "s," so that the sentence became "It a dog." Upon further investigation it was found that the "s" plural form of nouns—"rats," "cats"—was used consistently and correctly, as was the possessive form. In this instance, omission of the "s" in *it's* was not an articulation error but a linguistic one, due to an inability to use the rules of grammar to contract the words *it is* to form *it's*.

In addition to the linguistic characteristics there is usually evidence of perceptual malfunction in one or more of the sensory modalities, especially hearing and vision, but also in taction and proprioception. There may be a loss of hearing as measured by objective audiometry, but hearing function for practical purposes, that is, comprehension and association of verbal stimuli, is much more severely impaired (Eisenson, 1968).

Children with developmental aphasia very often manifest adaptive behavioral characteristics as well as the specific language and perceptual disorders described above. Some of these are perseverative behavior, emotional lability, hyperactivity, catastrophic behavior, visual-motor perceptual disturbances, and gross motor incoordination (Berry, 1969; Eisenson, 1968, 1972; Wood, 1964).

In recent years more emphasis has been placed on analyzing the characteristics of the specific behavioral deficiencies in language rather than on attaching a label to the child. Vignette 6.1, about a boy with the characteristics of developmental aphasia, illustrates how one "team" recognized that educational planning for the child and his particular way of learning was more important than the label attached.

Vignette 6.1 A Boy with Characteristics of Developmental Aphasia

Steven, a friendly six-year-old in the first grade, was noted by the teacher to have difficulty following classroom instructions, manipulating pencil and scissors, and grasping concepts presented. He showed difficulty also with language expression and misarticulated several speech sounds.

The teacher referred Steven to the school psychologist for a battery of tests and to the speech clinician for an assessment of speech and language skills. Formal tests were considered unreliable as Steven's responses were erratic and inconsistent. When a picture articulation test was given, Steven was unable to name the pictures and usually responded with the function rather than a name. When shown a picture of a broom, he replied, "Uh – – uh, you sweep with it," and when questioned about the name, he answered, "Uh – – – I know but I can't say it." When asked if it was a broom he said, "Yeah – – – it's a broom." He responded to nearly every item presented in the same way. The teacher, principal, psychologist, and speech clinician met to discuss the observations made during the attempted testing procedures and to formulate educational plans for Steven. In regard to oral language expression, it had been observed that when shown a picture of a "house" and encouraged to name it, Steven had replied "roof," and when shown a "lamp," he replied "room," giving an associated name but not the specific one. He sometimes used a rhyming word as "fish" for "dish," or one with the same initial sounds, as "swim" for "swing." Another frequently noticed characteristic was that once Steven had learned to say the correct name of an object, he used the same name for other objects (perseveration). He would then say, "No, that's not right," showing awareness of the error.

Although these language patterns and others led to the diagnosis that Steven was indeed a developmental aphasic, especially displaying amnesic characteristics, the team preferred to focus on the best educational handling of the boy—keeping all his learning characteristics in mind—rather than on the label. It was decided that Steven would be placed in a classroom for children with specific learning disabilities for half of each day, where he would receive diagnostic teaching as well as individual help on oral language expression. The techniques developed for Steven in that setting would be passed on to the classroom teacher through consultations and utilized by her during the other half day in the classroom, until such time when Steven could be wholly integrated into the regular classroom. The important point was made that regardless of the label, it was still the child and his particular way of learning which needed major consideration.

The aphasic child's inability to learn like other children in the classroom has forced us to look for ways that he can learn. Thus it is more important to know that the child has not learned the meaning of "dog," "run," or "fast," that he does not understand the meaning of "the dog runs fast," or that he searches and hesitates in attempting to find and use the correct words, than to identify him by the label *development aphasia*. The label does nothing for the child and it is questionable whether it does much for the parent, teacher, or speech clinician.

Language Disabilities of Economically Disadvantaged and Minority Group Children

In recent years, there has been a focus of attention on the development and education of children who live in economically disadvantaged areas, both urban and rural. In addition to the economically disadvantaged, there are groups of children who may or may not be economically poor, but whose culture differs from those in the mainstream of the population to the extent that they often encounter difficulties in formal education. In the following discussion, use of the terms *economically disadvantaged* and *culturally different* refer to children who have been deprived of quality experiences in the preschool environment resulting in an interference with the development of adequate speech and language usage. Specifically, it is assumed that there is no impairment of the central nervous system and that sensory deprivation due to a hearing loss or visual impairment is not a factor. Thus the apparent language difference is due to circumstances in the environment.

The relation between the "culturally different or disadvantaged language" syndrome and educational success is one of the most controversial present-day issues in education. The fact that there is disagreement among those concerned with the education of children is evidence enough that both the issue and the nature of the controversy are worth consideration. Essentially the disagreement seems to center around the argument as to whether the nonstandard English language of the culturally different is substandard (deficient) or nonstandard (different). On the one hand, it is held by one group that the oral language of disadvantaged children is substandard (Bereiter and Englemann, 1966; Bernstein, 1960; Deutsch et al, 1968; Hunt, 1968; Raph, 1967). Furthermore, it is argued by some that such language deficits will interfere with learning and academic achievement. On the other hand, many linguists, namely Baratz (1968), Labov (1970), Monsees and Berman (1968), and Shuy (1970), see the language of the culturally different (especially that of the urban ghetto black) as nonstandard rather than substandard. Therefore, language of the economically disadvantaged and/or culturally different is, for the most part, different but not deficient.

Speech and language characteristics. According to Bereiter and Englemann (1966), "culturally deprived" preschool children are typically retarded about one year in the language areas of vocabulary size, sentence length, and the use of grammatical structures. Raph (1967), in summarizing the work of several investigators, reported that disadvantaged children used a limited vocabulary which consisted predominantly of nouns and verbs sprinkled with the restricted use of a limited number of adjectives and adverbs. Typically, sentences are incomplete and the grammatical structure is marked by the perseverative use of the present tense of verbs even when the past tense is needed. Inflective endings of plurals and possessives are frequently omitted and many double negatives are used. One noticeable deficiency in syntax is the omission of auxiliary verbs, conjunctions, prepositions, and articles. In a comprehensive evaluation of 480 subjects ranging in age from three to eight years of age, Templin (1957) found that children in her lower socioeconomic status group performed significantly lower than those in her upper socioeconomic status group for measures of articulation skill, sound discrimination ability, variety of words in the vocabulary, length of verbalizations (average length of remark), and many other subcategories of these basic linguistic performances.

With respect to the concept of cultural differences and language, it seems clear that the language of low-income children differs from that of middle- or high-income children. Further, the educators, psychologists, and linguists generally agree that children with nonstandard language have difficulty in school. Whether nonstandard English, per se, accounts for the poor performance or whether there are other associated cognitive factors that are interrelated is questioned.

Speech Disabilities

Although many definitions of a speech disability appear in the literature, one of the most widely accepted is proposed by Van Riper (1972). He states: "Speech is defective when it deviates so far from the speech of other people that it calls attention to itself, interferes with communication, or causes its possessor to be maladjusted." This definition suggests that the criteria for acceptable speech makes allowances for some variability of speech production. Speech differences are expected just as other human individual differences, but when a difference is viewed as too extreme, the "difference" may also be viewed as a disability. Because of the recent interest in language and the interrelation of language and speech, the following definition is suggested: *A speech deviation may be considered a disability when there is an interference in the production of audible utterances of such proportion that it does not serve satisfactorily as the basic tool for oral expression.*

Neither of the foregoing definitions indicate to the teacher how much the speech should deviate at a given age for the child to need help. Age and severity of the deviation are important factors to be taken into consideration when planning remedial programs. The utterance "I see duh wed cah" (I see the red car) coming from an eleven-year-old boy obviously would be conspicuous. However, the same utterance produced by a four-year-old would raise few eyebrows because such misarticulations are acceptable at this age. Similarly, a child between the years of two and a half and four may exhibit periods of disfluent speech. Since this occurs in a large number of children and disappears in most of them eventually, it is considered to be an acceptable phase in the acquisition of speech and language. The second factor, severity, ranks along with age as another consideration. Certainly, not every speech deviation warrants intervention. Society will accept a wide range of differences in the production of speech sounds and in a person's fluency and voice. For example, the "s" sound may be produced in a variety of ways, differing from each other, but all acceptable. From an intervention point of view, the label "speech disability" is attached when the difference is great enough that speech correction is needed to bring the total speech pattern into the range of acceptability.

Disabilities of speech fall into several different categories. There are disabilities of (1) articulation, in which speech sounds are omitted, replaced by a substitute sound, or distorted; (2) voice problems, in which pitch, loudness or quality of the voice is affected; and (3) stuttering. These conditions are found not only among individuals with no special handicapping conditions but also among those with impaired hearing, cerebral palsy, cleft palate, and mental retardation. Often a child with a disability in oral language exhibits deviations in articulation and may, of course, have a problem of voice or fluency.

Articulation

There are numerous common terms which have been used in the description of an articulation disability: "baby-talk," "lalling," and "lazy tongue." These terms tend to denote either a reflection of the child's overall developmental pattern or to emphasize the tongue itself as the culprit, neither of which is necessarily true. In a general way, the articulation disturbance presents a pattern which can be described as a form of *mispronunciation* involving a part or all of the word or words. The most consistently found types of articulation disability are (1) omissions, (2) substitutions, and (3) distortions of consonants or vowels or both.

1. *Omissions* In this type of error certain speech sounds are omitted, resulting in the production of only a part of the word, for example, "-oat" for "goat," or "po-y" for "pony." To illustrate this point further, notice the effect on the overall speech pattern when the following sentence is repeated with the omission of each "s" and "r": "The squirrel ran across the lawn."

2. *Substitutions* This error involves utterances such as "wun" for "run," "tate" for "cake," and "thome" for "some." Repeat the following sentence,

substituting "w" for each "l" and "r," and "t" for each "c" or "k": "Laurie likes chocolate cookies." One can easily understand how incomprehensible a child's speech would be if a substitution were used for each consonant sound. Some of the most common sound substitutions found among children in the early grades are "t" for "k" or "k" for "t," "b" for "v," "f" for "th," "th" for "s," and "w" for "l" or "r." The "th" for "s" substitution is frequently referred to as a "lisp," although there are other deviations of "s" and "z" often included in this category.

3. *Distortions* A distorted sound is a substitute sound which cannot be identified as any known consonant or vowel in the language. This error is a much debated form of articulation deviation. Van Riper and Irwin (1958) argue that there is no justification for including the distortion error as a separate class. Their rationale is that all distortions are forms of sound substitutions which the speaker does not ordinarily use, although this same sound may be quite acceptable in another language. Be that as it may, the classification of some erred sounds as "distortions" is a distinct aid in describing the severity of a disorder. One example of a sound distortion is that of an "s" produced by sucking air in between the teeth. This is a difficult distortion for the normal speaker to reproduce but occasionally a child is found who misarticulates the "s" in that fashion.

The three types discussed above are all referred to as articulation errors, and any degree of severity of any of the three types of errors can exist within a given child's speech pattern. In fact, a single child's speech may exhibit one or a combination of all three of these types of errors. For instance, in the sentence, "Yesterday was my birthday," a child may omit the "t" and "d," substitute "uh" for "r," and distort the "s" by emitting the air from the sides of the teeth, resulting in a "slushy" sound. If one tests this combination of errors himself, one can readily discover the high degree of unintelligibility.

In the majority of children with articulation problems, it is almost impossible to pinpoint the causal factor. The misarticulations seem to occur due to some defect in the developmental process; however, there are instances in which specific conditions seem to be at the root of the problem. Some examples are a paralyzed tongue, dental malocclusions, or a lingual frenum (fold of mucous membrane under the tongue) which is tense or too short. McDonald (1964) states that even though compensations do develop which may allow "normal" articulation in isolated words, if the necessary compensatory movements of the articulators are too awkward to achieve, the articulation may be defective.

One important social or environmental factor which influences the development of correct articulation in the young child is the speech model set by adults, especially the parents. Every teacher has had the experience of being concerned about the lisp of a child only to confer with the parent who proves to have an even more severe lisp. A second environmental factor is sibling order. An older child may notice the attention a younger sibling receives with his infantile speech and may imitate this speech pattern until it becomes automatic. Lack of adequate speech stimulation in the home can also deprive the child of an opportunity to develop satisfactory articulation. Speech patterns seem to vary, too, with the socioeconomic level and ethnic and racial group. These factors tend to overlap and it is impossible to determine that any single factor is the cause.

Voice

Voicing (phonation), which is generated by the vibration of the vocal folds located in the larynx, is similar to singing because it has a "tonal" or "musical" quality, as previously mentioned. When the vocal folds do not vibrate, voicing does not take place and the air coming from the lungs merely passes out of the mouth cavity as a voiceless stream of exhaled air. Some examples of voiced and unvoiced sounds were given earlier in this chapter. Other examples are "l," "b," "z," "m," "j" (voiced), and "p," "s", "ch," "sh" (unvoiced).

There are five basic characteristics of any voice, namely, *pitch, loudness, voice flexibility, quality* and *duration*:

1. *Pitch.* Pitch is defined as the highness or lowness of the voice as related to the musical scale. Some children use a pitch level that is too high or too low and therefore inappropriate for their age. It would not be appropriate for an 18-year-old male to speak in the same high pitch he had used as an 8-year-old and it would be equally inappropriate for a 10-year-old girl to speak in a heavy, low-pitched voice. Either voice would be noticeably unpleasant and would be regarded as a voice disorder involving pitch.

2. *Loudness.* This characteristic denotes the strength or weakness of the voice and is related to the amount of energy or volume used. A voice that is too loud can be disturbing to the listener and one that is too weak can interfere with communication.

3. *Voice flexibility.* Variability of pitch and loudness levels during ordinary conversation is typical of a good speaking voice. Many of the subtle meanings of speech and often the emotional state of the individual are perceived through the use of variations in pitch and loudness. When the voice is monotonously weak the articulation generally lacks precision, which compounds the problem of oral communication.

4. *Quality.* The characteristic of voice, independent of pitch and loudness, that provides a basis for differentiating two voices is referred to as quality. Disturbances of voice quality are found among school children more often than any other type of voice disorder. Fairbanks (1960) described four categories of voice quality disorders: breathiness, harshness, hoarseness. and nasality. The breathy voice appears to be similar to a whispered voice. This type of voice is generally weak and lacks some of the desirable characteristics heard in voices that are more clearly phonated. The harsh voice is discordant, raspy, low-pitched, and louder than normal. Hoarseness is typical of laryngeal irritation which may result from excessive yelling or

acute infections in the throat region. The hoarse quality has important health implications as it is an indicator of laryngeal pathology and, if persistent, should receive medical attention. In nasal quality (hypernasality) too much of the sound passes through the nasal cavities and out through the nose. When this happens the typical impression of "talking through the nose" results. The term "denasality," often confused with "hypernasality," is applied to a voice disorder in which the speech has a muffled quality, giving the impression that the person has a head cold.

5. *Duration.* The total length of time that phonation exists is called duration. A voice disorder involving significant deviations of duration occurs when the phonation periods of speech are either abnormally long or short. In either instance speech sounds, especially vowels, may be distorted.

Although there are a number of factors reported in the literature that are related causally to voice disturbances, misuse of the voice is probably responsible for most problems in children. Misuse occurs when children scream or yell excessively, imitate voice patterns that are unnatural for them or otherwise use their voices in such a way that the voice mechanism is extended beyond its physical limits. Misuse frequently leads to abuse which results in physical damage to the structures of the larynx. Boone (1971)points out that there are a number of local irritants such as smog and dirt that can maintain laryngeal problems. The fact that air pollution has become so prevalent in our overcrowded cities may account for the apparent increased number of school children with voice disorders in recent years.

Articulation and Voice

In the literature very little attention has been given to the relation between articulation and voice, although, strangely enough, we have been aware of it for many years. For example, almost 30 years ago Williamson (1944) reported that voice quality problems can be improved by concentrating on the correction of a coexisting articulation deviation. Logically, there is an interrelation between the two phenomena because some of the same structures of the speech mechanism are responsible for both articulation and voice production. Thus, when articulation is disturbed for any reason the voice also should be affected to some degree; conversely, a disturbance of voice production should be accompanied by some deviation of articulation. However, the nature and extent of this interrelation has not been explored systematically although results from the National Speech and Hearing Survey indicate that the relation between articulation and voice performance is closer than we had suspected previously. For example, a very large proportion of the school children who were found to have extreme deviations of articulation also exhibited some disturbance of voice and vice versa. Results of the study also showed that the proportion of children with extreme voice deviations was significantly greater in the group of children with extreme articulation disturbances than in the group judged to have acceptable articulation. These findings do not reveal the nature of the interrelation, but they strongly suggest that articulation and voice should be considered together as an extremely complex phenomenon rather than as separate entities of speech performance. In a sense one can view the speech mechanism as a group of complex anatomic structures that function to produce the very unique linguistic symbols called speech. It is convenient to discuss articulation and voice problems separately, as has been done in this section. However, those teachers and speech clinicians working with children who have speech problems should listen for both articulation and voice disturbances so that a more effective intervention program can be planned. Past experience has shown that children with handicapping problems cannot be grouped into neat little disability categories if their educational problems are to be solved. The trend in the direction of determining the kinds of problems children have and how they affect educational, social, and vocational success, observed in the 1960s, has freed the educators and, more important, the child from the restrictions brought about by labeling. Thus, in the future, it is foreseen that teachers and speech clinicians, working as a team, will concentrate on the interrelation of not only articulation and voice disabilities but also other aspects of oral communication behavior as they relate to the child's total performance in the mainstream of education.

Stuttering

Stuttering is a complex behavior. It is a matter of speech disfluency (interruptions in the smooth flow of speech), but as Johnson et al. (1967) point out, disfluent speech occurs with many who are not considered stutterers; therefore, disfluency alone does not adequately describe stuttering. As discussed earlier in this chapter, young children become disfluent in the early acquisition of language and any "normal" speaker will also be disfluent at times. It is not until disfluencies occur frequently and severely enough to become noticeable to the listener and an irritant to the speaker that the condition is called stuttering. Detailed discussions of stuttering and its nature can be found in the writings of Ainsworth (1970), Bloodstein (1960a, 1960b, 1961), Brutten and Shoemaker (1967), Goldiamond (1968), Johnson et al. (1967), and Van Riper (1971).

In the early stages disfluent speech is usually considered to be "stuttering" when it is characterized by excessive prolongations and repetitions of sounds and hesitations in the general speech pattern. In more advanced stages prolongations of such severity occur that the speaker may be unable to begin talking because the first sound in the word is abnormally prolonged. Such prolongations may also occur on the first sound of a syllable or word interrupting the flow of speech at any point. In the sentence, "Come to my party," the tongue or other speech structures may not move from one position to another; thus the speaker would be "stuck" and unable to go ahead. The sentence would sound like this: "C | —ome | toooo | mmy | p—arty." Repetitions of sounds, syllables, words, and sometimes phrases accompanied by hesitations and pauses between many elements of a connected speech pattern also disrupt the flow of speech. Therefore, "Come to my party" becomes "C-c-come——t-t-too——my-my-my——p-p-p-party."

Essentially stuttering is a developmental phenomenon in that it passes through stages of increased severity over a period of time. Bloodstein (1960b) described the development of stuttering in an individual as a four-phase phenomenon in which the four phases are related to age levels. Bloodstein's four phases are summarized as follows:

Phase one. The most common age of onset of this phase is in the early preschool years. Typically there are alternating periods of fluent speech and stuttering. The stuttering generally occurs on the first word of a sentence and also on such words as prepositions, conjunctions, and pronouns.

Phase two. This phase usually begins at about seven or eight years of age or even earlier. The stuttering periods are longer than before and there are fewer periods of fluent speech. Usually the child tends to stutter when he attempts to talk fast or when excited. Stuttering occurs more frequently on the more important words of the sentence rather than the "little" parts of speech as was characteristic of phase one.

Phase three. This phase has very broad age limits, sometimes beginning as early as eight years of age and, on occasion, extending into adulthood. The stutterer is well aware of the increased amount of difficulty he experiences in certain situations. He has now begun to use word substitutions and speech-starting devices to help promote fluent speech. He is fully aware of his stuttering yet he does not avoid speaking situations.

Phase four. This phase of stuttering also may have a broad age range but is usually found in late adolescence and adults. This is the last phase of the development of stuttering and it has now become a personal problem. The stutterer avoids certain speaking situations and frequently uses word substitutions and circumlocution. He is embarrassed, fearful, and sensitive about his speech and how others react to it. In this phase, the behaviors found in the earlier phases are also present so that there seems to be a cumulative effect in the development of stuttering.

Van Riper (1971) described stuttering as a developmental phenomenon, but his concept differs from Bloodstein's four-phase approach. He conceives of stuttering as developing in four different ways, which he refers to as tracks. Each track represents the development of stuttering from the time of onset to the "advanced" or "confirmed" stage at which time it is fully established. In his analysis of 300 case folders of stutterers which had been seen first in childhood, Van Riper was able to identify four relatively distinct patterns of progressive change in stuttering behavior which occurred over a period of several years. He found that 77 percent of the 300 stutterers fell into these four major patterns of change, while the remaining 23 percent could not be placed into any of the four tracks. Some of the developmental characteristics which distinguished the four tracks are presented here:

Track I. Stuttering began early, at about two and one-half to four years of age. There were frequent oscillations of stuttering, sometimes very pronounced and at other times absent. This was more characteristic of track I than of the other tracks. Ultimately these children developed "word fears" and attempted to disguise the stuttering.

Track II. The onset of stuttering was often later than in track I, but speech was disfluent when the child began to talk. In the later stages of development "word fears" were not a part of the behavior and there was no attempt to disguise the stuttering.

Track III. The age of onset was later than for track I stutterers and it also began suddenly rather than gradually. Awareness, frustration, and struggle behavior developed early and eventually these children would not attempt to talk.

Track IV. Stuttering usually began later than for children in the other three tracks. The beginning of stuttering was preceded by several years of fluent speech. One of the characteristics which distinguished track IV from the other three tracks was that the behavioral changes were minimal with the passage of time. Track IV children talked freely, developed very little avoidance behavior, and stuttered very openly at the "confirmed" stage.

As Van Riper (1971) very carefully points out, his four-track system describing the development of stuttering was based on a particular method of clinical observation (analysis of case folders covering a period of over 30 years). Such observations, as Van Riper states, may not meet the criteria of longitudinal research which is sorely needed if we are to obtain important information about the nature of stuttering. The results of Van Riper's analysis, however, do indicate that there is some sequential patterning of changes in stuttering over a long period of time. Furthermore, the four-track system indicates that not all children develop stuttering in the same way.

Stuttering is a variable inconsistent behavioral phenomenon. Every child who stutters does not stutter on each utterance, and the circumstances under which he stutters one day may not precipitate stuttering the next. The severity of stuttering for a given child can vary extensively from one day to another, from one speaking situation to another, and from word to word. Sometimes stuttering severity will vary with different emotional and physical states. Usually, the higher the degree of verbalization initiated by the stutterer, the greater the chances are that stuttering will occur.

During the last 50 years many theories regarding the cause of stuttering have been proposed. Formerly stuttering theories tended to hold to a single factor which was responsible for the condition. However, in recent years experts in the field have made an attempt to place the different theories into major groups. For example, Brutten and Shoemaker (1967) list four groups of theories which are related to or rely on specific concepts and factors: (1) physical and neurological concepts (constitutional factors), (2) psychological factors, (3) interaction between physiogenic and psychogenic factors, and (4) current learning theory. Similarly, Van Riper (1963) divides the theories into three groups: (1) constitutional differences, (2) neurosis, and (3) learning theory.

Since space does not permit even a cursory review of these three or four theories, one which has had considerable impact will be described here—the theory proposed by the late Wendell Johnson of the University of Iowa. Johnson et al. (1967) hypothesized that stuttering develops as a problem which involves an interaction between the young child who exhibits disfluent speech patterns while talking and an authority figure (generally a parent) who listens and reacts to the speech. The child perceives the listener's response as disapproval of his speech and of him. Because of this, he attempts to change to the speech pattern which he thinks is the one expected of him. Such attempts fail and he then develops unsuccessful behavioral patterns in an effort to avoid the disfluent speech which caused the chain reaction in the first place. According to Johnson's theory, such a series of interactions may result in stuttering; therefore, the reasons for the onset of stuttering should be sought primarily "in the parent's attitudes and reactions to the child, and especially, to the way the child speaks."

Speech and Language Disabilities Related to Other Conditions

Over a period of several years the teacher will occasionally find children in her class who have physical, neurological, or developmental problems in which speech and language disabilities will be found as a result of the total condition. Although these conditions may occur without any noticeable speech or language disability, communication is affected often enough so that some space should be given to the subjects. In these conditions, any one or more of the previously described speech or language deviations may be found varying from mild to severe in degree.

Impaired Hearing

A child with a hearing loss is affected both in language and speech development according to the kind, severity, and age at onset of the hearing loss. McConnell (Chapter 7) discusses the language development of the hearing impaired child in his section on "Behavioral Characteristics," in which he points out the tremendous barrier that deprivation of hearing has on language learning.

Not only is there an interference with the reception and expression of language but the manner in which the sounds are voiced and articulated are particularly disturbed. A child with a hearing loss in the speech-frequency range will probably have some problems in developing speech sounds. As the loss becomes more severe, the accurate production of speech sounds becomes more difficult. According to Frisina (1967), if the child has a mild loss of hearing, the sounds "s," "sh," "z," "th," "t," "k," "ch," and "f," which are of high frequency and low-acoustic power, are those most likely to be mis-articulated. The voice may be weak, nasal, and breathy, but the child does develop nearly normal pitch, rate, and inflection. The child, with proper training, can develop acceptable, intelligible speech. The author points out, however, that the infant with a severe hearing loss does not develop speech spontaneously, and the speech is characterized by a wide variety of misarticu-lations, abnormal patterns of breathing, voicing, rhythm, and rate. Even so, in a child whose hearing is severely impaired, with highly specialized teach-ing speech is often developed as a useful tool for communication.

Cerebral Palsy

Wilson (Chapter 9) shows that approximately 50 percent of children with cerebral palsy have speech defects. It is difficult to differentiate between speech and language behavior in many children with such severe impair-ments, but it is safe to say that many language disorders are included within the 50 percent figure. The fact that brain lesions are frequently widespread indicates that marked language disturbances are often present. The child may also exhibit perceptual disturbances of the visual, auditory, and tactile-motor modalities which will interfere with the development of language concepts. The neuromuscular involvement will limit the child's opportunity to move about in his environment and result in a restriction of linguistic development as well as general experience.

Voice and articulation problems, and occasionally the overt symptoms of stuttering, are also found in children with cerebral palsy. The severity of speech disorders ranges from unintelligible "grunts" to mild articulation errors and from aphonia (no voice) through disturbances of pitch, loudness, and resonance.

Hearing loss is also found among these children. In the type of cerebral palsy diagnosed as *athetosis*, there is a relatively high rate of high-frequency hearing loss which affects the child's ability to discriminate between speech sounds and interferes with normal language acquisition.

In some cerebral palsied children, the disability is so extreme that speech correction procedures are of little help. In others, depending on severity and type of problem, careful instruction can bring about much improvement in the child's oral communication.

Cleft Palate

The condition *cleft palate* and/or *cleft lip* refers to a split or opening in the roof of the mouth (palate) and/or the upper lip which usually exists at birth. These conditions are due to a failure of the bones and soft tissues of the palate and the soft upper-lip structures to fuse properly during the early growth and development of the embryo. The split in the palate creates an abnormal opening between the mouth and nasal cavities which allows a dis-proportionate amount of air to be emitted through the nose. The incidence of cleft palate and cleft lip is approximately one in 700 live births (Olin, 1963).

The earliest difficulties encountered by the child with a cleft palate are those of chewing, sucking, and swallowing, which interfere with nutrition as well as speech development. Corrective surgery to close the structural defect is generally required for most children, although an artificial palate or some other prosthodontic aid is sometimes necessary when surgery is not possible. Even with successful surgery, speech correction is often necessary before the child can be expected to acquire acceptable speech.

The typical characteristics of cleft palate speech are *hypernasality, nasal emission*, and *misarticulation* (Morley, 1967; McDonald and Baker, 1951; Spriestersbach, 1955; and Westlake and Rutherford, 1966). Thus the cleft palate condition causes primarily deviations of voice quality (hypernasality) and articulation performance. Language deficits have also been noted. Morley (1967) (shown later in Table 6.4) has estimated the prevalence of speech disturbances to be much higher in the cleft palate group than in the normal population. The oral communication disorder is complicated further by the higher than usual occurrence of a hearing loss in these children. Because of the nature of the structural deviation, children with a cleft palate are subject to more than the usual number of nasopharyngeal infections which lead to secondary middle-ear infections via the Eustachian tube (see McConnell, Chapter 7).

Mental Retardation

Very little can be added to Dunn's (Chapters 2 and 3) discussion of speech and language disabilities related to reduced cognitive abilities. Spradlin (1963) reviewed the literature on mental retardation and concluded: (1) between 57 and 72 percent of institutionalized retarded individuals have speech disorders, (2) 72–82 percent of the severely retarded children in parent-sponsored day schools have speech defects, and (3) 8–26 percent of children in public school special classes have speech disabilities, much lower than for institutionalized individuals. In a study involving 516 institutionalized mentally retarded residents, Schlanger and Gottsleben (1957) found the prevalence of articulation disorders to be 78 percent, voice 47 percent, and stuttering 17 percent. By comparing the above prevalence figures with those in Table 6.2, one can see that the prevalence of speech disabilities of all types is much greater in the retarded population than in the total population. The relation of language disabilities to retardation is also very high, as Dunn (Chapter 3) has pointed out. With respect to educational success, the high rate of existing language deficiencies among retarded children is much more damaging than the presence of speech disorders.

PREVALENCE

Over 50 years ago, Blanton (1916) reported the prevalence of speech disorders to be 5.69 percent of a sample of Wisconsin school children. Subsequently, over 100 surveys designed to estimate prevalence have been conducted throughout the United States and Canada. Typically most surveys have been conducted in restricted geographical areas with selected samples and have employed diverse data-collection techniques. As a result, there have been large discrepancies between the figures reported by the different surveys. There are several factors responsible for the wide range of reported prevalence estimates. One of these is the criteria used to define the various speech and language problems. Unfortunately, even agreement among speech clinicians regarding the characteristics that define speech disorders is not high. The standard strategy has been to classify an individual as having or not having a speech defect. Such dichotomies are forced choices and generally hazardous. In an effort to avoid the problem of using a preconceived definition of a speech disorder, Hull et al. (1971) collected prevalence data on a national sample of 38,000 public school children using a different approach. In this study, known as the National Speech and Hearing Survey (NSHS), the child's speech performance was compared to predetermined speech standards and rated in terms of deviation from that standard. No attempt was made to label a performance as "defective" or "normal." Instead, a scale which included the rating categories "acceptable speech," "moderate deviation," and "extreme deviation" was used to establish gross levels of performance. Subsequent analyses of the data provided criteria for identifying relatively how many precise levels of speech performance extended from "acceptable speech" to "extreme deviation."

A second factor is the important role that maturation plays in the quality of speech performance. For example, as will be shown later, results from the NSHS show that the percentage of children judged to have articulation and voice deviations drops sharply during the first two years of school and continues to become smaller through the twelfth grade. Therefore, prevalence estimates can be misleading unless they somehow reflect the improvement in speech performance that takes place as the age level increases, which indicates the influence of maturation. The fact that speech problems as a group are less pronounced in older children raises the question as to how many of the younger children actually have a speech difference that needs immediate direct speech-correction services. This question will be discussed in more detail later in the chapter.

A third factor is related to the relatively high prevalence of speech and language deficiencies among other types of exceptional children groups. For example, frequently articulation, voice, rhythm, and oral language function are adversely affected by other disabling conditions such as impaired hearing, cerebral palsy, cleft palate, mental retardation, and brain damage. It is helpful to include this kind of information in prevalence estimates, but the overall figures should not be inflated because of it.

The estimated prevalence of articulation and voice deviations and stuttering which are summarized in Table 6.2 were compiled from the NSHS data. In Table 6.2 the category *articulation impairment* designates a group of subjects who were judged to have articulation patterns which deviated extremely

TABLE 6.2 Estimated Prevalence of Articulation and Voice Impairments and Disabilities and Stuttering of School-age Children for Grades 1-12, Expressed in Percentages

Grade Level	Articulation Impairment			Articulation Disability			Voice Impairment			Voice Disability			Stuttering		
	M	F	T	M	F	T[a]	M	F	T	M	F	T[a]	M	F	T[a]
1	4.85	2.81	3.87	6.89	4.51	5.75	4.61	2.94	3.81	2.51	1.11	1.84	1.74	.39	1.10
2	3.59	1.65	2.64	2.67	1.14	1.93	4.26	3.62	3.95	2.31	1.08	1.71	2.13	.51	1.34
3	1.39	.96	1.18	1.03	.51	.78	4.78	3.28	4.05	1.39	.45	.94	1.21	.90	1.06
4	1.05	.72	.90	.88	.20	.56	3.86	2.09	3.03	.88	.39	.65	1.05	.78	.93
5	1.18	1.13	1.16	.53	.27	.41	3.07	1.53	2.35	1.06	.40	.75	1.71	.67	1.22
6	.50	.55	.53	.44	.18	.31	2.71	1.65	2.18	.69	.31	.50	.88	.25	.56
7	.60	.25	.43	.36	.31	.34	2.87	1.38	2.15	.30	.06	.18	1.31	.25	.80
8	.42	.19	.31	.06	.44	.25	2.65	1.07	1.87	.48	.25	.37	1.39	.25	.83
9	.60	.38	.49	.30	.13	.22	1.38	.82	1.11	.42	.51	.46	1.08	.32	.71
10	.24	.37	.31	.24	.19	.21	1.09	.68	.89	.42	.12	.28	.72	.25	.49
11	.24	.32	.28	.35	.06	.22	1.01	.77	.89	.12	0.00	.06	.59	.38	.49
12	.12	.26	.19	.48	.13	.31	.78	.77	.77	.30	.06	.19	.72	.06	.40
Overall Average	1.23	.79	1.02	1.19	.66	.93	2.75	1.71	2.25	.91	.39	.65	1.21	.41	.82

[a] See Figure 6.1.

SOURCE: NSHS data

from the predetermined speech standard; *articulation disability* designates a group of subjects who also deviated extremely from the standard, but to a greater degree than the *articulation impairment* group. The impairment category includes those subjects who have observable deviations that may or may not require immediate direct-corrective services, and the disability category includes those children who have an articulation deviation that will require immediate direct-corrective services. Percentage figures for males (M), females (F), and totals (T) are shown for each of the 12 grades, and the average total (overall average) for the 12 grades is combined under each category of rated speech performance.

As seen in Table 6.2, the average overall prevalence of *articulation impairments* was found to be 1.02 percent and the prevalence of *articulation disabilities* was .93 percent. The information in Table 6.2 also points up two important trends regarding the prevalence of articulation impairments and disabilities. First, the prevalence of articulation impairments and disabilities is much greater in the lower grades than in the higher grades. Of particular interest is the fact that the rate of improvement for the articulation-disability group is greater during the first two years of school than during the following ten years. This distinct trend is shown more clearly in Figure 6.1, where the prevalence figures for the "total" column of Table 6.2 are displayed graphically. From these data one concludes logically that the apparent influence of maturation with regard to the improvement of articulation, even among children with severe deviations, cannot be ignored, especially in the first two grades when children are about six to eight years of age. However, tempting as it may be, these findings do not suggest that teachers and speech clinicians should ignore the first- and second-grade child with extreme articulation deviation. We do not have reliable means for predicting which children in the early school years will "grow out" of their problem. Until such predictions are possible, children who are to receive speech-corrective services must be selected carefully because, as seen in Table 6.2, there are some high school students who have severe articulation deviations. Procedures for case selection will be discussed later in this chapter. Second, the prevalence of both severity levels of articulation deviation was greater for boys than for girls at most grade levels. The overall sex ratio (average for 12 grades) was 1.6 to 1 for the articulation impairment category and 1.8 to 1 for the articulation-disability category.

The *voice-impairment* and *voice-disability* categories in Table 6.2, as with the articulation categories, also represent two levels of voice-deviation severity. The average overall prevalence figure was 2.25 percent for the voice impairment category and .65 percent for the voice disability category. The prevalence of the two voice-severity categories becomes smaller with increasing age, but the changes during the first two grades are not as dramatic as noted for the articulation-severity categories. These results suggest that maturation does not affect changes in voice deviations in quite the same way that it does articulation, especially in the voice-impairment category. How-

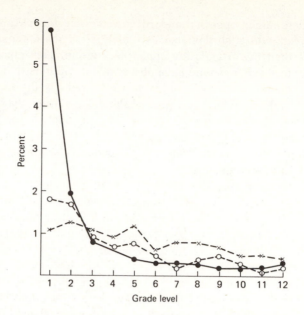

FIGURE 6.1 *Estimated prevalence of articulation and voice disabilities and stutter-*
ing showing percentage figures for each of the 12 grades. The curves
are plots of the values from the "totals" columns in Table 6.2. Key:
•————————• *Articulation disability;* o————o *voice disability;*
x————x *stuttering.*

ever, the configuration of the voice-disability curve in Figure 6.1 is quite
similar to the articulation-disability curve. The percentage of voice deviations
was greater for boys than for girls at all grade levels. The overall sex ratio
was 1.6 to 1 for the voice impairment category and 2.3 to 1 for the voice
disability category.

The prevalence of stuttering is shown as a single level of severity in
Table 6.2. Therefore, a total of .82 percent of the school-age population
sampled were found to have disfluent patterns of speech which satisfied
the requirements of true stuttering behavior. The percentage of male stutterers
exceeded females by a ratio of 3 to 1. Although the prevalence of stuttering
is greater in the first five grades when compared to the last seven grades, the
configuration of the curve showing the relation of prevalence to increasing
grade level (Fig. 6.1) is much different from those for articulation and voice.
Apparently the effects of maturation on stuttering are different from those on
articulation and voice problems.

The estimated prevalence of speech and language problems of children
in the United States and Canada is summarized in Table 6.3. These figures
were accumulated from a number of sources, including Johnson (1959), the
NSHS data, and authors of other chapters in this text.

The reliability of the .05 percent figure for oral language disabilities
which was taken from Johnson (1959) is questionable for at least two

TABLE 6.3 *Estimated Prevalence of Oral Communication Disorders among Children in the United States and Canada*

Type of Disorder	Estimated Prevalence of Speech and Language Impairment (Percent)	Estimated Prevalence of Speech and Language Disability (Percent)
Delayed speech and language	.05[a]	.05
Articulation	1.02[b]	.93[b]
Voice	2.25[b]	.65[b]
Stuttering	.82[b]	.82[b]
Total	4.14	2.45

[a] Does not include nonstandard English.
[b] Preliminary results from NSHS data.

reasons. First, as noted, nonstandard English is not included because the definitional criteria are so variable that the prevalence figure is more like a "guesstimate" rather than an "estimate." If all the children who use a non-standard form of English grammar were to be included, the prevalence figure could easily be increased by tenfold. Second, many children who have oral language problems also may exhibit deviations of reading and writing. Therefore, some should be included in the learning disabilities group, a move that merely would add more confusion to the question of a reliable prevalence estimate. Johnson's (1959) .05 percent estimate very likely includes delayed speech and language developmental problems as well as those associated with brain damage of some kind, including developmental aphasia.

The percentage of speech and language problems associated with impaired hearing, cerebral palsy, cleft palate, and mental retardation is shown in Table 6.4. As noted, 9.49 percent of the children found to have a hearing loss, defined as a best binaural average (BBA) of 25 decibels (dB)[2] or more, also were judged to have an extreme articulation deviation. The prevalence figure of 25 percent for speech problems associated with cleft palate which was reported by Morley (1967) for children in the age range of six to eight years is too conservative. Dunn (see Chapter 3) reported the prevalence of speech and language disorders among children with mild cognitive disabilities to be 8–37 percent. When the moderately and severely retarded groups are added the figure will increase to as much as 94 percent (Matthews, 1971). The percentage of speech and oral language disabilities accompanying multiple handicaps was not included in the prevalence figures discussed above. For example, children with cerebral palsy, in addition to being physically handicapped, may also be mentally retarded, emotionally disturbed, and partially hearing and exhibit symptoms of learning disabilities and visual disturbances as well as problems of articulation, voice, stuttering, and receptive and expressive language disturbances. Obviously such children

[1] See Chapter 5 for a definition of decibel (dB).

present an almost overwhelming challenge to the classroom teacher, special educator, speech clinician, and others who are responsible for providing a satisfactory educational opportunity for them.

TABLE 6.4 *Estimated Prevalence of Oral Communication Disorders Accompanying Other Types of "Handicapping" Conditions*

Type of Condition	Prevalence (Percent)
Partially Hearing	9.49^a
Cerebral Palsy	50.00^b
Cleft Palate	25.00^c
Mild Mental Retardation	$8-37^d$
Moderate Mental Retardation	94^e

[a] From NSHS data.
[b] From Wilson (see Chapter 9).
[c] From Morley (1967).
[d] From Dunn (see Chapter 3).
[e] From Matthews (1971).

SOCIAL AND VOCATIONAL IMPLICATIONS

Most young children are not rejected by their peers because of a speech or language disability alone. However, the child's reaction to his problem may lead to some personality disturbances causing difficulties in social adjustment. A young child with a deviant speech pattern is not particularly aware of the deviancy, whether it is one of voice, articulation, or stuttering. Later, when speech is used as a social tool, the adolescent may become much more aware of his inadequacies in oral communication. Adolescence is a period of serious self-reevaluation; thus some junior and senior high school students, who were not concerned about speech performance before, are now disturbed by a lisp or defective "r." For the adolescent who stutters social success may be very difficult to achieve because of the frustration he feels as he agonizes to talk fluently. Repeated frustrating experiences of this kind can result in the adolescent's negative self-evaluation, which damages his self-esteem; this may lead to social withdrawal or hostility. Social success does not seem to be an area of major difficulty for the young child or the adolescent with a cleft palate or lip that has been successfully repaired by surgery. In these days of highly skilled plastic surgeons, the cosmetic problems due to surgical scarring of the lip and other facial structures are practically nonexistent. In addition, the speech at this stage of the child's growth usually is acceptable to society. Society accepts the less fortunate individual today much more readily than in the period preceding the 1950s and 1960s. Through the radio, television, and newspaper media we are continuously reminded that those who do not fit into the mold of normalcy are nevertheless human beings and deserve to be treated as such. Therefore, even if the individual with an oral communication problem limps a little socially, he is usually accepted on the basis of what he is and what he does rather than on his ability to talk like his peers.

In most instances vocational success can be achieved by those with an oral communication disorder, although the avenues open to them may be somewhat restricted. Fortunately remedial services for children with speech and language disabilities combined with the continuous influence of maturation help to reduce the number of adults with severe problems to a minimum. For those who must adjust to some type of speech disturbance the opportunities are good, although the goals must be realistic. For example, it would not be wise for a confirmed stutterer to choose radio announcing as a career. However, several stutterers have been successful in professions and business enterprises that require a certain amount of speaking skill for success.

Expert vocational guidance and counseling are extremely important for the high school student with a speech disturbance who is undecided about his future. Therefore, it is imperative that the teacher most familiar with the student's problem, the speech clinician, and the counselor work together to help the student in choosing realistic vocational goals.

IDENTIFICATION

Procedures for identifying children with speech and/or language disabilities must be implemented before intervention programs can be initiated. Sommers (1969) stressed that methods chosen for finding these children should meet the criteria of "effectiveness" and "efficiency." He stated that "effectiveness" refers to successfully reaching the goal of finding those children who need remediation, and "efficiency" refers to the use of procedures which do not waste time, effort, or information. A number of methods have been developed for finding children in the schools with speech disabilities, and of these four have been in rather wide use. One procedure, described by Edney (1956), is a method in which the speech clinician visits classrooms and listens and observes children as they recite. The "class visitation," as it is termed, has been found to be cumbersome, and although "effective," certainly not "efficient." In addition, it does not utilize the teacher who is already in the classroom where she can listen to and observe the children over a long period of time. A second procedure, described by Irwin (1965), requires the teacher to fill out a "questionnaire-inventory" for each child she finds in her class with a speech deviation which she considers serious enough to require the services of the speech clinician. The questions refer to articulation, voice, and fluency as well as to other problems which might relate to speech disabilities. This method can certainly be effective, but it is time consuming for the teacher who also has many other forms and questionnaires to complete, and therefore the method is somewhat inefficient. A third method, described by Ainsworth (1948), is the survey, which involves the use of brief speech screening procedures with each child in the entire school (when a speech correction program is being initiated) or in certain selected classes (when a speech correction program is on-going). A fourth is the teacher referral method, in which the teacher listens to and observes the children and refers those with noticeable deviations for further screening and testing procedures to determine the specific problems.

As a part of a nation-wide study, Roe et al. (1961) asked school speech clinicians to indicate which of these four types of identification procedures they most frequently used. The results of the study showed that the survey method and the referral method were much more widely used than either of the other two. These two methods, often used in combination, probably most closely approach the criteria of "effectiveness" and "efficiency" than any other. Because of their widespread use, these two methods will be discussed in further detail.

The Speech Survey

The survey method consists of a brief, personal interview with each child. During the interview the child's speech is screened for deviations of articulation, voice, and fluency. The screening is organized to require only a few minutes and consists generally of questions designed to elicit a sample of the speech of each child as well as repetition of sentences, counting, and sometimes specific sounds. As mentioned earlier, if a speech correction program is being introduced for the first time in a school, it may be necessary to screen the speech of each child enrolled. In school systems with well-established speech correction programs, however, a survey of a selected grade, conducted in the beginning of each school year, combined with teacher referrals from other grades, serves well in finding children with speech problems. In some school systems the first grade or even kindergarten is selected for class screening. This practice can be considered acceptable if differences in child development and age are kept in mind. It may also be helpful in identifying serious problems needing early intervention. Unfortunately, all too often children whose speech will become acceptable through maturation alone are scheduled for speech lessons simply because many states require the speech clinician to carry a specified and unrealistically large number of children on the caseload.

More and more second or third grades are being chosen for class screening, since, as indicated in Table 6.1, speech development in both boys and girls is generally nearing completion between six and eight years of age. At these ages, too, deviations of voice and patterns of disfluency requiring intervention are sometimes found.

Teacher Observation and Referral

Whether a child with a speech problem is found through a class survey or referred by the teacher, the teacher's careful observations should be of the greatest importance in the assembling of information concerning a child's oral communication ability. In making informal observations, the teacher should listen carefully as each child speaks, not only to the content but to how he sounds when he speaks. Through such observations the teacher will keep several things in mind, which are appropriate for students in all grade levels:

1. Listen to the sounds he uses and how they compare with his age mates as well as with the standards set forth in the developmental chart in Table 6.1

2. Listen to the rate and fluency of his speech.

3. Listen to the pitch, quality, and degree of loudness he uses. If a deviation is heard, the voice should be observed on several different occasions to establish whether or not the condition is temporary—such as hoarseness due to a sore throat.

4. Observe the overall coordination of the child and the suspicion of any structural deviation related to speech.

5. Estimate the general intelligibility of his speech.

6. Listen to the grammar, vocabulary, and overall ability in oral expression, the correctness of recall and repetition of sentences, and the ability to follow directions.

7. Listen to the amount of talking exhibited. If he is silent during the normal talking periods he may only be a little shy and talk more as he gains confidence. However, he may be avoiding one or more problems; he may be covering up a disturbing articulation deviation, fearing that he will stutter if he speaks, he may have a hearing problem, or possibly he does not speak or understand English. Then, too, there is the possibility that speech or language is not the problem but the silence is due to an emotional problem which might be indicated in other ways also and would require another kind of help. The silent child should be observed carefully over a long enough period to attempt to find the reason.

The teacher should listen to and observe the student in several settings: the classroom, halls, playground, in conversation with others and with herself. Most of these observations can be carried out in a very casual way with only a little structuring to determine certain items, such as the repetition of a few sentences. As the teacher begins to identify children about whom she is concerned, she should make some notes and continue observing until she has assembled her information.

When the teacher concludes, on the basis of her observations, that the child does appear to have a speech and/or language problem, the referral should be made to the speech clinician. The speech clinician may decide that the deviation is a mild one which could be handled effectively in the classroom with some consultation between the teacher and the speech clinician; however, in the case of a child with a more serious handicap, the decision would be to conduct formal tests. Following this, the child would likely be placed on the speech correction schedule. In some instances, such as those indicating medical problems or suspected emotional overlay, the speech clinician may also decide upon further referral to other members of the school team—the nurse (and subsequently to the child's doctor) and/or the school psychologist. Teachers can become both "effective" and "efficient" in their referrals by developing skills in observation of speech and language and by becoming well informed on the nature of speech and language disabilities. In this way formal testing and individual speech correction sessions can be reserved for the most seriously speech-handicapped children.

Formal Testing Procedures

When tests for articulation are indicated, the speech clinician has several choices. Basically, most tests of articulation assess the spontaneous production of each consonant sound in three positions—initial, medial, and final—by means of pictures. Two examples of such tests are the *Hejna Developmental Articulation Test* (1959) and the *Goldman-Fristoe Test of Articulation* (1969). The *Templin-Darley Tests of Articulation* (Revised) (1960) are also excellent but require more time as more areas are tested in detail. The *McDonald Deep Test of Articulation* (1964) is for a more specific purpose—that of testing consonant sounds in relation to other consonant sounds to determine in which contexts sounds are produced correctly or incorrectly, and what percentage of the time a sound is correct or incorrect. An added advantage is that the erred sound will be found nearly correct in one of the tested contexts and thus provide a springboard for speech remediation. A *Predictive Screening Test of Articulation* (PSTA), devised by Van Riper and Erickson (1969), is a useful tool which was designed to identify children in the first grade who may achieve correct articulation spontaneously. These children are not given speech remediation but are followed by periodic rechecks.

During the administration of the tests for articulation and a period of conversation, the speech clinician will make some assessment of the pitch, quality, and loudness of the voice. The presence of voice problems usually indicates physical problems which require medical diagnosis and/or treatment before speech remediation is initiated. Therefore the condition should be discussed with the teacher and parents and the parents consulted regarding a medical referral.

Formal testing is unnecessary to determine a problem in stuttering. The teacher's observations are probably the best indicators of the existence of the problem. It is better to confirm stuttering through consultation with teachers, other school personnel, and the parents than singling the child out and bringing further attention to him.

REMEDIATION PROCEDURES

The most important consideration in planning remediation procedures is the child himself—the needs of the child who has the language or speech disability—not schedules, programs, the teacher, or the speech clinician. It is easy to become involved in processes and details of organization and planning and forget the child—the central reason for the planning. The child's feelings and his possible responses must be considered as well as the future consequences regarding any plans made for his remediation. The question should be asked: Is this the best plan for helping this child as an individual to participate as completely and fulfillingly as possible in the educational process and in life?

Certain procedures used for the screening, observing, and testing of speech and/or language disabilities have been dealt with in the preceding section of this chapter. Following identification of the children, decisions regarding remediation must be made. At this time, several items should be considered by the speech clinician and discussed with the teacher: (1) Is the deviation in language and/or speech a disability or does it seem to be one which will disappear as the child matures? (2) Is it a disability which could interfere with education and life adjustment? (3) If it seems to be a disability requiring remediation to overcome, how will the child respond to intervention? Does he seem open to help? Does he appear to need some other kind of intervention first, that is, medical, psychological, or social work? (4) What are the reactions of the parents when consulted regarding the findings? What further insights can they provide? (5) If conditions seem favorable for remediation, what type of programing would be best for him? Should he stay in the classroom with the speech clinician serving as consultant to the teacher? Should he be taken out for individual help by the speech clinician, utilizing teacher assistance for carry-over?

When these points and perhaps others have been discussed and resolved, the final decision regarding remediation will be made. This decision is the responsibility of the speech clinician, since that individual is ultimately responsible for the remediation program. This is true whether the program is carried out in the classroom by the teacher in consultation with the speech clinician or whether the child is taken for direct corrective services. The following parts of this section will offer some suggestions concerning the teacher's role, the speech clinician's role, and their cooperative efforts and those of other individuals who are concerned in helping the child in the remediation program.

The Teacher's Role

The classroom teacher's role with the child in need of speech and/or language remediation is an important one. Whether she is carrying out a program of remediation in the classroom or is reinforcing the work of the speech clinician, the teacher's manifested attitude toward the speech-handicapped child influences the child's feelings about himself as well as those of his peers. Complete acceptance of this child will build his confidence and be noted by his classmates. Some specific techniques which the classroom teacher can use in helping to improve or correct a child's speech problem will be discussed in this section.

Language Disabilities

Language development programs for the teacher to use in the classroom are used in many school systems as a part of prereading, or reading readiness, programs. The major goal of language development and stimulation programs is to develop the receptive and expressive language skills necessary for learning. Such programs expose children to a variety of experiences and sensations in the development of concepts, vocabulary, and linguistic construction. Designed primarily for classroom use with children whose early childhood experiences have been limited, who show substantial language deficit, or with culturally different children who are learning English as a second language, they are also interesting, stimulating, and enriching for other children.

It is important for the teacher to understand some of the problems that arise when a young child is accustomed to nonstandard English patterns or is learning English as a second language. In such instances, a language "gap" can occur between the child's conversational grasp of English and the more complex English patterns he needs as a tool for education.

Some suggestions for helping the child who learns standard English as a second language are mentioned here. The teacher should:

1. Be sure the child understands the meanings of words used in directions. If he appears to misunderstand, interpret the instruction in terms he does understand.
2. Observe the nature of the vocabulary and grammar the child uses and the syntactical constructions he omits so you can understand his "language," but also continue to build on and teach him new word meanings and syntax more appropriate for his education.
3. Avoid implications that his language is "wrong"; rather, stress that there are several ways of saying the same thing.
4. Avoid interpreting any relation between the child's intellectual ability and his oral language, which might contribute to his educational detriment and lack of self-esteem.

The teacher may find a child in her class who exhibits some of the characteristics of "aphasia." Time and patience are important in dealing with this child.

1. The teacher should speak slowly and simply in giving instructions and may need to repeat and demonstrate what is wanted.
2. Give the child time to ask questions if he does not understand; however, remember that he may have difficulty in asking the question because oral expression is difficult. He may need to demonstrate what he is asking through actions.
3. The teacher should look for whatever language strengths the child may have and encourage their use.
4. Do everything possible to give the child a feeling of success and accomplishment.
5. As the teacher observes and works with this child, she should also be seeking help from others—the school psychologist and, if available, a specialist in learning disabilities.

Articulation

There are certain activities which the classroom teacher can use with students in the improvement of articulation. Before attempting any corrective measures, the teacher should consult with the speech clinician. The clinician may recommend sources for the standard production of consonants and vowels. Experimentation by watching in the mirror and observing movements of the tongue, lips, and jaw and comparing voiced and voiceless sounds will demonstrate to some extent the way sounds are made. For the teacher who is interested in the specifics of sound production, a textbook on phonetics will be helpful, for example, Carrell and Tiffany (1960).

One useful and effective procedure a teacher can use in introducing the sound to be learned involves "listening" rather than requiring the student to reproduce the sound. This is a process of auditory training or "ear training" as described by Van Riper (1972). The purpose of this procedure is to teach the student to recognize when the sound is correct and when incorrect. The procedure consists of four basic steps which are briefly outlined here with examples of activities. It is hoped that the teacher can use the examples provided as a springboard for further activities of her own invention.

1. *Isolation.* The student learns to isolate the sound from the whole word.

Activity for young children. The teacher can show the class a colorful picture that includes many items. The children are asked to find in the picture as many words as possible containing the sound to be learned. As the children find the words, the teacher will say them slowly enough for the children to hear the sound as she says it.

Activity for older students. The teacher can present a list of words to the student, some of which contain the sound to be learned. The student is then asked to underline the key sound each time it occurs. He is then asked to read each word, omitting the underlined sound.

2. *Stimulation.* The student is bombarded with the sound by frequent repetition.

Activity for young children. The teacher says the sound repeatedly, but at irregular intervals stops saying the sound, s – s – s – s – – – – – s – s – – – – s – s – s –, and so on. As long as the children hear the sound they leave their hand up. When the sound stops, the hands are lowered.

Activity for older students. The teacher repeats the new sound using varying rhythm patterns. As the student listens, he marks the rhythm on a sheet of paper, as – –– – –– –.

3. *Identification.* In this step the teacher provides an association for the child. In the school setting, the best association for the spoken sound is the letter symbols. For example, the letter "S" sounds like sssssss(a hissing sound).

4. *Discrimination.* This step involves a comparison and contrast of the correct and incorrect sounds and is no doubt the most important of all the steps. The acoustic differences are so slight between some sounds that it is very difficult to discriminate between them without visual cues, for example, "f" and "th."

Activity for young children. The teacher may read a list of words, all beginning with the new sound. The teacher uses the correct sound part of the time but substitutes the incorrect sound on some words. The children are asked to signal (by clapping, raising hands, etc.) when the correct sound is heard.

Activity for older students. The teacher can use the same activity as described above, but read aloud material on the older child's level and he may signal the correct sound by a check mark on paper as the sound is heard.

The area of auditory discrimination is considerably more complex than it appears as described in this section. Lindamood and Lindamood (1969) have developed a program specifically designed for teaching auditory discrimination as a basic aid to the development of auditory perception, reading, spelling, and speech skills.

Some children will be able to say the new sound correctly following the use of auditory training procedures. If the sound still is spoken incorrectly, it may be necessary for the teacher to show the child how to move the articulators for the correct production. At this point the teacher may wish to consult the speech clinician for more detailed teaching of the correct sound.

Once the correct sound is learned, it must be incorporated into the total speech pattern. This achievement is reached in a series of steps and requires "self-monitoring" or "self-listening" by the individual. Often the first step involves correct repetition of the isolated sound, although this step is not always necessary. Practicing the sound in syllables is usually the second step. The sound is then practiced in words, with the sound occurring in initial, medial, and final positions. The words are next practiced in sentences. At each step the sound should be well stabilized before proceeding.

When the child is able to use the sound consistently in these structured steps, he is ready to carry over the new sound into his conversation. The carry-over phase is difficult, since the newly learned sounds are not as well established as the old error patterns. Whether the teacher has taught the sound herself or is reinforcing the work of the speech clinician, she can be of great assistance at this point. Here are some suggestions for this *transitional* step:

1. The child can be asked to repeat sequences while monitoring his newly learned sound—as counting, days of the week, and months of the year.
2. The child may practice an oral message which he will deliver to another person, being sure he uses his new sound correctly each time it occurs.
3. For the child who can read, it is helpful to read passages aloud, noting and monitoring the correct sound.
4. Short periods of conversation can be arranged, first with the teacher, then gradually involving one, two, or three other children. In these periods the child will monitor his speech and then repeat some of the words from the conversation which contained the new sound.

As the teacher works with the child she will think of other situations in which the child can use the sound in a gradually expanding environment. It must be remembered that the new sound will not become a part of the child's speech pattern all at once—rather, the shift will be a gradual one from inconsistent to consistent carry-over of the new sound to conversation.

Several publications are available to the teacher which can be used in helping the child improve his articulation (Berry and Eisenson, 1956; Black, 1964; Egland, 1964).

Voice

Suggestions for the teacher in handling disorders of the voice are necessarily limited due to the possible physical reasons for the disorder. If the child's voice sounds breathy, hoarse, nasal, or denasal, the teacher can discuss the condition with the child's parents and suggest that the child be referred to his physician or otolaryngologist to ascertain any physical reason for the deviation. If the child's voice is too loud or too soft, a medical referral may also be made. If no physical reason is found which prohibits practice in using the voice, the teacher may invent various ways for the child to increase the loudness of his voice by "projecting" or focusing on a certain point where he wants his voice to be heard. In the case of an overly loud voice, he could also be taught to listen to his own voice and to make judgments of loudness and softness and the degree of loudness needed in various situations.

Sometimes teachers notice that a child's voice lacks flexibility or sounds "monotonous," indicating that there is very little pitch change. In this case, if there is no evidence of hearing loss, the teacher could demonstrate how various pitches can change the meaning of phrases and let the children make up and practice their own examples. For example, say the sentence, "He wants to go" with the voice pitched higher on "He" than on "wants to go." Repeat the same sentence with the voice pitched higher on "wants" than on "He" and "to go" and notice how the meaning has changed. Other voice patterns and meanings can also be demonstrated in the same sentence.

Stuttering

The kind of stuttering which the teacher will encounter in a child in the kindergarten and first years of school is characterized by prolongations, hesitations, and repetitions in which the child usually shows no awareness or anxiety about speaking. Older children who stutter exhibit stuttering symptoms of struggle behavior as they attempt to push through blocks and are very much aware, anxious, and troubled about speaking.

One of the first things for the teacher to remember is that the child who stutters does not stutter all the time. Basically, he can talk—it is usually only at certain times and under certain conditions that the child has trouble speaking. As pressures in the environment and on the child increase, so does the amount and severity of the disfluency tend to increase. One very important goal, then, for the teacher with a young stutterer in her class is to create a warm, accepting, noncritical classroom climate—conditions which also will be favorable for all children. The prevailing atmosphere of the classroom starts with the personality and manner of the teacher. One who welcomes all children, who recognizes individual differences in abilities, appearances, and behavior, and who handles the class with an easy confidence will certainly provide an excellent environment for the stuttering child, as well as for all children. If a teacher knows that he is a somewhat tense and exacting individual, he may still be able to bring about some changes in his own manner which would help the stuttering child; however, if there is another class available where the teacher feels the child would be under less pressure, then to request such a change would certainly be an ethical move.

The attitude of the other pupils in the class is a second very influential factor related to the stuttering child. As a general rule, young children tend to accept differences and deviations, and frequently show compassion and helpfulness to children with an obvious handicap. Occasionally, though, there will be a child in the class who will laugh at and tease the stuttering child and perhaps others will join in. This is more likely to happen if there is something in the stuttering child's personality which is not likable. If such a situation occurs, the teacher can prearrange an errand for the stuttering child which will send him to another room and then openly discuss the situation with the children in the class. The teacher can compare speech differences with other disabilities people have, and perhaps a real question and answer session can evolve in which the children arrive at some good solutions concerning acceptance of other people. Some elementary schools have counselors who are skilled in conducting such sessions, and the problem of accepting the stuttering child can be turned into one of benefit for all the children.

There are a number of fairly specific techniques which the teacher can use with the young stutterer which will contribute to favorable conditions for speaking:

1. Give this child enough time to say what he has to say. If he is to recite orally, avoid "surprising" him—let him know a little in advance when his turn will come.

2. Really listen to the content of what he is saying rather than to the trouble he has in speaking.

3. Give the child classroom responsibility—a position which gains respect for him from his classmates.

4. See that this child experiences success in a variety of ways, but help him to accept his failures. His speech, too, is a series of successes and failures.

5. Watch for his "good" days and give him special opportunities to recite when he is fluent.

6. Try to establish a regular routine for the child. Avoid rushing him through any task. He should be expected to conform to the same school rules as any child, which may require some pressure, but pressure should never be put on his speech.

7. Avoid saying anything to him which will create anxiety about his school work or his performance. Try to build his confidence in his abilities.

8. This child should not be allowed to use his stuttering to avoid a class assignment. If the required task is oral and he feels he cannot do it, he should be required to submit the work in written form.

9. Avoid any kind of a "label." He may have heard himself called a stutterer, but perhaps not. In any case, labeling does not help him.

There are some directions which well-meaning persons have given stutterers for years in an attempt to bring about fluent speech. These directions are usually expressed as "slow down," "start over," "stop and think," "take a deep breath before you start," "try another word if you can't say that one," and so on. Perhaps there is some success with some of these instructions occasionally, but they do not really solve the problem. It is far more likely that eventually the stutterer will become so apprehensive about what he will be told to do that he will begin to try some "tricks" of his own to overcome the problem and only perpetuate the difficulty.

The suggestions listed above apply particularly to the young child in the earlier phases in the development of stuttering. The teacher will be the central person in working with this child, but will consult with the speech clinician, the school counselor, and perhaps the psychologist and social worker. Certainly there will be counseling with the parents, as the home environment and attitudes there are of great importance. The speech clinician in most cases will not take the young child in the first phase of stuttering out of the classroom—an indirect approach of consultation is preferred.

Many of the suggestions for the teacher of the child in the first phase of stuttering are applicable to the junior or senior high school student in the third or fourth phase, especially those pertaining to a decrease in pressure and anxiety. The following are suggestions which might allow the stutterer in secondary schools to participate more fully in school life:

1. Find out whether the stutterer enjoys singing, since many stutterers can sing without stuttering. If he enjoys singing, encourage his participation in a choral group.
2. If a stutterer can recite memorized material, such as poetry, he could be encouraged to do so in an English or drama class when appropriate. He might also enjoy taking a part in a play.
3. Many stutterers can read aloud fluently. This ability, if present, could be utilized in many classes.
4. By interviewing the stutterer directly, the teacher can gain considerable insight concerning speaking situations which are either "easy" or "difficult." With some understanding also of the stutterer's particular interests, it should be possible to channel him into activities which could be enjoyable and also give him some degree of speaking success.

In addition to the indirect handling through consultation, the speech clinician also will probably hold private or group sessions with the older stutterer, involving specific techniques for coping with the complexities of his speech.

Other Conditions

Certain conditions affecting speech and language are complex and usually require direct services from the speech clinician; however, the teacher with some knowledge of these conditions will certainly be better prepared to help with adjustment problems of these children in the classroom.

Impaired hearing. Children with a hearing loss severe enough to cause a disturbance of articulation and oral language development are classified as deafened or partially hearing and require special remediation programs as discussed by McConnell (Chapter 7). Many children with hearing losses are able to function in the regular classroom, but there are some things the teacher can do to help him participate more fully. Eisenson and Ogilvie (1963) suggest that the child be seated where he can best see and hear the speakers in the room; that he move about the room in order to be where he can hear best; that the light should be on the speaker's face; that the speaker should not distort his speaking, but speak naturally; that the teacher write key thoughts on the chalkboard; and that the teacher should watch for signs indicating that the child does not understand so that the teacher can explain the information in another way.

The high school partially hearing student may have difficulty comprehending enough of the lecture material to take notes. In this case, the teacher can ask a student who takes good notes to use carbon paper in order that a copy may be made for the partially hearing student. This provides the additional benefit of possibly developing a friendly feeling between the helping student and the partially hearing student.

Cerebral palsy. Helping the cerebral palsied child to develop speech and oral language skills in the classroom is a most challenging undertaking for the teacher because of the multiplicity of problems these children have (see Wilson, Chapter 9). What and how much the teacher can do will depend on the severity of the neuromuscular involvement. For example, many children find it extremely difficult to coordinate the movements of the speech mechanism to produce even the simplest speech sounds. The basic principles of articulation and voice training described in an earlier section can be used; however, progress will be much slower than for children who do not have this kind of handicap. Early verbal stimulation and "formal" speech and language training before the child begins the first grade will make the classroom teacher's task much easier. Since damage to the central nervous system is irreparable, long-term goals as well as the immediate remedial program must be planned and coordinated carefully. Regardless of the child's placement in the school program, the services of several specialists will be needed; some of these are the audiologist, physical therapist, physician, and psychologist as well as the teacher and speech clinician.

Cleft palate. In most schools the speech clinician will assume the major responsibility for the remedial speech program for children with cleft palate speech. However, with some understanding of the complexities of cleft palate speech the teacher may be able to assist in the carry-over phase of remediation and help the child use as good speech as possible in the classroom.

Following surgical or dental intervention, structural deviations involving the roof of the mouth still may exist so that the child is unable to correctly articulate speech sounds that require a continuous flow of air; some of these are "s" (soup), "z" (zoom), and "th" (think). Also he may have difficulty in producing the explosive sounds such as "p" (paper), "b" (baby), "t" (toe), and "d" (mad) which normally are acquired early through maturation. When the child with a cleft palate attempts to use many of the above-mentioned sounds the air may be expelled through the nose rather than the mouth. The child will learn in sessions with the speech clinician that the air is to be expelled through the mouth when he produces the sounds "s," "t," and so forth. The teacher can assist in carry-over in the classroom by asking the child to imitate words containing the desired sounds while he determines for himself whether the air is coming out of the mouth or nose by placing a finger on the upper lip. The problem of hypernasality which is due to voiced sounds, such as the vowel "ah" and the consonant "b" being emitted through the nose, can be approached in a similar manner. The child will feel the "vibrations" coming through his nose by touching it on the side. If he can learn to direct the airstream correctly, procedures similar to those described earlier in the section on articulation disabilities can be used.

Mental retardation. One of the most disabling disturbances associated with mental retardation is the deficiency in oral language. Since language function is so closely related to cognitive abilities and therefore educational progress, remedial programs which concentrate on improving these basic skills should rank high on the list of things to be done for such children. The fact that these children may also manifest articulation and voice disorders as well as stuttering is of secondary importance. Therefore the classroom teacher should concentrate on developing the child's oral language skills. Many children will be assigned to a special teacher part of the time, in which case both the regular teacher and the special education teacher should work closely with one another to assure that their efforts are coordinated. The role of the speech clinician as a member of the team should be flexible; serving as a consultant to the overall program or, at times, working directly with the child to improve his speech skills.

Dunn has discussed educational and training programs for the mentally retarded child extensively in Chapters 2 and 3. As these children are moved into the educational mainstream to a greater degree, the regular classroom teacher's responsibility for carrying out the oral language and speech development program will increase.

The Speech Clinician's Role

There are three broad areas in which the speech clinician can be of service in the total educational program. The first role is to serve as a resource person by providing *consultant* services to the classroom teacher and other staff members in regard to the improvement of communication skills in the classroom. The second is to provide *direct services* for students with significant speech disabilities. The third role is as a program *administrator* working with the school administration in planning and operating the speech correction program.

Consultant Services

In the role of *consultant*, the speech clinician should serve as a member of a team in planning cooperatively for a student with a specific problem.

When a student's speech is creating a problem for him personally and educationally, the teacher can call together individuals who might pool their skills and resources in order to provide service and better education for the student. The story of Gary shows how the team approach was used for an adolescent with an articulation disorder.

Vignette 6.2 A Senior in High School with an Articulation Problem

Gary, a senior in high school, found that he was scheduled for "Public Speaking," a required course for graduation from high school and one which he had avoided for the last two years. This course was regarded with dismay by many adolescents but for Gary it spelled disaster. Good-looking, six-foot-one Gary had an undeniable tongue-protrusion lisp on the "s" and "z" sounds. He had always managed to minimize the problem by restricting his speaking to close friends and family. He told the teacher that he would not and could not make speeches and, if forced, threatened to drop out of school. As he spoke, the teacher became acutely aware of the reason.

Gary was referred to his counselor, who stated that the requirement might be met in a different way. During the interview, Gary revealed that he had never had remediation for his speech problem and, when questioned, replied that he would like to eliminate the lisp but did not think it possible. It must be stressed that this young man was not malingering. The counselor had known him for the previous two years and had noticed his reticence in speaking and his lisp, but she had no indication that it was affecting Gary and his education in a negative way.

During a staffing with the teacher, the counselor, and the school's speech clinician, a plan was evolved in which Gary would participate in all written and listening activities of the class. In addition, he would be scheduled for one 40-minute individual speech correction session per week. The plan was presented to Gary and he accepted it, although he obviously doubted that he could alter the lisp, as did the teacher, the counselor, and the speech clinician because of Gary's age and negative feelings.

Fortunately the lisp did yield to corrective techniques, and as progress was made Gary became motivated to practice the sounds in the grocery where he had an after-school job, though he still did not believe he could ever talk "that way." By the end of the school year, the new sounds had become habituated and Gary spoke freely with the teacher, the counselor, and the speech clinician. Although he did not reach the level of presenting a prepared speech before the class, Gary did begin to volunteer a few comments during class discussion. He reported later that he felt "real good" about using the newly learned sounds.

Indirect remediation is another way in which the speech clinician can serve as a consultant. The term "indirect remediation" refers to a type of intervention in which the speech clinician does not take the child out of the classroom for sessions but does extensive planning, rechecking, and follow-up to determine that the child is being helped and making progress. One example, mentioned earlier, is the indirect service provided the young stutterer in which the speech clinician does confer and plan often with the teacher. Other examples are the carry-over phase in articulation remediation and periodic rechecks of children in the early grades who misarticulate some sounds, many of whom will improve through maturation. If not, these children can be scheduled later for direct remediation.

In the role of consultant, the speech clinician can also serve as a resource person who can be helpful to the classroom teacher in locating and providing materials for use in a general speech improvement program for the primary grades. For example, Byrne (1965) has developed a program for speech improvement in the kindergarten and first grades which focuses on sounds most commonly missed by five- and six-year olds and which stresses the use of auditory discrimination techniques. In this program, the speech clinician could demonstrate a few lessons, with the classroom teacher taking over the remainder of the lessons and incorporating them into her daily plans. The *Goldman-Lynch Sounds and Symbols Development Kit* (1971) is another program designed for use in group speech improvement programs. This kit, suitable for group work, serves to introduce phonics and reading as a part of the overall speech and language program.

Direct Remediation

If the consultant part of the oral communication program is well planned and operating effectively, only students with the most significant speech disabilities should be taken out of the classroom for direct remediation. How one selects students with the "most significant speech disabilities" is a matter of great concern for all speech clinicians. As was seen in Table 6.2, extreme articulation and voice deviations, as well as stuttering, improve with age. Therefore, many children who apparently have significant problems in the first grade will have improved enough by the time they reach the third or fourth grade that direct remedial services will not be needed. A wise approach in case selection would be to determine to what degree the speech deviation affects academic performance and personal adjustmnt in the school setting. Certain types of speech disabilities require such specific techniques that it would be distracting and ineffective to attempt any type of class or group work. By developing a good consultant program, there should be time for scheduling lessons as often and on as flexible a basis as needed in order to give a strong program to the students with severe speech disabilities.

New approaches and techniques are being developed and applied in all areas of remedial work, which is true also in speech remediation. Many of these can be used only, or at least to the best advantage, in an individual setting. One example of this is the use of operant conditioning techniques as applied in the modification of stuttering behavior with the advanced stutterer. Other examples of handicapped students requiring direct services are those with voice disorders and severe articulation problems who can benefit from specific techniques; hearing-impaired students needing auditory training, lip-reading, and articulation work; and children whose conditions are complicated by structural or neurological complications. With these children a cooperative exchange of information between the teacher and the speech clinician to insure progress in carry-over is very helpful.

Program Administration

The speech clinician is usually responsible for working with the school administration in organizing, planning, and effecting any changes which are needed in the speech correction program. Although school districts differ in the organization of speech correction programs, a general pattern was developed in the 1940s and has been widely used since that time.

Essentially, the speech clinician is responsible for screening, testing, scheduling, follow-up, and consultation on any children with speech problems in assigned schools. In the traditional role, the speech clinician is itinerant and works at more than one school each day. For example, one school may be attended on Monday and Wednesday mornings and another on Monday and Wednesday afternoons. Tuesdays and Thursdays may be scheduled in the same way so that four schools would be attended twice weekly. Each half day is divided into several 20- or 30-minute lesson periods. During each session the clinician works with children in small groups, usually varying in size from two to six children, or occasionally with one child individually. In this way each child may receive two lessons each week. The total caseload varies from district to district, but traditionally it ranges from 75 to 100 or more children on the schedule per week, although a trend began to develop in the 1960s toward lower caseloads, as will be discussed later. The fifth day of the week is sometimes used by the clinician for serving variously as consultant or resource teacher in testing, follow-up, and in additional sessions for children who may need more intensive help. Another system of scheduling, called the block system, has also been used to some extent. In the block system, the speech clinician concentrates time in one or two schools for intensive remediation daily for a selected number of weeks, perhaps five weeks. For the second block one or two other schools are attended for a five-week period, and so on. Eventually the clinician returns to the first block, and thus each school is attended for intensive periods two or three times during the school year. This type of scheduling, too, is subject to many variations.

The speech clinician is also responsible for various kinds of reports required by the state department of education as well as the local school administration in accounting for the services. In addition to required reports, the speech clinician keeps records of screening, evaluations, and progress reports available to persons on the staff directly involved in helping the children.

TRENDS AND GOALS

In the past decade some important trends have emerged that are changing the concept of interventive services in public schools for children with oral communication disabilities. These changes are encouraging since they ultimately will improve the quality of services. There are also some changes, not yet evident to any marked degree, that should be made. The following are some trends which will continue in the future and some changes which must come about eventually if we are to be successful in our efforts to guide the exceptional child down the mainstream of education.

1. *The speech clinician should be more active in the general education program.* The speech clinician should be integrated more completely into the total educational program as an active participant in overall planning rather than as a peripheral specialist who provides unique services only "when indicated." Services for the child with an oral communication disturbance should be planned jointly by the speech clinician and the teacher. Ainsworth (1965) urged that the speech clinician be a "participant" in the school program rather than a "separatist." In his argument, Ainsworth points out that a speech clinician is in a better position to help the child when he can obtain the cooperation of other school personnel; this is more easily accomplished if the speech clinician actively participates in the total educational program.

2. *The classroom teacher should participate more actively in the remediation program.* The classroom teacher should assume the responsibility for the total remediation program, with the speech clinician serving as a consultant much of the time. This arrangement is desirable especially for children in the first and second grades who have mild speech disturbances. The goal in special education is, as Dunn (Chapter 1) has stated, to reduce educational segregation to the minimum. Thus we must exert our efforts toward keeping all exceptional children in the stream of general education. Referring to Dunn's inverted pyramid, we see that children with speech and language disabilities can be classified as TYPE II EXCEPTIONAL CHILDREN, receiving Level IV services (regular day class supplemented with direct special itinerant or school-based tutorial instruction). Hopefully, in the future many of these children will move up to at least Level III services and in some instances TYPE I, Level III services, especially for junior high and senior high school students who can do much on their own with minimal assistance from either the teacher or the speech clinician. One of the challenges for the teacher and the speech clinician is to devise a plan that will start children at a higher level than TYPE II, Level IV services and move them up sooner than has been done in the past. How well this is done will depend on the professional credentials and motivation of both the teacher and speech clinician. In any case, the needs of the child cannot be sacrificed; continuous evaluation of the program must be an integral part of it.

3. *The caseload of the speech clinician should be reduced.* Although the caseload of the speech clinician was reduced during the 1960s, it must be reduced even more if maximum quality services are to be realized. Steer et al. (1961) reported the average caseload for public school speech clinicians to be 130. A caseload of 82 was reported nationally for public school speech clinicians by the U.S. Office of Education in 1968–1969 (see Dunn, Chapter 1). O'Toole and Zaslow (1969) describe much smaller caseloads in which direct services are provided daily for longer periods for each individual on the schedule. These individuals are partially hearing and their programs include speechreading and auditory training practice; vocabulary and language building; and speech correction. In another program they report the speech clinician has a caseload of 45 individuals per week; the more severely handicapped are seen four times a week while the others are seen three and two times a week depending on severity and needs. An "ideal" caseload size cannot be predetermined. When this is done, children are made to fit into a plan rather than a plan being designed to fit the needs of the children. On the one hand, if the speech clinician is to be responsible for direct services for only the severe problems, the number might be small. On the other hand, if the speech clinician is to serve as the consultant to the teacher for the milder problems, time must be allowed for such activities. It is suggested here that the caseload number for direct services have no lower limit, but an upper limit could be set at approximately 40. There should be other ways of accounting to the public for the services rendered than in terms of numbers of children on the schedule. Flexibility of the program is more important than firm numbers.

4. *Language disturbances of economically disadvantaged and minority group children need more attention.* There has been increased emphasis on the educational problems related to language disturbances during the past decade. This is especially true with respect to the nonstandard English patterns that are used by inner-city children. This trend will continue in the future; it must if we are to provide these children with a realistic opportunity to obtain a quality education.

We must push forward on research designed to gain a better understanding of the nonstandard English pattern used by culturally deprived children and how it relates to educational success.

5. *Efficacy of remediation services needs to be evaluated.* For many years we have used numerous methods in remedial programs to alleviate the symptoms of speech and language disorders, yet there has been very little research reported that attempted to evaluate objectively the efficacy of our efforts. The research of Irwin (1962, 1963) and Sommers et al. (1961), three studies on the effectiveness of speech remediation for first- and second-grade children, is contradictory. Irwin found that speech remediation for articulation disorders was not effective for first- and second-graders while Sommers found that it was. These contradictory findings suggest that we need to continue our efforts to find answers.

6. *Use of professional aides should be increased.* As we increase our efforts to bring services to small isolated schools scattered throughout the nation, speech and language programs must be organized to meet these demands at a minimum cost without wasting valuable manpower. Information from the U.S. Office of Education, *Education Directory* (1965), shows that approximately 50 percent of the identified school districts in the United States have enrollments of fewer than 300 pupils. In most such school districts there are neither enough students with significant speech and language disabilities nor sufficient funds to justify a trained full-time speech clinician. In an effort to solve the problem, several small towns have banded together and employed a speech clinician and other specialists to establish certain special services for their schools. By sharing specialists each of the schools derives some benefit from special services. However, the program will be more effective if professional aides living in the individual communities can be utilized to provide a continuous service. Although it is hoped that teachers will become increasingly active in the areas of speech and language development and improvement, they too are overburdened and aides could benefit this program by assisting both teachers and speech clinicians. The itinerant speech clinician would supervise the aides assisting the teacher in carrying out suggested activities. Alpiner (1968), reporting on a pilot study for training and utilization of supportive personnel in speech correction, concluded that such aides can be useful in a variety of activities associated with long-term speech and language remedial programs. The speech aides in the pilot study program underwent a three-week training program. In this program they were given a survey of speech correction procedures in the schools, and they received specific instruction in duties expected of them as assistants to speech clinicians.

Although some very significant strides have been taken during the past decade to improve the quality of services for the speech and language problems of children in the schools much still remains to be done. In the public school setting one of the major tasks for the future is to devise realistic service programs that are flexible enough to provide quality service for all levels of severity without moving to an expensive tutorial system.

7. *Professional training for speech clinicians and language specialists should be broadened.* Within the past 10 years universities and colleges throughout the United States have broadened their training programs for speech and language specialists by increasing the emphasis in the areas of learning theory, language development, linguistics, and language disorders of all types so that trained professionals will be better equipped to meet the new challenges which we must meet in the total education of the exceptional child. Again, as in other areas of change within the field, this trend will continue to develop. We must learn more about the educational implications of nonstandard English if we are to help the culturally different child in our public education system.

SUMMARY

During the late 1960s and the early 1970s two of the most important trends in public education in the United States were the increased emphasis on language disturbances of children and the concern for the education of children who speak nonstandard English. This emerging change has affected both the speech and hearing field as a whole and also the trained speech and language specialists working in the public schools. The definition of language disturbances has been broadened to include nonstandard English used by inner-city blacks, Mexican-Americans, American Indians, Eskimos in Alaska, pidgin-speaking Hawaiians, and whites in our economically depressed areas. Although not everyone agrees that nonstandard English should be labeled as a language disorder, there is general agreement among educators, linguists, and psychologists that it does interfere with the child's educational success. This represents progress because we now have become concerned about a problem which has existed for many years. The next step is to develop the educational methods and teaching skills needs to provide these children with an opportunity to obtain a good education.

The trend regarding practical approaches to the management of speech and oral language disorders which emerged in the 1960s is well established now. In the future, the planning of remedial programs for children with oral communication disturbances will be incorporated into the school curriculum to a greater extent than has been done so far. This means that the role of the speech clinician has changed and will continue to do so in the future as new and better educational methods emerge. The public school speech clinician now serves as a consultant to the regular and special education teacher, provides direct and indirect remedial services for children with many types of oral communication disturbances, and often teaches English as a second language. In short, the speech clinician functions as a member of a team of experts whose goal is to educate all children. The discussion in this chapter does get at this concept in order to show how the team approach can be used to plan and carry out the delivery of special services in the school. However, success of the team approach will depend on the people involved in the total educational program. The teacher, special educator, psychologist, and speech clinician all have much to offer in the total educational program for the exceptional child. When the skills of these specialists are coordinated as a team effort the chances for success are increased immeasurably.

Much has been learned about oral communication in the past 10 years. Yet we continue to learn more—and what is more important, we are learning how to use the knowledge to improve our skills in helping children with oral communication disabilities. The increasing activity in all areas of research regarding language development, linguistics, language disorders and their impact on education, and the relation of cognitive behavior to language will no doubt yield information which will take us closer, in the next decade or two, to the solution of many problems faced by educators throughout the nation.

Resources

Additional information concerning oral communication disorders can be obtained by writing: Executive Secretary, American Speech and Hearing Association, 9030 Old Georgetown Road, Washington, D.C. 20014.

The association publishes the *Journal of Speech and Hearing Disorders, Journal of Speech and Hearing Research, Asha, ASHA Reports, ASHA Monographs, ASHA Trends, Language, Speech and Hearing Services in Schools*, and special reports of professional interest.

For many years the American Speech and Hearing Association has actively supported the improvement of professional services in the United States. The association has within its structure a professional certification committee that certifies the clinical competency of its qualified members. In addition, the American Board of Examiners in Speech Pathology and Audiology evaluates and certifies clinical services programs and professional training programs of service agencies and training institutions in the nation. A list of certified members, service programs, and professional training programs is maintained in the central office.

In addition to the national organization, there are many state speech and hearing associations that serve as sources of information at the local level. Most state organizations publish a periodic bulletin or journal containing information of a professional nature. Most state departments of education have a special services division which can furnish information about services for exceptional children throughout the state.

References

Ainsworth, S. *Speech correction methods.* Englewood Cliffs, N.J.: Prentice-Hall, 1948.

Ainsworth, S. The speech clinician in public schools: "Participant" or "separatist"? *Asha,* **7,** 495–503.

Ainsworth, S. Report and commentary. In *Conditioning in stuttering therapy: Applications and limitations.* Pub. No. 7. Memphis, Tenn.: Speech Foundation of America, 1970.

Alpiner, J. G. The utilization of supportive personnel in speech correction in the public schools. Pilot project supported by the Colorado State Department of Education, Title VI, ESEA, Bureau of the Handicapped, U.S. Office of Education, 1968.

Baratz, J. C. Reply to Dr. Raph's article on speech and language deficits in culturally disadvantaged children. *Journal of Speech and Hearing Disorders,* 1968, **33,** 299–300.

Bereiter, C., and Englemann, S. *Teaching disadvantaged children in the preschool.* Englewood Cliffs, N.J.: Prentice-Hall, 1966.

Bernstein, B. Language and social class. *British Journal of Psychology,* 1960, **11,** 271–276.

Berry, M. F. *Language disorders of children: The bases and diagnoses.* New York: Appleton-Century-Crofts, 1969.

Berry, M. F., and Eisenson, J. *Speech disorders.* New York: Appleton-Century-Crofts, 1956.

Black, M. E. *Speech correction in the schools.* Englewood Cliffs, N.J.: Prentice-Hall, 1964.

Blanton, S. A survey of speech defects. *Journal of Educational Psychology,* 1916, **7,** 581–592.

Bloodstein, O. The development of stuttering: I. Changes in nine basic features. *Journal of Speech and Hearing Disorders,* 1960, **25,** 219–237. (a)

Bloodstein, O. The development of stuttering: II. Developmental phases. *Journal of Speech and Hearing Disorders*, 1960, **25**, 366–376. (b)

Bloodstein, O. The development of stuttering: III. Theoretical and clinical implications. *Journal of Speech and Hearing Disorders*, 1961, **26**, 67–82.

Boone, D. R. *The voice and voice therapy.* Englewood Cliffs, N.J.: Prentice-Hall, 1971.

Broca, P. Remarques sur le siège de la faculté du langage articulé suivé d'une observation d'aphémie. *Bulletin Societé Anatomique de Paris*, 1861, **36**, 331. Cited by J. M. Wepman, *Recovery from aphasia.* New York: Ronald Press, 1951, 9.

Brutten, G. J., and Shoemaker, D. J. *The modification of stuttering.* Englewood Cliffs, N.J.: Prentice-Hall, 1967.

Byrne, M. C. *The child speaks.* New York: Harper & Row, 1965.

Carrell, J., and Tiffany, W. R. *Phonetics: Theory and application to speech improvement.* New York: McGraw-Hill, 1960.

Carrow, M. A. The development of auditory comprehension of language structure in children. *Journal of Speech and Hearing Disorders*, 1968, **33**, 99–111.

Davis, E. A. Mean sentence length compared with long and short sentences as a reliable measure of language development. *Child Development*, 1937, **8**, 69–79.

Davis, E. A. Developmental changes in the distribution of parts of speech. *Child Development*, 1938, **8**, 309–317.

Deutsch, M., Katz, I., and Jensen, A. R. (Eds.) *Social class, race, and psychological development.* New York: Holt, Rinehart and Winston, 1968.

Edney, C. W. The public school remedial speech program. In W. Johnson, S. F. Brown, J. F. Curtis, C. W. Edney, and J. Keaster, *Speech handicapped school children.* New York: Harper & Row, 1956.

Egland, G. O. *Speech and language problems. A guide for the classroom teacher.* Englewood Cliffs, N.J.: Prentice-Hall, 1964.

Eisenson, J. Development aphasia: A speculative · view with therapeutic implications. *Journal of Speech and Hearing Disorders*, 1968, **33**, 3–13.

Eisenson, J. *Aphasia in children.* New York: Harper & Row, 1972.

Eisenson, J., and Oqilvie, M. *Speech correction in the schools.* (2nd ed.) New York: Macmillan, 1963.

Fairbanks, G. F. *Voice and articulation drillbook.* (2nd ed.) New York: Harper & Row, 1960.

Frisina, D. R. Hearing disorders. In N. G. Haring and R. L. Schiefelbusch (Eds.), *Methods in special education.* New York: McGraw-Hill, 1967.

Goldiamond, I. Stuttering and fluency as manipulatable operant response classes. In H. N. Sloane Jr., and B. D. MacAulay (Eds.), *Operant procedures in remedial speech and language training.* Boston: Houghton Mifflin, 1968.

Goldman, R., and Fristoe, M. *Goldman-Fristoe test of articulation.* Circle Pines, Minn.: American Guidance Service, 1969.

Goldman, R., and Lynch, M. E. *The Goldman-Lynch sounds and symbols development kit.* Circle Pines, Minn.: American Guidance Service, 1971.

Hejna, R. J. *Developmental articulation test.* (Rev.) Ann Arbor, Mich.: Speech Materials, 1959.

Hull, F. M., Mielke, P. W., Jr., Timmons, R. J., and Willeford, J. A. The national speech and hearing survey: Preliminary results. *Asha*, 1971, **13**, 501–509.

Hunt, J. McV. Environment, development, and scholastic achievement. In M. Deutsch, I. Katz, and A. R. Jensen (Eds.), *Social class, race, and psychological development.* New York: Holt, Rinehart and Winston, 1968.

Irwin, O. C. Infant speech: Consonantal sounds according to place of articulation. *Journal of Speech and Hearing Disorders*, 1947, **12**, 397–401.

Irwin, O. C. Infant speech: Development of vowel sounds. *Journal of Speech and Hearing Disorders*, 1948, **13**, 31–34.

Irwin, R. B. Speech therapy and children's linguistic skills. *Journal of Speech and Hearing Research*, 1962, **5**, 377–381.

Irwin, R. B. The effects of speech therapy upon certain language skills of first-grade children. *Journal of Speech and Hearing Disorders*, 1963, **28**, 375–381.

Irwin, R. B. Speech and hearing therapy. Pittsburgh, Pa.: Stanwix House, 1965.

Johnson, W. *Children with speech and hearing impairment*. Washington, D.C.: U. S. Office of Education Bulletin, No. 5, 1959.

Johnson, W., Brown, S. F., Curtis, J. F., Edney, C. W., and Keaster, J. *Speech handicapped school children*. (3d ed.) New York: Harper & Row, 1967.

Labov, W. The logic of nonstandard English. In F. Williams (Ed.), *Language and poverty*. Chicago: Markham, 1970.

Lee, L. L. Developmental sentence types: A method for comparing normal and deviant syntactic development. *Journal of Speech and Hearing Disorders*, 1966, **31**, 311–330.

Lindamood, C., and Lindamood, P. *Auditory discrimination in depth (A.D.D. Program 1)*. Boston: Teaching Resources, 1969.

Matthews, J. Communication disorders in the mentally retarded. In L. E. Travis (Ed.), *Handbook of speech pathology and audiology*. New York: Appleton-Century-Crofts, 1971.

McCarthy, D. Language development in children. In L. Carmichael (Ed.), *Manual of child psychology*. New York: Wiley, 1954.

McDonald, E. T. *A deep test of articulation*. Pittsburgh, Pa.: Stanwix House, 1964 (a).

McDonald, E. T. *Articulation testing and treatment: A sensory-motor approach*. Pittsburgh, Pa.: Stanwix House, 1964 (b).

McDonald, E. T., and Baker, H. K. Cleft palate speech: An integration of research and clinical observations. *Journal of Speech and Hearing Disorders*, 1951, **16**, 9–20.

Metraux, R. W. Speech profiles of the preschool child 18–54 months. *Journal of Speech and Hearing Disorders*, 1950, **15**, 37–53.

Monsees, E. K., and Berman, C. Speech and language screening in a summer Headstart program. *Journal of Speech and Hearing Disorders*, 1968, **33**, 121–126.

Morley, M. E. *Cleft palate and speech*. (6th ed.) Baltimore: Williams and Wilkins, 1967.

Olin, W. H. Incidence of cleft lips and cleft palates in Iowa. *Cleft Palate Bulletin*, 1963, **13**. Cited by H. Westlake and D. Rutherford, *Cleft palate*. Englewood Cliffs, N.J.: Prentice-Hall, 1966, p. 4.

O'Toole, T. J., and Zaslow, E. Public school speech and hearing programs: Things are changing. *Speech and hearing services in schools*, Vol. 1. Published by American Speech and Hearing Association. Reprinted from *Asha*, 1969.

Raph, J. B. Language and speech deficits in culturally disadvantaged children: Implications for the speech clinician. *Journal of Speech and Hearing Disorders*, 1967, **32**, 203–214.

Roe, V. I., Hanley, C. N., Crotty, C. M., and Mayper, L. R. Clinical practice: Diagnosis and measurement. In Public school speech and hearing services. *Journal of Speech and Hearing Disorders*, Monograph Supplement 8, U. S. Office of Education, Coop. Research Project No. 648 (8191), (M. D. Steer, Project Director), July 1961.

Schlanger, B. B., and Gottsleben, R. H. Analysis of speech defects among institutionalized mentally retarded. *Journal of Speech and Hearing Disorders*, 1957, **22**, 98–103.

Shuy, R. W. The sociolinguists and urban language problems. In F. Williams (Ed.), *Language and poverty*. Chicago: Markham, 1970.

Sommers, R. K. Case finding, case selection, and case load. In R. J. Van Hattum (Ed.), *Clinical speech in the schools*. Springfield, Ill.: Charles C Thomas, 1969.

Sommers, R. K., Cockerille, C. E., Paul, C. D., Bowser, D. C., Fichter, G. R., Fenton, A. K. and Copetas, F. G. Effects of speech therapy and speech improvement upon articulation and reading. *Journal of Speech and Hearing Disorders*, 1961, **26**, 27–37.

Spradlin, J. E. Language and communication of mental defectives. In N. R. Ellis (Ed.), *Handbook of mental deficiency*. New York: McGraw-Hill, 1963.

Spriestersbach, D. C. Assessing nasal quality in cleft palate speech of children. *Journal of Speech and Hearing Disorders*, 1955, **20**, 266–270.

Steer, M. D., Doerfler, L. G., Eisenson, J., Johnson, K. O., Johnson, W., Matthews, J., and Schubert, E. D. Public school speech and hearing services. *Journal of Speech and Hearing Disorders*, Monograph Supplement 8, U.S. Office of Education, Coop. Research Project No. 649 (8191), (M. D. Steer, Project Director), July 1961.

Templin, M. C. *Certain language skills in children*. Minneapolis: University of Minnesota Press, 1957.

Templin, M. C., and Darley, F. *The Templin-Darley tests of articulation*. Minneapolis: University of Minnesota Press, 1960.

U.S. Office of Education. *Education Directory 1964–65*. Part 2, Public School Systems. Superintendent of Documents, Catalog No. FS 5.220: 20005–65/pt. 2. Washington, D.C.: Government Printing Office, 1965.

Van Riper, C. *Speech correction: Principles and methods*. (4th ed.) Englewood Cliffs, N.J.: Prentice-Hall, 1963.

Van Riper, C.: *The nature of stuttering*. Englewood Cliffs, N.J.: Prentice-Hall, 1971.

Van Riper, C. *Speech correction: Principles and methods*. (5th ed.) Englewood Cliffs, N.J.: Prentice-Hall, 1972.

Van Riper, C., and Erickson, R. A. A predictive screening test of articulation, *Journal of Speech and Hearing Disorders*, 1969, **34**, 214–219.

Van Riper, C., and Irwin, J. V. *Voice and articulation*. Englewood Cliffs, N.J.: Prentice-Hall, 1958.

Weisenberg, T., and McBride, K. *Aphasia*. New York: Commonwealth Fund, Oxford University Press, 1935.

Wernicke, C. *Der aphasische symptomenkomplex*. Breslau: Taschon, 1874. Cited by C. Osgood and M. Miron (Eds.), *Approaches to the study of aphasia*. Urbana: University of Illinois Press, 1963, p. 47.

Westlake, H., and Rutherford, D. *Cleft palate*. Englewood Cliffs, N.J.: Prentice-Hall, 1966.

Williamson, A. B. Diagnosis and treatment of eighty-four cases of nasality. *Quarterly Journal of Speech*, 1944, **30**, 471–479.

Wood, N. E. *Delayed speech and language development*. Englewood Cliffs, N.J.: Prentice-Hall, 1964.

Opposite: Language and communication skills for a child with a severe hearing disability are best stimulated under intensive tutorial instruction where the teacher has the complete attention and involvement of the pupil. (Photo courtesy Bill Wilkerson Hearing and Speech Center, Nashville, Tenn.; photographer, B. A. Hanners.)

children with
hearing disabilities

chapter outline

From the beginning of life the growing child adapts to his environment on the basis of the experiences he perceives through his sense modalities. While each of the five sensory receptors responsible for the functions of hearing, sight, touch, taste, and smell plays an important role in the manner in which the developing child perceives a given experience, the two that are most crucial for acquiring information about the world are hearing and vision. Of these two, the sensory deprivation of hearing results in a more serious educational handicap, for in the absence of hearing, language symbols are not perceived and learned. The ability to use a symbolization process enabling us to remove ourselves from the world of the here and now is the chief advantage man holds over the rest of the animal kingdom. Thus, an individual *without a language system* indeed would be reduced to a level of functioning much closer to that of the lower species of animals.

Not to be able to hear is a condition which most of us as hearing individuals can never fully understand nor appreciate. We can close our eyes and gain some notion of what it might be like not to see, but we cannot close our ears, for they are always open and always at work—even when we sleep. That is why the mother of a newborn child is able to hear and be awakened by the crying of the infant, even though she may not awaken to traffic or other night-time noises. It is through hearing that we constantly monitor our environment, filtering out automatically sounds such as the air conditioner or the wind outside our window which we do not need to hear and listening selectively to the many sounds telling us that people and things are moving about and all is well with our world. Thus, it is hearing that provides us with a continual source of information about happenings within our immediate physical environment, as well as with warning signals that are important to our physical safety.

To teach children who hear only partially or not at all is truly an educational challenge. One need only watch a television program without the sound, or with very faint and distorted sound, to gain some realization of what hearing-impaired children experience in the classroom. In this chapter, the nature of auditory disability is discussed in detail as it relates to the education of such children.

DEFINITIONS AND CLASSIFICATION SYSTEMS

An *auditory disability* having educational significance exists when a defect in one or more parts of the ear and its associated nerve pathways leading from the ear to the brain prevents the child from adequately hearing, perceiving, or attending to either faint speech, ordinary conversational speech, or loud speech. Educators generally prefer an operational definition which indicates how much the hearing impairment has affected the language development of the child, since this factor is the one most closely related to the instructional programing that will be required. Within this context, the definitions most commonly used and understood are the following:

1. The *deaf*—those whose hearing loss is so severe at birth and in the prelingual period (before two to three years of age) that it precludes the normal, spontaneous development of spoken language.

2. The *partially hearing*—those whose hearing loss in the prelingual period or later is not of sufficient severity to preclude the development of some spoken language, and those who have normal hearing in the prelingual period but acquire hearing loss later. (The term "partially hearing," which is used extensively in the United Kingdom, and the term "hard of hearing," which is more frequently used in the United States, are interchangeable.)

While many persons today point out the inadequacy of the terms *deaf* and *partially hearing*, there have not emerged any consistent substitute terms which recognize the existence of the many variables associated with auditory defects in children. We are faced with the problem of providing educational programs specifically designed to alleviate the sensory deprivation of hearing in the twentieth century using terms more applicable to the state of knowledge in the previous century. The older terminology fails to account for the fact that some children with only moderately severe hearing loss will, without early and effective intervention, always remain educationally deaf (virtually nonauditory). Other children with similar degree of hearing loss, when provided appropriate help in the first years of life, are able to learn to use their hearing effectively so that by school age they can enter public schools as partially hearing children wearing hearing aids. Since identification of these children is occurring much earlier today and there is increasing awareness of the value of early intervention for *all* handicapped children, the number of such children detected in the first year of life or soon thereafter is steadily increasing. The sooner detection and intervention occur, the greater the potential for the child to become eligible for the *partially hearing* rather than the *deaf* classification.

The two preceding definitions are related primarily to sensory impairment, although those who are familiar with hearing-impaired children will recognize that problems of perception and attending are common even when amplification of sound has substantially alleviated the loudness factor. There is yet another group of children with auditory disabilities who in fact may, and often do, have hearing acuity within the normal range, but who have difficulty processing and obtaining meaning from auditory stimuli. Such children may be observed to exhibit poor performance in one or more of the following tasks: (1) identifying the source of sounds; (2) discriminating among sounds or words; (3) reproducing pitch and rhythm patterns; (4) sorting significant from nonsignificant sounds; (5) blending speech sounds into words; (6) understanding the meaning of environmental sounds in general (Chalfant and Scheffelin, 1969). The educational problems presented by this group are also common to other areas of handicap treated in other chapters. Hence, the major emphasis in this chapter will be on those auditory disabilities which result from sensory rather than central impairment of hearing.

It becomes apparent that to define the various types of auditory impairments in children is indeed not a simple matter, since a wide range of variable and interrelating factors may be operating in a given instance. Table 7.1 presents four basic factors which must be considered in defining and classifying any hearing impairment. While the first classification is most relevant to educational handling, the second factor (time) interacting with degree of impairment would weigh heavily in terms of resultant delay in language development, which would influence both educational and other rehabilitative or habilitative treatment.

TABLE 7.1 *Factors on Which Hearing Loss Classifications Are Based and Their Resulting Classification Systems*

Factors	Resulting Classification System
1. Degree of impairment	Deaf/partially hearing. Slight/mild/marked (or moderate)/severe/extreme (or profound).
2. Time (age at onset)	Congenital/acquired.
3. Cause	Genetically transmitted or endogenous (hereditary)/adventitious or exogenous (by disease, accident, or injury).
4. Physical origin (site of anomaly or lesion)	Conductive/sensorineural/central.

SOURCE: Adapted from Myklebust (1964).

Degree of Impairment

Although it is clear a number of factors must influence the way in which we think of children who are *deaf* or *partially hearing*, the factor of greatest importance to the educator still remains degree of impairment, despite the fact that these terms have many shades of meaning. It is true that a child may shift from one classification to the other, depending upon the type of audiologic, parent, and educational handling available at different periods of life. Table 7.2 provides six classes of hearing handicap based on the degree of hearing loss in decibels (dB), with accompanying interpretation on how the ability to hear speech is affected. Prevalence figures from a study of hearing levels found in school children in regular classes are included as they relate to the various classes of handicap. Since these classes of handicap are based only on the intensity levels of spoken voice, they reflect the handicap accruing to adults with established language and do not take into consideration such factors as age at onset. Teachers should find this particular grouping quite useful, however, if it is related to the audiograms of children in their classes.

Age at Onset

As already indicated, hearing impairment may also be categorized on the basis of age at onset, which is particularly relevant to the degree of language handicap that may be anticipated. Normally the loss of hearing which

TABLE 7.2 *Classes of Hearing Handicap with Accompanying Prevalence Figures in Percent for School Children, Ages 5-10, in Pittsburgh Study*

Hearing Level in dB (ISO 1964[b])	Class	Degree of Handi-cap	Average Hearing Level for 500, 1,000, and 2,000 Hz in Better Ear[a]		Ability To Understand Speech	Prevalence Figures in Percent for 4,064 Children Ages 5-10
			More Than	Not More Than		
	A	Not signifi-cant		25 db (ISO)	No significant difficulty with faint speech	98.3
25						
	B	Slight	26 dB (ISO)	40 dB	Difficulty only with faint speech	0.9
40						
	C	Mild	41 dB	55 dB	Frequent difficulty with speech at normal loudness	0.5
55						
	D	Marked	56 dB	70 dB	Frequent difficulty with loud speech	0.2
70						
	E	Severe	71 dB	90 dB	Can understand only shouted or amplified speech	0.05
90						
	F	Extreme	91 dB		Usually cannot understand even amplified speech	

[a]Whenever the average for the poorer ear is 25 dB or more greater than that for the better ear in this frequency range, 5 dB are added to the average for the better ear. This adjusted average determines the degree and class of handicap. For example, if a person's average hearing-threshold level for 500, 1,000, and 2,000 Hz is 37 dB in one ear and 62 dB or more in the other, his adjusted average hearing-threshold level is 42 dB and his handicap is Class C instead of Class B.

[b]dB reference level, International Standards Organization, 1964.

SOURCES: Adapted from Davis (1970c); Silverman and Lane (1970); Subcommittee on Hearing in Adults of the Conservation of Hearing Committee of the American Academy of Ophthamology and Otolaryngology (1965).

occurs at or before birth or in the first year or two of life before language develops is most handicapping of all because of the effects on language acquisition. However, educators must not overlook those acquired hearing problems which are not manifested until the school-age years. Such conditions, even though they may be relatively mild, affect the child's educational and social progress when they are unrecognized and untreated for an indefinite period of time.

The Committee on Nomenclature of the Conference of Executives of American Schools for the Deaf recognized more than 30 years ago the practicality of considering the importance of age at onset, as well as ability to speak and to hear, in their definitions of deaf and hard of hearing (Silverman and Lane, 1970). They spoke of the *congenitally deaf* as those born deaf, but in whom the sense of hearing is "nonfunctional for the ordinary purposes of life," and the *adventitiously deaf* as those born with normal hearing, but in whom the sense of hearing becomes nonfunctional later through accident or illness. They also defined the *hard of hearing* (partially hearing) as those in whom the sense of hearing, although defective, is functional with or without a hearing aid.

Causal Factors

Hearing impairment may also be categorized according to causal factors by use of the terms *endogenous* and *exogenous*. The first term refers to conditions which have their origin in the genetic characteristics of the individual, while the second includes all causes other than factors of heredity. This is to say that an endogenous-type auditory defect is transmitted from parents to child as an inherited trait, while exogenous defects result from disease, toxicity, accident, or injury which inflicts damage on any part of the auditory system, thus affecting its capacity to receive and transmit sound. A number of hereditary conditions may manifest themselves long after birth and as late as middle age or older; for example, otosclerosis, a disease of the middle ear causing bony fixation of the stapes footplate, is known to be hereditary, but it rarely occurs before young adulthood (*acquired but endogenous*). On the other hand, there are external agents such as German measles virus (rubella) which affect the unborn child's hearing system so that hearing loss is present at birth (*congenital but exogenous*). Such an impairment is acquired by factors outside the genes, just as would be true of impairment in a school child who fell victim to meningitis (*acquired and exogenous*).

Physical Origin

For purposes of medical management, there is a need for a classification system which indicates the site of the lesion that has occurred in the auditory system. If there are anomalies or lesions in the middle or outer ear, the type impairment is spoken of as *conductive*, which implies an obstruction to transmission of sound vibrations through the sound-conducting apparatus of the ear. If damage occurs to the nerve endings in the inner ear, or cochlea, the type hearing loss is known as *sensorineural*, which indicates the sensory receptor area of the ear is involved. Auditory impairments which are the result of damage to the auditory nerve pathways leading through the brain stem to the auditory area of the cortex of the brain represent *central auditory dysfunction* and may exist independent of any others. Such hearing impairment is referred to by Davis (1970a) as central dysacusis and reflects a defect in auditory processing mentioned earlier.

PREVALENCE

Data pertaining to the prevalence of auditory impairment in children are frequently reported from the results of mass testing surveys among school children and thus may vary considerably because of differences in the definition of hearing impairment, as well as in techniques, apparatus, and conditions of testing. Table 1.1 gives a prevalence estimate indicating that 0.58 percent of all school-age children in the United States are affected by educationally handicapping hearing loss. This total includes 0.08 percent deaf and 0.5 percent partially hearing. Since it has been demonstrated that hearing impairment exists in many degrees of severity, caution is indicated in interpreting prevalence figures. Silverman and Lane (1970) estimate on the basis of the extensive and detailed study of Pittsburgh school children that 5 percent of school-age children have hearing levels *outside the range of normal in at least one ear* and that 0.5–1.0 percent require some form of special education attention. This study, by the way, did *not* include children who were enrolled in special schools and classes for the hearing impaired. The results confirmed earlier estimates by O'Connor (1954) and Hardy (1952) that up to 1½ percent of school-age children are at least minimally handicapped educationally. Prompt medical assistance should be adequate for the remaining 3½–4 percent who fail screening tests so that their condition can be remedied before it causes handicap. While children with hearing losses designated by Classes B and C in Table 7.2 would normally not be enrolled in special classes or schools, they are educationally handicapped so that, depending upon individual circumstances, some kind of special management—ranging from special seating in the classroom to supplementary tutoring from an itinerant teacher in development of communication skills—is indicated.

STRUCTURE AND FUNCTION OF THE AUDITORY SYSTEM

The peripheral hearing mechanism consists of three clearly defined structures known as the *outer,* the *middle,* and the *inner* ear (see Fig. 7.1).

The *outer ear* includes the externally visible portion shown as the *pinna* and the ear *canal,* which ends at the *eardrum,* forming the boundary between the outer and the middle ear. The pinna helps to collect sound waves from the atmosphere to be conveyed inward through the outer canal to impinge upon the eardrum.

The resulting vibrations of the eardrum are transmitted directly to the cavity of the *middle ear,* which houses the three tiny bones called ossicles (*malleus, incus,* and *stapes*). They constitute an intricate lever system across the middle ear, transmitting sound waves from the eardrum to the *oval window* opening into the inner ear or *labyrinth,* which is the portion encased in bone to the right of the middle ear cavity in Figure 7.1. The first of the three ossicles, known as the *malleus (hammer),* is connected to the eardrum along its handle. It articulates with the body of the *incus (anvil),* which is joined to the head of the *stapes (stirrup).* The footplate of the stapes fits into the frame of the oval window to which it is connected by fibrous tissue,

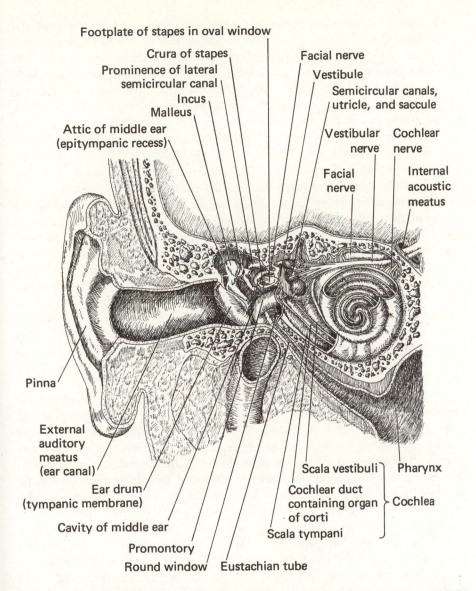

Footplate of stapes in oval window

Crura of stapes

Prominence of lateral
semicircular canal

Incus

Malleus

Attic of middle ear
(epitympanic recess)

Facial nerve

Vestibule

Semicircular canals,
utricle, and saccule

Vestibular   Cochlear
nerve   nerve

Facial   Internal
nerve   acoustic
                 meatus

Pinna

External
auditory
meatus
(ear canal)

Ear drum
(tympanic membrane)

Cavity of middle ear

Promontory

Round window   Eustachian tube

Scala vestibuli   Pharynx

Cochlear duct
containing organ   Cochlea
of corti

Scala tympani

FIGURE 7.1 *Cross section of the hearing mechanism. Adapted from D. Myers, W. D. Schlosser, and R. A. Winchester. Otologic diagnosis and the treatment of deafness. Clinical Symposia. Summit, N.J.: CIBA Pharmaceutical Corporation, 1962,* **14.** *Copyright 1962 CIBA Pharmaceutical Company. Reproduced with permission from the Clinical Symposia, illustrated by Frank H. Netter, M.D.*

allowing both inward and outward movement of the footplate to correspond with the phase patterns of incoming sound waves.

It may be seen further in Figure 7.1 (lower right corner) that the middle ear is connected by means of the *Eustachian tube* to the back of the nose and throat (*pharynx*), forming the upper portion of the respiratory system. This is the only direct opening for air from the outside atmosphere. Muscular action performed in chewing, swallowing, and yawning causes the Eustachian tube to open at its lower end. This action permits outside air to enter the ear, thereby providing equal air pressure on both sides of the eardrum, which is essential to its vibratory responsiveness and normal functioning.

The *inner ear*, or *labyrinth*, comprises the true end organ of hearing, for it is here the acoustic nerve fibers terminate. Figure 7.1 depicts the bony labyrinth situated in the portion of the temporal bone which extends inward from the outer skull, forming a floor to the brain cavity just above it. The central portion, known as the *vestibule*, has an opening off the middle ear by means of the oval window, which connects the inner and middle ear sound transmission systems. In response to sound waves transmitted from the eardrum membrane by way of the ossicular chain, a corresponding wave motion is set up in the inner ear fluids at the vestibule. This fluid vibration is thence transmitted into the *cochlea* (see Fig. 7.1), in which are located thousands of nerve fibers, each of which is attached to the base of a hair cell. The sensation of hearing occurs when these auditory nerve fibers are energized as a result of movement from the sound pressure patterns that act as traveling sound waves in the fluid of the inner ear. For a more detailed description of the anatomy and physiology of hearing, the reader is referred to Davis (1970b).

While sensation of hearing (the biological detection of a signal by the organism) is a function of an intact periphery of hearing made up of the three parts of the ear just described, the recognition, perception, and integration of a heard stimulus is dependent upon that portion of the auditory system situated in the central nervous system (CNS). In other words, sensation of hearing occurs as the auditory stimulus travels through the outer and middle ear and is electro-mechanically transduced into a nerve impulse at the level of the cochlea in the inner ear. From there the impulse travels through the VIIIth nerve to the juncture of the nerve with the brain stem, and it is beyond that point that the central processes of hearing are handled. The newborn child, for example, if he has a normal hearing mechanism, is quite able to *hear* sound in the sense that excitation of nerve impulses in the cochlea occurs. If his central nervous system is intact, the nerve impulse will travel, uninterrupted and undistorted, to be received at the auditory cortex. Yet it cannot be said that he has learned either to attend, listen to, or perceive those sounds which surround him on the first day of life, insofar as he is able to associate meaning with them. This hierarchical level of sensation is demonstrated by the Language Development model included by Hull in Chapter 5, which shows that the sensation for a given auditory experience precedes the more complex functions of audition involved in language acquisition.

TYPES AND CAUSES OF AUDITORY IMPAIRMENT

The sensory process of hearing depends first of all on an intact peripheral mechanism, which implies normal functioning of the three parts of the ear—outer, middle, and inner—as well as the nerve fibers extending from the inner ear to the central nervous system. Hearing loss, either partial or complete, may result from damage to or maldevelopment of any part of this system. The perceptual process of hearing is a function of the central auditory pathways passing through the brain stem and terminating at the receptor area of the brain, the auditory cortex. In the following section the various causes of hearing loss which affect the ear are briefly reviewed.

Conductive Hearing Loss

Conductive hearing loss occurs as a result of obstruction to the passage of sound waves through the external canal or by way of the ossicular chain through the middle ear. A common obstruction in the outer ear is excessive secretion of ear wax; another is insertion of objects such as beans, peas, and other such foreign bodies into the canal by young children. Such obstructions will cause mild hearing losses, which are detected frequently by hearing-screening programs, particularly among children in kindergarten and primary levels.

Inspection of Figure 7.1 will show that the middle ear cavity is very readily subject to invasion by bacteria or viruses from the Eustachian tube extending from the middle ear cavity into the back of the nose and throat. It is very probable that almost every individual suffers ear infection at least one or more times in his life even though he or his parents may not be able to remember such an occurrence and even though he is left with no residual damage. The structure of the infant's face, in particular the jaw alignment, is such that the Eustachian tube runs almost horizontally to the middle ear cavity from the nasopharynx, thus allowing infection from this region to proceed readily into the child's ear when in a prone position, as the infant most frequently is during the first year.

Another cause for the high prevalence of ear infections in the young child is the tendency toward adenoids, which form a spongy mass around the nasopharyngeal opening of the Eustachian tube, sometimes completely obstructing it. Blockage of this tube creates a vacuum in the middle ear, which in turn prevents proper ventilation of the middle ear cavity. The secretion of fluid by the mucous membrane lining of the middle ear cannot then drain out normally and thus soon becomes a readily available medium for invasion of bacteria from the nasopharynx. An acute ear infection can then occur, sometimes in just a few hours in the case of young children. While damage to hearing does not necessarily occur with each ear infection, the probability of such damage increases with each successive infection. Chronic or repeated infections are apt to form deposits of adhesive scar tissue on the eardrum itself and around the joints of the ossicular chain, making the sound transmission system much less flexible. This stiffening can depress hearing levels from mild to moderate degrees depending upon the amount of such formations. Teachers who are alert to such transient hearing problems in their classrooms should encourage parents to seek medical assistance, which, if begun at the first signs of ear infection, can often circumvent the likelihood of permanent serious hearing loss (Guilford, 1967; Davis and Fowler, 1970).

Sensorineural Hearing Loss

Hearing loss which occurs as a result of damage to the inner ear structures is classified as sensorineural. The causes of hearing loss which result from injury to or maldevelopment of nerve fibers and hair cells in the inner ear are myriad. First, children who are subject to frequent ear infections and those in whom this condition becomes chronic often begin to show added components of sensorineural damage, apparently from invasion of the infectious-bearing agent in the middle ear into the cochlear system where the nerve endings are situated. Bacterial, viral, and toxic agents may enter the inner ear through either the lymph or the pathways leading to the inner ear from the cranial cavity (Davis, 1970a). Diseases such as meningitis, measles, influenza, mumps, and, in fact, almost any infectious disease affecting the upper respiratory system and accompanied by high temperatures can cause damage to the nerve fibers in varying degrees. While relatively little is known about the effects of maternal infections while the child is *in utero*, it is well established that maternal rubella (German measles) can seriously affect not only the hearing of the unborn child but the cardiac, vision, and mental functions as well. Even less is known about the pathologies incurred in the fetal auditory system from various drugs taken by the mother during pregnancy (Subcommittee on Human Communication and Its Disorders, National Institute of Neurological Diseases and Stroke, 1969).

Another major cause of hearing loss in children may be increasing as a result of the many antibiotics that have been developed in the past two decades. Drugs such as streptomycin, dihydrostreptomycin, kanamycin, and neomycin are known particularly to have degenerative effects on the structures of the inner ear (Hawkins, 1967). Unfortunately, even less is known about the dosage amounts which may cause damage to the hearing of infants compared to adults.

An ecological origin of hearing loss today is frequent exposure to very high-intensity noise, as occurs in many occupational and other environments. Since children are not usually exposed to such noise levels on a regular basis, major hearing problems in school children probably should not be ascribed to this cause. Nevertheless, it is well to point out that toys have come on the market in recent years which have been shown to produce noise levels sufficiently high to cause damage to hearing. Certain types of cap guns and toy rockets and missiles may be in this category. Children who accompany their parents on snowmobile rides and skeet and rifle shoots will be subjected to hazardous noise levels. Furthermore, rock and roll music in public places is routinely played at intensity levels well above the damage-risk criterion levels that have been established (Lipscomb, 1969). Over the years, hearing-conservation programs have routinely shown a higher occurrence of hearing damage, particularly for the high-frequency sounds, in boys than in girls. It is usually conjectured that this finding results from the greater amount of exposure to tractors, machinery, firearms, firecrackers, and other such sound sources more likely to characterize the life environment of boys as compared to girls.

In summary, it has been said that the sensory mechanism of hearing is more vulnerable to damage and insult than any of the other sense organs. The early childhood years are extremely important ones for hearing-conservation measures to be in effect. Although medical science has advanced remarkably in its management of hearing problems, it is unfortunate that many underprivileged children still are not provided the medical help that if available to them early in life would in many instances prevent their entering school with a serious educational handicap.

Auditory Perceptual Disturbances

Detailed information on the nature and manifestations of disorders of the central auditory nervous system is very sparse and thus represents a whole area for which there is a great knowledge gap. Among the numerous causes of this type of disability, which is infinitely complex and more difficult to diagnose and to provide habilitative and proper educational treatment for, are such diseases and injuries as encephalitis, meningitis, cerebrovascular accidents, multiple sclerosis, carbon monoxide poisoning, and prolonged asphyxiation, as well as brain tumors, cysts, and abscesses. Birth trauma, particularly lack of oxygen, are considered to be a common etiology for central disturbances involving language and learning processes. For further treatment of this problem the reader is referred to Dunn, Chapter 1; the Hulls, Chapter 6; and Wilson, Chapter 9.

MEASUREMENT OF HEARING

Sound as a Physical Stimulus

Sound is a form of energy for which the most common source is a vibrating solid body. The sounds the ear perceives result from the alternate condensation and rarefaction of the molecules in the atmosphere which are set into motion by the vibrating body. Sound waves, however, do not travel undirectionally from the source to the ear of the receiver, but rather the patterns of vibration radiate in all directions. Most analogous to this wave motion in the atmosphere is the common visual experience observed by all of us as youngsters upon throwing a stone into a body of water, producing ripples on the surface of the water. These wave patterns travel from the point of impact of the stone in all directions; with increasing distance they may be seen gradually to subside until they can no longer be perceived.

Sound waves creating sensation of hearing in the human ear have two main characteristics, *intensity* and *frequency*, both of which are determined by the nature of the source. If we view sound waves as alternating patterns of disturbance in the atmosphere, we can consider *intensity* to represent the amplitude or extent of the disturbance. (This physical dimension is perceived by the ear as *loudness*.) The unit of measure for intensity is expressed by the *decibel* (dB). It is derived from a logarithmic scale; that is, each increase of 10 decibels on an audiogram indicates a tenfold increase in sound intensity. Thus, 20 dB would indicate a sound 10 times the intensity of 10 dB, or 100 times that for the starting point (zero dB on the audiogram); at 30 dB, the intensity is 10 times that at 20, or 1,000 times the intensity of the starting point. By the time one has increased a given sound to 60 decibels, the intensity for that stimulus is one million times that for the just-audible level at zero dB. As an estimate of the tremendous range of intensity the human ear can accommodate, a riveter drilling on a concrete pavement about 35 feet away produces a sound the intensity of which is 100 dB, or 10 billion times the intensity of a sound that is just barely audible. The upper limits of intensity are reached when levels as high as 130–140 decibels occur, at which point pain is experienced, and permanent damage to the ear results if exposed for any considerable length of time. The intensity level in dB for some of our more common environmental sounds are shown in Table 7.3, as adapted from Tonndorf (1965) and Broch (1967).

TABLE 7.3 *Sound Pressure Levels of Some Commonly Encountered Noises in Reference to Hearing Thresholds*

Hearing-threshold Levels	Decibels	Environmental Sounds
Threshold of pain	140-	
Threshold of discomfort		
	-130	
	120-	Pneumatic chipper
		Loud auto horn (3 ft.)
	-110	Automatic punch press (3 ft.)
	100-	Inside subway train
	-90	Inside motor bus
	80-	Average traffic on street corner
	-70	
Conversational speech (3 ft)	60-	
	-50	Private business office
	40-	Living room, suburban area
		Library
	-30	Bedroom at night
Whisper (5 ft.)	20-	Broadcasting studio
	-10	
Threshold of hearing	0-	

SOURCES: Adapted from Broch (1967) and Tonndorf (1965).

The other main dimension of sound is frequency, or wavelength. The closer the waves are together, the shorter the wavelength and the more rapidly these waves will strike the eardrum of the individual in the area where the sound disturbance occurs. The frequency of a given sound stimulus, therefore, is the term used to designate the rapidity of the vibration. From the top of one wave to the top of the next is a single cycle; frequency (or number of vibrations per second) is spoken of as cycles per second (cps), which is synonymous with a more recent designation, which will be seen on audiograms written as Hertz (Hz). This physical dimension is an important determinant of how our ears perceive a given sound stimulus. The more rapid the vibration (thus, the shorter the wavelength), the higher is the perceived pitch of sound. Although the audiogram routinely provides for measuring hearing threshold (or hearing level) at frequencies from 125 through 8,000 Hz, the human ear can respond to sounds over a very wide range of frequencies, extending downward to 16–20 Hz at the lower range and upward as high as 20,000–30,000 Hz. The ear has maximum sensitivity for the higher ranges in early childhood with a gradual decrease thereafter. The normal adult would have difficulty hearing frequencies greater than 10,000–12,000 Hz.

Pure-tone Audiometry

Basically, the pure-tone audiogram is a chart plotting hearing-threshold levels in intensity for a given individual as a function of frequency. With other tests in an audiologic battery, it helps to answer these questions: How much hearing loss does this person have? Which part of the auditory system is most likely to be the site of the lesion resulting in damage to hearing? Which etiologic factor or factors are most closely associated with the particular audiometric configuration obtained? What prognostications can be made for medical restoration or alleviation, language development, educational progress, and vocational goals?

Air-conduction audiometry is administered through headphones to enable charting of hearing thresholds separately for each ear. Sampling is usually done at octave[1] intervals for frequencies from 125 through 8,000 Hz, which encompasses all speech sound frequencies and all other sounds relevant to one's functioning in his environment. The sounds of speech are without question the most vital of all sounds for man to be able to hear for optimum life functioning. Fortunately, speech is a highly redundant signal, comprising individual frequency components ranging across several octaves, but speech is intelligible for the most part if one hears normally in the range 500–2,000 Hz. Thus, the three frequencies in the midrange (500, 1,000, and 2,000 Hz) are known as the speech frequencies. It should be pointed out that there are single phonemic (sound) units of speech which are comprised of frequency components outside this range, but running speech (which

[1] An octave is the interval between two tones when they are separated by a frequency ratio of 2:1 or by a musical interval of 12 semitones.

provides many contextual clues) can be understood if one's hearing is normal at these three frequencies. For example, the telephone does not transmit many of the higher frequencies, yet we can understand most words in the context of sentences. Proper names that are unfamiliar may give us trouble. That is the reason the telephone operator may ask you, "*D* as in dog? or *P* as in papa?"

The reference point for normal hearing on the audiogram is represented by the zero decibel line. (See Figure 7.2 for a sample audiogram.) The audiometer is calibrated to emit pure-tone signals at each frequency to provide an intensity at the earphone to correspond to that level of intensity which is just audible, on the average, to the young adult in the age range 18–30 years (Davis, 1970c). Hearing for a particular individual at the various octave frequencies across the range is thus charted in relation to this *zero reference point*. The audiogram is constructed in such a way that hearing poorer than normal is charted on the descending scale. In terms of actual sound-pressure level, the human ear is most sensitive to those frequencies in the mid-range, and it requires greater physical intensity at the low and high ends of the frequency spectrum to reach threshold. For convenience in charting, however, the audiogram simply uses a straight horizontal line (zero dB) to represent this *minimum audible level*, so that the charting of a particular individual's threshold remains in reference to the amount of intensity (zero dB) necessary to elicit response in the normal-hearing person. The level plotted represents that which the person being tested can *just hear*, usually based on response to at least two of three presentations.

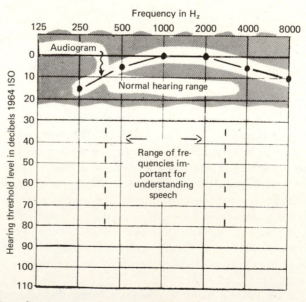

FIGURE 7.2 Sample copy of pure-tone audiogram.

Air-conduction thresholds are used to establish the level of hearing by frequencies at which a given individual functions, for it is by the air-conduction route that hearing occurs normally. For additional information about a hearing problem, an audiometric assessment also includes hearing levels by *bone conduction*. In testing for bone conduction, an oscillator attachment (vibrator) is placed firmly against the promontory of the mastoid process just behind the ear. Hearing by bone conduction is considered to occur when the vibratory pattern at the oscillator is transmitted directly through the skull to the inner ear without initiating air-borne stimuli at the outer or middle ear. In general practice, one may interpret the amount by which the threshold is reduced by bone conduction to be that amount of hearing impairment resulting from damage to the sensorineural mechanism of the ear (the cochlea). Thus, when a child's air and bone thresholds are equally reduced, his deficit is generally considered to reflect nerve damage, which most usually indicates permanent hearing loss.

When air-conduction thresholds are reduced but bone conduction has not been proportionately reduced or is normal, the air-bone gap shown by the audiogram suggests the obstruction to hearing lies in the mechanical transmission system of the outer or middle ear resulting in a conductive hearing loss. Such conditions as otosclerotic fixation of the stapes footplate, separation of the ossicular chain by a hard blow, impacted wax in the ear canal, a fluid-filled middle ear, and a scarred tympanic membrane are all factors which can reduce the ability to hear by air conduction in the presence of an intact inner ear. The loss in transmission of air-borne sound resulting from an upper respiratory infection which has invaded the middle ear cavity of a young child is illustrated by the air-bone gap in the audiogram for Jamie shown in Figure 7.3 (a). Following effective and prompt medical treatment, this child's hearing was restored to near-normal levels, as noted in Figure 7.3 (b), where the air-conduction hearing is approximately normal again (see Vignette 7.1). Examples of audiograms representing other types of conditions mentioned in this section are also shown in Figure 7.3, each of which is further explained in the accompanying vignettes.

Vignette 7.1 A Child with Medically Remediable Transient Hearing Loss

The audiograms for Jamie in Figure 7.3 (a) and 7.3 (b) illustrate the type of hearing loss resulting from middle ear infections common in young children, particularly during the winter and early spring months when upper respiratory infections occur frequently. Figure 7.3 (a) illustrates the depression in air-conduction hearing resulting from the accumulation of fluid and pus formation in the middle ear. This accumulation impedes action of the ossicles in transmitting sound vibrations to the inner ear, which had remained intact, as noted by the normal bone-conduction levels.

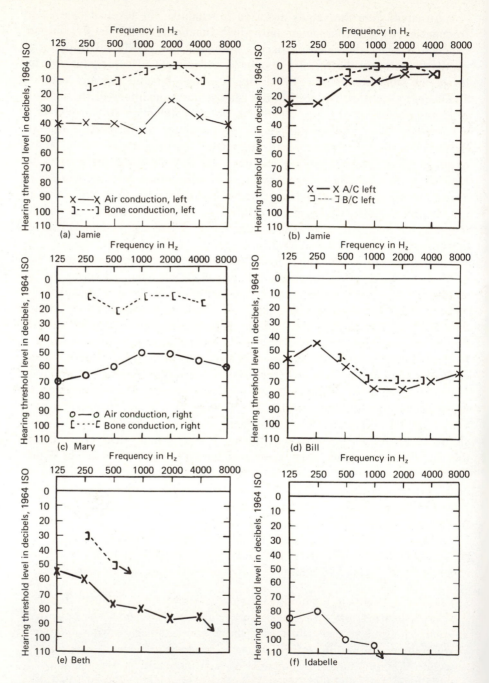

FIGURE 7.3 (a) Jamie—ear infection before medical treatment; (b) Jamie—ear infection after medical treatment; (c) Mary—chronic middle ear disease; (d) Bill—rubella; (e) Beth—postmeasles; (f) Idabelle—hereditary deafness.

Jamie, an eight-year-old second-grade child, suffered repeated colds in the winter months from which ear infections in both ears developed. His teacher noted he was listless and inattentive in class. Although able to hear at close range, he often failed to respond appropriately at a distance. When the parents were informed of the suspected hearing disability, they sought help promptly from a medical ear specialist, and Jamie's hearing returned to a normal level within a few weeks, as shown in Figure 7.3 (b), which demonstrates the obstruction to sound transmission in the middle ear has been removed. Jamie's classroom performance improved rapidly, and he experienced no further difficulty in hearing.

Vignette 7.2 A Partially Hearing Child with a Chronic Ear Condition

Mary's audiogram in Figure 7.3 (c) represents the same type of hearing problem described in Vignette 7.1, except that the condition represented had become chronic and possibly resistant to medical treatment. Mary was 11 years old and in the fourth grade in a rural school at the date of the audiogram. The school system in which she was enrolled made no provisions for hearing-screening tests on a regular basis. Mary was simply considered to be a slow child, poorly motivated and generally unresponsive to her environment. Through social promotions she had advanced to fourth grade, but was reading only at the second-grade level.

For such children skilled medical intervention may still enable restoration of hearing to occur as long as the bone-conduction levels are at or near normal, indicating the nerve fiber endings in the inner ear are still intact. The wasted years in school, the sense of defeat suffered by such children, and the poor self-image developed are usually much harder to overcome than the medical problem. Such children need special class placement for partially hearing children where they can obtain individualized remedial instruction, moving toward integration into regular classes as soon as they can compete successfully.

Vignette 7.3 A College Youth with Sensorineural Hearing Loss and Auditory Perceptual Impairment

Bill, whose audiogram is shown in Figure 7.3 (d), was a victim of maternal rubella, which apparently affected both his peripheral hearing (nerve endings in the cochlea) and his ability to process and integrate auditory stimuli (auditory pathways in the central nervous system). Despite this dual handicap, he was able to achieve surprisingly well as a result of his family's concern and their ability to translate it into positive action in his behalf. Upon failure to develop speech and language at the normal age, the family sought the help of a well-known private clinic and school, where he remained through completion of eighth-grade studies. Prompt acquisition of a wearable body-type hearing aid and help in learning to use it on a full-time basis, together with his good potential of residual hearing, evidenced by thresholds across the frequency range giving him the potential to hear most speech sounds with amplification, enabled him to develop quite adequate oral language. (The trough-shaped audiogram has been observed to be characteristic of the type shown by rubella children.)

Bill attended a public high school for five years to complete his secondary education. He enrolled in a hearing college, but has experienced serious difficulties in maintaining an adequate level of performance. His family, who are people of means, would like to see him graduated from college, which is probably an unrealistic goal in view of his hearing difficulty and added learning disabilities assumed to be of central origin. His personal-social contacts are now mainly with hearing young people, and he is an unusually poised and outgoing young man despite his communicative handicap and slight speech defect of misarticulation of consonant sounds. Vocational-technical training would apparently be his best route educationally. Since he has overcome the hurdles in the past sufficiently well to show that he has an amazing degree of ego strength and inner resources, there is no reason failure in college should prevent him now from becoming a fully independent and contributing citizen in competition with hearing peers.

Vignette 7.4 Junior High Student with Severe Sensorineural Hearing Loss from Infancy

Beth (audiogram shown in Figure 7.3 (e)) was first noticed to fail to respond to sound at about 15 months following a severe attack of measles a month or two earlier. First hearing tests showed a level of hearing better than the one in the illustration, but within a year her thresholds had progressed downward to the level shown, representing a not uncommon result following measles. Fortunately, Beth's parents were alert to their child's condition and sought professional help at a speech and hearing center immediately. By 18 months she had been fitted with her own body-type hearing aid, and her parents were seen regularly to assist in the auditory-stimulation and language-development program recommended.

Beth had intensive instruction from three to six in an educational program for preschool deaf children. Her language development progressed well from the beginning, and at age six she entered regular school where she has continued into senior high. She is achieving at grade level and communicates freely in spontaneous oral language. She is seen periodically by an audiologist to assist in the hearing aid management program and is on the itinerant schedule of a speech clinician in the schools for assistance in production of some misarticulated consonant sounds.

Beth's case is an illustration of the great savings in tax dollars effected by an early intervention program that prevented the development of the need for a long-term full-time special education program.

Vignette 7.5 A Profoundly Deaf Child with No Oral Language

Idabelle (audiogram in Figure 7.3 (f)) was less fortunate than those children described in the preceding case studies. She and two siblings were profoundly deaf from birth as the result of an hereditary factor.

She was born into a large family to parents of lower socioeconomic level and of limited intellectual resources, who were simply unable to provide her the support and kind of special help she needed. With such a severe loss, prognosis for adequate oral language would be guarded under the best of circumstances. (Note that her thresholds drop out completely at 1,000 Hz.) Idabelle received no special help other than a clinic visit about once a year until she was enrolled at age six in the state residential school. Unable to hear the spoken voice, and little other than the loudest of sounds, Idabelle had long since ceased any attempts at vocalization. She was dependent upon gestures and some manual language for her very limited communication. Her progress in school has been steady but slow. At age 15, she is now able to achieve academically at about the third-grade level. She is likely to require extensive assistance from public funded agencies upon leaving school, and intensive vocational guidance and training will be necessary to help her maintain an independent level of functioning.

Speech Audiometry

The use of speech-stimulus material in hearing measurement was developed in the 1940s in an effort to determine if hearing for speech could be correlated with pure-tone hearing levels (O'Neill and Oyer, 1966). Speech-hearing tests assess not only the ability of the individual to hear speech but also to understand, or comprehend, it. The first of these measures is known as the Speech Reception Threshold (SRT), measured in decibels, while the second is the speech discrimination function, expressed in a percent correct score.

The speech-reception threshold yields in a single score the hearing level in decibels representing a person's ability to hear speech as compared to the normal hearing population. There is a strong interdependence between the pure-tone average in the speech-frequency range (500 through 2,000 Hz) and the SRT thus established. Thus, when the results of the two tests are in close agreement, one can assume confirmation of one for the other. An equally if not more important hearing function is the clarity with which one hears speech when it is made comfortably loud. To assess this ability, a test is administered using phonetically balanced monosyllabic word lists, each of which is representative of the individual sounds or phonemes in the English language in about the same proportion as they occur in everyday conversation. The test is scored on a percentage basis, with scores of 90 percent or better denoting normal discrimination ability. The conductive-loss patient, for example, usually is expected to have normal discrimination, for one has only to override the existing obstruction to sound transmission to enable him to distinguish between these fine differences in speech sounds with clarity. In contrast, for the individual with sensorineural impairment, many speech sounds may not be audible regardless of their intensity. The audiometric configuration typified by sloping high-frequency loss, for example, yields this lowered discrimination because many of the consonantal beginnings and endings of words are comprised of the frequency components in the area for which the patient has little or no capacity to respond.

The speech-discrimination score is especially significant educationally, since it deals with the *intelligibility of speech* for the listener. Modern acoustic amplification equipment, both headphone and wearable hearing aid types, makes it possible for the large majority of children who are either deaf or partially hearing to hear a signal comprised of speech material. Unfortunately, it does not at the same time permit them always to understand and distinguish between the various speech sounds they are hearing to enable them to piece together the meaning of what is being said. In other words, they may be hearing only a very garbled and indistinct message, very much as the normally hearing individual hears messages over poor-quality loudspeakers which produce high rates of distortion as well as high amplification. As with other aspects of handicap from hearing impairment, the degree of handicap is much greater for the child who was born with or acquired hearing loss early in life. While speech-discrimination testing is subject to many variables with hearing-impaired children, it does provide one with useful information on the adequacy of the child's ability to understand that which he hears through his hearing aid. As a very general kind of guideline, the child whose performance with his hearing aid is less than 50 percent correct for monosyllabic words used in speech-discrimination testing cannot be expected to understand spoken messages without visual supplementation of his hearing capacity through speechreading, even though his speech-reception threshold is improved to be near or within normal range.

Evaluating the Hearing of the Very Young Child

Measurement of hearing by the pure-tone and speech audiometer is a relatively uncomplicated task when one is attempting to evaluate school-age children with normal communication ability. The routine measures described above must be greatly modified, however, in their application to the infant or very young child who for some reason has not acquired speech and language at a level commensurate with his chronological age. The problem confronting the audiologist and/or language specialist is then one of differential diagnosis to determine the factors that may be producing either the complete absence of, or retardation in, language development. Both *auditory intake* and *oral speech output* must be considered together in the audiologic assessment of such children. These are the kinds of children for whom tests themselves may break down completely if we rely upon them to the exclusion of that all-important evaluative tool, careful observation of behavior; and auditory behavior follows certain patterns in both normally functioning children and in those with deviations in auditory capacities. When faced with a child who has not developed aural-oral language, there are four major conditions resulting in lack of language to consider: (1) hearing impairment, (2) mental retardation, (3) emotional disturbance, and (4) childhood aphasia (neurological language impairment).

First, the child with severe sensory deprivation of hearing does *not* learn to talk. The degree to which he acquires any speech is dependent upon many factors, but particularly and especially upon the residual hearing level. Thus, speech may be totally or partially absent—in the case of partial loss, perhaps a vocabulary age of two years when he is six, for example. Very few children are totally deaf, if by "total" we imply lack of hearing for *any* frequency at *any* intensity. The deaf child is reasonably consistent in a test situation and will give overt responses to sounds which are louder than his threshold for them. Reports from parents will indicate that the child does seem to notice environmental sounds of high intensity, such as a car horn, a dropped dish, or a low-flying airplane. Noisemakers, particularly percussion sounds, will often evoke a startle response. Eye movement, momentary cessation of activity, and turning toward the source as the sound breaks into the child's consciousness are the most classic modes of response. The young partially hearing child, on the other hand, is apt to be quite inconsistent in his responses to sound.

Second is mental retardation. Again, depending upon the degree of intellectual inadequacy, the child will have complete lack of or very meagerly developed oral language. The predisposition to classify all children without language as mentally retarded is very great in those who are either unfamiliar with or inexperienced in such problems. The severely retarded child tends to be erratic in his response to sound and requires an intensity usually considerably greater than his threshold in order to elicit a response. Pure tones, which are meaningless abstractions at best, since they are simply a "hum," are highly inappropriate when not combined with more meaningful stimuli or play-conditioning–type situations. Depending upon the degree of retardation, lack of attention alone can be the main reason for lack of response to sound. Alertness on the part of the examiner is very important, for very subtle evidences of hearing will be given many times which will not be repeated on retrial. Operant techniques have been used with some degree of success in recent years, though the amount of time required to obtain thresholds makes this method more feasible for the laboratory than for clinical practice.

The *third* cause is emotional disturbance. Severe psychoses, such as childhood schizophrenia and infantile autism, are also reflected in lack of language. Development of communicative behavior through speech is man's chief way of relating to others in his environment. The child with a severe emotional disturbance who wishes to withdraw from his world will certainly reject oral communication, the chief link which ties him to other humans. Parents of such children, however, will often say the child "sometimes seems to hear us." Pleasant sounds at low intensities are more apt to elicit response than sounds of high intensities, but many will not respond to sound even at pain-threshold levels. In other words, they tend to ignore all sensory stimuli.

The *fourth* condition is childhood aphasia, which as used here denotes the condition in a child who has suffered damage to certain areas of the brain, the brain stem, or its pathways as a result of prenatal, natal, or early postnatal disease or trauma. Severe disturbances of language are the result. Such a child may learn to talk inadequately or not at all. Distinguishing this child from either the hearing impaired, the mentally retarded, or the emotionally disturbed is usually quite difficult at best and requires an extended period of observation. Like the severely retarded child, he may also ignore all sounds except those with which he has learned to associate meaning. Usual sound stimuli produced by noisemakers may produce a response once or twice, but will quickly be ignored once the child is conditioned to the stimulus. Questioning parents to determine if there are any particular sounds to which the child will attend may yield effective results. For example, the writer recalls a postencephalitic child, severely involved, who responded neither to noisemakers nor to other test stimuli of any kind. Further questioning of the parents revealed she would respond to two speech phrases—"Give Daddy a kiss" and "Do you want a cookie?" When the first of these phrases was spoken at a very low conversational level six feet behind her, she turned immediately, ran to her father, and kissed him. Both the aphasoid and the mentally retarded child may be stimulated to produce verbalization by babbling ("buh-buh-buh") at very soft intensity levels near their ear. The emotionally disturbed child, on the contrary, will ignore such stimulation, as will the deaf.

HEARING-CONSERVATION PROGRAMS

The public schools have been the major vehicle by which programs of hearing conservation have been implemented, the availability of the school-age population being best assured through the schools. Moreover, it is in the early school-age years that middle ear conditions resulting in ear infections and subsequent permanent hearing impairment are highest in incidence.

Detection of these conditions through mass screening programs is the first step in referral of children for medical evaluation and treatment, which can often alleviate or cure the problem and permit subsequent possible restoration of hearing to normal levels.[2] The procedures by which these programs are carried out vary from state to state. For example, the program may be coordinated on a state-wide basis by either the Department of Health or the Department of Education. Local school systems often develop their own programs and through their leadership provide guidelines for the state. The minimum program is based on the belief that hearing defects should be found early in life or as soon as they occur. Unfortunately, programs carried out in the public schools cannot accomplish this goal, since educational programs rarely extend to children below five years of age except for children already known to be handicapped. In recent years considerable interest and activity have developed in screening the hearing of newborn babies in hospitals, particularly in the larger urban areas. Such screening tests, which are quite gross, detect only those children with severe losses at birth, and they do not provide means of identifying those who suffer hearing loss as a result of illness in the first year or two of life. For this reason, efforts are being made through some health departments to screen hearing about every six months from birth up to three or four years of age in well-baby clinics. There is no single plan, however, which would provide a means of checking the hearing of *every* preschool child under our present diverse plans of education and health in the various states and local communities. The increased attention that is being given the younger child in this regard can be expected to yield much better results in the future and should prevent many of the serious problems that now arise because the child has not been tested before he reaches school age.

Once the child has entered the school system, it would be desirable that he be tested immediately from the standpoint of early detection. It has been found impractical in many programs to subject the child in the first months of school to hearing-screening testing along with the many other kinds of examinations and observations to which he must adjust as a beginning pupil. An excessive number of false positives has resulted in instances where first-graders have been included in the hearing screening. Consequently, increasing sentiment is being expressed by persons in charge of state and local screening programs that it is preferable not to initiate mass hearing screening with pure-tone audiometers until second grade. A practical guideline is that at least three hearing-screening tests are provided three times while a child is progressing through the eight years of elementary school. Thus, if second, fifth, and eighth grades are chosen, the hearing-conservation staff will

[2] In Cleveland, Ohio, where a program was established as early as 1935, it was demonstrated that sound hearing-conservation measures conducted annually in the schools can markedly lessen the prevalence of ear disease in the school population (Kinney, 1951).

administer screening tests to each child enrolled in each of these three grades each year. Either individual or group screening techniques may be used. The audiometer level is set at a given intensity (for example, at the limits of normal—25 dB, and the child is requested to respond to each of the seven test frequencies for each ear. Children who cannot hear one or more of the pure-tone signals in either ear fail the screening test. The number of pure-tone signals a child may miss hearing and still pass the screening test varies from one to three in most programs. The procedures for each child are normally carried out in the following order:

1. First screening test.
2. Retesting at screening level all those who failed preset pass criteria for first screening.
3. Individual air- and bone-conduction audiogram for all those who fail retest screening;
4. Referral to medical ear specialist for examination and treatment all those in step 3 above whose hearing defect was confirmed by pure-tone audiometry.
5. Referral to audiology clinic all children for whom medical treatment is either not feasible or unsucessful in restoring hearing levels to normal limits.
6. Appropriate remedial and educational recommendations to school system (preferential seating in the classroom, itinerant services in speech, speech-reading, and/or auditory training, individual tutoring in language and school subjects, wearable hearing aid, special class placement or special school placement).

Perhaps the most comprehensive evaluation of hearing-conservation programs in the schools was that undertaken by Eagles, Wishik, Doerfler, Melnick, and Levine (1963) in Pittsburgh. This study included a thorough analysis of the various factors related to measuring hearing sensitivity in children. The findings should be carefully reviewed by all school systems and state departments undertaking such a program. For example, it was shown that some children who showed otoscopic[3] evidence of ear disease may have as sensitive hearing as children with normal findings. Thus, any effective hearing-screening program should include both audiologic[4] and otologic[5] personnel. Since it is not common for the otologist to participate until a child is referred to him because of the audiometric findings, it is possible for a child to have otologic abnormalities and still pass the screening test.

Findings from the Pittsburgh study regarding audiometers and their calibration are also a source of some dismay when one considers the complete lack of control of this factor in many programs. A further shortcoming

[3] *Otoscopic* refers to an instrument used by medical personnel for inspection of the ear.
[4] *Audiologic* refers to the nonmedical specialist (audiologist) who evaluates and offers habilitative and rehabilitative programs for those with impaired hearing.
[5] *Otologic* refers to the medical specialist (otologist) who evaluates and treats diseases of the ear.

in many programs conducted in the public schools is that children of junior high school age and above are not included. To be truly effective, hearing screening should be accomplished at regular intervals through senior high school. While the younger children may be expected to evidence greater incidence of ear infections, many of the more serious problems persisting into the older age group represent those which may not have received adequate attention earlier.

What are some of the signs which the regular classroom teacher should be able to recognize as indicative of auditory impairment? There are a number of symptoms which characterize the child with hearing disability, and when such symptoms appear, the teacher should by all means question whether a hearing problem may exist and refer such children to the appropriate personnel in the school system. Noting any of these common observable signs of hearing difficulty should alert the teacher to action:

1. Cupping hands behind ears when attempting to listen.
2. Turning one side of the head toward the speaker to favor better ear listening.
3. Unusual behavior in response to oral directions.
   a. Inattentive because the strain of listening causes the child to lose interest in what is being said.
   b. Obstinacy or apparent confusion because he does not hear clearly, and since he cannot tell what is expected of him, refrains from making any responses.
   c. Unacceptable responses or inappropriate responses given in his eagerness to please others.
4. Inadequate ability to do school work. May hear only a part of teacher's instructions and class discussion.
5. Reluctance to participate in class activities. Fear of failure because of not understanding.
6. Discipline problem in class because of attempts to overcompensate.
7. Defective speech patterns, particularly for consonant sounds at beginning and end of words.
8. Delayed language ability.

BEHAVIORAL CHARACTERISTICS OF THE HEARING IMPAIRED

Language Development

The greatest single handicap that results from sensory deprivation of hearing from the prelingual years is the barrier to language learning, which in turn is the main reason for the educational handicap. The child who hears only partially or not at all is unable to progress in the normal sequence of language mastery, which includes the capacity to comprehend verbal messages normally, to speak, to read, and to write. The normal child enters school at six with a rich background of heard language acquired gradually from the day he was born. Within a few weeks after birth he begins to perceive sounds in his environment, associating meaning and source of the stimulus.

In turn, as he continues to receive auditory stimulation, he begins his own vocal imitations, which emerge into words by about one year. By the time he starts school several years later and is expected to associate meaning with the visual symbols of language (learn to read), he has a well-established foundation of experience in hearing and producing words which he sees in print. The hierarchy of language development presupposes this natural order of events, and as educators of handicapped children, we can never ignore the basic tenet that language input *must* precede language output.

What then is involved in language learning? Stated very simply, it is achieving facility in the use of words which make up language and gaining control of its grammar, which governs the way in which words are put together to form ideas. Acquisition of vocabulary is a lifelong process related primarily to an individual's experiences and needs. At the same time that increasing numbers of words are being added to those he knows already, the young child must gradually become aware of the multiple meanings of words to express himself in different ways (Simmons, 1971). This ability to arrange the constituent elements making up vocabulary into a structure which will carry meaning (a sentence, clause, or phrase) is known as syntactical ability, and this element of language is grammar or syntax. For the hearing child, this syntactic process is developed automatically as words he hears tie together the daily events around him. The hearing-impaired child, however, may be familiar only with a single concept related to the verb "run" and adjective "little" in a sentence such as, "The *little* boy can *run* fast." When confronted with this same adjective and verb in a statement such as "The path will *run* a *little* to the right," he is completely confused and unable to make the transition in meaning for the same words when used as different parts of speech or in a different context.

In the development of language there is a natural sequence of receiving (input) and expressing (output), and each higher language skill is dependent upon mastery of the one preceding it. First is the mastery of heard (*receptive-auditory*) language followed by spoken (*expressive-oral*) language. These two skills are assumed to be well developed before the child is expected to read (*receptive-visual*) and last, to write (*expressive-motoric*), which is the highest level of language functioning. The hearing-impaired child who lags far behind in the first step (receptive-auditory) readily demonstrates that each of these skills is important to the one hierarchically above it. The task of learning to speak, read, and write is infinitely more complex when the child has not heard nor learned to speak in the same language symbols.

The essay in Vignette 7.6, which was written by a 16-year-old profoundly and congenitally deaf youngster of average intelligence, but *without* auditory language, demonstrates the difficulties in handling language encountered by the deaf child who has never had an opportunity to hear it. It is obvious that this young lady was attempting to convey an idea, the exact nature of which the reader can only conjecture. The types of errors in word order and morphology are fairly typical of, and to a large extent exclusive to, the written language of the deaf.

Vignette 7.6 Written Language Sample of Teen-age Student Profoundly Deaf from Birth

What America Means to Me

America mean to me for Freedom and not be slaves to the people. America have be to right speech and insult. American look like the people like Freedom. American will complain about the slave. The American won't become Freedom. American right the worship. American is our business and we can't error with the people. Our American is Freedom and speech.

Unfortunately, studies on the overall Language Age of hearing-impaired children are not available. A primary reason is that we do not have instruments to measure such a complex phenomenon as language, which in addition to the various modalities mentioned above, is further subdivided into phonemic, semantic, syntactic, and morphologic components. For practical purposes the reading-achievement level is frequently used to assess language function in hearing-impaired children, even though it provides information on only one narrow aspect of total language competence. Be that as it may, one can gain some idea of the language proficiency of such children by determining their visual-receptive language competence through their grade-level performance in reading. This retardation reflected by lowered performance in reading is characteristic of both deaf and partially hearing children. Johnson (1962) in a study of 56 partially hearing children with average hearing levels ranging from 30 to 69 dB found that two thirds of the group were retarded in Reading Age by amounts ranging from one to seven years. The degree of retardation is a function of the degree of hearing impairment, age at onset, and other factors. Hardison (1965), using a sentence-completion technique, compared the performance of a group of partially hearing children in special classes with a normal-hearing group of the same age on written and oral language. The mean number of written-language errors for the partially hearing group was 42.7 compared with 9.1 for the normal-hearing; the mean number of oral-language errors was 30.7 versus 3.8 respectively, for the same groups.

Educational Achievement

It is in the area of educational achievement that the results of hearing impairment become all too apparent in our educational programs for such children. The average amount of educational retardation for the deaf child is at least three to four years, while the partially hearing child is from one half to two years retarded in grade level. Results of academic achievement tests administered to approximately 19,000 hearing-impaired children enrolled in 290 different special education programs in the 1970–1971 school year have been reported by the Office of Demographic Studies, Gallaudet College (Annual Survey for Hearing Impaired Children and Youth, 1972). Table 7.4

TABLE 7.4 *Weighted Mean Grade Equivalents Attained from Stanford Achievement Tests Administered in Annual Survey of Hearing Impaired Children and Youth, 1970-1971*

Subject	N	Mean Grade Equivalent	Range of Means by Test Battery	Grade-level Expectancy for Normal Children
10-Year-Old Students				
Arithmetic Computation	1277	2.5	1.8-5.1	5
Total Arithmetic	1269	2.4	1.8-6.2	5
Paragraph Meaning	1290	2.2	1.8-6.4	5
Total Reading	1277	2.3	1.9-6.4	5
14-Year-Old Students				
Science	554	4.7[a]	4.2-8.0	9
Social Studies	442	5.3[a]	4.9-8.0	9
Spelling	532	6.3[a]	5.6-9.3	9
Arithmetic Computation	1560	4.5	1.9-7.9	9
Total Arithmetic	1550	4.0	1.9-8.2	9
Paragraph Meaning	1566	3.2	1.8-7.9	9
Total Reading	1566	3.1	2.0-7.9	9
18-Year-Old Students				
Science	629	5.3[a]	4.2-7.5	13
Social Studies	629	5.9[a]	5.0-7.7	13
Spelling	973	6.4	6.2-9.6	13
Arithmetic Computation	973	6.4	1.9-9.2	13
Total Arithmetic	972	5.6	1.9-8.6	13
Paragraph Meaning	974	4.3	1.9-7.4	13
Total Reading	974	4.3	2.0-7.4	13

[a]Approximately one third of the 14-year-old students were judged unable to take the Intermediate I battery or higher of the Science, Social Studies, and Spelling subtests; the total mean, therefore, represents the more advanced two thirds of the 14-year-old students taking the tests. About one third of the 18-year-old students were judged unable to take the Intermediate I battery or higher of the Science and Social Studies subtests.

SOURCE: Annual Survey of Hearing Impaired Children and Youth, Washington, D.C. Personal communication, 1972.

includes a sampling of these findings. Weighted means in grade equivalents for three age groups (10, 14, and 18 years) on the Stanford Achievement Tests are shown. For most of the subject-matter subtests the test battery included levels from Primary I and II through Intermediate I and II through Advanced. All children tested were first screened to assure that they took the particular battery appropriate to their level of educational functioning. It may be noted that a span of about one grade level for Total Reading and about two years in Total Arithmetic separated the 10-year-old students from the 14-year-old ones and the 14-year-olds from the 18-year-olds. The range of means for the different batteries (Primary I through Advanced) shows that the spread between the lowest- and highest-functioning groups was in some instances as much as eight years. The reading vocabulary of many deaf students at eighteen upon completion of their schooling may be as much as eight to nine years retarded. Although their overall achievement is not behind to that extent, the importance of reading as a tool subject for all other learning is reflected in most of the other areas. The end result is rather serious retardation in overall education level.

The rapid increase in early detection, infant and preschool education, and day-class programs of higher quality should result in greater numbers of children able to join the regular education system. The achievement of these children, unfortunately, is not reflected in the results derived from those still in special programs, many of whom have had fewer educational advantages. An example of more successful achievement is found in the study by O'Connor and Connor (1961), who reported on 21 pupils who had left the Lexington School for the Deaf to be integrated into regular classes. Nine were transferred upon parents' request, the remainder upon the school's recommendation. The average IQ for the group was 114.6, and the mean hearing level was 83.1 dB. Five years later 60 percent were enrolled successfully in grades corresponding to their age level, and eight were reading at grade level or above for their age. An accurate picture of achievement characterizing both deaf and partially hearing pupils cannot be obtained without including the growing numbers of good achievers who each year are integrated into regular educational programs.

Intellectual Development

The intelligence of hearing-impaired children has been studied extensively in the present century to determine if they differ significantly from normal-hearing children on this dimension. The validity of some of the earlier investigations (Pintner, 1941) suggesting that the average IQ of the deaf does not quite reach 90 was questioned when psychologists began stressing qualitative rather than quantitative differences in intelligence. When nonverbal- and performance-type tests are used in place of the earlier standardized tests, many of which are highly verbal in content, the deaf are found to approximate very closely the norms for the hearing population (Vernon, 1968).

Data from the 1969–1970 Annual Survey for Hearing Impaired Children and Youth shown in Table 7.5 demonstrate that when hearing impairment is not complicated by the presence of other handicaps, intellectual ability is normal (100.38 mean for over 19,000 children). Unfortunately, it is not possible to separate the deaf from the partially hearing children in this population, but 50 percent had hearing threshold levels greater than 85 dB (ISO) and 75 percent had hearing levels 65 dB or poorer. Thus, the majority would have been deaf children as defined earlier in this chapter. This category is further confirmed by the fact that more than 80 percent were enrolled in full-time special classes or schools for the hearing impaired.

Furth (1971), who reviewed research with deaf subjects from 1964 through 1969, concludes that the thinking processes of deaf children are

TABLE 7.5 *Intelligence Quotient Data on 29,113 Hearing Impaired Children Reported in the 1969-1970 Annual Survey of Hearing Impaired Children and Youth*

Group	N	Mean Nonverbal IQ	Number of Children in 80-119 IQ Range
Hearing impaired with no other handicap	19.698	100.38	9,024
Hearing impaired and emotional or behavioral disability	2,068	95.53	1,000
Hearing impaired and emotional or behavioral disability with other handicapping condition[a]	1,019	83.00	358
Hearing impaired with other handicapping condition, but not emotional or behavioral disability[a]	6,328	85.42	2,220
Total	29,113		

[a]Including mental retardation.

SOURCE: Annual Survey of Hearing Impaired Children and Youth, Office of Demographic Studies, Gallaudet College, Washington, D.C. Personal communication, 1972.

similar to those of hearing children and therefore must be explained without recourse to verbal processes. His review provides strong empirical support for Piaget's (Inhelder and Piaget, 1964) theory that language is not a constitutive element of logical thinking. Myklebust (1964) formulated the rationale that the deaf have altered perceptual skills because of the necessity for them to shift their utilization of the senses relative to normal, and that such altered perceptual skills result in altered abilities. He points out that both verbal and nonverbal functions are involved in Guilford's five types of mental operations (cognition, memory, convergent thinking, divergent thinking, and evaluation), and that while language limitations would influence each of these in some degree, a generalized effect does not occur. Finding that deaf children were indeed not inferior on *all* types of abstract abilities and conceptualizing processes, Farrant (1964) carried out an analytic study to discover whether deaf children's abilities merely differ in degree on the same factors emerging from factorial analysis of the results with hearing children, or whether the tests factorized differently for deaf and partially hearing. Since the median hearing loss of his 120 subjects was 85 dB, his hearing-impaired sample was more heavily weighted with deaf rather than partially hearing children. His results substantiated the finding that hearing-impaired children are retarded on tests involving the factor of verbal comprehension either directly or indirectly. This retardation in verbal ability manifested itself not only in tests of obvious verbal content but also on a number of tests in which the verbal factor was implicit. Further, he found the abilities of the deaf and partially hearing less intercorrelated (integrated) with each other than with the normal-hearing. In other words, the partially hearing were more similar to the normal-hearing than to the deaf. Farrant concludes that these findings are consistent with the sensory and intellective shift theory of deafness.

The present knowledge on the assessment of intelligence of hearing-impaired children strongly suggests that great caution is indicated in interpreting test results. Vernon and Brown (1964) have reviewed the types of intelligence tests more suited to hearing-impaired children. They stress that validity requires the use of a nonverbal instrument; otherwise, one may be measuring only language deficiency. Verbal instructions even for nonverbal tests are equally inappropriate, for hearing-impaired children often pretend to understand to avoid incurring displeasure. Assessment of the intellectual ability of the very young child (under school age) tends to be unreliable; frequent and periodic testing is needed before decisions affecting long-term management are made. Educators are reminded there is far more danger that the hearing-impaired child will score low on an IQ test rather than high, since few factors in tests lead to performance above capacity. Tests administered by those without experience with hearing-impaired children are subject to appreciably greater error, and group testing and timed tests are generally undesirable.

Personal-Social Development

The barrier created by lack of language development permitting use of normal channels of communication with one's peers would obviously be expected to play an important factor in the personal-social development of any human. In the infant period, when the child is highly egocentric in his communicative attempts, the hearing-impaired child is not easily distinguished from a hearing child by most observers. In fact, his deficit often goes completely unnoticed even by his parents and the physician who follows his physical development. At two, he deviates more, but still is not unlike a hearing child of the same age who is just beginning to use connected speech attempts. From that time on, when the normal child is expected to increase his spoken-language attempts in such a way that he learns it is a medium by which he can begin to control his environment and relate to others, the difference manifested by the deaf child becomes increasingly marked. By three to four years of age, when the mastery of connected speech normally occurs in hearing children, the differences marking the deaf child increase almost in snowball fashion. Differences in the partially hearing child are, of course, relative to the degree of handicap.

One of the most significant aspects of any handicap is the extent to which it causes increased dependency on others. Capacities and attainments in man are not necessarily correlated. Hence, it is how one *uses* what he has, as well as *what* he has, that becomes the criterion of value used by society. Doll (1947) used the term *social maturity* to designate this broad aspect of human behavior, and devised the Vineland Social Maturity Scale to assess it. Myklebust (1964), in reviewing the various investigations that have been done in this area, concluded that deaf children up to age 15 are approximately 10 percent retarded in social maturity compared to hearing children. Up to 15 years the greatest task confronting the child is attainment of ability in self-help and in self-direction. He implies that deaf children are not inferior in achieving self-help, but as higher levels of social competence become necessary as they increase in age, they find attainment more difficult, indicated by the gradual decline after 15. By age 21 the degree of inferiority is as great as 15–20 percent.

The influence of inadequate language and degree of hearing loss on social maturity was studied by Treacy (1955), who compared the social competence levels of profoundly deaf children in a day school with a group of partially hearing children in another department of the same school. Both groups were at approximately the same age level (9–10 years). The latter group, who had considerable residual hearing, used amplification well, and were less handicapped in language than the deaf group, achieved a mean Social Quotient of 97.5, denoting a level well within the average range, while the deaf children's mean SQ was 90.0, at the lower limits of normal. In view of the higher level of social competence achieved by Treacy's subjects, who were from a day-school setting compared to the level of social maturity reported by previous investigators for children in residential school,[6] one might imply children from day schools are superior in social competence to children from residential schools. Participation in the regular community of children in day schools may enable a child to achieve a higher level of competence. Other selective factors would need to be clarified in generalizing on the basis of the educational environment, although it is logical to expect that children in residential schools have greater isolation generally from demands made on the growing child who can circulate more freely in the community at large. At any rate, research findings today are substantially evident that the social maturity of those deaf from early life may be expected to be below normal. For the partially hearing child, this likelihood is much less, which emphasizes the importance of capitalizing upon and exploiting to the greatest extent possible the residual hearing of every young hearing-impaired child to maximize the possibility for him to function as a partially hearing rather than a deaf child.

The personality of the child who suffers sensory deprivation of hearing in early life is also subject to deleterious developmental effects. Meadow (1968) has pointed out that one of the most consistent findings in this area is that the deaf are less "mature" than the hearing. Verbal language is known to play an extensive and pervasive role as one of the early "organizers" of the psyche (Altshuler, 1962). The limitations and constraints imposed by inadequate language development thus modify and restrict the self-identifica-

[6] Vineland Social Quotient of 80.7 for 92 children (Bradway, 1937); 15–20 percent below normal (Myklebust and Burchard, 1945).

tion of the young child. This identity of self requires the knowledge that one's own feelings and attitudes are similar to those of his peers, in particular those of his same sex group. The inability to receive (to hear) the many nuances of language regarding sex roles and the interpersonal dynamics of family living creates serious problems for the deaf child. It is, after all, with the spoken word that we reach out to other human beings, and when these sounds that facilitate interpersonal relations are not heard, isolation results. It is with words that we monitor our own feelings and ideas about events around us by comparing our thoughts with those of others with whom we closely identify. We either receive support or are influenced to modify our own attitudes or thoughts in another direction if we encounter insufficient reinforcement. The deaf child, and to a less extent the partially hearing, lacks this constant sharing and, therefore, loses much of the essence of identifying with his peer group. While deafness itself does not result in mental illness, the adjustment process necessitates a different psychological organization and structure when deafness is present from infancy (Myklebust, 1964). Nevertheless, the overall effects of deafness from early childhood have a very durable impact on personality development, which is evidenced by the fact that the percent frequency of schizophrenia in the deaf population is about two and one-half times that in the hearing population (Altshuler, 1967).

As in all preceding sections of this chapter describing characteristics of the hearing impaired, it must be repeatedly stressed that hearing impairment exists on a continuum from total and profound hearing loss to hearing sensitivity within the normal range. Dependent upon the degree and type of hearing loss, the partially hearing exhibit characteristics which are similar to the characteristics of the deaf, but to a less degree. In the area of personality traits, the partially hearing may develop conflict as a result of inability to identify themselves as belonging to either the world of those who hear or those who do not hear. Partial hearing always is a confusing state. Adults who begin to lose their hearing often demonstrate severe personality conflict as their level of hearing deteriorates to that point at which consideration of a hearing aid or surgery begins to appear necessary. Thus, borderline hearing may create greater problems of personality than severer levels of hearing loss which can be helped in part with a hearing aid, restoring the psyche to the *auditory* world. All this is simply to say that degree of hearing loss will always be a relevant factor in personality development of hearing-impaired children.

It has been found that those children profoundly deaf from early life show the greatest emotional deviation as they grow older, males to a greater extent than females. These children tend to be unaware of their deafness as a handicap in the early years. It is not until about the age of puberty that they begin to view their problem as a handicap distinguishing them from their hearing peers. Adolescence is a particularly stressful period, since it is then that they begin to consider their role in the future as independent adults.

Myklebust (1964), comparing the personality characteristics of day-school children compared to those in residential schools, found the former showed more emotional stress, conflict, and frustration in comparison to the residential children. This finding may reflect the greater stress associated with a school situation which places the hearing impaired in competition with hearing children at an early age when their limitation in language prevents them from achieving success in the many school situations requiring language skills. For this reason, the residential setting is necessary for many children. The residential school strives to give the child the competence as well as the confidence preparing him for his adult life away from the school, but the inherent protective atmosphere is often a shelter that may be too prolonged to achieve the desired goals. The child remaining in a day program may have overcome much of the embitterment and frustration from the stressful competition earlier, so that he has acquired sufficient self-confidence by the time he leaves school to make a successful adjustment in vocational life.

Postschool Adjustment

Although the deaf are average in strength, mobility, and intelligence, they have a serious underemployment problem, reflecting directly upon their lower educational achievement and difficulty in communication. Reporting findings from an intensive study of occupational conditions among the deaf, Bigman (1960) found them to be concentrated most heavily in skilled and semiskilled manual occupations. It is important, however, to point out that despite the concentration of deaf workers in such occupations, small numbers of the deaf were found in many different employments, with about 400 distinct occupational titles being reported. While there are certain occupations which are not open to the deaf (for example, such as those which would require frequent use of the telephone), one of the major problems is in helping to change the attitudes of the public to give deaf people opportunities to perform in new areas of endeavor. The deaf constitute a subculture insofar as the employment world is concerned. As with other subcultures, we can expect to overcome economic barriers only if we can do a better job of overcoming educational barriers. For the deaf we must add language barriers, which are, of course, directly reflected in the educational handicap.

Comparable data on vocational status of the partially hearing and auditorially perceptually impaired are not available. The better ability in language and communication characterizing these two groups causes them to be obscured in the mainstream of the hearing world, and many of the partially hearing adult population acquire their hearing loss after they are well established in their vocational career. The degree to which the communication, language, and educational levels approach normal would be a major consideration in the vocational status of those who have had hearing loss throughout childhood. One may conjecture that because many such children are unable to reach their full potential, or because they may have multiple handicapping conditions, as with many of the auditorially perceptually impaired, there would be some underemployment among these groups as well.

EDUCATIONAL PROGRAMS

The educational system for children with hearing impairment is highly diversified from state to state. In some states there are virtually no facilities except the public residential school and the regular classroom for those whose hearing impairment is not of a severity that precludes their participation. A number of states, however, provide a variety of alternatives with a well-structured relation among them to meet the different individual needs of deaf and partially hearing children. Despite different approaches, there is a common element in most programs which purport to deal with the educational handicap accruing from hearing loss in childhood. In the preschool years efforts are directed toward the language deficiency secondary to hearing impairment so that the child may approach a level of language functioning required for him to participate in the more formal education of the school-age years. Throughout the elementary and secondary years the educational objectives are the same as for normal-hearing children in that the hearing-impaired student is expected to master the same skills and acquire the same knowledge as other children. Hence the curriculum objectives are not different, even though techniques must vary on the basis of the severity of the impairment. As basic guidelines which may be used to estimate the relation of the degree of hearing impairment to educational needs, the Illinois Commission on Children (1968) has presented the categories and types of programs listed in Table 7.6.

Special Curriculum Features for Hearing-impaired Children

Hearing Aids and Auditory Training

The process of emphasizing the auditory aspects of communication and learning by means of individual and group hearing aids is normally referred to as auditory training. In the early years and later, until such time as it has proved ineffectual for certain children, auditory training should permeate all the child's learning activities on a continuing basis. It should not be viewed as an exercise scheduled for a specific period each day after which auditory stimulation is forgotten and visual input substituted completely. The group auditory-training unit with headphones frequently has stronger acoustic output and a wider frequency range than the individual body-type or wearable hearing aid and is thus recommended for class instruction and particularly for speech training, since it allows for higher fidelity of the signal than may generally be attained through individual hearing aids. Individual hearing aids on a full-time basis, however, should become the goal, so that auditory stimulation throughout the day is a natural outcome. The individual hearing aid is an extremely valuable tool for learning for a large majority of all partially hearing children and to a more limited extent for deaf children. The guidelines below contain some practical measures and working concepts for the teacher who has children wearing hearing aids in her class:

TABLE 7.6 *Relation of Degree of Impairment to Educational Needs*

Average of the Speech Frequencies in Better Ear	*Effect of Hearing Loss on the Understanding of Language and Speech*	*Educational Needs and Programs*
Slight (26–40 dB)	May have difficulty hearing faint or distant speech. May experience some difficulty with the language-arts subjects.	Child should be reported to school principal. May benefit from a hearing aid as loss approaches 40 db (ISO). May need attention to vocabulary development. Needs favorable seating and lighting. May need speechreading instruction. May need speech therapy.
Mild (41–55 dB)	Understands conversational speech at a distance of 3–5 feet (face to face). May miss as much as 50 percent of class discussions if voices are faint or not in line of vision. May exhibit limited vocabulary and speech anomalies.	Child should be referred to special education for educational follow-up. Individual hearing aid by evaluation and training in its use. Favorable seating and possible special class placement, especially for primary children. Attention to vocabulary and reading. Speechreading instruction. Speech conservation and correction, if indicated.
Marked (56–70 dB)	Conversation must be loud to be understood. Will have increased difficulty in group discussions. Is likely to have defective speech. Is likely to be deficient in language usage and comprehension. Will have limited vocabulary.	Child should be referred to special education for educational follow-up. Resource teacher or special class. Special help in language skills: vocabulary development, usage, reading, writing, grammar, and so on. Individual hearing aid by evaluation and auditory training. Speechreading instruction. Speech conservation and correction. Attention to auditory and visual situation at all times.

TABLE 7.6 *Relation of Degree of Impairment to Educational Needs* (Continued)

Average of the Speech Frequencies in Better Ear	Effect of Hearing Loss on the Understanding of Language and Speech	Educational Needs and Programs
Severe (71-90 dB)	May hear loud voices about 1 foot from the ear.	Child should be referred to special education for educational follow-up.
	May be able to identify environmental sounds.	Full-time special program for deaf children, with emphasis on all language skills, concept development, speech reading, and speech.
	May be able to discriminate vowels but not all consonants.	
	Speech and language defective and likely to deteriorate.	Program needs specialized supervision and comprehensive supporting services.
		Individual hearing aid by evaluation.
		Auditory training with individual and group aids.
		Part-time in regular classes only as profitable.
Extreme (91 dB or more)	May hear some loud sounds but is aware of vibrations more than tonal pattern.	Child should be referred to special education for educational follow-up.
	Relies on vision rather than hearing as primary avenue for communication.	Full-time in special program for deaf children, with emphasis on all language skills, concept development, speechreading, and speech.
	Speech and language defective and likely to deteriorate.	Program needs specialized supervision and comprehensive supporting services.
		Continuous appraisal of needs in regard to oral and manual communication.
		Auditory training with group and individual aids.
		Part-time in regular classes only for carefully selected children.

SOURCE: Adapted from Illinois Commission on Children (1968).

1. After the child has received appropriate orientation to the hearing aid leading to its acceptance, he should be required to wear the aid *at all times*, unless he has a discharging or injured ear. If the hearing aid is out of order, call his hearing aid distributor and ask him to supply the child with a "loaner" while his own instrument is being repaired.

2. The teacher must understand what the hearing aid can and cannot do for the child. The hearing aid only makes sounds louder. Through the hearing aid, much as over the telephone, sounds seem "different." The aid does not hear for the child nor does it correct his speech.

3. The hearing aid also has its limitations. Therefore, the child should be within close proximity of all hearing situations. Allow him to assume a position in the room which best enables him to derive maximum benefit from his hearing aid.

4. Be patient with the hearing aid. It has to become "a part of the child," and this is frequently achieved only after a long period of adjustment.

5. Make certain that the child has an extra battery on hand in school. He should be allowed to leave the room if he so desires to change the battery as soon as his aid goes "dead." The teacher of very young children should acquire the necessary information which will enable her to render "first aid" (changing batteries, inserting cords, and so on) to the hearing aid. The special-skills teacher or the local hearing aid distributor can provide this information.

6. Accept the child with his hearing aid and help others to do so. Thus we help him overcome whatever feelings he may have against accepting the hearing aid based upon his impression of being "different" from other children. This may be accomplished by asking the child to demonstrate the use of the hearing aid to his classmates early in the school year. He can point out how the aid is turned on and off, how the volume and tone controls are adjusted, the function of both the microphone and the receiver, and how batteries are replaced. The hearing aid can be compared to a radio. In class groups beyond the primary grades, such a demonstration can be part of a science demonstration dealing with electronics. Such participation in the demonstration on the part of the hearing-impaired child does much toward helping him achieve status among the group.

7. The teacher should understand the effect background noise in the classroom may have on the child wearing a hearing aid. Classroom sounds such as pounding a desk, slamming a door or desk top, and dropping books frequently startle the child wearing a hearing aid and make it difficult for him to concentrate on the spoken voice and to interpret speech.

8. The child should know how to manage his hearing aid, but may not in some cases. If the aid starts whistling or squealing (due to feedback), he may not hear it. This will likely annoy others in the classroom. The whistling or feedback results from sound leaking from the earmold and coming in contact with a sound-reflecting surface. It can usually be corrected by adjusting the earmold so that it is properly positioned and fits more firmly into the ear, or by turning down the volume control slightly. If this fails to eliminate the whistling, the parents should call on the hearing aid dealer to solve the feedback problem.

9. Parents of children using hearing aids should not hesitate to call on dealers for needed service. The user is entitled to service and hearing aid dealers acknowledge this. If the child's hearing seems poor or appears to be deteriorating with the use of the aid, the parents should be encouraged to call on the dealer to have the instrument checked. The dealer will check for possible poor contacts, plugs due to dirty pins, weak microphones, broken cords, run down batteries, and so on.

Speech

The act of speaking is closely related to the act of hearing. All of us monitor our own voices as we speak to judge whether we have uttered the individual consonants and vowels with clarity and precision and have altered pitch and timing features appropriately to convey the intended meaning. The speech of deaf and partially hearing children reflects the degree to which they have been able to use this feedback system either with or without hearing aids to attain speech that is intelligibile to others. The greater the hearing loss from an early age, the more serious will be the speech handicap. Speech training is thus an integral part of the education process for hearing-impaired children. The following principles suggest ways for the teacher to reenforce desirable speech habits:

1. Teach the child the use of the dictionary to aid his pronunciation.
2. Speech, as well as reading, can be improved through emphasis on basic phonics.
3. Encourage the child to take part in oral recitations and expect him to use complete sentences when speaking.
4. The teacher should provide a good pattern of speech for the child to imitate. Remember that distinct articulation is more helpful to him than raising one's voice.
5. *Listen* to the child with interest and intent to understand. Don't take the joy out of talking by "speech nagging." However, words initially mispronounced should be corrected so as to avoid the development of faulty speech habits.
6. Praise and encourage the child, where justified, to give him a feeling of success which he needs in order to build up his confidence in his speaking abilities.

Speechreading

Children with any degree of hearing loss invariably will need to supplement their defective auditory sense by increased use of vision. All of us as normal-hearing persons find that when our environment makes hearing difficult, we find it helpful to watch the moving lips and facial expressions of the speaker. This art of interpreting the content of speech by concentrated visual attention is known as speechreading. Increasing dependency on this skill is directly related to the degree of hearing loss, and in cases of severe to extreme hearing loss, the visual sense becomes the lead sense with hearing supplementing vision rather than vice versa. It is fortunate for the hearing-impaired population that many of the sounds which are most difficult to hear (for example, consonants making up the beginnings and endings of words) are the easiest seen on the lips. Because the visual modality is an important channel of receiving information for all hearing-impaired children, the following principles should be helpful in working with such children:

1. So that the child with a hearing impairment may see your lips better:
(a). Do not stand in front of windows while talking. Take a position

where the light falls on your face and not in the pupil's eyes. Do not move about the room while talking. (b) Keep your hands away from your face while speaking so that your speech and other facial expressions may be better interpreted by the child. (c) Face the class while talking or explaining material which is on the chalkboard. (d) It is well to realize that a moustache on a man's upper lip makes speechreading difficult, while light application of lipstick on a woman's lips aids in this art.

2. Remember that many words look alike on the lips and many sound the same. Examples are "buy" and "pie." If the child appears confused by any such word, use it in a sentence to give some clue concerning its identity and meaning. We must realize that the child is handicapped by the speed of natural speech and the invisibility of many sounds.

3. Look directly at the child and speak naturally, not too slowly and not with excessive mouthing. Use natural gestures when they complement, not substitute for, speech.

4. When necessary, "cue" the child into the conversation with a written or spoken word or phrase so that he does not lose contact with the group.

Media Centers and Captioned Films

An important development in the sixties which has had a significant impact on the instruction offered in classes for hearing-impaired children on a nation-wide basis was the program offered by the Media Services and Captioned Films Branch of the Division of Educational Services of the Bureau of Education for the Handicapped. Through this program a wide array of instructional aids and audiovisual equipment have been made available without cost to any educational program serving hearing-impaired children. Filmstrips on a wide variety of topics and graded in series by order of difficulty can be obtained upon request along with numerous other prepared instructional materials. Four Regional Media Centers (RMC's) having primary emphasis on instructional materials for deaf and partially hearing children are also administered by the Media Services and Captioned Films Branch to serve their special educational needs.

The Preschool Years

Infancy and Prenursery

The connotation of the term "early" has undergone marked change in the past decade, in that formerly identification of the hearing-handicapped child by three to four years of age was thought of as being early. In recent years, however, increased importance has been placed upon identification and pre-educational programing prior to this time. Those interested in the acquisition of language have repeatedly stressed that the basic prerequisites, including the establishment of the strong interdependent relations among the various senses, are firmly instituted within the first year of life.

While special educators have been aware of the need for increased downward extension of their educational programs, the methods by which this approach to the very young child and his parents can be achieved have continued to be elusive because of the administrative complications entailed.

Nursery and kindergarten programs have been to a large extent provided through collaborative efforts with hearing and speech centers. Many of the most elaborate and well-equipped such centers, however, have neither the physical facilities, programs, nor personnel adequate for the kind of guidance that a hearing-impaired baby and his parents require. Moreover, neither the setting of a clinical center nor a school lends itself to an approach adequate for demonstrating the kinds of activities that are beneficial to the young child's development. The clinical setting necessarily has to rely on verbally instructing parents, offering only limited opportunities to observe the types of activities to be done; thus a gap exists between the teacher's description of an activity and the parents' ability to implement the activity later in the home from the description given previously. A number of programs have attempted to bridge this gap by providing a setting in which the parent can be guided in actively translating principles of pre-educational handling into action. Hence, the demonstration home concept has taken shape.

The John Tracy Clinic in Los Angeles, long a strong advocate of the parent teaching method with young deaf children, was among the first to demonstrate the model home setting for parent work. Other centers have developed programs with similar methods and goals, but using home visits by the teacher as a substitute for the centrally located demonstration home. The dire need for such educational services has been demonstrated by the distances parents have shown they are willing to travel to seek help for themselves and their child. In one program serving 94 families over a three-year period, a mean number of 65 miles was traveled for each visit, and more than one fourth of the parents came from outside the state in which the program was located (McConnell and Horton, 1970).

The goal in the parent-infant program is to develop a program of instruction for young hearing-impaired children and their parents to be carried out in a home environment, allowing for incorporation of language and auditory training into the more normal routine of home activities as compared to the programing typical of a clinical center or a preschool. It is in these first years that parents need immediate and continuing help in developing their child's ability to understand and use language in the period before he is ready to enter a more formal education experience, such as the nursery-kindergarten (Knox and McConnell, 1968). The home teaching program is a much differently oriented service, with its emphasis on everyday activities as a source of instructional material for development of speech and language skills (see Fig. 7.4). Such activities will emphasize the natural acquisition of language built around the child's daily experiences and needs. The purpose is not to make "teachers" of parents, but rather to help them capitalize on their natural way of interacting with their children to stimulate the development of aural-oral language in the critical early months and years of development. For more detailed content of such a parent teaching program the reader is referred to McConnell and Horton (1970).

The success of the program for children under three which stresses

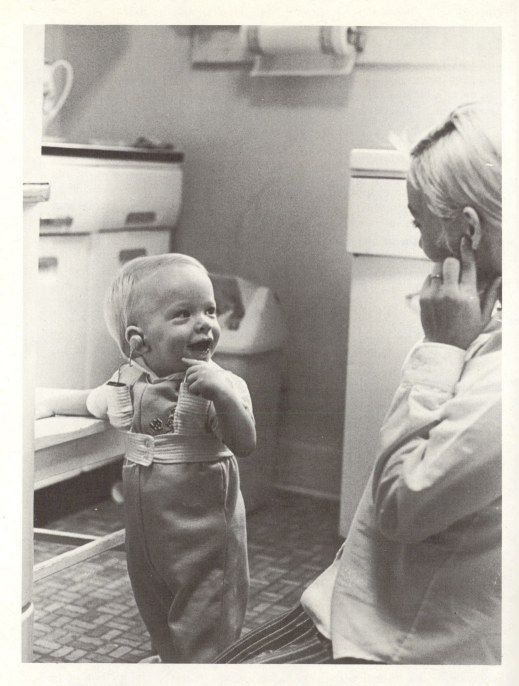

FIGURE 7.4 A deaf baby of 13 months shows his mother he can identify the source of the sound made by opening the refrigerator door in the kitchen of the parent-teaching home. (Photographer, Dana Thomas.)

early use of audition in acquisition of language is dependent not only upon highly skilled and competent teacher-counselors but also upon close coordination between the teacher and the audiologist. To capitalize upon residual hearing, individual hearing aid use is begun immediately, even as young as four to six months of age. It is in the period from birth to three that the importance of an interdisciplinary approach to the problem of hearing impairment is exemplified. If service is provided only by educators, the potential of the child's residual hearing may often be neglected. Inadequate management of the wearable hearing aid by the parents or the teacher can result in failure to take maximum advantage of audition, the most important avenue for learning. The longer the child by necessity is required to use the visual modality exclusively for intake of language concepts, the less readily will he shift to the other sensory modality when it is made available to him.

While parent-infant programs have not yet been widely practiced nor evaluated in the literature, results achieved in one such program are depicted in Figure 7.5. These data were accumulated on 28 four-year-old deaf children whose parents had had instruction in the years before three. It may be noted that Language Age growth was markedly accelerated with the onset of intervention, prior to which time the Language Age curve was increasingly separating from that for Performance Age. Another significant finding was that on the Peabody Picture Vocabulary Test these same children gained in vocabulary as much as eight months in their first eight months spent in the nursery school. In other words, their acquisition of vocabulary was linear with age. Such results suggest that early identification, individual hearing aids from the

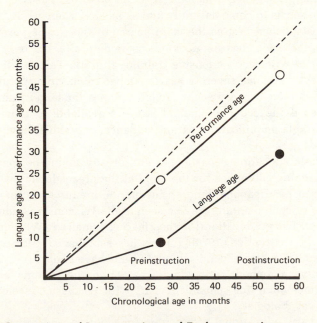

FIGURE 7.5 Comparison of Language Age and Performance Age.

first year of life, and concentrated parent instruction have much to offer in the best possible management of the hearing-impaired child's future educational programing. They further suggest that "deaf" is a term with more than one meaning. Most hearing-impaired children have some residual hearing despite the fact that they may be classified as deaf in accordance with the definition stated earlier in this chapter. Whether many of these children remain deaf or become partially hearing depends upon the *type of intervention* and *how soon* it is initiated. Those with extremely severe hearing losses and only fragmentary hearing thresholds are more likely to continue life as deaf children; those with marked to severe hearing loss may be able to function as partially hearing children dependent upon the factors just mentioned. For example, the necessity of visual supplementation as a channel for input of information for the deaf child has been such a strongly established educational tenet that many teachers of the deaf and other professional workers tend to behave automatically toward him as a "not-hearing" person. If his parents and others treat him only as "not-hearing," then he will indeed become so, despite the potential for hearing he may have. Therefore, it becomes necessary to emphasize to parents that their child may be able to hear a great deal without looking so they may avoid an overemphasis on vision.

This early attempt to give priority to hearing over vision is extremely important if we are to bring about the natural growth of language as nearly as possible as it occurs in the hearing child. Children who become good listeners will also use vision as necessary to become good speechreaders. Since the two events do not happen simultaneously, it is necessary to establish the acoustic channel as the primary input modality *if at all possible.* The use of the visual channel then seems to come naturally and as needed. Conversely, if the visual channel is established first as the main source of the child's perceptions and information, the use of hearing does not come naturally, but only laboriously and slowly and with much intensive training, if at all. This position does not ignore the fact that some severely hearing impaired children will be unable to use hearing as their primary sense modality, but a far larger number will be able to do so if the acoustic channel is made available to them very early through wearable amplification, parent guidance, and skilled audiologic management.

Some state education departments are already taking cognizance of the future by planning guidelines for the child at the preacademic level, which in the instance of handicapped children means the prenursery years. An excellent example of such planning may be seen in the Wisconsin Guidelines (Field Test Issue) on Early Education for the Hearing Impaired (Wisconsin Department of Public Instruction, 1970). Illinois has established pilot programs for parent teaching in which several school districts have cooperated to the extent of constructing a demonstration home to which the parents and hearing-impaired babies come for scheduled visits with teacher-counselors, audiologists, and a psychologist.

In summary, educational programing for children under three must take into account the nature of the impairment so that remediation is based on developmental constructs which are appropriate. Since legislative provisions extending the school's responsibility for the handicapped child down to infancy are very likely to become widespread in the years ahead, a whole new look at curriculum and personnel is necessary, and including the parents in the educational process becomes mandatory. To consider and treat a disability of a child of 18 months in the typical school setting separate from his parents is not likely to yield desired results. What is good for five-year-olds is not *a priori* good for two-year-olds. In the zeal for implementing needed programs, unfortunate practices can develop. May we be spared the sight of two-year-old hearing-impaired children with headsets strapping them around a table like so many telegraph operators, all trying to mouth the syllables, "uh-fish."

Nursery and Kindergarten

The emphasis on early detection of hearing loss together with the advent of electronic amplification devices and interest in aural habilitation have made possible notable advances in the development of nursery and kindergarten programs for hearing-impaired children. Prior to about 20 years ago such facilities for evaluating and providing special educational treatment for the very young deaf child were limited, either in schools or clinics. The emergence of audiology as a profession, with its emphasis on evaluation of the hearing impaired, naturally created a need for educational programs for preschoolers. Thus, many urban communities saw their first preschool classes for hearing-impaired children originate from the development of a hearing and speech center. Clinicians soon learned that the needs of a young deaf or partially hearing child far exceeded a few clinic visits a week. Consequently, many more far-sighted audiologists and speech pathologists initiated preschool classes for children in the age range of three to six, thereby demonstrating to the community at large the importance of such early education programs at a period in the child's life when he was not eligible for the state school and when there were no facilities locally. A number of programs have utilized the team teaching approach, using both a teacher of the deaf and a trained nursery teacher. In recent years such specialist personnel have worked hard at integrating hearing-impaired children with hearing children, even at the preschool level. The Mary E. Bennett School in Los Angeles, for example, has for a number of years had a program in which their children attend the special class for one-half day and the other one-half day the regular kindergarten or nursery. This arrangement would be best suited to the child four and a half to five years of age, since the younger child normally would not be in school that many hours.

Although some writers have raised questions concerning whether preschool education for deaf children has any value in terms of improved educational functioning later (Craig, 1964), the crucial element is probably not preschool education as such, but the *kind* of preschool education offered. If we simply extend our methods of working with children six years old and above to children who are three, four, and five, we may expect failure in the attempted objectives. Pollack (1970) favors a clinical-type program carried out with the family and the child together, while simultaneously placing the child in a suitable kindergarten environment with hearing children. She also emphasizes the auditory approach. Findings are further being accumulated which support the use of individual *binaural* amplification (two hearing aids, one for each ear) at the earliest possible time, accompanied by careful and frequent audiologic management as an integral part of the child's educational management (Callihan, 1971). Such programs, like those described for the children under three, stress intensified auditory learning and place high priority in the preschool years upon audition as the channel through which language, and subsequently speech, is learned.

It is extremely important that maximum flexibility be maintained throughout the preschool years. Those education systems which attempt infant and preschool education must not get locked into a system which prevents achieving what is best for a given child. Such programs must be highly individually oriented because of the wide differences occurring within any group of hearing-impaired children, such as degree of hearing loss, age at which habilitation was implemented, language and intellectual levels, and the family's capacity to reinforce the child's learning at home.

The curriculum should be essentially the same as that recommended for normal-hearing children, including a balance of content directed at language and speech development, intellectual including perceptual-motor and conceptual development, and personal-social development. Experience opportunities, equipment, and materials should be used which will assist the children to discover for themselves meaning and relations. Programing for three-year-olds must involve greater opportunities for free play, individual learning, and shorter teaching segments. Emphasis on parent counseling and involvement in the educational process has a high priority throughout. The more individualized-type program for the three-year-old will gradually emerge between three and four into more formalized kindergarten instruction suitable for older children. Programing for five-year-olds should provide for longer teaching segments, with specific attention to prereading and prewriting skills, greater elaboration of the language structures used, and inclusion of reasoning and problem-solving skills.

Innovative programs are also being developed which place emphasis on normal language experiences with hearing children by including an equal number of hearing-impaired and normal-hearing children together in each nursery and kindergarten class. Results have confirmed that such grouping accelerates language learning, as evidenced by greater changes in speech and language comprehension compared with hearing-impaired children not in class placements with hearing children.

At the same time, an educational philosophy in much evidence at the beginning of the seventies is that recommended by a considerable number of educators which holds that teaching finger spelling[7] (manual alphabet) and/or sign language[8] from the earliest period in life facilitates and greatly enhances the child's later speech and language. Stuckless and Birch (1966) published findings on children of manually communicating deaf parents who communicated with their children prior to two years of age, compared with children of hearing parents who did not use manual communication with their children in the preschool period. The children who had deaf parents scored higher on measures of reading, speechreading, and written language than the children of hearing parents. The authors concluded that early manual communication facilitates the acquisition of language skills as evidenced by reading comprehension and written expression later. There are, of course, a large number of variables which would have to be considered here. Obviously, parents who are themselves deaf would have less difficulty in accepting the deaf child; thus, the psychosocial climate would be a healthier one, which in itself would be an advantage to developing interpersonal communication. Further, there is little question that very early stimulation and intervention facilitates the child's learning and acquisition of specific skills in any one of a number of areas. The other very significant parameter to be pointed out in the Stuckless and Birch study is the control population—the children of hearing parents. These children came from the same schools as the children of deaf parents, and no information was given regarding the type of infant and preschool opportunities they had, if any. Presumably, the amount of aural-oral language stimulation was minimal, or at least had not yielded adequate results by school age to make possible an educational placement other than the residential school for the deaf. Hence, a highly selected population was described by these authors. Quite different results might have been obtained had the children for the control sample been taken from educational settings in which the children had been exposed to a strong auditory program from an early age. In fact, the variable of whether the parents were deaf or hearing might well become quite insignificant.

Programs are now being introduced in some of the public school systems which advocate the method of *total communication* for preschool children. Total communication reputedly combines finger spelling and sign language with speech, speechreading, and auditory training. The difference between the philosophy pervading these two kinds of approaches at the preschool level is one which involves the use of the auditory channel in educating hearing-

---

[7] Finger spelling is a form of symbolized language in which the sender of the message (speaker) uses a manual symbol for each letter of the alphabet and spells each word in rapid sequence. This method preserves the same vocabulary and syntactical patterns of spoken and written English.

[8] Sign language is a form of symbolized language which uses a manually formed sign to represent either a word or a whole idea. It does not conform to the structure of English which the child must master in read and written forms in school. It is easily learned, however, and for those deaf individuals who are unable to master English, it becomes the only available communication medium.

impaired children. It cannot be denied that a certain proportion of hearing-impaired children are profoundly deaf in the prelingual years and will not be able to obtain sufficient auditory language through the use of hearing aids to enable them to rely upon audition, even though a great deal of stress may be placed upon the auditory method. There is a far larger proportion of hearing-impaired children, however, who in their early years of life do have sufficient residual hearing to benefit markedly from wearable amplification introduced at the earliest possible time to make the auditory channel functional and to make the child an auditory child. The level of hearing alone is not the most important criterion for educational attainment. If each hearing-impaired child by virtue of being born educationally deaf were irrevocably destined to depend entirely upon vision, then there would be greater justification for the introduction of manual language at the preschool level. On the contrary, if one believes that a very substantial number of these children can learn through hearing, and that every hearing-impaired child should first be given an opportunity to do so, then the former method, which is the auditory approach espoused by Pollack (1970) and Ling (1964) is logical. Introduction of manual communication into the preschool period would seem to emphasize the visual modality over the auditory and for that reason can be seriously questioned for local public school systems if their aim is indeed, as usually stated, to integrate children successfully later on in their school life into regular classes.

The School-age Years

Hearing-impaired Children in Regular Classes

The goal of special education services for hearing-impaired children is to provide them the special help necessary to prepare them for participation in the regular classroom whenever possible. The time at which this placement becomes possible, *if at all*, is highly variable, dependent upon many of the factors previously discussed. Although the majority of children in classes B and C (see Table 7.2) will be educated in the regular school, it is not at all impossible that children in classes D, E, and F will be integrated with hearing children by the time they are ready for secondary school or before. The suggestions offered below should provide considerable help for the regular classroom teacher who has children in any of these categories in her class:

1. The child with impaired hearing *listens with his eyes as well as with his ears*. Therefore, assign the child a seat not more than five or ten feet from the teacher. The pupil can speechread best at this distance as well as make better use of his residual hearing.
2. Allow the child to find the seat most favorable for speechreading and hearing with efficiency and ease. Thus, he is better able to maintain contact with all class activities. Flexibility in seating arrangement, movable desks, and table and group arrangements all enable the child to observe and actively participate in class activities.
3. Ask the child an occasional question related to the subject under discussion to make certain that he is following the discussion and understands it.

4. Encourage the child to ask to have statements repeated when he does not understand what has been said. If the child fails to understand what has been repeated, *rephrase the question or statement.* Certain words are not easily recognized by speechreading. By using a substitute word, the intended meaning can be more readily conveyed.

5. It is desirable to have the child read ahead on a subject to be discussed in class so that he can become familiar with the vocabulary. Thus, he is better able to follow and participate in the discussion.

6. Before discussing new material, it is extremely helpful to place a list of words comprising the key vocabulary of the material on the chalkboard. Try to build the discussion around this key vocabulary.

7. To help the child follow instructions accurately, assignments should be written on the board so that he can copy them in a notebook used for this purpose. Give responsibility to a classmate who would make certain that the child is acquainted with all assignments made during the day.

8. Encourage active interest and participation in expressional activities such as reading, conversation, storytelling, and creative dramatics. Reading is especially important to the child. Information and knowledge gained through reading help compensate for what he may miss because of his hearing defect.

9. Teachers should remember that a child with impaired hearing is fatigued more readily than other children because of the continuous strain resulting from his efforts to keep up with and compete in classroom activities. However, he should be expected to complete regular class assignments.

10. As with other children having sensory defects, the child with impaired hearing needs individual attention. The teacher should be alert to every opportunity to provide individual help in order to fill gaps stemming from the child's hearing defect.

11. Visual aids help hearing-impaired children by providing the association necessary for learning new things.

Supplementary services for hearing-impaired children offered by many school systems are provided by itinerant teachers trained to work with hearing-loss problems and by speech correctionists. The itinerant teacher of the hearing impaired is frequently able to provide educational tutoring as well as speech, language, and auditory training. The number of children served is limited to 15 to 25 a week, so that time is available for individual work, parent counseling, and assistance to the classroom teacher. Speech-correction schedules often require one specialist to see as many as 75 children in one week, all with a variety of speech problems. Such a person often works entirely with small groups and concentrates on the speech process itself, with less opportunity for language work, supplementary educational tutoring, and strengthening defective auditory skills, all of which are very necessary for the hearing-handicapped child. In any case, either the itinerant teacher of hearing-impaired children or the speech correctionist may be called upon by the classroom teacher and can often be a most valuable resource person.

Day Schools and Day Classes

Although the first special education facilities for deaf and partially hearing children in this country were residential, the day-center movement under the leadership of Alexander Graham Bell had gained increasing momentum by the latter part of the nineteenth century (Wooden, 1963). This rapid growth of day facilities is evidenced by a comparison of figures reported in 1959 (Frisina, 1959) compared with those for 1970 (*American Annals of the Deaf*, 1970). Frisina's report showed that twice as many hearing-impaired children were enrolled in residential schools (16,523) as in day programs (8,792) only slightly more than ten years ago. The *American Annals of the Deaf Directory* for 1970 reported for the first time a larger proportion in day schools and classes in this country, with 53 percent of all children reported in day programs compared to 47 percent in residential programs. Information in Table 7.7 summarizes this rapid change in educational settings over a recent five-year period. A trend in the whole field of education of hearing-impaired children which is suggested here is that local school systems are now increasingly accepting responsibility for educating these children. It should be pointed out that the figures in this table include only those hearing-impaired children who were enrolled *in special classes*. The figure of 62,504 children included by Dunn in Table 1.2, which was reported by the Bureau of Education for the Handicapped (BEH), is listed as the number of hearing-impaired children *served* in special education programs in the United States in 1968–1969, not necessarily just those enrolled in special classes. The larger BEH figure would, therefore, include those children with hearing handicap who, though placed in regular classes, received supplementary assistance in the form of speechreading, speech and/or language training, and auditory training from itinerant personnel.

TABLE 7.7 *Enrollment in Schools and Classes for the Deaf and Partially Hearing, 1965 and 1970*

Type School	1964-1965[a]		1969-1970[b]		Percent of Increase in Enrollment
	No. of Units	No. of Children	No. of Units	No. of Children	
Residential Schools					
Public residential schools	69	17,563	64	20,159	14.7
Private residential schools	14	1,231	15	1,450	17.8
Total	83	18,794	79	21,609	
Day Schools and Classes					
Public day schools	15	2,021	34	4,045	100.0
Private day schools	10	328	30	1,608	390.2
Public day classes	281	9,648	547	17,677	83.2
Private day classes	49	1,217	112	2,069	70.0
Classes for multiply handicapped	17	257	51	738	187.2
Total	372	13,471	774	26,137	
Grand totals	455	32,265	853	47,746	45.7

[a]*American Annals of the Deaf*, 1965, 110, 278.
[b]*American Annals of the Deaf*, 1970, 115, 405.

The differentiation between the day-school and the day-class program is that a day school is in itself a separate school. Day-school pupils go home at night and return to the special school the next morning. Such an example would be the Horace Mann School in Roxbury, Massachusetts, which was the first day school developed in this country. Conversely, day classes are separate classes for hearing-impaired children located in the larger regular elementary schools. If a proper attitude prevails in the administration and working relations are carefully established, the hearing-impaired child, as he is able, may move out of the day classes for a certain period in the day to be integrated into the hearing classes, making later transition from the special class into the hearing class more easily possible. This flexibility is an advantage of the day class generally and is the reason for their being more prevalent than the day schools.

Day programs have rapidly increased in number because many parents feel inherently that their child should be educated at home and remain a part of the family unit. Family identification, competition wih society in which the child lives, and many other factors are immediately evident here. The degree of hearing loss, of course, also becomes important. If the hearing modality has had optimum development, many of these youngsters can compete successfully in hearing high schools and colleges. Ideally, in each state we should have the possibility of transferring children to and from the residential facilities based on their individual needs. Such individual cooperative programs are now possible in a number of states.

There are both advantages and disadvantages in day programs for the hearing impaired, some of which are listed in Table 7.8. Only through careful consideration of all the individual factors in a given instance can the most suitable placement be selected.

Residential Schools

The development of education for hearing-impaired children in this country, as well as abroad, has been traditionally in the residential-school setting, as has already been pointed out by Dunn in Chapter 1. Most states developed their own public residential schools in the nineteenth century. Although they were intended to meet the needs of the deaf, many partially hearing children were in the past also enrolled because of the lack of educational facilities for them at home. These schools are supported either directly or indirectly by state tax funds and are for the most part now under the control of state education authorities. There are also a number of private residential schools, some of them operated by religious groups, such as the Lutheran School in Detroit, while others are nondenominational, like the well-known Central Institute for the Deaf in St. Louis.

Deaf children at residential schools are housed in dormitories or cottages during the regular school year, returning to their homes during the summer months and also for the regular school holiday periods. In their living

TABLE 7.8 *A Comparison of the Advantages and Disadvantages of Educational Placement for Hearing-impaired Children in Day Schools or Classes*

Advantages	Disadvantages
1. Remaining in the home and participating in all aspects of family living under most circumstances should prepare the child for adult responsibilities more effectively. 2. Self-identity within the family unit and sexual identity are afforded better opportunities for development. 3. Participation in neighborhood and community living requires the hearing-impaired child to use his residual hearing and oral language to the maximum extent possible; the day class program, if properly organized, affords the daily stimulation of communicating with normal-hearing peers, which can be the most effective of all incentives to use his oral-aural language ability. 4. Competition with hearing children fosters development of independence and a more realistic perspective on the demands of adulthood.	1. Day programs much less frequently provide vocational-technical training opportunities in the educational program. 2. Daily competition with hearing children places much greater stress on the personality; if the family is not in a strongly supportive role, the child's frustration may exceed his tolerance to withstand such competition. 3. Social rejection by his classmates is much more likely to occur on the basis of his inability to communicate normally, and irrespective of other personality traits. 4. Opportunity to participate in the extracurricular activities of the school are much more limited.

quarters at the school they are under the supervision of house parents. Tuition and room and board are free in the public residential schools to residents of the state. In keeping with the trend toward day pupil enrollment, a number of the state residential schools have relaxed their regulations to permit students who are residents of the community in which the school is located to attend on a day basis if the families are willing to provide transportation to and from the school each day. Another trend has been the lowering of age-of-admission requirements in recognition of the value of preschool-level educational opportunity for hearing-impaired children. In a few instances children as young as age three are admitted to residential programs, although the majority have accepted children only down to four or five years of age.

Residential schools as a group place more stress on religious education and vocational training than do the day schools and classes. Some residential schools, particularly the private schools, use only the oral method of instruction, but the majority use the combined method (oral and manual). The vocational-training emphasis in many of the state schools has been highly valuable to the deaf young person entering the world of work upon completion of school. Employment or on-the-job training opportunities are enhanced by the practice of maintaining a close relation with state vocational rehabilitation counselors. This relation is fostered and encouraged by school personnel so that the students have had opportunity for vocational guidance during their teen-age years at the school.

By the time a hearing-impaired child has reached school age, his full-time educational placement must be chosen on the basis of a number of factors which take into consideration the extent of hearing loss, the status of his language development, and the adequacy of the educational facilities in the local school system. For children suffering severe to extreme hearing loss, the residential school will often be required simply because of the inadequacy of local school system provisions. Table 7.9 lists some of the advantages and disadvantages inherent in the residential setting.

TABLE 7.9 *A Comparison of the Advantages and Disadvantages of Educational Placement in Residential Schools*

Advantages	Disadvantages
1. Children with severe and profound hearing losses have more chance for successes in the classroom, in athletic events, in extracurricular activities, and in their personal-social life because they are competing only with others having the same handicap.	1. Dependency attitudes are fostered because of the sheltered nature of the residential school environment.
2. The greater emphasis on vocational training should prepare them better for later work experience and suitable vocational pursuits.	2. Use of hearing, oral speech, and language tends not to develop or to diminish in schools where the combined system is used; children with more hearing potential begin to behave more like those with extremely limited hearing toward whom the instructional program is directed.
3. Personality development occurs in a less stressful environment than that imposed in their home community where they are primarily among normal-hearing persons.	3. The child becomes more or less a stranger to his own family and is deprived of experiencing the dynamics within the family unit which foster his identity as an integral member of that unit.
4. The entire program around the clock each day is planned in consideration of the particular needs of the child who cannot hear.	4. Sexual identity is more difficult to establish outside the family constellation; house parents normally have too many children for whom they are responsible to be able to serve adequately as true parent surrogates to any one child.

Despite some of the inherent disadvantages of the residential school, it appears that we will always have a need for both types, residential and day, to serve all hearing-impaired children adequately. One growing program, which is now being instituted in many public residential schools, is one for the multiply handicapped deaf child. A number of these children are denied an education because they do not fit into any one category and they are apt to be placed in residential facilities for the mentally retarded or the mentally ill. We may expect that as educational opportunities for the hearing impaired improve and increase in number, they will be developed in local school systems to a much greater extent than in the past. In turn, the proportion of the multiply handicapped deaf in the residential school populations may be expected to increase as a larger proportion of hearing-impaired children who can do so enter day programs in their home communities.

Higher Education

The aim of educational programs for hearing-impaired children should be to prepare them to enter a secondary school and/or college if they have the abilities. Such a goal has long been the object, for example, of the Central Institute for the Deaf, many of whose students have attained academic, vocational, and communicative ability that has enabled them to compete successfully in regular high schools and colleges for the hearing. Many hearing-impaired children, however, who, because their language proficiency has never sufficiently developed, cannot take advantage of higher educational generally. Gallaudet College, founded more than 100 years ago in Washington, D.C., for the deaf has afforded the opportunity for a college education to young deaf people, not only from the United States and Canada but from many foreign countries. Yet, only a very small percentage of the graduates of the schools for the deaf each year can qualify for Gallaudet because the average graduate is not scholastically prepared to pass the entrance examinations. Moreover, Gallaudet is essentially a liberal arts college and does not offer a curriculum which is more suited to the average young deaf person whose linguistic and verbal skills are limited.

More recently the National Technical Institute for the Deaf (NTID) was founded as an integral part of a larger technical institute for the hearing, the Rochester Institute of Technology in Rochester, New York. Here special provisions are made to integrate deaf with hearing students; each deaf student is assigned a hearing student who assists him with class assignments and helps him to maintain his place in the program. The curriculum is of a technical nature and thus does not place such an emphasis on verbal and linguistic skills as the ordinary liberal arts college, but NTID is also a school for students with college potential. A pressing educational need is a vocational-technical school in every state that would be open to hearing-impaired students who cannot meet the higher entrance requirements of Gallaudet, NTID, or schools and colleges for the hearing.

EMERGING DIRECTIONS IN SPECIAL EDUCATION FOR CHILDREN WITH HEARING DISABILITIES

The educational management of children with auditory impairments, like that for children with other types of handicapping conditions, is undergoing many changes as a result of the transition in the whole field of special educaion. Such transition is not without its disturbing elements, and there has indeed been dispute and controversy among educators of the hearing impaired regarding method and philosophy. From this upheaval has come greater public interest in the hearing-handicapped child, and ultimately this in itself should work toward the betterment of his educational opportunites. If this is true, we should see a number of trends emerging which will assure the fundamental right to an appropriate public education for every auditorially impaired child in the future. Listed below are eight major trends which point in this direction:

1. Educational programs in the public schools will be extended to include deaf, partially hearing, and auditorially perceptually impaired children from birth, or as early as detected.

2. Teacher-preparation programs will be modified to provide for children at all age levels. Specialization in teacher-training programs will be developed for preparation of primary, middle, and secondary school teachers of auditorially impaired children. A new kind of teacher-counselor will be trained to handle the family and the child under three. This teacher will be knowledgeable in parent counseling, child development principles, and psychoacoustics. Nursery- and kindergarten-trained teachers will be added to the teaching team in special programs for children three to six years.

3. State departments of education will not only move toward certification of teachers for different age levels but also will certify school audiologists and language specialists to supplement the special programs provided for children with auditory impairments.

4. Day programs for partially hearing and auditorially perceptually impaired children will be developed in ever greater numbers in local school systems providing maximum special education instruction in the early years, followed by maximum integration with normal-hearing children as early as feasible, and ultimate placement in the regular class with resource help available from itinerant teachers of the hearing impaired.

5. Flexibility in programing will be developed to enable preschool hearing-impaired children to attend special classes, special classes with an equal number of normal-hearing children, private nursery schools and kindergartens for hearing children where desirable, with supplementary special language and audiologic assistance either in the school system or contractually provided through private or public speech and hearing centers.

6. The residential and day programs within states will develop a relation that will expedite the transfer of children from one type facility to another as needs of individual children dictate. Combined residential and day programs will result in larger proportions of day pupil enrollments in the residential type schools.

7. Deaf children in residential schools will be given increasing opportunities to participate in work-study programs in the community before completion of their academic program. Vocational and technical skills congruent with changes in society brought about by increased technical advances and automation will be made available in both their academic and post-academic training programs.

8. Units for multiply handicapped children with hearing impairment will be added to state residential schools for the deaf to provide for the growing numbers of such children who are not now eligible for any education program because they do not fit into a single category of handicap.

SUMMARY

In the past decade we have seen initial developments of a number of concepts outlined in the preceding section which augur well for the future of hearing-impaired children in the United States. A great deal of interest at the federal level has been focused on the need for programs of early detection and intervention, parent involvement, and nursery and preschool education for such children. The Bureau of Education for the Handicapped took steps to stimulate programs for preparation of teachers of the deaf and partially hearing, who had long been in acutely scarce supply.

The interest in screening the hearing of newborns and of preschool children has steadily grown. The audiologist and the educator have invaded newborn nurseries, well-baby clinics, day care centers, and Head Start Programs to identify children with auditory problems at an early age. The concept that the language barrier can best be alleviated by intervention in the same critical period of life when language development occurs for the normal-hearing child is now widely accepted by most educators, regardless of the methodology they espouse. The fact that wearable body-type hearing aids are now available to the very young child, providing him auditory experience on a full-time basis, is also a great step forward when one considers the improvements in hearing aid design that have occurred to make such devices possible, even for the infant.

There have also been increased educational advantages for school-age children through the federal programs which have made available captioned films and a large array of other audiovisual equipment and materials to all schools and classes for the hearing impaired upon request. The network of instructional materials centers and media centers has enabled deaf and partially hearing children throughout the nation to have access to modern equipment and materials in their classrooms.

All of these advances have occurred in the presence of continuing debate regarding the philosophy that should prevail in education of hearing-impaired children. It is doubtful that one method or philosophy can ever be presented which will be a panacea to prevent the serious educational handicap of auditory impairment in all instances. It is more important that we concentrate on providing every hearing-impaired child with the kinds of educational opportunities that have already been demonstrated to yield results. Let us not forget that many deaf people have achieved notably well educationally when they were availed of the proper opportunities in childhood, as evidenced by examples of congenitally deaf individuals who have achieved educationally through the Ph.D. degree. More research is needed to delineate the factors which have influenced such superior educational achievement for a few to help us accomplish far more with the many than we are now doing.

Resources

The Resource section at the end of Chapter 1 provides an annotated list of sources of information relating to exceptional children generally, with names of organizations and agencies to which inquiries may be directed. Here are presented organizations and agencies which deal specifically with the auditorially handicapped to which both the handicapped themselves and those who work with them may turn.

The Alexander Graham Bell Association for the Deaf, Inc., founded in 1890 by Bell himself, maintains its headquarters at 1537 35th Street, N.W., Washington, D.C. 20007. The official publication is The Volta Review, which is an important source of information to parents, teachers, and to the hearing impaired themselves on curriculum methods, communication skills, hearing aids, language, and problems of parents of hearing-impaired children.

The American Speech and Hearing Association is a professional organization, membership being confined to speech and language pathologists, audiologists, and educators of the deaf. Its headquarters are at 9030 Old Georgetown Road, Washington, D.C. 20014. Its journals include the Journal of Speech and Hearing Disorders, the Journal of Speech and Hearing Research, and ASHA.

The Conference of Executives of American Schools for the Deaf, founded in 1868, is an organization for administrative heads of schools for the deaf. The Conference emphasizes the educational and vocational needs of the severely and profoundly deaf, and it set standards for preparation of teachers of the deaf long before state education departments became involved in certification for such special educators. The Conference publishes an important monthly periodical, the American Annals of the Deaf, which is edited at Gallaudet College, Washington, D.C. 20002. The Convention of American Instructors of the Deaf is an affiliate organization of the Conference and represents the one professional organization which is comprised solely of teachers of the deaf.

The National Association of Hearing and Speech Agencies (NAHSA), formerly the American Hearing Society, is a type of voluntary health agency which has been in existence since 1919. Its headquarters are at 919 18th Street, N.W., Washington, D.C. 20006. Hearing and speech conservation and informing the public about the needs of the communicatively handicapped are among its major aims. A monthly publication, Hearing and Speech News, is published by NAHSA.

References

Altshuler, K. Z. Psychiatric considerations in the school age deaf. American Annals of the Deaf, 1962, **107**, 553–559.

Altshuler, K. Z. Theoretical considerations in development and psychopathology of the deaf. In J. D. Rainer and K. Z. Altshuler (Eds.), Psychiatry and the deaf. (Social and Rehabilitation Service, #VRA 67–32). Washington, D.C.: U.S. Department of Health, Education and Welfare, 1967.

American Annals of the Deaf. Directory of schools, classes, and clinics for the deaf in the United States and Canada. American Annals of the Deaf, 1965, **110**.

American Annals of the Deaf. Directory of Services for the deaf in the United States. American Annals of the Deaf, 1970, **115**.

Annual Survey of Hearing Impaired Children and Youth. Office of Demographic Studies, Gallaudet College, Washington, D.C. Personal communication, 1972.

Bigman, S. K. Occupations of the deaf. Rehabilitation Record, 1960, **1**, 23–26.

Bradway, K. Social competence of deaf children. *American Annals of the Deaf*, 1937, **82**, 122–140.

Broch, J. T. *The application of the Bruel & Kjaer measuring systems to acoustic noise measurements.* Copenhagen: Bruel & Kjaer, 1967.

Callihan, V. A comparison of binaural and monaural hearing aid performance of preschool children. Unpublished master's thesis, Vanderbilt University, 1971.

Chalfant, J. C., and Scheffelin, M. A. *Central processing dysfunctions in children: A review of research.* Bethesda, Md.: National Institute of Neurological Diseases and Blindness, 1969.

Craig, W. N. Effects of preschool training on the development of reading and lipreading skills of deaf children. *American Annals of the Deaf*, 1964, **109**, 280–296.

Davis, H. Abnormal hearing and deafness. In H. Davis and S. R. Silverman (Eds.), *Hearing and deafness.* (3d ed.) New York: Holt, Rinehart and Winston, 1970 (a).

Davis, H. Anatomy and physiology of the auditory system. In H. Davis and S. R. Silverman (Eds.), *Hearing and deafness.* (3d ed.) New York: Holt, Rinehart and Winston, 1970 (b).

Davis, H. Audiometry: Pure tone and simple speech tests. In H. Davis and S. R. Silverman (Eds.), *Hearing and deafness.* (3d ed.) New York: Holt, Rinehart and Winston, 1970 (c).

Davis, H. Hearing handicap, standards for hearing, and medicolegal rules. In H. Davis and S. R. Silverman, (Eds.), *Hearing and deafness.* (3d ed.) New York: Holt, Rinehart and Winston, 1970 (d).

Davis, H., and Fowler, E. P., Jr. The medical treatment of hearing loss and the conservation of hearing. In H. Davis and S. R. Silverman (Eds.), *Hearing and deafness.* (3d ed.) New York: Holt, Rinehart and Winston, 1970.

Doll, E. A. *Vineland Social Maturity Scale Manual of Directions.* Circle Pines, Minn.: American Guidance Service, 1947.

Eagles, E., Wishik, S., Doerfler, L., Melnick, W., and Levine, H. *Hearing sensitivity and related factors in children.* St. Louis, Mo.: The Laryngoscope, 1963.

Farrant, R. H. The intellective abilities of deaf and hearing children compared by factor analyses. *American Annals of the Deaf*, 1964, **109**, 306–325.

Frisina, D. R. Information concerning the deaf and hard of hearing in the United States, *American Annals of the Deaf*, 1959, **104**, 265–270.

Furth, H. G. Linguistic deficiency and thinking: Research with deaf subjects 1964–1969. *Psychological Bulletin*, 1971, **76**, 58–72.

Guilford, F. R. Surgical treatment of hearing losses in children. In F. McConnell and P. Ward (Eds.), *Deafness in Childhood.* Nashville, Tenn.: Vanderbilt University Press, 1967.

Hardison, L. N. A study of the expressive language ability of a group of hearing impaired children. Unpublished master's thesis, Vanderbilt University, 1965.

Hardy, W. G. *Children with hearing impairment.* Children's Bureau Publication No. 325. Washington, D.C.: Government Printing Office, 1952.

Hawkins, J. E., Jr. Iatrogenic toxic deafness in children. In F. McConnell and P. Ward (Eds.), *Deafness in childhood.* Nashville, Tenn.: Vanderbilt University Press, 1967.

Illinois Commission on Children. A comprehensive plan for hearing impaired children. Springfield, Ill.: Office of the Superintendent of Public Instruction, 1968.

Inhelder, B., and Piaget, J. *The early growth of logic in the child.* New York: Harper & Row, 1964.

Johnson, J. C. *Educating hearing-impaired children in ordinary schools.* Washington, D.C.: The Volta Bureau, 1962.

Kinney, C. The city's responsibility for hearing conservation. *Hearing News,* 1951, **19**, 2–18.

Knox, L. L., and McConnell, F. Helping parents to help deaf children. *Children,* 1968, **15**, 183–187.

Ling, D. Implications of hearing aid amplification below 300 cps. *Volta Review,* 1964, **66**, 723–729.

Lipscomb, D. M. Ear damage from exposure to rock and roll music. *Archives of Otolaryngology,* 1969, **90**, 545–555.

McConnell, F., and Horton, K. B. *A home teaching program for parents of very young deaf children,* Final Report, USOE. Bethesda, Md.: Educational Resources Information Center Document Reproduction Service, 1970.

Meadow, K. P. Early manual communication in relation to the deaf child's intellectual, social, and communicative functioning. *American Annals of the Deaf,* 1968, **113**, 29–41.

Myers, D., Schlosser, W. D., and Winchester, R. A. Otologic diagnosis and the treatment of deafness. In J. H. Walton (Ed.), *Clinical symposia.* Summit, N.J.: CIBA Pharmaceutical Company, 1962, **14**.

Myklebust, H. R. *The psychology of deafness.* (2d ed.) New York: Grune & Stratton, 1964.

Myklebust, H., and Burchard, E. A study of the effects of congenital and adventitious deafness on the intelligence, personality and social maturity of school children. *Journal of Educational Psychology,* 1945, **36**, 321–343.

O'Connor, C. D. Children with impaired hearing. *The Volta Review,* 1954, **56**, 433–439.

O'Connor, C. D., and Connor, L. E. A study of the integration of deaf children in regular classrooms. *Exceptional Children,* 1961, **27**, 483–486.

O'Neill, J. J., and Oyer, H. J. *Applied audiometry.* New York: Dodd, Mead, 1966.

Pintner, R. The deaf. In R. Pintner, J. Eisenson, and M. Stanton, *The psychology of the physically handicapped.* New York: Appleton-Century Crofts, 1941.

Pollack, D. *Educational audiology for the limited hearing infant.* Springfield, Ill.: Charles C. Thomas, 1970.

Silverman, S. R., and Lane, H. S. Deaf children. In H. Davis and S. R. Silverman (Eds.), *Hearing and deafness.* (3d ed.) New York: Holt, Rinehart and Winston, 1970.

Simmons, A. A. Language and hearing. In Connor, L. E. (Ed.), *Speech for the deaf child: Knowledge and use.* Washington, D.C.: Alexander Graham Bell Association for the Deaf, 1971.

Stuckless, E. R., and Birch, J. W. The influence of early manual communication on the linguistic development of deaf children. Part II. *American Annals of the Deaf,* 1966, **111**, 499–504.

Subcommittee on Hearing in Adults of the Conservation of Hearing Committee of the American Academy of Ophthalmology and Otolaryngology. *A guide to the care of adults with hearing loss.* (2d ed.) American Academy of Ophthalmology and Otolaryngology, 1965.

Subcommittee on Human Communication and Its Disorders. *Human communication and its disorders—An overview.* Bethesda, Md.: National Institute of Neurological Diseases and Stroke, 1969.

Tonndorf, J. Introduction to acoustics. In A. Glorig (Ed.), *Audiometry: Principles and practices.* Baltimore, Md.: Williams and Wilkins, 1965.

Treacy, L. A study of social maturity in relation to factors of intelligence in acoustically handicapped children. Unpublished master's thesis, Northwestern University, 1955.

Vernon, M. Fifty years of research on the intelligence of deaf and hard of hearing children: A review of literature and discussion of implications. *Journal of Rehabilitation of the Deaf,* 1968, **2**, 1–12.

Vernon, M. Potential, achievement, and rehabilitation in the deaf population. *Rehabilitation Literature,* 1970, **31**, 258–267.

Vernon, M., and Brown, D. W. A guide to psychological tests and test procedures in the evaluation of deaf and hard-of-hearing children. *Journal of Speech and Hearing Disorders,* 1964, **29**, 415–423.

Wisconsin Department of Public Instruction. *Early education for the hearing impaired: Wisconsin guidelines (Field Test Issue), Part II.* Teacher's Manual, U.S. Office of Education Project No. 00042 of Title VI of the Elementary and Secondary Education Act. Madison, Wis.: Department of Public Instruction, 1970.

Wooden, H. Z. Deaf and hard of hearing children. In L. M. Dunn (Ed.), *Exceptional children in the schools.* New York: Holt, Rinehart and Winston, 1963.

Opposite: Often an embossed model of the campus of a residential school for the blind will help students improve their travel and mobility skills by giving them a global view of the topography. (Photo courtesy Tennessee School for the Blind.)

chapter eight / randall k. harley, Jr.

children with
visual disabilities

chApTER ouTliNE

At some time or other, almost every sighted person has had to attempt to grope his way across a room or an outdoor area in the dark. Even this temporary experience sharpens an awareness of the inconvenience caused by reduced vision. In order to obtain some idea about the effects of blindness on ordinary daily living activities, some normally sighted college students have tried eating a meal or walking in a familiar environment while wearing a blindfold. A blindfolded person soon learns that reduced vision hinders him in obtaining important information about his environment and makes it more difficult to eat or move from one place to another. He may also learn that he is suddenly more dependent on his associates, or that they will treat him differently while he wears the blindfold. Similar results of the effects of reduced vision may be experienced by wearing thick-lensed glasses; or trying to read a book while viewing its image in a mirror. While such simulations of the loss of vison or difference in processing may help people to understand several of the problems of children with visual problems, it remains impossible to simulate the effects of a permanent visual loss.

DEFINITIONS AND CLASSIFICATIONS

Children with visual disabilities are those who differ from the average to such a degree that special personnel, curriculum adaptation, and/or additional instructional materials are needed to assist them in achieving at a level commensurate with their abilities. The terms "visual impairment," "vision loss," or "vision problem" refer to the physical loss of part or all of useful vision.

Pupils with visual disabilities are by no means a homogenous group with common learning characteristics. It is misleading to think of children with visual disabilities as a separate group when their basic educational needs are generally similar to those of normally seeing children. Recent special educational approaches which emphasize differences in individual learning characteristics within the group rather than a traditional categorical treatment of a mythical group recognize wide variance in abilities and needs. For instance, some children need only be provided special materials such as large-type or braille books, whereas other children need special teachers and special curricular adaptations in their school programs.

Pupils with visual disabilities may also have additional accompanying handicaps such as mental retardation, behavior disorders, defective hearing, or nonvisual learning disorders. A history of special education reveals that children with visual disabilities were at first pitied and protected in special classes and schools and later accepted and integrated with sighted children into regular schools (French, 1932).

For economic and legal purposes it has become traditional to define children with visual disabilities on a medical and physiological basis according to degree of visual acuity and the field of vision. Special teachers, books, and tangible apparatus are still allotted to schools on the basis of legal definition.

The legally *blind* are children who have central visual acuity of 20/200 or less in the better eye with corrective glasses (or children who have a peripheral field so contracted that the widest diameter of such a field subtends an angle of distance no greater than 20 degrees). The legal definition of the *partially seeing* are children who have remaining visual acuity between 20/200 and 20/70 in the better eye with the best possible correction. These two legal definitions have little utility to the educator because they do not tell him how the child functions in school. The treatment of legally blind and partially seeing children as separate groups is recognized as a result of tradition rather than as a function of extensive commonalities in educational needs.

For educational purposes a more functional definition is required. Educationally *blind* children are visually impaired children who principally read braille, whereas *partially seeing* children are visually impaired children who primarily read large print or regular print under special conditions. These definitions are sometimes misunderstood, because many braille readers learn to read print, and some children function in school using both print and braille materials. Children with special tactual and visual perceptual problems may not learn to read either braille or print, but may learn primarily through listening. In prescribing educational procedures for children with visual disablities, a number of factors must be considered in addition to visual acuity, such as visual efficiency, age at onset of visual impairment, experiential background, intellectual ability, and chronological age.

Labels should be avoided as much as possible. Blind may mean congenitally (disability occurring from birth) and totally blind (no useful remaining vision) to one author (Cutsforth, 1951) and a braille reader to another writer (Bateman, 1967). Perhaps, it would be better to describe the children according to the purpose of the identification. Why not use *braille reader* rather than blind if the purpose of the description is to convey the media of instruction? (The reason for retaining the conventional labels in this book is explained by Dunn in Chapter 1.)

THE CHILD'S EYE AND ITS COMMON DEFECTS

The human eye is a ball or globe which is an outgrowth of the brain (see Fig. 8.1). The functional parts of the visual system may be divided into four groups: (1) protective, (2) refractive, (3) directive, and (4) receptive. A disturbance to any part of the system by injury, disease, poisoning, or prenatal influence may cause temporary visual disfunctioning or permanent visual impairment.

1. The *protective* structures consist of the bony socket within the skull, the eyelids, eyebrows, eyelashes, and tears. Trachoma (a serious form of conjunctivitis or pink eye) is an example of a major cause of blindness which

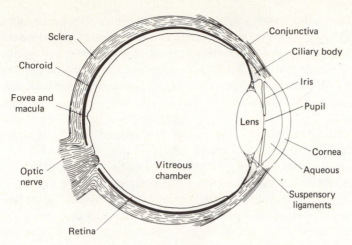

FIGURE 8.1 *Cross section of the human eye. From Principles of modern biology, fourth edition, by Douglas Marsland. Copyright 1945, 1951, © 1957, 1964 by Holt, Rinehart and Winston, Inc. Reprinted by permission of Holt, Rinehart and Winston, Inc.*

affects the eyelid as well as the cornea and conjunctiva of the eye. An early, typical sign of this disease is the drooping of the lids.

2. The *refractive* part of the system is designed to focus light on the retina by use of the cornea, aqueous, lens, and vitreous. Myopia, hyperopia, cataract, astigmatism, and glaucoma are common types of eye problems affecting the refractive media of the eye. Myopia (nearsightedness) is usually the result of the eyeball being too long. The lens is too far from the retina, causing the focus for rays of light from distant objects to fall in front of the retina. Hyperopia (farsightedness) is usually the result of the eyeball being too short. The lens is too close to the retina, causing the point of focus for rays of light from distant objects to fall behind the retina. A cataract is the result of an opacity of the crystalline lens. Astigmatism is a refractive error resulting from an irregularity of the cornea or lens of the eye. Glaucoma may cause damage to the eye due to increased pressure from accumulation of aqueous fluid.

3. The *directive* group consisting of six muscles connected to the outside of the eye is used to turn the eyes up, down, and to either side. Common examples of defective muscle functioning are strabismus, nystagmus, and amblyopia ex anopsia. Strabismus (crossed eyes, or squint) is the failure of both eyes to direct their gaze simultaneously at the same object because of faulty muscle coordination. Nystagmus is a rapid involuntary movement of the eyeball that may occur as a secondary characteristic of a variety of visual disorders and brain injury. Amblyopia ex anopsia is dimness of vision due to disuse of the weak eye from improper muscle balance.

4. The *receptive* part of the system includes the retina, optic nerve, and the part of the brain where vision takes place. Examples of common types of

impairments to this system are retrolental fibroplasia, retinitis pigmentosa, and optic atrophy. Retrolental fibroplasia is a condition of the retina caused by giving excessive oxygen to premature infants. It is characterized by scar tissue behind the lens of the eye. Retinitis pigmentosa is a hereditary degeneration and atrophy of the retina characterized by misplaced pigment. Optic atrophy is degeneration of the nerve fibers which connect the retina to the brain.

The visual process cannot function properly unless the occipital lobes, the seeing portion of the brain, can receive, interpret, and send messages. (The retina is a specialized part of the central nervous system and the optic nerve may be considered a nerve fiber tract.) The optic nerves (see Fig. 8.2) continue from the eye, crossing at the optic chiasm, to the visual cortex where the phenomenon of *seeing* takes place. Conditions affecting the seeing part of the brain or the area of the brain where memory and association occur can cause defective vision. Epilepsy, meningitis, hydrocephaly, multiple sclerosis, and brain tumors are examples of disorders of the central nervous system that may affect the visual process.

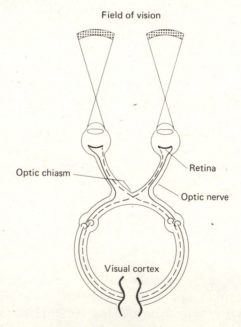

FIGURE 8.2 *Schematic representation of the visual paths.*

The most frequent causes of visual impairment at all ages have been listed by the Model Reporting Area for 1966 (U.S., 1970c). These data, compiled from 15 states, indicate that prenatal influence such as cataract and retinal degeneration impaired the vision of the young. Among children under 5 years, 47.8 percent of the new additions were visually impaired as a result of prenatal influence; for the age 5 to 19 group, the figure was 64.4 percent (see Table 8.1). Infectious disease (syphilis), injuries, poisonings (retrolental

TABLE 8.1 Additions to MRA Registers in 1966; Percent of Age Total by Etiology

Age Group	Total[a]	Infectious Diseases	Injuries, Poisonings	Neoplasms	Diabetes	Senile Degeneration	Vascular Diseases	Other General Diseases	Prenatal Influence	Multiple Etiologies	Unknown to Science	Not Reported or Determined
MRA total	100.0	2.5	2.8	1.1	11.6	33.0	3.0	1.4	13.7	4.9	11.8	14.1
Under 5	100.0	23.2	8.0	7.2	0	0	0.7	0.7	47.8	0.0	0.0	12.3
5 to 19	100.0	5.5	5.5	4.2	0	0.2	0.2	2.3	64.4	0.0	1.4	16.2
20 to 44	100.0	3.3	11.1	1.3	17.8	1.3	0.4	5.4	33.7	1.1	7.1	7.4
45 to 64	100.0	2.3	2.7	1.3	21.0	21.3	3.6	1.7	8.8	3.4	13.1	20.8
65 to 74	100.0	1.6	0.9	0.2	17.1	38.4	3.5	0.2	2.4	6.3	17.7	11.7
75 to 84	100.0	0.5	0.0	0.3	5.0	56.5	4.7	0.3	1.0	8.1	14.9	8.7
85 and over	100.0	0.0	0.2	0.2	2.3	70.1	2.3	0.2	0.8	8.9	8.3	6.8
Unknown	100.0	0.6	3.0	0.0	9.5	32.7	3.0	2.4	8.9	4.8	14.3	20.8

[a]Details may not add to total due to rounding.
SOURCE: U.S. Department of Health, Education and Welfare (1970c).

fibroplasia), and neoplasms (tumors) accounted for significant numbers of new additions to Model Reporting Area registers in the age 5 to 19 group (especially in the under-5 group). The largest numbers of visual impairments in legally blind children under age 5 added to the Model Reporting Area registers in 1966 were cataracts (23.9 percent), optic nerve atrophy (8.7 percent), other retinal affections (9.4 percent), and retrolental fibroplasia (8.0 percent).

Ferree (1967) predicted an increase in visual impairments from general diseases (diabetes) and prenatal influence and decreases in visual impairments from infectious disease, injuries, and poisoning. Unknown to science causes (myopia, glaucoma) would account for about 38 percent of new cases of visual impairment for all ages. Probably the most significant changes concerning visual impairments among school-age children in the fifties and sixties were the decline in numbers of retrolental fibroplasia children and the increase in numbers of rubella children.

The number of children with retrolental fibroplasia has been dramatically reduced through more careful control of oxygen therapy with premature infants. The rubella epidemic in 1964 produced many multiply impaired children with visual problems such as cataracts. The popular use of the rubella vaccine has drastically reduced the number of rubella children. However, large numbers of children with multiple impairments may result from new virus infections, drugs, poisons, and pollutants. A significant number of children with visual impairments due to hereditary causes and undetermined origin is also expected.

The largest number of visual impairments in partially seeing children, according to Kerby (1958), are refractive errors such as myopia and hyperopia. Developmental anomalies such as cataract and albinism rank second, and defects of muscle function such as squint and nystagmus rank third.

SCREENING AND IDENTIFICATION
OF VISION PROBLEMS

The location of visually impaired school children who need special educational services invokes more than the mere mechanical application of a visual screening device. The identification of visual problems requires teamwork of educational, medical, and other personnel such as volunteer workers. The teamwork consists of vision screening of all children, continuous classroom observation for behavioral and physical symptoms, referral of some children for comprehensive eye examinations, and follow-up to carry out recommendations. An adequate program of identification requires the carrying out of each step in a carefully planned systematic effort.

Most vision-screening procedures are based on the use of the Snellen chart plus careful observation of symptoms of eye trouble in the classroom. The Snellen chart is the most commonly used chart for measurement of distant, central field acuity (see Fig. 8.3). The standard letter chart may be used for literate children, but the symbol (E chart) is especially suitable for young children. The testing distance for distant visual acuity is set at 20 feet (6 meters) because rays of light are practically parallel at this distance. It is believed that the muscle controlling the shape of the lens in the normal eye is generally in a state of rest when viewing objects at this distance. Visual acuity is recorded in the form of a fraction in which the test distance (usually 20 feet) is recorded in the numerator. The denominator represents the distance at which the smallest letters seen should be read by the normal eye. A visual acuity of 20/200 indicates that the child reads at 20 feet the line which should be read by a normally seeing eye at a distance of 200 feet.

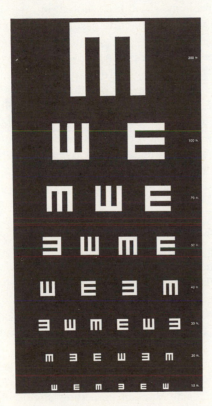

FIGURE 8.3 Snellen symbol chart. Courtesy of the National Society for the Prevention of Blindness, Inc., New York.

The National Society for Prevention of Blindness (1969) recommends screening according to the following criteria:

Three-year-olds: failure to achieve a visual acuity of 20/40 or better.
Four-, five-, and six-year-olds; vision of 20/40 or less.
Kindergarten through third grade: vision of 20/40 or less.
Fourth grade and above: vision of 20/30 or less.

It is important that visual-acuity screening be done under standardized conditions. The chart must be clean and properly placed according to background and eye height. Correct illumination of chart and room is important, since glare or insufficient lighting can alter the results of the examination. The child must stand at the specified distance from the chart, and his position during the examination must be carefully observed. A standardized administration procedure based on recommendations of the National Society for the Prevention of Blindness should be followed.

The screening process should include careful observation of the behavior of the child during the measurement of visual acuity from the Snellen chart, in addition to a history of visual complaints and illnesses. Certain signs and symptoms of eye problems should be noted by the teacher and Snellen tester for correlation with visual-acuity results before referral to an ophthalmologist. For example, crusts on eyelids or among eyelashes, red or swollen eyelids, watery eyes or discharges, sensitivity to light, reddened conjunctiva, and lack of coordination in focusing the two eyes should be noted. The child may rub his eyes frequently or attempt to brush away blur. He may experience headaches and/or nausea following visual close work, or he may complain of itchy, scratchy, or burning eyes. The child may have to move extremely close to the chalkboard or books to discriminate pictures, words, or diagrams. Any unusual visual behavior or symptoms should be noted on the child's screening record.

For children who are having reading difficulties or other visual learning problems (or who have medical problems such as diabetes or cerebral palsy), a professional eye examination is needed in addition to the general physical examination. It must be emphasized that no screening procedure, regardless of its nature, can be as valuable as a complete professional eye examination.

Some children may be handicapped due to restriction of the field of vision. The field of vision is the entire area which can be seen while the eye remains fixed upon one point. When the widest angle of the central field is restricted to 20 degrees or less in the better eye with correction, the person is considered legally blind, even though he is usually able to read ink-print materials.

Some screening procedures call for the use of other measures in addition to the Snellen chart. Factors such as parental attitude, community resources, and efficiency of the basic Snellen screening should be considered before adding other special screening tests. Special tests which are often used to supplement the Snellen chart include the convex lens distance-vision test for farsightedness, tests for vertical and horizontal muscle balance, and a depth-perception test when needed for vocational placement. The Massachusetts Vision Test includes a test for visual acuity, with convex lens and muscle-balance supplementary tests. Although no manufacturer is currently producing a device bearing this name, several companies have marketed binocular measuring instruments which incorporate these tests as well as other tests for specific purposes (American Optical Company, Bausch and Lomb Optical Company, Titmus Optical Company).

PREVALENCE

Screening programs are useful in revealing the prevalence of children with visual impairments requiring special education services. Prevalence information is useful in determining the extent of services needed in a particular local school system or in checking the adequacy of the screening program in locating children with visual impairments. Unfortunately, estimates of the prevalence of educationally blind and partially seeing children in all situations are not reliable. Prevalence of visual impairments varies extensively from state to state according to age and socioeconomic level. The degree of visual loss necessary to require special educational services is also difficult to define.

In Chapter 1, using figures from the U.S. Office of Education, Dunn estimated that 0.15 percent of children had visual impairments requiring special educational services. He indicated that prevalence estimates included 0.14 percent as partially seeing and 0.01 percent as blind. Applying these prevalence estimates to the total population of school-age children, there were about 5,000 blind and 71,000 partially seeing children in 1968.

Prevalence estimates of legally blind and educationally blind children could be projected from the registration of legally blind pupils at the American Printing House for the Blind. Nolan and Bott (1971) reported a registration of 20,512 children in January 1969. Since the U.S. Office of Education (U.S., 1970a) reported 50,761,000 children enrolled in kindergarten through twelfth grade in 1968, a prevalence of 0.04 percent is indicated for legally blind children. The number of unregistered legally blind children is uncertain, but the 0.04 figure should be relatively accurate in representing the percentage of legally blind children in the population who need special services. Since braille readers constituted 39 percent of the group, a prevalence of almost 0.02 is indicated for educationally blind children.

Jones and Collins (1966) analyzed reports from 353 local public school programs which employed one or more full-time teachers of visually impaired children and from 54 residential schools for these children. They found that one out of every 1,000 children (0.1 percent) in average daily membership was classified as visually handicapped by local school systems with special programs for these children. Using the results of this survey and the data from Nolan and Bott regarding braille readers, the projected prevalence would indicate approximately 0.02 percent as educationally blind and 0.08 percent as partially seeing.

The prevalence of mild defects is relatively high. Data from the National Health Survey of Visual Acuity of Children (U.S., 1970b), using a sample of 7,119 children representing 24 million noninstitutionalized children (6–11 years of age), showed 6 percent of children at 20/70 or less vision. The children were screened for uncorrected binocular vision on the Master Ortho-Rater (a device consisting of a viewing box and two illuminated sets of test slides). The survey indicated that 0.8 percent of the children tested had less than 20/200 vision under the same conditions. This information regarding uncorrected visual acuity does not indicate the prevalence of visually impaired children for special educational services, but it does provide useful data on the number of children who may need a professional examination by an eye specialist.

Although the prevalence figures represent some slight discrepancies, the reader may draw several conclusions: (1) the number of visually impaired children constitutes the smallest group of exceptional children; (2) the prevalence of partially seeing children is much greater than the prevalence of educationally blind children; (3) approximately one per thousand children have visual impairments that require special education services; (4) the prevalence of children needing professional eye examinations is much greater than the prevalence of children needing special education services.

BEHAVIORAL CHARACTERISTICS

Cognitive Processes

Concept development of the congenitally blind child may be restricted due to lack of vision which causes limitations in kind and quantity of sensory input. Kind of sensory input is different because the lack of vision causes the totally blind child to rely solely on his other senses to gain information about his environment. The quantity of sensory input may be restricted due to inaccessibility of parts of the environment or lack of opportunity to explore the parts that could be made available to him. Bateman (1967) hypothesized that neither total blindness nor partial blindness decreased the ability to process information, but did impose limitations on the sensory data available to the visually impaired person. Thus, if the sensory data were unduly limited because of deprivation, lack of opportunities to explore, or poor mobility, the visually impaired child could lag behind sighted children in cognitive development.

The range of types of experiences for a totally blind child is restricted to a much smaller segment of his environment than the range for a normally seeing child. Many of these restrictions in observation are imposed upon partially seeing children depending upon the degree of remaining useful vision. Visually impaired children observe those items which are accessible to them through use of their remaining senses—by feeling, listening, tasting, smelling, and using remaining vision. Some items, such as the sun, moon, and stars, are inaccessible. Some items are too large to be observed with understanding by touch, such as a volcano or a skyscraper; others are too small, such as an amoeba or a blood cell. Some items are too fragile, some are moving too fast, some are too dangerous to handle, and some are difficult to touch because they are contained behind glass, such as liquids in thermometers or needles on voltmeters.

The frequency of contact needed to identify objects and validate generalizations may cause more conceptual errors among severely visually impaired than among children with normal vision. A relatively higher frequency of contact may increase the probability of incidental learning for normally see-ing children. For example, a normally seeing child may see a rabbit at a pet store. Subsequently this child may see a picture of a rabbit at school, or he may see a rabbit run across his yard at home. A visually impaired child may see a rabbit at the pet store by tactually exploring parts of the rabbit. He may not be able to see the rabbit again until he returns to the pet store. Verbal learning without appropriate foundation in concrete experience has been frequently mentioned in the literature as one of the major problems in educa-tion of visually impaired children (Harley, 1963).

The space perception of totally blind children differs from the space perception of normally seeing children. Senden (1960) reported observation of pre- and postoperative behavior of congenitally blind subjects who were able to see after the removal of cataracts. He concluded that a totally blind person was unable to acquire an awareness of space merely by tactual per-ception, but that this was solely dependent on visual perception. Senden argued that spatial depth to the totally blind person comes from the use of time when traversing by foot. The use of time to examine spatial relations is confirmed in research by Worchel (1951) in which 33 totally blind students and a matched group of sighted subjects with blindfolds were led along two sides of eight right triangles and asked to return without guidance via the hypotenuse to the starting point. Although the totally blind subjects were inferior to the sighted subjects due to angular deviations, the totally blind subjects were able to estimate distance by the use of time. The use of sound to teach orientation and spatial organization was mentioned by Garry and Ascarelli (1960). Fraiberg, Siegel, and Gibson (1966), in contrast to Senden, believed that the congenitally blind person did possess spatial concepts based on his knowledge and control of his body and its movement capability. McReynolds and Worchel (1954) studied the ability of totally blind residential school pupils to orient themselves for near and distant places. They con-cluded that visual imagery was not necessary for geographic orientation. The lack of visual imagery causes difficulties for totally blind children in space perception, but there is evidence to indicate that they can develop an aware-ness of spatial relations through the use of their other sensory modalities.

Integration of a sequence of touch sensations which are given by an object when an individual explores it with his hands is often called the *haptic* sense. Revesz (1950) concluded that totally blind people have the ability to perceive space haptically and that a necessary condition is move-ment of the body. Lowenfeld (1970) studied creative art activities with con-genitally blind subjects. His observations indicated that the congenitally blind are capable of achieving simultaneously spatial images through an act of integration of successively perceived tactual impressions.

A difference in spatial relations of severely visually impaired and nor-mally seeing persons can be found in illustrative studies by Juurmaa (1967) and Hartlage (1968). Juurmaa explored tactual spatiality, tactual discrimina-tion, and several other cognitive abilities of 228 educationally blind individ-uals. With respect to degree of blindness, a negative relation was found with spatial ability and tactual discrimination. Hartlage, in a study of 200 children from grades two, three, five, seven, and twelve, found visually impaired subjects inferior to their paired seeing subjects on items of a spatial nature.

Recent research studies point up the difficulties that visually impaired children have in abstract thinking. Zweibelson and Barg (1967) found visually impaired subjects inferior to seeing subjects in abstract concepts. Singer and Steiner (1966) found that seeing children were significantly higher in imaginativeness of play, spontaneous fantasy, and dreams, whereas the visually impaired children showed greater concreteness and lack of flexibility. Kenmore (1965) found that visually impaired children were inferior to seeing children in dealing with random shapes and distorted objects. Boldt (1969), in analyzing protocols of 103 visually impaired children, explained that the haptic and aural senses offer few opportunities for exact conception of functional and causal relations especially of distant phenomena, leading to uncritical verbalism. Tillman (1967) compared 110 educationally blind and an equal number of seeing children on the Wechsler Intelligence Scale for Children. It was concluded that the visually impaired children have a tendency to approach abstract conceptualization problems from a concrete and functional level and as a result fall behind sighted children. Miller (1969) found that on three Piagetian tests of conservation the partially seeing did better than the children with more limited vision and concluded that visual intactness may be an important determinant in the development of reasoning abilities.

The results of the previously cited research should more forcibly emphasize that visually impaired and especially totally blind children need a unique program in order to help them to learn simple concepts that seeing children can more readily develop through use of vision. The results have indicated that the visually impaired child is at a disadvantage in observing objects as a whole and in relating these objects to other parts of his environment. He is deficient in the unifying sense of vision which draws experiences with these objects together as a whole. A program unique in concrete and practical experience is desirable for clarifying and strengthening basic concepts before moving into abstractness.

A rich, stimulating environment is especially needed for children with limited backgrounds of experience. The seeing child is stimulated by vision. He sees an object and moves to it to explore the item more completely with his other senses. The visually impaired child lacks this natural excitation from the visual sense. He is not stimulated by vision to traverse to the object. This stimulation could be provided from listening, feeling, tasting, and smelling. The implications point to use of instructional methods to include stimulation through the use of remaining sensory modalities. The teacher must take the child on numerous field trips and bring a vast quantity of objects to the classroom for him to explore with his remaining senses. A school curriculum which provides a maximum number of real, vivid, practical experiences is vital to the development of meaningful concepts for the visually impaired child.

Intelligence

The intelligence of visually impaired children and normally sighted children has been compared to determine if the mental faculties of the visually impaired are affected in any way due to reduced vision.

Hayes (1941) has provided the earliest and most extensive study of intelligence of visually impaired children. He developed the Interim Hayes Binet for testing visually impaired children based on the 1937 Revision of the Stanford-Binet. His intensive, long-term study of intelligence of legally blind children indicated that these children in residential schools in the 1940s compared favorably with sighted children on the verbal items (1963). Smaller percentages of visually impaired children were found at both the superior and inferior levels, but the percentages in the inferior range were consistently higher than in the superior range. Hayes also found in an earlier study of 137 legally blind and partially seeing pupils in nine schools for the blind an inverse relation between vision and intelligence, that is, intelligence decreases as vision increases. He found no correlation between intelligence and age of onset of the visual loss.

The intelligence of partially seeing children in special class programs in public schools is reported as in the normal range. Bateman (1963) reported a mean Binet intelligence of 100 for 131 partially seeing children in public school grades one through four. The mean IQ for the mild defect group was 95.0 compared to 101.1 for the moderate defect group and 106.1 for the severe defect group. Her results tend to confirm the conclusion by Hayes that intelligence decreases as vision increases for the visually impaired children selected for special education services. Birch, Tisdall, Peabody, and Sterrett (1966) obtained a mean intelligence of 95.83 for 792 partially seeing children in grades five and six. There were only 44 subjects with IQ's of 75 or lower. A near-average intelligence could be expected, since 42 percent of local school programs required average or above-average intelligence for admission to special education programs for partially seeing children (Jones and Collins, 1966). Many of the children noted in the Bateman and Birch studies were from segregated special classes.) School practices that set eligibility requirements high enough to screen out children with accompanying additional impairments and segregate moderately impaired children in special classes must be questioned.

The data on intelligence testing of visually impaired children must be understood to have certain limitations:

1. The tests have been adapted from tests for seeing children and may not represent adequately the characteristics of visually impaired children.
2. The tests are predominately based on verbal rather than performance items.
3. The data represent children from specialized school programs which eliminated many visually impaired children who did not meet the intellectual criteria established for admission to these programs.

However, certain conclusions can be reached in regard to the intelligence of visually impaired children:

1. Mental retardation is not a necessary consequence of visual impairment.

2. The physical anomalies which impair vision can also impair intellectual development.

3. The retarded intellectual development of some visually impaired can be the result of inadequate opportunity to explore their environment.

School-achievement Characteristics

The educational achievement of visually impaired children in special education programs has generally shown some academic retardation. Evidence of retardation has been indicated in studies of both large-type and braille readers using achievement-test and age-grade comparisons with normally seeing children. Accurate comparisons are difficult, since testing-time limits are relaxed to accommodate the slower rate of enlarged print and braille reading. Birch and others (1966), in a study of school achievement and effect of type size on reading involving 903 partially seeing children in grades five and six, noted that these children were over age in grade placement by one year and nine months, and, in addition, they were academically retarded by one year and 11 months. They found that underachievement was the most important characteristic of the sixth grade partially seeing child. An interesting result of this study showed that the average sixth-grader had been in a special education program (usually a special class or resource room) for 5.4 years of the 7.9 years he had been in school. An important question to raise is, Would these same children have achieved as well in the regular classroom without a special program? No such comparison study was found in the literature.

Bateman (1963) found that the reading-achievement scores of a small sample of partially seeing children from grades three and four were less than one-half month below grade placement, according to national norms. However, when reading-achievement scores were compared with mental ages, reading achievement was 5.2 months below M.A. with the third-graders and 6.5 months below with the fourth-graders. The very small retardation in reading was attributed to the mildness of the visual defects.

Hayes (1941) noted that visually impaired children without multiple impairments have generally been shown to measure the same on achievement tests as seeing pupils in the same grade. However, he pointed out that the visually impaired child is at least two years older than seeing children in the same grade.

Lowenfeld, Abel, and Hatlen (1969) also found age-grade differences between braille readers and normally seeing students in a braille-reading study involving 200 subjects from the fourth and eighth grades. The fourth grade braille readers were 0.8 years older in local schools and 1.2 years older in residential schools than normally seeing children. There were only small differences between braille readers and seeing students on the eighth grade level.

The results of a few very limited research studies indicate varying degrees of academic retardation for both partially seeing and educationally blind children. Some evidence indicates that the retardation is definitely related to underachievement. The apparent educational retardation for visually impaired children is probably due to a variety of causes: (1) slower acquisition of information from observation as a result of the visual impairment; (2) slower reading rates; (3) lack of concreteness in instructional procedures; (4) loss of time in school due to surgery or treatment of eye conditions; (5) late provision of special education services. Much research is still needed for a better understanding of the nature of the educational retardation of visually impaired children in order to provide appropriate special educational services for them. However, important implications point to the need for early identification of visually impaired children and the necessity to provide effective remedial education.

Personal and Social Adjustment

The personal and social adjustment of visually impaired and normally sighted children have been compared to determine if the behavioral adjustment of visually impaired children is affected in any way due to loss of vision. Myerson (1971) postulated that variation in physique is unrelated to psychological maladjustment, but that emotional problems may develop in physically impaired persons due to the reaction of the social environment to the variation in physique.

The visually impaired person lacks a fully intact tool (vision) needed for behavior in his culture. Other individuals notice this deficiency and devalue the person for it. The visually impaired person may accept the judgment of others and devalue himself, which can lead to adjustment problems. Cutsforth (1951) charged that society's negative reaction to blindness was entirely responsible for the emotional problems of totally blind persons. Although he may have overstated his case, he did identify an important cause of behavioral maladjustment among some severely visually impaired persons.

Cowen, Underberg, Verrillo, and Benham (1961) studied the adjustment to visual disability in adolescence using 167 youths in the seventh through twelfth grades divided into three groups—the visually impaired in local day school programs, the visually impaired in residential schools, and a group of comparable seeing children. The visually impaired were defined as having visual acuity of 20/70 or less, visual loss established before school age, and no other functional disability. No differences in adjustment were found among the three groups using seven basic adjustment measures. There was a tendency for adjustment difficulties to be associated with the partially seeing, although no significant differences were found between groups divided according to severity of visual loss. The researchers concluded that "*any prior beliefs about inevitable contingencies between visual disability and maladjustment are severely challenged by the findings of the present investigation"* (Cowen and others, 1961, p. 176).

Sommers (1944), using the California Personality Test, questionnaires, and case studies, found five patterns of parental reaction to their 143 educationally blind adolescent children; (1) acceptance, (2) denial, (3) overprotectiveness, (4) overt rejection, and (5) disguised rejection. Frustrating attitudes were formed when blindness was considered as a symbol of punishment, a result of social disease of the parent, a result of negligence, or a personal disgrace. The subjects showed six patterns of adjustive reactions which were closely related to the parental reactions. Since no consistent behavior deviations were found among the group, it was concluded that adjustment must be related to factors other than blindness.

The results of the illustrative studies of personal adjustment generally indicate that adjustment must be related to factors other than the physical anomaly causing loss of vision. A more significant factor that can cause maladjustment is a result of negative self-concepts imposed upon the visually impaired child by attitudes of seeing persons in his home, school, and community.

Kim (1970) hypothesized that the force that drove visually impaired people to form their own institutions comes from the opposition of the sighted majority group to integration. Using six attitude scales in interviews with 85 visually impaired persons from ages 20 to 75, it was found that the partially seeing person did not identify with the community of the "blind" as intensively as did severely visually impaired persons. He noted that the higher the status of the position attained by the subject in his community, the less firmly the subject identified with the "blind" community. A major finding was that the more negatively the visually impaired person perceived the attitudes of the seeing toward the "blind," the more strongly he identified with the "blind" community.

The standards of conduct which visually impaired persons receive from their primary social environment effectively contribute to their role performance. Lukoff and Whiteman (1970), using interviews of 498 legally blind persons (relatively few subjects were totally blind or had only light perception), found that variance in expectations for independence depended on such variables as education, intelligence, sex, residual vision, social class, and parental attitudes. Visually impaired persons with dependent self-standards were likely to adapt to whatever expectations they encountered, whereas independently oriented visually impaired persons were likely to defy dependent expectations. The children who attended special schools tended to choose visually impaired friends after leaving school, regardless of the degree of their remaining vision and age of onset of their impairment. It was concluded that attendance at residential schools was the most important discriminating factor influencing the social role and lifelong patterns of the children.

Bauman (1964) compared a group of 150 boys and girls attending residential schools to an equal number attending integrated classes using a self-report personality inventory. She found differences according to degree of remaining useful vision, type of school setting, and sex. The moderately visually impaired adolescents showed significantly higher anxiety and insecurity than the severely visually impaired. The residential school subjects were higher in anxiety and insecurity, in difficulties related to the home and parents, and in problems of social and emotional adjustment than the integrated group. It may be safely concluded that more research is needed before definite conclusions can be drawn about the direct effects of the residential school environment upon the emotional development of the students. However, the results of the illustrative studies by Bauman and by Whiteman and Lukoff certainly raise questions concerning the impact of special school experience upon social and emotional characteristics of visually impaired children.

The social adjustment of visually impaired children has been studied to determine if a relation exists between social acceptance and degree of remaining useful vision. Bateman's (1964) study, using teacher evaluations for a group of 259 partially seeing children in special classes and resource rooms, found that the moderate-defect group (visual acuity 20/70-20/200) was found to be the lowest in social acceptance and the severe-defect group (20/200) the best accepted of the three groups rated on a severity-of-visual-loss scale. However, Bateman and Wetherell (1967) used questionnaire responses from 31 teachers of 297 partially seeing children from grades one through twelve. The mildly impaired tended to show higher adjustment than the severely impaired, though both were rated higher than the moderately impaired group. Although social adjustment was significantly related to intelligence, no significant relations were found between vision and social adjustment. Spivey (1967), using sociometric techniques with 57 integrated classes, each containing a visually handicapped child, found that moderately impaired children were less well accepted than severely impaired children. Research has failed to show the cause of the apparently lower social acceptance of moderately impaired children. It is sometimes hypothesized that children with moderate impairments function as borderline individuals. They function as seeing children in the classroom reading print materials, but they function on the playground as visually impaired children, unable to participate competently in games requiring normal vision. The resulting inability to meet the expectations of seeing children causes lowered social acceptance of the moderately impaired children.

Visually impaired children may be physically integrated but socially segregated in the classroom because of negative stereotypical attitudes of their seeing peers. Gowman (1957) used a questionnaire to explore attitudes of high school seniors toward blindness. A comparison with other impairments revealed that blindness was considered the most difficult handicap to accept, either for oneself or one's prospective mate. Jones, Gottfried, and Owens (1966), using a social-distance scale in seven interpersonal situations, reported that severely visually impaired individuals were among the least well accepted of 12 groups of exceptional children by 186 high school students, whereas the partially seeing children were generally among the higher groups on the acceptance scale. However, definitions of exceptional children were not given to the subjects, and no information was compiled concerning the previous experience of the subjects with exceptional children in this small midwestern community. Stereotypes directed toward visually impaired children may result in extensive social adjustment problems and sometimes may induce negative self-regarding attitudes in visually impaired children.

Stereotypical attitudes toward blindness can be improved. Bateman (1962, 1964) explored factors that would produce a more positive attitude. It was found that seeing children who had known and attended school with visually impaired children were more positive in their appraisal of the abilities of the visually impaired than those lacking experience with these children. It was also found that personal contact with visually impaired persons failed to affect the sighted adult's perceptions of abilities of the visually impaired. However, information-giving techniques increased the positiveness of their attitudes. The educational implications of the studies by Bateman are: (1) integration of visually impaired children is needed to develop more positive attitudes among seeing children toward their visually impaired peers; and (2) inservice programs designed to give information about the abilities of visually impaired children are needed to develop more positive attitudes among teachers in the integrated schools.

Vignette 8.1 John

John is enrolled in the fifth grade in a small rural school system. His visual acuity has been evaluated as light projection from congenital cataracts, but he is normal in other respects. His parents are very accepting of the impairment. Two of his siblings have the same condition. John enjoys playing outside his mountain cabin with his brothers and sisters. He rides the horse, climbs trees, and swims in a nearby pond. John is helpful to his mother in pouring milk, setting the table, and washing dishes. He also helps his father with such chores as feeding the hogs, digging potatoes, and milking the cows. At school John is able to type his class assignments, but he has considerable difficulty in writing his own name with a pencil. Although he cannot play basketball very well, he enjoys games like tug-of-war, hide-and-seek, kick-ball, and wrestling with his sighted classmates. John easily learned to ride a bike across an open field and roller skate on the sidewalks of school. Although John's vision is deficient, he appears to have gained a relatively high degree of independence even without the aid of a special teacher.

Much of the research on attitudes has tended to confirm earlier beliefs concerning stereotypes and attitudes of the sighted toward those who are visually impaired. Few studies have been reported in which attempts were made to change attitudes toward severely visually impaired and partially seeing children. One of the major problems in the education of children with visual impairments continues to be the social effects of sightlessness. The social consequences derived from stereotypes and the reactions of visually handicapped persons to them constitutes an important area to be considered by all professional personnel who deal with visually impaired children. The most hopeful sign of a breakthrough in earlier beliefs is the trend toward increased integration of children with visual impairments with normally seeing children.

If any general conclusions can be reached in regard to the relation between visual impairment and personal or social adjustment, it is believed that the development of more wholesome attitudes toward the handicap by the parent, school, and community would effect a more satisfactory development of the personality of the visually impaired child. It is also thought that society's negative reaction to blindness as well as the social-adjustment problems of children with moderate visual impairments may result from the frustrations caused by expecting these children to perform visual tasks that are too difficult for them.

EDUCATIONAL PROCEDURES

Historical Background

The first programs for educationally blind children began in residential schools in Europe about 200 years ago. French (1932) gives an account of the first residential school started by Valentin Hauy in Paris in 1784. Residential schools in the United States enrolled their first pupils in 1832.

Howe (1965) advocated that residential schools reject all children who could be taught in "common schools." He especially believed that "seeing blind" or partially seeing children do not belong in a school for the blind and that they should attend the common schools and "learn what they could."

Day school programs for the educationally blind in the United States began in 1900 in Chicago, and in 1913, the first special class for partially seeing children was established in Roxbury, Massachusetts (Hathaway, 1966). The first local day school programs were generally set up as special classes with very little integration of visually impaired with sighted children.

Extent and Types of Special Education Services

School Programs

Five types of administrative plans have been implemented for children with visual impairments. In recent years a sixth type has gained increasing recognition, popularly called the teacher-consultant plan. The plans are usually flexible and vary in structure depending largely on the philosophy and the needs of the local school system. Most programs employ teachers prepared to serve both educationally blind and partially seeing children. Some programs separate educationally blind from partially seeing children while others incorporate visually impaired pupils with children having other impairments. The plans are listed in order of degree of integration, with the most integrated programs listed first.

1. The *teacher-consultant* plan enables children to enroll in the regular classes in schools near their homes with provision of direct or indirect services as needed by a teacher consultant.

2. The *itinerant-teacher* plan is similar to the teacher-consultant plan in organization, but the itinerant teacher gives more time to individual instruction and less time to indirect services than the teacher consultant.

3. The *resource-room or resource-teacher* plan is an organizational pattern in which children do virtually all of their work within the regular class, but go to the resource teacher in a special room for help and materials as the need arises.

4. The *cooperative class* is an organizational pattern in which children are registered with the special teacher but attend regular classes during a sizable portion of each day.

5. The *special class* is organized as a separate unit in which children are instructed by the special teacher throughout the school day in a self-contained room.

6. The *residential school* plan provides a complete educational program with residential facilities for children.

The changing nature of the population of visually impaired pupils attending residential schools has been most notable in recent years. An increase in numbers of multiply handicapped children in residential schools has occurred. An increase of 29 percent was reported for the three-year period from 1966 to 1969 by Nolan and Bott (1971). If the trend continues, residential schools will increasingly serve a large proportion of visually impaired pupils with accompanying impairments.

At one time Lowenfeld (1959) advocated services of the residential school for four groups of pupils: (1) the multiply impaired; (2) children without local services; (3) children from broken homes; and (4) children whose parents prefer a residential school. Later Lowenfeld (1969), reporting in a study of multiply impaired blind children in California, recommended that as many "normal" visually impaired children as possible be placed in day schools. The child without local services could be served by cooperation of adjoining counties to provide local school services. Foster home placement in a community with local provisions for visually impaired children was recommended for the children from broken homes. The parents preferring a residential school should be assisted in placing their children in local schools. Residential services, including a diagnostic center, training and adjustment centers, guidance, and counseling services for the parents were recommended for multiply impaired children with vision defects.

The residential school is often a part of a state-wide cooperating plan designed to provide services from both residential and local public schools according to indivdual needs of the children. For example, New Jersey provides services for its visually impaired children primarily in regular schools, but supplements these services by utilizing residential school provisions in other states. Oregon provides a cooperative plan between day and residential schools within the state. Children may obtain the basic skills in the residential school and later enroll in local day school programs where continued special services are available. Some residential schools provide boarding facilities for visually impaired children who are integrated in special academic and vocational classes in local public school programs. Many states (such as California) are redesigning the residential school programs for visually impaired children to meet the needs of the multiply impaired population.

Certain recommendations are made in regard to choice of an administrative plan:

1. Flexibility of services on a continuum basis is needed to provide for the individual needs of the children. Some children may operate from the beginning quite independently, needing very little assistance except for special aids and materials. Other children may need very specialized services in a self-contained unit for a period of time until they can move out to a more integrated environment. The children with severe multiple impairments may need long-term placement in a special class.

2. Labeling of children should be avoided regardless of the amount of specialized services needed.

3. Administrative plans are not as important as the content of the total program and methods of instruction and adequacy of the teaching staff.

4. Innovations in administrative plans, based on the needs of the children, the philosophy of the local school program, and the nature of the community, should be attempted.

The prevalence of children with visual disorders within a community should be considered. Arrangements in a large metropolitan area will differ from those in a small rural setting. One of the most important goals of special education for visually impaired children is the adequate preparation of as many children as possible for integration into the general school program and into the community where they will be participating as adults.

Although the value of integrated education of children with visual disorders was stressed by Howe (1965) in 1865 and by the American Foundation for the Blind in 1954 in the Pine Brook report (AFB, 1954), surveys in recent years have indicated that segregated education in the public schools is still widespread for many visually impaired children. Birch and others (1966) found that a large proportion of their partially seeing subjects in the elementary grades were enrolled in full-time special classes in a national study involving large-type readers. Forty-four percent of the children were in special classes, 33 percent in resource rooms, and 19 percent in itinerant programs. However, the smaller local programs were omitted in the sample. The more segregated classes were selected largely because of ease in administration of the tests.

One of the most surprising results of this study was that in spite of recommendations cited the intelligence of the group was average, and a very small percentage of multiple impairments was reported by the teachers. The results indicated that many partially seeing children with no accompanying disability were being segregated from the mainstream of general education.

Jones and Collins (1966) noted a trend toward more complete integration of visually impaired children in regular public classes and more provision for multiply impaired children in local and residential school programs. More local school programs had initiated itinerant-teacher organizational patterns than any other type of plan. Only 16 percent of local public school systems in the nation used the full-time special class plan for partially seeing children. The reported increase in provisions for multiply impaired children may require segregated classes for those who are low functioning and are unable to make satisfactory progress in a regular classroom. With the reported increase in functional and flexible pupil placement, children should be able to move from segregated to more integrated plans according to their abilities and needs (see Chapter 1).

Vignette 8.2 Lydia

Lydia has been having problems in communication because of combination hearing and visual impairments. She is now 14 years old with a mental age of about 12.0 and loss of vision from hyperopia. She is bused across town to a school containing several classes of children with hearing impairments. An itinerant teacher of visually impaired children is helping her in typing lessons for two periods each week. Lydia's scores on an achievement test place her at the second-grade level in reading, spelling, and arithmetic. Since she has difficulty in understanding speech sounds, she seldom participates in social activities outside her home. She has learned to use the manual alphabet quite effectively with her mother, although its use is generally discouraged at school.

Lydia complains of headaches, has a limited attention span, and often is noted to be gazing out the window. She reads work on the chalkboard or bulletin board quite readily, but she tires very easily of reading books, flash cards, or any other kind of printed materials.

The efficacy of special classes for partially seeing or educationally blind children has really never been tested. It seems that visually impaired children with normal or above intelligence, with no additional impairments, should be able to function adequately in regular classes without need of special rooms. Such questions as the following need to be answered: When are special classes really needed for the children with visual disabilities? Why are partially seeing and educationally blind served in separate classes? Why are partially seeing and educationally blind children with below average IQ excluded from special classes for visually impaired children?

Preschool Programs

The importance of preschool provisions for children with visual disorders cannot be overemphasized. The increasing interest in the early identification and education of visually handicapped children, as shown by research, is encouraging. The research of Norris, Spaulding, and Brodie (1957) indicated that retardation need not necessarily accompany a visual handicap if adequate social and environmental experiences are provided. A positive parental attitude is especially important in securing the kind of environment that will allow, encourage, and provide the child opportunities to develop as normally as possible.

The following suggestions are presented to parents and teachers for helping children minimize visual problems:

1. *Take full advantage of professional services.* Many communities provide professional services which should serve to strengthen the relation between the parents and the child and give the parents information and skill that would enable them to meet the child's special needs. Examples of such services include diagnostic and counseling clinics in medical and educational centers, home counseling programs, special and integrated preschool programs, and parent institutes. If possible, visually impaired children should be enrolled in a regular nursery program to provide experience with normal children.

2. *Obtain books and articles that have been published for parents of preschool visually impaired children.* Lowenfeld's (1971) *Our Blind Children* is primarily addressed to parents, with advice regarding such practical matters as learning to eat, toilet training, sleeping habits, learning to dress, learning to walk, and learning to talk. Buktenica (1968) made suggestions for parents on visual discrimination, visual-motor development, figure-ground perception, spatial relations, and perceptual constancy. Halliday (1970) developed a booklet for parents and teachers for visually impaired children of preschool age. Her booklet includes (1) a description of the specific needs of visually impaired children; (2) an outline of special helps needed by visually handicapped children to circumvent or minimize their visual problems; (3) an outline of the developmental sequences through which children pass before admission to a formal school program; and (4) a list and description of educational materials especially suited for visually handicapped children in the early developmental sequences.

3. *Stimulate the child to use his remaining senses, including any remaining vision.* Stimulation through the remaining senses can enhance language and communication development, physical development, mobility skills, and

social development. Provide rich, stimulating, concrete experiences, such as trips to the grocery store, farm, pet shop, and other places in the community. Encourage the child to explore in the kitchen, garage, or attic at home.

The major areas of development which require special attention for pre-school visually impaired children are (1) language development (especially concept development); (2) orientation and mobility; (3) self-help skills (toileting, eating, dressing); (4) social and emotional development; and (5) physical development. Progress in any of these areas requires effective use of the remaining sensory modalities.

Adaptations of Curriculum, Media, Methods, and Materials

Some educators believe that the curriculum and methods of instruction for visually impaired children are the same as those for seeing children and that only the media differ. Others think that differences are so great that segregated classes and schools are necessary for children with visual disorders to function properly. Neither extreme is true. A media difference is evident from the necessity of providing large-type, braille, and audio materials. A curriculum difference is illustrated by the need for orientation and mobility and for daily living skills by children with little remaining useful vision. In addition, adaptations of general educational methods and provisions of special aids and equipment in areas such as mathematics and science are necessary for some visually impaired children to function effectively in coping with their physical and social environment.

If a child with a visual disability gains a knowledge of his environment, he will naturally depend on the information received through his sense organs —the visual, tactual, kinesthetic, auditory, olfactory, and gustatory stimuli. If he were to depend upon the visually oriented learning materials and activities designed for sighted children, he would obviously be deficient in achieving this goal. He would need to learn to utilize effectively any remaining vision to gain information from visual stimuli. Sight-utilization procedures enable the visually impaired child to gain a knowledge of his environment through maximum use of his remaining visual modality.

Sight Utilization

Most visually impaired children have enough remaining vision to read ink print. In recent years, medical specialists have increasingly emphasized the importance of using vision rather than saving it. The barriers to use of vision of partially seeing children have largely come from the myth that use of the eyes would tend to cause further damage, whereas limited use would save the vision and protect the child from further loss. Actually, effective use of the visual sense for interpreting visual stimuli is learned by use.

Jones (1961) noted that 92 percent of children with 20/200 vision in local schools read print while only 50 percent did so in residential schools. Nolan and Bott (1971) found that the proportions of legally blind registered at the American Printing House for the Blind had decreased in residential schools. However, braille students outnumbered the large-print readers by about two to one in the residential school programs, but the print users outnumbered the braille users by about two and a half to one in local day school programs. The overall percentage of students using ink print (regular type) increased from 11 percent in 1966 to 16 percent in 1969. If the present trend continues, a higher percentage of children will be integrated into local school programs and a higher percentage of legally blind children will be reading large print and regular print materials.

Research has indicated that even very low-vision children can learn to use their vision more efficiently through training in recognition and discrimination. Low-vision children are children with very limited visual acuity, usually defined as less than 5/200.

Barraga (1964) studied the effects of specialized instruction on the visual behavior of children using 10 matched pairs of visually impaired children with low vision (6/200 or less). The experimental group received 30 hours of intensive and individualized teaching using a progressive sequence of lessons for visual discrimination proceeding from tactual and visual stimulation of geometric forms to visual stimulation for discrimination of word symbols. Substantial gains were found in the ability to use remaining vision on a discrimination test among children in the experimental group. Ashcroft, Halliday, and Barraga (1965) replicated the study with 41 children, confirmed the previous results, and recommended a treatment for use with low-vision children. It should be noted that no increase in visual acuity was found in the studies. Reactions of teachers indicated that the children gained increased confidence in their ability to use their remaining vision. This research information has been disseminated through teacher-training programs, special in-service workshops, and special teaching aids provided through federally sponsored special education instructional materials centers.

Print Reading

Seeing is affected by factors such as (1) brightness, (2) size of image, (3) contrast, (4) time, and (5) distance. Generally, if any of these factors is increased beyond the minimum required to make vision possible, seeing becomes easier.

1. *Brightness* or proper illumination is one of the most important factors in helping visually impaired children to be successful in visual tasks. To be effective, lighting must be of the proper quantity and quality and yet be variable to meet individual needs of the children. Some children will be able to see better with a decrease of normal lighting. For example, children with albinism are particularly sensitive to high levels of illumination. Children with myopia usually profit from a much higher degree of illumination for tasks requiring visual discrimination. Glare can be reduced by using shielding

devices such as blinds or shades and by using pastel-colored paints with proper reflectance values. Proper seating in the regular classroom can help by placing children away from glare that may be present near the windows. The teacher should stand and sit in positions which direct pupils' vision away from the windows. No pupil should face a window or work in his own shadow. Portable bulletin boards and classroom furniture can be used to shield the light-sensitive child from uncomfortable intensities of illumination. The minimum intensity of lighting varies among individuals and among visual tasks. For example, activities such as typing, sewing, drafting, and speech-reading usually require lighting of higher intensity than activities such as playing games, walking through a corridor, or eating lunch. Recommended minimum lighting levels in schools can be obtained from the Illuminating Engineering Society or the National Society for the Prevention of Blindness.

2. The *size of image* or size of print symbols is certainly important to children with visual disorders. Birch and others (1966), studying the effects of type size on achievement of partially seeing children, found that one fifth of the group earned their highest test scores in each of the five type sizes. The type size needed by visually impaired children will vary according to the individual eye problem. Standards have been set by the National Accreditation Council (1970) for a minimum type size of 16 points. The most popular type size is 18 points, and examples range up to 30 points (see Fig. 8.4). Books in large type may be obtained using original typesetting or photo enlargement from the American Printing House for the Blind or a number of private publishers. Day school programs needing small numbers of large-print books often use microfilm duplication and enlargement services or hand production using volunteer typists at large-print typewriters.

Optical-aids magnification is very useful and more versatile than large-print production to many visually impaired children. Spectacles and hand magnifiers are more common examples of arrangements for enlarging the retinal image of the child. More complex arrangements such as mounted magnifiers, telescopic lenses, and projection magnifiers are sometimes used. Closed circuit television has been used for magnification of regular print. A manual developed by Sloan (1971) catalogs the findings of a 10-year study of optical aids, including clip-on reading lenses, distance magnifiers, and testing equipment (see Fig. 8.5). Gibbons (1963) reported on the use of low-vision aids among 500 low-vision persons in 40 clinics. Thirty-five percent of the subjects showed significant improvement in vision and continued to use their special lenses. Robertson (1963) described a survey of 42 low-vision clinics and indicated that more than half of the examined children received optical aids and that preschool children were seen in a majority of the clinics. Although low-vision lenses enable many visually impaired people to read print, the reading field is reduced and the reading distance is usually much less than the normal distance for reading.

The amount of *contrast* between an object and its background is also a factor in the visual task. Contrast depends on the relation of the reflectances

14 Point Type

Few parents realize that during the progress of these
diseases the eyes of the patient may develop serious

18 Point Type

Few parents realize that during the progress of these diseases the eyes of the patient

24 Point Type

Few parents realize that during the
progress of these diseases the eyes of

30 Point Type

Few parents realize that during the progress of the

FIGURE 8.4 Examples of large type sizes set in Baskerville.

of an object and its background—the greater the contrast, the more easily the object is seen. Nolan (1961) stated that black on white or white on black offered the greatest contrast for partially seeing children, although buff-colored paper was preferred by teachers because of less glare. The frustration of many visually impaired children could be avoided by duplicating tests and instructional materials in black on white rather than using a light blue or green ink on poor-quality paper. Chalkboards offer much more contrast when clean and in good repair. Fiber-tipped pens with black ink are often used for better contrast. Unglazed cream-colored paper with light green lines three fourths to one inch apart and soft heavy lead pencils are used with young children learning to write.

4. *Time* is an important factor in seeing for visually limited children. The fact that more time is required for low-vision children is recognized by extension of time limits on standardized tests. More time is needed because the field of vision is usually small and frequent eye rest periods are needed for some pupils. Birch and others (1966) found that fatigue, the need for rest

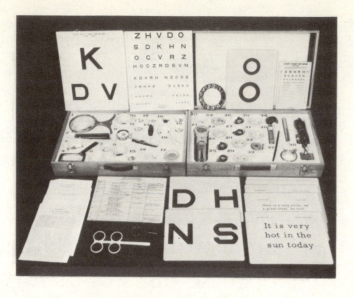

FIGURE 8.5 Test kit containing essential equipment for prescribing reading aids. From Louise L. Sloan, Recommended aids for the partially seeing. New York: National Society for the Prevention of Blindness, Inc., 1971. Courtesy of the Society.

periods, and restriction in eye use were the most educationally significant attributes of partially seeing children. The time required for discrimination of shapes and details will vary among pupils. The photochemical processes in the retina require time. If there is enough time, small details may be seen under rather low light levels that could not be seen with too short exposure. An analogy is the time-exposure picture made with a camera.

5. *Distance* is a factor in seeing that should be considered in providing an enlarged image for visually impaired children. The child can be moved closer to the front of the room, chalkboard, or screen in order to see more effectively. A book can be brought closer to the eye without doing any harm when enlargement is necessary. Even with the best lighting, optical magnification, contrast, and plenty of time, some very low-vision pupils may need to move the book much closer to the eye than the normal distance of 14 inches, and should be encouraged to do so. Correct posture and physical comfort can be enhanced by placing reading materials on special adjustable desks, easels, and book or copy stands.

Braille Reading

Braille was developed in 1829 by Louis Braille as an improvement for raised-line lettering, which was first used in embossing materials for the blind. Braille is a system of touch reading for those unable to see well enough to read print. It employs embossed dots arranged in quadrangular spaces

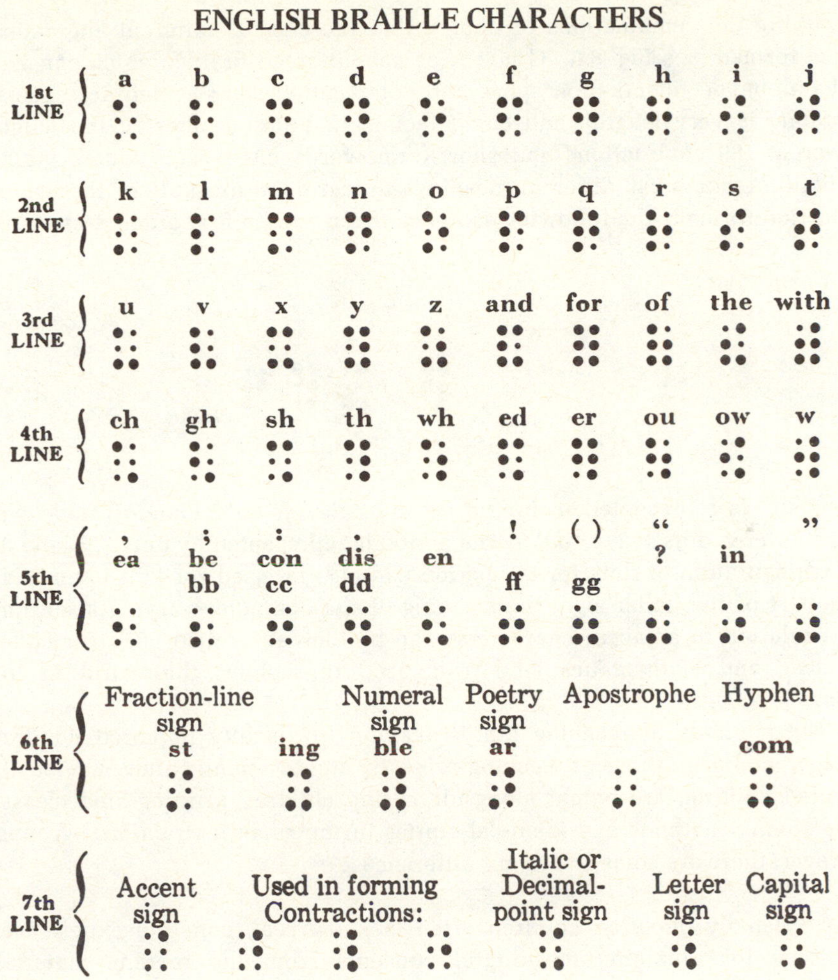

ENGLISH BRAILLE CHARACTERS

	a	b	c	d	e	f	g	h	i	j
1st LINE										

	k	l	m	n	o	p	q	r	s	t
2nd LINE										

	u	v	x	y	z	and	for	of	the	with
3rd LINE										

	ch	gh	sh	th	wh	ed	er	ou	ow	w
4th LINE										

	,	;	:	.		!	( )	" ?	_	"
5th LINE	ea	be	con	dis	en				in	
		bb	cc	dd		ff	gg			

	Fraction-line sign			Numeral sign	Poetry sign	Apostrophe		Hyphen	
6th LINE	st		ing	ble	ar			com	

	Accent sign	Used in forming Contractions:			Italic or Decimal-point sign	Letter sign	Capital sign
7th LINE							

FIGURE 8.6 Standard English Braille, Grade II.

called cells. Each cell contains space for six dots, three dots high and two dots wide. For convenience in describing the braille characters, the raised dot positions are numbered on the left downward 1, 2, 3 and on the right downward 4, 5, 6:

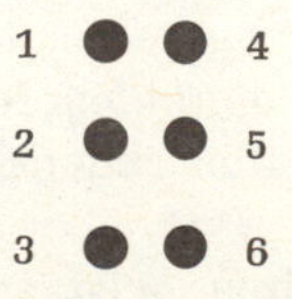

By varying the combinations of dots within the cell, 63 different characters can be formed (see Fig. 8.6). Grade 1, or uncontracted braille, which consists of the alphabet, punctuation signs, and composition signs which are special to braille, is very lengthy and cumbersome. In order to shorten the length of words, 189 contractions and short-form words have been added, giving the braille readers 246 different meanings to learn. An example of the use of contracted forms is the following sentence taken from a first grade preprimer:

I can go up.

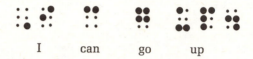

I   can   go   up

"Can" is represented in braille by the letter *c*, dots 1 and 4, and "go" by the letter *g*, dots 1, 2, 4, and 5. The period is represented by dots 2, 5, and 6. The configuration of dots for the period can also be used for "dis" and "dd" or as part of the dollar sign, the meaning of the character varying according to its relation to adjacent characters. The braille cell is also used for codes in music and mathematics, and it is used throughout the world in the various languages.

The methods of teaching braille reading to visually impaired children are very similar to those of teaching print reading to seeing children. Visually impaired children are taught alongside seeing children in integrated classes using similar methods and identical stories in the same instructional groups. However, there are some important differences:

1. Visually impaired children often lack the real, concrete experiences necessary for obtaining meaningful concepts from the reading material. A teacher may be surprised to learn that Johnny hasn't yet seen a bird, but she wants Johnny to read a story about a bird. The resourceful teacher will learn to supplement the experiential background of the child by bringing in objects to the classroom or taking the child out to the objects. For example, Helen Keller learned botany from her teacher while sitting in a tree. Language development may often be retarded in visually impaired children because of deprivation in preschool years due to lack of experience.

2. Visually impaired children need tactual-readiness materials just as seeing children need visual-readiness materials. Tactual understimulation may have occurred before the child reaches school. The material used to teach reading to visually impaired children usually consists of embossed copies of the material used for sighted children. The visual emphasis of the primary reading series provides a problem for the visually impaired child who cannot see the pictures and illustrations referred to in the stories and exercises.

3. Visually impaired children need activities to develop gross motor

tasks before moving to fine motor tasks such as the discrimination of braille dots.

4. Recent research (cited below) indicates that whole-word reading is not characteristic of braille readers, and the perceptual unit in word recognition is the braille cell. A synthetic approach may be more appropriate for visually impaired children than the analytic approach which is used with sighted readers.

Contrasting methods of teaching braille reading to visually impaired children have been found by researchers. Lowenfeld, Abel, and Hatlen (1969) found that approximately two thirds of the teachers in local and residential schools began teaching reading using the word or sentence method, whereas one third of the teachers began with the braille alphabet. Maxfield (1928) advocated using the word method rather than the letter or letter-word method. She favored phonetic training for visually impaired children, saying that visually impaired children must build up the whole from the observation of the parts. However, new evidence suggests a different approach. The most important result of a series of nine studies by Nolan and Kederis (1969) indicated that the braille character is the perceptual unit in reading and that word recognition is the result of step-by-step (sequential) integration of information from the individual characters (C-A-T reads cat). The principle evidence for this conclusion came from the finding that the recognition of braille words requires 16–96 percent more time than the sums of the times required to recognize the individual characters. Harley and Rawls (1970) found that phonemic braille could be used successfully with beginning braille readers. Braille characters were assigned to 44 sound symbols which were used to make up the phonemic code. The subjects using the phonemic braille made the transition to Grade 2 braille by the end of the academic year. A comparison of Grade 1, Grade 2, and the phonemic approach is shown in Table 8.2.

TABLE 8.2 A Comparison of Grade 1, Grade 2, and a Phonemic Braille

Total Signs	
	Grade 1
46	The foundation of the fountain is really very strong.
	Grade 2
26	The foundation of the fountain is really very strong.
	Phonemic[a]
34	The foundation of the fountain is really very strong.

[a]The curved line under groups of letters indicates substitution of a braille symbol.

In order to conserve space, braille symbols have been assigned multiple meanings which depend on position within the braille cell and on the context of the symbol in the reading material. Contractions may stand for from two to five letters. Abbreviations and symbols for whole words add to the complexity of the problem.

The first research in braille reading was related to the mechanics for tactile reading. Burklen (1932), in studying the mechanics for touch reading, found that the vertical arrangement of six dots is the best condition for touch reading. He found that the index fingers of both hands are the most predominantly used reading fingers. Good readers use little up-and-down motion, exert slight and uniform pressure, and read with both hands. Maxfield (1928), in the first book dealing with methods of teaching braille reading, stressed such things as relaxation; correct posture; light pressure of the fingers; use of both hands; a minimum of up-and-down movement of the finger tips; acute angle of the fingers with the book; and encouragement to use hands independently while moving from line to line.

Touch reading is slow and this slowness has helped to retard braille readers in their educational progress. Henderson (1966), using subjects from grades three through six, found that special instruction increasing the speed and accuracy of recognition of the braille code increased the efficiency of the total reading process. Umsted (1970) obtained similar results with high school subjects. The implications point to the need for individualized instruction to improve the efficiency of braille readers at both elementary and high school levels.

Another problem in braille reading occurs when the visually impaired child is introduced to contractions and short forms too rapidly. Rex (1970) noted that the majority of signs, abbreviations, and contractions of standard English braille were employed in the reading vocabularies of children in the first grade. Special reading materials based on a systematic introduction of contractions using the principles of linear programed instruction were developed. Special braille reading materials can also be developed according to the experiential background of each child whose visual limitations eliminate print reading. A number of teachers use the experience approach in teaching reading to visually impaired children, developing experience charts and homemade books based on field trips and learning experiences of their children.

Vignette 8.3 Sallie

Sallie is an 11-year-old girl with congenital loss of all useful vision from retrolental fibroplasia. Her father, an insurance salesman, moved his family to the community of a residential school for visually impaired children in order that Sallie could become a day pupil. Sallie's verbal IQ of 87 is indicative of her intellectual functioning in school for the past five years.

Sallie's teacher found that Sallie could not identify many items which she could define quite readily. For example, a fish hook was defined as something to put in the water to catch fish, but Sallie identified a fish hook as a safety pin. Sallie related that a chicken is a farm animal which lays eggs, but she identified a chicken as a cat. She said that a saw is used to cut down a tree, but she mistook a saw for a knife. She could not identify many other objects such as violin, rabbit, apron, rice, hoe, or kite. However, she was able to discuss these words quite readily when they appeared in her reading book.

Touch reading is limited by the amount of material that can be made available in embossed form. The cost of production of small quantities and the storage space needed for large books are problems that limit the quantity of books that can be transcribed into braille. A vest pocket dictionary requires six to seven thick volumes with pages much larger than the pages of a regular print book. Day school teachers may spend a large part of their time obtaining embossed copies of books, tests, and other reading materials needed by the child in the regular classroom.

Technological advances may help to solve many of these problems. The Optacon (Bliss and Crane, 1969) is a portable electronic device with a small camera that converts print materials to vibrating letter images through a photochemical- to mechanical-energy–conversion process. The visually impaired person slides a small probe containing photocells across the printed page with one hand and reads the vibrating reed letters by a finger on the other hand. The photocell signals are used to drive circuits which activate the tactile stimulators. The major difficulty has been the inability to gain speed in reading. Although this instrument is still experimental, it offers hope for overcoming dependence on sighted readers and volunteers to transcribe special materials from print into braille.

Listening Skills

A recent trend of special educational programs for children with visual disorders is the increasing emphasis on listening as a means of providing information about the environment. The development of listening skills begins in infancy when sound localization enables the child to explore his environment and when sound interpretation helps him to understand speech. It continues into school age and adulthood when listening provides a means of increasing learning efficiency through substitution and supplementation of embossed and large-type reading materials.

Listening has recently gained more recognition for school-age visually impaired children and youth because of the increased learning efficiency of listening over large-type and braille reading materials. Nolan (1959) reported that children in grades four to twelve, using large print, had a reading rate of about 100 words per minute, less than half the rate of their seeing peers. Talking Books and other recorded material provide speeds of about 180–200 words per minute. Nolan (1963) compared learning through listening with learning through braille reading using braille-reading subjects from grades six to ten. It was found that information could be obtained through listening in one third of the braille-reading time without loss of comprehension. Morris (1966) summarized the results of a media study involving 1,152 legally blind subjects from grades four, five, six, and high school. Amounts learned were expressed in terms of time required to listen or read in braille or large type. It was noted that learning through listening appeared to be 155–360 percent more efficient than learning through reading in braille or large type.

An extensive programmatic research study of aural systems for the visually handicapped has been undertaken at the American Printing House for the Blind to study the process of learning through listening and to develop a system—playback equipment, textbook formats, and study techniques—designed for this purpose. Among the general findings have been that children with low braille or enlarged-print reading speed and comprehension can profit more from listening than children with high braille-reading speed and comprehension. Message length has not yet been shown to affect comprehension. No difference has been found between learning from massed or distributed practice for easy or difficult material for high school students (Nolan and Morris, 1969).

Listening has utility for the following visually impaired groups:

1. Visually impaired adults. Library of Congress circulation indicates that listening materials are by far the most popular for the adults who lose vision in adulthood and therefore have not acquired effective braille-reading skills.

2. Visually impaired college students. Readers, talking books, and tape recorders are needed by college students. Braille and large-print copies of college texts are almost nonexistent, and information processing is much faster with listening.

3. Visually impaired slow-learning children. Nolan and Kederis (1969) recommended listening over braille reading for pupils below an IQ of 85.

4. Visually impaired school-age pupils. Listening is generally more efficient than either braille or large-print reading. (An exception would be mathematical and scientific materials employing formulas and tables; they may be easier to comprehend in braille or large print.)

5. Children and adults with visual perceptual disorders. The Library of Congress now loans listening materials to people who are unable to read conventional print materials because of physical limitations or learning disabilities.

The improvement of listening comprehension of partially seeing children can be accomplished by special instruction. Bischoff (1967) divided 63 partially seeing pupils from grades four through nine into two experimental groups and one control group. Each experimental group received two 15-minute listening lessons per week for 10 weeks, one from My Weekly Reader Listening Comprehension Paragraphs and the other from SRA Listening Lessons. The experimental group which received listening-comprehension lessons increased in listening efficiency, but the control group actually showed a decrease. Teachers should become aware that listening efficiency could be improved by instruction and that with increased listening efficiency recorded materials could better supplement reading materials in the classroom.

The speed of information processing attained by listening at approximately 175 words a minute is relatively slow when considering the speed of reading attained by high school and college students. For this reason much effort has been focused on increasing the speed of aural materials. Accelerated or compressed speech can be used to speed up information processing by listening. Popular methods of accelerating speech include (1) speaking rapidly, (2) increasing the playback speed of tape or record, and (3) sampling segments of the speech signal. Speaking rapidly is limited, since only a moderate increase in rate of articulation of speech sound by the speaker is possible. Increasing the speed of a tape or record results in a higher pitch, making intelligibility difficult at high speeds. A speech compressor has been developed that electronically returns the pitch to the original range. (See Fig. 8.7). An electromechanical apparatus can be used to reproduce periodic samples of a recorded tape. The unreproduced samples are short enough so that a discarded sample cannot contain an entire speech sound. Speech compression is limited if it eliminates periodically and unselectively, thereby discarding parts of critical consonants as well as longer vowel sounds. A speech compressor has been devised that selectively shortens pauses and vowel sounds while retaining consonant sounds in their true duration.

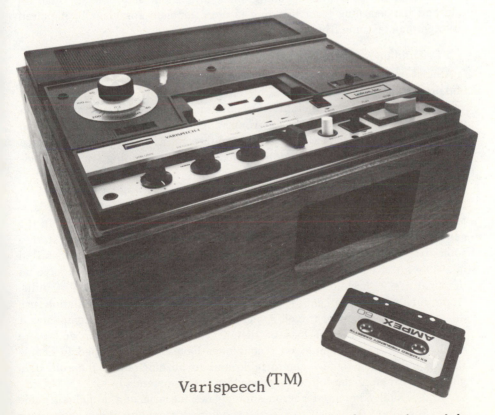

Varispeech(TM)

FIGURE 8.7 Varispeech-I, a time compression tape recorder manufactured by Lexicon, Inc., of Waltham, Massachusetts.

The research studies have been concerned primarily with intelligibility and comprehension of accelerated speech materials produced by various methods and the characteristics and training of the listeners. For example, compression beyond 275 words per minute has resulted in a sharp decline in retention of information (Foulke, 1966). Nolan and Morris (1969) reported that high school students learned significantly more at 175 words per minute than at 225 words per minute. Foulke found no statistically significant difference in favor of either the speech sampling of the speed-changing method in an experiment using visually impaired children who were accustomed to reading by listening. Comprehension apparently depended on the difficulty of the selection and the vocal characteristics of the reader. One major problem in learning by listening is the development of training programs to increase comprehension of the aural materials.

Research related to listener variables that affect listening comprehension does not offer sufficient evidence to warrant many conclusions except that there has been considerable variation in the ability of listeners to comprehend accelerated speech and that efficient training methods for improving the comprehension of accelerated speech have yet to be determined. However, the evidence indicated that listening efficiency can be improved by instruction and that learning from listening is more efficient for visually impaired children than learning from braille or enlarged type.

Orientation and Mobility

A most important task of the educator is to maximize the severely visually impaired child's ability to explore his environment. This job requires mental orientation and physical mobility. Orientation is the visually impaired person's ability to understand his environment—to recognize surroundings and their relation to himself. Mobility is the ability to move from place to place through the use of specific techniques, making use of remaining senses, including vision.

Although visually impaired persons have learned to use canes, dogs, or sighted human guides since biblical times, teaching of orientation and mobility by professionally trained teachers is a relatively new concept in the education of visually impaired children. The dog-guide movement was started soon after World War I, and the teaching of the use of the cane was started in 1943 with visually impaired veterans of World War II. Dog guides have no practical use with children in school and have very limited use with adults. Approximately 2–6 percent of the visually impaired adult population use dog guides as a means of travel. A sighted human guide often accompanies a person with a significant loss of distant vision so that faster and more efficient travel can be employed. Techniques have been developed to enable the sighted person to feel comfortable and to be efficient in the role of a guide. For example, the following procedure is recommended:

The visually impaired person should take the arm of the sighted guide above his elbow and walk half a step behind the guide. When going into narrow or dangerous places, the sighted guide should always lead the way. The sighted guide should never take the visually impaired person's arm and propel him by the elbow. In guiding a visually impaired person to a chair, lead him to a point at which he touches it and knows which direction it faces.

Orientation and mobility travel techniques were developed, and the prototype of the current long cane was engineered at Valley Forge Army Hospital (Malamazian, 1970). A special program for visually impaired veterans of World War II was developed at the Veterans Hospital in Hines, Illinois. Graduate programs for the purpose of training orientors or mobility specialists (peripatologists) were established at Boston College in 1960 and Western Michigan University in 1961. Although the programs were set up initially to train instructors of visually impaired adults, provisions were soon made to prepare instructors to teach children with visual impairments.

Basic instruction in orientation and mobility programs is concerned with body orientation, sensory training, concept and language development, posture, balance, gait, and development of special mobility skills such as squaring off, trailing, direction taking, and using shorelines and landmarks. Travel skills include learning to use the long cane effectively as a bumper and probe to navigate in a variety of settings.

An effective program of orientation and mobility begins at home. The specific needs of the child depend on factors such as degree of visual loss, age of onset, intelligence, motivation, hearing ability, tactual-kinesthetic ability, and physical health. A protective and restrictive attitude of the parents can seriously retard the development of independence in travel for the young visually impaired.

Obstacle perception is an important skill needed by the independent visually impaired traveler. Supa, Cotzin, and Dallenbach (1944) found in research on the perception of obstacles by the visually impaired that obstacle perception can be learned and that aural stimulation is a necessary and sufficient condition for the perception of obstacles. Ammons, Worchel, and Dallenbach (1953) found that object perception could be taught by a systematic course in perceptual recognition and detection of objects. Juurmaa (1970) found that visually impaired subjects could learn to discriminate differences in distance, size, and material of objects using natural auditory functions, but that distance could be judged more accurately by use of a special ultrasonic aid which showed differences in distance by fluctuations in audible sound. Obstacle sense correlated significantly with pitch discrimination and audiometric variables (Worchel, 1951). Rice, Feinstein, and Schusterman (1965) found that the greater the distance, the larger the target needed for visually impaired subjects who used echoes from tongue clicking or throat clearing to detect metal targets.

The perception of gradient (uphill and downhill) and veering tendency was explored by Cratty (1967) using 164 educationally blind and partially seeing subjects between the ages of 8 and 86 and a sighted control group. Subjects with blindfolds and earplugs were instructed to walk in a straight line on a large field which had uphill and downhill areas. Congenitally blind subjects veered less on incline and decline than did the older or younger adventitiously visually impaired subjects. It was concluded that learning is important in determining amount of veer. Cratty (1971) developed a training sequence for spatial orientation of blind children. The body-image training sequence was organized about four phases: body planes, parts and movements; left-right discriminations; body-object relationships; and body parts and movements of another person.

Scales have been developed to measure orientation and mobility components in young children. Lord (1969), using 173 visually impaired children ages 3–12, standardized a scale for appraisal of orientation and mobility skills based on five major subscales: (1) self-help in relation to travel, (2) formal precane orientation and mobility skills, (3) movement in space, (4) use of sensory cues in travel, and (5) use of direction and making turns. The scale could be very useful in planning an individual program in orientation and mobility for a young visually impaired child.

Vignette 8.4 Clem

Clem enrolled in a regular class for kindergarten children at the age of five. Although he appeared normal in most respects. Clem was totally blind. During the year in this program, he learned some important self-help skills in such areas as dressing, feeding, and especially orientation and mobility. An itinerant teacher taught him to use a "trailing" technique which became his main avenue for independent travel within the school. He trailed by extending his hand against the wall about a foot ahead of his body. He followed walls, lightly touching his hand against the wall with his fingers relaxed, palm down and thumb folded near the palm for protection. He can travel to the boys' room, cafeteria, and playground independently if given enough time.

Clem's special teacher describes his main problem as one of receiving too much help, which is always readily available from sympathetic and curious children and sometimes from the teachers. Clem frequently uses his lack of vision as a means to gather assistance and attention from those about him. The special teacher has difficulty in getting the children and teachers to treat him like any other kindergarten child.

The use of electronic travel aids still remains in the experimental stages. Three of the best-known devices are the Ultra-Sonic Aid, the Russell Pathsounder, and the laser cane. These devices are designed to give additional data regarding terrain changes and objects and are most effective in combination with the long cane. For example, the Ultra-Sonic Aid consists of a torch, power supply, and receiver. When the aid is switched on, its transmitter begins sending out a beam of ultrasonic energy. When this beam strikes an object within its range, a portion of the beam is reflected and picked up by the aid's detector and converted to signals that can be heard through the receiver and interpreted by the human listener (Gissoni, 1966).

Although research has failed to produce an electronic device that is practical for common usage, the research in orientation and mobility has been one of the most promising areas related to education of visually impaired persons. Most encouraging improvements in recent years are the training of teachers with mobility skills in local and residential schools for the blind, the increasing numbers of mobility specialists in local school programs, and the expanding services to preschool and multiply impaired children with limited vision.

Daily Living Skills

Daily living skills such as skills in eating, dressing, bathing, grooming, doing household chores, dialing a telephone, making change, lighting a cigarette, or pouring a drink are important to visually handicapped children and youth. Task analysis and programed instruction have been useful in teaching a child how to tie a shoe or take a bath. Guides and manuals have been developed for parents of preschool children (Lowenfeld, 1971) and for visually impaired adults (American Foundation for the Blind, 1970). Although much has been written concerning the importance of daily living skills to the visually handicapped child, very little research can be found concerning the most effective methods of teaching these skills. An example of verbal instructions for cutting meat is illustrated below:

> Locate the edge of the meat using the fork with the prongs downward and the index finger along the back of the fork. Slightly lift the fork and slide it over the edge of the meat, enter it about one half. Stick the fork into the meat and cut around the fork being careful not to cut the meat loose from the fork. This may be done by cutting one-half inch from the fork and also by angling the knife's cutting edge away from the rear of the fork.

Physical Education

The school-age child with defective vision may especially need individual attention in physical education because of such factors as (1) overprotection of parents and teachers; (2) inability to successfully compete in games with normally seeing peers; (3) lack of sensory stimulation to move about in his environment; (4) fatigue from excessive strain produced in reading print or braille; and (5) complications from multiple disabilities.

Overprotected visually impaired children often enter school with retarded motor and muscular development due to confinement to a playpen, a bedroom, or a house. Buell (1966) found that overprotected educationally blind and partially seeing children perform far below the norms of other visually impaired children on activities such as running, jumping, and throwing. Using the Iowa Brace Test and selected track and field events with

865 subjects ages 10–20, he found that partially seeing children generally performed better than children without useful vision; both groups performed below seeing children. Inability to compete in games with normally seeing children may contribute to the dislike of sports and outdoor activities by visually impaired children who are deficient in distant vision.

Fatigue is frequently mentioned as a characteristic behavior of visually impaired children. Lack of motor stimulation and motivation for physical activity of the visually impaired preschool child may retard his physical-motor development. Fatigue is inevitable in the young child when stress is placed on the task of learning a fine motor activity such as reading braille too early in his neuromuscular development. The excessive use of the ciliary muscle in the accommodation for near vision required by children with hyperopia often causes fatigue. Physical activities requiring gross motor movements, such as running, jumping, and wrestling, are vital to the physical and mental health of these children.

Teachers may often fear accidents or underestimate the ability of visually impaired children to actively participate in games with normally seeing children. Physical education activities can be adapted for children with visual disabilities in integrated school programs. Some activities need little or no adaptation, such as bowling, rope climbing, tug-of-war, hiking, roller skating, swimming, or wrestling. Games may be modified with the use of special aids such as the placing of a bell in the ball for baseball or kickball. An audible goal locater or a box with an electric beeper is sometimes used in basketball. The primary task in obtaining a vigorous and useful physical education program for visually limited children is the development of positive attitudes toward the abilities of these children.

The increasing numbers of visually impaired children in local schools demand that more attention be given in general teacher-training programs to the development of positive and realistic attitudes toward children with physical impairments.

Multiply Impaired

One of the most significant changes in education of children with visual impairments occurred as a result of the rubella epidemic in 1964–1965 (see Chapter 1). Children with congenital rubella were found to have multiple defects; cataracts, glaucoma, heart disease, and hearing defects were the most common. Many of the children also had motor and neurological problems. Significant developments in education of multiply impaired children were:

1. The establishment of highly specialized preschool and school programs with supplementary services.
2. The development of diagnostic and adjustment centers for children and counseling services for parents.
3. The establishment of more teacher-education programs.
4. The stimulation of additional research. In addition, federal legisla-

tion was passed providing for special assistance in the development of regional centers to provide the services needed for education and rehabilitation of deaf-blind persons.

Increasing interest in school programs for multiply impaired children occurred in the middle and late sixties. Jones and Collins (1966) reported that 94 percent of 353 local programs served visually impaired children who also had additional handicaps. However, only 19 percent of the residential schools accepted children in the 25–50 IQ range, and only 17 percent accepted children classified as deaf. Wolf (1967) noted that 46 percent of residential school administrators believed that providing services for the multiply disabled blind child will become the major role of the residential school. An example of this thinking is exhibited in the program in California which was cited earlier in this chapter. Lowenfeld (1969), reporting on a survey of educational, residential treatment and other facilities in California, found that visually impaired children with no accompanying disabilities were outnumbered by multihandicapped children with visual disorders by 19 to 11. The multiply impaired children (exclusive of deaf-blind) had a combined average of 3.0 impairments per child, with mental retardation, emotional disabilities, and speech problems leading in order of frequency of occurence.

The curriculum for multiply impaired children usually gives particular emphasis to the development of language and communication, motor and mobility skills, object and self-concept, and self-help skills. Work with children having combinations of hearing and visual impairments has had the most influence on curriculum development. Although a minority of the children are profoundly deaf or totally blind, they have been labeled deaf-blind. Samuel Gridley Howe was responsible for teaching the first deaf-blind child in the United States. His work with Laura Bridgman formed the basis for the program for deaf-blind children at Perkins Institute in Watertown, Massachusetts and for the procedures used by Ann Sullivan Macy with Helen Keller. Robbins (1963) described a beginning speech and language program for parents of deaf-blind children. She explained a popular method used in communication by deaf-blind persons called the Tadoma, or vibration, method, in which the child's hand is placed on the face of the speaker with his thumb lightly on the speaker's lips and his fingers spread on the speaker's neck and cheek. Robbins and Stenquist (1967) related the nonverbal and verbal stages of language development for children with auditory and visual impairments resulting from maternal rubella. Guldager (1970) designed a body-image scale for multiply handicapped rubella children based on the child's abilities to imitate body movement and to demonstrate object concept from the theories and observations of Jean Piaget. Hart (1971) developed a manual to help parents and teachers in the development of motor and self-help skills in multiply handicapped children. The systematic sequential steps in the teaching of basic skills in eating, dressing, toileting, and grooming are outlined in detail. Evaluation of behavior for each skill is provided by extensive checklists, with a rating scale for each task.

Programed instruction and precision teaching have apparently been sweeping the country in special education, but very little research or actual practice using operant-conditioning techniques has been reported in the literature in relation to young visually impaired children. Larsen (1970) suggested the use of operant techniques in sensory assessment. Hart (1969) reported using behavior modification and programed instruction for young multiply impaired children of ages three to nine years in a pilot study emphasizing self-help skills, motor skills, language and speech skills, and adaptive behavior. Bricker and Bricker (1970) described a sequence of language-training procedures for the severely language- and mentally handicapped child using behavior-modification techniques. Larsen and Bricker (1968) developed a manual for parents and teachers of severely and moderately retarded young children in which behavior-modification principles and methods for those low-functioning children are applied to deaf and visually impaired children.

Calvert, Reddell, Jacobs, and Baltzer (1972) used operant-conditioning techniques with 20 preschool children who were legally deaf and blind from maternal rubella. A food-reward unique for each child in the project was used as a primary reinforcer. Light was introduced later as a secondary reinforcer. Behavior profiles were obtained from observation of the child at home and in the San Francisco Hearing and Speech Center in such areas as feeding, dressing, toilet training, muscle tone, locomotion, and play. After four years, it was concluded that operant-conditioning procedures have limited value for testing and training of deaf-blind children, but hold promise for those children having good organization of the central nervous system.

The importance of orientation and mobility for multiply impaired children has been emphasized in the literature. The young infant needs to explore his environment. Moore (1970) found that short-term instruction was effective in developing orientation, mobility, social competency, and body-awareness skills in preschool-age multiply impaired children. Case studies by Seelye and Thomas (1966) indicate that orientation and mobility instruction can improve the ability of the school-aged multiply impaired child to move about in his environment.

One of the greatest problems for deaf-blind children is their difficulty in communication. Zumalt, Silver, and Kramer (1972) used the Deaf-Blind Communication Aid with six deaf-blind people to teach 10 monosyllabic words. The instrument, developed by General Electric Company, divides words spoken into the microphone into various sound frequencies and through five circuits activates finger-sized vibrators mounted in a small box. The deaf-blind person feels the vibrations produced by the spoken words by placing his hands on the vibrators.

Though much remains to be done, the outlook is promising for the visually limited child with multiple impairments. More interest has been expressed through surveys, legislation, and provision of services to meet their special needs. The rubella wave of the sixties helped to generate a fresh look at appraisal techniques and the designing of educational procedures appropriate for these children. However, the most promising aspect of the new interest has been the trend toward acceptance of all children for public education regardless of their level of functioning.

Special Material and Equipment

Visually impaired children sometimes have special difficulties in the physical sciences and mathematics. Tangible aids such as relief maps, computational and measuring devices, and a wide variety of models have been developed to supplement the instructional materials used with normally seeing children. Nolan and Morris (1964) demonstrated in a study of 42 junior high students that the use of the Japanese abacus is an efficient approach for overcoming computational problems encountered by educationally blind persons. The students used a special pocket size adaptation called the Cranmer abacus, which was specially designed for the use of persons with limited vision. Brothers (1972), noting the low achievement in arithmetic computation of 269 pupils in grades three, four, six, and eight, recommended providing an opportunity for abacus proficiency by completion of grade six.

Franks (1970) adapted and tested some measurement devices such as the ruler, thermometer, dial-spring balance, and pan balance with 70 pupils from grades four to nine. The instruments were designed to illustrate basic measurement concepts in seventh, eighth, and ninth grade science books. He found that 86 percent of the measurements and simple experiments were successfully performed by the subjects. Franks and Baird (1971) presented plastic land forms which represented environmental features from relief maps to students in grades one to four. The results indicated that raised-surface land forms could be effectively used as classroom aids in the teaching of geographical concepts to visually impaired children as early as first grade.

Many other special aids have been designed to assist the visually impaired person in communication, travel, daily living skills, and concept development. Braille writers, slates and styli, large-print typewriters, variable-speed cassette players, handwriting equipment, easels to hold books, optical aids, canes, serving and kitchen aids, watches, games, and audible compasses are among the many kinds of special devices available. Listings of commercially available instructional materials useful with visually impaired children can be obtained from the Instructional Materials Reference Center of the American Printing House for the Blind.

Future Directions

Several trends in general education appear very likely to affect the future education of visually impaired children. The increased acceptance and integration of exceptional children into local day school programs will certainly require more individualization of instruction. More teacher consultants with special skills and knowledge about visually impaired children will be needed to advise the regular classroom teacher. The increasing influx of children with multiple impairments will require teachers with more specialized skills. Increased use will be made of diagnostic and prescriptive teaching techniques to provide for the individualized instruction needed by the children. Clinical approaches which use carefully determined behavioral objectives to design appropriate programed lessons will provide a more systematic system of instruction. Parent counseling and diagnostic services for preschool children, coordinated with medical and social services, will provide the young visually impaired child with opportunities to develop needed concepts and basic skills. Behavior-modification techniques will be used more frequently to shape behaviors of preschool multiply impaired children.

Some trends involving children with visual disabilities in particular are the following:

1. Increased use will be made of technological aids developed to make more information available and to enable the visually impaired person to receive it at a faster rate.

2. More positive attiudes toward blindness and visual limitations will result in an increased variety of employment opportunities.

3. Increased use will be made of special teacher aides and materials as well as research information through the IMC network.

4. Prevention of visual impairments will be emphasized through the use of vaccines, family counseling, and the provision of adequate food and health services.

5. Research will continue on artificial vision as a possible visual prosthesis that could be implanted in the visual cortex to perceive light and serve some of the functions of the eye.

6. More research will be undertaken using engineering techniques to develop teaching aids and materials.

7. Increased research will be conducted related to spatial relations and concept development of the person with severe visual limitations.

8. Research will be initiated to determine the effectiveness of special classes for visually impaired children.

9. Increased services will be available for visually impaired children in the developing countries of Asia, Africa, and South America.

10. Increased numbers of children with visual perceptual disorders will be served by teachers now serving partially seeing and educationally blind children.

11. Increased numbers of visually impaired children and multiply impaired children will attend local schools.

12. Greater numbers of children with severe multiple impairments will alter the nature of most residential schools and segregated classes as they currently exist.

SUMMARY

1. Functional descriptions of the behaviors of visually impaired children are more useful for educational purposes than traditional labels.

2. A disturbance of any part of the visual system (protective, refractive,

directive, receptive) may cause sufficient visual disfunctioning to require special education.

3. Visual impairment from retrolental fibroplasia and rubella are decreasing, but impairments may increase in the future from virus infections, drugs, poisons, and pollutants.

4. The Snellen test is the most popular visual screening procedure, but the test should be used to locate visually impaired children rather than to make educational classifications or decisions for the children.

5. Approximately one per thousand children have visual impairments which require special education services.

6. If the sensory perceptual data is unduly restricted, the visually impaired child will lag behind sighted children in cognitive development. A preschool and school program which provides a rich, stimulating environment is necessary for the development of meaningful concepts for the child with limited vision.

7. Retarded intellectual development is not a necessary consequence of visual impairment, but it may result from inadequate opportunity to explore the environment.

8. The characteristic underachievement and fatigue of partially seeing children are important considerations in planning remedial programs for these children.

9. Reduced vision is not a direct cause of any personal or social maladjustment, but adjustment problems may result from negative attitudes toward loss of vision by seeing persons.

10. Employment opportunities for visually impaired persons may be restricted due to negative attitudes toward visual impairments by employers.

11. More visually impaired children are being integrated in local day schools, and more multiply impaired children with visual disorders are being accepted in segregated classes and residential schools.

12. The visually impaired child usually needs stimulation so that he will use effectively his other sensory modalities to explore his environment.

13. The visually impaired child needs to learn to use his remaining vision more efficiently to interpret visual stimuli.

14. Information receiving can be increased through the development of listening skills.

15. The development of meaningful concepts for visually impaired children requires a maximum number of concrete, vivid, and practical experiences.

16. Special curricular adaptations are needed to provide for special needs in spatial relations, motor development, mobility, and daily living skills.

17. Special media are needed for some visually impaired children in the form of large type, braille, and audio books and materials.

18. Special aids and equipment may be needed to compensate for lack of vision, especially in communication, computation, measurement, concept development, travel, and daily living skills.

19. The educational needs of visually impaired children are served in a variety of ways, from the mere provision of special books and aids for the more independent children in integrated classes to the extensive use of special teachers for the more dependent children in segregated classes.

Resources

The American Printing House for the Blind (1839 Frankfort Avenue, Louisville, Kentucky 40206) was established in Louisville to aid the education of the visually impaired through the production of educational materials. Federal assistance has helped to finance its operations, which include (1) the transcription of braille, large-print, and recorded publications; (2) the manufacture of tangible apparatus such as braille writers and mathematical aids; (3) the conducting of research related to the design and use of the materials transcribed and manufactured for its customers, the visually impaired children and youth in school programs. The American Printing House provides catalogs of braille, large-type, and recorded books and tangible apparatus. The results of the research are published in numerous reports and journal articles. A Central Catalog of Volunteer Transcribed Books provides services to teachers who desire to secure copies of volunteer-transcribed books. The federally supported Instructional Materials Center for Visually Handicapped Children at the Printing House develops and disseminates information on special aids and materials for use with visually impaired children.

The American Foundation for the Blind (44 East 23d Street, New York, New York 10010) is a privately supported service and research agency concerned with the education and welfare of visually handicapped persons. It has assisted in stimulating and supporting research projects and in the publishing and dissemination of research information. It has provided consultant services in the states and abroad to encourage the development of school programs for children and professional training programs for teachers. It conducts the following special services: publishes the *New Outlook for the Blind, Talking Book Topics,* special monographs, articles, and newsletters; maintains a library loan service from a special library on blindness; develops and sells special aids and appliances; sponsors institutes, workshops, and conferences related to teacher training and research; provides support to the National Accreditation Council for Agencies Serving the Blind and Visually Handicapped.

The National Society for the Prevention of Blindness, Inc. (79 Madison Avenue, New York, New York 10016), is a privately supported agency which concentrates on activities related to prevention of blindness such as public education and research. Among its publications are the *Sight-saving Review,* the *Wise Owl,* pamphlets and reprints of journal articles on the education of partially seeing children, vision-screening materials, and public information films.

Recording for the Blind (205 East 58th Street, New York, New York 10022) is a national voluntary organization which provides recorded educational books to visually impaired students who require reading material in their professional or vocational preparation. This recording service, the largest of its kind in the world, provides a national library service of books in all major fields of study, including technical subjects. Tapes are provided free on loan to all eligible borrowers, and raised-line drawings are supplied with some books. A revised catalog of books is published each year.

A number of strategically located regional centers comprise the Special Education Instructional Materials Center Network for Handicapped Children and Youth. These centers provide information to teachers and administrators of handicapped children and youth, including those who are deaf-blind or visually impaired. They assist state departments of education to develop and implement state plans for local provisions of instructional materials, including braille, large-type, and recorded materials. Regional centers that specialize in materials development for visually impaired pupils and their teachers are located in Illinois, Michigan, and at the American Printing House for the Blind.

The Library of Congress, Division for the Blind and Physically Handicapped (Washington, D.C. 20542), provides reading materials to visually impaired persons in the form of braille publications and tape and talking-book recordings which are distributed through regional libraries. The Division offers a correspondence course in braille writing for persons desiring to become volunteer braille transcribers.

The Division for the Visually Handicapped of the Council for Exceptional Children (1411 S. Jefferson Davis Highway, Arlington, Virginia 22202) holds special sectional meetings at the annual convention of the parent organization. It also publishes a quarterly newsletter for teachers, the *DVH Newsletter*.

The Association for Education of the Visually Handicapped (711 14th Street, N.W., Washington, D.C. 20005) is a professional organization of educators of children with visual impairment. It publishes a journal, *Education of the Visually Handicapped*, and a newsletter, *Fountainhead*. The association also publishes the proceedings of its biennial convention.

Science for the Blind (221 Rock Hill Road, Bala-Cynwyd, Pennsylvania 19004) is a nonprofit organization that provides two unique service programs for visually impaired scientists, technicians, and laymen. This organization circulates tapes of periodicals, and it creates and distributes special tools and instruments designed for use by persons with limited vision in the laboratory, shop, or home.

References

American Foundation for the Blind. The Pine Brook report: Natonal work session on the education of the blind with the sighted. *AFB Publications,* Group reports No. 2, 1954.

American Foundation for the Blind. *A step-by-step guide to personal management for blind persons.* New York: Author, 1970.

Ammons, C. H., Worchel, P., and Dallenbach, K. M. Facial vision: The perception of obstacles out of doors by blindfolded and blindfolded-deafened subjects. *American Journal of Psychology,* 1953, **66**, 519–553.

Ashcroft, S. C., Halliday, C., and Barraga, N. Study II: Effects of experimental teaching on the visual behavior of children educated as though they had no vision. Report to U.S. Office of Education, Grant No. 32-52-0120-1034. Nashville, Tenn.: George Peabody College for Teachers, 1965.

Barraga, N. *Increased visual behavior in low vision children.* New York: American Foundation for the Blind, 1964.

Bateman, B. Sighted children's perceptions of blind children's abilities. *Exceptional Children,* 1962, **29**, 42–46.

Bateman, B. Reading and psycholinguistic processes of partially seeing children. *CEC Research Monograph,* Series A, No. 5. Arlington, Va.: Council for Exceptional Children, 1963, pp. 1–46.

Bateman, B. The modifiability of sighted adults' perceptions of blind children's abilities. *New Outlook for the Blind,* 1964, **58**, 133–135.

Bateman, B. Visually handicapped children. In N. C. Haring and R. L. Schiefelbusch (Eds.), *Methods in special education*. New York.: McGraw-Hill, 1967.

Bateman, B., and Wetherell, J. L. Some educational characteristics of partially seeing children. *International Journal for the Education of the Blind*, 1967, **17**, 33–40.

Bauman, M. K. Group differences disclosed by inventory items. *International Journal for the Education of the Blind*, 1964, **13**, 101–106.

Birch, J. W., Tisdall, W., Peabody, R., and Sterrett, R. School achievement and effect of type size on reading in visually handicapped children. Cooperative Research Project No. 1766, Contract No. OEC-4-10-028. Pittsburgh, Pa.: University of Pittsburgh, 1966.

Bischoff, R. W. Improvement of listening comprehension in partially sighted students. *Sight Saving Review*, 1967, **37**, 161–165.

Bliss, J. C., and Crane, H. D. Tactile perception. *AFB Research Bulletin*, 1969, No. 19, pp. 205–230.

Boldt, W. The development of scientific thinking in blind children and adolescents. *Education of the Visually Handicapped*. 1969, **1**, 5–8.

Bricker, W. A., and Bricker, D. D. A program of language training for the severely language handicapped child. *Exceptional children*, 1970, **37**, 101–111.

Brothers, R. J. Arithmetic computation by the blind: A look at current achievement. *Education of the Visually Handicapped*, 1972, **4**, 1–8.

Buell, C. E. *Physical education for blind children*. Springfield, Ill.: Charles C Thomas, 1966.

Buktenica, N. A. *Visual learning*. San Rafael, Calif.: Dimensions, 1968.

Burklen, K. *Touch reading of the blind*. Trans. by F. K. Merry. New York: American Foundation for the Blind, 1932.

Calvert, D. R., Reddell, R. C., Jacobs, U., and Baltzer, S. Experiences with preschool deaf-blind children. *Exceptional Children*. 1972, **38**, 415–421.

Cowen, E. L., Underberg, R., Verrillo, R. T., and Benham, F. G. *Adjustment to visual disability in adolescence*. New York: American Foundation for the Blind, 1961.

Cratty, B. J. The perception of gradient and the veering tendency while walking without vision. *AFB Research Bulletin*, 1967, No. 14, pp. 31–51.

Cratty, B. J. *Movement and spatial awareness in blind children and youth*. Springfield, Ill.: Charles C Thomas, 1971.

Cutsforth, T. D. *The blind in school and society: A psychological study*. New York: American Foundation for the Blind, 1951.

Ferree, J. W. The blind population: 1967–1977. *New Outlook for the Blind*, 1967, **61**, 290–295.

Foulke, E. Comparison of comprehension of two forms of compressed speech. *Exceptional Children*, 1966, **33**, 169–173.

Frailberg, S., Siegel, B. L., and Gibson, R. *The role of sound in the search behavior of a blind infant*. In R. S. Eissler, et al. (Eds.), *The psychoanalytic study of the child*. New York: International Universities Press, 1966, **21**, 327–357.

Franks, F. L. Measurement in science for blind students. *Teaching Exceptional Children*, 1970, **3**, 2–11.

Franks, F. L., and Baird, R. M. Geographical concepts and the visually handicapped. *Exceptional Children*, 1971, **38**, 321–324.

French, R. S. *From Homer to Helen Keller*. New York: American Foundation for the Blind, 1932.

Garry, R. J., and Ascarelli, A. Teaching topographical orientation and spatial orientation to congenitally blind children. *Journal of Education*, 1960, **143** (2), 1–48.

Gibbons, H. Low-vision aids—the educator's responsibility. *International Journal for the Education of the Blind*, 1963, **12**, 107–109.

Gissoni, F. My "cane" is 20 feet long. *New Outlook for the Blind*, 1966, **60**, 33–38.

Gowman, A. G. *The war blind in American social structure.* New York: American Foundation for the Blind, 1957.

Guldager, V. Body image and the severely handicapped rubella child. *Perkins Publication*, No. 27. Watertown, Mass.: Perkins School for the Blind, 1970.

Halliday, C. *The visually impaired child: Growth, learning, development— Infancy to school age.* Louisville, Ky.: American Printing House for the Blind, 1970.

Harley, R. K. Verbalism among blind children: An investigation and analysis. *AFB Research Series*, 1963, No. 10.

Harley, R. K., and Rawls, R. Comparison of several approaches for teaching braille reading to blind children. *Education of the Visually Handicapped*, 1970, **2**, 47–51.

Hart, V. The blind child who functions on a retarded level: The challenge for teacher preparation. *New Outlook for the Blind*, 1969, **63**, 318–321.

Hart, V. A manual for the development of self-help skills in multiply handi- capped children (Unpublished experimental edition). Paper presented at the Special Study Institute, Professional preparation of teachers of the multiply handicapped with special concern directed toward the child with both auditory and visual impairments. Conducted by the Department of Special Education of the University of Pittsburgh, Pittsburgh, Pa., Summer 1971.

Hartlage, L. C. *The role of vision in the development of spatial ability.* Doc- toral dissertation, University of Louisville, Louisville, Ky., Ann Arbor, Mich.: University Microfilms, 1968, No. 69-443.

Hathaway, W. *Education and health of the partially seeing child* (4th ed. by F. M. Foote, D. Bryan, and H. Gibbons). New York: Columbia University Press, 1966.

Hayes, S. P. *Contributions to a psychology of blindness.* New York: Ameri- can Foundation for the Blind, 1941.

Hayes, S. P. Measuring the intelligence of the blind. In P. A. Zahl (Ed.), *Blindness: Modern approaches to the unseen environment.* New York: Hafner, 1963. (Originally published by Princeton University Press, Prince- ton, N.J., 1950.)

Henderson, F. The rate of braille character recognition as a function of the reading process. 48th Biennial Conference of the American Association of Instructors for the Blind, Washington, D.C.: American Association of Instructors of the Blind, 1966, pp. 7–10.

Howe, S. G. Reprint of an address delivered at the ceremony of laying the cornerstone of the New York State Institute for the Blind at Batavia, Sept. 6, 1866. In *AAWB 1965 Annual.* Washington, D.C. American Asso- ciation of Workers for the Blind, 1965.

Jones, J. W. *Blind Children: Degree of vision: Mode of reading.* Washington, D.C.: U.S. Office of Education, Bulletin 1961 (OE-35026), No. 24.

Jones, J. W., and Collins, A. P. *Educational programs for visually handicapped children.* U.S. Office of Education, Bulletin 1966 (OE-35070), No. 6.

Jones, R. L., Gottfried, N. W., and Owens, A. The social distance of the exceptional: A study at the high school level. *Exceptional Children*, 1966, **32**, 551–556.

Juurmaa, J. Ability structure and loss of vision. *AFB Research Series*, 1967, No. 18.

Juurmaa, J. On the accuracy of obstacle detection by the blind, Parts 1 & 2. *New Outlook for the Blind*, 1970, **64**, 65–72, 104–118.

Kenmore, J. R. *Associative learning by blind versus sighted children with words and objects differing in meaningfulness and identifiability without vision.* Doctoral dissertation, University of Minnesota. Ann Arbor, Mich.: University Microfilms, 1965, No. 66-8903.

Kerby, C. E. Causes of blindness in children of school age. *Sight-Saving Review*, 1958, **28**, 10–21.

Kim, Y. H. The community of the blind: Applying the theory of community formation. *AFB Research Series*, 1970, No. 22.

Larsen, L. A. Behavior modification with the multihandicapped. *New Outlook for the Blind*, 1970, **64**, 6–15.

Larsen, L. A., and Bricker, W. A. A manual for parents and teachers of severely and moderately retarded children. *IMRID Papers and Reports.* **5**, No. 22. Nashville, Tenn.: George Peabody College for Teachers, 1968.

Lord, F. E. Development of scales for the measurement of orientation and mobility of young blind children. *Exceptional Children*, 1969, **36**, 77–81.

Lowenfeld, B. The role of the residential school in the education of blind children. In Concerning the education of blind children compiled by G. L. Abel. *AFB Publications*, 1959, Educational Series No. 12.

Lowenfeld, B. Multihandicapped-blind and deaf-blind children in California. *AFB Research Bulletin*, 1969, No. 19.

Lowenfeld, B. *Our blind children, growing and learning with them* (3rd ed.) Springfield, Ill.: Charles C Thomas, 1971.

Lowenfeld, B., Abel, G. L., and Hatlen, P. H. *Blind children learn to read.* Springfield, Ill.: Charles C Thomas, 1969.

Lowenfeld, V. *Creative and mental growth.* (5th ed.) New York: Macmillan, 1970.

Lukoff, I. F., and Whiteman, M. The social sources of adjustment to blindness. *AFB Research Series*, 1970, No. 21.

Malamazian, J. D. The first 15 years at Hines. Blindness: *1970 AAWB Annual*, 1970, pp. 59–77.

Maxfield, K. E. *The blind child and his reading, A handbook for teachers of primary braille reading.* New York: American Foundation for the Blind, 1928.

McReynolds, J., and Worchel, P. Geographic orientation in the blind. *Journal of General Psychology*, 1954, **51**, 221–236.

Miller, C. K. Conservation in blind children. *Education of the Visually Handicapped*, 1969, **1**, 101–105.

Moore, M. E. *Developing body image and skills of orientation, mobility and social competence in preschool, multiplyhandicapped blind children.* Doctoral dissertation, University of Pittsburgh. Ann Arbor, Mich.: University Microfilms, 1970, No. 70–20, p. 338.

Morris, J. E. Relative efficiency of reading and listening for braille and large type readers. 48th American Biennial Conference of the American Association of Instructors of the Blind, Washington, D.C.: American Association of Instructors of the Blind, 1966.

Myerson, L. Somatopsychology of physical disability. In W. M. Cruickshank (Ed.), *Psychology of exceptional children and youth.* (3d ed.) Englewood Cliffs, N.J.: Prentice-Hall, 1971.

National Accreditation Council. Standards for production of reading materials for the blind and visually handicapped. National Accreditation Council for Agencies Serving the Blind and Visually Handicapped. Project chairman, T. J. Carroll, Washington, D.C., U.S. Office of Education, OEG 0-9-422151-3709 (607), 1970.

National Society for the Prevention of Blindness. *Visual screening in schools.* Publication No. 257. New York: National Society for Prevention of Blindness, 1969.

Nolan, C. Y. Readability of large types: A study of type sizes and type styles. *International Journal for the Education of the Blind,* 1959, **9**, 41–44.

Nolan, C. Y. Legibility of ink and paper color combinations for readers of large type. *International Journal for the Education of the Blind,* 1961, **10**, 82–84.

Nolan, C. Y. Reading and listening in learning by the blind. Exceptional Children, 1963, **29**, 313–316.

Nolan, C. Y., and Bott, J. E. Relationships between visual acuity and reading medium for blind children 1969. *New Outlook for the Blind,* 1971, **65**, 90–96.

Nolan, C. Y., and Kederis, C. J. Perceptual factors in braille word recognition. *AFB Research Series,* 1969, No. 20.

Nolan, C. Y., and Morris, J. E. The Japanese abacus as a computational aid for blind children. *Exceptional Children,* 1964, **31**, 15–17.

Nolan, C. Y., and Morris, J. E. Learning by blind students through active and passive listening. *Exceptional Children,* 1969, **36**, 173–181.

Norris, M., Spaulding, P. J., and Brodie, F. H. *Blindness in children.* Chicago: University of Chicago Press, 1957.

Revesz, G. *Psychology and art of the blind.* Trans. by H. A. Wolff. London: Longmans Green, 1950.

Rex, E. A study of basal readers and experimental supplementary instructional materials for teaching primary reading in braille. Part I: An analysis of the braille features in basal readers. *Education of the Visually Handicapped,* 1970, **2**, 97–101.

Rice, C. E., Feinstein, S. H., and Schusterman, R. J. Echo-detection ability of the blind: Size and distance factors. *Journal of Experimental Psychology,* 1965, **70**, 246–251.

Robertson, C. H. Services to children reported by optical aids clinics. *International Journal for the Education of the Blind,* 1963, **13**, 59–61.

Robbins, N. Speech beginnings for the deaf-blind child: A guide for parents. *Perkins Publication,* No. 22. Watertown, Mass.: Perkins School for the Blind, 1963.

Robbins, N., and Stenquist, G. The deaf-blind "rubella" child. *Perkins Publication,* No. 25. Watertown, Mass.: Perkins School for the Blind, 1967.

Seelye, W. S., and Thomas, J. E. Is mobility feasible with multiply handicapped blind children? *Exceptional Children,* 1966, **32**, 613–617.

Senden, M. von. *Space and sight: The perception of space and shape in the congenitally blind before and after operation.* Trans. by P. Heath. Glencoe, Ill.: Free Press, 1960.

Singer, J. L., and Steiner, B. F. Imaginative content in the dreams and fantasy play of blind and sighted children. *Perceptual and Motor Skills,* 1966, **22**, 475–482.

Sloan, L. L. *Recommended aids for the partially sighted.* (2d ed.) New York: National Society for the Prevention of Blindness, 1971.

Sommers, V. S. *The influence of parental attitudes and social environment on the personality development of the adolescent blind.* New York: American Foundation for the Blind, 1944.

Spivey, S. A. The social position of selected children with a visual loss in regular classes in the public schools of Atlanta, Georgia. Unpublished Ed. S. independent study. Nashville, Tenn.: George Peabody College for Teachers, 1967.

Supa, M., Cotzin, M., and Dallenbach, K. M. "Facial vision": The perception of obstacles by the blind. *American Journal of Psychology*, 1944, **57**, 133–183.

Tillman, M. H. The performance of blind and sighted children on the Wechsler Intelligence Scale for Children, Study 1 & 2. *International Journal for the Education of the Blind*, 1967, **16**, 65–74, 106–112.

Umsted, R. G. *Improvement of braille reading through code recognition training.* Doctoral dissertation, George Peabody College for Teachers. Ann Arbor, Mich.: University Microfilms, 1970, No. 71-4255.

U.S. Office of Education. *Statistics of trends in education.* National Center for Educational Statistics, Washington, D.C.: Government Printing Office, 1970. (a)

U.S. Public Health Service, Health Services and Mental Health Administration. *Visual acuity of children in the United States.* National Center for Health Statistics, Public Health Service Publication No. 1000, Series 11, No. 101. Washington, D.C.: Government Printing Office. 1970. (b)

U.S. Department of Health, Education and Welfare, Public Health Service, National Institutes of Health. *Statistics for 1966 on blindness in the model reporting area.* Washington, D.C.: Government Printing Office, 1970. (c)

Wolf, J. M. The blind child with concomitant disabilities. *AFB Research Series*, 1967, No. 16.

Worchel, P. Space perception and orientation in the blind. *Psychological Monographs*, 1951, **65** (Whole No. 332).

Zumalt, L. E., Silver, S., and Kramer, L. C. Evaluation of a communication device for deal-blind persons. *New Outlook for the Blind.* 1972, **66**, 20–25.

Zweibelson, I., and Barg, C. F. Concept development of blind children. *New Outlook for the Blind*, 1967, **61**, 218–222.

Selected Films

Before We Are Six. 16 mm., color and sound. Twenty-two minutes. $125. Available on loan without charge. A film to prepare professionals and volunteers to screen the vision of preschool and school children using the Snellen Test. The National Society for the Prevention of Blindness.

Current films about blindness are available for purchase or for loan without charge. Listings of these films may be obtained from the American Foundation for the Blind.

The Legacy of Anne Sullivan. Color and Sound. Free loan basis. A documentary film showing the work of Ann Sullivan with Helen Keller. Campbell Films, Academy Avenue, Saxtons River, Vermont 05154.

For Blind Children of the World. 16 mm., color and sound. Available on loan without charge. A film showing visually impaired children in school and at play in Holland, Thailand, Ceylon, and Taiwan. Helen Keller World Crusade for the Blind, 22 West 17th Street, New York, N.Y. 10011.

Opposite: It is easier for some children with neuromotor disorders who use creepers and crutches to work at instructional materials framed on the floor rather than placed on table tops or chalkboards. (Photo courtesy San Juan, Calif., Unified School District; photographer, Mack Law.)

children with crippling and health disabilities

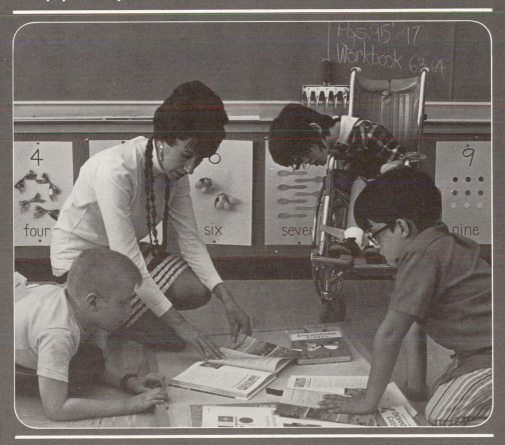

chapter outline

The great variety of conditions found among neuromotor, crippled, and health-impaired children makes it extremely difficult either to define, classify, or describe them, or to specify precisely how many with these disabilities are in need of special education services. This is the most medically oriented as well as the most heterogeneous of the categories into which exceptional children are traditionally classified; therefore, it is the least useful for educational purposes. However, because physical conditions do affect learning, it is advantageous for an educator to understand them, to be able to interpret health reports of pupils, and to realize the implications for teaching that such information supplies in providing for the total welfare of children. Thus there is some justification for using medical classifications in the first part of this chapter. The extreme heterogeneity among the children included here precludes much general discussion of them. Consequently, with the exception of brief, general statements on definition, prevalence, and classification of the total group, physical disabilities will be considered under the particular types of impairment. Medical details about specific disabling conditions have been put into tables for quick reference, and the text includes only that information which applies to education.

Problems of personal, social, and vocational adjustment possibly related to physical impairment and having implications for education are discussed in the second section of the chapter. The third part of the chapter focuses on educational provisions. Children with neuromotor and other physical impairments vary so greatly in intellectual capacity, learning characteristics, and type and degree of disability that they will be found in all of the types of special education programs, as well as in all of the three levels discussed by Dunn in Chapter 1. A large majority of the children who have the disabilities described in this chapter are not classified as exceptional for education. They are able to learn as other children learn, and their condition is not handicapping in a classroom when adjustments for individual problems are made in facilities, equipment, and materials. Some of them may need additional assistance, such as speech or physical therapy, and perhaps augmented psychological and social services. Those children who require more specialized education will be primarily in one of three types of programs: (1) special day schools or classes; (2) hospital classes; and (3) programs for the homebound. Some severely impaired children with multiple handicaps may receive their education in residential and boarding schools.

DEFINITION

One of the major problems of defining the group of children discussed here lies in delineating a category and classifying individuals according to it. The kinds of physical problems are as varied as the children who have them, and no one term can apply to all. They have been described as crippled, orthopedically handicapped, chronically ill, delicate, homebound, hospitalized, and physically impaired, or said to have low vitality, motor disabilities, or neurological impairments. The only escape from this dilemma is to substitute delimitation for definition. Therefore, this chapter deals with childhood physical handicaps that are not sensory in nature, such as blindness and deafness, and also excludes speech impairments.

PREVALENCE

The difficulties encountered in an attempt to determine the number of children with neuromotor and other physical impairments who need special education have been discussed by Dunn in Chapter 1. One of the problems is that the diagnostic label usually is affixed for medical rather than special education purposes. In addition, prevalence figures for individual disabilities are misleading because many children have multiple handicaps and are counted more than once. However, total and comparative figures are useful in estimating the relative number of children with specific types of impairment who might need educational services. Dunn, in Chapter 1, indicates prevalence for the group as 0.36 percent, approximately half of whom have cerebral palsy and other crippling conditions and the other half chronic health problems (see Table 1.1).

In a study of approximately 45,000 children in a six-county area in Iowa to determine the prevalence of educationally and psychologically relevant physically handicapping conditions among school-age children, Friedman and MacQueen (1971) found 195 physically handicapped children. This number constitutes .44 percent of the total group, comparable to the Dunn estimate. On the basis of the principal handicap, the children were placed in one of five categories. Table 9.1 shows the number of children per 1,000 in each of these.

TABLE 9.1 Type and Number of Physically Handicapped Children in a Six-County Area in Iowa

Source of Handicap	Number of Children per 1,000
Cerebral palsy	1.70
Polio	0.85
Disease and trauma	0.83
Congenital anomalies	0.44
Other (not classified)	0.58
Total	4.40

SOURCE: R. J. Friedman and J. C. MacQueen, Psychoeducative considerations of physical handicapping conditions in children. *Exceptional Children,* 1971, **37** (7), 538-539.

Health service agencies report an increase of children with physical impairments over the last two decades. Although improvement in identification and services accounts for a good proportion of the growth in numbers, part also results from additional numbers of impaired children. The National Society for Crippled Children and Adults (1967) reported that the total number of crippled children served through federal and state programs increased

87 percent between 1950 and 1963. In 1964 there was an increase of 5.7 percent. A report of various impairments of children under 15 years of age by the U.S. Department of Health, Education and Welfare (DHEW) (1971c) showed an increase in the prevalence of orthopedic impairments of approximately 5 per 1,000 over a 10-year period. In 1966–1967 there were more children listed with such impairments than visual, hearing, and speech defects combined (see Table 9.2). These figures appear to be in general agreement with those reported elsewhere, except that the number of speech impairments shown in the table compared to orthopedic conditions is extremely low according to figures quoted by Dunn in Chapter 1. However, note that the cases reported here probably are only those with an organic basis, or which are of concern to the medical profession. Also the great difference in the number of physically handicapped children of 4.4 per 1,000 in the Friedman and MacQueen Study (Table 9.1) and 21.0 per 1,000 in the Public Health Service report (Table 9.2) demonstrates again that the majority of children with nonsensory physical disorders have medically but not educationally relevant disabilities.

TABLE 9.2 *Prevalence of Physical Impairments, 1958-1967*

	1957-1958 Rate per 1,000	1966-1967 Rate per 1,000
Orthopedic	16.3	21.0
Speech	10.8	9.1
Hearing	6.0	7.8
Visual	3.4	5.5

SOURCE: U.S. Department of Health, Education and Welfare, Children and youth: Selected health characteristics, United States, 1958 and 1968. *Vital and Health Statistics, 1971,* **10** (62)

CLASSIFICATION AND DESCRIPTION OF CONDITIONS

Children with nonsensory physically handicapping conditions can be divided into a number of different types of classifications. Functionally, it would be more useful to divide them into categories on the basis of the educational modifications they need. Actually, this is not feasible because of the many variations among the individuals who make up the total group, the overlapping conditions, the great difference in educational needs, and the necessity for shifting from one type of program to another as physical conditions change. Division into groups on a medical basis has its limitations and disadvantages, but this method will be used in the first part of the chapter because the sources of information about specific conditions and classifications used in describing them are primarily medical. In reporting on the numbers of children who received physicians' services under crippled children's programs, the U.S. Department of Health, Education and Welfare (1971a) used the following classifications: (1) diseases of the nervous system; (2) diseases of the musculoskeletal system; (3) congenital malformations; and (4) other crippling and health conditions. For purposes of showing comparative numbers this classification system has value. Understandably, the categories do overlap. There are instances in which a particular condition may fall into more than one group; for example, clubfoot, which is both a musculoskeletal deformity and a congenital malformation.

Children with Disorders of the Nervous System

Impairments that involve the nervous system generally are more handicapping educationally than other types of nonsensory physical disabilities and chronic health conditions. Although the manifestations may be motor, this is rarely the sole extent of the problem. Since the nervous system is the activating mechanism of the total human organism, no matter how healthy and intact the body may be, none of its systems function without adequate performance of the nervous system. The capability of the central nervous system to react to environmental influences; to receive and conduct nerve impulses; to interpret, store, integrate, and process information; and to activate responses is essential in the learning process, which is the concern of education. Because impairment of learning ability as well as physical functioning is often associated with neuromotor disability, children with this handicap present one of the most complicated problems with which the special educator must deal. Children whose handicaps are primarily physical usually can attend regular classes and learn by the same methods used with the majority of children, but children with neurological involvement may need special teaching methods, materials, and facilities.

Cerebral Palsy

Definition Cerebral palsy is an impairment of the nervous system that cannot be considered a disease in the usual sense. Rather, the term designates a number of types of neuromuscular disabilities which are characterized by disturbances of motor function resulting from damage to the brain and central nervous system. Some of the symptoms of cerebral palsy include muscle weakness or flaccidity, excessive involuntary motion, postural imbalance, and spasticity. The manifestations of the disorder differ according to the site and extensiveness of the main lesion and may vary from extremely mild motor incoordination to virtually complete helplessness.

Causes The damage to the central nervous system which causes cerebral palsy may take place (1) prenatally (before birth); (2) paranatally (at the time of birth); or (3) postnatally (during the early years of life). Prenatal factors that may predispose the fetus to damage include (1) blood-type incompatibility, especially the Rh factor; (2) maternal infections, particularly rubella, and occasionally other virus diseases; (3) toxemia, a condition associated with presence of toxic substances in the blood of the mother; (4) conditions that cut off the supply of oxygen to the brain of the fetus or affect the oxygen-carrying properties of the mother's blood, such as severe anemia; (5) prematurity; (6) diabetes; and (7) X-ray therapy. At the time of birth the conditions which can cause brain damage are (1) prolonged labor; (2) difficult or abnormal birth, such as breech birth; (3) the cord twisted around the throat; (4) precipitant brith; (5) excessive birth weight; and (6) obstetrical procedures, such as forceps delivery. Contrary to public opinion, a relatively small proportion of brain injuries can be attributed to the last factor. Factors that may be responsible for damage in the early years of life are (1) infections of brain tissue, such as encephalitis; (2) mechanical damage to the brain; (3) poisons, such as lead poisoning; and (4) progressive neurological disorders. Only that damage to the central nervous system that affects motor coordination and occurs during the developmental years is classified as cerebral palsy. Therefore, damage later in life that impairs motor function already established is not considered a cause.

Prevalence Estimates of the prevalence of cerebral palsy vary according to the definition and classification, the area of the study, the age group studied, and other factors. Prevalence appears to be lower according to some estimates than in the past. In a study conducted in Georgia in 1954, Wishik (1956) estimated five children with cerebral palsy under 21 years of age for every 1,000 persons in the general population. This is quite different from the 1.7 per 1,000 children with cerebral palsy in need of special education reported by Friedman and MacQueen (1971) (see Table 9.1). Morgenstern (1964) reported a figure between these two, which is probably a more accurate reflection of the present situation. He estimated prevalence as three persons in 1,000. Presumably, not all of these would need special education. Woods (1963) observed an apparent trend toward a lower incidence of cerebral palsy in recent years and an increase in milder, subclinical cases than there were previously, although all the factors responsible for this trend have not been determined. However, Kershaw (1969) stated that more cases of cerebral palsy are appearing and that the average age of diagnosis is earlier because parents are more aware of the condition and more hopeful that something can be done.

Classification and characteristics A number of types of cerebral palsy have been identified. Classification is generally based on the kind of motor involvement, but there are also systems that use other criteria, such as degrees or location of physiological impairment (Crothers and Paine, 1959; Minear, 1956; Perlstein and Barnett, 1952). The more widely accepted categories will be used here: (1) spasticity; (2) athetosis; (3) ataxia; (4) rigidity; and (5) tremors. These five types of cerebral palsy, the principal area of the brain lesion, and the major motor manifestations of each are shown in Table 9.3. While the types can generally be identified by these characteristics, numerous mixed conditions occur, making accurate differential diagnosis and classification difficult. The principal areas of the brain referred to in the table are shown in Figure 10.1. Neurological damage is rarely confined to a discrete area but usually affects many parts. Therefore, pure types of cerebral palsy are the

TABLE 9.3 Classification of Types of Cerebral Palsy by Principal Area of Brain Lesion and Major Motor Manifestations

Type and Proportion	Principal Area of Brain Lesion	Major Motor Manifestations
Spasticity (50%)[a]	Motor cortex and pyramidal tracts	Involuntary contraction of affected muscles when they are suddenly stretched—called stretch reflex—resulting in tenseness and difficult, inaccurate voluntary motion
Athetosis (25%)[a]	Basal ganglia and extra pyramidal tracts	Involuntary contraction of successive muscles resulting in marked incoordination and almost constant motion of the extremities
Ataxia (25%)[a]	Subcortical, probably in cerebellum	Uncoordinated movement, impaired balance, and sense of orientation in space
Rigidity (rare)[a]	Diffuse	Widespread continuous muscle tension or "lead-pipe" stiffness
Tremor (rare)[a]	Basal ganglia	Rhythmic, involuntary, uncontrollable motions limited to certain muscle groups

[a]M. Morgenstern, Psychoeducational and vocational problems of the cerebral palsied child. In J. Hellmuth (Ed.), *The special child in century 21*. Seattle: The Special Child Publications of the Sequin School, 1964.

exception rather than the rule, and the manifestations of the damage to the brain and nervous system are different for each individual.

In addition to the types of cerebral palsy, other terms that indicate the part of the body affected are used to describe more clearly the child's condition. *Monoplegia* refers to involvement of only one limb. Relatively few cerebral palsied are monoplegic. Involvement of one side of the body is termed *hemiplegia*, found to the greatest extent among spastics. As a rule, the arm is more severely involved than the leg. When the lower part of the body is affected, the condition is called *paraplegia*. *Quadriplegia* refers to paralysis or incoordination of all four extremities. Athetoids and spastics both fall into this category, spastics usually with greater involvement of the legs and athetoids of the arms.

Treatment Since the damaged areas of the brain cannot be repaired or replaced, treatment must be aimed at the symptoms rather than the cause. The process circumvents the areas which are damaged and utilizes unimpaired areas to perform the necessary functions. The child with cerebral palsy must learn to relax those muscles that become tense and prevent motion, to synchronize muscle groups for smoothness of movement, and to bring uncontrolled movement under voluntary control. The place of nonmedical therapies in assisting with this is discussed later. Other procedures and devices help the child overcome the motor incoordination. Braces and other aids are prescribed to support affected muscles, prevent permanent contractures, and control excess movement. Operations can lengthen contracted tendons or transplant an operating muscle to perform the work of an impaired one. Other symptoms can sometimes be relieved through operations on the brain itself. Masland (1967) reported on such advances in the treatment of cerebral palsy which have resulted from studies at the National Institutes of Neurological Diseases and Blindness (NINDB) and elsewhere. There have been encouraging results from alleviation of extreme hypertonicity by surgery in the cerebellar region. Another encouraging procedure is electric stimulation to the brain to create therapeutic lesions. The extent to which these medical treatments are effective in alleviating the symptoms of cerebral palsy cannot be predicted, either for individuals or groups. Improvement usually does occur, but how much results from growth and maturation and how much from treatment procedures is uncertain. In educational situations, teachers and other individuals must teach the child in spite of his disabilities and must assist him to make the most of his potentials—both intellectually and physically—regardless of handicaps.

Secondary handicaps Most children with cerebral palsy have other multiple handicapping conditions which complicate the educational problem. Some conditions that cause damage to the brain and nervous system and result in motor incoordination may also impair sensory, receptive, and integrative functions. Particular kinds of secondary defects are more common in one type of cerebral palsy than another, due largely to both site and cause of the damage. The most prevalent secondary handicaps in cerebral palsied children are speech impairments and mental retardation. The classic New Jersey study by Hopkins, Bice, and Colton in 1954 (Hopkins et al., 1954) and that by Taylor (1961) estimate that approximately half the children with cerebral palsy are mentally retarded, with IQ scores below 70. A larger proportion have speech defects, and visual and auditory impairment are common (see Table 9.9).

Other difficulties may cause educational problems for children with cerebral palsy. Many of them have seizures. About one fourth of the children in the New Jersey study lacked firmly established hand dominance. Many studies indicate that hand dominance plays an important part in learning to read (Harris, 1970), although there is considerable disagreement on this point. Coupled with poor coordination and lack of eye-hand coordination, this added deviation can impair learning.

Because of the many handicapping conditions found among children with cerebral palsy, an accurate appraisal of their educational potential is extremely difficult. A question about whether the potential of the cerebral palsied child can be assessed with the same intelligence tests used with unimpaired children exists, but much can be said in favor of the position stated by Allen (1960) that "evaluating the cerebral palsied in terms of the picture of the nonhandicapped group eventuates in a more realistic appraisal of strengths and weaknesses as these traits enter into the individual's everyday life (p. 203)." These are indeed, as Allen concluded, "the hard facts of life." Haeussermann (1958) and Taylor (1961), among others, have developed procedures for adapting test items for evaluating the potential of children with severe and multiple disability. They contend that these procedures give a more accurate picture of capabilities than can be obtained by standardized test administration.

Since cerebral palsy is the result of neurological impairment, many of these children demonstrate characteristics described under the heading of minimal brain damage by McIntosh in Chapter 10, such as tactual and kinesthetic impairment, disturbances of spatial orientation and judgment, or difficulty in discriminating figure and background. Problems of conceptualization also are prevalent in children with cerebral palsy. In the light of such multiple problems it is important to evaluate extensively and individually both the educational and psychological aspects of performance of the cerebral palsied, to determine their potentiality to achieve scholastically in comparison with other pupils, and to plan educational programs accordingly.

Convulsive Disorders (Epilepsy)

Definition   There is some difference of opinion concerning the use of the terms *epilepsy* and *convulsive disorders*. Some authorities view the two as synonymous and list convulsions as one of the symptoms of the epilepsy syndrome (Lorenze, 1965). Others apply the term *convulsive seizures* to all conditions, including very temporary ones, in which convulsions occur and classify as epilepsy the more permanent chronic or persistent condition. In this discussion, "convulsive disorders" will be used as the generic term and the convulsive or epileptic state will be defined as "a sudden onset and sudden offset of phenomena affecting consciousness and/or sensory-motor or autonomic functions (Torres, 1969, p. 152)." A diagnosis of epilepsy, according to Torres, is based on (1) an observation of seizures, (2) a complete individual and family history, and (3) an electroencephalogram (EEG). The EEG may show characteristic brain wave patterns, but it is also possible for an individual to have epilepsy without any indication of abnormality in the pattern, or vice versa. A spinal puncture may be necessary to rule out meningitis or other diseases of the nervous system as causes of the seizure.

Causes   Epileptic, or convulsive, seizures result from spontaneous, uncontrolled firing of neurons in the brain. Although the exact mechanism is not known, there is evidence that lesions which cause this seizure may be either organic or biochemical and may stem from some structural defect in the brain itself or from a defect in cellular metabolism. Seizures may be indicative of (1) more or less permanent physical conditions such as injury to the brain from metabolic disorders, nutritional deficiencies, genetic factors, accidents, or prenatal or birth injury; or (2) temporary conditions including digestive upsets, high temperature, or acute infection. They often accompany mental retardation, cerebral palsy, and other neurological disorders.

Prevalence   Convulsive disorders are relatively common among young children. Tower (1960) estimated that one child in 100 is afflicted with epilepsy. Torres (1969) also stated that approximately 1 percent of the population suffers from convulsions. He indicated that this is an increase over some previous prevalence figures, part of which is a real increase and part of which is due to the tendency to classify as epilepsy a larger variety of episodic disturbances that used to be in other categories.

Classification and characteristics Epilepsy may be classified in two broad categories: (1) *symptomatic* if it is due to a specific organic disease or damage; and (2) *idiopathic* when there is no known cause. These classifications based on etiology are too general to be of much use either in management or treatment. Therefore, the common groupings have been based on types of seizures. *Grand mal* is the term used for the major seizure usually associated with epilepsy in the minds of the general public and *petit mal* for the minor type. Although the majority of seizures are one of these two varieties, many other kinds have been recognized, particularly in recent years, and a number of systems of categorization have been tried. Torres (1969) stated that although classification systems are innumerable, with none completely satisfactory, some classification is important for purposes of treatment. He proposed a system based upon a number of interdependent factors: (1) clinical characteristics; (2) electrical manifestations; and (3) response to treatment. The types of seizures are divided into two main groups, those that are generalized over the entire body and those that are focal. While the classification is not all-inclusive, it appears to be useful and workable and is the one that is referred to here (see Table 9.4).

TABLE 9.4 *A Classification of Convulsive Disorders*

Major Category	Types	Clinical Manifestations
Seizures generalized from the onset	Grand mal	Generalized seizure with tensing of muscles and/or twitching and tremors with loss of consciousness
	Petit mal	Brief lapse of consciousness (3–10 seconds), sometimes rhythmic 3-second blinking
	Akinetic-myclonic	Sudden generalized jerk or loss of tone without detectable alteration of consciousness
Seizures focal at the onset (any of these can progress to a generalized major motor)	Motor	Rhythmic movement of one part of body, stationary or progressing to other parts (Jacksonian). May be generalized from beginning
	Sensory	Somatosensory, visual, auditory, olfactory, or dizzy manifestations. May rapidly spread to become major motor, masking the aura
	Psychomotor	Feeling of unreality, visual delusions or hallucinations, with alteration of consciousness
	Autonomic	Paroxysmal abdominal pain, diarrhea, vasomotor changes

SOURCE: F. Torres, Convulsive disorders: A working classification and guidelines for diagnosis and treatment. *Medical Times*, 1969, 97, 152–156.

Medical treatment Medical treatment for epilepsy varies according to the type and the specific cause. In some cases of symptomatic epilepsy in which there is a known brain lesion, operations can be successful in removing pressure from tumors or other causes and seizures are alleviated. However, since in the large majority of individuals epilepsy is idiopathic, removal of the cause of the seizure is not possible. The procedure then becomes treatment of symptoms with drugs or occasionally with dietary modification to control the seizures. The specific drug or combination of drugs must be individually determined and administered under medical supervision. Drugs successful in controlling one type of seizure may trigger another type. It is sometimes necessary for a child to spend time in the hospital while the proper drug therapy is worked out.

The effectiveness of anticonvulsive treatment varies with individuals and types. Psychomotor and other types of focal seizures usually are more difficult to control than petit mal or grand mal. Millichap and Aymat (1967) reported that control of grand mal seizures is possible in about 60 percent of the cases. In petit mal seizures, complete control with drug therapy is successful in 39 percent. For an additional 25 percent of epileptics with petit mal seizures, control can be achieved the majority of the time. Crowther (1967) added that most early pure petit mal seizures respond initially to medication. Some such seizures, which may be difficult to control during childhood, tend to abate after puberty. However, physiological changes at this time also are apt to result in an onset of seizures, particularly with girls, who often experience an onset or increase of seizures with the beginning of menstruation. Torres (1969) warns that anticonvulsive drug treatment should be used only when a diagnosis of epilepsy has been established, because the drugs may have some toxic effect, and that effects of their use should be checked regularly because hypersensitivity may develop, as well as side effects such as anemia. Failure to respond to drug treatment may indicate some organic lesion. Wilson (1969) recommended that although anticonvulsant medication can usually be discontinued after two or three seizure-free years, children with epilepsy should be urged to continue taking the pills into the late teens because of the tendency for seizure control to relapse during adolescence. He also suggests that parents need counseling about the drugs. They should be warned that success with drug therapy may not be immediate and that changes in treatment may be necessary without predicting a poor prognosis. In addition, he states that "with current concern over drugs parents need a lot of reassurance that . . . anticonvulsants are not drugs of addiction, nor do they lead to moral turpitude (p. 476)."

In spite of the hopeful prognosis for the majority of epileptics, there remain important problems of education and adjustment. Medication often results in drowsiness, lack of concentration, or incoordination which can be disruptive to school work. However, there is no reason why the child with epilepsy cannot function in regular classrooms. Teachers should be aware of any possible difficulties either in the accomplishment of school tasks or in relations with peers and adults and be ready to help the child meet these problems successfully.

Management of seizures A seizure witnessed for the first time can be very upsetting. This is particularly true in the case of grand mal. The tendency is to overreact, which only makes the situation worse. If one knows what to expect and remains calm, the management of the seizure is simple. For this reason a teacher should always be apprised of epilepsy, its type, and whether medication is being used.

A *grand mal* seizure is often preceded by a strange sensation known as an aura, and often by a shrill cry. Some individuals with this type of epilepsy have the aura far enough in advance of a seizure that they can get to a place to lie down before losing consciousness. The seizure of violent jerks usually lasts a minute or two but may last longer. When he recovers, the child may be dull or disoriented. He may want to sleep for some time. Consequently, his school program is disturbed and normal progress is impaired. When such a seizure occurs, the teacher should not attempt to hold the person to reduce the jerking. Instead, he should (1) ease the child to the floor and (2) see that he is not apt to injure himself by striking furniture or sharp corners while in convulsions. Turning the child's head to one side and carefully placing, but never forcing, a folded handkerchief or similar soft object between the back teeth is sometimes advised. A pencil or other solid object should never be used, as the teeth and gums may be injured. Other than these procedures there is nothing a teacher need do aside from providing a place for the child to sleep if he wants to when the seizure is over. A grand mal seizure need not be too disturbing for the other children in a classroom when they are prepared for it and it is handled properly. If a seizure occurs during a class period, some explanation to the students will be necessary, but their attitude toward the situation will largely reflect the teacher's. The teacher should help classmates accept the convulsion calmly and understand that there is nothing contagious or harmful about it.

The child who has a *petit mal* seizure may drop things, appear to be staring straight ahead, or stand still unaware of what is going on around him. The teacher may often think he is just not "paying attention." He quickly recovers, usually in seconds, and goes on with what he was doing. If such seizures occur frequently the child is apt to be handicapped by gaps in continuity. The teacher should watch for signs that indicate a child is having a seizure and check to see that he has understood what was going on in the class.

Other types of epilepsy are not so well known or as easily recognized. In fact, they may often go undiagnosed by a physician if he is not well acquainted with the child and has not actually seen him in a seizure. Any strange and persistent behavior by the child should be called to the physician's attention. *Psychomotor* seizures, in particular, have been under investigation recently because it is suspected that some kinds of deviant behavior in children can be attributed to a seizure state. The individual with this type of epilepsy often acts automatically for a short time; his actions may appear to be purposeful but are really irrelevant. He may even act violently and upon recovery not remember what he has done. Such a seizure may be dismissed as "bad behavior" or a "temper tantrum." Some kinds of so-called delinquent behavior may actually be manifestations of psychomotor epilepsy. A teacher who observes recurrent behavior of this kind should call it to the attention of the school nurse for investigation.

Multiple Sclerosis

Multiple sclerosis is a disorder of the central nervous system characterized by hardening or scarring (sclerosis) of the myelin sheath, the protective covering on certain nerve fibers. Breakdown of the sheath may result from a chronic virus infection or disorder of the immunity system of the body (Freeman and Mckhann, 1969). Primarily a disease of older adolescents and adults, it also concerns educators involved with junior and senior high school pupils. Symptoms include muscle weakness, spasticity of the extremities, tremors, unsteady gait, and visual and other sensory complications. Progress is generally downhill, spontaneous remissions or partial recoveries often occur with or without subsequent regression. Eventual total disability and death may result, usually from such secondary complications as pneumonia or other respiratory diseases or infections. However, the condition can become static and the individual may be able to live a fairly normal life for considerable periods. There is no known cure for multiple sclerosis, but some progress has been made in finding causes of the disease which may lead to treatment procedures (National Multiple Sclerosis Society, 1971). Drugs and physical therapy may help the afflicted maintain activity. The child should remain in regular school as much as possible with home-teaching help during periods of regression. Emotional and adjustment problems may need consideration along with the physical condition. Alexander, Berkeley, and Alexander (1961) stressed that the management of multiple sclerosis should accomplish (1) realistic, encouraging interpretation of the disease to the patient; (2) a protective regimen or way of life least likely to provoke attacks; and (3) treatment to relieve attacks and/or chronic progression between attacks.

Children with Musculoskeletal Conditions

Musculoskeletal malformations in children affect primarily the upper and lower limbs, spine, and joints. Such disabilities may handicap a child in walking, sitting, standing, or using his hands. They may be either congenital or acquired as a result of infectious diseases, developmental disorders, or accident (see Table 9.5).

Clubfoot

Clubfoot is the most prevalent of the impairments of the foot. It accounts for 25 percent of the congenital anomalies seen in crippled children's clinics, and 75 percent of those involving the feet. Usually discovered and corrected in the early years of a child's life, the condition is rarely an educational problem.

Scoliosis

There are a number of kinds of *curvature of the spine* of which *scoliosis,* a lateral curvature, is the most common. When severe, it can cause limitation of movement, which might affect school progress.

TABLE 9.5 Summary Description of Disorders of Musculoskeletal System

Condition	Cause	Characteristic Manifestations	Treatment
Clubfoot	Congenital	One or both feet turned downward and outward at ankle	Casting and bracing during infancy and early childhood
Scoliosis	Congenital or acquired from poor posture, accidents, or disease which weaken muscle	Lateral curvature of spine; body thrown out of alignment, resulting in irregular growth and deformities	Casting and bracing to correct or prevent deformity
Legg-Perthe's disease	Probable circulatory disturbance caused by injury or strain	Flattening of head or femur, or hip bone; destruction of bone tissue; pain, muscular spasm; limping	Rest from strain or weight-bearing until evidence of repair and no pain or muscle spasm
Juvenile rheumatoid arthritis	Unknown; may follow acute systemic infection; may involve localized pressure on digital or peripheral nerves; tends to be familial	Inflammation of joints, tendons, and tendon sheaths; may also be in muscle; joint pains, swelling, stiffness, later muscle weakness, atrophy, and joint deformity. Severe weakness and fatigue; rash, fever; inflammation of the eyes; cardiac enlargement	Rest with supervised exercise and massage; treatment of local infections; well-balanced diet; relief from worry and anxiety. Aspirin, cortisone, or ACT therapy
Osteomyelitis	A pyogenic, or pus-forming, organism; majority stapholococcus	Acute inflammatory symptoms; pain, fever, generalized weakness, swelling, tenderness in affected area; destruction of bone; draining sinuses; weakness, irritability	Antibiotics; diet high in calories and vitamins; surgical drainage and removal of dead bone; protection from injury
Muscular dystrophy	Unknown; possibly faulty metabolism, malfunction of endocrine glands, or deficiency of peripheral nerves; some sex-linked	Deterioration, degeneration, and wasting away of muscle tissue; in pseudohypotrophic type displacement of muscles by fatty and connective tissue, giving outward appearance of healthy muscle	Early orthopedic care to maintain functional motion and prevent deformities; physical therapy, occasionally surgery, to prolong mobility and other motor functions

SOURCES: W. E. Nelson, V. C. Vaughn, III, and R. J. McKay (Eds.), *Textbook of pediatrics*. Philadelphia: Saunders, 1969; and A. R. Shands, *Handbook of orthopedic surgery* (5th ed.). St. Louis, Mo.: Mosby, 1959.

Legg-Perthe's

Legg-Perthe's disease is developmental rather than infectious. It occurs most frequently among boys between the ages of 3 and 12 years. Recent treatment procedures include the use of crutches or other supports which enable the child to get about much more freely than formerly. It may make it necessary for the child to be taught in the hospital or at home for a period of time.

Rheumatoid Arthritis

Although arthritis is generally considered a disease of older people, many children suffer from *rheumatoid arthritis*. Clark (1959) estimated that 30,000 children a year were afflicted with this disease, 16,000 of them to the extent that they needed medical care in many cases as extensive as treatment for paralytic polio. Ten years later Calabro (1970) estimated that 175,000 American children had rheumatoid arthritis. It occurs more often among girls than boys. At puberty, for reasons not clearly understood, children with rheumatoid arthritis tend to improve. One of the most serious complications is inflammation of the eyes. Blindness is reported as a threat in 5 to 15 percent of the cases. Serious eye inflammation appears to be most prevalent in those children with the mildest disease. Calabro (1970) contended that with good treatment normal development is now possible for most children who have this type of arthritis. Children afflicted often must stay at home or in the hospital and may receive educational services there.

Osteomyelitis

Osteomyelitis affects mainly the long bones, most often in the lower extremities. It has been so successfully controlled by antibiotics that it is very rare among children and is no longer an educational problem.

Progressive Muscular Dystrophy

Progressive muscular dystrophy includes several forms of disease characterized by gradual degeneration and wasting of muscles. The commonest type among children, generally considered the typical juvenile form, is called *pseudohypertrophic muscular dystrophy* because it causes apparent growth of muscles. The onset of this type usually occurs between one and four years of age, and often by ten the child will be in a wheelchair. Although progressive with no known cure, treatment can alleviate some of the symptoms. Both psychologically and physically the child with muscular dystrophy benefits from remaining in school and participating in normal activities as long as possible. The child can usually achieve adequately in school, though in the later stages he is impaired by weakness.

Children with Congenital Malformations

Congenital malformations are defects with which a child is born (see Table 9.6). They may be hereditary or may be caused during pregnancy by diseases or other conditions of the mother.

TABLE 9.6 Summary Description of Congenital Malformations

Condition	Cause	Characteristic Manifestations	General Treatment
Congenital malformations of heart	Maternal infection, radiation, and drugs; other undetermined factors; tends to be familial	Impaired pulmonary blood vessels leading to or from heart; impaired valves or walls of heart, resulting in malfunction and progressive damage to heart; reduced strength, vitality, and stamina	Surgical repair of damage; restriction of activity; prevention and treatment of dehydration; balanced diet with iron and vitamins; treatment for infections
Congenital dislocation of hip	Probably a genetic factor; tends to be familial	Head of femur, or thigh bone, displaced in hip socket	Cast and/or brace to hold femur in place until bone and socket grow properly
Spina bifida	Not known; may have genetic basis	Defect of closure of spinal cord, protrusion of nerve fibers and other contents of cord into exterior sack; paralysis of lower limbs and internal organs below defect from cutting off of nerve supply	Surgical treatment of meningoce and hydrocephalus. Orthopedic care to maintain straight spine, legs, feet, and mobility of joints
Hydrocephalus	Blockage of passages carrying spinal fluid from brain; defective absorption or secretion of spinal fluid	Excessive pressure on brain and skull resulting in greatly enlarged head; damage to brain tissue, eventual brain deterioration; loss of ambulation; severe mental defect; early death	Surgical shunt or tube, from cerebral cavity to heart, jugular vein, or other part of body to relieve excessive pressure

SOURCE: W. E. Nelson, V. C. Vaughn, III, and R. J. McKay (Eds.), *Textbook of pediatrics.* Philadelphia: Saunders, 1969.

Malformations of the Heart

Malformations of the heart comprise approximately half of the congenital malformations treated in crippled children's programs. They also account for about 40 percent of organic heart diseases in children. The development of operations to correct these defects has received much attention recently, and many children who would have died early or have been limited in their activity for life have been given normal lives.

Dislocation of the Hip

Congenital dislocation of the hip is one of the most prevalent of the malformations of bones and joints. Early correction of this impairment has been successful to the extent that it is seldom seen except in the very young. Therefore, it is rarely a school problem.

Limb Deficiencies

Congenital amputations or malformations of the extremities came into prominence recently because of the many children who were deformed through the use of the drug Thalidomide by their mothers during pregnancy. Many other prenatal factors can also cause absence or deformities of limbs. Some of these children are permanently severely handicapped and may need special class facilities, while others may spend periods at home or in hospitals while prosthetic devices are developed and fitted, but will then be able to attend regular classes.

Spina Bifida

Spina bifida, a term for a variety of conditions in which there is a defect of closure in the bony spinal cord, is one of the more common congenital malformations. In fetal growth the two halves of the spinal cord develop and fuse at the midline. This closure begins at the middle and proceeds toward the head and feet "like a double zipper, until the tube is open only at either end (Kilfoyle, 1967)." At times something goes wrong and the spinal tube either fails to close or is blown open by pressure in the spinal tube. Lack of fusion of the two halves of the body is also seen in cleft hip and cleft palate (see Hull, Chapter 6). In spina bifida there may be a protrusion of the nerve fibers and other contents into a sack outside the spine, the contents of which are the bases of the classifications of the condition. The nerves to the lower limbs and internal organs, particularly the bladder and kidneys, below the defect may be cut off, causing paralysis and lack of function. Various abnormalities of the skeletal system such as clubfoot, dislocated hips, and unsegmented vertebrae, as well as anomalies of the heart, bowel, or brain, may also be present. Hydrocephalus, or "water on the brain," caused by obstruction of the normal flow of cerebral spinal fluid, is sometimes a complicating factor. It may be present at birth or develop later, usually during the first year.

The mortality rate of children with spina bifida is fairly high during the early years. Improvement in care has lowered the death rate considerably, although many severely impaired children still do not survive. Orthopedic care should begin at birth, and although normal function of lower limbs is not always possible, the child is enabled to get about with crutches or braces. Hand and arm use are usually good. Unless hydrocephalus causes mental retardation, mobility and possible lack of bowel and bladder control will be the principal problems to be solved in school.

Hydrocephalus

Hydrocephalus, mentioned above as a frequent complication of spina bifida, is a common cause of mental deficiency. The deficiency may be severe or there may result only a slight loss in intellectual functioning, making possible average school progress in the regular grades.

Children with Other Crippling and Health Conditions

In this category are a wide variety of physical disabilities that cause impairment of function or vitality. Crippling conditions generally are considered to be impairments which affect bones, joints, and muscles and thus limit ability to move about, sit, stand, or manipulate the tools of daily living. This context appears to have broadened, and the term "crippled" is sometimes applied to other than these orthopedic disabilities. In 1969 the more prominent impairments were cystic fibrosis, spina bifida, and other congenital problems (Ronayne, 1969). The classification used here is more in line with the older traditional categories, and "crippling" is applied to conditions of skeletal and muscular systems caused by (1) accidents; (2) infectious diseases; and (3) birth injuries. Health conditions include those that result from (1) diseases of the various internal body systems; (2) allergic, metabolic, and nutritional factors; and (3) neoplasms, or new growths.

Miscellaneous Crippling Conditions

Accidents that cripple (including child abuse) Accidents cause considerable crippling among children. Though the accidental death rate in the United States has decreased in the past few years, the rate of reduction is less than that of the other main causes of death. The number of individuals involved in nonfatal accidents in the United States in 1958 as compared with 1968 (U.S. Department of Health, Education, and Welfare, 1971c) is shown in Table 9.7. Some of these injuries cause permanent damage directly to the skeletal system, as in amputations, while others result in injury to nerves and muscles which often lead to crippling. Although many accidents involving children are vehicular, a large proportion of accidental injuries occur at home. Poisonings from medicines, insecticides, cleaning materials, and similar substances are a major cause of deaths and injuries among children. Injuries that result in lack of adequate motion or in the absence of upper extremities are the most handicapping for school work. In addition to permanent impairments,

TABLE 9.7 Number of Nonfatal Injuries, 1958-1968

Age Levels	1958	1968
	Number per 1,000 per year	
0-4 years	291	311
5-14 years	325	292
15-24 years	334	299
Total	950	902

SOURCE: U.S. Department of Health, Education and Welfare, Children and youth: Selected health characteristics, United States, 1958 and 1968. *Vital and Health Statistics,* 1971, **10** (62).

ones that necessitate modifications of school programs during periods of convalescence also require provision of services.

Of growing concern in this area is *child abuse.* Child abuse, or the "battered child syndrome," as it has been called, has become one of the commonest forms of violence as a cause of physical impairment in children. With increasing frequency, child deaths, permanent brain damage, or physical disability resulting from punishment administered by parents or guardians are brought to the attention of physicians, social workers, and children's agencies. There are probably no overall national figures that adequately reflect the prevalence of child abuse, but Anderson (1969) cites the estimates of the American Humane Society that 10,000 children are beaten, burned, "boiled," and deliberately starved in the U.S. each year by parents, relatives, and guardians. This is in addition to those similarly mistreated in institutions.

The reasons for child abuse are not clearly understood, but regardless of the cause of the problem, the protection and well-being of the children must be the major concern. How best to accomplish this task remains a question, but certainly the school has some responsibility to do everything possible to insure that children arrive in the classroom in a physical condition conducive to learning. School problems will be discussed later in the chapter.

Infectious diseases which cripple Crippling conditions resulting from infectious or parasitic diseases have been a major cause of physical impairments in children. However, modern methods of prevention and treatment have virtually eliminated them from the picture. This is the case with poliomyelitis, tuberculosis of the bone and joints, and osteomyelitis.

Poliomyelitis has been one of the most publicized and best known as well as most feared of the neuromotor diseases. In 1955, before immunization techniques were perfected, there were 28,985 cases of acute polio in the United States (U.S. Department of Commerce, 1971). Since that time immunization for this disease has been so successful that it appears to be joining the "almost unknown" category of smallpox. diphtheria, and scarlet fever. In 1969, according to the above report, figures from the Center for Disease Control showed 20 cases of paralytic polio in the United States. However, in 1970 there were outbreaks of the disease among unvaccinated children, pointing up the necessity of continued emphasis on the need for the immunization of children, particularly in city slums where many children do not receive the vaccine.

A brief medical description of poliomyelitis is given in Table 9.8. In addition to treatment shown here, surgery and physical and other therapies can help to restore use of weakened muscles and to provide aids and devices to help movement. Since the disease does not affect intellectual functioning or ability to learn, most children can attend regular class if adequate facilities and equipment can be provided to accommodate wheelchairs, crutches, or braces.

Tuberculosis of bones and joints usually is contracted from a pulmonary infection and principally attacks the spine (Pott's disease), then the hips and lower extremities (see Table 9.8). It can cause severe crippling unless treated promptly. The necessity of immobilizing the affected part for a time may interfere with school progress and require home or hospital teaching.

Birth injuries that cripple The term "birth injuries" in this context usually refers to mechanical damage at the time of birth, such as *Erb's palsy,* which affects the shoulder and forearm, and torticollis, or deformity of the neck. Relatively few children sustain permanent severe damage from this cause which greatly impairs their educational functioning.

Miscellaneous Health Conditions

Rheumatic fever Rheumatic fever, particularly recurrent attacks, has been greatly reduced by the prevention of infection through regular treatment with penicillin and other antibiotics over a period of years (see Table 9.8). As a result, the danger of permanent heart damage from prolonged attacks has been lessened. Furthermore, the long bed rest formerly prescribed for rheumatic fever patients has been modified so that children are seldom confined at home for long periods as they once were. Therefore, the educational problem has been greatly minimized. However, in cases in which permanent heart damage has been sustained, it is important that a physician be asked what activities the child can have in school.

Cystic fibrosis Cystic fibrosis (see Table 9.8) was recognized as a disease only fairly recently, probably because of the wide range of manifestations and the difficulty of diagnosis. About half the children who have it die by age 10, and 80 percent by age 20, usually from pulmonary complications. If puberty is reached, the condition becomes fairly stable as a chronic lung disease. Teicher (1969) reported that cystic fibrosis rivals cancer as a cause of death among children under 15. However, improved treatment has increased the lifespan until at present about one third of the patients who have it are over 12. This increase in the number of school-age people with the disease has focused attention on educational problems. Excessive coughing and frequent bowel movements present difficulties. The afflicted child also may have to spend some time in the hospital, and school routine is interrupted. The school may need to help the child accept himself and his limitations and

TABLE 9.8 Summary Description of Miscellaneous Crippling and Health Conditions

Condition	Cause	Characteristic Manifestations	Treatment
Poliomyelitis	Poliovirus which attacks nerve cells in the spinal cord	Damage to nerve cells in grey matter of spinal cord and/or areas of brain, resulting in pain, spasticity, weakened and paralyzed muscles; skeletal deformities	Acute stage relief of pain; analgesics, sedatives; hot packs, bed rest, avoidance of exertion, good diet; physical therapy
Tuberculosis of bone and joint	Tubercule bacilli	Formation of tubercles, destruction and disintegration of bones and joints; pain, swelling; muscle spasm, rigidity, and atrophy	Antibacterial therapy, isoniazid, streptomycin; well-balanced diet, high vitamin content; rest, immobilization of affected part
Rheumatic fever	Unknown, but generally follows streptococcus infection	Chronic infection of connective tissue, affecting joints, heart and blood vessels; arthritic, abdominal, and chest pain; skin rash; shortage of breath; chorea (St. Vitus dance); heart damage from continued or prolonged attacks	Acute stage, rest and limitation of activity; anti-inflammatory drugs, sedatives, aspirin; prevention of reinfection by penicillin therapy
Cystic fibrosis	Basic defect unknown; generalized dysfunction of exocrine glands (sweat, tear, salivary); hereditary	Impaired digestion and absorption, chronic pulmonary disease; respiratory tract allergies; recurrent, excessive coughing; heat prostration; excessive sweating; usually progressive deterioration	Respiratory assistance, oxygen, aerosol solutions; antibiotic therapy, high calorie diet; physical therapy to promote bronchial drainage
Pulmonary tuberculosis	Tubercule bacilli	Infection of respiratory system; cough, chest pains, fever, loss of weight, tiredness	Antimicrobial therapy—isoniazid; maintenance of nutrition, avoidance of fatigue; bed rest until substantial evidence of improvement
Hemophilia	Lack of clotting element in blood; hereditary, sex-linked	Bleeding into tissues and joints; can result in permanent crippling; health problems and lack of vitality from loss of blood	Prevention of injury; control of hemorrhage; blood transfusion; orthopedic care to prevent a permanent deformity of joints

Condition	Cause	Symptoms	Treatment
Asthma	Susceptibility to various allergenics; contributed to by emotional stress, excess exertion, climate or temperature, infection, endocrine factors	Spells of coughing; heart and respiratory rates increased; difficulty in breathing; restlessness, fatigue, sweating; abdominal pain, possible vomiting	Relief of acute symptoms, vapor inhalants, drug therapy, antihistamines; desensitization agents, allergenic substances; dietary and occupational regulation; control of infection
Diabetes	Insufficient production of insulin to enable body adequately to utilize glucose or sugar; tends to be familial	Loss of weight, increased appetite, excessive thirst, listlessness, lack of vitality; irritability, restlessness, inattention; complicating factors such as impaired vision, skin lesions, paralysis, heart conditions	Balanced regime of diet, exercise, and insulin treatment
Nephritis	Unknown; often preceded by a streptococcal infection	Puffiness about eyes and other parts of body; vomiting, fever, loss of appetite; anemia, high blood pressure, headache, drowsiness, often convulsions; possible damage to kidneys; enlargement of heart	Diet regulation, fluid balance; reduction of blood pressure; rest and curtailment of activity; antibiotics
Infectious hepatitis	Virus spread by direct contact or through contaminated food and drinking water	Fever, loss of appetite, feeling of weariness, nausea, abdominal pain, headache; jaundice, bile pigment in liver; enlargement and tenderness of liver	Diet, high protein, no fat; bed rest until liver functioning is normal; reduction of discomforts of pain and fever
Infectious mononucleosis	Probably a virus; method of transmission uncertain	Fever, sore throat, chills, headache, abdominal pain; initial enlargement of lymph nodes; body rash and occasional jaundice; possible involvement of central nervous system	Reduction of discomforts; rest and restriction of activity

SOURCE: W. E. Nelson, V. C. Vaughn, III, and R. J. McKay (Eds.), *Textbook of pediatrics.* Philadelphia: Saunders, 1969; and L. Spekter, *The pediatric years.* Springfield, Ill.: Thomas, 1955.

improve relations with his peers. In addition, it can guide parents to accept genetic counseling.

Pulmonary tuberculosis Pulmonary tuberculosis (see Table 9.8) is the infection of the respiratory system generally thought of as tuberculosis by laymen. It is a low-vitality condition formerly of concern to the special educator because of the required restriction of activity and the long periods of convalescence which have been a part of the treatment. However, the outlook has changed appreciably in the last two decades. Not only has the prevalence of the disease been reduced by effective control and treatment with drugs but children who have it are returning to school sooner after infection. Consequently, special educational programs for the tubercular, common years ago, have virtually disappeared.

Hemophilia Hemophilia (see Table 9.8) can be very limiting to a school child or young person because of the danger of accidents that might start the excessive bleeding characteristic of the disease. It may also require periods of hospitalization. Other than this, functioning in school is not affected. Progress in isolating the blood-clotting element promises increasingly effective treatment.

Asthma Asthma and other *allergic conditions* (see Table 9.8) are found frequently on lists of handicapping disabilities among young people. Figures from the U.S. Department of Health, Education and Welfare (1971b) indicate that among individuals under 17 years of age who have some degree of limitation of activity and mobility due to chronic conditions, there are as many who suffer from asthma and hay fever as from all other conditions combined. Severe asthmatic conditions may require a child to spend some time in a hospital or clinic or to attend a special class where the allergins can be controlled. Otherwise the child with asthma should be able to attend regular school.

Diabetes Diabetes (see Table 9.8) is a metabolic condition which may result in a loss of alertness and vitality affecting progress in school. Diabetes mellitus, the type ordinarily associated with the general term, is more prevalent in adults over 40 years of age. Of the estimated 3 million diabetics in the United States, approximately 4 percent are under 15 (U.S. Department of Health, Education and Welfare, 1967). In the initial stages, hospitalization may be necessary until a treatment program has been worked out. Once this has been done, a child can participate in normal activities and perform his school tasks without interference or inconvenience. The teacher should be informed of the prescribed routine and be aware of the consequences if the child fails to eat properly, neglects the insulin, or overexercises. He may go into insulin shock, become dizzy and lightheaded, suffer abdominal pain, and show other diabetic symptoms described. A piece of candy, lump of sugar, or glass of orange juice usually will quickly restore him to normal. Most diabetic children are taught to care for themselves, and there is no reason why they should need special placement of any kind. It is only when the school personnel are unaware of the diabetic condition that situations such as the one described in Vignette 9.1 may arise.

Vignette 9.1 A Third-grade Pupil with Diabetes

When he entered the third grade Allan was an eight-year-old whose physical and mental development appeared normal for his age. His academic achievement was somewhat below the average of his classmates, although his records showed that his intellectual capacity was well within the normal range. On the cumulative school record there were no indications of serious health problems. He had had several common childhood diseases and an accident in kindergarten in which he had broken his arm, but none of these had resulted in complications. The only negative comments were that he was often listless and inattentive, and both of his previous teachers had remarked that he was "lazy" and needed to be prodded and encouraged to finish his assignments. The investigations of his third-grade teacher had disclosed nothing which would account for his lack of ambition and low performance. In fact, she was completely unprepared when he suddenly lost consciousness in the middle of the arithmetic lesson.

Neither the teacher nor the school nurse could revive Allan, and it was some time before any of his family could be located. It was then that it was discovered that he had diabetes. Allan was taken to the hospital where he was given emergency treatment for a diabetic coma. It became evident that although his problem had been known by his family and their physician for two years, no one else was aware of it. Insulin had been prescribed and diet instructions had been given to his mother, but neither of these programs had been followed consistently.

When Allan returned from the hospital the school nurse worked with the mother and impressed upon her the need to follow the doctor's directions regarding the administration of insulin, the special diet restrictions, and the necessity for regular meals and a healthy daily routine of exercise and sleep. Notes on Allan's condition were added to his school health record and his teacher was informed of his diabetes. She was advised to be alert to changes in his condition, to watch for the signs that indicated he might be going into insulin shock after he had been playing hard at recess, and to see that he had a piece of candy or other sweet available and took it immediately upon recognizing the signs of impending difficulty.

Allan's family got him a small identification bracelet that told of his condition and gave the necessary information in case he should have problems away from home. They also reacted favorably to the suggestion that he be allowed to go to a camp for diabetic children the following summer where he could learn to make his own tests, to administer the insulin himself, and to make the dietary adjustments that were needed to live a normal life. Equally important, he would learn that there were others who had to live with the same restrictions that he did and that none of them were "freaks," as he had often considered himself.

Malnutrition   Malnutrition can decrease strength and alertness to the extent that progress in school is affected. Although the severe nutritional conditions found in Africa, India, and other underdeveloped countries are not prevalent in the United States and Canada, except in extremely deprived areas, others such as rickets are still listed as health problems.

Leukemia   Leukemia and other forms of cancer usually are more acute and progress more rapidly in children than in adults. Leukemia, sometimes called "cancer of the blood," may be either chronic or acute and almost without exception is fatal. Much research on etiology and treatment is being conducted and some advances have been made in prolonging the lives of afflicted children. In the meantime, treatment is aimed at keeping the child comfortable, interesting him in the world around him, and keeping him active as long as possible.

Other diseases of body systems   Three diseases of body systems *nephritis, infectious hepatitis,* and *infectious mononucleosis* (see Table 9.8), which affect the kidneys, liver, and other internal organs, have not yet been brought under control. As other health conditions have decreased in prevalence because of improved methods of prevention and treatment, these three diseases have assumed a relatively more important position in special education programs for children and young adults. The true incidence of acute *nephritis* is not known, but it occurs most frequently in young boys. *Hepatitis* has the highest incidence rate of any disease among school-age children and remains the leading unconquered viral disease in the United States (Kaye, 1969). *Mononucleosis* is particularly prevalent among high school and college students, but is not uncommon among children of 2 to 10 years (Blattner, 1969). All three of these diseases may limit to some extent the ability of a pupil to perform, and in severe cases the child may be on a program for the homebound and hospitalized.

Children with Multiple Handicaps

Definition and Classification

Any child with more than one disabling condition can be classified as multiply handicapped. These children usually have been placed for purposes of education on the basis of their one most severe disability. This practice may be satisfactory for some children, but for many others such an arrangement fails to meet their needs because of inadequate physical facilities or lack of training and experience of those who work with them. Examples of children for whom this is especially true are deaf-blind, mentally retarded with severe vision or hearing problems, or blind or deaf children who are also retarded or severely disturbed. Such multiply handicapped children are also discussed elsewhere in a number of chapters in this book. For children with multiple handicaps the trend in special education to eliminate more or less rigid categories and to deal with the whole child on the basis of his individual learning problems has been particularly advantageous.

Identification and Prevalence

Identification of multiple handicaps often fails until after placement in some facility for care or education. Sometimes one impairment such as cerebral palsy, deafness, or blindness may so predominate that other disabilities are extremely difficult to assess and are ignored or undetermined. For this reason and also because of the fact that one individual may be listed in several disability categories, prevalence figures may be misleading or hard to evaluate.

In the survey of physically handicapped school-age children by Friedman and MacQueen (1970), referred to earlier in the chapter, many were found to have secondary handicaps, with mental retardation being the most prevalent. Of the 195 children, 43 percent were mentally retarded, with IQ's below 80. Retardation was most frequently associated with cerebral palsy, with over two thirds being retarded to some extent. Speech problems were identified in 37 percent of the physically handicapped, again mostly among those with cerebral palsy. Psychological examinations indicated a higher prevalence of maladjustment than in the general population. A similar pattern of multiple disabilities is shown in Table 9.9, which gives the percentage of secondary handicaps among children enrolled in classes for the orthopedically handicapped and other health-impaired children in California (California State Department of Education, 1972).

The high prevalence of multiple handicaps among school-age children is largely because of two factors. As has been pointed out by Dunn (Chapter 1), multiply handicapped children are receiving more attention because of a shift of philosophy; furthermore, there is a real increase caused by medical advances which have prevented or ameliorated many types of single disabilities and have saved many who would have died at birth or not have been born.

Causes

The most promising study of the causes of neurological damage, usually responsible for multiple handicaps, and its relation to conditions of pregnancy and birth is the *Collaborative Perinatal Research Project* (Masland, 1967) being conducted under the direction of the National Institute of Neurological Diseases and Blindness of the National Institutes of Health. Through 14 medical centers throughout the country, 55,000 mothers and their offspring are being studied. Detailed obstetrical and pregnancy histories are kept, and the children are followed for eight years through regular examinations. The purpose is to determine whether neurological defects may have resulted from unfavorable events of pregnancy. Information gathered includes illnesses and infections of the mother during pregnancy, accidents, drugs taken, and the circumstances during birth. The first findings reported when the children were seven years of age indicated definite relations between evidences of potential damage and certain factors such as (1) prematurity; (2) birth weight; (3) drugs and anesthesia administered to the mothers; and (4) health conditions of the

TABLE 9.9 *Secondary Problems among Children Enrolled in California Special Day Classes for the Orthopedically Handicapped and Other Health Impaired (Including Teleclasses), 1971-1972*

Type of Physical Defect	Numbers of Cases	Total with Defect	Mental Retardation	Speech	Vision	Hearing	Seizures	Social Behavior
Cerebral palsy	3,079	48%	60%	52%	35%	5%	13%	27%
Muscular dystrophy	387	6%	32%	12%	8%	0.52%	1%	19%
Other	2,986	46%	37%	26%	19%	3%	9%	20%
Total	6,452		47%	37%	26%	4%	11%	24%

SOURCE: Minors with orthopedic and other health impairments enrolled in special day classes (including teleclasses), 1971-1972. Mimeographed Report, Sacramento, Calif., State Department of Education, 1972.

mothers, including diabetes mellitus, nephritis, convulsions, and vaginal bleeding. Through such detailed information the perinatal study should contribute greatly to the prevention of neurological damage through (1) the maintenance of good health of pregnant mothers; (2) measures to prevent prematurity; (3) prevention of disease and infection; (4) alertness to damage from rubella and other diseases; and (5) tests of blood incompatibility. The latter two conditions have received considerable attention and will be discussed in more detail.

Rubella When contracted by pregnant mothers during the first trimester, rubella has been one of the major causes of multiple impairment in children. The disease itself is usually mild and does not last long in either children or adults, but as one of the virus diseases that cause prenatal damage it is particularly virulent. Approximately 20,000 to 30,000 children born in the United States after the rubella epidemic of 1963–1964 (Hardy, 1970) had handicaps including visual impairment, cardiac disorders, deficits in hearing, problems of basic biological development, general retardation, and lack of thriving. A typical case of multiple handicap caused by rubella is described in Vignette 9.2. The recently developed vaccine for rubella shows indications of controlling the disease and thus preventing the deformities it causes. It is discussed later in the chapter under medical advances.

Vignette 9.2 Larry, a Multiply Handicapped Teenager

Larry's mother apparently had German measles during pregnancy, although she was unaware of it at the time. She had few symptoms and recovered completely in two or three days. There were no complications during the remainder of the pregnancy and Larry was born only three weeks prematurely. At the time of birth he appeared to be a normal infant with no severe observable defects. However, early examinations by the pediatrician disclosed that he had congenital cataracts. In addition, muscle tone appeared to be abnormal, he was limp and flaccid, and some of his reflexes were weak. It became evident that he had sustained some prenatal brain damage.

During his early years Larry was operated on for removal of the cataracts and fitted with glasses. He responded fairly normally to visual stimuli, although he often held small things close to his eyes to see them. He babbled during his first year, but as he grew old enough to begin to say recognizable words he still could not be understood. His mother concluded that, since he obviously heard sounds, he was merely slow in developing speech. His flaccid condition did not improve and he was unable to sit, pull himself up with his hands, or crawl. He gradually learned to hitch himself along the floor to get around. He was a contented baby and seldom cried or fussed.

As Larry grew older and did not learn to sit alone or to walk, his mother was advised to take him to a physical therapist who immediately began treatment to improve his muscular condition. He learned to sit, to operate pedal toys, and to pull himself up and stand with support. He was later fitted with crutches, and even though his progress was always slow and labored he was able to get about in most situations. Larry's speech did not improve greatly and even at the age of nine was completely unintelligible except to those who had learned his type of jargon. He was a very sociable, friendly child, understood speech well, and responded to others with a flow of animated syllables which had little resemblance to English words.

As Larry grew older it became apparent that he was retarded beyond what might be expected even for a child with his several disabilities. Shortly before he was enrolled in a special class at the age of nine his mother took him to an otologist, who discovered that he had a severe hearing loss in some frequencies. He was fitted with a hearing aid that helped a little, and after some time at school with the assistance of a speech therapist he became more understandable, though he never developed clear articulation. He was started on a preacademic school program and became an eager and persistent pupil.

At 13 years of age Larry can read a simple first-grade book and recognizes common words and signs in his environment. He does simple arithmetic but has not mastered even the rudiments of dealing with money. He does recognize some coins. He prints his name, though he often reverses it completely, as well as a few other simple words. Reversals also show up in his art work, and he will draw an automobile upside down or a girl lying on her side. He can take care of his own personal needs and is able to help his mother around the house with such tasks as dusting or drying the silverware. He is still a pleasant and engaging person most of the time, but very recently he has begun to have periodic severe headaches which worry his mother. It is difficult to determine what the future will bring.

Rh blood incompatibility Rh incompatibility is another major cause of multiple disabilities in children. The facts about blood types and the danger of transfusions of the wrong type of blood are well known. The threat in many instances is to the receiver whose own blood reacts to a different type. However, in some kinds of blood incompatibility the damage is done to an unborn child. This is the case with the Rh blood factor. In about 85 percent of all human beings the component called the Rh factor is present. These people are Rh positive. In the remaining, the factor is missing and they are Rh negative. A mother who has Rh negative blood is likely to have an Rh positive baby. If for some reason the blood of the fetus enters the blood of the mother her body builds up antibodies to fight the invading factor. This is not detrimental to the mother. However, in subsequent pregnancy, the antibodies may have built up to a high level and the mother's blood may get into the bloodstream of the fetus with serious consequences. The ponderous term *erythroblastosis fetalis* is applied to the condition of the affected fetus or newborn infant. Jaundice, a yellow coloring of the skin, is a symptom of the condition in the newborn. Since the major part of the damage takes place shortly before or after birth, the principal method of preventing brain damage has been to give the infant a complete blood transfusion. Other procedures of prevention are discussed later under recent medical advances.

Drug abuse Drug abuse by the mother is also a cause of impairment resulting in multiple handicaps. The tragic crippling of thousands of children whose mothers had been given the drug Thalidomide during pregnancy is an example of the consequences that can result from the use of a drug that was intended for beneficial medical purposes. The wide use of drugs of all kinds, many of which have not been adequately tested, has become so much a part of present-day custom that potentially harmful drugs are available to anyone, from the small child who swallows the aspirin tablets to the adult who tries the sedative prescribed for someone else, both often with tragic results. The problem of the effects of drug use by women on their unborn children is receiving considerable attention.

Evidence of *chromosomal abnormalities due to drug abuse,* which may result in a variety of impairments, is not yet conclusive. However, indications are that a definite cause and effect relation may be established. At present LSD appears to be one of the most damaging drugs. Warren, Rimoin, and Sly (1970), in reporting on the effect of prenatal exposure to LSD, stated that although the drug is known to produce congenital malformation in rodents, its effect upon the human fetus is uncertain. They indicate that in a number of cases infants with limb malformations have been born to mothers who were using LSD, but that other studies of such mothers have shown no effects. Since LSD users often take other drugs such as amphetamines, and also since LSD as it is purchased is often mixed with other substances, it is difficult to determine the effect of a specific drug. Hsu, Strauss, and Hirschhorn (1970) reported chromosomal abnormalities associated with multiple physical deformities in the child of an LSD user. Although there have been questions raised as to the validity of the conclusions in the above report (Hoey, 1970), other researchers have found evidence of chromosomal damage in users of this drug. Egozcue, Irwin, and Maruffo (1968) studied 50 mothers who were users of LSD, almost half of whom had also used marijuana during pregnancy and had experimented with other drugs. These researchers suggested that a possible danger from damage to chromosomes would be an increase in leukemia and other types of neoplasms (new growths such as cancer), physical abnormalities, and stillbirths and stunting. However, Judd, Brandkamp, and McGlothin (1969) found no significant difference in chromosomal breakage rates among three groups, including some LSD users who had continued to use the drug, others who had been heavy users but had discontinued, and a third group of drug-free subjects.

Evidence of prenatal and postnatal damage to the offspring of users of other types of drugs has been found in a number of other studies. A British study by Neuberg (1970) showed that among heroin users there was a much greater incidence of premature births, breech births, and fetal deaths than among a control group of nonusers.

An unforeseen consequence of the use of a generally beneficial drug that may have harmful effects was reported by Herbst, Ulfelder, and Poskanzer (1971). A number of cases of a rare vaginal cancer (adenocarcinoma) were found in several young women, ages 15 to 22, whose mothers had been given the drug diethylstilbestrol, a synthetic hormone, 15 to 20 years earlier during pregnancy. The results of the study convinced Herbst to conclude that there is a highly significant association between the treatment of mothers with diethylstilbestrol during pregnancy and the subsequent development of adenocarcinoma in their daughters.

Not only is there evidence of chromosome breakage and malformations in babies born to drug users but infants of drug abusers have been found to be addicted and have shown evidence of withdrawal symptoms after birth. Some effects on babies have been seen when only the mates of the mothers were drug abusers. Desmond, Schwanecke, Wilson, Yasunaga, and Burgdorff (1972) reported withdrawal symptoms in infants whose mothers had taken barbiturates during pregnancy. In addition, there are indications that some commonly used tranquilizers can have deleterious effects on infants when they are taken by mothers during pregnancy.

The evidence of the consequences of drug abuse as a cause of multiple impairment in children is not all in and is by no means conclusive, but it is convincing enough to indicate that it is indeed a serious social problem that will be extremely difficult to solve. Coupled with rubella, Rh incompatibility, and other possible causes of damage to children, it presents an alarming picture to the special educator, who must envision swarms of multiply handicapped pupils invading the classroom. However, the outlook is not completely discouraging. Medical advances discussed later in the chapter show promise of preventing some of the predisposing causes of physical disabilities.

Pregnant School-age Girls

An increasing area of concern for educators is that of the pregnant school-age girl. Whether or not this should be considered with health problems and whether it is the specific responsibility of special education to handle the problem is open to question. Traditionally it has been viewed more as a social than a medical problem, and the girls have been eliminated from school and usually taught at home. However, the health of the young mother as well as the child should be considered and the school becomes involved in providing adequate health and other services.

Prevalence

For numerous reasons accurate prevalence rates among pregnant teenagers are difficult to ascertain, but a number of studies give indications of their number and characteristics. Wurtz and Fergen (1970) stated that nearly 150,000 girls become pregnant out of wedlock each year with an annual approximated increase of 30,000 unmarried pregnant school-age girls. In an article in *Today's Education* (National Education Association, 1970), it was estimated that in 1970 200,000 girls under 18 years in the United States would give birth to children, approximately one third of whom were unmarried. Pregnancy is the largest known single cause of dropout from school. The problem is greatest for girls under 16 years of age.

Among young mothers there is a greater incidence of premature births and more cases of toxemia and other complications. Many also have some degree of anemia, high blood pressure, and excess weight during pregnancy. Thus the problem involves not only the health of the mother but also of the unborn child. Without doubt, the scope and pertinency of the problem of pregnant teenagers require that schools cooperate with other community agencies to provide the needed health, educational, and social services. The question of the responsibility of the school is discussed later under educational provisions.

PROBLEMS OF ADJUSTMENT

Personal and Social Adjustment

One of the important factors that influence an individual's ability to achieve in academic areas and to develop his intellectual potential is the degree to which he is able to acquire and maintain a state of personal and social adjustment. A physical disability can place limitations on achievement, but so can feelings of inadequacy and insecurity, attitudes of rejection on the part of parents, or the isolation and ridicule of peers. Such factors may change a disabling condition into a major handicap. Therefore, these problems must be the concern of the school if it is to help pupils reach the limits of their capabilities. Nothing indicates that a physically handicapped person will automatically be maladjusted. In fact, general agreement seems to be with Wright (1960) that there is no substantial evidence that groups with impaired physiques differ from the unimpaired in general or overall adjustment or that types of physical disability relate to particular personality and adjustment characteristics.

On the other hand, there is no question that physically disabled persons sometimes have adjustment problems. Richardson, Hastorf, and Dornbusch (1964) studied children with handicapping conditions that were not severe, including cerebral palsy, diabetes and postpolio, cardiac, and various orthopedic disabilities, who were attending a camp for the underprivileged. Although serious maladjustment generally was not apparent, it was found that the handicapped children showed some signs of maladjustment in terms of personal relations and negative and aggressive behavior. Rutter, Tizard, and Whitmore (1970) studied the psychiatric aspects of physical disability and concluded that, in general, children with chronic physical disorders evidenced psychological disturbance only slightly above the rate of the general population. They suggested that the effects of bodily disorders on brain function found in such severe conditions as anemia, cyanotic heart disease, low blood sugar, hormone imbalance, and neurological disorders might contribute to emotional disturbance. Children with asthma demonstrated mild signs of emotional upset but did not differ significantly from those with other miscellaneous disorders. However, there was evidence that disturbing emotional experiences might be important in precipitating attacks of asthma. The researchers concluded that there was an indirect relation between physical disorders and psychological disturbance, but no association between the severity of handicap and the proportion of the children showing psychiatric disorders.

In a psychological study of children with *cerebral palsy,* Neilson (1966) compared spastics with nonimpaired children and found them to have significantly more signs of moderate or severe personality disorders. Moed and Litwin (1963), in a study of cerebral palsied individuals, found that psychosocial adjustment was related to (1) extent to which the person exaggerated his degree of ability; (2) interest in and ability to maintain relations with other handicapped; (3) the ability of the parents to permit social independence commensurate with physical capabilities; (4) parental understanding that independence is not synonymous with self-sufficiency; (5) parents' own attitudes and adjustment; (6) degree of isolation because of inability to travel resulting from physical and social restrictions; and (7) early emphasis on total rehabilitation rather than medical therapy alone.

Emotional maladjustment of a mild to severe nature may be a problem with *epileptics.* Although the idea of a typical epileptic personality is no longer accepted, attitudes of others toward the epileptic, legal restrictions (on driving cars, employment, and marriage), and prejudices of employers can cause personality and adjustment difficulties, particularly in teenagers and young adults. Social pressure during adolescence often brings problems. The young person may feel embarrassed about his condition and attempt to hide it or withdraw from social contacts so that it will not be discovered. He may also chafe under restrictions and become defiant or aggressive.

Studies indicate that individuals with *psychomotor epilepsy* are especially apt to have psychiatric disturbances. In an investigation comparing subjects with grand mal and psychomotor seizures with a group that had chronic medical problems, Guerrant, Anderson, Fischer, Weinstein, Janos, and Deskins (1962) found that in half or more of the group with seizures emotional disturbances tended to be severe. They concluded that the convulsive groups not only had a higher incidence of psychiatric symptoms than the group with chronic health problems but that the problems of the psychomotor group far exceeded those of the subjects with grand mal seizures. Rutter, Tizard, and Whitmore (1970) also found psychomotor epilepsy to be strongly associated with a high rate of psychological disorder.

Gingras, Mongeau, Moreault, Dubois, Herbert, and Corriveau (1964) in a study at the Rehabilitation Institute of Montreal found no evidence of major emotional disorders in individuals with *congenital anomalies of the limbs,* many the results of Thalidomide. Conflicts tended to be intensified by physical anomalies, and the attitudes of the subjects were influenced by the degree of acceptance of parents and by the general emotional state of the environment, but no direct relation could be demonstrated between the disability and emotional adjustments. Children with abnormalities showed no marked distortion of body schema in the early years, and body image developed as normally as in the nonhandicapped.

Diller et al. (1969) studied the psychological and educational development of children with *spina bifida* as compared with amputees and nondisabled children. The children with spina bifida who also had hydrocephalus had more problems in these areas, while the nondisabled group and those with spina bifida but not hydrocephalus seemed to show normal social awareness. *Hemophilia* has been found to be associated with psychosocial problems. Hurt (1966) states that mothers of boys with hemophilia are often excessively anxious and overprotective and sometimes have a sense of shame and guilt that may affect the child. The afflicted boy may regard the mother's overprotection as domination and may take unnecessary risks in rebellion or to compensate for his fears. Fathers may resent the boy's close association with the mother and blame the mother or child for negligence when accidents happen. The father may also withdraw from and tend to deny the problem, and, because of a feeling of disappointment in the boy, devote a disproportionate amount of time to the unhandicapped siblings. Consequently the boys themselves, Hurt concluded, often grow up with a sense of inadequacy, low self-esteem, poor academic preparation, tendencies to withdraw from action and responsibility, and a lack of preparation for the adult world. Malikin (1971) states that a child with hemophilia may develop emotional problems because he is deprived of the conflict situations vital for the development and strengthening of ego. Malikin contends that the hemophiliac needs to be given opportunities to learn his own limits and tolerances, to be more active, and to participate in testing situations that promote ego maturation.

Collier (1969) studied junior and senior high school students with *diabetes* and found that adjustment appeared to be somewhat affected. Both counselors and parents reported that diabetes limited social activities, although the pupils did not see this to the same extent.

As with other fatal diseases, *cystic fibrosis* patients are inclined to resent or reject the constant therapy and to blame their parents if something goes wrong with the treatment (Teicher, 1969). Many children are averse to attending school because they do not have the stamina for strenuous physical activity and may be teased by classmates. Consequently problems of social adjustment may develop.

For children with *muscular dystrophy* the psychological and social problems sometimes associated with the condition may be of more vital concern to the educator than the physical ones. Boys particularly may display hostility, aggressive and destructive behavior, and stubbornness. Some children may employ other defenses such as withdrawal, often as a result of a change in the regular program of activities brought about by the deterioration in physical ability (Gucker, 1967). By nature the disease may cause the child to develop overdependence, self-pity, and hopelessness. Solow (1965) stated that the extent to which psychological aspects are important in the treatment and management of the child with muscular dystrophy depends upon the limitations imposed upon the child by loss of strength and on the length of time he has had the disease. Feelings of guilt and isolation in the parents and the value they put upon such skills as athletic competence may affect the child's adjustment.

Even though it has been found that individuals with physical impairment may tend to be emotionally disturbed, the disability is not necessarily the cause of the disturbance. A disability, Meyerson (1971) states, is a social judgment rather than an objective thing in a person. He contends that the two concepts which relate directly to the adjustment of the physically disabled are (1) new psychological situations and (2) overlapping psychological roles. The reasons, then, that individuals with physical disabilities tend to be more severely maladjusted than the unimpaired are that (1) they are placed in situations that are new to them more frequently and the "newness" is more pronounced; and (2) they live in two psychological worlds, one of the disabled, the other of the "normal" individual. Solutions to these problems lie in (1) helping the handicapped person to increase his tolerance for frustration, teaching him skills that will reduce the newness of situations, and facilitating his acceptance as a person; and (2) minimizing the forces that impel him to strive for goals that are unobtainable and inaccessible and thus reduce the frequency of overlapping excluding role situations. Meyerson suggests that behavior-modification techniques, which do not take into account or omit as unnecessary the complexities of the person and his environment and place little emphasis on the person's perception of his problem, offer possibilities for solving adjustment problems.

Postschool Occupation Adjustment

The problem of what the physically impaired person is able to do when he has completed his formal education and how he is able to adjust in a world that seldom makes allowances for his disability is of vital concern to educators and other community agencies. In the world of work there is often little room for the individual that cannot operate at maximum efficiency. Preparation for productive employment should begin in the preschool and kindergarten and continue to be a major objective throughout the remainder of the school years. Good basic working traits should be consistently fostered, including (1) an understanding and acceptance of the handicapping condition and its limitations; (2) an image of oneself as a worthwhile, productive individual capable of making a contribution to others; (3) a sense of responsibility to carry one's share of the burdens of living; (4) a respect for work no matter how menial or insignificant it may appear; (5) the ability to accept directions and to work well with other people; and (6) efficient habits of work, caring for materials, completing a task, punctuality in meeting commitments, neatness, and cleanliness. The cultivation of these attributes is one of the primary goals of special education. However, the extent to which individuals with severe motor and health impairments can be prepared for employment is often limited. Some of them can become partially or completely self-sufficient, but others will never be able to move out of the sheltered workshop or home environment where they can earn enough to contribute to their care, and many can never become independent. Physical conditions are not always the limiting factors in successful employment. Personality factors may be the primary consideration. In addition, the prejudices of employers often deprive capable persons of the opportunity to demonstrate that they can handle a job.

It is estimated (President's Committee on Employment of the Handicapped, 1965) that 10 percent of the people of the United States are limited to some extent in what they can do in providing for their needs through employment because of physical disability or chronic illness. Recently there has been a marked increase in the willingness of government agencies and private industries to employ the physically handicapped. In 1967 placement of disabled persons in local public employment was the highest in 20 years, with 17,000 employed by the federal government alone (President's Committee on Employment of the Handicapped, 1967). In a study by the Division of Rehabilitation Services, 279 firms surveyed indicated that 93 percent of the employers judged the impaired to be average or better in job stability, and 90 percent said they were average or above in adjustment to working conditions and trainability.

Studies indicate that attempts to prepare the physically impaired for vocational adjustment have met with varying degrees of success. Brieland (1967) conducted a follow-up study of orthopedically handicapped graduates of a children's hospital school and found the employment rate for the group to be 40 percent, higher among women than men. Intelligence and the further education they had obtained were significantly related, as were IQ scores and general well-being and social contacts outside the family, their hobbies, and posthigh school education. One interesting and pertinent finding was that the longer the subjects had been in school, the less favorable was their attiude toward leaving it and going to work.

The two physically disabled groups that seem to have the greatest difficulty finding employment are the cerebral palsied and the epileptics. Part of the problem stems from the reluctance of employers to hire them and part from the severity of their impairment. Four hundred thousand epileptics of working age and 200,000 with cerebral palsy were reported upon by the President's Committee on Employment of the Handicapped (1967). The rate of unemployment of the epileptic was 15 to 25 percent, and only a handful of the cerebral palsied were employed. Efforts to rehabilitate epileptics generally have met with greater success than has been the case with the cerebral palsied. Moed and Litwin (1963) reported on two studies to determine the employability of persons with cerebral palsy. The first was conducted with ambulatory individuals over a five-year period for the purpose of establishing practical methods of work evaluation. Three basic movements in manual dexterity were found to be related most to employability. Other important factors were (1) verbal IQ; (2) handwriting; (3) vocational adjustment; (4) severity of gait defect; (5) ability to travel independently; (6) performance IQ; and (7) speech intelligibility. Of those subjects in the study who were already employed, approximately half were in unskilled jobs and one fourth in clerical work. The latter tended to stay on the job longer and were the more stable employees. Those who had been evaluated during high school were more stable than those who went to work after a period of idleness. Employment chances appeared best if the first job was found within eight months.

In the second study Moed and Litwin (1963) evaluated young cerebral palsied adults from vocational centers in the United States. They concluded that over 50 percent of persons with cerebral palsy whom they studied needed sheltered workshop employment and estimated that 60 to 70 percent of the cerebral palsied population are marginal workers without the capacity for regular employment.

Machek, Hardin, and Collins (1960) described a project for comprehensive evaluation and classification of the vocational potential of individuals with cerebral palsy. Slightly less than half of the individuals screened were judged to have vocational potential. For the severely involved, the vocational potential was found to be poor. Only a quarter of the group could be placed on jobs, and the great majority appeared to be able to be productive only in a sheltered workshop, since the tensions of regular employment tended to increase motor problems and multiply emotional defects. An interesting sidelight was that those from smaller communities and those who had had less agency exposure were inclined to do better work and to adjust more readily. The researchers concluded that the most important factors in predicting vocational success were not IQ or sample job performance but motivation and emotional stability. Many of the young people were found to have low level of maturity, an unrealistic attitude toward employment, and lower chances for vocational rehabilitation. Results of the study stressed the placement of emphasis on the total adequacy of the individual, including qualities that pertain to the practical application of functional intelligence.

Although *epileptics* often have difficulty in obtaining employment, those whose seizures are controlled have been found to be more careful than average, to have fewer accidents on the job, and less absence. They are not deterred from Civil Service employment if they can compete in the regular examinations.

In discussing the vocational development of individuals with *hemophilia,* Rusalem (1969) found problems to exist at a higher rate than might be expected. Only a small proportion of the pupils with hemophilia on whom he reported had had access to any specialized vocational counseling and generally lacked vocational readiness.

Cantoni (1960) gives a number of guidelines on the vocational rehabilitation of children with *heart conditions*: (1) vocational rehabilitation should begin at the time of diagnosis; (2) those working with the child should know the energy requirements of various tasks and be able to relate the calorie-per-minute expenditure for specific jobs to the severity of the heart condition; (3) a graded activity program should be provided; (4) there should be an impartial evaluation of work; (5) it may be desirable to have a waiver of right to workman's compensation for an employee; and (6) a team should prepare the cardiac child for work from the time of diagnosis. In a study of rehabilitation counseling with *cardiac* children, Kir-Stimon (1967) reported that although most of the subjects were able to participate in normal activity, many had limited social experience and cultural impoverishment in addition to inadequate educational background and often exhibited unrealistic aspirations. These factors were a greater handicap than the cardiac condition, according to the researcher.

EDUCATIONAL PROGRAMS

Administrative Provisions

General Problems and Trends

As has been noted previously, children with neuromotor and other crippling and health disabilities will be found in all of the types of special education programs discussed by Dunn in Chapter 1. Physical facilities may need to be adapted for them, but modification of curriculum, methods, and materials probably will be necessary only when (1) the disability is severe and permanent and will greatly influence future vocational and social competency; (2) lack of normal experiences, absences from school, and the necessity of functioning at reduced speed may extend the amount of time required to complete prescribed courses; and (3) intellectual capacities and learning deficits may require the use of special methods and materials. For a large majority of these children their physical condition is not handicapping in a regular classroom when certain minor adjustments are made. Others will require the services of consultants and itinerant or resource teachers. The remainder of the children who need special education traditionally have been placed in one of three general types of programs: (1) special boarding or day schools or day classes; (2) hospital classes; and (3) programs for the homebound. Administrative problems related to these programs, such as teacher competencies and preparation, class size and teacher load, transportation, and modification of facilities will be discussed later under each program and only general problems will be considered here.

One of the major administrative problems is that of *placement of pupils*. In Chapter 1 Dunn presented a comprehensive discussion of this problem with administrative guidelines for specific situations. Therefore, it is necessary only to call attention to a number of criteria for special placement which apply directly to children with nonsensory physical impairments. Four of these appear to be particularly applicable:

1. The child needs some kind of special equipment or adjustment of physical facilities impossible in a regular classroom. This reason for special placement should not be used freely without careful consideration of all alternatives.

2. The physical and/or learning needs of the child require a disproportionate amount of the teacher's time and attention with resultant neglect of other children in the room. This problem, too, should be thoroughly studied and not be used as an excuse for special placement by teachers and administrators who do not want to be bothered with a handicapped child. Often the guidance of a consultant can help to solve this difficulty in a manner satisfactory to everyone concerned.

3. The child requires some type of therapy or treatment which can be provided only in a special facility.

4. The child's physical impairment causes emotional problems so severe that placement in a special class is desirable, or rejection by his classmates creates an emotional condition that makes segregation preferred. Often placement for this reason can be temporary, and the child can gradually be helped to adjust to more normal situations.

A number of *trends* and *changes* in special education have affected the roles and responsibilities of administrators. Dean and Barbour (1965) discuss the administrative problems that result from the changing role of the home and hospital teacher. Such trends include the change from a relatively small number of different illnesses and diseases of long-term patients to shorter-term illness, disease, and injury and the inclusion in programs of unwed mothers. In addition, some states, have changed existing laws to include the teaching at home and in hospitals of children with marked learning or behavioral disorders and significant discrepancies between ability and achievement. The inclusion of these students with specific learning disabilities, or the educationally handicapped, as they are designated in some areas, in home-teaching programs or in day and residential psychiatric hospital units brings about the need for a shift of approach, new training for teachers, and changes in relations of professional teams. Carr (1965) noted that the trend toward postelementary programs for severely crippled students places new demands on administrators and teachers. Teaching at the secondary level not only requires a command over a wide range of academic subjects but also a smooth articulation with the elementary school program and functional prevocational training. The teacher must work effectively with community agencies in providing the needed services and in planning and implementing work-study programs.

Newer Concerns

Two problems related to the physical condition of pupils, which have not been discussed previously, have become of increasing concern to educators and require the consideration of administrators. These involve the responsibility of the school in dealing with (1) abused children and (2) school-age pregnant girls. As social problems neither of these is new. There have always been pupils whose ability to function normally in school has been affected by one of these conditions. However, the tremendous increase in the number involved in these areas in the last decade has forced educational systems to take a new look at their role. Whether special education has the prerogative to handle the problems is open to question, particularly for abused children. However, if its function is to provide for needs beyond those of the majority of the pupils in the classroom, then the individuals in these two categories logically come, to some extent at least, under the jurisdiction of special education services. This is especially true of pregnant school-age girls, since traditionally many of them have been included in programs for the homebound. Both of these groups are discussed briefly here.

Abused or "battered" children The question of whether or not school administrators have any responsibility in the *problem of child abuse* was investigated by Rochester, Ellis, and Sciortino (1968). Questionnaires were sent to elementary school principals and guidance counselors in a Midwest metropolitan area. Approximately half indicated that they had dealt with one or more cases of abuse. The three most common forms of abuse reported, in order of prevalence, were (1) child beating, (2) malnutrition, and (3) cruel punishment. Of the persons inflicting the abuse, a slightly higher number were mothers than fathers. Stepmothers and grandparents were reported in several cases. The major action taken by the school was a conference with the counselor or principal and the abused, the abuser, or both. Some cases were referred to social workers, juvenile authorities, or superintendents for further action. As a result of the investigation, approximately half of the abused children were left in their present environment after corrective measures, and about one third were provided with protective services. A small number were placed in each of several facilities outside the home; foster homes, institutions, private schools, and homes of relatives. Only in 11 cases was legal action taken. Neither the legal nor the medical professions yet have devised adequate means for handling the problem, and it is apparent that the schools must join with other social agencies in finding ways of coping with it.

Pregnant school-age girls The need for expanded programs for pregnant school-age girls has brought additional problems and responsibilities to administrators. Wurtz and Fergen (1970) surveyed 48 state departments of education to determine the extent and type of the services provided for pregnant girls. Of the 17,000 school districts surveyed, 5,450 had programs which ranged from homebound instruction to regular school classes. The trends noted by the researchers were: (1) districts are moving away from home teaching toward special or regular classes; (2) states are providing increased funds for programs; (3) state departments are assuming greater leadership in establishing and maintaining programs; and (4) rehabilitation has become the keynote in long-range planning. McMurray (1970), in reviewing community action in behalf of pregnant school-age girls, stated that in 1966–1967, 1,568 students in New York City schools were discharged from school because of pregnancy, approximately half of whom received home instruction provided by maternity homes and other agencies. During the same period more than 6,000 girls under 17 years gave birth. She estimated that about 85 percent of these had dropped out of school of their own volition and probably were not known to the school authorities as being pregnant. The following year school board policy was changed to allow girls to remain in school. Five full-time schools were established for pregnant students, with a public agency that was responsible for coordination of health, educational, and social services.

The growing trend is to allow pregnant school-age girls to remain in school. The expense of special programs has contributed to this trend. The legal question of the right of a girl to remain in school even though pregnant has also been a factor. A number of school systems have had a policy concerning the fathers of children of pregnant girls, some requiring the withdrawal of known fathers from school, at least until after the delivery, and others of involving fathers with the mothers in special programs.

As an alternative to educational provisions in regular classes or in a program for the homebound, some school districts have transported pregnant girls to central classes. A program of this kind is obviously more economical than individual home teaching. The girls have the benefit of more hours of schooling and also the services of a social worker, public health nurse, and home economist as well as the maternity clinic facilities.

Karnes (1965), in discussing programs for school-age pregnant girls, states that to be successful (1) close contact must be maintained with the school, (2) students must be highly motivated, and (3) every effort must be made to have them return to school when they are able. Wolinsky (1970) suggests that programs for pregnant girls require school systems to (1) explore patterns of professional training of teachers of the homebound; (2) examine the dimensions of the sociology of exclusion from school; (3) evaluate realistically the one-to-one teaching situation; (4) reexamine the role and function of continuing education for teachers; and (5) review the whole structure of certification and professional standards. Most of these points apply with equal pertinence to administrative responsibility in making instructional provisions for pupils with physical impairments.

Instructional Provisions

Provisions in Regular Classes

The children who are able to receive an adequate education in the regular classroom are those who (1) have physical impairments that are only mildly handicapping, correctible, periodic, or able to be controlled; (2) have little or no impairment in intellectual functioning and no severe learning disabilities which would necessitate teaching methods unusable in the regular class; (3) do not need extreme modifications of physical facilities and equipment not feasible in the regular school or classroom; and (4) require no drastic curriculum revisions with respect to content, type of educational experiences, length of time spent in schooling, or ultimate goals.

Physical facilities   Changes in physical facilities in regular school buildings that can be made to compensate for physical impairments include modifications in buildings such as (1) a short ramp up a number of steps for children in wheelchairs or on crutches; (2) a hand bar by a drinking fountain, in a toilet stall, or near a section of blackboard; (3) the removal of desks to make room for a wheelchair; (4) modification of furniture to provide for a child with braces; or (5) rubber mats over slippery floors. Other building features for the safety of handicapped students are discussed by Graham (1961), Connor (1962), and Mullen (1965). The problems of the child with poor hand coordination may be solved by such procedures as (1) taping paper to the desk; (2) devising means of keeping pencils and crayons from rolling to the floor; and (3) providing book holders or mechanical page turners. In buildings of more than one story, and particularly in secondary schools in which students change classes frequently, the problem is somewhat complicated. In some cases transfer of a student to another building or a change in scheduling may solve the difficulty. Larger school districts usually plan at least one regular school building with ramps or elevators to which handicapped pupils can be transported. Adjustments in buses can be made to accommodate wheelchairs and crutches and to assist students in getting off and on.

Adjustment of teachers and pupils   The presence of a physically impaired child in the regular class need not be detrimental to the child, to the other pupils, or to the well-being of the teacher. It can be a rewarding and humanizing experience for everyone concerned. The disabled child can learn to accept his limitations, to compensate for them in many ways, and at an early age to solve problems of living and competing in a world of unimpaired people. The other pupils can come to realize that the impairment of the disabled child is only a relatively insignificant part of his total personality; that he has the same interests, desires, and ambitions that they have; and that he has a unique contribution to make to the group. Whether the handicapped child or his classmates actually acquire this understanding of each other will depend in large measure on the teacher. As an increasing number of children with handicapping conditions are placed in regular classrooms, a vital part of the preparation of every teacher should be aimed at helping her to understand and provide for the educational needs of every child who comes under her guidance, no matter what his limitations. Teacher-training institutions generally have been negligent in orienting the student to the problems of exceptional children. A good survey course on the characteristics and educational needs of the exceptional child will not prepare a teacher to solve all the problems she is apt to meet, but it can help her to accept the child who is different, to know where to look for help, to familiarize her with some of the special techniques she will need, and to gain confidence in her ability to handle the unexpected. Equipped with these abilities, she can more effectively guide the pupils to the same kind of understanding and acceptance of each other.

The teacher has an ever-increasing number of resources to assist her in this task. Teaching materials for the individualization of instruction appear almost faster than they can be evaluated and utilized. Evaluation facilities, learning centers, and instructional media centers are becoming more available. But of as much or more importance is the attitude of the teacher herself toward the exceptional child in her classroom. As she thinks, feels, and acts, so to a great extent will her pupils react. Attitudes and values can be influenced by warm, open acceptance of pupils' differences, through frank discussion of situations that arise in the classroom and of books and motion pictures that help children to "put themselves in the other person's shoes."

Role of the school counselor and psychologist In the past the training of counselors and psychologists often has been no more adequate in preparing for the needs of the exceptional child than has that of teachers. Recent years have seen improvements in this respect, but many school counselors and psychologists still feel unequipped to evaluate or counsel the exceptional pupil and ill at ease in advising teachers concerning his management and adjustment. School psychologists often do not have the time or the training to administer the number and variety of evaluative measures needed to assess the child with poor communication or motor coordination. Such a child should not be denied a chance for an education on the strength of an intelligence test alone if there are other indications that he is capable of doing school work, nor should selection or rejection for a class be based on purely physical or medical criteria. More physically disabled students could succeed in regular classrooms if more teachers felt that they could request and obtain the assistance of school psychologists and counselors in correctly evaluating pupils. Fortunately, the trend in the preparation of these members of the team is to provide them with an ever-widening range of abilities which makes it possible for them to accomplish these goals.

Role of the principal No one person is more important than the principal in making it possible for the child with physical impairments to attend a regular class. It is he who must decide on problems on placement, make provisions for transportation and adjustments in physical facilities and materials, and mediate problems with parents. However, he has an even more vital role in setting the emotional tone of the school, ensuring that the staff is aware of the problems and needs of the exceptional pupil and prepared to accept and include him in the school activities. As with the teacher, his own attitudes and understanding are the factors that determine to a large extent the success or failure of the exceptional pupil in his school.

Provisions in Special Education Programs

Dunn, in Chapter 1, has presented the various types of special education programs and discussed their strengths and weaknesses. Those aspects of the programs which apply specifically to children with neuromotor, crippling, other health conditions, and multiple handicaps will be considered here.

Special schools and classes Traditionally many of the children with neuromotor and other crippling and health problems have been educated in special schools and classes. In the United States and other countries in the past there have been large schools for crippled children and special day classes for those with cerebral palsy, heart conditions, asthma, and other chronic health conditions. The trend has been away from such specialized facilities except for the severely and multiply handicapped. Some of the children in the latter group have been in *residential* or *boarding schools*, sometimes for periods of from three months to a year for thorough diagnosis and evaluation and in other instances as permanent placement. Often such placement has been on the basis of other major handicaps such as blindness, deafness, or mental retardation. Frequently the school is equipped to deal only with the blindness, deafness, or retardation but not the physical condition. The residential facility seldom is prepared to deal with more than one of the handicapping conditions. Too often a blind individual or one with cerebral palsy can be found stagnating in a residential facility because it was not staffed or equipped to deal with the multiple problem. This situation has not been so prevalent in residential schools for the deaf and blind because they have refused to admit children with other severe physical problems. However, many residential schools are recognizing their responsibility and are providing the special facilities and trained personnel required. Increasingly such children are being moved into special day schools and classes closer to their homes where they can receive their education in a less segregated situation. In most urban areas a large proportion of the pupils in these programs have been children with cerebral palsy, with a smaller number with other severely handicapping physical conditions. In small districts and rural areas the handicapped have been placed in the heterogeneous groups with pupils with other disabling conditions, in programs for the homebound, or in some cases left without any educational provisions.

There has been a trend on the part of smaller urban and rural school districts to set up special schools for physically and multiply handicapped students who have been considered ineligible for other public school special programs. Private organizations also provide special schools for severely handicapped children who have been eliminated from public schools.

Special schools and centers to provide *early education* for multiply handicapped children appear to be on the increase. Such a program for young and severely handicapped children was initiated in 1961 by the California Department of Public Instruction (Los Angeles Unified School District, 1969) for those children not old enough or mature enough to attend school, or whose conditions are so severe that they are ineligible for other public school programs. These Developmental Centers for Handicapped Minors were instigated partly as a result of the German measles epidemic in the early 1960s, when it was estimated that there would be about five times the usual number of children with multiple handicaps in need of such programs. Children are admitted at age three and may be able to move on to other special education programs or may remain in the Center. Besides activities in motor and perceptual development, self-care skills, language and speech training, and socialization and adjustment supervised by the teachers, ancillary services are provided by social workers, speech specialists, physical and occupational therapists, and a family counseling staff.

In keeping with the trend to extend rehabilitation services to include a much broader range of handicapping conditions and ages, some rehabilitation centers are also beginning to provide early education services to very young children.

Obviously the *competencies of the teachers* in such programs and in special schools and classes for cerebral palsied and multiply handicapped students are of utmost importance. However, studies of teacher competencies to date have been concerned largely with skills and abilities for working with pupils in one area of exceptionality, and in most of these there has been no indication that teachers of children with one disability have skills which equip them to handle other impairments. The solution of the problem does not lie in having teachers "observe" children with multiple handicaps nor even in having them take course work in two or more categories of exceptionality. The special procedures employed in teaching a child with one type of disability are not appropriate when that disability combines with another impairment. Teacher-training institutions need to become more involved in developing innovative programs for preparing special education teachers for the multiply handicapped. Even though experience or research has provided little data on the abilities and characteristics of a successful teacher of multiply handicapped children, it is apparent that among these must be (1) skill in assessing potential for learning and in determining avenues of accessibility; (2) ability to evaluate and apply varied teaching techniques as appropriate; (3) a working knowledge of innumerable teaching media; (4) flexibility in approaching the teacher-learning situations; and (5) imagination and creativity far beyond that required in "normal" teaching. Perhaps it is impossible to specify particular competencies required for any given teacher of a group of severely and multiply handicapped pupils, and teachers will need to be selected more on the basis of personality traits than specific abilities. In any case, with the trend away from discrete categories and the increase in multiple handicaps it is imperative that considerable attention be given to providing competent teachers for such children.

Physical facilities and equipment in both special schools and classes are designed to accommodate the child with severe physical involvement and to allow for freedom of movement and independent living. Some features to be considered are (1) wide doorways; (2) nonskid floors; (3) handrails; (4) rounded corners; and (5) protected coat hooks. Play areas, toilet facilities, and drinking fountains should be planned for wheelchairs and crutches. Desks and other furniture should be planned with the handicaps of the children in mind and be flexible enough to be adapted to various individual needs.

Regular school furniture can sometimes be modified by (1) adjusting seats to turn to the side so that a child with braces can sit more easily; (2) providing foot rests; (3) adding hinged extensions to the desk with a cut-out for the child that has poor sitting balance; and (4) eliminating protruding parts over which a child might trip. For children with special problems of sitting or standing, equipment such as special adjustable chairs, stand-up tables, stabilizers, or cut-out tables may be necessary. Only very general statements may be made about teaching equipment required in special schools and classes since the variety and complexity of the disabilities which may be present among even a small class of children make it necessary for the teacher to have available many of the special devices and materials that are used in teaching not only pupils with physical impairments but those with visual, auditory, and other disabilities as well. In addition, much of the equipment must be modified to meet individual needs. Each specific combination of disabilities requires its own modifications. Therefore, in addition to the electric typewriters, page turners, book stands, and pencil-holding devices that may be needed to accommodate physical handicaps, specialized equipment described in other chapters of the book may be needed. Even though class load is small, classrooms need to be as large or larger than regular classrooms to accommodate the special equipment. Further information and descriptions of such equipment may be found in references, particularly those that deal with the education of children with cerebral palsy.

Class load will depend on the age and degree of severity of disabilities. Eight pupils who are very young or severely disabled may be all that a teacher can manage in one group. Because of the difficulties of handling these children and the need of helping them with toileting, eating, and other self-care activities, the teacher of a class of severely handicapped children usually is assisted by an attendant or teacher aide, often both. Class size for less handicapped and older children might be as high as 10 or 12.

Classroom management of children with cerebral palsy and neuromotor impairments is important because they may display some of the same behavioral characteristics as those with minimal brain dysfunction (see McIntosh, Chapter 10). They may tend to be hyperactive and easily distracted by surrounding stimuli. If this is the case, measures to reduce stimuli and control behavior may be necessary. Fassler (1969) compared the effect of reduced auditory input on the performance of children with cerebral palsy with normal hearing acuity. Compared with a normal control group the cerebral palsied showed greater change in performance on a test of attention but no significant differences on other tasks. It was suggested that more experiments be conducted to determine if quieter classrooms would encourage greater attention and concentration in pupils with cerebral palsy.

Behavior-shaping techniques have been experimented with in the management of both the motor and behavioral problems of children with cerebral palsy. Although the small number of children involved and the limited amount of research reported in this area do not provide conclusive evidence of the effectiveness of this procedure, the indications are that productive results may be possible. Stone (1970) reports on the use of the method with a small group of boys with cerebral palsy who demonstrated evidence of diffuse minimal motor problems. An alarm clock to time periods of quiet, controlled behavior, and a system of individual record charts and tangible rewards resulted in an improvement of behavior during the school year, although the procedure did not bring about self-control without the need for the rewards.

The *curriculum* for pupils with cerebral palsy and other multiple disabilities will depend to a great extent upon what the student is going to be able to do with his education when he leaves school. Because the educational process for these pupils is so complex, valuable time is apt to be wasted on unnecessary courses and unproductive procedures. During the early years of life it may be impossible to determine the extent to which a child will be able to overcome his handicap. Nevertheless, it is important to scan the future and to prepare each individual for the fullest possible life. Careful appraisal of potential is extremely important, especially when pupils reach secondary school where decisions regarding future schooling and vocational possibilities must be made. On the basis of extensive and continuous evaluation of each student the curriculum content and school experiences should be planned. The educational program should emphasize enrichment of experience to compensate for limited environment. Provisions should be made for (1) extensive involvement with and utilization of school and community facilities; (2) physical and recreational activities; and (3) opportunities for leadership and initiative. Such enrichment is difficult to provide for children who, without a great deal of assistance, cannot browse through the library, take a nature walk, visit a fire department, participate in the student council, or plan a school program, but with the cooperation of teachers, principals, therapist, parents, and volunteer workers these activities can be a part of the school program of children with handicaps.

Methods of teaching the basic tool subjects should emphasize the development of functional skills and the use of meaningful material. The importance of reading skills for the child with cerebral palsy and other multiple handicaps can scarcely be overemphasized. Reading for pleasure, for stimulating creative thinking, and for keeping in touch with the world can mean much to the person who has limited firsthand experience. However, secondary handicaps such as sensory defects and conceptual and perceptual problems which accompany cerebral palsy often make the acquiring of these skills difficult. It often is advisable to teach reading to children with multiple handicaps by methods that minimize the amount of muscular coordination involved, focusing primarily on silent reading. Extensive oral reading employed for normal children may be an added burden to the child with severe problems in speaking.

It is vitally important that children with cerebral palsy and other multiple impairments develop adequate basic skills in the language arts other than reading. Speech and language development should be stressed. Inability to communicate is extremely frustrating and can lead to increased tension, which further aggravates the physical problems of these children. The acquiring of understandable speech is a long and tedious task in many cases and for some children will never be accomplished. A more detailed discussion of speech difficulties in children with cerebral palsy is given by Hull in Chapter 6. While formal speech correction must be done by a trained specialist (see Hull, Chapter 6), the classroom teacher can accomplish a great deal. Games and exercises that stimulate auditory discrimination or the production of specific sounds can be incorporated into lessons in spelling, phonics, reading, and other subjects. When good speech is not possible, written communication becomes extremely important. If the cerebral palsied person can learn to carry on conversation with others, tension will be considerably relieved. "Conversation boards" containing pictures of common objects for the child who has not yet learned to read and the letters of the alphabet for the older child are devices that have been used successfully. By merely pointing to the proper item or letters, the child can make himself understood. Older nonoral students can often get satisfaction from learning the Morse code and using it to communicate with the teacher and other pupils by blinking their eyes or tapping on the desk for dots and dashes. McCann (1966) developed and evaluated a number of adaptive electronic communication devices for the severely handicapped child.

Handwriting is difficult for many children with cerebral palsy and others with severe impairments of arms and hands. Prewriting activities such as tracing, coloring within lines, and activities in space orientation may be necessary. Children who have extreme difficulty writing should be taught to type.

Specific language deficits in understanding, formulating, or expressing ideas often are found in multiply handicapped children. Myers (1965) studied the language disability patterns of children with cerebral palsy to determine effective methods of instruction. She concluded that there were basic differences in the language structure of two groups of cerebral palsied children. Spastics were superior on the automatic sequential items of the Illinois Test of Psycholinguistics, which have to do with the grammatical and syntactical aspects of language; the athetoids were superior on the representational or meaning level of the language process. These findings emphasize the need of differential diagnosis of learning difficulties and the use of teaching procedures aimed at utilizing specific strengths and correcting particular deficits. A suggested instructional program included in the report of the above study gives useful suggestions.

Since many children with multiple disabilities, particularly those with cerebral palsy, may have the kinds of learning problems discussed in the section on minimal brain dysfunction, many of the same teaching techniques and materials can be profitably used with both groups (see McIntosh, Chapter 10). Suggestions resulting from a study aimed at developing teaching methods for brain-injured children conducted in Montgomery County, Maryland (Cruickshank, Bentzer, and Ratzeburg, 1961), are particularly applicable for the child with multiple handicaps. The recommendation was made that in teaching reading the exact nature of the perceptual problem be identified by determining whether the child has the ability to perform such tasks as (1) distinguishing form and color; (2) recognizing spatial relations; (3) differentiating between high and low or loud and soft sounds; (4) seeing a picture as a whole; or (5) following simple directions. Materials are developed and training given in those areas in which the child is deficient.

Conceptual as well as perceptual difficulties will necessitate using special methods and materials. Particular attention may need to be given to help pupils advance beyond the concrete stage of learning, in arriving at generalizations, and in seeing broad relations. Helpful learning experiences include (1) arranging objects in suitable categories; (2) deciding which items are relevant to a certain situation; or (3) matching objects on the basis of specific relations. These skills are vital in learning to read and should be acquired as part of the readiness program.

Teaching materials must be adapted to the needs of students on the basis of their physical problems as well as their perceptual and other learning difficulties. Modifications often need to be made in school materials and equipment to enable a child to hold a book, turn pages, write, or use other educational materials. Children who cannot hold an ordinary pencil may be able to manage one that has been built up with tape or inserted in a plastic or rubber holder. Electric typewriters can be fitted with a plastic guard with cutouts for keys and bars. Thus a child who does not have the coordination to get his fingers in the proper place is sometimes able to use a piece of dowel to which a handle has been attached for this purpose. Pupils in pre-academic classes use many manipulative materials in learning to match colors and shapes, distinguish between objects of different sizes and textures or develop concepts of number through manipulative games and devices that develop eye-hand coordination. Some of the materials that can be made or obtained commercially are (1) pegboards; (2) snap blocks; (3) lock boxes; (4) coordination boards; (5) take-apart toys; (6) color cones; (7) jumbo boards; and (8) puzzles. Many variations of these materials will need to be devised to increase motivation and minimize boredom.

The problems inherent in teaching basic academic skills to children with multiple handicaps often result in the failure of such pupils to achieve to the extent to which they are capable. Concern with physical problems, lack of experience, and limited social contacts can become so pressing that a disproportionate amount of time is given to these areas to the neglect of essential academic skills. All aspects of the child's development are important, but in examining the goals of education for a severely handicapped person it is necessary to look at all the alternatives. It may be more vital to his happiness and successful adjustment to be able to read, spell, and do arithmetic well enough to be employed in a job that will enable him to become even partially self-supporting than to walk on crutches.

Aspects of *physical development* as a part of the total educational program are of major importance for children with cerebral palsy and other physical handicaps, but physical development should always accompany academic and social growth, not supersede it, if the student is to make adequate use of his education. It is important to educate the child's mind without neglecting his body so that at the completion of his schooling he can use his learning either for his own satisfaction or for making a living. The alert, imaginative teacher can find many ways to develop physical coordination during academic learning. Special equipment can be devised with the assistance of the physical or occupational therapist so that training begun in the therapy sessions can be carried over into the classroom. To cooperate fully with the therapist in a consistent program, the teacher should understand the therapist's purposes and general procedures. Therapists should also be aware of the educational goals and cooperate in working toward their attainment.

Ancillary Services

Teachers in special schools and classes generally have a number of ancillary services to assist with the educational program. In fact, the availability of such paraprofessionals may justify placing some children in a special education program. The school psychologist and counselor may contribute very important assistance in assessment, curriculum planning, classroom management and help toward personal, social, and vocational adjustment of the pupils. Adequate social services maintain good relations between the school and the family and community. Teachers for the homebound and hospitalized should also have access to these services.

Services provided even more directly to pupils are those of the speech, physical, and occupational therapists. Some programs also receive assistance from a recreational therapist. The speech correctionist is discussed by Hull in Chapter 6. The others are described briefly here.

Physical and occupational therapists always work under the direction of a physician and can assist the teacher in carrying out his recommendations for the pupils' physical comfort and development. A child will work more effectively if he is comfortable, maintaining correct sitting or standing posture, and if he has maximum hand use. Through close cooperation with therapists, the teacher receives guidance in managing the child who, for example, should work part of the day in a standing position to develop leg and trunk strength and coordination or who will benefit by restrainers to control involuntary motions and improve his hand use.

Hospital program Programs for the hospitalized and the homebound have some characteristics in common but also some essential differences. A major purpose of each is to teach the ill or physically impaired child temporarily until he can return to school. The problems of the hospital teacher are much the same as those of the teacher of the homebound because the same types of children are encountered by both. Obviously many of the students will move from the hospital into their homes for convalescence. However, the *daily class load* of the hospital teacher is more variable. This variability increases as the length of time spent by patients in the hospital decreases. The variability is not only in numbers but also in age range and types of disability, since some hospitalization conditions are seasonal. It is not feasible to constantly change teachers either for times when there are fewer pupils to teach or when the majority of the students shift from primary to secondary grades. Although large hospitals will have a number of teachers for various grade levels, the hospital teacher still must be prepared to handle a wide variety of grades and subjects. The number of students she can manage at one time will depend upon (1) variability in age; (2) types and degree of disability; (3) variation in amount of schooling; and (4) facilities in the hospital for group instruction. These factors also will influence the amount of instruction time that each pupil will receive.

The hospital teacher faces *problems of scheduling* instruction complicated not only by shifting population, varying age groups, and individual needs but also by the necessity of fitting the teaching into the hospital routine. The child is hospitalized for medical treatment, and the teacher needs to realize that clinic and therapy sessions, medications, and other such procedures have first call. This adds to the complexity of the program, but it must be accepted and planned for accordingly. The teacher should cooperate closely with doctors, nurses, therapists, and other professionals and keep well informed of the child's condition, progress, needs, and capabilities.

One of the advantages of hospital teaching over the homebound program is the opportunity for the students to learn in group situations. Physicians emphasize the importance of helping the child to develop a feeling of independence and trust in himself and in his own health through companionship with others his own age. One of the greatest values of group activity is to provide reassurance about one's condition and an opportunity to discharge tension. The satisfaction parents have from knowing their child is happy and contented with others is of additional value.

The teacher's *relation with parents* is quite different from that of the teacher of the homebound, since generally she will have few direct contacts with them. If she meets the child's parents at all, it is usually only briefly and casually. She is not apt to become involved in the parents' problems or feel called upon to give them advice and support. However, she does need to be aware of the possible effect of the parents' anxiety, oversolicitousness, or uncertainty upon the child and his performance.

The child in the hospital is apt to be more physically ill and emotionally upset than the one who is recovering at home. Hospitalization is traumatic for a great many children. Adequate preparation for the hospital experience can alleviate anxiety by alerting the child as to what to expect in procedures and treatment. Wolinsky (1971), in an article on materials to prepare children for hospital experiences, emphasizes that in spite of changes in hospital procedures and the fewer days spent there, hospitalization is still frightening. She lists excellent, inexpensive materials from hospitals and volunteer organizations that can be given to children to prepare them for hospital routine and to help reduce the trauma. Sources for obtaining some of these materials are given in the list of resources at the end of the chapter. Geist (1965) also presents suggestions for preparing a child for the hospital and management procedures while he is there that minimize the trauma. One of the ways suggested for preventing emotional disturbances is to continue with a school program that is as normal as possible. While providing the program, the teacher must recognize and deal with emotional problems as they arise. As a rule, these problems decrease in both frequency and severity with age, but occasionally even the teenager needs support and reassurance. The teacher must be able to give the child a feeling of security and adequacy without becoming overly solicitous and too sympathetic.

In general, the *educational objectives and curriculum* for hospitalized children are similar to those for homebound pupils. The primary purpose is to maintain continuity in the child's education. Close cooperation with the pupils' regular schools is desirable but not always possible. Instruction must frequently be given to children from widely scattered school districts. It is often impossible for the teacher to be well acquainted with the courses, textbooks, or school experiences provided previously. She may have access to very little information about each child's potential, achievement level, or school background. In such a situation she will have to make decisions on the basis of the information she can gather herself. Therefore, she needs skill in educational diagnosis to determine a child's level of functioning and plan a program based on his needs and capabilities.

Methods of teaching in the hospital also are similar to home teaching in that they differ little from good methods employed in regular classrooms, except for specialized procedures necessary in teaching children with neurological damage and multiple handicaps. Though the students can work in groups on units in the various subject areas, much of the instruction must be individualized because few of the pupils will be at the same level of achievement.

Teaching materials and equipment in the hospital usually are not the problem that they are in home teaching. An increasing number of modern hospitals have specially designed and equipped classrooms and storage facilities. Libraries, small stages for performances, movie and slide projectors, and play equipment contribute to a varied and rich curriculum. Ambulatory children can be brought into the classrooms for group instruction and for socialization through music, arts, crafts, storytelling, and dramatic play. Occupational, speech, and recreational therapists are available to assist in planning or providing materials for these activities. Thus the hospital program can be almost as full and diversified as that in the regular school. However, in less ideal situations there is no central school room, and storage and availability of supplies are more of a problem. Even with classroom space not all children can be moved and some must be taught in their rooms or wards. Then teaching materials must be moved to the bedside, and the curriculum becomes more limited, though small groups can be formed by moving beds.

Since children are usually placed in wards on the basis of approximate age, this presents no problem. Connor (1964) gives a comprehensive discussion of the educational program of the hospitalized child with many very helpful suggestions to teachers. The program for the homebound also is covered in this excellent publication.

Homebound program A number of problems of management of the program for the homebound must be solved at the administrative level. One of these is the length of time a pupil must expect to be confined at home to be allowed in the program. A minimum time usually is set by the school district, and regulations require that schooling be provided only for those who are apt to be absent from school for a longer period. The lower limit is often three months. The *class load* of the teacher of the homebound is another problem that may be determined on a district level. Five or six pupils would be the maximum number that a teacher can handle if she spends one hour each school day with each pupil. In some instances the class size is doubled by having the teacher visit pupils only two or three times a week. Travel time between pupils must also be taken into consideration. State or local departments of education may set minimum and maximum amounts of time to be spent in instruction as well as limits on the number of pupils. These limits may be in terms of specific teaching hours per week or in the amount of instruction time that constitutes a day's attendance for purposes of financial support.

Although the amount of instruction may be determined on a district level, the teacher of the homebound usually is responsible for the *scheduling* of pupils on an hourly or weekly basis. Sometimes older pupils are able to work independently and can be given long-term assignments and consequently can be seen less often.

The *competencies of the teacher* of homebound children are of utmost importance. She must be versatile, for she will encounter a variety of situations. She will teach children with widely different educational backgrounds and with many kinds of disabilities and will have to know something of the limitations each imposes upon a child. She will go into many types of homes, some of which provide an atmosphere that is conducive to learning, others that have the opposite effect. Perhaps the best preparation she can have for her task is breadth of teaching experience and skill in public relations.

One important problem with which the teacher must be prepared to cope is that of *parent relations*. A teacher finds herself in a very special relation with the child's mother, which is quite different from that in any other teaching situation. The mother cares for the child all day and is often weary and anxious and wants reassurance and advice. The teacher is sometimes caught in a difficult position as a result of the need to give support to the mother without robbing the pupil of time and attention. It is important for her to have the friendly cooperation of the mother in providing a quiet place for study and in following through on assignments. Some teachers set aside a little time for counseling the mother, but this should be kept to a minimum.

Curriculum will vary to some extent for each individual, but in the main will not differ drastically from that for the regular student. The physical condition of the pupil will have some effect upon the school activities, and the medical prognosis will largely determine the long-term educational goals. For those who will return to school, one of the principal objectives of home teaching is to enable them to progress through the grades at the same rate as their classmates. The permanently disabled, severely impaired student, who may never be able to attend a classroom, presents a somewhat different problem. Here the aim is to provide educational activities that will enable him to develop to the maximum despite his handicap. Breadth of experience is desirable, but keeping abreast of the regular school curriculum is of secondary importance. Teaching that will help him acquire skills in reading, listening, and communicating, exercise his creative powers, and enjoy the natural world around him may be more vital to his happiness than more purely academic learning. For some, economic self-sufficiency will never be entirely possible. However, independence in self-care, usefulness around the home and some degree of self-support are realistic goals.

With few exceptions there are no special *teaching methods* peculiar to homebound students. However, some conditions complicate the learning problem to such an extent that specialized procedures are necessary. Included in this group are children with cerebral palsy and related disorders, multiple handicaps, and learning and behavior problems resulting from minimal brain damage, which have been discussed elsewhere in the book. Other information on methods and materials can be found in the list of resources at the end of the chapter. The individualization of learning is one of the advantages of home teaching, though home instruction is certainly not an ideal arrangement for students who can participate in a classroom, as children taught individually are deprived of the social contacts with their peers important to the development of well-rounded personalities. Many socializing experiences and activities that enrich the lives of pupils in regular classrooms can be used successfully in teaching the homebound. These include crafts, puppetry, educational games, science experiments, collections, and nature projects, all of which provide a basis for relating successfully with other children. Rooke (1962) and Connor (1964) give helpful suggestions for teachers.

Management of *teaching materials, textbooks, and equipment* is often a problem. A home teacher may sometimes feel that she needs a small truck to get supplies from place to place. She will find that careful planning is necessary so that she will have everything she needs. One of the limitations of the program is that materials such as large maps and charts, science equipment, sets of encyclopedias, and other reference material are difficult to transport and cannot easily be brought into the home. Therefore, instruction sometimes is limited to the textbook, and the curriculum is confined to the academic subjects.

Dunn, in Chapter 1, discusses the advantages of extending and enlarging contacts and the curriculum of the child who is homebound through the *telephone* and the *teleclass.* These methods do not take the place of the home teacher, but can add to her effectiveness and may reduce the amount of time she spends with the pupil. They are particularly useful in areas where much of a teacher's time would be spent in traveling.

One medium, which has many possibilities for home instruction, is *programed instruction.* Teaching machines and well-programed materials enable the child at home to work by himself and progress at his own rate, skipping his proficient areas and spending more time on his deficiencies. Instruction can be truly individualized. Many times students are able to learn faster and more efficiently in this way than in the classroom. The home teacher is not replaced by the machine but remains important in personalizing the situation. Inexpensive machines are available in which teacher-developed materials can be used. The preparation of the lessons or program to be used in the machine initially requires a great deal of time and effort, but once prepared the programs can be used again with different students. Commercially prepared programs are not available in all subjects and at all levels of difficulty, but this should not deter teachers and administrators from utilizing this teaching medium.

FUTURE DIRECTIONS IN THE EDUCATION OF CHILDREN WITH NEUROMOTOR AND OTHER CRIPPLING AND HEALTH CONDITIONS

The problem of providing an educational program for children with neuromotor and other crippling and health impairments has changed greatly over the last quarter of a century, and indications are that it will continue to change drastically. A number of factors are responsible for this change, some of which have resulted in increased numbers of children with some of these disabilities and others which show promise of reducing the number of impairments. Several of these factors have been discussed in this and other chapters of the book. They are summarized here, and a number that have particular application to the specific conditions covered in the chapter are enlarged upon.

Medical Advances with Implications for Special Education

The major trends that have been responsible for the *increase* in the number of children with neuromotor, crippling, and multiple disabilities are: (1) improvement in maternal care and obstetrical practices, which have saved many children who otherwise would not have survived; (2) impairments resulting from accidents of all sorts, including the battered child; and (3) drug abuse. Developments that have brought a *decrease* in the prevalence of disabling conditions are (1) the great reduction in the chronically ill and those crippled from infectious diseases, such as poliomyelitis, osteomyelitis, and tuberculosis; and (2) early detection and treatment of congenital conditions, such as clubfoot, that will virtually eliminate certain handicapping impairments.

Several medical advances that as yet have not resulted in great reduction in impairment but appear to have tremendous possibilities are:

1. Obstetrical practices for reducing the damaging effects of anoxia and blood incompatibility.
2. The development of vaccines to prevent maternal infections such as rubella and procedures for desensitization of mothers to Rh blood incompatibility.
3. Increased knowledge of genetic factors related to certain impairments resulting in prevention of some disabling conditions through genetic counseling of parents.

In addition, improved methods of treating inborn errors of metabolism and related conditions through dietary regulation and other procedures should reduce their damaging effect.

Prevention of Anoxia

Advances in obstetrical practice may prevent impairment from anoxia, or deprivation of oxygen to the cells, one of the conditions which accounts for a major proportion of neurological damage in the fetus or newborn child, since brain cells are particularly sensitive to lack of oxygen. One such obstetrical technique which is being researched with the possibility of reducing neurological damage to infants is the so-called "baby bubble" (Heyns, 1959; Heyns, Samson, and Graham, 1962; Quinn and McKeown, 1962). The technique is still somewhat controversial, and while it is generally accepted that it does no harm, there are still doubts about its efficacy. Other studies of anoxia by Steer and Bonney (1968) have led to the conclusion that perhaps oxygen deprivation and other obstetrical abnormalities are the result and not the cause of cerebral palsy. Some infants may have a genetic defect that results in limited ability to withstand anoxia and therefore suffer damage to the central nervous system. Newly developed procedures make it possible to detect oxygen deprivation in the fetus, and through early detection and efficient treatment for anoxia the incidence of cerebral palsy should be reduced.

Prevention of Impairment from Rubella

Immunization against rubella has become possible through the development of a vaccine to prevent the disease. The vaccine is given (1) to school-age children, not so much to keep them from getting the disease themselves as to eliminate the possibility of exposing their mothers to it; (2) to teenage girls; and (3) to women of child-bearing age before they become pregnant. However, even if this disease should become as rare as smallpox or diphtheria, multiple handicaps will continue to occur and will remain an educational problem.

Immunization and Treatment of Rh Incompatibility

Research in blood compatibility has resulted in the development of procedures for immunization and treatment of Rh incompatibility to prevent damage to babies. Chinn and Mueller (1971) summarized recent advances in the treatment of Rh negative incompatibility in both mothers and infants. Injections of an immune gammaglobulin have been found effective in preventing sensitization to Rh positive antibodies. Further research may be necessary to determine whether the globulin will have an adverse effect on the maternal immune system, but at present the procedure appears to be very effective. Diamond (1968) stated that with the use of anti-Rh gammaglobulin "there is now reason to hope that in another generation most of the possible cases of erythroblastosis fetalis will have been prevented and this disease may become only of historic interest." (p. 4) Other kinds of preventive treatments discussed by Chinn and Mueller, which are given to the baby that is threatened with neurological damage rather than to the mother, are (1) the injection of blood not laden with antibodies into the abdomen of the fetus; (2) exchange blood transfusion *in utero* early in the gestation period; and (3) treatment of the affected infants by the use of natural or artificial ultraviolet rays which break down the bilirubin molecules in the blood that are responsible for the damage.

Detection of Prenatal Factors

Amniocentesis, which was discussed by Dunn in Chapter 3, shows promise of providing information about several of the disabling conditions discussed in this chapter which could lead to the prevention and the treatment in prenatal and neonatal stages of some types of impairments (Fuchs and Cederqvist, 1970; Nadler, 1969; Nelson, 1970). Among these possibilities are the (1) prediction of sex-linked diseases such as hemophilia and some types of muscular dystrophy by ascertaining the sex of the fetus; (2) examination of chromosomes to determine inborn errors of metabolism, which result from the lack of certain enzymes, breakage from use of LSD and other drugs, and abnormalities found in cystic fibrosis; (3) detection of damage from rubella and other viral diseases; and (4) assessment of fetal age and condition, which might indicate the need of terminating the pregnancy early in cases of diabetes.

For the present generation of children, the positive developments in the prevention and treatment of disabling conditions have not yet reached the point where they outweigh the negative ones. Therefore, for the next decade at least, special educators will need to plan for an increasing number of severely and multiply impaired children. Wald (1971), in a report of the West Point Institute on crippled and other health-impaired (COHI) children, conducted by Teachers College, Columbia University, summarized the significant changes in this population of children over the past 5 to 10 years and the implications for education. The report noted that children in this category are younger than previously, and also that those now in school are more severely involved with complicating factors such as multisensory deficits, perceptual disturbances, communication barriers, mental retardation, and social and emotional problems. Complex hereditary, congenital, or traumatic disorders were given as causative factors in these multiply handicapped children. In discussing educational provisions, the Wald report pointed out that a large proportion of COHI children are in a regular class setting or receive education in a home or hospital. However, they seldom have had normal environmental experiences, which contributes to their retarded academic achievement. It was recommended that steps be taken to close the gap between potential and achievement, which is so often characteristic of their performance. It was suggested further that they should be described in terms of what they can do, what they have learned, and under what conditions they can best respond, taking into account behavioral deficits as well as achievement limitations. The report concluded, "Concern with identifying a primary physical or medical impairment may be restrictive to future educational planning. This is a multiply disabled population." (p. 2) Increased understanding of the learning process and of means of facilitating it should result in improved educational programs for this group of children.

Advances in Instructional Procedures

Techniques that have been developed primarily to aid and enchance the learning process are being used with increasing efficiency not only in this area but also in alleviating and correcting physical problems that interfere with learning. Two such procedures are (1) electronic technology and (2) behavior modification and other instructional techniques. (See Dunn, Chapter 2.)

Electronic Technology

The use of electronic technology in correcting physical problems and assisting learning is discussed by Hedrich (1972). She describes devices and techniques developed by a team of neurophysiologists, electrical engineers, electronics technicians, and other skilled persons. These include (1) an artificial sensory device that helps a child learn to move and control a severely damaged arm and (2) a plastic gravity-sensitive helmet which, when worn by a child with poor head control, gives off clicks corresponding to the degree of tilt whenever the head falls out of correct alignment and alerts the child to return to a neutral position. These aids provide a means of individualizing instruction, of gearing it to specific problems, and of modifying behavior through conditioning techniques.

Instructional Techniques

In discussing future trends in special education, Martin (1972) cites two broad concepts which, in the newer interpretation, will have a vital impact. The first of these, *individualism*, has both positive and negative implications for the education of the exceptional pupil. The trend toward individulization in both the regular and special class emphasizes the need for teaching based on the relevant behavior of the child and the type of process to be learned rather then on the etiology of the handicapping condition. Conversely, the individual tutoring model, aimed at a specific condition rather than at the wholeness of the child, is not only costly but denies social and psychological stimulation. It also requires a great variety of learning resource systems for salf-teaching and individualized learning. Martin warns that individualism can contribute to the ignoring of skills in interpersonal relations, which are very important for children with disabilities. The second broad concept of *behaviorism,* Martin contends, must be viewed in relation to the output in terms of child behavior rather than to the input, and as a part of a variety of learning and personality theories rather than merely operant conditioning and reinforcement. He concludes that the increased emphasis on these two concepts in special education demands more definitive goals for the education of the handicapped, earlier as well as extended educational planning, and a greater role of the special educator outside as well as within the school.

Meyerson, Kerr, and Michaels (1967) note that often the traditional methods used to correct physical defects and improve function have been ineffective because they are so difficult and unpleasant that disabled individuals lack motivation or actively resist following the prescribed treatment. Psychologists often have done little to assist teachers with the problem beyond confirming observations or stating them in psychological terms that are even less useful. Meyerson recommends that psychologists cooperate with and assist the physical therapist and others in manipulating the environment through *behavior-modification* techniques to restore functional use of disabled parts of the body. Such procedures, he contends, would be far more valuable and feasible than attempting to deal with feelings of inadequacy, dependency, and inferiority through psychotherapy alone.

In view of these trends and advances, educators concerned with special education programs must take into consideration the following factors: (1) the necessity for earlier and more effective programs of evaluation and intervention, and more extensive use of interdisciplinary teams in assessing potential and planning educational procedures; (2) the increased need for more adequate educational facilities for children with multiple handicaps, and the development and utilization of more innovative and efficient means of enhancing learning; (3) the utilization of more flexible and individualized programs based on precise prescription; (4) the extension of special education programs for young children; and (5) more effective parent counseling and involvement in the educational programs.

SUMMARY

It has been emphasized throughout this chapter that the children classified in the general category of neuromotor and other crippling and health impaired make up a very heterogeneous group. This great diversity of disabilities, capabilities, and degrees of handicap make it impossible to summarize their educational needs in a brief, comprehensive statement. However, one broad generalization has been stressed which applies to the majority of them: they can learn as unimpaired children learn, and with some modification of physical facilities or temporary placement in special programs, they can succeed in regular classes. The small proportion of the group who do need specialized services—the severely physically impaired, the cerebral palsied, and other multiply handicapped—present the most complex problems in the field of special education. The fact that this group is increasing in number, and will probably continue to do so for the next few years makes it necessary that special schools or day classes and ancillary services to alleviate some of the handicapping conditions continue to be provided for them. Their problems of personal, social, and vocational adjustment will require the services of qualified personnel. When they leave school they will need vocational assistance if they are to be employed and sheltered workshops where they can be partially self-sufficient if they are not. Making these provisions is not the principal problem, however. The most difficult aspect is finding adequate techniques for teaching children who have more than one avenue of learning that cannot be fully utilized. Teachers of special classes for children with cerebral palsy are well aware of this problem. It is no simple matter to choose one teaching approach or even a combination of methods best suited to the child whose learning difficulties are multiple. A teacher may know how to teach a blind child to read, but how does she apply this knowledge if the child has poor coordination which makes it difficult to move his fingers smoothly across a line of braille or if he has an impairment of tactile perception which limits his ability to perceive dots? How much more complicated the problem becomes if the child also has a hearing loss. For some severely involved multiply handicapped children it may be enough to provide adequately for their physical needs, teach them self-care and social skills, and enable them to perform useful tasks in sheltered workshop situations. However, for the others who are capable of doing more than this but who are prevented by the multiplicity of their handicaps, we are not fulfilling our obligations as special educators until we have found better ways of evaluating and developing their potential. This is a difficult and challenging task but one that eventually must be accomplished.

In attempting to reach this goal it is important to remember that it is not the facilities or equipment that make a good program. In fact, there is real danger that special provisions for children with nonsensory physical impairments may be made too specialized and that students may become so surrounded with "gadgetry" designed to make things easier for them that they never learn to cope with the world outside the classroom walls. More vital to the realization of each child's goals than his physical environment is the attitudinal climate in which he learns. The determining factor is not where the child is but how he and others think and feel about him. He can become dependent and insecure or be rejected and isolated in any type of program.

The school has not fulfilled its responsibility to the physically impaired pupil until it has helped him to accept himself as he is, to view his assets and limitations realistically, to strive for attainable goals, to develop independence in thought and action, and to find a place for himself among his peers. Nor has the school accomplished its purposes unless it has assisted those with whom the child associates—his classmates, parents, neighbors, teachers—to accept him as a worthy individual and to see beyond his defect to the person that is there.

References

Alexander, L., Berkeley, A. W., and Alexander, A. M. *Multiple sclerosis: Prognosis and treatment.* Springfield, Ill.: Charles C Thomas, 1961.

Allen, R. M. Intellectual evaluation in cerebral palsy. *Exceptional Children,* 1960, **27**, 202–204.

Anderson, J. Child abuse: A national scandal? Salt Lake City, Utah, *Deseret News,* Nov. 24, 1969.

Blattner, R. J. Infectious mononucleosis. In W. E. Nelson, V. C. Vaughn, III, and R. J. McKay (Eds.), *Textbook of pediatrics.* Philadelphia: Saunders, 1969.

Brieland, D. A follow-up study of orthopedically handicapped high school graduates. *Exceptional Children,* 1967, **33**, 555–562.

Calabro, J. J. Management of juvenile rheumatoid arthritis. *Journal of Pediatrics,* 1970, **77** (3), 355–365.

California State Department of Education. Minors with orthopedic or other health impairments enrolled in special day classes (including teleclasses) 1971–1972. Mimeographed report. Sacramento, Calif.: The Department, 1972.

Cantoni, L. J. Can cardiacs work? *Vocational Guidance Quarterly,* 1960, **8**, 239–240.

Carr, D. B. Planning educational programs at the post-elementary level for severely crippled children. In *New frontiers in special education: Selected convention papers.* Washington, D.C.: Council for Exceptional Children, 1965.

Chinn, P. C., and Mueller, J. M. Advances in treatment of Rh negative blood incompatibility of mothers and infants. *Mental Retardation,* 1971, **9** (1), 12–15.

Clark, W. S. *Arthritis.* New York: The National Foundation, 1959.

Collier, B. N. The adolescent with diabetes and the public school: A misunderstanding. *Personnel and Guidance Journal,* 1969, **47**, 753–757.

Connor, F. P. Safety for the crippled child and child with special health problems. *Exceptional Children,* 1962, **28**, 237–244.

Connor, F. P. Education of homebound and hospitalized children. New York: Teachers College Press, Columbia University, 1964.

Crothers, B., and Paine, R. S. *The natural history of cerebral palsy.* Cambridge, Mass.: Harvard University Press, 1959.

Crowther, D. L. Psychosocial aspects of epilepsy. In J. G. Millchap (Ed.), *Pediatric clinics of North America.* Vol. 14, No. 4. *Pediatric neurology.* Philadelphia: Saunders, 1967, 921–931.

Cruickshank, W. M., Bentzen, F. A., Ratzeburg, F. H., and Tannhauser, N. T. *A teaching method for brain-injured and hyperactive children.* Syracuse, N.Y.: Syracuse University Press, 1961.

Dean, M. J., and Barbour, R. Administrative problems with the changing role of the home and hospital teacher. *New frontiers in special education:*

Selected convention papers. Washington, D.C.: Council for Exceptional Children, 1965.

Desmond, M. M., Schwanecke, R. P., Wilson, G. S., Yasunaga, S., and Burgdorff, I. Material barbiturate utilization and neonatal withdrawal symptoms. *Journal of Pediatrics,* 1972, **80**, 190–197.

Diamond, L. K. Protection against Rh sensitization and prevention of erythroblastosis fetalis. *Pediatrics,* 1968, **41** (1), 1–4.

Diller, L., et al. *Psychological and educational studies with spina bifida children. Final report.* Washington, D.C.: Office of Education, Bureau for the Handicapped, 1969.

Egozcue, J., Irwin, S., and Maruffo, C. A. Chromosomal damage in LSD users. *Journal of the American Medical Association,* 1968, **204**, 214–218.

Fassler, J. Reduced auditory input aids cerebral palsy children. *R. & D. News,* 1969, **1**, 1–3, Teachers College, Columbia University, 1969.

Fenner, M. S. (Ed.) Pregnant teenagers. *Today's Education,* 1970, **59**, 26–29, 89.

Freeman, J. M., and McKhann, G. M. Degenerative disease of the central nervous system. In I. Schulman (Ed.), *Advances in pediatrics,* Vol. 16, 1969, pp. 121–169.

Friedman, R. J., and MacQueen, J. C. Psychoeducative considerations of physical handicapping conditions in children. *Exceptional Children,* 1971, **37** (7), 538–539.

Fuchs, F., and Cederqvist, L. L. Recent advances in antenatal diagnosis by amniotic fluid analysis. *Clinical Obstetrics and Gynecology,* 1970, **13** (1), 178–201.

Geist, H. A child goes to the hospital. Springfield, Ill.: Charles C Thomas, 1965.

Gingras, G., Mongeau, M., Moreault, P., Dubois, M., Herbert, B., and Corriveau, G. Congenital anomalies of the limbs: Psychological and educational aspects. *Canadian Medical Association Journal* 1964, **91**, 115–119.

Graham, R. Safety features in school housing for handicapped children. *Exceptional Children,* 1961, **27**, 361–364.

Gucker, T., III. Muscular defects. In J. T. Shaw (Ed.), *Pediatric clinics of North America.* Vol. 14, No. 2. *Musculoskeletal disorders,* I. Philadelphia: Saunders, 1967, pp. 439–459.

Guerrant, J., Anderson, W. W., Fischer, A., Weinstein, M. R., Janos, R. M., and Deskins, A. *Personality in epilepsy.* Springfield Ill.: Charles C Thomas, 1962.

Haeussermann, E. *Developmental potential of preschool children.* New York: Grune & Stratton, Inc., 1958.

Hardy, J. B. Rubella and its aftermath. *Children,* 1970, **16**, 91–96.

Harris, A. J. *How to increase reading ability: A guide to developmental and remedial methods.* New York: McKay, 1970.

Hedrich, V. Applying technology to special education. *American Education,* 1972, **8**, 23–25.

Herbst, A. L., Ulfelder, H., and Poskanzer, D. C. Adenocarcinoma of the vagina: Association of maternal stilbestrol therapy with tumor appearance in young women. *New England Journal of Medicine,* 1971, **284**, 878–881.

Heyns, O. S. Abdominal decompression in the first stages of labor. *Journal of Obstetrics and Gynecology of the British Empire,* 1959, **66**, 220–228.

Heyns, O. S., Samson, J. M., and Graham, J. A. C. Influence of abdominal decompression on intra-amniotic pressure and fetal oxygenation. *Lancet,* 1962, **1** (7224), 289–292.

Hoey, J. LSD and chromosome damage. *Journal of the American Medical Association,* 1970, **212**, 1707.

Hopkins, T. W., Bice, H. V., and Colton, K. C. *Evaluation and education of the cerebral palsied child.* Washington, D.C.: Council for Exceptional Children, 1954.

Hsu, L. Y., Strauss, L., and Hirschhorn, K. Chromosomal abnoramility in off-spring of LSD user: Ditrisomy with D/D translocation. *Journal of the American Medical Association*, 1970, **211** (6), 987–990.

Hurt, C. A total program for the patient with hemophilia: Psychosocial problems. *Journal of the American Physical Therapy Association*, 1966, **46**, 1282–1284.

Judd, L. L., Brandkamp, W. W., and McGlothlin, W. H. Comparisons of the chromosomal patterns obtained from groups of continued users, former users, and nonusers of LSD 25. *American Journal of Psychiatry*, 1969, **126**, 626–635.

Karnes, M. D. A team approach to the education of homebound pregnant girls. In *New frontiers in special education: Selected convention papers*. Washington, D.C.: Council for Exceptional Children, 1965.

Kaye, R. Infectious hepatitis. In W. E. Nelson, V. C. Vaughn, III, and R. J. McKay, (Eds.), *Textbook of pediatrics*. Philadelphia: Saunders, 1969.

Kershaw, J. Cerebral palsy, an index of progress. *Developmental Medicine and Child Neurology*, 1969, **11**, 545–546.

Kilfoyle, R. M. Myelodysplasia—Spina bifida. In J. I. Shaw (Ed.), *Pediatric clinics of North America*. Vol 14, No. 2, *Musculoskeletal disorders*, I. Philadelphia: Saunders, 1967, pp. 419–437.

Kir-Stimon, W. Rehabilitation counseling with cardiac children. *Personnel and Guidance Journal*, 1962, **40**, 551–556.

Lorenze, E. J. The central nervous system: Disorders of the brain. In J. S. Myers (Ed.), *An orientation to chronic disease and disability*. New York: Crowell-Collier-Macmillan, 1965, pp. 216–257.

Los Angeles Unified School District. *Status 68: Report of the Special Education Branch*. Los Angeles: Los Angeles Unified School District, 1969.

Machek, M. D., Hardin, A., and Collins, M. A. Preliminary report of evaluating and classifying the vocational potential of the cerebral palsied. *Archives of Physical Medicine and Rehabilitiation*, 1960, **41**, 434–437.

Malikin, D. Hemophilia. Psycho-social aspects. *Journal of Rehabilitation*, 1971, **37**, 36–38.

Martin, E. W. Individualism and behaviorism as future trends in educating handicapped children. *Exceptional Children*, 1972, **38**, 517–525.

Masland, R. L. National Institute of Neurological Diseases and Blindness (NINDB) research profile No. 13—Cerebral palsy. Public Health Service Publication No. 1671, 1967.

McCann, C. *Development and evaluation of adaptive communicative devices for the severely handicapped child*. Greenfield, N.H.: Crotched Mountain Foundation, 1966.

McMurray, G. L. Community action on behalf of pregnant school-age girls: Educational policies and beyond. *Child Welfare*, 1970, **69**, 342–346.

Meyerson, L. Somatopsychology of physical disability. In *Psychology of exceptional children and youth*. W. M. Cruickshank (Ed.), Englewood Cliffs, N.J.: Prentice-Hall, 1971.

Meyerson, L., Kerr, N., and Michael, J. L. Behavior modification in rehabilitation. In *Child development: Readings in experimental analysis*. S. W. Bijow and D. M. Baer (Eds.), New York: Appleton, 1967.

Millichap, J. G., and Aymat, F. Treatment and prognosis of petit mal epilepsy. In J. G. Millichap (Ed.), *Pediatric clinics of North America*. Vol. 14, No. 4. *Pediatric neurology*. Philadelphia: Saunders, 1967, pp. 905–917.

Minear, W. L. A clasification of cerebral palsy. *Pediatrics*, 1956, **18**, 841–852.

Moed, M., and Litwin, D. The employability of the cerebral palsied. *Rehabilitation Literature*, 1963, **24**, 266–277.

Morgenstern, M. Psychoeducational and vocational problems of the cerebral palsied child. In J. Hellmuth (Ed.), *The special child in century 21*, Seattle:

The Special Child Publications of the Sequin School, 1964.

Mullen, F. A. How to keep the handicapped child in your classroom safe. *School Safety*, 1965, (1) 25–27.

Myers, P. A study of language disabilities in cerebral palsied children. *Journal of Speech and Hearing Research*, 1965, **8**, 129–136.

Nadler, H. L. Prenatal detection of genetic defects. *Journal of Pediatrics*, 1969, **74** (1), 132–143.

National Education Association. Pregnant teen-agers. *Today's Education*, 1970, **59** (7), 26–29, 89.

National Multiple Sclerosis Society. *Annual Report 1970*. New York: The Society, 1971.

National Society for Crippled Children and Adults. *Trends affecting program planning in Easter seal societies*. Chicago: The Society, 1967.

Neilson, H. H. *A psychological study of cerebral palsied children*. Munksgaard, Copenhagen, Denmark: Scandinavian University Books, 1966.

Nelson, M. M. Amniotic fluid: Its use in antenatal diagnosis. *Nursing Times*. 1970, **66**, 1106–1108.

Nelson, W. E., Vaughn, V. C., III, and McKay, R. J. (Eds.), *Textbook of pediatrics*. Philadelphia: Saunders, 1969.

Neuberg, R. Drug dependence and pregnancy: A review of the problems and their management. *Journal of Obstetrics and Gynaecology of the British Commonwealth*, 1970, **77**, 1117–1122.

Perlstein, M. A., and Barnett, H. E. Nature and recognition of cerebral palsy in infancy. *Journal of the American Medical Association*, 1952, **148**, 1389–1397.

President's Committee on Employment of the Handicapped. Application for employment: To American industry from the physically handicapped. Washington, D.C.: The Committee, 1965.

President's Committee on Employment of the Handicapped. Action: A program guide 1967–1968. Washington, D.C.: The Committee, 1967.

Quinn, L. J., and McKeown, R. A. Abdominal decompression in the first stages of labor. *American Journal of Obstetrics and Gynecology*, 1962, **83**, 458–463.

Richardson, S. A., Hastorf, A. H., and Dornbusch, S. Effects of physical disability on a child's description of himself. *Child Development*, 1964, **35**, 893–907.

Rochester, D. E., Ellis, M. A., and Sciortino, S. C. What can the schools do about child abuse? *Today's Education*, 1968, **57**, 59–60.

Ronayne, E. Case finding and placement of the crippled child. *CEC Selected Convention Papers*, 1969. Washington, D.C.: Council for Educational Children, 1969.

Rooke, M. L. Aids for home and hospital teaching. *Exceptional Children*. 1962, **28**, 261–265.

Rusalem, H. Problems in the vocational development of the hemophiliac individual. Vocational Guidance Quarterly, 1969, **18**, 115–118.

Rutter, M., Tizard, J., and Whitmore, K. (Eds.) *Education, health and behavior: Psychological and medical study of child development*. New York: Wiley: 1970.

Shands, A. R., and Raney, R. B. *Handbook of orthopaedic surgery*. St. Louis: Mosby, 1967.

Solow, R. A. Psychological aspects of muscular dystrophy. *Exceptional Children*, 1965, **32**, 99–103.

Spekter, L. *The pediatric years*. Springfield, Ill.: Charles C Thomas, 1955.

Steer, C. M., and Bonney, W. Obstetric factors in cerebral palsy. *American Journal of Obstetrics and Gynecology*, 1968, **83**, 526–531.

Stone, M. C. Behavior shaping in a classroom for children with cerebral palsy. *Exceptional Children*, 1970, **36**, 674–677.

Taylor, E. M. *Psychological appraisal of children with cerebral defects.* Cambridge, Mass.: Harvard University Press, 1961.

Teicher, J. D. Cystic fibrosis in children and adults. *California Medicine,* 1969, **111**, 408–409.

Torres, F. Convulsive disorders: A working classification and guidelines for diagnosis and treatment. *Medical Times,* 1969, **97**, 152–156.

Tower, D. B. *Neurochemistry of epilepsy: Seizure mechanisms and their management.* Springfield, Ill.: Charles C Thomas, 1960.

U.S. Department of Commerce, Bureau of the Census. Statistical abstracts of the United States, 1971. Washington, D.C.: Government Printing Office, 1971.

U.S. Department of Health, Education and Welfare. Current estimates from the health interview survey, United States, 1968. *Vital and Health Statistics,* 1970, **10** (60).

U.S. Department of Health, Education and Welfare. Children who received physicians' services under crippled children's programs: Fiscal year 1969. Rockville, Md.: Public Health Service, U.S. Department of Health, Education and Welfare, 1971a.

U.S. Department of Health, Education and Welfare. Chronic conditions and limitations of activity and mobility, United States, July 1965–June 1967. *Vital and Health Statistics,* 1971b, **10** (61).

U.S. Department of Health, Education and Welfare. Children and youth. Selected health characteristics, United States, 1958 and 1968. *Vital and Health Statistics,* 1971c, **10** (62).

Wald, J. The crippled and other health impaired and their education: Report of the West Point Institute. Unpublished mimeo paper, Council for Exceptional Children Convention, Miami, Fla., 1971.

Warren, R. J., Rimoin, D. L., and Sly, W. S. LSD exposure in utero. *Pediatrics,* 1970, **45**, 466–469.

Wilson, J. Drug treatment of epilepsy in childhood. *British Medical Journal,* 1969, **4**, 475–477.

Wishik, S. M. Handicapped children in Georgia: A study of prevalence, disability, needs, and resources. *American Journal of Public Health,* 1956, **46**, 195–203.

Wolinsky, G. F. A special education problem: Home instruction: Status, issues, and recommendations. *Exceptional Children,* 1970, **36**, 673–674.

Wolinsky, G. F. Materials to prepare children for hospital experience. *Exceptional Children,* 1971, **37** (7), 527–528.

Woods, G. E. A lowered incidence of infantile cerebral palsy. *Developmental Medical Child Neurology,* 1963, **5**, 449–450.

Wright, B. A. *Physical disability: A psychological approach.* New York: Harper & Row, 1960.

Wright, M. K. Comprehensive services for adolescent unwed mothers. *Children,* 1966, **13**, 170–175.

Wurtz, F., and Fergen, G. Boards still duck the problem of pregnant school girls. *American School Board Journal,* 1970, **157**, 23–24.

Opposite: Some youth have such major specific learning disabilities in the areas of auditory and visual perception for speech sounds and their symbols that they may first need to learn to read word symbols (or rebuses).(Photo courtesy Honolulu Junior Academy; photographer, Robin Kaye.)

children with major specific learning disabilities

chApTer ouTliNe

DEFINITIONS, TERMINOOGY, AND PREVALENCE
  The Strauss Syndrome Definition
  The Minimal Brain Dysfunction Definition
  The Specific Learning Disabilities Definitions
    The Initial Definitions
    A Proposed Definition
THE BRAIN
  Brain Parts and Functions
  Localization versus Mass Action
THE BASIC DIAGNOSTIC-REMEDIATION PROCESS
  The Traditional Models
    The Interdisciplinary Team Model
    The Individual School Psychologist Model
  The Emerging Model
    Initial Selection and Screening
    Noneducational Child Study and Treatment
    Environmental Assessment and Treatment
    Special Education Assessment and Intervention
DIAGNOSIS AND REMEDIATION OF MAJOR SPECIFIC LEARNING DISORDERS
  Major Motor Disorders
  Major Visual Discrimination Disorders
  Major Auditory Discrimination Disorders
  Major Oral Language Disorders
  Major Reading Disorders
  Major Spelling Disorders
  Major Handwriting Disorders
  Major Mathematics Disorders
ORGANIZATIONAL PLANS AND THEIR EFFECTIVENESS
  Boarding School Instruction
  Hospital Instruction
  Child Guidance, Mental Health, Remedial Reading, and Learning Resource Centers
  The Special Day Class Plan
  The Resource-Room Plan
  The Helping-Teacher Plan
  The Preschool Plan
EMERGING DIRECTIONS FOR THE FIELD

By the 1950s, the field of special education for handicapped pupils had grown and consolidated to the point where 10 types of children had been delineated: the blind, partially seeing, deaf, partially hearing, speech impaired, emotionally disturbed, socially maladjusted, mentally retarded, crippled, and children with chronic health problems. Since then, special educators have questioned the use of these traditional categories on three accounts. First, such related areas as the blind and the partially seeing are not discretely different. As a result there has been a steady movement to combine these categories, as was noted in earlier chapters of this text. Second, these 10 traditional handicapping labels resulted largely from the diagnostic efforts of physicians and psychologists and thus tended to emphasize etiology rather than educational significance. In their search for a more appropriate system of terminology, special educators have turned to such terms as learning problems or disabilities. Third, these 10 handicapping labels excluded from special education many children with fairly serious learning problems who did not fall neatly into one of these 10 categories. A new area of special education, now known as *specific learning disabilities* (SLD), has evolved to encompass these children. This chapter provides an overview of this emerging field. The point of view expressed will be that it be restricted to pupils with *major* specific learning disabilities.

DEFINITIONS, TERMINOLOGY, AND PREVALENCE

Terminology has already passed through three stages. Children were first classified as brain injured, later as having a minimal brain dysfunction, and most recently as having a specific learning disability. Definitions and prevalence estimates have changed along with terminology. These three stages are reviewed below.

The Strauss Syndrome Definition

The genesis of the term "specific learning disabilities" leads back to Strauss, a physician, and to Lehtinen, a special educator. In their classic text *Psychopathology and Education of the Brain-Injured Child*, Strauss and Lehtinen (1947) described specifically a particular type of brain-injured (exogenous) child that has since been labeled the Strauss syndrome child by Stevens and Birch (1957). The basic Strauss and Lehtinen definition was rather broad:

> A brain-injured child is a child who before, during, or after birth has received an injury to or suffered an infection of the brain. As a result of such organic impairment, defects of the neuromotor system may be present or absent; however, such a child may show disturbances in perception, thinking, and emotional behavior, either separately or in combination. These disturbances can be demonstrated by specific tests. These disturbances prevent or impede a normal learning process. Special education methods have been devised to remedy these specific handicaps. (p. 4)

The authors refined this general definition and arrived at the following seven criteria for classifying a child as brain injured, the first four being behavioral and the last three biological in nature: (1) *perceptual disorders*—such children, when viewing pictures, see parts instead of wholes and make figure-ground distortions; (2) *perseveration*—they continue at an activity once started and have great difficulty in changing sets; (3) *thinking or conceptual disorders*—they organize materials and thoughts differently from most average individuals; (4) *behavioral disorders*—they display such characteristics as hyperactivity, as well as explosive, erratic, and uninhibited behavior; (5) *slight neurological signs*; (6) *a history of a neurological impairment*; and (7) *no history of mental retardation in the family.* The last three biological signs could be negative and still the child could be diagnosed as having the Strauss syndrome on the basis of the four behavioral characteristics. Therefore "brain injury," thus described, can be seen as a pseudomedical term. It will be noted that a low IQ score was not a necessary prerequisite for the Strauss label, yet a majority of such children do have depressed scores in this area.

During the fifties, considerable emphasis was placed on special education services specifically designed for pupils with the Strauss-type syndrome. The Lehtinen techniques (Strauss and Lehtinen, 1947) formed the basis for the teaching procedures used in these programs. Six of the guiding principles were as follows:

1. A nondistracting school environment should be provided by sound-proofing and by making the classroom as bare as possible. Ground floor windows were covered with opaque material. Teachers were dressed plainly and refrained from using ornaments.
2. Instruction should be individualized as much as possible, with the maximum class size 10–12 students who were widely separated from one another. For individual work, pupils faced a wall, were placed in cubicles, or were otherwise screened off from the others.
3. An elemental rather than a global approach to teaching should be used. For example, in reading, the pupil was first required to learn individual letters; later, these letters were assembled into words, and still later into phrases, sentences, paragraphs, and stories. No use was made of the project or unit method.
4. The pupils' attention should be focused on the relevant materials through the use of colors, dividers, cut-outs, and so forth.
5. Such motor activity as tracing, copying, and cutting and sorting should be used to enhance academic learning. From the outset cursive writing was used to give smooth, flowing movements.
6. The emphasis should be on the basic tool subjects. Social activities, group learning, oral language, social studies, and science were given only incidental and secondary consideration.

As will be pointed out later in the chapter, research has not universally substantiated the claim made in the basic definition that these strategies do, in fact, remedy the specific handicaps associated with the Strauss syndrome. In addition, as will also be discussed later in the chapter, childhood hyperactivity is not necessarily a symptom of brain injury.

Since there are few such children in the public schools, it is estimated that no more than about one fifth of 1 percent of the school population would fit neatly into the Strauss-syndrome category. This percentage is quite low compared to most prevalence estimates of brain injury in children because the generic term "brain injury" includes many neurologically impaired children who do not display Strauss-syndrome behavioral characteristics.

Elaine in Vignette 10.1 is fairly typical of Strauss children who can be found today in many schools.

Vignette 10.1 Elaine: A Pupil Classified as Having a Strauss-type Syndrome

Elaine was the only child of fairly wealthy Anglo parents who lived in a suburban area of a large city. Her mother reported a normal pregnancy and birth. Walking and talking began within normal limits. However, Elaine had an early history of excessive crying, temper tantrums, hyperactivity, and clumsiness. At age 6, in the 1950s, she was retained for two years in the first grade because she failed to make adequate progress in the areas of reading, spelling, and arithmetic, and her social adjustment was unsatisfactory. She hit other children and threw items around the room. Occasionally she was pleasant, but usually the opposite.

As was the tradition during the 1950s, at the request of her first-grade teacher, she was eventually referred to a diagnostic clinic with an interdisciplinary team made up of a physician, psychologist, social worker, and speech and hearing therapist. A psychologist found her to have a verbal intelligence quotient on the WISC of 80, with a performance quotient of 70. He also found Elaine to display soft signs of brain injury on the psychometric tests he administered, but the physician could find no firm signs of neurological impairment. Nevertheless, the diagnostic team classified her as a Strauss-syndrome child, largely because her temper tantrums were diagnosed as catastrophic reaction, symptomatic of organic brain injury rather than of emotional disturbance.

Elaine was placed in a self-contained special class for brain-injured children, modeled after the Lehtinen guidelines. In this setting she made some academic progress. Her parents also took her to a very expensive private mental health clinic for over a year of play therapy to reduce her temper tantrums, but little improvement was noted. Throughout the remainder of her school career Elaine was placed in a series of self-contained special classes. At one time drug therapy was used to reduce hyperactivity, but this dulled her still more. This program was terminated after adolescence when her Strauss-syndrome characteristics diminished somewhat. She is now a young adult who continues to be cared for by her parents, even though she has learned to read a newspaper and otherwise become minimally literate.

The Minimal Brain Dysfunction Definition

During the 1960s, *minimal brain dysfunction* (MBD) became the broadened label to include both the Strauss-type child and other children with perceptual and learning problems. This shift in terminology resulted largely from the efforts of Clements (1966), who served as project director for Phase I of a three-phase project jointly sponsored by the U.S. Department of Health, Education and Welfare and the National Society for Crippled Children and Adults (designated throughout this chapter as the HEW/NSCC Project). Phase I concentrated on terminology and identification of minimal brain dysfunction in children. The condition was defined in the Clements report (1966) as follows:

> children of near average, average, or above average general intelligence with certain learning or behavioral disabilities ranging from mild to severe, which are associated with deviations of function of the central nervous system. These deviations may manifest themselves by various combinations of impairment in perception, conceptualization, language, memory, and control of attention, impulse, or motor function . . . these aberrations may arise from genetic variations, biochemical irregularities, perinatal brain insults or other illnesses or injuries sustained during the years which are critical for the development and maturation of the central nervous system, or from unknown causes. (pp. 9–10)

This basic definition had much in common with the one of Strauss and Lehtinen. In one respect, it was more restrictive in that only children of near average, average, or above average intelligence could be included in this category, thus eliminating all those with low IQs. Strauss and Lehtinen placed no such limitation in their definition. In terms of the behavioral manifestations, it was broadened to include language and motor disorders.

Like Strauss and Lehtinen, Clements (1966) went on to elaborate on the characteristics his MBD children displayed, arriving at 15 somewhat overlapping categories. These make clear that he defined his group much more broadly than did Strauss and Lehtinen. For example, both hypoactivity and hyperactivity in children were included. Also, pupils with a variety of scholastic disabilities in reading, arithmetic, spelling, writing, and oral language came under the rubric. In fact, it would be difficult to find a child who did not possess some of the qualities listed by Clements. Thus the "minimal brain dysfunction" label became somewhat of a catch-all. Couched as it was in words such as "central nervous system disorders," "biochemical irregularities," and "genetic variations," which assume an organic impairment, this was a pseudomedical term, as was "Strauss-type brain injury." In reality, the symptoms were largely behavioral in nature, as were those with the Strauss syndrome. Although this definition was adopted by some special educators in the 1960s, it was never widely accepted. As a result, the term "minimal brain dysfunction" did not become popular in special education.

Two other documents which grew out of the HEW/NSCC Project were published in 1969. They reported on Phase II and III of that project and were both directed by special educators. The Phase II report (Haring, 1969) was devoted to (1) educational identification, assessment, and evaluation procedures; (2) educational administration and classroom procedures; (3) professional preparation for the education of children with learning disabilities; and (4) legislation. The Phase III report (Chalfant and Scheffelin, 1969) provided a review of the research related to the behavioral consequences of central nervous system processing dysfunctions in children. The report addressed itself to an analysis of auditory, visual, and haptic processing; and to dysfunctions in the synthesis of sensory information, in the interpretation of multiple stimuli, in short-term memory and in symbolic operations in the areas of language and quantitative thinking. A great change in emphasis took place after Task Force I. Task Forces II and III were specifically concerned with the educational needs of children with learning disorders.

Using the broad Clements definition, it is estimated that at least 1.0 to 2.0 percent, and probably many more, school-age children could be classified as having minimal brain dysfunction.

Allyn, in Vignette 10.2, is an example of a pupil who was classified as having minimal brain dysfunction but who did not fit the classical Strauss syndrome.

Vignette 10.2 Allyn: A Pupil Classified as Having Minimal Brain Dysfunction

Allyn, a lethargic boy, was the youngest of the five children of lower middle income parents who lived in a small town. After being socially promoted through the elementary school, his sixth-grade teacher referred him to the school psychologist because she recognized he was not ready for the regular junior high school work. In the case study which followed, Allyn was found to be near average on individual intelligence tests, but with considerable subtest scatter. In academic performance he displayed reading, spelling, and arithmetic disabilities, with strengths in the areas of handwriting and science. Even though he had adequate motor coordination, he had mixed lateral dominance. Referral to the physician yielded the information that he had no major physical defects but an abnormal electroencephalogram pattern. On the basis of these findings, the school psychologist classified Allyn as having minimal brain dysfunction.

Since a new junior high school resource room was being initiated in the fall, Allyn was promoted into the seventh grade and was recommended to receive assistance from the resource teacher. For one hour a school day he was tutored in the resource room in written language and mathematics, with all other instruction being obtained in the regular classroom. He is likely to continue on the same schedule throughout his stay in the junior high school. By that time the community hopes to have another resource teacher available at the senior high school level, as well as a work-study program. With this extra assistance, hopefully Allyn will gain enough scholastic and vocational skills to function, at least marginally, as a self-sufficient adult.

The Specific Learning Disabilities Definitions

The Initial Definitions

Even before the reports of the HEW/NSCC Project began to appear, there was a groundswell of reaction among special educators against labels that connotated a medical etiology. Increasingly they realized the necessity for developing terms and definitions that had greater educational relevance. Examples include such terms as "educationally handicapped," "language disorders," and "perceptually impaired." To demonstrate how educators were hard at work on substitute terminology, Kirk (1962) coined the label "learning disability" some four years before Clements (1966) published his report using the term "minimal brain dysfunction". Both men employed very similar definitions.

The Kirk position stated:

A learning disability refers to a retardation, disorder, or delayed development in one or more of the processes of speech, language, reading, spelling, writing, or arithmetic resulting from a possible cerebral dysfunction and/or emotional or behavioral disturbance and not from mental retardation, sensory deprivation, or cultural or instructional factors. (p. 263)

This tended to include all of the school-related learning problems that were not included before under the 10 traditional handicapping areas listed at the beginning of this chapter. Like Clements' minimal brain dysfunction, this definition was broader than the Strauss definition of the exogenous type, brain-injured child. In fact, Kirk's definition was very nearly the educational equivalent for Clements' "minimal brain dysfunctioning." If anything, it was somewhat broader, since he specified that the disabilities may exist as a disturbance in one or more processes, whereas Clements saw them as existing in combinations. Here we see the first inclusion of the notion of *specific* learning disabilities. Although this qualifier was not used by Kirk in the 1962 edition of his text, it became a chapter heading in his second edition of *Educating Exceptional Children* a decade later (Kirk, 1972). It is interesting to note that neither the Clements nor the Kirk definition dealt with the problem of degree of severity of the learning disorder to qualify for inclusion. No attempt was made to arrive at the demarcation between special and remedial education. Thus they opened the door for the category to become a "catch-all" for any and all children who had not been eligible under the traditional handicapping conditions.

Three years after Kirk's 1962 definition, and before the Clements report was published, Bateman (1965a), a former Kirk student, published a definition of learning disorders which added a completely new dimension, namely the necessity for a difference to exist between capacity and achievement. It stated:

> children who have learning disorders are those who manifest an educationally significant discrepancy between their estimated intellectual potential and actual level of performance related to basic disorders in the learning process, which may or may not be accompanied by demonstrable central nervous system dysfunction, and which are not secondary to generalized mental retardation, educational or cultural deprivation, severe emotional disturbance, or sensory loss. (p. 220)

While echoing the Strauss and Kirk contention that a child *may or may not* have an accompanying central nervous system dysfunction, and while adding little to restrict the field to severe disorders, Bateman borrowed an important dimension from the definitions of remedial education cases. For example, Harris (1970) has updated his classic descriptive definition of a reading disability as follows:

> *Reading disability* applies to retarded readers whose reading is significantly below expectancy for their age and intelligence and is also disparate with their cultural, linguistic, and educational experience. It is sometimes differentiated into *primary* (constitutional in origin) and *secondary* (environmental in origin). (p. 11)

Further, in elaborating on his basic definition, Harris included dyslexia (severe impairment in ability to read due to assumed brain injury) as an example of a reading disability. Thus, the problem was opened up of the overlap between remedial and special education for the learning disordered. In fact, he states that as many as 10 percent of school children are in need of remedial education. Special educators were not only borrowing children from remedial educators but also definitional ingredients.

When the U.S. Office of Education became involved in providing financial support for the special education of children with learning disorders, it was obvious that a definition would be needed by that organization. The National Advisory Committee on Handicapped Children (1968) of the U.S. Office of Education, headed by Kirk, in its first annual report, tendered one that was later incorporated into the initial authorizing legislation used by that agency, entitled Public Law 91-320, The Learning Disabilities Act of 1969. This definition stated:

> Children with special (specific) learning disabilities exhibit a disorder in one or more of the basic psychological processes involved in understand-

ing or in using spoken or written language. These may be manifested in disorders of listening, thinking, talking, reading, writing, spelling, or arithmetic. They include conditions which have been referred to as perceptual handicaps, brain injury, minimal brain dysfunction, dyslexia, developmental aphasia, etc. They do not include learning problems which are due primarily to visual, hearing, or motor handicaps, to mental retardation, to emotional disturbance, or to environmental disadvantage. (p. 14)

This definition can be viewed as a refinement and elaboration of Kirk's, since it spelled out examples of the conditions to be included, such as dyslexia and developmental aphasia, among others. The inherent problems in the USOE definition center around the following six related issues:

1. The definition is loose, with no quantitative restriction on the degree of severity of the learning disabilities to qualify for special education services; thus it does not differentiate between remedial and special education for SLD children.

2. The Bateman contribution from remedial education of a differential between capacity and achievement is not included.

3. The term "specific" tends to conflict with "one or more" in the definition.

4. The miscellaneous collection of children and conditions included in the definition precludes a classical syndrome, or even common characteristics, to make the group a cohesive whole.

5. The types of conditions included under the definition are left open; only examples are given.

6. Children with traditional handicapping conditions are completely excluded, yet such pupils could also have one of the specific learning disabilities; while the primary disability of certain children may be emotional disturbance or mental retardation, the definition just given does not recognize that these pupils with traditional disability labels may also have a major specific learning disability such as reading.

It would appear that the U.S. Office of Education definition was dictated more from administrative than professional considerations, keeping as it does the areas of exceptionality mutually exclusive so as to reduce conflict and competition.

As for the prevalence estimates which follow from the U.S. Office of Education definition, clearly they could vary widely depending on how inclusively the definition is applied. The U.S. Office of Education is using the definition rather restrictively, since it advocated a 1.0 percent figure in 1971–1972 (see Table 1.1).

A number of other prevalence estimates of SLD children are to be found in the literature, with very few running as low as 1 percent. The Commission on Emotional and Learning Disorders in Children (1970) in Canada found that 1.6 percent of regular classroom pupils had learning disabilities, and a further 4.2 percent had a combination of emotional and learning problems. The Rocky Mountain Education Laboratory study (Meier, 1971) found approximately 15 percent of the children were two years or more below grade expectancy on various screening instruments; 6 percent were two years or more below using both screening and more precise educational diagnosis; and 4.7 percent were two years or more below using screening and medical diagnosis.

To enlarge the prevalence estimate picture, three indications of the extent of remedial reading cases are presented. In reporting on reading disorders in the United States, the U.S. Department of Health, Education and Welfare (1969) stated that 13.3 percent of the school population were underachieving in reading. Newbrough and Kelly (1962) cited a somewhat similar figure, namely, that 14 percent of a school population was achieving in reading two years below grade level. However, Bruininks and Weatherman (1970) found only 5.8 percent of the school population to be two grades below expectancy in reading. Such gross inconsistencies as these caution against the use of specific prevalence estimations, especially inflated ones.

Shirley, in Vignette 10.3, is an example of a pupil classified during the early seventies as having a specific learning disability. In this case, a diagnostic teacher working as a helping teacher-consultant to Shirley's regular third-grade teacher successfully corrected and/or compensated for the child's auditory perceptual problem in just over a year.

Vignette 10.3 Shirley: A Pupil Classified as Having a Specific Learning Disability

Shirley lived in a large city with her parents who provided her with an above-average environment in which to grow. In the 1970s, she was enrolled in a regular kindergarten where she had a successful year. She was then placed in an elementary school that utilized the three-on-two approach (two classes of students to three teachers). While her social adjustment was good, she almost immediately began to evidence difficulty in learning to read. The school district had adopted a phonics-oriented program and Shirley could not learn how to make the sounds of letters, nor could she sound-blend when the letter sounds were made for her. At the same time she was learning in arithmetic and spelling very slowly. By the time Shirley reached the third grade, her reading and arithmetic problems were so severe that her third-grade teachers became concerned. Through informal diagnostic evaluations, they discovered that Shirley was reading at only the middle first-grade level, with even less mathematical skills. The child was referred to Miss Haussman, a special education diagnostic teacher who did a more detailed educational evaluation on her. Shirley obtained an IQ score of 110 on screening tests. She evidenced adequate visual perceptual and motor skills, but marked weaknesses in auditory perception. Miss Haussman then referred Shirley to the speech and hearing clinic for a more thorough work-up. Among other measures, she was given the Illinois Test of Psycholinguistic Abilities. Results indicated she was average or above in the representational levels, but fairly low in grammatic closure, visual closure, auditory sequential memory, and visual sequential memory. In addition, she scored lowest of all on the supplemental tests of auditory closure and sound blending (see page 571 for a description of the ITPA subtests).

Miss Haussman classified Shirley as having a specific learning disability in the auditory perception area, and designed an instructional program to remediate the weaknesses. She then joined the regular teacher as a teacher-consultant to implement it. The Fernald kinesthetic whole-word written language program, which combined reading, writing, and spelling, was used (see page 576). Arithmetic was also taught by the Fernald kinesthetic approach. At the same time, Miss Haussman developed and taught specific drills to build up the weaknesses Shirley had shown on the ITPA.

With this intensive individualized instruction, Shirley reached grade level in school achievement in just over a year. Then, the special education program was phased out.

A Proposed Definition

The following somewhat more restrictive definition of SLD children is proposed to bridge the gap between the initial ones, which were rather open-ended, and an even more definitive one, which is clearly needed. Its goals are to prevent large numbers of pupils from being labeled as having specific learning disabilities and to provide a more functional basis for this new field to mesh with remedial education and the more traditional areas of special education. Obviously, this proposed definition is far from operational in nature, but it moves in that direction. It deals with some but not all of the six problems which the U.S. Office of Education definition has presented and will form the basis for the remainder of the discussion in this chapter.

Children with major specific learning disabilities (MSLDs) are those 1.0 to 2.0 percent of the school population (1) who display one primary severe or moderately severe discrepancy between capacity and performance in a specific basic learning process involving perception, conception, or expression associated with the areas of oral and written language or mathematics; (2) yet whose MSLDs are neither mental retardation nor any of the other traditional handicapping conditions; (3) but who may have one or more additional, secondary traditional or specific learning disabilities to a milder degree; (4) none of whom have MSLDs that can be adequately treated in the regular school program when only remedial education is provided as an ancillary service; (5) not more than one half of whom have MSLDs that can be adequately treated in the regular school program even when special education consultant-helping teacher services are extensively provided; (6) half or more of whom, therefore, will require more intensive special education instruction under such administrative plans as the resource room, the combined resource room and special class, the special class, and the special day and boarding school; and (7) yet any of whom may also require other remedial and special education services to deal with their secondary traditional or specific learning disabilities.

It will be immediately noted that this definition (1) has built in a low prevalence figure to restrict the field; (2) has adopted the term "major specific learning disability" (MSLD) to leave a place for associated secondary traditional and specific learning disabilities; (3) has not implied any neurological dysfunctions; (4) and has specified that cases which can be handled by remedial education should not be classified as MSLD. Thus, this new proposed definition is designed to encompass primarily children with severe learning disorders who were traditionally assumed by physicians and psychologists to have neurological dysfunctions. These medical or pseudomedical labels included the following: (1) Strauss syndrome; (2) aphasia (severe inability to understand receptive and/or to recall needed expressive oral language); (3) dysarthria (voice control disability); (4) visual perceptual disability, including visual agnosia (disorder of identification, organization, or interpretation of visual stimuli); (5) auditory perceptual disability, including auditory agnosia (disorder of identification or interpretation of auditory stimuli); (6) dyslexia (severe reading disorder); (1) dysgraphia (extreme handwriting problem); and (8) dyscalculia (disorder in quantitative thinking).

A prevalence figure for MSLD pupils of 1.0 to 2.0 percent of the population has been built into the definition. This implies that children formerly placed into each of the above eight classical categories would be a very small group indeed. However, severe reading disorders—the modern counterpart of dyslexia—probably would be the largest single group. Judging from past findings (Mumpower, 1970), it is anticipated that approximately 70 percent of the pupils classified as MSLD will be boys.

In the years ahead one of the most serious challenges confronting special and remedial education will be to establish a compatible interface. Already there are signs in Sweden and Canada that special education is encroaching on remedial education, especially in the areas of reading disabilities (see Chapter 1, page 16). If this pattern becomes established, then the 1.0 to 2.0 percent prevalence estimate is insufficient. It should be raised to at least 3.5 percent, and perhaps even higher in light of the Harris 10 percent figure for reading disability cases cited earlier in this chapter .The next decade should see one of three possibilities developing: (1) special educators could make additional inroads in taking over cases usually served by remedial educators; (2) there could be a rather well-defined wall established between them; or (3) there could be a melding of these two related fields. One can only hope that this last option will come about.

Assuming that the third choice is pursued, and an attempt made to establish a rather clear division line, then there is at least a quarter of a century of effort to call upon wherein attempts have been made to differentiate between remedial and general education. These efforts have concentrated on determining how much a pupil's reading achievement needs to lag behind his reading capacity before he is eligible for remedial reading. *Reading achievement* has been operationally defined as reading age or reading grade (RA or RG) on a nationally standardized achievement test of reading, usually individually administered. *Reading capacity* has been operationally defined by reading expectancy formulas, which include such ingredients as chronological age or years in school and mental age or IQ on nationally standardized individual intelligence tests. For example, Harris (1970) has used the following expectancy formula:

$$\text{Reading Expectancy Age} \atop \text{(R.Exp.A.)} = \frac{2MA + 1CA}{3}$$

A reading expectancy quotient was then obtained by using this formula:

$$\text{Reading Expectancy Quotient} \atop \text{(R.Exp.Q.)} = \frac{RA}{R.Exp.A.} \times 100$$

Harris went on to define a reading disability case as any pupil with a R.Exp.Q. below 90. Gunderson (1971) also stated that a reading-disabled child is one who has a reading age less than 90 percent of his expectancy age level. No lower limit was included, but one would need to be established if a demarcation line is to determine the difference between remedial and special education. Thus, the question arises: If a R.Exp.Q. of 90 and below yields 10 percent of the school population, as Harris (1970) has suggested, what quotient will yield about 0.5 percent—perhaps a value of between 50 and 67?

Now let us examine a second question: Is a 15-year-old boy a remedial reading case when entering the 10th grade with an IQ score of 85 (and therefore a mental age of 12.75) and a reading age of 9.0?

$$\text{R.Exp.A.} = \frac{2(12.75) + 15}{3} = 13.5 \text{ years}$$

$$\text{R.Exp.Q.} = \frac{9.0 \times 100}{13.5} = 67 \text{ percent}$$

With a R.Exp.Q. of 67, this boy is clearly a reading disability case, according to both Harris and Gunderson. The key question is whether a dull normal youth in the 10th grade, who is reading only at the beginning fourth-grade level, should be provided with about three hours of remedial reading a week, or whether he should be classified as MSLD and given more intensive special education. Clearly, this boy represents a marginal case between remedial and special education, and perhaps factors other than age, grade placement, intelligence, and reading achievement need to be considered in arriving at an appropriate classification. In any event, if these two related fields elect to remain separate, some demarcation formula such as the above will need to be found.

THE BRAIN

The inclusion of even this brief section on the brain in a chapter on specific learning disabilities may be viewed as controversial. As already stated, the field of special education is still recuperating from an era of domination by the medical model with its physiological labels and their actual or implied medical etiologies and treatments. More specifically, because the medical model has so little educational utility, the terms "brain injury" and "minimal brain dysfunction" were replaced with "specific learning disorders," which does not imply neurological impairment. Even though there is considerable agreement that there must be central nervous system dysfunctioning in many cases of major specific learning disabilities, no doubt there are also many other important contributing factors. Furthermore, as yet it can be argued that so little is firmly established about the complex relationships between specific learning disabilities and specific types of neurological impairment that a discussion of the brain at this stage of knowledge is premature. Nevertheless, the topic is included here for two main reasons. First, some discussion of the brain was considered necessary in this introductory text on special education, and it was arbitrarily agreed to place it here so that other contributing authors could refer to it. Second, while much remains to be learned, a considerable amount is already known about the functioning and dysfunctioning of the central nervous systems (CNS), and these facts cannot be ignored. Figure 10.1 illustrates the various parts of the brain and some of the functions and dysfunctions that have been established or hypothesized for them.

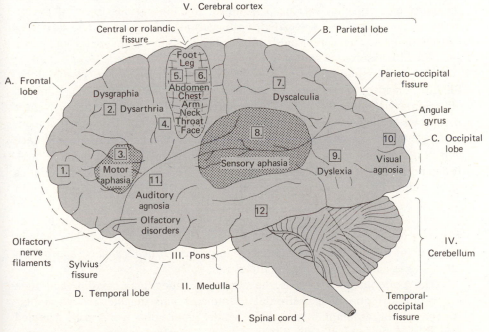

FIGURE 10.1 Exterior, right lateral view of the human brain indicating some of the established and hypothetical functions and dysfunctions of the various areas of the cerebral cortex. Key: 1—Thought association, reasoning, and idea generation; 2—written expression; 3—Broca's speech-expression area; 4—voice and articulation control; 5—voluntary-movement expression; 6—body-surface sensations; 7—arithmetic understanding; 8—Wernicke's speech-understanding area; 9—reading recognition and comprehension; 10—visual sensations; 11—auditory sensations; 12—information organization, interpretation, and storage.

Brain Parts and Function

The major role of the *spinal cord* is to carry signals to and from all parts of the body through its many nerves. The *medulla oblongata,* or, more briefly, the medulla, is a short extension of the spinal cord at the base of the brain. It controls involuntary muscle movements such as respiration and heartbeat. Above the medulla is an oval-shaped structure known as the *pons.* It serves as a bridge between the medulla and the higher brain centers up through the *midbrain* and *diencephalon* (tween-brain), which are not shown in Figure 10.1. The medulla, pons, and midbrain are sometimes referred to as the brain stem or basal ganglia. The extrapyramidal tracts are located in this area. The *cerebellum,* which is also called the little brain, is the second largest division of the brain and is located at the lower back of the head. It controls such muscular functions as balance and coordination, qualities many brain-injured children lack.

By far the largest and most important division of the human brain is called the *cerebral cortex,* or *cerebrum.* It consists of two hemispheres separated vertically by a deep groove, across which many nerve fibers run. The cerebrum is the center for consciousness and higher-thought processes, including memory and learning. It follows that the various types of severe learning disorders are associated with various types of cerebral cortex dysfunctioning. The cerebrum is divided into four major parts or lobes, separated by fissures, as shown in Figure 10.1.

The chief motor areas of the cerebral cortex are in the *frontal lobe.* Slightly ahead of the central, or Rolandic fissure, is the strip that controls all voluntary body movements. This is often called the motor cortex. Nearer the crown of the head are the centers that control the foot, leg, and abdomen; and nearer the ear are the centers that control the neck, throat, and face muscles, including voice control. Thus, dysarthria results from damage here. It should be noted that all persons with dysarthria have some characteristics of stutterers or stammerers, but all stutterers do not have brain damage in this area.

Ahead of this voluntary body-control area is the region responsible for written expression. Therefore, brain damage in this location would result in dysgraphia. Below that is the crucially important *Broca's speech expression area.* Damage here would precipitate motor aphasia.

The *prefontal lobe area* is the center of thought association and idea generation. At one time prefrontal lobotomies and lobectomies were performed on the assumption that they would reduce the worry and troubled thoughts of the mentally ill. But it is most important for special educators to know that problems in oral and written language expression are associated with frontal lobe malfunctioning.

The *parietal lobe* monitors and interprets a number of sensations. The strip immediately behind the central, or Rolandic fissure, receives body-surface sensations of touch and temperature from the various parts of the body. In terms of specific functions, the motor and sensory strips are mirror images of one another. The *occipital lobe,* at the back of the cerebral hemisphere, monitors visual sensations. Damage to this lobe results in visual perceptual disorders, including visual agnosia and hallucinations (Lashley, 1930–1942; Chow, 1952). According to Nielson (1946), damage to the occipital cortex can also result in spatial disorganization. Auditory and olfactory sensations are received and interpreted in the *temporal lobe.* Auditory and olfactory agnosia and hallucinations result from dysfunctions here. A large area of the temporal lobe is devoted to information correlation, organization, interpretation, and storage. A second area of speech, and the largest one, falls across both the parietal and temporal lobes and is therefore called the parieto-temporal area. This is known as Wernicke's speech area and has to do primarily with the reception and understanding of speech sensations (Wernicke, 1874). Damage here results in sensory aphasia. It should now be clear why a person can have sensory aphasia but little motor aphasia, and vice versa, in that different lobes and areas are involved. It is not surprising that areas adjacent to Wernicke's speech area appear to be centers that control arithmetic understanding, reading recognition, and comprehension. The arithmetic area is probably at the top of the parietal lobe, where damage would result in dyscalculia. The reading area is at the juncture of the occipital, parietal, and temporal lobes, where damage results in dyslexia. So we see, while the frontal lobe deals with expression, all the other three major lobes—the parietal, occipital, and temporal—receive, interpret, and store sensory information. Here is the center of oral and written language reception. Generally, the left hemisphere controls both receptive and expressive language for persons who are right-side dominant. This is why the left hemisphere is displayed in Figure 10.1. But when one hemisphere is damaged, the other one eventually takes over some of its functions. Thus, the question arises: To what degree is there localization of brain functions, or is there much mass action? The above discussion would suggest a great deal of localization of functions. Perhaps this has resulted from an oversimplified description of an extremely complex organ.

Localization Versus Mass Action

Although major interest in brain-injured children did not develop until the late 1940s, the groundwork was laid many years before that with the study of brain-injured animals and adult humans. In the nineteenth century, Broca demonstrated one type of localization of central nervous system functioning in human beings by showing that lesions located in Broca's area (see Fig. 10.1) of the frontal lobe of the cerebral cortex caused expressive language problems. Since then, many scientists, such as Penfield and Roberts (1959), have mapped out additional locations of brain function.

In contrast to the "localization of function" approach, Franz and Lashley (1917) and Lashley (1929) conducted some classic studies involving maze learning and retention with rats, which led them to formulate the "mass action principle." They found that capacity of rats to learn or relearn a maze pathway was reduced roughly in proportion to the amount of cerebral tissue that they destroyed, regardless of the area ablated. This finding has been replicated repeatedly. Up to that point, the localization theory had been in vogue. Now the notion of nonspecificity of function, or mass action, came into existence.

The work on human beings by Hebb (1939, 1942, 1949), a Canadian neuropsychologist, is relevant at this point. From his research he proposed a "cell assembly" theory, which stated that when the same sensation is experienced repeatedly, a particular set of cortical nerve cells becomes integrated and organized into a single functional unit, called a cell assembly. This initial learning is a function of repeated specific sensory excitations of these cell tracks. Early systematic stimulation is seen as especially important to form these essential connections. Cell assemblies become integrated through experience. According to his theory, the time of brain injury is very important. Impairments present at birth or occurring in early infancy produce the most serious problems, since they interfere with the formation of these essential cell assemblies. Brain injury, after the cell assemblies are formed, is viewed as less damaging. By then, key concepts and connections are formed and generalized. Therefore, Hebb hypothesized, there is less dependence on specific pathways. Later brain injury impairs the formation of new cell assemblies more than it eradicates earlier established learnings. In terms of the localization of function versus mass cortical action theories, Hebb tends to accommodate both positions. In initial learning there is great specificity, but later there is less dependency on one track. However, the reader is reminded that both the Lashley and Hebb positions are theoretic generalizations rather than universal facts. For example, their data are not completely compatible. Lashley found, with rats, that a lesion did more harm to retention of a maze habit already formed than to the ability to learn a new one or relearn the same one. Hebb found the opposite with human beings. It is not surprising that research on rats and human beings yields conflicting results. Much of the learning in man is verbally mediated—a tool not available to rats. This overriding strategy provides man with a higher mental thought process of a completely different order than that available to nonlinguistic lower animals. Therefore, both Hebb's and Lashley's findings could be essentially correct. There is little doubt but that many areas of the brain have quite specific purposes. Also, it is evident that many parts of the brain are called into action to perform one task. A malfunction in an area not directly related to the task being performed may still inhibit successful completion of the task at hand. Conversely, the brain is apparently capable of some compensation—but within limits. How much will depend on the location and extent of the brain injury and the nature of the task to be learned. At this point, since solid basic principles about the functioning of the human brain are still not available, instructional programs based on a neurophysiological foundation are likely to be controversial if not fallacious. Hopefully, future brain research will change the picture.

THE BASIC DIAGNOSTIC-REMEDIATION PROCESS

The procedures for identifying children as having specific learning disabilities for special education purposes have undergone substantial changes in the last decade or so. At the same time, methods of determining and implementing special education interventions have been refined. The traditional and emerging diagnostic-remediation models are discussed below.

The Traditional Models

In the past, two diagnostic models have dominated the field: (1) the interdisciplinary team and (2) the individual school psychologist.

The Interdisciplinary Team Model

When the terms "brain injury" and "minimal brain dysfunction" were in vogue, the ideal team, typically, consisted of such individuals as a pediatrician, a neurologist, a psychologist, a social worker, a speech therapist, a special educator, and, on occasion, the child's classroom teacher. All were expected to bring an area of expertise to the group and to share equally in decision-making. However, this rarely happened. Since neurological impairment was being studied, usually the physician or psychologist dominated the team as its chairman. This interdisciplinary-team approach rarely resulted in useful educational recommendations other than those having to do with classification and school placement. At least three factors dictated against this strategy: (1) it was very costly in terms of dollars and manpower; (2) professions outside of education were making educational decisions; and (3) the emphasis was on finding weaknesses and speculating on their possible causes. Nevertheless, this strategy is still in use today and is often found in "diagnostic and prescriptive teaching centers," both in public schools and in private clinics. A number of articles critically examine this technique (Gunderson, 1971; Millman, 1970; Rice, 1970; Abrams, 1969; Barsch, 1968).

The Individual School Psychologist Model

Many school systems could not assemble either the financial or manpower resources to utilize the interdisciplinary team, desirable as it was considered to be. Instead, a single school psychologist assumed responsibility for classifying and certifying pupils as eligible for special education SLD services. He usually spent two to three hours in administering a psychometric test battery to the child and in interviewing parents and teachers. When possible, other disciplines were asked to contribute data to build up a more complete case study. Then, a psychological report was prepared and submitted to the school authorities. In addition to having the same last two weaknesses as the team approach, the individual school psychologist model had the added one of placing too much responsibility in the hands of one person—and a noneducator at that—though most school psychologists would argue that they are educators or have an educational background. Recently this approach came into disfavor among special educators and psychologists.

The latter no longer see themselves as primarily psychometricians and argue that psychoeducational tests, including individual intelligence tests, could be more appropriately administered by trained educational diagnosticians. In this way, they would be free to serve other roles to be presented shortly.

The Emerging Model

The emerging trend is for teachers to do much of their own diagnosis and to be at the center of the educational assessment process. However, neither regular nor special educators have often been trained as skilled diagnosticians. This shortcoming is being corrected through preservice and inservice training, especially among special educators. As a result, the trend is to adopt the model presented in the flow chart in Figure 10.2. This scheme will provide the framework for the discussion to follow.

Initial Selection and Screening

Perhaps before too long, a comprehensive individual psychoeducational assessment will be routinely and recurringly given to all children from pre-school and on to find those in need of special help. Until this occurs, some less desirable referral mechanism will be needed. As shown in Figure 10.2, both regular teachers and parents should be allowed to request special education evaluation-prescriptive work-up services for children suspected of having major learning disorders. The suggestion that parents be allowed to refer their children directly when they become concerned about lack of school progress may be viewed as controversial, and certainly it will result in over-referral. Nevertheless, it is included to increase the referral options and the accountability of the schools.

It is recognized that regular teachers will also tend to overrefer. For example, through a mail questionnaire, a group of K through 3 teachers identified 41.4 percent of their pupils as having one or more learning problems (Rubin and Balow, 1971). As the authors indicated, such preposterously large referrals suggest that the need is as great to investigate the teaching personnel as it is to study the children the teachers feel they cannot teach. Nevertheless, Ferinden and Jacobson (1970) reported that kindergarten teachers were quite accurate in determining which children would have learning problems in the first grade. This is not surprising. Teachers interact and observe their pupils for many hours throughout each school day, and thus should be aware of the scholastic strengths and weaknesses of each of them. The problem is not their failure to recognize children in trouble but their willingness to turn excessive numbers over to others to teach. Many techniques could be used to reduce the number of referrals. Among these would be less reliance on subjective judgment and greater reliance on more objective behavioral checklists, if not actual tests of pupil progress.

Since there will be a tendency for both the school and the home to over-refer children for a diagnostic workup, the first step needed will be an initial screening (see Fig. 10.2). For this purpose, Table 10.1 lists as examples three individual tests of scholastic aptitude and two wide-range individual tests of

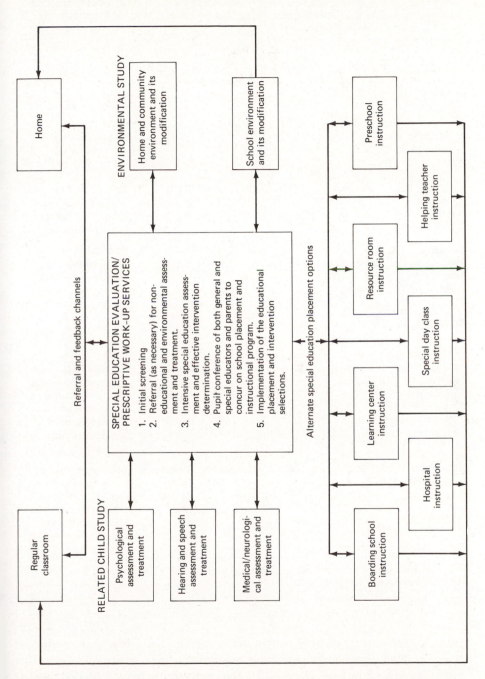

FIGURE 10.2 Flow chart for special education and ancillary referral, assessment placement, and intervention services for children with specific learning disabilities (including restudy, recycling, and replacement when indicated).

TABLE 10.1 *Representative Teacher-Administered Individual Screening Tests Useful for Children Suspected of Having Specific Learning Disabilities*

Test	Author	Data	Administration Time	Range	Description[1]
SCHOLASTIC APTITUDE					
Slosson Intelligence Test	R. L. Slosson	1964	10-20 min.	Birth to adult	Wide range, based in part on Stanford-Binet and Gesell scales
Peabody Picture Vocabulary Test	L. M. Dunn	1959	10-15 min.	1-9 to adult	Measurement of verbal intelligence through hearing vocabulary for standard English
Columbia Mental Maturity Scale	B. B. Burgemeister L. H. Blum I. Lorge	1972 revision	15-20 min	3-6 to 9-11	More culture-fair nonverbal measure of reasoning ability involving same and different, and relations
SCHOOL ACHIEVEMENT					
Peabody Individual Achievement Test	L. M. Dunn F. C. Markwardt	1970	30-40 min.	Kindergarten through adult	Untimed wide-range screening test with 5 subtests and total score giving picture of overall level of achievement; no written work required
Wide Range Achievement Test	J. Jastak S. R. Jastak	1965 revision	15 min.	Kindergarten through adult	Short wide-range screening of spelling, reading, arithmetic achievement; useful as a quick estimate of level of scholastic functioning

[1] More detailed information on these instruments and others may be found in the Buros *Mental Measurement Yearbook* series.

school achievement, each of which can be given in a fairly short period of time. At least screening tests such as these, if not more comprehensive examinations, should be given to all referred pupils. In addition, screening visits should be made to both the child's regular classroom and home. With these data, it should be possible to determine if there is a need to go further in the evaluation and prescription-determining process.

Noneducational Child Study and Treatment

At any time during the initial screening or the in-depth educational assessment, the pupil may be referred for one or more types of noneducational analysis and treatment where indicated (see Fig. 10.2). In some school systems, the student is referred out to other professionals only when symptoms suggest that this is desirable. In others, this is more routinely done if the money and manpower are available. Discussed below are psychological, hearing and speech, and medical-assessment factors. Some of the factors in these areas which may need attention most frequently are listed in the first three columns of Table 10.2. The section closes with a brief examination of "hyperactivity," including drug control. While this condition often falls within the province of medicine, it is also a concern of educators and psychologists.

Psychological assessment and treatment. In being relieved of the routine appraisal of scholastic aptitude and achievement, school psychologists who have sufficient training would be freed to assume even more complex roles, as shown in the first column of Figure 10.2. In terms of assessment, information is very often helpful on motivational factors, learning characteristics, and personal adjustment patterns of children referred as potential SLD cases.

Previously, a differential diagnosis among brain injury, emotional disturbance, and mental retardation was given considerable attention by psychologists, with psychometric test batteries used to make the judgmental distinctions. A major problem was the poor validity of these instruments. After critically reviewing the research literature on adults and children, Yates (1954) and Klebanoff, Singer, and Wilensky (1954) concluded that these tests usually differentiate out from the normals, as one single group, the organically impaired, the mentally retarded, and the emotionally disturbed. However, their record for differentiating among the three groups was appallingly poor. It was even worse for individual cases. These negative results on finding subtle signs of organicity using psychometrics are not surprising, especially for children. For one thing, children only rarely have a specific brain lesion. This is more an adult phenomenon. Many children traditionally classified as having a minimal brain dysfunction (and more recently as having specific learning disabilities) have not even had any hard signs of neurological impairment. Furthermore, Dunn (1968) has reported that three different clinical teams, depending on their biases, preoccupations, and training, labeled the same child brain injured, emotionally disturbed, or mentally retarded. It became increasingly apparent that making a valid differential diagnosis was often impossible. More recently, special educators have raised the question: How important is it to make such a differential diagnosis among children? As far as they are concerned, it is not. No matter which label is attached to the child, the educational intervention will probably be to detect specific troublesome behaviors and remediate them. Etiologies and categories have little influence on this process. Thus, concern about making category distinctions is fast fading.

TABLE 10.2 Some Areas Related to, and Specific Types of, Severe Learning Disorders Needing Consideration and Possibly Intensive Investigation and Attention

Areas for Investigation

Child-centered Variables				Environmentally Centered Variables	
Psychological Factors	Hearing and Speech Factors	Medical/Neurological Factors	Specific Learning Disability Areas	Home & Community Factors	School Factors
1. Differential diagnosis among brain injury, emotional disturbance, and mental retardation 2. Detection of neuropsychological signs of brain damage 3. Motivational factors 4. Learning characteristics	1. Diagnosis of type and degree of hearing impairment 2. Diagnosis of type and degree of speech disorder	1. Hearing acuity deficit 2. Visual-acuity deficit 3. Eye-movement problem 4. Chronic illness 5. General health, nutrition, sleep, and rest problems 6. Metabolic or glandular problems 7. Endocrine dysfunction 8. Brain dysfunction 9. Drug addiction 10. Laterality problem 11. Incoordination 12. Activity level	Diagnosis and remediation in one or more of the following categories: 1. Motor 2. Visual perceptual 3. Auditory perceptual 4. Oral language 5. Reading 6. Spelling 7. Writing 8. Arithmetic	1. Ineffective parents (child neglect or excessive pressure) 2. Family instability and deterioration 3. Parent uninterested in education 4. Inadequate home language models 5. Inadequately educated parents 6. Lack of cultural opportunities 7. Lack of educational materials in the home 8. Excessive migrant behavior 9. Poverty and slum conditions	1. Poor instructors 2. Inappropriate curriculum 3. Inappropriate methods and materials 4. Teacher/pupil rejection 5. Failure experiences 6. Segregation 7. Truancy 8. Lack of ancillary services
Some Intervention				**Options**	
1. Mental health consultation 2. Learning and motivation consultation 3. Research consultation 4. Psychotherapy for emotional disturbances	1. Consultation on treatment of children with hearing problems 2. Consultation on treatment of children with speech disorders 3. Actual therapy for hearing and/or speech disorders	1. Corrective devices 2. Surgery 3. Medication		1. Parent counseling 2. Parent education 3. Financial support 4. Foster home placement 5. Community services	1. Teacher, pupil, or school transfers 2. Provision of ancillary services (including remedial instruction) 3. Provision of out-of-school supplementary tutoring, therapy, etc.

With regard to psychological treatment, four major ones that psychologists can provide are listed at the bottom of Table 10.2. Depending on their areas of expertise, the psychologists can be helpful as consultants in the areas of mental health and learning, including behavior modification, and research. Furthermore, a number of children with major learning disorders will also have severe behavior disorders for which psychotherapy may be effective.

Hearing and speech assessment and treatment. A fair number of pupils referred for a major learning disorder have significant hearing and/or speech problems. It is extremely important, therefore, for SLD special educators to cooperate closely with hearing and speech personnel. In Chapter 7, McConnell discussed hearing losses and their assessment. The Hulls, in Chapter 6, dealt with speech disorders, with aphasia being the most central one to the SLD area. This condition will again be mentioned when oral language is discussed later in the chapter. Only through close collaboration of hearing and speech with special education personnel is it likely that children with learning disorders will gain optimal efficiency in receptive and expressive language. In certain cases hearing and speech personnel may provide actual therapy to the children involved. In nearly all cases, they will provide invaluable consultation on how to work best with the child who is discovered to have a hearing or speech problem (see column 2, Table 10.2).

Medical/neurological assessment and treatment. The medical diagnosis can be most helpful if it leads to the findings of physical problems that can be treated by that profession through surgery, medication, or corrective devices. Examples are a hearing loss corrected by surgery, seizures controlled by medication, and faulty vision corrected by glasses. In determining whether or not a pupil is to be provided with special SLD education, an important step is to study and treat, where possible, physical defects such as those listed in column 3 of Table 10.2. While medicine can work miracles in curing or alleviating some of these factors, it cannot, as yet, stimulate, regenerate, or replace damaged central nervous system tissue.

Childhood hyperactivity. There has been no section in this chapter on the characteristics of SLD children such as there has been in nearly all the previous ones. This is because these children are not sufficiently homogeneous to fall into a single group or even into subgroups, except for the Strauss syndrome. Yet some characteristics of Strauss-type children and of some other SLD pupils have been of great concern to educators, namely, childhood hyperactivity. Therefore, in spite of this condition not being a universal characteristic among SLD children, it is now singled out for special attention. This phenomenon, which is also known as hyperkinesia, has been extensively researched for over 25 years. Excellent reviews of the literature and provided by Cromwell, Baumeister, and Hawkins (1963), Werry (1968), Werry and Sprague (1969), and, more recently, by Keogh (1971). Here are five generalizations gleaned from this material:

  1. Only about 20 percent of school children classified as brain injured, or some such synonym, will display noticeable hyperactivity. Further-

more, capable persons across the full intellectual spectrum will demonstrate this same characteristic at times. Thus all hyperactivity pupils are not brain-injured, just as all brain-injured pupils are not hyperactive.

2. Hyperactivity, while a somewhat persistent trait, usually fluctuates with the situation. A pupil may be far more hyperactive in the classroom than at home watching T.V. or in her sleep. And children tend to outgrow hyperactivity as they reach adolescence.

3. It is not just the amount but the timing and type of hyperactivity that leads the teacher to refer the pupil for classification as brain injured, minimal brain dysfunction, or SLD.

4. The six behavioral characteristics most frequently attributed to hyperactive children are: (1) restlessness; (2) inattentiveness; (3) distractibility; (4) excitability; (5) management problem; and (6) lack of frustration tolerance.

5. In terms of school work, hyperactive children tend to be erratic. Further, they often make reversal and mirroring errors in writing.

These five major findings led Keogh (1971) to speculate that there may be at least three different types of hyperactivity with different etiologies which suggest different educational interventions. She carefully pointed out that these three types are not mutually exclusive and are only hypothetical constructs needing empirical testing.

1. Hyperactivity in some children may be but one aspect of *a basic impulsive habit pattern*. Such pupils make hasty decisions and, as a result, their school work is slapdash. In areas of high-response uncertainty, they are likely to have heightened eye and body movement as they search for a *modus operandi*. The implication for education is that they need to be taught to be more reflective. Behavior-modification techniques have been found successful and herefore support this hypothesis. Freibergs and Douglas (1969) found 100 percent reinforcement more successful than a 50 percent schedule for hyperactive children in learning new concepts. It could be argued that continuous reinforcement increased caution and attention to tasks, and thus reduced impulsivity.

2. Hyperactivity, in some other children, may simply reflect *information seeking* among those who are limited in intelligence. This hypothesis also suggests the need for behavioral management with the goal to teach the child how to select relevant information, how to learn, and how to solve problems.

3. Hyperactivity, in still other children, may reflect a *neurological impairment*. This hypothesis leads to medication as a therapeutic agent. Wender (1971), a child psychiatrist, is one of the strong advocates of drug management. In fact, if there is a suspicion of minimal brain dysfunction, he argues that the child should be given trial medication. If this reduces hyperactivity and its correlates, he believes one has sufficient evidence for classifying the child as MBD. Thus, the drug becomes the major diagnostic tool.

Since well over half of the pupils classified as having SLD are required to take drugs to make them behave better, the topic needs some attention.

For these children, the preferred medications are the amphetamine-type stimulant drugs. Paradoxically, while these stimulate (pep up) average persons, they have the reverse consequence on many of the hyperactive because of a curvilinear effect where individuals already overaroused will exhibit a decrease in arousal following the administration of this medication. In much rarer instances, tranquilizers are used to reduce temper tantrums, boisterousness, and destructiveness. In still rarer cases, mood-changing drugs, such as antidepressants, are used, but usually for hypoactive children classified as having minimal brain dysfunctioning.

How effective have such drugs been with these children? In his review of the literature, Freeman (1966) concluded that learning was improved in about one third of the cases and behavior was improved in nearly one half. While they do not improve general intelligence, memory, or visual-auditory perception, drugs do reduce some cases of inattentiveness, behavior disorders, and learning problems and thus promote classroom peace. However, their widespread use on children raises basic ethical problems in a society already plagued by widespread drug abuse and dependency.

What are the possible costs of drug usage? Ladd (1970) has examined this issue in some detail and has outlined five risks: (1) the addiction problem; (2) the disguising of other serious problems; (3) contribution to the drug culture; (4) the provision of an artificial crutch rather than training the child to regulate his own behavior; and (5) the issue of the child's rights. Concerning the latter, there are many things school children do that teachers and principals consider disruptive but that may be within their legal rights. These points argue against many physicians being so cooperative in supplying drugs for hyperactive children, especially when parents request them at the urging of teachers who are seeking relief from discipline problems. For drugs to be accepted as a treatment for hyperactivity they must meet at least three criteria: first, they must have a calming effect on the child; second, they must not cause excessive drowsiness or dullness; and third, they must at least, not impede school learning.

One management question about hyperactivity, aside from drug therapy, still remains: Does a classroom environment with reduced extraneous stimuli, such as was proposed by Strauss and Lehtinen (1947), lower the activity level of hyperactive children and facilitate learning? With a group of institutionalized retarded children, Gardner, Cromwell, and Foshee (1959) demonstrated that hyperactivity decreased rather than increased with stimulus bombardment. Carter and Diaz (1971) compared the performance of 42 brain-injured and 42 normal sixth-graders on achievement tests while using both visual and auditory distractors. The increased visual and/or auditory distraction did not significantly lower the scores of either group. Another study sheds further light on the question. Burnette (1962) compared the relative effectiveness of a Strauss-Lehtinen-type restricted classroom environment with that of a standard classroom environment on the learning ability of hyperactive versus nonhyperactive mildly retarded children in a state residential facility. All subjects were classified as educable mentally retarded.

Four groups were constituted: (1) high active-restricted environment; (2) high active-standard environment; (3) average active-restricted environment; and (4) average active-standard environment. The task consisted of recognizing and reading aloud the names of 45 previously unknown words following repeated drill. Results indicated that neither hyperactive nor nonhyperactive retardates learned any faster in the restricted environment. This sample of literature casts considerable doubt on the necessity of the Strauss-Lehtinen classroom environment for hyperactive and/or brain-injured children. However, until studies are conducted with classical Strauss-syndrome children, the case is not closed.

Environmental Assessment and Treatment

The previous discussion focused on child study by noneducators and some of the various interventions they can provide for SLD pupils. But of equal importance is an examination of the environment of the child to determine to what degree it is contributing to his learning problems. Home, community, and school factors will now be briefly examined, as reflected in Figure 10.2 and the last two columns in Table 10.2.

The home and community environment. It is normally the responsibility of the school social worker to provide services in this area. A number of factors related to home and community can contribute to severe learning disabilities. Some of these are listed in column 5 of Table 10.2.

Most SLD definitions rule out cultural and environmental disadvantages as the prime causative factors, yet they may be secondary or contributing influences. Slum children, especially from ethnic and linguistic minorities, develop language differences that impede school learning (Deutsch, 1965; Bernstein, 1964). Further, they live in a noise-filled environment and lack educationally stimulating materials. Toward the end of the chapter, the need for preschool instruction to compensate for these factors will be discussed.

Other home factors such as child neglect and excessive pressure cut across all ethnic and socioeconomic groups. In fact, it is interesting to note that an excessive proportion of SLD pupils initially came from the middle and upper class, while comparable children of the poor tended to be classified as educable mentally retarded. But it must be assumed that this classification should be represented approximately equally across all racial, ethnic, and socioeconomic groups. On the one hand, children should not be given the SLD label just because they come from an environment that does not stimulate them educationally. On the other hand, children of poor parents can and do have specific learning disabilities that demand focused attention. For that matter, because of poor health and nutrition, one could expect more CNS dysfunctioning and, therefore, more SLD problems among the poor than among the wealthy. Thus the future should see a more equitable proportioning of SLD pupils across social class and ethnic groups.

The school environment. When a student is failing in school, as much attention needs to be given to analyzing his school situation as is directed to studying the child himself. Listed at the top of the last column of Table 10.2 are some of the school correlates of pupil failure. To a large degree any investigation of the regular school program will need to be conducted by general education supervisors and consultants, in cooperation with the principal of the school and the regular teacher herself. When indicated, other central office educators may need to be involved, including psychologists, counselors, and truant officers. With a willingness to make changes, it is probable that one or more needed alterations will be found desirable in each case studied. Some of the possible intervention options are listed at the bottom of the last column of Table 10.2. In addition, the obvious first choice is for the homeroom teacher to make the needed changes to correct the learning problems encountered by the pupil she has referred.

Special Education Assessment and Intervention

The third step in Figure 10.2 in the special education evaluation-prescriptive work-up is the intensive educational assessment, including the determination of an effective intervention. Many of the details on the diagnosis and remediation of each of the eight specific learning disorders listed in the fourth column of Table 10.2 are discussed later in the chapter. However, before that, some general comments on the following related special education assessment-prescription determining strategies are introduced here. First, the different approaches advocated for teaching SLD pupils are presented, followed by a brief mention of the last two stages in the special education work-up, namely, pupil conferences and program implementation.

Special education diagnostic testing and teaching. Desirable diagnostic testing and teaching practices in special SLD education have been valued differently by different persons at different times. In fact five, if not six, strategies have been practiced. The first three of these are various versions of "diagnostic," "prescriptive," or "clinical" teaching. All of them involve child study and individualized instruction through the implementation of the classic "test-teach-retest" paradigm. It can be argued that all good general and special educators conduct hundreds of their own test-teach-retest sequences on each of their pupils in connection with their day-to-day teaching. Sometimes these teachers have treated the three stages rather discretely by using formal tests before and after a unit of instruction. More often they have relied on informal questions and feedback throughout a dialectic teaching sequence to implement the model. Besides holding to this classic paradigm for day-to-day teaching, special SLD education has adopted modified versions of it. Below are presented the five different approaches to educational intervention practiced with SLD pupils.

1. A number of authorities have favored some version of the traditional approach to "diagnostic teaching" as borrowed from remedial education. For purposes of pupil classification and placement, the sequence was originally: (1) the physician or psychologist tested; next (2) the special educator

taught; and then (3) the physician or psychologist retested on demand. As special educators have assumed greater responsibility for their own diagnosis, two choices of implementation of this particular version of diagnostic teaching have been available to them. On the one hand, because so few special SLD teachers are as yet skilled diagnosticians, the widely utilized strategy has been: (1) the high-level diagnostic teacher tests and determines an effective intervention; next (2) the special education tutor teaches; and then (3) the diagnostic teacher retests regularly. Under this version, an educational diagnostic test battery which yields a profile of abilities and disabilities is administered in the pupil's area of suspected weakness. Next, the educational report is written, pointing out the weaknesses to the tutor and making recommendations on how to alleviate them. This report and the pupil are then turned over to the remedial tutor to implement the predetermined program of instruction. This is largely the pattern being followed in special SLD education in the early seventies. On the other hand, while this diagnostic teacher as the tester but not as the tutor model is a marked improvement over the noneducator as the tester, it still has one glaring weakness. The tester and the tutor are separate persons. Therefore, as special SLD teachers gain greater diagnostic skills, the pattern is shifting to: (1) the special teacher tests; (2) the same special teacher teaches; and then (3) same special teacher retests. This version of diagnostic teaching can be implemented to the degree that the special SLD teacher is able to diagnose specific learning disabilities and plan interventions to correct them. The major characteristic of this strategy is first to detect weaknesses and then to teach to remediate, correct, or alleviate them.

2. A few rare authorities favor a reversal of this basic diagnostic teaching strategy. Instead of determining and teaching to weaknesses, they advocate the opposite, namely, determining and teaching to and through strengths for better motivation and greater learning. The Mills Learning Methods Test (p. 573) is a device that implements this approach.

3. A growing number of others in the field reject both of the above traditional versions of diagnostic teaching, mainly on two counts. First, they view the testing and teaching as separate operations which should be combined. Second, they argue that "norm-referenced" or "standardized" tests are too global to be useful in diagnostic teaching and that a profile analysis of subtest difference is unreliable because of the high positive intersubtest correlations which indicate they are measuring substantially the same phenomenon. To overcome these weaknesses, such critics have moved to an adaptation of behavior modification. Instead of detecting and teaching to weaknesses, they argue that they are determining the level at which a pupil is functioning in his area of specific disability and then that they are applying behavior-modification techniques to advance his skills in a step-by-step fashion. (The eight steps in this version of "diagnostic" teaching were listed in Chapter 3.) Perhaps this approach might more appropriately be called developmental rather than diagnostic teaching.

The key philosophical position underlying this approach is that assessment and instruction are one operation. An educator cannot be simply an educational diagnostician. Instead, the instructional process itself becomes the relevant diagnostic measure. The distinct advantages of this strategy are that evaluation is ongoing, and that failures are viewed as teacher-programer failures rather than pupil failures. The upshot is that present-day special SLD teachers have rediscovered the classical classroom ongoing process of test-teach-retest mentioned at the outset of this section, but they now have new labels to attach to it and improved techniques for implementing it—in the form of small sequential steps and immediate positive reinforcement.

Because behavior modification has tended to emphasize the terminal step in the diagnostic teaching process, namely, the positive reinforcers (the consequences), many special educators are now shifting their attention to the antecedent stages, especially the task to be performed. The terms that are growing in favor are "task analysis," "behavioral objectives," and "mini-lessons." A teaching sequence begins with the establishment of a terminal behavioral objective, which is specific in its direction, narrow in orientation, and written in operational terms. Next, a task analysis is made for the purpose of developing small sequential steps (or component behaviors) that will help the pupil attain the terminal behavioral objective. The entry behavior of the pupil, the step at which the instruction must begin, is determined at this point. One child would start on step five if he has mastered the previous four, while another child would have to begin at step one. In this way, formal norm-referenced tests are replaced with informal criterion-referenced tests, which are aimed simply at finding out what behaviors a pupil has attained leading toward the terminal behavioral objectives, and toward the ultimate criterion or goal. At this point a minilesson is constructed to move the student through the series of steps required to reach this terminal behavior. An exemplary minilesson illustration in reading is found in Chalfant and Scheffelin (1969), with a modification of it presented in Table 10.3. In this case the terminal behavioral objective for the pupil is to say the word "cat" correctly after he has seen it in print and sounded it out in a five-step operation. If the child fails at any step, the teacher can immediately begin remediation at that point. A number of texts give clear and concise instructions on preparing behavioral objectives and making task analyses (Mager, 1962; Glaser, 1965; Popham, 1969; Gronlund, 1970; Plowman, 1971).

At this point some of the problems of the behavior-modification strategy need to be pointed out. As with the first approach, almost universally it is aimed at remediating weaknesses, though it would work as well or better to advance strengths. Another problem relates to the atomistic, spoon-feeding nature of this process. This charge especially holds when the emphasis is on small-step-by-small-step pacing to attain a discrete terminal behavior. Another problem is created when there is a preoccupation with extrinsic reinforcers. Many thoughtful persons worry because this tends to dehumanize education. For these reasons, the behavior-modification strategy should be viewed as only one useful method to employ in diagnosing and teaching SLD children.

4. A few dissenters decry all three of the individualized diagnostic teaching strategies described above. Instead, they favor a more global approach to curriculum and instruction for SLD pupils, arguing that such pupils need a broad, balanced course of study as much as average children. Mann (1971) has been one of the leaders arguing for this strategy. Like those in favor of behavior modification, he too has been critical of the use of standardized (or norm-referenced) tests, pointing out that subtests on existing psychoeducational tests are highly intercorrelated. Thus subtest scores cannot be used to "pinpoint" reliably weaknesses, since only the overall scores have much meaning. While Mann rejects narrow programs of instruction based on profile analysis using present psychoeducational tests, instead of a shift to behavior modification and the use of informal criterion-referenced tests, he advocates the broad, standard global curriculum for children with learning disabilities just as for children who make adequate progress in the regular grades. This attack on diagnostic teaching, which has become almost the sacrosanct instructional model in special SLD education, is probably a very healthy development.

5. Many of the more able practitioners do not rely exclusively on any of the above four strategies. Instead, they adopt an eclectic approach calling on all of these various options as necessary, depending on the characteristics and needs of their pupils and the settings in which they find themselves. This last elective seems a wise one, since no studies have been done as yet on the relative effectiveness of these various procedures for teaching SLD pupils. Just as practitioners in the field need to call on a variety of intervention strategies, so those responsible for the work-up we have been describing need to employ the same flexibility in their search for an effective intervention.

Pupil conference and program implementation. As seen in Figure 10.2, the last two steps in the special educational work-up are a pupil conference followed by a program implementation. While a series of conferences throughout the child-study period would be desirable, a final one at the end of the case study is the minimally essential. By then the various steps presented on the previous pages will have been completed. In addition, a diagnostic-intervention–determining work-up will have been conducted in one or more of the specific learning disability areas listed on page 563. It is essential that parents be full partners in decision-making conferences, that all child-study data be divulged, and that the pupil's rights be respected, especially if a disability classification and a special education placement is being considered. The eight guidelines presented in Chapter 3 for classifying and placing children with mild general learning disabilities apply equally in the case of SLD pupils (see p. 141).

Hopefully, many of the pupils referred for work-ups will not need to be classified SLD and provided with special education services. Only when all requested treatment by the other professional groups have been implemented, when all environmental changes possible have been made, and when a special educational intervention has been at least successfully piloted, should such services be recommended. Seven options are depicted in Figure 10.2. As indicated early in this chapter, in up to half the cases who require special education this will probably take the form of helping-teacher instruction to supplement regular education. With the even more severe SLD cases, a more classic special education placement may be needed. As can readily be seen in Figure 10.2, there are no 'blind alleys" in this plan. Each child can be referred for further evaluation, recycled, and reassigned when so indicated.

DIAGNOSIS AND REMEDIATION OF MAJOR SPECIFIC LEARNING DISORDERS

Eight of the specific learning disorders most frequently encountered by teachers of SLD children are dysfunctions in the following areas: (1) motor; (2) visual perception; (3) auditory perception; (4) oral language; (5) reading; (6) spelling; (7) handwriting; and (8) arithmetic.[1] Below are brief discussions of each, including examples of typical diagnostic and remediation techniques. This presentation will serve to make two very important points. First, while the term "specific learning disabilities" has been in existence only about a decade, each of these eight conditions has had professional attention for a much longer period of time. In the academic areas, much of the literature has been developed by remedial educators. In fact, some of the material presented below is also covered in such remedial education texts as Harris (1970) and Harris and Smith (1972) in the case of reading, and in Otto and McMenemy (1966) in terms of a broader treatment of corrective teaching. Second, while special educators see themselves as concentrating on pupils with severe learning disorders, as yet most of the instructional procedures ·are not specifically designed for this group. At best, they are designed for remedial education. In some cases, they are only adaptations of regular instructional techniques used in a standard developmental school program. Hopefully more specific interventions for pupils with major specific learning disabilities will be developed in the next decade or so. In the meantime, it must be observed that there is little as yet that is mystical or remarkably unusual about existing tests and teaching tools in this area of special education

Table 10.4 lists a number of tests that can be used to determine the specific weakness of children. A teacher with a modest amount of training in tests and measurement should be able to draw educational inferences from scores on these measures, if not administer them validly. For ease of reading, they are classified under seven of the eight disability areas listed above. Oral language has been omitted since the most popular test in this area, the Illinois Test of Psycholinguistic Abilities (ITPA), which will be discussed in considerable detail on page 571, is considered to require more test sophistication to administer.

---

[1] It will be noted that these are ordered somewhat in the sequence in which they emerge.

TABLE 10.3 A Five-Step Task Analysis and Minilesson for Teaching the
Recognition of the Printed Word "Cat" Using the
Sound-Blending System

Terminal Behavioral Objective: When presented with the printed word "cat" the
child will say the word aloud correctly.

Step	Activity Sequence	Response
I.	Attends to the single printed word "cat" when requested: Look at this.	Eyes fixate on the printed word
II.	Acknowledges the stimulus as a printed word when asked: What is this?	It's a word
III.	Identifies stimulus as a sequence of three discrete speech sounds when asked: How many sounds in this word?	Three
IV.	Retrieves and expresses aloud each of the three sounds when asked.	1st 2nd 2d (/k/) - (/ae/) - (/t/)
V.	Repeatedly sound blends the three phonemes in closer and closer proximity until the familiar word "cat" is recognized and said aloud	(/k/ /ae/ /t/) (/k/ae/t) "cat"

SOURCE: J. C. Chalfant and M. A. Scheffelin (Eds.), Central processing dysfunctions in
children: A review of research, Phase III. *NINDS Monograph No. 9,* Washington, D.C.:
Government Printing Office, 1969.

Major Motor Disorders

In recent years, motor development has been recognized as a basic
foundation for later learning. A number of children classified as having
major learning disorders lag so far behind the acceptable pattern that remediation of the motor disorder is often necessary before other more advanced
skills are likely to develop. Frequently these pupils have especially serious
difficulties with spatial orientation, balance, eye-hand coordination, and
body image. The areas of the brain most likely to be affected are the motor
cortex and other portions of the frontal lobe, and the occipital lobe in the case
of fine hand-eye coordination (see Fig. 10.1).

The diagnosis of motor disorders may be approached from three directions. First, there are measures of *gross motor* abilities such as crawling,
jumping, running, skipping, throwing, and balancing. Second, there are tests
of *fine motor* skills, including tying, threading, cutting, coloring, folding, bead
stringing and drawing. Third, there are items to assess *body image, orientation* and *laterality,* including body-parts identification and location, and body
positioning. Listed in Table 10.4 are three popular tests which focus on these
different aspects of motor development. O'Donnell (1969) provides a very
adequate treatment of the diagnosis of motor and haptic disabilities, including
many informal checklists and test that teachers should find helpful.

Three exemplary programs for the remediation of severe motor disorders are introduced to illustrate the approaches being used. Doman and Delacato have delineated the most extreme and controversial procedures (Delacato, 1966). It is based on the old theory that ontogeny recapitulates phylogeny. Children with problems are taken back and patterned through the stages: rolling over; crawling; creeping; and finally walking. As yet, research results have not supported this method. A study by Robbins (1966) on second-grade children suggests that reading achievement is not related to neurological organization and that the Delacato motor training does not even aid in the development of laterality. Kershner (1968) gave many of the Doman-Delacato exercises to a group of retarded children and found primarily that only creeping and crawling were improved. O'Donnell and Eisenson (1969) have also researched this method with second- to fourth-grade children who scored below the 25th percentile on the Stanford Reading Tests. In terms of reading achievement and visual motor integration, they found a regular physical education program just as effective as various combinations of cross-pattern creeping and walking, visual pursuit exercises, and reading free of extraneous stimuli. Studies such as these do little to support or refute the Doman-Delacato approach, since none of them were done with groups who were diagnosed as brain-injured or SLD children.

Kephart (1963, 1970), who co-authored an earlier book with Strauss (1955), and who devised the Purdue Perceptual Motor Survey with Roach, developed corrective training programs for children with severe motor disorders. Instead of emphasizing creeping and crawling, his program was designed to develop body image, space orientation, balance, and eye-hand coordination through the use of the walking boards, balanced boards, trampolines, stunts, and games. Chalkboard exercises were developed to enhance form perception. Kephart's key argument was that teaching basic school subjects before fundamental motor control was solidly established would result in fragmented of splintered skills. Alley and Carr (1968), who studied the effectiveness of the Kephart sensory-motor training program over a two-year period with educable mentally retarded children, concluded that it had no advantage over a more traditional program of physical activity in developing visual perception, sensory-motor or concept-formation performance. However, again this study does not provide information on the effectiveness of the Kephart approach with SLD children.

Barsch (1965), who also worked with Strauss, developed the "movigenics model" involving a study of the nature of movement patterns necessary for learning effectiveness. Again, this is simply saying in another way what Kephart advocated. Barsch, too, emphasized the development of muscular strength; dynamic balance; spatial awareness; body awareness; visual, auditory, and tactile dynamics; and rhythmics. Research evidence was not found to support Barsch's claim that work in such areas increases academic learning. However, Painter (1966) found that the movigenic curriculum significantly increased the scores of kindergarten children on selected subtests of the Illinois Test of Psycholinguistic Abilities.

While strong research evidence is yet to be forthcoming, no doubt all three of these corrective training programs have a place with *selected* children who have severe motor disorders. It is very improbable that most will need to be taken back to the Doman-Delacato creeping and crawling stages. Larger numbers are likely to need the Kephart or Barsch programs, which are essentially the same.

Major Visual Discrimination Disorders

A good deal of research has demonstrated that many neurologically impaired children have visual perceptual difficulties, even though their visual acuity is adequate (Cohen, 1959; Luria, 1966; Cruickshank, Bice and Wallen, 1957). The medical term for extreme cases is visual agnosia (see Fig. 10.1). During the sixties, the identification and correction of visual-perception problems received considerable attention because skills in this area were considered especially basic to successful early reading when the look-say method was in vogue. In fact, a number of special classes for the so-called perceptually impaired were initiated in the first breath of enthusiasm.

A number of tests of visual perception are available; two examples are listed in Table 10.4. Buktenica (1968) describes and discusses various other methods for assessing visual abilities which should prove helpful to teachers.

One of the most widely used training programs in this area is the program for the development of visual perception developed by Frostig and Horne (1964). Training exercises in visual perception consist of providing a series of workbooks that emphasize the same five areas as the Frostig test measures. Since evidence indicates that these subtests do not measure discrete areas but rather a common visual perceptual function (Stuart, 1967; Olson, 1968; Boyd and Randle, 1970), one could expect the remedial exercises on any one to generalize to the whole process. Research has indicated that training on the Frostig exercises will improve performance on the Frostig test, which is understandable, since the training program largely teaches to the test. There is little evidence, however, that this generalizes to school achievement or oral language development (Forgnone, 1966).

Getman, an optometrist, and his associates (1966, 1968), have developed a "physiology of readiness" program based on visual-motor stimulation. It emphasizes body balance and control, form recognition, and visual memory utilizing the tachistoscope. No research was found on the efficacy of this approach.

Other visual-perceptual training programs are available. The Fitzhugh (1966) program consists of self-correcting workbooks designed for the development of spatial orientation, language, and numbers. The emphasis is on aiding children in working with shapes and objects in space and time. Buktenica (1968) has described other training programs as well as offering a number of excellent instructional suggestions in the area of visual discrimination, and spatial relations.

While visual-perception skills appear to be largely developmentally determined, there are a few SLD children who have severe problems in this area that could benefit from corrective attention. Preoccupation with mild perceptual disorders in a cross section of SLD children, however, is not likely to prove fruitful. Furthermore, in reviewing the research on perceptual motor activities in the treatment of severe reading disabilities, Balow (1971) found no experimental evidence to support their use for correction or prevention of serious disabilities in reading or the other basic school subjects.

Major Auditory Discrimination Disorders

Auditory discrimination, especially of speech sounds, has been an important part of the literature on specific learning disabilities for many years, most often as it relates to reading (Robinson, 1946). Recently there has been a renewed interest in this topic. Just as visual perception was popular when the look-say reading method was in its heyday, so today auditory perception is in vogue now that phonic and linguistic methods are widely used in teaching initial reading. There is a large amount of research that relates brain damage to auditory discrimination problems (Luria, 1966; Semeritskaya, 1945; Nielsen, 1946; Penfield and Roberts, 1959). In many severe cases the problems are probably in the temporal lobe (see Fig. 10.1). Extreme forms of auditory perception disorders are known as auditory agnosia.

A number of tests are available to help teachers detect auditory discrimination or other related problems. Three of these are outlined in Table 10.4. Zigmond and Cicci (1968) list a number of other tests that can be used to assess auditory learning, along with a brief description of each. One brief word of caution is advised in administering these instruments. As Berry and Eisenson (1956) have stated, auditory discrimination items presented orally means the results of the tests are quite dependent upon the testor being consistent and correct in presenting the stimuli.

Although auditory discrimination is considered by many to be the key to successful reading and spelling, there are fewer remedial programs in this area than in the visual perceptual area. The "auditory discrimination in depth" (ADD) program (Lindamood and Lindamood, 1969) was designed to teach children sequentially how to discriminate out and make all of the 44 sounds of standard English and how to blend these sounds into words. The program was designed for use in conjunction with almost any phonic-oriented reading program. No research was found to substantiate its value.

The *Goldman-Lynch Sound and Symbols Development Kit* (Goldman and Lynch, 1971) also provides exercises to stimulate auditory discrimination of speech sounds and visual discrimination of their printed symbols in the form of letters of the alphabet. Children are given sound-blending training and instruction in the proper articulation of sounds, words, and sentences. This program should aid in correcting articulation problems and provide systematic phonic-attack reading-skills training. Again, no research is as yet available on its efficacy.

Johnson and Myklebust (1967) have outlined an early training program of auditory stimulation. Comprehension is taught before expression. The program is begun with single words that are systematically built up into

TABLE 10.4 *Representative Teacher-Administered Tests Useful for Diagnosing Areas of Specific Weaknesses in Children Suspected of Having Specific Learning Disabilities*

	Test	Author	Date	Administration Time	Range	Description[1]
MOTOR SKILLS	Lincoln-Oseretsky Motor Development Scale	W. Sloan	1956	30–60 min.	6-14 years	Revision of the original Oseretsky test. Many items deal with hand-eye coordination.
	Purdue Perceptual Motor Survey	E. G. Roach N. C. Kephart	1966	Untimed	Grades 1-4	Indication of child's visual, perceptual, and motor development.
	Harris Tests of Lateral Dominance	A. J. Harris	1958	Untimed		Specialized test that provides a measure of hand and eye preference. Also uses writing to help determine the preference
VISUAL SKILLS	Beery Buktenica Visual Motor Integration Test	K. E. Beery N. A. Buktenica	1967	10–15 min.	1-9 to 15-11 separate norms for males & females	Form copying; manual includes discussion of development of visual-motor integration
	Frostig Developmental Test of Visual Perception	M. Frostig	1961	15–20 min.	3-0 to 10-0+ years	Pencil and paper test; measures eye-motor coordination, figure-ground, form constancy, position in space, spatial relations
AUDITORY SKILLS	Auditory Discrimination Test	J. M. Wepman	1958	2-3 min.	5-0 to 8-0 years	Auditory-discrimination ability for speech sounds in single words, consonant vowel consonant patterns, 3-5 letter words; requires concept of same and different
	Goldman-Fristoe Test of Articulation	F. Goldman M. Fristoe	1969	10 min.	2 years and above	Diagnosis of defects in speech sounds and articulation. Uses pictures. Three measures: sounds in sentences, sounds in words, and stimulability
	Roswell-Chall Diagnostic Reading Test of Word Analysis Skills	F. G. Roswell J. S. Chall	1959	5-10 min.	Grades 2-6	Knowledge of letter sounds and their combinations into words; ability to apply phonic rules
READING SKILLS	Mills Learning Methods Test	R. E. Mills	1965	15 min. a day for 5 days	Primer to third grade	Determines a pupil's ability to learn new words using a visual phonic, auditory, kinesthetic, or combination method

[1] More detailed information on these instruments and others may be found in the Buros *Mental Measurement Yearbook* series.

READING SKILLS (Continued)	Gates-McKillop Reading Diagnostic Tests	A. I. Gates A. S. McKillop	1962	Untimed	Grades 1-8	Oral reading, flash and untimed presentations of words and phrases, word-part knowledge, word-attack skills, visual forms of sounds, auditory blending.
	Durrell Analysis of Reading Difficulty	D. D. Durrell	1955	30-45 min.	Grades 1-6	Tests of oral and silent reading, listening comprehension, word recognition and analysis, naming letters, visual memory of words, auditory analysis and learning rate.
SPELLING SKILLS	Gates-Russell Diagnostic Test	A. I. Gates D. H. Russell	1937-1940	Untimed	Grades 2-6	Nine separate scores: oral spelling; word pronunciation; letter-for-letter sounds; spelling one syllable; spelling two syllables; reversals; spelling-attack skills; auditory discrimination; visual, auditory, kinesthetic, and combined study methods
	Lincoln Diagnostic Spelling Test	A. L. Lincoln	1962	Untimed	Grades 2-12	Three overlapping levels of spelling words; organized to detect problems in pronunciation, enunciation, and use of rules
HANDWRITING SKILLS	Thorndike Scale for Handwriting	E. L. Thorndike	1910	Untimed	Grades 2-8	Clarity, uniformity of line, and artistic quality are used as criterion measures
	Ayres Measuring Scale for Handwriting	L. P. Ayres	1912	10-15 min.	Grades 2-8	Measures legibility in terms of speed at which handwriting specimens can be read by trained recorders as matched against samples
ARITHMETIC SKILLS	Schonell Diagnostic Arithmetic Tests	F. J. Schonell	1946	Untimed	Ages 7-13	Twelve subtests. First four involve basic number combinations in four fundamental operations. Fifth concentrates on more difficult combinations. Subtests 6 through 11 have combination problems of gradual increasing difficulty. Twelfth is based on old British measurement system
	Diagnostic Tests and Self-Helps in Arithmetic	L. J. Brueckner	1955	Untimed	Grades 3-12	Four screening tests and 23 diagnostic tests. What and why of basic facts, fundamental operations, whole numbers, common fractions, decimal fractions, percentage, and measurement

complete sentences. Simple nouns are taught first, followed by simple verbs, prepositions, adjectives, adverbs, and pronouns. New words are taught using oral presentations, visual aids, verbal instruction, or kinesthetics. Drills in rapid naming are used. The last step is helping the child use syntax and vocabulary for expression of thought and feeling. This program, like the others cited, combines receptive and expressive oral language training.

There are other sources of information on auditory perceptual training. A book by Barry (1961) on young aphasic children contains many ideas for developing auditory memory and perception. Valett (1967) offers a number of useful recommendations for the teaching of auditory skills. Berry and Eisenson (1956) have developed word lists, poems, and a variety of activities to encourage auditory discrimination. The Kirk and Kirk (1971) exercises to remediate auditory reception weaknesses are also very much on target.

While the programs listed above have not been well researched, the role of auditory processes in learning has. A number of investigators have found that children who are retarded in reading also evidence some sort of auditory deficit, be it auditory memory, discrimination deficits, auditory closure, sound blending, or auditory sequential memory (Shephard, 1967; Zigmond, 1969; Golden and Steiner, 1969; Kass, 1966). In addition, Templin (1957) and Berry and Eisenson (1956), among others, have found auditory and articulation problems to be related. Furthermore, Kronvall and Diehl (1954) found a positive relation between articulation disorders and reading disabilities. Because of these close relations, auditory training certainly cannot be underrated in working with selected SLD children.

Major Oral Language Disorders

Chapter 6 considered a variety of oral communication disabilities in detail. Perhaps the most difficult ones to correct are language disorders such as aphasia, which are related to central nervous system impairment. Also discussed briefly in Chapter 6 were both sensory (receptive) and motor (expressive) aphasia (see Fig. 10.1). Eisenson (1972) has provided a more complete description of the complex procedures which need to be followed in arriving at a differential diagnosis among developmental aphasia, emotional disturbance, and mental retardation. The three conditions are understandably correlated because all may be symptoms of central nervous system dysfunction. He goes on to outline an instructional program for aphasia based on the following two basic principles: (1) build on strengths; and (2) vary the presentation and materials to prevent rigid speech patterns from developing. In her concise and useful manual, McGinnis (1963) has described an association method for teaching aphasic children. Words are first broken down into their phonic elements, and correct articulation of each sound is stressed. Next the words are taught, and only then are they combined into sentences. More and more aphasic children are becoming a responsibility of SLD teachers, since speech correctionists are finding that the few hours a week of therapy, which is all they can usually provide any one pupil, is insufficient.

In contrast with the aphasic children who have severe receptive and/or expressive oral language dysfunction, many SLD children have milder and more subtle psycholinguistic problems which can often be detected with the 1968 revision of the Illinois Test of Psycholinguistic Abilities (ITPA) (Kirk, McCarthy and Kirk, 1968). While this instrument is too complex for most SLD teachers to administer, they will often be called upon to develop exercises to stimulate the processes tapped by each of its 12 subtests. Therefore, they are listed below in brief descriptive form:

1. *Auditory reception:* the ability to comprehend the spoken word in the form of questions. *Example item:* The S responds "yes" or "no" to: Do ponies shave?
2. *Visual reception:* the ability to gain meaning from pictures of objects. *Example item:* S is shown a picture of a can on a first page, and then is asked to point to another picture of a different type of can when included with three picture decoys on another page.
3. *Auditory association:* the ability to complete orally verbal analogies. *Example item:* grass is green; sugar is _____.
4. *Visual association:* the ability to identify pictures of objects that go together. *Example item:* a plate containing five pictures, where the S is to point to one of four pictures which goes with the central stimulus picture, such as a dog goes with a bone.
5. *Verbal expression:* the ability to express elaboratively verbal concepts. *Example item:* The S is shown an actual nail, and is asked to tell the examiner all about it.
6. *Manual expression:* the ability to express ideas manually. *Example item:* S is asked to demonstrate manually the use of a pictured hammer.
7. *Grammatical closure:* the ability to use oral language redundancies to express correct syntactical and grammatical inflections. *Example item:* S is shown a plate with one bed pictured on one side and two on the others and is asked to complete the statement: Here is a bed; here are two _____.
8. *Visual closure:* the ability to recognize objects from only part of a picture. *Example item:* S is shown a picture of a busy construction scene and is asked to point to as many partially exposed hammers as possible in 30 seconds.
9. *Auditory sequential memory:* the ability to repeat digit series of increasing length when they are presented orally. *Example item:* Listen, say "3-7-4-2."
10. *Visual sequential memory:* the ability to reconstruct sequences of nonmeaningful figures from memory after a visual presentation of the series. *Example item:* S is shown a picture of a series of geometric designs, and is then asked to reproduce them from memory in order, using plastic chips on which these same geometric designs have been imprinted.
11. *Auditory closure:* the ability to recognize words presented orally in units when one or more of the units is omitted. *Example item:* S is to say "bottle" when he hears "bo/le."
12. *Sound blending:* the ability to blend sounds presented orally into

whole words with and without picture clues. *Example item:* S is to say "dog" when he hears the two speech sounds "d—og" presented orally with a pause between each.

Bateman (1965b) has compiled much of the extensive research on the 1961 experimental edition. Paraskevopoulos and Kirk (1969), and Kirk and Kirk (1971) also cover many of these same studies, plus some on the 1968 revision. Different traditional groups of handicapped children have rather characteristic ITPA profiles. The same cannot be said of SLD children, which argues again that no such single syndrome exists.

As their prime instructional strategy, Kirk and Kirk (1971) have proposed the remediation of weaknesses displayed by the ITPA profile. They describe exercises for each of the 12 subtests, as have Bush and Giles (1969). Too, Karnes and her associates (1968) have classified their activities for preschool disadvantaged children by ITPA functions. In addition, Rupert (undated) has compiled lists of commercial instructional materials by ITPA subtests.

The ITPA has been criticized by Weener, Barritt, and Semmel (1967), who have pointed out that while total test-retest reliability coefficients are reasonably high, there is also a fairly high positive correlation across subtests, indicating that they tend to measure a common phenomenon. In addition, the ITPA is highly correlated with the Stanford-Binet and the Wechsler tests of intelligence, indicating that psycholinguistics and verbal intelligence have much in common. Cautious experimentation with the ITPA profile analysis approach to differential diagnosis and remediation appears prudent.

While the strategy of remediating specific weaknesses identified by the ITPA lends itself best to individual tutoring of SLD pupils, other oral language stimulation programs are designed for group instruction. Two examples are briefly described below.

The Peabody Language Development Kits by Dunn, Smith, and Horton (1965, 1966, 1967, 1968), which are available at four levels that extend from the kindergarten through the third grade, stimulate oral language globally rather than focus on the remediation of weaknesses. The daily lessons combined in these kits were designed primarily for use with average and linguistically disadvantaged children rather than for SLD pupils. Thus, unless children have delayed language or a restricted language code, it is doubtful that the PLDK exercises would be of any great value. (For SLD children who have very uneven oral language skills, the teacher may wish to select out only certain of the activities rather than follow the complete sequence of structured daily lessons.)

Distar (Engelmann et al., 1969c; 1969d), another oral language stimulation program, is much more highly structured than the PLDK. It emphasizes patterned drills to develop the correct syntactical and grammatical skills for standard English among black slum children at the kindergarten and first-grade levels. Teachers are required to use the exact language pattern prescribed in the book; improvisation is not encouraged. The child's language development is continuously monitored by reviews and tests spaced through-out the lessons. Like the PLDK, Distar is not designed for SLD children. Fur-thermore, there is, as yet, no research available on its efficacy.

Many other commercial and experimental oral language stimulation pro-grams have been developed, especially for black slum children, ages five through seven. Parker et al. (1970) has described a number of these. It is doubtful that many white, native-born children from middle class standard English-speaking homes who are classified as having specific learning disabili-ties will need these systematic programs of oral language stimulation. How-ever, selected SLD pupils from nonstandard English backgrounds might well profit from parts of them.

Major Reading Disorders

Reading disorders are the major source of referrals for children who are later classified as having specific learning disabilities—simply because a child who cannot read has little chance of success in school. Brain damage is often suspected when a severe reading problem appears. Dyslexia is pur-ported to result from damage to a juncture of the occipital, parietal, and temporal lobe (see Fig. 10.1). Damage to areas of the brain that control speech, hearing, and vision can also manifest itself in a reading problem.

As a first step in the diagnosis of reading difficulties it is recommended that an informal reading inventory, such as the one developed by Johnson and Kress (1965), be administered. Comprehension, types of errors, and word-attack skills can all be observed informally as the child reads from a series of basal readers. Three reading-recognition levels may also be determined: (1) *independent level*—at least 98 percent word recognition; (2) *instructional level*—90 to 98 percent word recognition; and (3) *frustration level*—less than 90 percent word recognition.

Next, the teacher may wish to give the student an informal series of mini-lessons to try out the relative effectiveness of each of the three basic ap-proaches to teaching beginning reading: phonics linguistics; whole word; or kinesthetics. The Mills Learning Methods Test (see Table 10.4) determines which approach is most effective in a more formal manner. The interpreta-tion of the results is difficult because one cannot know whether a pupil performed best on a particular approach because his natural aptitudes are so inclined or because he was taught that way in the past. As an alternative or supplementary strategy, Boder (1968) has suggested analyzing the child's spell-ing errors on informal or formal tests for clues as to whether an auditory or visual approach might best be used in reading instruction. She argues that those with strong auditory tendencies use a phonic organization, while those with strong visual tendencies often have all the letters written out for the word, but in the incorrect order. But again one does not know the reason the child displayed a particular style of preference.

Three examples of a number of individual diagnostic tests of reading disabilities are listed in Table 10.4. These devices are more useful than group tests, since they allow the examiner more opportunity to observe and probe intensively the actual reading processes. Included are measures of oral and silent reading, comprehension, word recognition, identification of consonant and vowel sounds, and blends. In essence, they try to zero in on the major stumbling blocks the child is encountering in learning. When these are discovered, almost universally the recommended instruction intervention is focused on correcting them. This is the reverse strategy to the Mills test, which focuses on the pupil's strengths.

There are a number of methods of teaching beginning reading. The *phonics-linguistic* strategy teaches word-attack skills, but is dependent upon the child's ability to hear and to discriminate among speech sounds. Furthermore, sounding out one word at a time is a slow procedure. The *whole word* method allows the child to gain a sight vocabulary quickly, but severely limits his word-attack skills. In this approach adequate visual-perceptual skills are a prerequisite. The *kinesthetic* procedure is the slowest of the three and mainly involves a combination of arm movement and vision. The pronunciation of the whole word is part of this process; sound blending is not practical. These three developmental approaches, or some combination of them, are all used with SLD children. Some of the favorite specific methods are briefly outlined below.

The *Gillingham-Stillman Phonic Method* (1970) teaches the sounds which are later built into words, using the visual, auditory, and kinesthetic modalities. The child traces and copies the individually printed letters as he memorizes them. Drill cards are used for consonant and vowel sounds. Blending sounds into words, spelling words, and finally story writing follow. This program is rigid. Furthermore, introduction of rule exceptions can also cause problems. It does, however, seem to be very effective with a number of SLD children with adequate auditory skills who have difficulty learning to read.

The *Spalding Unified Phonics Method* (1962) also emphasizes speech sounds, while concentrating on handwriting and spelling. (This program could just as easily be included in the spelling section because of the great emphasis on this area.) Seventy phonograms which represent the 44 sounds of English speech are taught. Sounds and not letter names are learned. Nonphonic sounds are learned from memory later. No books are used until the child has developed substantial word-attack skills. Since this approach emphasizes audition, it should not be used on a child with a deficit in this area unless one is committed to teaching to weaknesses.

The *Hegge-Kirk-Kirk Remedial Reading Drills* (1936) were designed for slow-learning children with severe beginning reading problems. The consonant sounds and the vowel "a" sound are taught first, followed by blending at least three sounds together. Drill-word lists are introduced to present systematically all the sounds and their symbols. The presentation uses phonics so that a child with insufficient auditory skills would have problems using this approach, as he would with the two methods described above.

The *Initial Teaching Alphabet*, designed by Pitman, in England, is a phonetic alphabet, not a method. It consists of 44 sound symbols, rather than the regular 26-letter alphabet, each representing one of the 44 speech sounds of standard English. (ITA has been used as the basis for not only phonic-oriented reading programs but those which use an eclectic approach.) The children make a transition into traditional orthography (the regular 26-letter alphabet) gradually at the second- to third-grade reading level. Because the ITA has one written letter for each speech sound, it simplifies beginning reading and thus may be effective with selected SLD pupils.

Words-in-Color, developed by Gattegno (1966), is also not a method but another attempt to make the 26-letter alphabet more phonetic. Each phoneme is represented by color coding the standard alphabet. Bannatyne (1966) also has a phonics system in which letters and letter combinations in the traditional orthography are coded so that each color idenifies a sound. Both ITA and the color code systems are examples of attempts to develop an early one-to-one correspondence between speech sounds and printed symbols. Other systems use still other symbols or less radical cues such as diacritical marks. For example, Engelmann and Bruner (1969a) have developed Distar Reading programs which employ a highly structured phonetic-linguistic approach to reading where the 26 standard printed letters carry diacritical marks to convey the sounds which the letters are making.

At the opposite extreme to the phonic strategies is the Peabody Rebus Reading Program (REBUS) developed by Woodcock (1967). Instead of beginning with the traditional 26-letter alphabet, pictograms or rebuses are used to represent words. The pupil first learns to read a series of these, which are arranged to form assertive sentences or questions. Later, there is a gradual transition from pictograms to the traditional 26-letter alphabet. Clearly, this approaches the ultimate in a sight-vocabulary method. Therefore, it should be useful with SLD pupils who have extreme auditory learning problems.

While many other reading programs besides the basal readers are commercially available, it is interesting to note that very few of a remedial nature use the whole-word approach, the classic exception being the Fernald kinesthetic whole-word method, which combines the teaching of reading and spelling, and so will be presented in the next section. Texts such as Harris (1970) and Harris and Smith (1972) describe a number of other reading programs which may be effective with selected SLD children.

Some teachers tailor their reading programs for individual SLD students. As the pendulum in general education swings from the extreme emphasis on the whole word to the extreme emphasis on the phonic strategy, more children will be referred to special SLD teachers because they have experienced repeated failure in this latter approach. In such cases, the special educator is likely to find more helpful modifications of the kinesthetic approaches to be presented in the next section, or experience units, where the pupil helps create words, sentences, and stories about events that are highly interesting and relevant to him. Finally, it must be observed that there is little chance that the SLD teacher will succeed without an extensive array of reading approaches. Since there are so many causes of reading disabilities, the challenge is to find the most effective method for each individual pupil.

Major Spelling Disorders

Many children who have reading problems also have spelling difficulties because the two are closely related. However, there is not a one-to-one relation between reading and spelling. In fact, the hypothesized brain center for spelling difficulties (dysgraphia) is located in the junction of the occipital-parietal-temporal lobe area (see Fig. 10.2). Thus, some pupils could be adequate readers, especially silent readers, but be poor spellers, and vice versa. Otto and McMenemy (1966) and Brueckner and Bond (1955) provide good reviews of the multiple causes of, and factors related to, spelling difficulties.

While teachers may use informal teacher-made tests to ferret out spelling problems, a number of more formal diagnostic instruments are also available. Two of these are listed as examples in Table 10.4.

When spelling is the only specific learning disability, it is likely that fostering improved motivation and learning habits, combined with some good systematic instruction, will yield positive results. When it is only one symptom of many other difficulties, then more intensive diagnosis and correction will be required. Most SLD children are of the latter variety.

Orton (1937), a neuropathologist, developed a combined visual, auditory, and kinesthetic approach for teaching reading and spelling to dysgraphic children. As in other phonic approaches, associations between letter symbols and speech sounds were first taught by the teacher presenting the sounds and symbols in unison. Then the sound was repeated and the child was asked first to trace, then to copy, and finally to produce from memory, the letter symbol. Later, words were presented by sounding them out orally to the child who was asked to write them. Orton recommended this strategy for children he classified as having streptosymbolia (twisted symbols). These were pupils with mixed lateral dominance who displayed excessive reversals and often mirror writing.

The Fernald (1943) kinesthetic, whole-word, combined spelling and reading method grew out of the Orton approach. It is probably the best-known and most used method for remediating severe spelling disabilities. Story writing is the goal, and the method employs the visual, auditory, and kinesthetic neural pathways. There are four stages, each passed through at the child's own pace. In Stage I, the child informs the teacher of any word he does not know, but needs to learn. The word is written out cursively by the teacher on a 4-inch by 11-inch strip of paper, using a crayon to give roughness. The pupil then traces the word with his finger, saying but not spelling it out at the same time. The paper is then turned over and the pupil writes the word *from memory* on the back. Correctness is checked, and the process is repeated as necessary. (Tracing in sand, and so forth, are used in very complex cases.) The Stage II method of learning new words is the same as above, except tracing is dropped as no longer necessary. Stage III and IV move the child up to the point of looking in the dictionary for words and then carrying through the self-teaching sequence on his own. This method works equally well with phonetic and nonphonetic words. However, it does not build phonic word-attack skills; it is time consuming; and it requires one-to-one instruction until the pupil reaches the self-teaching stages.

Durrell (1956) has devised a method of teaching the correct spelling of nonphonetic words which draws heavily on both Orton and Fernald. Any word not known is placed on a card. The child simply closes his eyes to picture it, then writes it from memory and compares it to the original, repeating as often as necessary.

Three final points. First, spelling rules are of little use to most SLD children because of the memory detail involved. Second, spelling should be restricted to words the child wants or feels he needs to know. Third, spelling and reading should be combined. Learning spelling in isolation is highly inappropriate.

Major Handwriting Disorders

Among children classified as being brain injured, minimal cerebral dysfunctioning, or specific learning disabled, writing disorders are almost universal. A child who has very poor handwriting is said to have dysgraphia, with brain injury in the frontal lobe implied (see Fig. 10.1). Myklebust (1965) takes the position that poor handwriting is usually due to poor motor control rather than faulty auditory or visual skills. That different lobes of the brain are assumed to control these functions lends support to his contention. Nevertheless, written expression should be seen as a complex act involving cognitive and motor factors as well as visual monitoring.

For diagnosticians who may wish to determine possible causes of poor handwriting, Myklebust (1965) and Blair (1956) provide lists of related factors. To determine how much below standard a pupil is performing in legibility and speed, two rather ancient handwriting scales are listed in Table 10.4.

The commercial materials used to teach handwriting in the regular grades follow a "look-trace-copy-write from memory" format. Most of the programs begin with manuscript and later make the transition to cursive writing at about the third-grade level of functioning. Lehtinen, in Strauss and Lehtinen (1947), and Johnson and Myklebust (1967) have comprehensive plans for teaching writing to children with dysgraphia which elaborates on the standard formula used in the commercial materials. Lehtinen, especially, stresses the importance of handwriting to develop visual-motor skills, and to learn to read. She usually omits manuscript writing with most SLD pupils since the cursive approach lends itself better to developing a kinesthetic perception of word forms.

There is little agreement among general educators about the importance of legibility in handwriting, and there is less among special teachers of SLD children. All agree that handwriting is an important part of a complete written language curriculum and is central to a number of methods of teaching reading and spelling to SLD pupils. When legible handwriting seems beyond the abilities of a SLD child, some persons have recommended the substitution of typewriting. Campbell (1968), in addition to reviewing the literature comprehensively, compared the relative effectiveness of typewriting and handwriting in teaching beginning reading to children with severe learning disorders. Both appeared to be effective, with a modest tendency for the typewriter to be superior. Thus, when the remediation of handwriting proves extremely difficult, the typewriter should be viewed as a viable alternative for handwritten expression. At some point, even the die-hards need to give up on attempting to correct a weakness, especially when it is not an essential skill.

Major Mathematics Disorders

With SLD pupils, the development of number concepts has not been of as great a concern to teachers as the development of reading skills. That this area deserves serious attention becomes clearer when mathematics is viewed more as the development of quantitative thinking and the ability to abstract, rather than the memorization of number facts. It is in this area of visual-spatial relations and understanding that most children with major mathematics disorders have their greatest trouble. A severe case of mathematics dysfunction assumed to be due to brain injury is known as dyscalculia, with the damage located at the top of the parietal lobe (see Fig. 10.1).

In evaluating major mathematics disorders, a study of the areas of visual perception and thinking disorders should be illuminating. Otto and McMenemy (1966), Brueckner and Bond (1955), and Johnson and Myklebust (1967) suggest a number of other factors to study a diagnosing arithmetic disorders. For those desiring to examine specific types of errors made in fundamental arithmetic, the two tests listed in Table 10.4 will be useful.

Six of a number of methods or devices for teaching beginning arithmetic to SLD pupils are introduced below:

1. Lehtinen, in Strauss and Lehtinen (1947), especially emphasizes the need for comprehension which must be specifically taught to SLD pupils, though it is often discovered spontaneously by average children. She begins with simple perceptual tasks of sorting and matching. Then semiconcrete materials and the kinesthetic method are used to teach the numbers and the number symbols through six. Next, addition and then subtraction are taught with the heavy use of the abacus. Understanding through the solving of problems is stressed throughout. Only later is more abstract number work begun.

2. Johnson and Myklebust (1967) also advocate the use of concrete materials and minute sequential steps. They stress developing the auditory and visual modalities simultaneously. Shape and form are taught first, followed by size and length. Next, work is sequentially done on one-to-one correspondence, counting, conservation of quality, visualization of groups, language of arithmetic, process signs, alignment and arrangement, sequencing of steps, and problem solving and reasoning.

3. Fernald (1943) has developed a method which focuses on learning

the number combinations. Concrete objects such as beads, buttons, and rulers are used to help the child work these out. Meaning rather than rote memorization is emphasized, and shortcuts are left to the pupil to develop.

4. Engelmann and Carnine (1969b) have a Distar arithmetic program for teaching beginning quantitative concepts using a programed format with oral sentences the mode of instruction. Quantitative terms and counting operations are emphasized. Understanding through story problems is stressed.

5. Stern and her associates (1965) developed the Structured Arithmetic kits for teaching beginning arithmetic in the regular classroom at the first- and second-grade levels. These kits, with their extensive manipulative materials, can be adapted for use with SLD children.

6. The Cuisenaire rods, designed in one to ten centimeter lengths, each of a different color, are useful in teaching selected SLD pupils to add, subtract, multiply, and divide.

The following four instructional principles are suggested for teaching quantitative concepts to SLD children: (1) concrete materials should be used whenever possible; (2) great effort must be taken to set up a carefully paced sequential program, with each step completed satisfactorily before moving on; (3) understanding of the process must be emphasized; and (4) whenever possible the pupil should be allowed to discover the various mathematical relations for himself, though often much assistance will be necessary.

ORGANIZATIONAL PLANS AND THEIR EFFECTIVENESS

The various types of administrative plans for educating exceptional children were presented in Chapter 1. This section provides a short elaboration on those that have been favored for SLD pupils (see bottom of Fig. 10.2), including the available evidence on their effectiveness.

Boarding School Instruction

For years boarding schools have provided instruction for some children with quite severe brain injury. Traditionally, most state residential facilities for the retarded have taken in a number of children of this type when they were beyond the resources of the family and community. In most cases, the treatment has tended to be largely custodial. However, presented below are two exemplary studies of what can happen when such schools have been given extensive special education services.

Gallagher (1960) conducted the classic experimental study for SLD children at a state school for the mentally retarded in Illinois. The subjects were a miscellaneous collection of brain-injured subjects (not all Strauss syndrome), ages from seven to nine years and with WISC IQ scores of from 58 to 106. The experimental group was given one hour a day of individual tutoring, based on each child's own pattern of strengths and weaknesses. It was a crash program of perceptual, conceptual, and language-development exercises; there was no attempt to follow the Lehtinen approach per se. In contrast to a matched control group, Gallagher's experimental subjects improved in intellectual development, increased in attention span, and achieved more in verbal than in nonverbal skills. He concluded:

> It is quite likely that history will also record that we have been entirely too pessimistic about the possible training potential of brain-injured children, and that this pessimism has prevented us from giving them the intellectual and educational stimulation that we wish for all our children. (p. 168)

This is evidence that the Strauss-Lehtinen techniques are not necessary to achieve moderately good results with neurologically impaired pupils.

In a follow-up of his subjects to determine the effects of removal of the special tutoring, Gallagher (1962) discovered that the gains were lost within a year after the tutoring ceased. He claimed that this probably was a result of the unstimulating environment of the residential facility and that the gains would likely have been more permanent if the children had been living in a more normal community setting. Finally, he pleaded for an extensive, individualized approach to build conceptualization skills among young neurologically impaired pupils rather than almost exclusive devotion to the development of social skills, as has too often been the case.

Vance (1956) conducted a similar study, also on children in a state residential school for the retarded. She provided daily, highly structured educational programs in reading readiness for three and one-half hours a week over an eight-month period, on matched groups of nonbrain-injured and neurologically impaired children. The range of IQ scores on the subjects was 40 to 70, with an age range of 7 to 13 years. She found that both groups learned equally well under the treatment she provided. This study demonstrated that a highly structured instructional program, quite similar to that proposed by Strauss and Lehtinen, works as well for nonbrain-injured residential retardates as it does for those classified as brain injured.

Such studies as these two reminds the field that the genesis of special education for present-day SLD children began with experimentation for brain-injured children in state residential facilities for the retarded. It points out again the futility of failing to acknowledge that severe brain injury, severe learning disorders, and mental retardation are positively correlated. Furthermore, it would be unrealistic to fail to recognize that a number of severe learning- and behavior-disordered children, who may or may not have frank brain damage, will need to be placed in boarding schools. This will be demanded by parents who can no longer cope with them.

Hospital Instruction

Instruction of this type has been available to some brain-injured children. For example, wards are provided in a few hospitals for children with chronic brain syndromes. Here the emphasis is on intensive, interdisciplinary treatment. An example is the one at the Medical Center of the University of California at San Francisco. Whitsell and Whitsell (1968) have described this comprehensive program for brain-injured children who function intellectually down into the quite severely retarded range. While the program is dominated by physicians, nevertheless, clinic teachers interact daily with them and with the nurses, social workers, psychologists, and others to provide a cooperative program of therapy.

Long-term medical treatment in a hospital raises a very basic concern. As yet there is simply no effective medical treatment for developmental brain injury in children except for drug control. The logic of having these young people in hospitals has yet to be explained. Short-term stays for specific medical diagnosis and treatment make more sense.

Child Guidance, Mental Health, Remedial Reading, and Learning Resource Centers

Centers of this type have long been involved in providing community treatment for children with learning problems. Present-day learning resource centers are largely the equivalent of traditional child study and remedial reading clinics. They generally provide services to children on released time during school hours, after school, on Saturdays, and during vacation periods. The team approach to diagnostic teaching is widely advocated. Essentially all such centers emphasize the high-level psychoeducational diagnostic work-up (McCarthy, 1969). Valett (1970), in discussing learning-resource centers, sees a place for psychoeducational specialists, educational psychologists, and demonstration teachers. No study was found in the literature contrasting the efficacy of this strategy with others.

The Special Day Class Plan

This plan has traditionally been the most popular one for extending special education services to SLD children. During the 1950s, these pupils were enrolled in classes for the educable mentally retarded, usually in higher socioeconomic neighborhoods. During the 1960s, the special classes were designated for brain-injured, perceptually impaired, or educationally handicapped children. The present and emerging trend is to consider them as serving children with major specific learning disabilities. Fragmented though it is, there is a growing body of studies on the effectiveness of these special classes.

Jolles (1956) conducted a three-year study, without a control or contrast group, on one of the first special day classes for brain-injured children located in Joliet, Illinois. The subjects were 10 students ages 6 to 10 years, selected jointly by the neurologist and clinical psychologist, who were functioning intellectually in the educable mentally retarded range. The teacher was given a year's training in the Strauss-Lehtinen method for teaching brain-damaged children. Emphasis was on reading, arithmetic, writing, and visual perception, with the classroom designed to reduce distracting stimuli. Intelligence, school achievement, and social development tests—along with cumulative studies, anecdotal records, and interviews with the family and child—were used to assess pupil progress. While the gains varied considerably, Jolles believed them to have been greater than would have been the case had the children remained in the regular grades. After three years, five of the pupils had been recommended for a return to regular class placement, three for a special class for the educable mentally retarded, and the other two for continuance in the special class of brain-injured children.

Perhaps the most widely cited study of the efficacy of special classes utilizing the Strauss and Lehtinen techniques was conducted by Cruickshank, Bentzen, Ratzeburg, and Tannhauser (1961). This was a two-year demonstration with 40 subjects diagnosed as brain injured and emotionally disturbed. Their IQ scores ranged as low as 50. The brain injured were detected not only by neurological tests but also by signs of hyperactivity and aggressiveness. A typical Lehtinen-type classroom environment was created for at least the experimental groups. The investigators concluded as follows:

> While still further evidence needs to be obtained, it is the opinion of the authors that hyperactive children in a nonstimulating environment and structured program demonstrate sufficient progress to warrant continuation of this approach with such children. (p. 421)

It is difficult to accept their conclusions in light of the following concerns. First, one has difficulty in ascertaining whether the subjects were brain injured, emotionally disturbed, hyperactive, or all three. Second, teachers of the contrast groups were allowed to set up any type of treatment they wished, and many of them chose to adopt the Lehtinen techniques similar to those used in the experimental classes, confounding the treatments. Third, there is little statistical evidence in the final report that the experimental groups made greater progress than the controls. However, if one wishes to accept the conclusions of the authors, we have some support for the use of the Lehtinen procedures with hyperactive pupils.

Frey (1961) conducted a retrospective study that tested the Lehtinen teaching technique with Strauss-type children. He selected a group of 20 neurologically impaired retarded children, who on psychological tests also exhibited perceptual disorders, and who had been in a special program using the Lehtinen techniques. These were compared with 20 nonbrain-injured retarded children of similar age and intellect who had been attending conventional programs in regular and special classes. In his survey of the reading behavior of these two groups, Frey found the Strauss-type group to be superior in silent-reading tests and in sound-blending ability, with a normal profile of reading errors, while the nonbrain-injured group showed excessive numbers of faulty vowels, faulty consonants, omissions of sounds, and omissions of words. This study has importance because it demonstrates that the Lehtinen technique appears to work, at least in reading, for the Strauss-type child. However, clearly, the study has the weakness of confounding types of subjects with treatments, in that the nonbrain-injured did not get the special treatment. Nevertheless, until research is accumulated to the contrary, on the basis of the Frey study, teachers will apparently be on fairly safe ground in experimenting with special classes for the Strauss-type pupil.

Again, the three studies reported here were conducted on brain-injured children with depressed IQ scores down as low as 50. No comparable studies were found in the literature on children who meet the present-day definition of specific learning disabilities. It must be recognized that many SLD children have been placed and will continue to be placed in largely self-contained special classes unless legal action is taken to prevent it. Most of these children are far harder for the regular teacher to manage and teach than children traditionally classified as culturally familial, educable mentally retarded pupils.

The Resource-Room Plan

Programs of this type have been advocated of late as a substitute for self-contained special classes. The most potent arguments for such a room are: that pupils need specialized help in certain specific areas, yet can function quite effectively in the regular classroom in many other areas; that more intensive individualization of instruction can be provided there than in the regular program; and that there can be a centralization of teacher talent and instructional materials in the resource class.

The resource teacher is expected to be a high-level educational diagnostician, a creative developer of instructional programs and materials, an able educational therapist, a respected consultant, a parent counselor, and an accepted liaison person between the schools and the many other professions concerned with each of her pupils. Yet usually she has only a fifth-year or master's degree, and frequently not even that. Also rather large case loads of up to 18 are given her. Some of the problems of this resource-room plan were outlined in Chapter 1. Above all, many SLD children will experience more failure in the regular classroom and more success in the resource room. As a result, they will display increasing amounts of noxious behavior in the former setting to insure spending almost full time in the resource room. These problems caution against wholesale initiation of resource rooms as the program of choice for SLD children. Furthermore, no studies were found in the literature on their effectiveness.

The Helping-Teacher Plan

This is a plan that is also becoming popular for providing special education services to SLD children. This preference reflects a movement toward keeping children with learning disabilities in a regular classroom on a full-time basis. Hopefully, it will reduce the social stigma, especially if the helping teacher is available to tutor all children with special learning needs in a regular classroom, whether they are labeled or not. With both the regular and helping-teacher team teaching together in the one classroom, there is greater opportunity to devise a wholly integrated instructional program for the pupil, since the regular and special work can be more meaningful by coordinated. Even more than the resource teacher, however, the special helping teacher must meet a high level of teacher competence—which will be difficult to attain. Truly, the helping teacher needs to have all the qualities of a resource teacher, plus superb interpersonal relations. These high-level persons need to be experienced master regular classroom teachers. Such an array of qualities suggests that only a limited number of helping teachers are likely to qualify. It becomes apparent that this is a very threatening plan for both the special and regular teacher. It is so new that its efficacy has yet to be researched. However, it is likely to work best with children who have milder learning disorders. Thus the question needs to be asked: Is this a job for special or remedial education? The answer is probably largely the latter, unless these two closely related areas join forces.

The Preschool Plan

Children have usually been classified as having a specific learning disability and provided with special education after having failed in the regular grades. Preschool programs are aimed at preventing such school failure. Therefore, currently, there is a great interest in such services for SLD children or those who at an early age indicate that there may be a need for specialized programs once they reach school. The problems are usually in the areas of language, audition, and perception. The challenge is to detect and remediate them before the child begins formal academic instruction. Models for accomplishing this are beginning to appear in the literature. Abrams and Pieper (1968) have described a preschool program for neurologically impaired children who were enrolled in regular nursery school programs in their own neighborhood. In addition, they spent two afternoons a week in a special learning center. The center utilized a play-school strategy in which sensorimotor tasks were presented in a developmental sequence. Group counseling for mothers was also provided once a week. Kenney (1969) has also described a preschool screening and treatment program. Its three goals were: (1) to diagnose developmental problems of children through observation and tests of emotional, visual, motor, and auditory levels of development; (2) to develop a planned school program that would enhance the strengths of the child and would help to compensate for the weaknesses; and (3) to work with the parents to help the child to function more effectively in both home and community life. Once the child was suspected of having a deficit in any area, he was referred to a special preschool where remediation was immediately provided.

As services move downward from kindergarten to nursery school and day care for all children, there will be opportunities, as never before, for the early detection and amelioration of school-learning disorders. Thus, preschool services for potential SLD children could be one of the most exciting and profitable developments for the field in the decade ahead.

EMERGING DIRECTIONS FOR THE FIELD

Throughout this chapter it has been pointed out that specific learning disabilities is the newest area of special education. Thus the field has little in the way of a tradition. Instead, it finds itself still in its initial stage of flux. This makes it especially difficult to discern accurately emerging directions. Nevertheless, the following trends appear to be developing:

1. Divergent forces are at work in delimiting the SLD field. On the other hand, for some persons it is becoming the "term of choice" to define broadly all school children with learning problems. On the other hand, many others recognize that this category will become a catch-all and infringe on remedial education unless it is restricted to major nontraditional learning disorders. The latter group appears to be in the ascendancy.

2. The trend is presently toward attempting to serve increased numbers of SLD pupils in more integrated programs with the helping teacher-consultant and resource-room plans. However, this trend is likely to be reversed when it is recognized that children with severe learning disabilities need much more intensive and extensive special education than can be provided by integrated programs. Boarding and special day schools, not to mention special classes, have a larger role to play than is presently thought to be the case.

3. The more emphasis there is on integrated programs, the more pressure is placed on the SLD special educator to fill the role of the master diagnostician, tutor, consultant, and counselor. Only a limited number of special educators are so endowed by natural ability, experience, training, or inclination. As the field proliferates, it will be difficult to insist on quality rather than quantity.

4. As, and if, large numbers of children are classified as SLD pupils, there will be administrative pressure for SLD instructors to run their pupil-teacher ratios up higher and higher. If this happens, there will be a tendency to choose pupils least in need of intensive remediation and to provide them with limited amounts of tutoring to the neglect of those with major learning disorders in need of extensive assistance. It is hoped that the SLD area is not forced to play this "numbers game," but rather that an in-depth intensive and extensive remediation program will be provided to children who most need the services.

5. Psychodiagnostics aimed at detecting weaknesses has dominated the emerging SLD field. During the next decade this preoccupation is likely to subside in favor of providing the unlikely combination of a more global comprehensive curriculum for groups of children, including SLD pupils, plus especially designed minilessons based on task analyses which determine the sequential steps needed to arrive at behavioral objectives for individual students. Conventional standardized tests of cognitive development, psycholinguistic processes, school achievement, or perceptual skills do not provide the basis for such a curricular approach.

6. Traditionally SLD special education services have been restricted to those who have already failed in the regular grades. An emerging trend is toward diagnosis and prevention in the preschool years with the main concerns being oral language, auditory and visual perception, and motor development. Too, remediation programs at the junior and senior high school levels are likely to become more prevalent.

7. The preparation of SLD teachers is likely to shift upward from the undergraduate and beginning graduate levels to advanced graduate work. The emerging reduction in school enrollments, the oversupply of teachers, and the availability of substantial federal scholarship funds will combine to make this realistic for the first time. Required will be regular teacher experience plus at least a year of internship in special education programs for SLD pupils.

SUMMARY

In addition to its even earlier roots in remedial education, special education for pupils with specific learning disabilities (SLD) had its inception in the 1940s when Strauss, a physician, and his associates, including Lehtinen, a special educator, initiated a boarding school for a small, somewhat homogeneous, group of children. These pupils displayed hyperactive, distractible, and perceptually impaired behavior and were labeled exogenous or brain injured because of assumed neurological impairment. More recently such children have been classified as having the Strauss syndrome. During the 1960s, the category was broadened considerably to include a much more heterogeneous collection of behavioral impairments in activity level, perception, conceptualization, language, memory, and attention. Led by physicians and psychologists who were still preoccupied with organicity, these pupils were said to have minimal brain dysfunctions to suggest that biochemical disorders as well as actual brain damage might be a possible cause. In contrast to Strauss, who placed no such restriction on his group, only children with average or near-average intelligence were included so as not to overlap with the traditional handicapping areas, especially mental retardation. ·At about the same time, Kirk, a special educator, coined the label specific learning disabilities as an educationally relevant nonmedical and less noxious ter . He also included essentially all children with learning problems that had not been encompassed by the traditional handicapping areas. In this chapter the SLD term has been adopted, but with the recommendation that the field be restricted to include only that 1–2 percent of the school population with *major* learning disorders. These children are defined on the basis of a significant negative discrepancy between performance versus capacity in one or more of the following areas: (1) motor; (2) visual perception; (3) auditory perception; (4) oral language; (5) reading; (6) spelling; (7) handwriting; and (8) arithmetic skills. Thus SLD is not one unitary syndrome but rather an umbrella that covers a wide variety of children with many different learning problems.

Traditionally, in this area, physicians and psychologists took prime responsibility for diagnosis aimed at labeling with a view to special educational placement. More recently educators have assumed this responsibility, calling on noneducational experts for assessment and treatment in their areas of expertise. One example is referral of hyperactive children to physicians for drug control. Now, excessive medication has become a serious enough problem to raise pupil-rights issues that demand attention. For such pupils, it is proposed that teachers apply behavior modification and other environmental controls as a substitute for drugs to a much greater extent than in the past.

Five, if not six, different approaches to educational intervention are practiced with SLD pupils. Some authorities favor the traditional strategy of "diagnostic teaching," borrowed from remedial education, wherein psycho-educational-diagnostic tests .are first administered to provide a profile of abilities and disabilities, followed by instruction aimed at correcting weaknesses. Others, who view such norm-referenced tests as too global and who consider an analysis of subtest differences as unreliable, define diagnostic teaching as the educational adaptation of behavior modification with diagnosis and instruction seen as one integrated operation. The procedure is to establish a specific behavior objective for a pupil, to analyze and set down the small sequential steps necessary to attain it, to determine the pupil's entry behavior along this continuum, and to use minilessons to reach the objective. Still others advocate a combination of these two diagnostic-teaching strategies. A few authorities recommend still another approach to diagnostic teaching, namely, to determine and teach to and through strengths for better motivation and greater learning. A few dissenters decry all four of these individualized, tutorial approaches and propose that SLD pupils need a broad, balanced course of study as much as average children. Many of the more able practitioners adopt an eclectic approach. They call on all of these various options as necessary, depending on the characteristics and needs of their pupils and the setting in which they find themselves, since no studies have been done as yet on the relative effectiveness of these various approaches to teaching SLD pupils. However, some earlier research is available that tests different teaching techniques with brain-injured children. While treatments and subjects were often confounded, the literature tends to support the conclusions that brain-injured children can learn considerably more than originally thought possible, that the Lehtinen restricted classroom environment is probably not necessary for the brain-injured hyperactive children, and that elemental instructional approaches are effective in teaching basic concepts to such children.

In addition to the prevention of later SLD problems through early childhood education, a challenge for the 1970s will be to determine the division line between remedial education and special SLD education. If mild and moderate cases are reserved for remedial educators, as this chapter has proposed, then such teachers are likely to serve almost exclusively as individual tutors, helping teachers, or consultants. But, as special educators move more to normalized instruction for SLD pupils, they too are inclined toward these more integrated plans. However, these strategies are likely to prove insufficient if the role of special education is restricted to serving pupils with major learning disabilities. These children will often require at least the resource-room plan, if not special day classes and boarding schools or even occasional hospital instruction during short periods of major medical treatment.

Resources

In 1968, a separate division called the *Division for Children with Learning Disabilities* (DCLD) was created within the Council for Exceptional Children (CEC) whose address was given in the Chapter 1 resources. Membership is open to interested CEC members. This division does not have a regular journal or publication, but useful materials are released each year and will be supplied upon request. This is the main professional organization for special educators of SLD children.

The major national parents' organization is known as the *Association for Children with Learning Disabilities* (ACLD), 2200 Brownsville Road, Pittsburgh, Pennsylvania, 15210, so organized in 1963. However, it grew out of parent organizations for the brain injured, neurologically impaired, and perceptually handicapped initiated during the 1950s. A newsletter is distributed periodically by the SCLD headquarters. The proceedings of the ACLD annual convention are published by Academic Therapy Publications, 1543 Fifth Avenue, San Rafael, California, 94901. There is also an ACLD directory that lists public and private agencies with varying amounts of interest in serving SLD children. Membership in ACLD and its local chapters is open to parents, professionals, students, and interested laymen.

There is a branch on "learning disabilities" within the Bureau of Education for the Handicapped of the U.S. Office of Education. The address is: Regional Office Building, 7th and D Streets, S.W., Washington, D.C. 20201.

Besides the special education publications mentioned in Chapter 1 resources, there are two professional journals that deal exclusively with learning disabled children. These are the *Academic Therapy Quarterly* and the *Journal of Learning Disabilities*.

While the field of special learning disabilities is new, a great deal of interest is developing in the field. As it does, the number of organizations and publications will increase. A rather complete list of publishers which distribute materials designed for SLD children will be found in an appendix to Lerner (1971).

References

Abrams, J. C. An interdisciplinary approach to learning disabilities. *Journal of Learning Disabilities*, 1969, **2**, 575–578.

Abrams, N., and Pieper, W. Experiences in developing a preschool program for neurologically handicapped children—a preliminary report. *Journal of Learning Disabilities*, 1968, **1**, 394–402.

Alley, G. P., and Carr, D. Effects of systematic sensory-motor training on sensory motor, visual perception, and concept formation of mentally retarded children. *Perceptual Motor Skills*, 1968, **27**, 451–456.

Balow, B. Perceptual-motor activities in the treatment of severe reading disabilities. *Reading Teacher*, 1971, **24**, 513–525.

Bannatyne, A. D. The color phonics system. In J. Money (Ed.), *The disabled reader: Education of the dyslexic child.* Baltimore, Md.: Johns Hopkins University Press, 1966.

Barry, H. *The young aphasic child; evaluation and training.* Washington, D.C.: Alexander Graham Bell Association for the Deaf, 1961.

Barsch, R. H. *A movigenic curriculum.* Madison, Wisc.: State Department of Public Instruction, 1965.

Barsch, R. H. Perspectives on learning disabilities: The vectors of a new convergence. *Journal of Learning Disabilities*, 1968, **1**, 4–20.

Bateman, B. D. An educator's view of a diagnostic approach to learning disorders. In J. Hellmuth (Ed.), *Learning disorders*, Vol. I. Seattle, Wash.: Special Child Publications, 1965. (a)

Bateman, B. D. *The Illinois Test of Psycholinguistic Abilities in current research: Summaries of studies.* Urbana, Ill.: University of Illinois Press, 1965. (b)

Bernstein, B. Elaborated and restricted codes: Their social origins and some consequences. *American Anthropologist*, 1964, **66**, 55–69.

Berry, M. F., and Eisenson, J. *Speech disorders; principles and practices of speech therapy.* New York: Appleton-Century-Crofts, 1956.

Blair, G. M. *Diagnostic and remedial teaching; a guide to practice in elementary and secondary schools.* New York: Macmillan, 1956.

Boder, E. Developmental dyslexia: Diagnostic screening patterns based on three characteristic patterns of reading and spelling. *Claremont Reading Conference*, 1968.

Boyd, L., and Randle, K. Factor analysis of the Frostig Developmental Test of Visual Perception. *Journal of Learning Disabilities*, 1970, **3**, 253–255.

Brueckner, L. J., and Bond, G. L. *The diagnosis and treatment of learning difficulties.* New York: Appleton-Century-Crofts, 1955.

Bruininks, R. H., and Weatherman, R. F. *Handicapped children and special education program needs in Northeast Minnesota,* Department of Special Education, University of Minnesota, 1970.

Buktenica, N. A. *Visual learning.* San Rafael, Calif.: Dimensions, 1968.

Burnette, E. Influences of classroom environment on word learning of retarded with high and low activity levels. Unpublished doctoral dissertation. Nashville, Tenn.: Peabody College, 1962.

Bush, W. J., and Giles, M. T. *Aids to psycholinguistic teaching.* Columbus, Ohio: Charles E. Merrill, 1969.

Campbell, D. D. Typewriting compared with handwriting in teaching beginning reading to children with severe learning disorders. Unpublished doctoral dissertation. Nashville, Tenn.: Peabody College, 1968.

Carter, J. L., and Diaz, A. Effects of visual and auditory background on reading test performance. *Exceptional Children*, 1971, **38**, 43–50.

Chalfant, J. C., and Scheffelin, M. A. (Eds.) Central processing dysfunctions in children: A review of research, Phase III *NINDS Monograph No. 9.* Washington, D.C.: U.S. Government Printing Office, 1969.

Chow, K. L. Further studies on selective ablation of associative cortex in relation to visually mediated behavior. *Journal of Comparative & Physiological Psychology*, 1952, **45**, 109–118.

Clements, S. D. (Ed.) Minimal brain dysfunction in children: Terminology and identification: Phase one of a three phase project. *NINDS Monograph No. 3.* (U. S. Public Health Service Publication No. 1415). Washington, D.C.: U.S. Government Printing Office, 1966.

Cohen, L. Perception of reversible figures after brain injury. *AMA Archives of Neurology*, 1959, **81**, 765–775.

Commission on Emotional and Learning Disorders in Children. *One million children.* Toronto, Ont.: Leonard Crainford, 1970.

Cromwell, R. L., Baumeister, A., and Hawkins, W. F. Research in activity level. In N. R. Ellis (Ed.) *Handbook of mental deficiency,* N.Y.: McGraw-Hill, 1963.

Cruickshank, W. M., Bentzen, F., Ratzeburg, F. H., and Tannhauser, M. T. *A teaching method for brain-injured and hyperactive children.* Syracuse, N.Y.: Syracuse University Press, 1961.

Cruickshank, W. M., Bice, H. J., and Wallen, N. E. *Perception and cerebral palsy.* Syracuse, N.Y.: Syracuse University Press, 1957.

Delacato, C. H. *Neurological organization and reading.* Springfield, Ill.: Charles C Thomas, 1966.

Deutsch, M. The role of social class in language development and cognition. *American Journal of Orthopsychiatry,* 1965, **35**, 78–88.

Dunn, L. M. Minimal brain dysfunction: A dilemma for educators. In H. C. Haywood (Ed.) *Brain damage in school age children.* Arlington, Va.: Council for Exceptional Children, 1968.

Dunn, L. M., Smith, J. O., and Horton, K. *Peabody Language Development Kits, Levels 1, 2, 3, and P.* Circle Pines, Minn.: American Guidance Services, 1965, 1966, 1967, 1968.

Durrell, D. *Improving reading instruction.* Yonkers, N.Y.: World Book, 1956.

Eisenson, J. *Aphasia in children.* New York: Harper & Row, 1972.

Engelmann, S., and Bruner, E. C. *Distar reading I and II: An instructional system.* Chicago: Science Research Associates, 1969. (a)

Englemann, S., and Carnine, D. *Distar arithmetic: An instructional system.* Chicago: Science Research Associates, 1969. (b)

Englemann, S., and Osborn, J. *Distar Language II; An instructional system.* Chicago: Science Research Associates, 1969. (c)

Engelmann, S., Osborn, L., and Engelmann, T. *Distar Language I: An instructional system.* Chicago: Science Research Associates, 1969. (d)

Ferinden, W. E., and Jacobson, S. Early identification of learning disabilities. *Journal of Learning Disabilities,* 1970, **3**, 589–593.

Fernald, G. M. *Remedial techniques in basic school subjects.* New York. McGraw-Hill, 1943.

Fitzhugh, K. B., and Fitzhugh, L. *The Fitzhugh plus program.* Galien, Mich.: Allied Education Council, 1966.

Forgnone, C. Effects of visual perception and language training upon certain abilities of retarded children. Unpublished doctoral dissertation. Nashville, Tenn.: Peabody College, 1966.

Franz, S. I., and Lashley, K. S. The effects of cerebral destruction upon habit formation and retention in the albino rat. *Psychobiology,* 1917, **1**, 71–140.

Freeman, R. D. Drug effects on learning in children: A selective review of the past thirty years. *Journal of Special Education,* 1966, **1**, 17–44.

Freibergs, V., and Douglas, V. L. Concept learning in hyperactive and normal Children. *Journal of Abnormal Psychology,* 1969, **74**, 388–395.

Frey, R. M. Reading behavior of brain-injured and non-brain-injured children of average and retarded mental development. *Dissertation Abstracts,* 1961, **22**, 1096–1097.

Frostig, M., and Horne, D. *The Frostig program for the development of visual perception, teacher's guide.* Chicago: Follett, 1964.

Gallagher, J. J. *Tutoring of brain-injured mentally retarded children.* Springfield, Ill.: Charles C Thomas, 1960.

Gallagher, J. J. Changes in verbal and non-verbal ability of brain-injured mentally retarded children following removal of special stimulation. *American Journal of Mental Deficiency,* 1962, **66**, 774–781.

Gardner, W. I., Cromwell, R. L., and Foshee, J. G. Studies in activity level II. Effects of distal visual stimulation in organics, familials, hyperactives and hypoactives. *American Journal of Mental Deficiency*, 1959, **63**, 1028–1033.

Gattegno, C. Words in color: I. The morphologico-algebraic approach to teaching reading. In J. Money and G. Schiffman (Eds.), *The disabled reader; education of the dyslexic child*. Baltimore, Md.: Johns Hopkins University Press, 1966.

Getman, G. N., Kane, E. R., Halgren, M. R. and McKee, G. W. *The physiology of readiness programs*. Chicago: Lyons & Carnahan, 1966.

Getman, G. N., Kane, E. R., and McKee, G. W. *Developing learning readiness: A visual-motor tactile skills program*. Manchester, Mo.: Webster Division, McGraw-Hill, 1968.

Gillingham, A., and Stillman, B. *Remedial training for children with specific disability in reading, spelling and penmanship*. (8th ed.) Cambridge, Mass.: Educators Publishing Service, 1970.

Glaser, R. (Ed.) *Teaching machines and programed learning, II; data and directions*. Washington, D.C. National Education Association, 1965.

Golden, N. E., and Steiner, S. R. Auditory and visual functions in good and poor readers. *Journal of Learning Disabilities*, 1969, **2**, 476–481.

Goldman, R., and Lynch, M. E. *Goldman-Lynch sounds and symbols development kit*. Circle Pines, Minn.: American Guidance Services, 1971.

Gronlund, N. E. *Stating behavioral objectives for classroom instruction*. New York: Macmillan, 1970.

Gunderson, B. V. Diagnosis of learning disabilities—the team approach. *Journal of Learning Disabilities*, 1971, **4**, 107–113.

Haring, N. G. (Ed.) Minimal brain dysfunction in children: Educational, medical, and health related services, Phase II of a three-phase project. *U.S. Public Health Service Publication No. 2015*. Washington, D.C.: U.S. Government Printing Office, 1969.

Harris, A. J. *How to increase reading ability* (5th ed.) New York: David McKay, 1970.

Harris, L. A., and Smith, C. B. *Reading instruction through diagnostic teaching*. New York: Holt, Rinehart and Winston, 1972.

Hebb, D. O. Intelligence in man after large removals of cerebral tissue: Report of four left frontal lobe cases. *Journal of Genetic Psychology*, 1939, **21**, 73–87.

Hebb, D. O. The effect of early and late brain injury on test scores and the nature of normal adult intelligence. *Proceedings of the American Philosophical Society*, 1942, **85**, 275–292.

Hebb, D. O. *The organization of behavior*. New York: Wiley, 1949.

Hegge, T. G., Kirk, S. A., and Kirk, W. D. *Remedial reading drills*. Ann Arbor, Mich.: George Wahr, 1936.

Johnson, D. J., and Myklebust, H. R. *Learning disabilities: Educational principles and practices*. New York: Grune & Stratton, 1967.

Johnson, M., and Kress, R. *Informal reading inventories*. Newark, Del.: International Reading Association, 1965.

Jolles, I. A public school demonstration class for children with brain damage. *American Journal of Mental Deficiency*, 1956, **60**, 582–588.

Karnes, M. B., Hodgins, A., Hertig, L., Solberg, C., Morris, J., Heggemeier, M., and Lorez, C. *Activities for developing psycholinguistic skills with preschool culturally disadvantaged children*. Arlington, Va.: Council for Exceptional Children, 1968.

Kass, C. E. Psycholinguistic disabilities of children with reading problems. *Exceptional Children*, 1966, **32**, 533–539.

Kenney, E. T. A diagnostic preschool for atypical children. *Exceptional Children*, 1969, **36**, 193–199.

Keogh, B. K. Hyperactivity and learning disorders: Review and speculation. *Exceptional Children*, 1971, **38**, 101–109.

Kephart, N.C. *The brain injured child in the classroom.* Chicago: National Society for Crippled Children and Adults, 1963.

Kephart, N. C. *The slow learner in the classroom* (2d ed.) Columbus, Ohio: Charles E. Merrill, 1970.

Kershner, J. R. Doman-Delacato's theory of neurological organization applied with retarded children. *Exceptional Children*, 1968, **34**, 441–450.

Kirk, S. A. *Educating exceptional children.* Boston: Houghton Mifflin, 1962.

Kirk, S. A. *Educating exceptional children.* (2d ed.) Boston: Houghton Mifflin, 1972.

Kirk, S. A., and Kirk, W. D. *Psycholinguistic learning disabilities*: Diagnosis and remediation. Urbana, Ill.: University of Illinois Press, 1971.

Kirk, S. A., McCarthy, J. J., and Kirk, W. D. *The Illinois test of psycholinguistic abilities* (rev. ed.) Urbana, Ill.: University of Illinois Press, 1968.

Klebanoff, S. G., Singer, J. L., and Wilensky, H. Psychological consequences of brain lesions and ablations. *Psychological Bulletin*, 1954, **51**, 1–41.

Kronvall, E. L., and Diehl, C. F. The relationship of auditory discrimination to articulatory defects of children with no known organic impairment. *Journal of Speech and Hearing Disorders*, 1954, **19**, 335–338.

Ladd, E. T. Pills for classroom peace? *Saturday Review*, November 21, 1970.

Lashley, K. S. *Brain mechanisms and intelligence.* Chicago: University of Chicago Press, 1929.

Lashley, K. S. *The mechanism of vision.* Vol. I–XVII. Provincetown, Mass.: Journal Press, 1930–1942.

Lerner, J. W. *Children with learning disabilities.* New York: Houghton-Mifflin, 1971.

Lindamood, C. A., and Lindamood, P. C. *Auditory discrimination in depth.* New York: Teaching Resources, 1969.

Luria, A. R. *Higher cortical functions in man.* New York: Basic Books, 1966.

Mager, R. F. *Preparing instructional objectives.* Palo Alto, Calif.: Fearon, 1962.

Mann, L. Psychometric phrenology and the new faculty psychology: The case against ability assessment and training. *Journal of Special Education*, 1971, **5**(1), 3–14.

McGinnis, M. A. *Aphasic children. Identification and education by the associative method.* Washington, D.C.: Alexander Graham Bell Association for the Deaf, 1963.

McCarthy, J. M. Providing services in the public schools for children with learning disabilities. In J. Arena (Ed.) *Management of the child with learning disabilities.* San Rafael, Calif.: Academic Therapy Publication, 1969.

Meier, J. H. Prevalence and characteristics of learning disabilities found in second grade children. *Journal of Learning Disabilities*, 1971, **4**, 1–16.

Millman, H. L. Minimal brain dysfunction in children-evaluation and treatment. *Journal of Learning Disabilities*, 1970, **3**, 89–99.

Mumpower, D. L. Sex ratios found in various types of referred exceptional children. *Exceptional Children*, 1970, **36**, 621–622.

Myklebust, H. R. *Development and disorders of written language.* New York: Grune & Stratton, 1965.

National Advisory Committee on Handicapped Children. *First Annual Report.* Washington, D.C.: U.S. Office of Education, 1968.

Newbrough, J. R., and Kelly, J. G. *A study of reading achievement in a population of school children.* In J. Money (Ed.), *Reading disability; progress and research needs in dyslexia.* Baltimore, Md.: Johns Hopkins Press, 1962.

Nielsen, J. M. *Agnosia, apraxia, aphasia; their value in central localization* (2d ed.) New York: Hafner, 1962.

O'Donnell, P. A. *Motor and haptic learning.* San Rafael, Calif.: Dimensions, 1969.

O'Donnell, P. A., and Eisenson, J. Delacato training for reading achievement and visual-motor integration. *Journal of Learning Disabilities,* 1969, **2**, 441–447.

Olson, A. V. Factor analytic studies of the Frostig Developmental Test of Visual Perception. *Journal of Special Education,* 1968, **2**, 429–433.

Orton, S. T. *Reading, writing, and speech problems in children.* New York: Norton, 1937.

Otto, W., and McMenemy, R. A. *Corrective and remedial teaching. Principles and practices.* New York: Houghton Mifflin, 1966.

Painter, G. The effect of a rhythmic and sensory motor activity program on perceptual motor spatial abilities of kindergarten children. *Exceptional Children,* 1966, **33**, 113–116.

Paraskevopoulos, J. N., and Kirk, S. A. *The development and psychometric characteristics of the revised Illinois Test of Psycholinguistic Abilities,* Urbana, Ill.: University of Illinois Press, 1969.

Parker, R. K., Ambron, S., Danielson, G. I., Halbrook, M. C., and Levine, J. A. *An overview of cognitive and language programs for 3, 4, and 5 year old children.* Atlanta, Ga.: Southeastern Educational Laboratory, 1970.

Penfield, W., and Roberts, L. *Speech and brain mechanisms.* Princeton: Princeton University Press, 1959.

Plowman, P. D. *Behavioral objectives. Teacher success through student performance.* Chicago: Science Research Associates, 1971.

Popham, W. J. *Instructional objectives.* Skokie, Ill.: Rand McNally, 1969.

Rice, D. Learning disabilities: An investigation in two parts. *Journal of Learning Disabilities,* 1970, **3**, 149–155, 193–199.

Robbins, M. P. A study of the validity of Delacato's theory of neurological organization. *Exceptional Children,* 1966, **32**, 517–523.

Robinson, H. M. *Why pupils fail in reading.* Chicago: University of Chicago Press, 1946.

Rubin, R., and Balow, B. Learning and behavior disorders: A longitudinal study. *Exceptional Children,* 1971, **38**, 293–299.

Rupert, H. A. *A sequentially compiled list of instructional materials for remediational use with the ITPA.* Greeley, Colorado: University of Northern Colorado Rocky Mountain Special Education Instructional Materials Center, undated.

Semeritskaya, F. M. *Rhythm and its disturbance in various motor lesions.* Candidate dissertation, Institution Psychological, Moscow, 1945.

Shephard, G. Selected factors in the reading ability of educable mentally retarded boys. *American Journal of Mental Deficiency,* 1967, **71**, 563–570.

Spalding, R. B., and Spalding, W. T. *The writing road to reading* (Rev. ed.) New York: Whiteside & Morrow, 1962.

Stern, C., Stern, M., and Gould, T. *Structural arithmetic program.* Boston: Houghton Mifflin, 1965.

Stevens, G. D., and Birch, J. W. A proposal of clarification of the terminology and a description of brain-injured children. *Exceptional Children,* 1957, **23**, 346–349.

Strauss, A. A., and Kephart, N. C. *Psychopathology and education of the brain-injured child: Progress in theory and clinic.* Vol. II. New York: Grune & Stratton, 1955.

Strauss, A. A., and Lehtinen, L. E. *Psychopathology and education of the brain-injured child.* Vol. I. New York: Grune & Stratton, 1947.

Stuart, I. R. Perceptual style and reading ability: Implications for an instructional approach. *Perceptual Motor Skills,* 1967, **24**, 135–138.

Templin, M. C. *Certain language skills in children: Their development and interrelationships.* Minneapolis, Minn.: University of Minnesota Press, 1957.

U. S. Department of Health, Education and Welfare. *Reading disorders in the United States: A report of the National Advisory Committee on dyslexia and related reading disorders.* Washington, D.C.: U.S. Government Printing Office, 1969.

Valett, R. E. *The remediation of learning disabilities.* Palo Alto, Calif.: Fearon, 1967.

Valett, R. E. The learning resource center for exceptional children. *Exceptional Children,* 1970, **36**, 527–530.

Vance, H. S. A psychological and educational study of brain-injured and non-brain damaged mentally retarded children. *Dissertation Abstracts,* 1956, **17**, 1033.

Weener, P., Barritt, L. S., and Semmel, M. I. A critical evaluation of the Illinois Test of Psycholinguistic Abilities. *Exceptional Children,* 1967, **33**, 373–380.

Wender, P. H. *Minimal brain dysfunction in children.* New York: Wiley-Interscience, 1971.

Wernicke, C. *Der aphasische symptomene complex.* Breslau, Poland: Cohen & Weighert, 1874.

Werry, J. S. Developmental hyperactivity. In H. Bakwin (Ed.), Developmental disorders of mobility and language. *The Pediatric Clinics of North America,* 1968 *15(3),* 581–599.

Werry, J. S., and Sprague, R. L. Hyperactivity. In C. G. Costello (Ed.) *Symptoms of psychopathology.* New York: Wiley, 1969.

Whitsell, A. J., and Whitsell, L. J. Remedial reading in a medical center. *Reading Teacher,* 1968, **21**, 707–711.

Woodcock, R. W. *Peabody Rebus Reading Program.* Circle Pines, Minn.: American Guidance Services, 1967.

Yates, A. J. The validity of some psychological tests of brain damage. *Psychological Bulletin,* 1954, **51**, 359–379.

Zigmond, N. K. Auditory processes in children with learning disabilities. In L. Tarnopol (Ed.) *Learning disabilities: Introduction to educational and medical management.* Springfield, Ill.: Charles C Thomas, 1969.

Zigmond, N. K., and Cicci, R. *Auditory learning.* San Rafael, Calif.: Dimensions, 1968.

uthor index

subject index